*Foundations of
Financial Markets
and Institutions*

# Foundations of Financial Markets and Institutions

## Frank J. Fabozzi

*School of Organization and Management*
*Yale University*

## Franco Modigliani

*Sloan School of Management*
*Massachusetts Institute of Technology*

## Michael G. Ferri

*School of Business Administration*
*George Mason University*

Prentice Hall Inc., Englewood Cliffs, NJ 07632

**Library of Congress Cataloging–in–Publication Data**

Fabozzi, Frank J.
   Foundations of financial markets and institutions / Frank J.
Fabozzi, Franco Modigliani, Michael G. Ferri.
      p.    cm.
   Includes index.
   ISBN 0-13-328980-X
   1. Finance. 2. Financial institutions. I. Modigliani, Franco.
II. Ferri, Michael G.  III. Title.
HG173.F29 1994
332.1—dc20

                                            93-22585
                                          CIP

Acquisitions editor: Leah Jewell
Production editor: Joanne Palmer
Interior and cover design: Donna Wickes
Prepress buyer: Trudy Pisciotti
Manufacturing Buyer: Patrice Fraccio
Editorial assistant: Eileen Deguzman
Cover art: Roy Weimann / The Image Bank

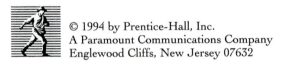 © 1994 by Prentice-Hall, Inc.
A Paramount Communications Company
Englewood Cliffs, New Jersey 07632

Printed in the United States of America

10  9  8  7  6  5  4  3  2  1

ISBN 0-13-328980-X

Prentice-Hall International (UK) Limited, London
Prentice-Hall of Australia PTY, Limited, Sydney
Prentice-Hall Canada Inc., Toronto
Prentice-Hall Hispanoamericana, S.A., Mexico
Prentice-Hall of India Private Limited, New Delhi
Prentice-Hall of Japan, Inc., Tokyo
Simon & Schuster Asia Pte. Ltd., Singapore
Editora Prentice-Hall Do Brasil, Ltda., Rio de Janeiro

To my parents, Alfonso and Josephine Fabozzi.
*Frank J. Fabozzi*

To all of my students, wherever they are.
*Franco Modigliani*

To my wife, Mary.
*Michael G. Ferri*

# Contents

# *Preface*

In the last 30 years, a profound, exciting, and irreversible revolution has occurred in the world's financial markets and institutions. The hallmarks of this radical change are *innovation*, *globalization*, and *deregulation*. New financial instruments are available, and there are new markets where these instruments are traded. Old markets have significantly changed their operations and have established new linkages with one another. Investors can now use innovative investment strategies as well as new techniques for guarding against always-present risks. The global integration of financial markets and institutions has been dynamic and irresistible. Securities trade on exchanges in different countries, firms and governments issue securities in their home markets as well as in foreign markets, and investors move funds across international boundaries with ease. In most cases, governments have accepted multi-faceted globalization and, in some cases, they have even welcomed and promoted it.

Our purpose in writing this book is to instruct students about this fascinating revolution. In this text, we describe the wide array of financial instruments available in today's markets for investing, financing operations, and controlling the various kinds of financial risk. To understand the nature and uses of these instruments, students must first realize that the instruments are responses to the needs of borrowers, lenders, and investors. These financial practitioners manage assets and liabilities in a complicated environment of varying interest rates and asset prices, regulatory constraints, accounting rules, and international competition and opportunities. Our book devotes a considerable amount of time to explaining how the world's key financial institutions manage their assets and liabilities and how the innovative instruments support that management. Also, our text gives the student a thorough introduction to financial regulation and to the major developments in international finance.

Undoubtedly, the forces that have shaped today's instruments and markets will lead to other new financial instruments and institutions in the future. Our comprehensive approach to explaining the developments that dominate today's financial scene provides students with the institutional structure and analytical tools for understanding the financial innovations that will surely occur during their careers and affect the financial world in which they will be working.

Our coverage of institutional investors and financial instruments is as up-to-date as possible in the current situation of frequent change. We have made a major effort to get the latest information on the players in the financial game and the changes in the rules by which it is played in all the important arenas of the world. We think our focus on the actual practices of financial institutions helps students more fully to comprehend the changes that have recently occurred, the changes happening now, and the changes that will inevitably take place in the future.

We believe that our book differs, in several key ways, from the standard text in financial institutions and markets. In order to introduce our book, we will now outline those differences.

*The first difference is our commitment to giving the students an extensive introduction to the international or global aspects of contemporary finance.* To this end, we explain in depth how the world's major financial markets and institutions interact with one another. Our discussions range across a wide field, encompassing markets for bonds and stocks as well as mutual funds in Tokyo, London, Frankfurt, and Paris, among other places. Further, our text gives some detailed explanations about the operations, structure, and regulations of these major markets and institutions. Just a glance at the table of contents reveals that this book covers the international topics which today's students must know in order to function in the globalized financial system and internationally integrated markets where they will soon be working.

*The second difference is our book's extensive coverage of the markets for derivative securities, such as options, futures, swaps, customized agreements for controlling interest rate risk, and so on.* These derivative securities and their markets are increasingly important parts of the integrated, global financial system. Though often characterized as "exotic" by the popular press and some poorly informed politicians, derivatives actually help financial practitioners to control risk and the cost of funding. Because of these instruments, financial markets in the United States and throughout the world are more efficient and can contribute more to economic development and growth.

Our discussion of options naturally contains an explanation of the theoretical principles of pricing these instruments. But we frequently show that option pricing theory also applies to a variety of complex securities that have embedded options. For example, many kinds of bonds have embedded options: issuers may exercise some of those options and the holders may exercise others. Students must understand option pricing theory if they are to understand the valuation of many of today's important securities.

Our treatment of derivatives has a specific purpose: we offer fundamental information about the structure of these instruments, the markets where they are traded, the principles for pricing them, and the applications to which financial practitioners can put them. Because this text does not offer a specialized treatment of derivative markets, it does not delve deeply into the complexities of trading strategies and the nuances of pricing models. However, we believe that this text contains a good deal of information that is lacking from many textbooks on derivative markets and is suitable as a supplementary text in a course on those instruments.

*A special feature of this text, and the third major difference between it and many texts in financial markets and institutions, is its lengthy coverage of the mortgage market and the securitization of assets.* Securitization is the process by which a security, whose collateral is the cash flow from a pool of assets, is created and sold in the capital markets. Asset securitization is a major innovation of the last 20 years and represents a radical departure from the traditional system for financing the acquisition of assets. The mortgage-backed security is the prime example of this process and accounts for the largest part of the market for securitized assets.

We do not believe that a teacher has the time in a single semester to treat all the topics covered by this book. The following table contains our suggestions for the chapters that should be included in a one-semester course on financial institutions and markets. The table also identifies the chapters that make the text useful as a supplement for a course in investments or one in derivative securities.

In conclusion, we want to inform those of you who adopt this book that we are eager to hear about your experience with it. Please, let us know where you find the book helpful and where it needs changing. Also, we would like to see the outline of the course in which you use this text. We have spent many, many hours on this effort and definitely want to know how profitable that expenditure is to the people who use our product. If all goes well, and there is a second edition of this book, we want it to be better in every possible way. For that, we will need your help. For your help, we will all be grateful.

POSSIBLE USAGE AND COVERAGE OF CHAPTERS FOR SELECTED COURSES

| Chapter | One Semester Course On Institutions And Markets | Supplement For Course: On Derivative Securities | On Investments |
|---|---|---|---|
| 1. Introduction | x | | |
| 2. Financial intermediaries and financial innovation | x | | |
| 3. The role of the government in financial markets | x | | |
| 4. Depository institutions: activities and characteristics | x | | |
| 5. Central banks and the creation of money | x | | |
| 6. Monetary policy | x | | |
| 7. Insurance companies | x | | |
| 8. Investment companies | x | | |
| 9. Pension funds | x | | |
| 10. Properties and pricing of financial assets | (a) | (a) | x |
| 11. Determinants of the level and structure of interest rates | x | x | x |
| 12. The term structure of interest rates | x | x | x |
| 13. Risk and return, and asset pricing models | (a) | (a) | x |
| 14. Primary markets and the underwriting of securities | x | | x |
| 15. Secondary markets | x | | x |
| 16. Treasury and agency securities markets | x | | x |
| 17. Municipal securities market | x | | x |
| 18. Common stock markets | x | | x |
| 19. Non-U.S. stock markets | x | | x |
| 20. Markets for corporate senior instruments: I | x | | x |
| 21. Corporate senior instruments: II | x | | x |
| 22. The markets for bank obligations | x | | |
| 23. Mortgage market | x | | x |
| 24. Mortgage-backed securities market | x | | x |
| 25. Financial futures markets | x | x | x |
| 26. Options markets | x | x | x |
| 27. Pricing of futures and options contracts | x | x | x |
| 28. The applications of futures and options contracts | | x | x |
| 29. Interest rate swap and interest rate agreement markets | | x | x |
| 30. The market for foreign exchange rate risk control instruments | | x | x |

*Note:* (a) This chapter should be covered if the students have not learned this material in another course.

# ACKNOWLEDGMENTS

We are indebted to many individuals for providing us with various forms of assistance in this project. Laurence Siegel (R.G. Ibbotson Associates) reviewed many chapters and offered insightful comments, as well as encouragement. Others who read portions of the manuscript and provided feedback include: Anand Bhattacharya (Prudential Securities), Steve Boxer (State Street Bank), David Canuel (Aetna Life and Casualty), Mark Castelino (Rutgers University), Daniel T. Coggin (Virginia Retirement System), Bruce Collins (Western Connecticut State University), Dessa Fabozzi (Merrill Lynch Capital Markets), Gary L. Gastineau (Swiss Bank Corporation), Frank J. Jones (Guardian Life Insurance Company), K.C. Ma (Investment Research Corporation and Texas Tech University), Ed Murphy (Merchants Mutual Insurance Company), and Uzi Yaari (Rutgers University).

We also benefited from discussions with the following individuals: Robert Arnott (First Quadrant), Peter L. Bernstein (Peter L. Bernstein Inc.), Michael Coppola (Merrill Lynch Money Markets), John H. Carlson (Lehman Brothers), Andrew S. Carron (First Boston), John Crockett (George Mason University), Peter E. Christensen (PaineWebber), Ravi Dattatreya (Sumitomo Bank Capital Markets), Henry Gabbay (Blackstone Financial Management), Sean Gallop (J.P. Morgan Securities), Gerald Hanweck (George Mason University), Jane Howe (Pacific Investment Management Company), David P. Jacob (J.P. Morgan Securities), Andrew Kalotay (Fordham University), Robert Kieschnick (George Mason University), Barbara Laico (Merrill Lynch Money Markets), Scott Pinkus (Goldman Sachs), Mark Pitts (Lehman Brothers), Sharmin Mossavar-Rahmani (Goldman Sachs Asset Management), Frank Ramirez (Alex. Brown & Sons), Chuck Ramsey (Alex. Brown & Sons), Dexter Senft (EJV Partners), George Wang (Commodity Futures Trading Commission), Richard Wilson (Fitch Investors Service), Jot Yau (George Mason University), and David Yuen (Alex. Brown & Sons).

In our end-of-chapter questions, we used excerpts from *Institutional Investor* and several weekly publications of Institutional Investor Inc., *Wall Street Letter*, *Bank Letter*, *BondWeek*, *Corporate Financing Week*, *Derivatives Week*, *Money Management Letter*, and *Portfolio Letter*. We are grateful to Lauren Marrus of Institutional Investor and Tom Lamont, editor of the weekly publications, for permission to use the material. Simon G. Davidson of Ferguson & Co. (Washington, D.C.) provided data on the largest U.S. bank holding companies reported in Chapter 4. The data source for the world's largest banks, reported in the same chapter, is EURASTAR, a division of Sleigh Corporation (Franklin Lakes, N.J.). Kate Jones of Morgan Stanley supplied us with information from various publications of *Morgan Stanley Capital Perspective* which we used in Chapter 19. Beth Preiss of Freddie Mac furnished information from the *Secondary Mortgage Market* that we used in Chapters 23 and 24.

In addition, the authors would like to thank the following reviewers: Robert Nagy, University of Wisconsin at Green Bay; Antony C. Cherin, San Diego State University; Rose M. Prasad, Central Michigan University; William Doyle Smith, University of Texas at El Paso, Inayat U. Mangla, Western Michigan University; Suzanne Paranjpe, Wayne State University; David R. Durst, University of Akron; Shane A. Johnson, Bowling Green State University; David A. Schauer, University of Texas at El Paso; Paul S. Nadler, Rutgers University; and Tony Plath, University of North Carolina at Charlotte.

Administrative and copyediting assistance was provided by Steve Arbour, Chris Palaia, and Toni Zuccarini. Patricia Peat edited the manuscript. Leah Jewell and Joanne Palmer of Prentice Hall were helpful at numerous steps in the long process of getting the book published. Joseph Garvie and Vinodh Srikanth of George Mason University were research assistants for portions of the text. Marie Southwick of MIT gave us a great deal of assistance, and we are all very grateful to her.

Finally, we wish to thank our families for their patience and support.

Frank J. Fabozzi
Franco Modigliani
Michael G. Ferri

# Biographical Sketches

FRANK J. FABOZZI is Adjunct Professor of Finance at the School of Organization and Management at Yale University and editor of the *Journal of Portfolio Management*. From 1986 to 1992, he was a full-time member of the Finance faculty at the Sloan School of Management at MIT. Dr. Fabozzi has authored and edited several widely acclaimed books in finance. He is on the board of directors of the BlackRock complex of closed-end funds and the Guardian Park Avenue Portfolio family of open-end funds, and on the board of supervisory directors of two offshore funds. He earned a doctorate in Economics in 1972 from The Graduate Center of the City University of New York and is a Chartered Financial Analyst.

FRANCO MODIGLIANI is Institute Professor and Professor of Finance and Economics at MIT. He is an Honorary President of the International Economic Association and a former President of the American Economic Association, the American Finance Association, and the Econometric Society. He is a member of several academies, including the National Academy of Science. Professor Modigliani has authored numerous books and articles in economics and finance. In October 1985, he was awarded the Alfred Nobel Memorial Prize in Economic Sciences. He has served as a consultant to the Federal Reserve System, the U.S. Treasury Department, and a number of European banks, as well as to many businesses, and is on several Boards of Directors. Professor Modigliani received a Doctor of Jurisprudence in 1939 from the University of Rome and a Doctor of Social Science in 1944 from the New School for Social Research, as well as several honorary degrees.

MICHAEL G. FERRI is a Professor of Finance at George Mason University in Fairfax, Virginia, and he is the holder of the GMU Foundation Chair in Finance. He received his doctorate in Economics from the University of North Carolina at Chapel Hill in 1975. His numerous articles on financial markets and investments have appeared in a variety of financial and economic journals. He is on the editorial board of the *Journal of Portfolio Management* and is a vice-president of the Financial Management Association. Professor Ferri has served as a consultant to agencies of the U.S. government and to several major financial institutions.

*Foundations of*
*Financial Markets*
*and Institutions*

CHAPTER ONE

# *Introduction*

## LEARNING OBJECTIVES

*After reading this chapter you will understand:*

- what a financial asset is and the principal economic functions of financial assets.
- the distinction between financial assets and tangible assets.
- what a financial market is and the principal economic functions it performs.
- the distinction between debt instruments and equity instruments.
- the various ways to classify financial markets.
- the differences between the primary and secondary markets.
- the participants in financial markets.
- reasons for the globalization of financial markets.
- the distinction between an internal market and an external market.
- the distinction between a domestic market, a foreign market, and the Euromarket.
- the reasons why entities use foreign markets and Euromarkets.
- what a derivative instrument is and the two basic types of derivative instruments.
- the role of derivative instruments.

In a market economy, the allocation of economic resources is the outcome of many private decisions. Prices are the signals operating in a market economy that direct economic resources to their best use. The types of markets in an economy can be divided into (1) the market for products (manufactured goods and services), called the *product market*, and (2) the market for the factors of production (labor and capital), called the *factor market*.

Our purpose in this book is to focus on one part of the factor market, the market for financial assets, or, more simply, the *financial market*. In this chapter we will look at the role of financial markets, the "things" that are traded (i.e., bought and sold) in financial markets, and the reasons for the integration of world financial markets.

## FINANCIAL ASSETS

We begin with a few basic definitions. An *asset*, broadly speaking, is any possession that has value in an exchange. Assets can be classified as *tangible* or *intangible*. A tangible asset is one whose value depends on particular physical properties—examples are buildings, land, or machinery. Intangible assets, by contrast, represent legal claims to some future benefit. Their value bears no relation to the form, physical or otherwise, in which these claims are recorded.

Financial assets are intangible assets. For financial assets, the typical benefit or value is a claim to future cash. This book deals with the various types of financial assets, the markets where they are traded, and the principles for valuing them. Throughout this book we use the terms financial asset, *financial instrument*, and *security* interchangeably.

The entity that has agreed to make future cash payments is called the *issuer* of the financial asset; the owner of the financial asset is referred to as the *investor*. Here are just seven examples of financial assets:

- a loan by Citibank (investor) to an individual (issuer/borrower) to purchase a car
- a bond issued by the U.S. Treasury
- a bond issued by General Motors Corporation
- a bond issued by the City of New York
- a bond issued by the government of Japan
- a share of common stock issued by IBM
- a share of common stock issued by Honda Motor Company, a Japanese company.

In the case of the car loan, the terms of the loan establish that the borrower must make specified payments to the commercial bank over time. The payments include repayment of the amount borrowed plus interest. The cash flow for this asset is made up of the specified payments that the borrower must make.

In the case of a U.S. Treasury bond, the U.S. government (the issuer) agrees to pay the holder or the investor the bond interest payments every six months until the bond matures, then at the maturity date repay the amount borrowed. The same is true for the bonds issued by General Motors Corporation, the City of New York, and the government of Japan. In the case of General Motors Corporation, the issuer is a corporation, not a government entity. In the case of the City of New York, the issuer is a municipal government. The issuer of the Japanese government bond is a central government entity.

The common stock of IBM entitles the investor to receive dividends distributed by the company. The investor in this case also has a claim to a pro rata share of the net asset value of the company in case of liquidation of the company. The same is true of the common stock of Honda Motor Company.

### Debt versus Equity Claims

The claim that the holder of a financial asset has may be either a fixed dollar amount or a varying, or residual, amount. In the former case, the financial asset is referred to as a *debt instrument*. The car loan, the U.S. Treasury bond, the General Motors Corporation bond, the City of New York bond, and the Japanese government bond cited above are examples of debt instruments requiring fixed dollar payments.

An *equity claim* (also called a *residual claim*) obligates the issuer of the financial asset to pay the holder an amount based on earnings, if any, after holders of debt instruments have been paid. Common stock is an example of an equity claim. A partnership share in a business is another example.

Some securities fall into both categories. Preferred stock, for example, is an equity claim that entitles the investor to receive a fixed dollar amount. This payment is contingent, however, and due only after payments to debt instrument holders are made. Another "combination" instrument is a convertible bond, which allows the investor to convert debt into equity under certain circumstances. Both debt and preferred stock that pays a fixed dollar amount are called *fixed-income instruments*.

### The Price of a Financial Asset and Risk

A basic economic principle is that the price of any financial asset is equal to the present value of its expected cash flow, even if the cash flow is not known with certainty. By cash flow we mean the stream of cash payments over time.[1] For example, if a U.S. government bond promises to pay $30 every six months for the next 30 years and $1,000 at the end of 30 years, then this is its cash flow. In the case of the car loan by Citibank, if the borrower is obligated to pay $500 every month for three years, then this is the cash flow of the loan. We elaborate on this principle throughout this book as we discuss several theories for the pricing of financial assets.

Directly related to the notion of price is the expected return on a financial asset. Given the expected cash flow of a financial asset and its price, we

---

[1] Accountants use the term cash flow in a different way. An accountant defines cash flow as the net income after taxes plus noncash outlays such as depreciation. Financial economists define cash flow as simply the cash expected to be received.

can determine its expected rate of return. For example, if the price of a financial asset is $100, and its only cash flow is $105 one year from now, its expected return would be 5%.

The type of financial asset, whether debt instrument or equity instrument, and the characteristics of the issuer determine the degree of certainty of the expected cash flow. For example, assuming that the U.S. government never defaults on the debt instruments it issues, the cash flow of U.S. Treasury securities is known with certainty. What is uncertain, however, is the purchasing power of the cash flow received.

In the case of the Citibank car loan, the ability of the borrower to repay presents some uncertainty about the cash flow. But, if the borrower does not default on the loan obligation, the investor (Citibank) knows what the cash flow will be. The same is true for the bonds of General Motors and the City of New York.

In the case of the Japanese government bond, the cash flow is known if the Japanese government does not default. The cash flow, however, may be denominated not in U.S. dollars but in the Japanese currency, the yen. Thus, while the cash flow is known in terms of the number of yen that will be received, from the perspective of a U.S. investor, the number of U.S. dollars is unknown. The number of U.S. dollars will depend on the exchange rate between the Japanese yen and the U.S. dollar at the time the cash flow is received.

The holder of IBM common stock is uncertain as to both the amount and the timing of dividend payments. Dividend payments will be related to company profits. The same is true for the cash flow of the common stock of Honda Motor Company. In addition, because Honda will make dividend payments in Japanese yen, there is uncertainty about the cash flow in terms of U.S. dollars.

While there are various types of risks that we will discuss in this chapter and those to follow, we can see three of them in our examples. The first is the risk attached to potential purchasing power of the expected cash flow. This is called *purchasing power risk*, or *inflation risk*. The second is the risk that the issuer or borrower will default on the obligation. This is called *credit risk*, or *default risk*. Finally, for financial assets whose cash flow is not denominated in U.S. dollars, there is the risk that the exchange rate will change adversely, resulting in less U.S. dollars. This risk is referred to as *foreign-exchange risk*.

## *Financial Assets versus Tangible Assets*

A tangible asset such as plant or equipment purchased by a business entity shares at least one characteristic with a financial asset: both are expected to generate future cash flow for their owner. For example, suppose a U.S. airline purchases a fleet of aircraft for $250 million. With its purchase of the aircraft, the airline expects to realize cash flow from passenger travel.

Financial assets and tangible assets are linked. Ownership of tangible assets is financed by the issuance of some type of financial asset—either debt instruments or equity instruments. For example, in the case of the airline, suppose that a debt instrument is issued to raise the $250 million to purchase the fleet of aircraft. The cash flow from the passenger travel will be used to service the payments on the debt instrument. Ultimately, therefore, the cash flow for a financial asset is generated by some tangible asset.

## *The Role of Financial Assets*

Financial assets have two principal economic functions. The first is to transfer funds from those who have surplus funds to invest to those who need funds to invest in tangible assets. The second economic function is to transfer funds in such a way as to redistribute the unavoidable risk associated with the cash flow generated by tangible assets among those seeking and those providing the funds. However, as we will see, the claims held by the final wealth holders are generally different from the liabilities issued by the final demanders of funds because of the activity of financial intermediaries that seek to transform the final liabilities into the financial assets that the public prefers.

We can illustrate these two economic functions with three examples.

1. Joe Grasso has obtained a license to manufacture Teenage Mutant Ninja Turtles wristwatches. Joe estimates that he will need $1 million to purchase plant and equipment to manufacture the watches. Unfortunately, he has only $200,000 to invest, and that is his life savings, which he does not want to invest, even though he has confidence that there will be a receptive market for the watches.
2. Susan Carlson has recently inherited $730,000. She plans to spend $30,000 on some jewelry, furniture, and a few cruises, and to invest the balance, $700,000.
3. Larry Stein, an up-and-coming attorney with a major New York law firm, has received a bonus check that after taxes has netted him $250,000. He plans to spend $50,000 on a BMW and invest the balance, $200,000.

Suppose that, quite by accident, Joe, Susan, and Larry meet at a social function. Sometime during their conversation, they discuss their financial plans. By the end of the evening, they agree to a deal. Joe agrees to invest $100,000 of his savings in the business and sell a 50% interest to Susan for $700,000. Larry agrees to lend Joe $200,000 for four years at an interest rate of 18% per year. Joe will be responsible for operating the business without the assistance of Susan or Larry. Joe now has his $1 million to manufacture the watches.

Two financial claims came out of this meeting. The first is an equity instrument issued by Joe and purchased by Susan for $700,000. The other is a debt instrument issued by Joe and purchased by Larry for $200,000. Thus, the two financial assets allowed funds to be transferred from Susan and Larry, who had surplus funds to invest, to Joe, who needed funds to invest in tangible assets in order to manufacture the watches. This transfer of funds is the first economic function of financial assets.

The fact that Joe is not willing to invest his life savings of $200,000 means that he wanted to transfer part of that risk. He does so by selling Susan a financial asset that gives her a financial claim equal to one-half the cash flow from the business. He further secures an additional amount of capital from Larry, who is not willing to share in the risk of the business (except for credit risk), in the form of an obligation requiring payment of a fixed cash flow, regardless of the outcome of the venture. This shifting of risk is the second function of financial assets.

▶ KEY POINTS THAT YOU SHOULD UNDERSTAND BEFORE PROCEEDING:

1. The difference between tangible assets and financial assets and how they are related.
2. The difference between debt instruments and equity instruments (or equity claims).
3. What is meant by the cash flow of a financial asset.
4. Three types of risks associated with investing in financial assets: purchasing power or inflation risk, default or credit risk, and exchange-rate risk.
5. The two economic functions of financial assets.

## FINANCIAL MARKETS

■ ■ ■ ■

A financial market is a market where financial assets are exchanged (i.e., traded). Although the existence of a financial market is not a necessary condition for the creation and exchange of a financial asset, in most economies financial assets are created and subsequently traded in some type of financial market. The market in which a financial asset trades for immediate delivery is called the *spot* or *cash market*.

### Role of Financial Markets

We explained above the two primary economic functions of financial assets. Financial markets provide three additional economic functions.

First, the interactions of buyers and sellers in a financial market determine the price of the traded asset. Or, equivalently, they determine the required return on a financial asset. As the inducement for firms to acquire funds depends on the required return that investors demand, it is this feature of financial markets that signals how the funds in the economy should be allocated among financial assets. This is called the *price discovery process*.

Second, financial markets provide a mechanism for an investor to sell a financial asset. Because of this feature, it is said that a financial market offers *liquidity*, an attractive feature when circumstances either force or motivate an investor to sell. If there were not liquidity, the owner would be forced to hold a debt instrument until it matures and an equity instrument until the company is either voluntarily or involuntarily liquidated. While all financial markets provide some form of liquidity, the degree of liquidity is one of the factors that characterize different markets.

The third economic function of a financial market is that it reduces the cost of transacting. There are two costs associated with transacting: *search costs* and *information costs*.

Search costs represent explicit costs, such as the money spent to advertise one's intention to sell or purchase a financial asset, and implicit costs, such as the value of time spent in locating a counterparty. The presence of some form of organized financial market reduces search costs. Information costs are costs associated with assessing the investment merits of a financial asset, that is, the amount and the likelihood of the cash flow expected to be generated. In an efficient market, prices reflect the aggregate information collected by all market participants.

## Classification of Financial Markets

There are many ways to classify financial markets. One way is by the type of financial claim, such as debt markets and equity markets. Another is by the maturity of the claim. For example, there is a financial market for short-term debt instruments, called the *money market*, and one for longer-maturity financial assets, called the *capital market*.

Financial markets can be categorized as those dealing with financial claims that are newly issued, called the *primary market*, and those for exchanging financial claims previously issued, called the *secondary market* or the market for seasoned instruments.

Markets are classified as either *cash* or *derivative instruments* markets. (The latter is described later in this chapter.) A market can be classified by its organizational structure: it may be an *auction market*, an *over-the-counter market*, or an *intermediated market*. These structures are described in Chapter 15.

All these classifications are summarized in Table 1-1.

## Market Participants

Participants in the global financial markets that issue and purchase financial claims include households, business entities (corporations and partnerships), national governments, national government agencies, state and local governments, and supranationals (such as the World Bank, the European Investment Bank, and the Asian Development Bank).

Business entities include non-financial and financial enterprises. Non-financial enterprises manufacture products—for example, cars, steel, and computers—and/or provide non-financial services—including transportation, utilities, and computer programming. The roles in financial markets played by financial enterprises and a special type of financial enterprise called a financial intermediary are described in Chapter 2.

Finally, while we have focused on market participants that create and/or exchange financial assets, a broader definition of market participants would include regulators of financial markets. We discuss regulation in Chapter 3.

| TABLE 1-1 |
|---|
| **SUMMARY OF CLASSIFICATION OF FINANCIAL MARKETS** |
| **Classification by nature of claim:** |
| Debt market<br>Equity market |
| **Classification by maturity of claim:** |
| Money market<br>Capital market |
| **Classification by seasoning of claim:** |
| Primary market<br>Secondary market |
| **Classification by immediate delivery or future delivery:** |
| Cash or spot market<br>Derivative market |
| **Classification by organizational structure:** |
| Auction market<br>Over-the-counter market<br>Intermediated market |

▶ KEY POINTS THAT YOU SHOULD UNDERSTAND BEFORE PROCEEDING:

1. The three economic functions of financial markets are to improve the price discovery process, enhance liquidity, and reduce the cost of transacting.
2. There are various ways that financial markets can be classified.
3. The market participants include households, business entities, national governments, national government agencies, state and local governments, supranationals, and regulators.

## GLOBALIZATION OF FINANCIAL MARKETS

Because of the globalization of financial markets throughout the world, entities in any country seeking to raise funds need not be limited to their domestic financial market. Nor are investors in a country limited to the financial assets issued in their domestic market. Globalization means the integration of financial markets throughout the world into an international financial market.

The factors that have led to the integration of financial markets are (1) deregulation or liberalization of markets and the activities of market participants in key financial centers of the world; (2) technological advances for monitoring world markets, executing orders, and analyzing financial opportunities; and (3) increased institutionalization of financial markets.

Global competition has forced governments to deregulate (or liberalize) various aspects of their financial markets so that their financial enterprises can compete effectively around the world. We discuss deregulation in Chapter 3.

Technological advances have increased the integration of and efficiency of the global financial market. Advances in telecommunication systems link market participants throughout the world, with the result that orders can be executed within seconds. Advances in computer technology, coupled with advanced telecommunication systems, allow the transmission of real-time information on security prices and other key information to many participants in many places. Therefore, many investors can monitor global markets and simultaneously assess how this information will impact the risk/return profile of their portfolios. Significantly improved computing power allows the instant manipulation of real-time market information so that arbitrage opportunities can be identified. Once these opportunities are identified, telecommunication systems permit the rapid execution of orders to capture them.

The U.S. financial markets have shifted from domination by retail investors to domination by financial institutions. By *retail investors* we mean individuals. For example, when you or I buy a share of common stock, we are referred to as retail investors. Examples of financial institutions are pension funds, insurance companies, mutual funds, commercial banks, and savings and loan associations. We describe these financial institutions in Section III of this book. Throughout this book we will refer to these financial institutions as *institutional investors*.

The shifting of the financial markets from dominance by retail investors to institutional investors is referred to as the *institutionalization* of financial markets. The same thing is occurring in other industrialized countries. Unlike retail investors, institutional investors have been more willing to transfer funds across national borders to improve portfolio diversification and/or exploit perceived mispricing of financial assets in foreign countries. The potential portfolio diversification benefits associated with global investing have been documented in numerous studies, which have heightened the awareness of investors about the virtues of global investing.[2]

## Classification of Global Financial Markets

While there is no uniform system for classifying the global financial markets, an appropriate schematic presentation appears in Figure 1-1. From the perspective of a given country, financial markets can be classified as either *inter-*

---

[2] For a review of these studies, see Bruno Solnik, *International Investments* (Reading, MA: Addison-Wesley, 1988), Chapter 2.

FIGURE 1-1

CLASSIFICATION OF GLOBAL FINANCIAL MARKETS

*nal* or *external*. The internal market is also called the *national market*. It can be decomposed into two parts: the *domestic market* and the *foreign market*. The domestic market is where issuers domiciled in a country issue securities and where those securities are subsequently traded.

The foreign market in any country is where the securities of issuers not domiciled in the country are sold and traded. The rules governing the issuance of foreign securities are those imposed by regulatory authorities where the security is issued. For example, securities issued by non-U.S. corporations in the United States must comply with the regulations set forth in U.S. securities law. A non-Japanese corporation that seeks to offer securities in Japan must comply with Japanese securities law and regulations imposed by the Japanese Ministry of Finance. Nicknames have developed to describe the various foreign markets. For example, the foreign market in the U.S. is called the *Yankee market*. The foreign market in Japan is nicknamed the *Samurai market*, in the United Kingdom the *Bulldog market*, in the Netherlands the *Rembrandt market*, and in Spain the *Matador market*.

The *external market,* also called the *international market*, allows trading of securities with two distinguishing features: (1) at issuance securities are offered simultaneously to investors in a number of countries, and (2) they are issued outside the jurisdiction of any single country. The external market is commonly referred to as the *offshore market*, or, more popularly, the *Euromarket*.[3]

---

[3] The classification we use is by no means universally accepted. Some market observers and compilers of statistical data on market activity refer to the external market as consisting of the foreign market and the Euromarket.

## *Motivation for Using Foreign Markets and Euromarkets*

There are several reasons why a corporation may seek to raise funds outside its domestic market. First, in some countries, large corporations seeking to raise a substantial amount of funds may have no choice but to obtain financing in either the foreign market sector of another country or the Euromarket. This is because the fund-seeking corporation's domestic market is not fully developed and cannot satisfy its demand for funds on globally competitive terms. Governments of developing countries have used these markets in seeking funds for government-owned corporations that they are privatizing.

The second reason is that there may be opportunities for obtaining a lower cost of funding than is available in the domestic market, although with the integration of capital markets throughout the world, such opportunities have diminished. Nevertheless, there are still some imperfections in capital markets throughout the world that may permit a reduced cost of funds. The causes of these imperfections are discussed throughout the book. A final reason for using foreign or Euromarkets is a desire by issuers to diversify their source of funding so as to reduce reliance on domestic investors.

*Corporate Financing Week* asked the corporate treasurers of several multinational corporations why they used nondomestic markets to raise funds.[4] Their responses reflect one or more of the reasons cited above. For example, the director of corporate finance for General Motors said that the company uses the bond sector of the Eurobond market (discussed in Chapter 21) with the objective of "diversifying funding sources, [and to] attract new investors and achieve comparable, if not cheaper, financing." A managing director of Sears, Roebuck stated that the company "has a long-standing policy of diversifying geographical [funding] sources and instruments to avoid reliance on any specific market, even if the cost is higher." He added that "Sears cultivates a presence in the international market by issuing every three years or so."

In a survey conducted by the Economic Council of Canada of Canadian borrowers who raised funds outside of Canada, 85% cited as a primary reason the lower cost of funding.[5] The other reasons cited by the participants in the survey were: diversification of the investor base (50%); ease of borrowing funds (37%); the presence of a subsidiary, parent, or affiliate in the country of borrowing (43%); the ability to attract new investors (30%); and publicity for the corporation's name (30%).

---

[4] Victoria Keefe, "Companies Issue Overseas for Diverse Reasons," *Corporate Financing Week*, November 25, 1991, Special Supplement, pp. 1 and 9.

[5] A. Nigam, *Canadian Corporations and Governments, Financial Innovation and International Capital Markets*, a paper prepared for the Economic Council of Canada, 1989.

▶ KEY POINTS THAT YOU SHOULD UNDERSTAND BEFORE PROCEEDING:

1. The three major factors that have integrated financial markets throughout the world.
2. What is meant by the institutionalization of financial markets.
3. What is meant by an internal market (or national market), domestic market, foreign market, and external market (or international market, offshore market, or Euromarket).
4. The motivations for U.S. corporations to raise money outside the United States.

## DERIVATIVE MARKETS

■ ■ ■ ■

So far we have focused on the cash market for financial assets. With some contracts, the contract holder has either the obligation or the choice to buy or sell a financial asset at some future time. The price of any such contract derives its value from the price of the underlying financial asset. Consequently, these contracts are called *derivative instruments*.

### *Types of Derivative Instruments*

The two basic types of derivative instruments are *futures/forward contracts* and *options contracts*. A futures or forward contract is an agreement whereby two parties agree to transact with respect to some financial asset at a predetermined price at a specified future date. One party agrees to buy the financial asset; the other agrees to sell the financial asset. Both parties are obligated to perform, and neither party charges a fee. The distinction between a futures and forward contract is explained in Chapter 25.

An options contract gives the owner of the contract the right, but not the obligation, to buy (or sell) a financial asset at a specified price from (or to) another party. The buyer of the contract must pay the seller a fee, which is called the option price. When the option grants the owner of the option the right to buy a financial asset from the other party, the option is called a *call option*. If, instead, the option grants the owner of the option the right to sell a financial asset to the other party, the option is called a *put option*. Options are more fully explained in Chapter 26.

Derivative instruments are not limited to financial assets. There are derivative instruments involving commodities and precious metals. Our focus in this book, however, is on derivative instruments where the underlying asset is a financial asset, or some financial benchmark such as a stock index or an interest rate, or foreign exchange. Moreover, there are other types of derivative instruments that are basically "packages" of either forward contracts or option contracts. These include swaps, caps, and floors, all of which are discussed in Chapter 29.

## *The Role of Derivative Instruments*

Derivative contracts provide issuers and investors an inexpensive way of controlling some major risks. While we will describe these risks in later chapters of this book, here are three examples that clearly illustrate the need for derivative contracts:

1. Suppose that General Motors plans to obtain a bank loan for $100 million two months from now. The key risk here is that two months from now the interest rate will be higher than it is today. If the interest rate is only one percentage point higher, General Motors would have to pay $1 million more in annual interest. Clearly, then, issuers/borrowers want a way to protect against a rise in interest rates.

2. IBM pension fund owns a portfolio consisting of the common stock of a large number of companies. (We describe the role of pension funds in Chapter 9, but for now the only thing that is important to understand is that the pension fund must make periodic payments to the beneficiaries of the plan.) Suppose the pension fund knows that two months from now it must sell stock in its portfolio to pay beneficiaries $20 million. The risk that IBM pension fund faces is that two months from now when the stocks are sold, the price of most or all stocks may be lower than they are today. If stock prices do decline, the pension fund will have to sell off more shares to realize $20 million. Thus, investors, such as the IBM pension fund, face the risk of declining stock prices and may want to protect against this risk.

3. Suppose Sears, Roebuck plans to issue a bond in Switzerland and the periodic payments that the company must make to the bondholders are denominated in the Swiss currency, the franc. The amount of U.S. dollars that Sears must pay to receive the amount of Swiss francs it has contracted to pay will depend on the exchange rate at the time the payment must be made. For example, suppose that at the time Sears plans to issue the bonds, the exchange rate is such that one U.S. dollar is equal to 1.5 Swiss francs. So, for each 7.5 million Swiss francs that Sears must pay to the bondholders, it must pay U.S. $5 million. If at any time that a payment must be made in Swiss francs, the value of the U.S. dollar declines relative to the Swiss franc, Sears will have to pay more U.S. dollars to satisfy its contractual obligation. For example, if one U.S. dollar at the time of a payment changes to 1.25 Swiss francs, Sears would have to pay $6 million to make a payment of 7.5 million Swiss francs. This is U.S. $1 million more than when it issued the bonds. Issuers/borrowers who raise funds in currency that is not their local currency face this risk.

The derivative instruments that we describe in Section IX of this book can be used by the two borrowers (General Motors and Sears, Roebuck) and the one investor (IBM pension fund) in these examples to eliminate or to reduce the kinds of risks that they face.

As we will see in later chapters, derivative markets may have at least three advantages over the corresponding cash (spot) market for the same financial asset. First, depending on the derivative instrument, it may cost less to execute a transaction in the derivatives market in order to adjust the risk exposure of an investor's portfolio to new economic information than it would cost to make that adjustment in the cash market. Second, transactions typically can be accomplished faster in the derivatives market. Third, some derivative markets can absorb a greater dollar transaction without an adverse effect on the price of the derivative instrument; that is, the derivative market may be more liquid than the cash market.

The key point here is that derivative instruments play a critical role in global financial markets. Unfortunately, derivative markets are too often viewed by the general public—and sometimes regulators and legislative bodies—as vehicles for pure speculation (that is, legalized gambling). Without derivative instruments and the markets in which they trade, the financial systems throughout the world would not be as integrated as they are today.

▶ KEY POINTS THAT YOU SHOULD UNDERSTAND BEFORE PROCEEDING:

1.  The two basic types of derivative instruments: futures/forward contracts and options.
2.  The principal economic role of derivative instruments.
3.  The potential advantages of using derivative instruments rather than cash market instruments.

## SUMMARY

In this chapter we have explained the role of financial assets and financial markets. A financial asset (or financial instrument or security) entitles the owner to future cash flows to be paid by the issuer as well as to the liquidation value of the asset. The claim can be either an equity or debt claim. The price of any financial asset is equal to the present value of the cash flow expected. Because of uncertainty about the cash flow, in nominal and inflation-adjusted dollars, there is risk in investing in financial assets.

The two principal economic functions of a financial asset are (1) transferring funds from those who have surplus funds to invest to those who need funds to invest in tangible assets, and (2) transferring funds in such a way that redistributes the unavoidable risk associated with the cash flow generated by tangible assets among those seeking and those providing the funds.

Financial markets provide the following three additional functions beyond that of financial assets themselves: (1) they provide a mechanism for determining the price (or, equivalently, the required return) of financial assets, (2) they make assets more liquid, and (3) they reduce the costs of exchanging assets. The costs associated with transacting are search costs and information costs.

There are various ways to classify financial markets: money (or short-term) versus capital markets, debt versus equity markets, primary versus secondary markets, and cash versus derivative markets. Another classification is based on the type of organizational structure: auction versus over-the-counter versus intermediated markets.

The increased integration of financial markets throughout the world can be attributed to three factors: (1) deregulation or liberalization of major financial markets (market deregulation and institutional deregulation); (2) advances in telecommunications and computer technologies; and (3) institutionalization of financial markets. Global financial markets can be classified as the national market of a country, consisting of the domestic market and foreign market, and the external market (overseas or Euromarket).

A derivative instrument is a contract whose value depends on the value of the underlying financial asset. The chief economic function of a derivative instrument is to provide ways to control risk. Derivative markets may offer three advantages over cash markets: (1) lower transactions costs; (2) faster speed at which transactions can be completed; and (3) greater liquidity.

## GLOSSARY

**Asset:** Broadly speaking, any possession that has value in an exchange.

**Call option:** An option that grants the owner of the option the right to buy a financial asset from the other party.

**Capital market:** The financial market for equity instruments, and for debt instruments with a maturity greater than one year.

**Debt instrument:** The claim that the holder of a financial asset has that is a fixed dollar amount. Loans and bonds are examples.

**Default risk (also called credit risk):** The risk that the issuer or borrower will default on its obligation.

**Derivative instrument:** A contract that gives the contract holder either the obligation or the choice to buy or sell a financial asset at some future time. Options and futures are examples.

**Domestic market:** A classification of the global financial market. It is the financial market of a country where issuers domiciled in the country issue securities and where those securities are subsequently traded. It is part of the internal or national market.

**Equity instrument:** A financial asset in which the issuer agrees to pay the holder an amount based on earnings, if any, after holders of debt instruments have been paid. Common stock is an example of an equity claim.

**External market (also called the international market, the offshore market, or the Euromarket):** Classification of the global financial market. This financial market includes securities with the following distinguishing features: (1) at issuance they are offered simultaneously to investors in a number of countries, and (2) they are issued outside the jurisdiction of any single country.

**Financial asset (or intangible asset):** An asset that represents a legal claim to some future benefit. The terms financial asset, financial instrument, and security are used interchangeably.

**Financial market:** A market where financial assets are exchanged (traded).

**Fixed-income instrument:** Debt instruments and preferred stock that pay a fixed dollar amount.

**Foreign-exchange risk:** For financial assets whose cash flow is not denominated in U.S. dollars, this is the risk that the exchange rate will change adversely, resulting in fewer U.S. dollars.

**Foreign market:** A classification of the global financial market. It is the financial market of a country where the securities of issuers not domiciled in the country are sold and traded. It is part of the internal or national market.

**Information costs:** Costs associated with assessing the value of a financial asset.

**Internal market (also called national market):** A classification of a global financial market. It can be decomposed into two parts: the domestic market and the foreign market.

**Money market:** The financial market for short-term debt instruments.

**Price discovery process:** An economic function of financial markets that signals how the funds in the economy should be allocated among financial assets.

**Purchasing power risk (also called inflation risk):** The risk attached to potential purchasing power of the expected cash flow.

**Search costs:** Costs in locating a counterparty to a transaction.

**Secondary market:** A market in which outstanding or existing securities are traded among investors.

**Spot market (also called cash market):** The market in which a financial asset trades for immediate delivery.

**Tangible asset:** An asset whose value depends on particular physical properties—examples are buildings, land, or machinery.

**QUESTIONS**

1. What is the difference between a financial asset and a tangible asset?
2. What is the difference between the claim of a debtholder of General Motors and an equityholder of General Motors?
3. a. What is the basic principle in determining the price of a financial asset?
   b. Why are the characteristics of an issuer important in determining the price of a financial asset?

4. What are the two basic roles of financial assets?

5. In September 1990 a study by the U.S. Congress, Office of Technology Assessment, entitled "Electronic Bulls & Bears: U.S. Securities Markets and Information Technology," included this statement:

   Securities markets have five basic functions in a capitalistic economy:

   1. They make it possible for corporations and governmental units to raise capital.
   2. They help to allocate capital toward productive uses.
   3. They provide an opportunity for people to increase their savings by investing in them.
   4. They reveal investors' judgments about the potential earning capacity of corporations, thus giving guidance to corporate managers.
   5. They generate employment and income.

   For each of the functions cited above, explain how financial markets (or securities markets, in the parlance of this Congressional study) perform each function.

6. Explain the difference between each of the following:

   a. Money market and capital market.
   b. Primary market and secondary market.
   c. Domestic market and foreign market.
   d. National market and Euromarket.

7. Give three reasons for the trend toward greater integration of financial markets throughout the world.

8. What is meant by the "institutionalization" of capital markets?

9. a. What are the two basic types of derivative instruments?
   b. "Derivative markets are nothing more than legalized gambling casinos and serve no economic function." Comment on this statement.

# CHAPTER TWO

# Financial Intermediaries and Financial Innovation

*After reading this chapter, you will understand:*

- the business of financial institutions.
- the role of financial intermediaries.
- the difference between direct and indirect investments.
- how financial intermediaries transform the maturity of liabilities and give both short-term depositors and longer-term, final borrowers what they want.
- how financial intermediaries offer investors diversification and so reduce the risks of their investments.
- the way financial intermediaries reduce the costs of acquiring information and entering into contracts with final borrowers of funds.
- how financial intermediaries enjoy economies of scale in processing payments from final users of funds.
- the nature of the management of assets and liabilities by financial intermediaries.
- how different financial institutions have differing degrees of knowledge and certainty

about the amount and timing of the cash outlay of their liabilities.

- why financial institutions have liquidity concerns.
- the primary reasons for financial innovation.
- the nature of asset securitization.
- the pivotal role of financial intermediaries in securitization.
- the benefits to issuers, investors, financial markets, and borrowers of securitization.

This chapter serves several purposes. The first is to introduce the financial intermediary. Intermediaries include commercial banks, savings and loan associations, investment companies, insurance companies, and pension funds. The most important contribution of intermediaries is a steady and relatively inexpensive flow of funds from savers to final users or investors. Every modern economy has intermediaries, which perform key financial functions for individuals, households, corporations, small and new businesses, and governments. Germany has large and regional commercial banks, as well as savings banks and credit cooperatives. Japan has nationally branched banks, local banking firms, and trust banks that specialize in savings and investment. Investors in Britain and Italy can choose from among numerous investment companies.

The chapter's second purpose is to convey a sense of the dynamic nature of contemporary finance and financial institutions. We live in a time marked by an unusually rapid pace of financial innovation. This innovation both reflects and responds to two historically significant events in today's world: the arrival of sophisticated telecommunications and computer technology, and the globalization of business, especially finance. In a sense, this entire book is a treatise on financial innovation. This chapter provides a brief overview of some of the reasons for and benefits of innovation.

Finally, the chapter calls attention to a special kind of innovation that originates with financial institutions. This innovation is the process by which financial intermediaries pool traditional assets (car loans, mortgages, and so on) and sell securities backed by these loan pools in the capital markets. This process of "securitization" is affecting all kinds of financial institutions and assets today, and it is taking hold in all business centers of the world. Before long, investors will have opportunities to buy bonds based on car loans in India, farm loans in Poland, credit card loans in France, and truck loans in (just maybe) Russia. Clearly, this is an exciting development and one that needs to be understood well.

# FINANCIAL INSTITUTIONS

■ ■ ■ ■

Business entities include non-financial and financial enterprises. Non-financial enterprises manufacture products (e.g., cars, steel, computers) and/or provide non-financial services (e.g., transportation, utilities, computer programming). Financial enterprises, more popularly referred to as *financial institutions*, provide services related to one or more of the following:

1. Transforming financial assets acquired through the market and constituting them into a different, and more widely preferable, type of asset—which becomes their liability. This is the function performed by *financial intermediaries*, the most important type of financial institution.
2. Exchanging of financial assets on behalf of customers.
3. Exchanging of financial assets for their own accounts.
4. Assisting in the creation of financial assets for their customers, and then selling those financial assets to other market participants.
5. Providing investment advice to other market participants.
6. Managing the portfolios of other market participants.

Financial intermediaries include depository institutions (commercial banks, savings and loan associations, savings banks, and credit unions), which acquire the bulk of their funds by offering their liabilities to the public mostly in the form of deposits; insurance companies (life and property and casualty companies); pension funds; and finance companies. Deposit-accepting, or depository institutions, are discussed in Chapter 4. The other financial intermediaries are covered in Chapters 7 through 9.

The second and third services in the list above are the broker and dealer functions, which are discussed in Chapters 14 and 15. The fourth service is referred to as underwriting. As we explain in Chapter 14, typically a financial institution that provides an underwriting service also provides a brokerage and/or dealer service.

Some non-financial enterprises have subsidiaries that provide financial services. For example, many large manufacturing firms have subsidiaries that provide financing for the parent company's customer. These financial instions are called *captive finance companies*. Examples include General Motors Acceptance Corporation (a subsidiary of General Motors) and General Electric Credit Corporation (a subsidiary of General Electric).

▶ KEY POINTS THAT YOU SHOULD UNDERSTAND BEFORE PROCEEDING:

1. The services provided by financial institutions.
2. The special role played by the financial intermediary when it transforms assets acquired from customers or the market into its own liabilities.

## ROLE OF FINANCIAL INTERMEDIARIES

As we have seen, financial intermediaries obtain funds by issuing financial claims against themselves to market participants, and then investing those funds. The investments made by financial intermediaries—their assets—can be in loans and/or securities. These investments are referred to as *direct investments*. Market participants who hold the financial claims issued by financial intermediaries are said to have made *indirect investments*.

Two examples will illustrate this. Most readers of this book are familiar with what a commercial bank does. Commercial banks accept deposits and may use the proceeds to lend funds to consumers and businesses. The deposits represent the IOU of the commercial bank and a financial asset owned by the depositor. The loan represents an IOU of the borrowing entity and a financial asset of the commercial bank. The commercial bank has made a direct investment in the borrowing entity; the depositor effectively has made an indirect investment in that borrowing entity.

As a second example, consider an investment company, a financial intermediary we focus on in Chapter 8, which pools the funds of market participants and uses those funds to buy a portfolio of securities such as stocks and bonds. Investors providing funds to the investment company receive an equity claim that entitles the investor to a pro rata share of the outcome of the portfolio. The equity claim is issued by the investment company. The portfolio of financial assets acquired by the investment company represents a direct investment that it has made. By owning an equity claim against the investment company, those who invest in the investment company have made an indirect investment.

We have stressed that financial intermediaries play the basic role of transforming financial assets that are less desirable for a large part of the public into other financial assets—their own liabilities—which are more widely preferred by the public. This transformation involves at least one of four economic functions: (1) providing maturity intermediation; (2) reducing risk via diversification; (3) reducing the costs of contracting and information processing; and (4) providing a payments mechanism. Each function is described below.

### *Maturity Intermediation*

In our example of the commercial bank, two things should be noted. First, the maturity of at least a portion of the deposits accepted is typically short-term. For example, certain types of deposit are payable upon demand. Others have a specific maturity date, but most are less than two years. Second, the maturity of the loans made by a commercial bank may be considerably longer than two years. In the absence of a commercial bank, the borrower would have to borrow for a shorter term, or find an entity that is willing to invest for the length of the loan sought, and/or investors who make deposits in the bank would have to commit funds for a longer length of time than they want. The commercial bank by issuing its own financial claims in essence transforms a longer-term asset into a shorter-term one by giving the borrower a loan for the length of time sought and the investor/depositor a financial asset for the desired investment horizon. This function of a financial intermediary is called *maturity intermediation*.

Maturity intermediation has two implications for financial markets. First, it provides investors more choices concerning maturity for their investments; borrowers have more choices for the length of their debt obligations. Second, because investors are naturally reluctant to commit funds for a long period of time, they will require that long-term borrowers pay a higher interest rate than on short-term borrowing. A financial intermediary is willing to make longer-term loans, and at a lower cost to the borrower than an individual investor would, by counting on successive deposits providing the funds until maturity (although at some risk—see below). Thus, the second implication is that the cost of longer-term borrowing is likely to be reduced.

### Reducing Risk via Diversification

Consider the example of the investor who places funds in an investment company. Suppose that the investment company invests the funds received in the stock of a large number of companies. By doing so, the investment company has diversified and reduced its risk. Investors who have a small sum to invest would find it difficult to achieve the same degree of diversification because they do not have sufficient funds to buy shares of a large number of companies. Yet by investing in the investment company for the same sum of money investors can accomplish this diversification, thereby reducing risk.

This economic function of financial intermediaries—transforming more risky assets into less risky ones—is called *diversification*. While individual investors can do it on their own, they may not be able to do it as cost-effectively as a financial intermediary, depending on the amount of funds they have to invest. Attaining cost-effective diversification in order to reduce risk by purchasing the financial assets of a financial intermediary is an important economic benefit for financial markets.

### Reducing the Costs of Contracting and Information Processing

Investors purchasing financial assets should take the time to develop skills necessary to understand how to evaluate an investment. Once those skills are developed, investors should apply them to the analysis of specific financial assets that are candidates for purchase (or subsequent sale). Investors who want to make a loan to a consumer or business will need to write the loan contract (or hire an attorney to do so).

While there are some people who enjoy devoting leisure time to this task, most prefer to use that time for just that—leisure. Most of us find that leisure time is in short supply, so to sacrifice it, we have to be compensated. The form of compensation could be a higher return that we obtain from an investment.

In addition to the opportunity cost of the time to process the information about the financial asset and its issuer, there is the cost of acquiring that information. All these costs are called *information processing costs*. The costs of writing loan contracts are referred to as *contracting costs*. And there is another dimension to contracting costs, the cost of enforcing the terms of the loan agreement.

With this in mind, consider our two examples of financial intermediaries — the commercial bank and the investment company. People who work for these intermediaries include investment professionals who are trained to analyze financial assets and manage them. In the case of loan agreements, either standardized contracts can be prepared, or legal counsel can be part of the professional staff that writes contracts involving more complex transactions. The investment professionals can monitor compliance with the terms of the loan agreement and take any necessary action to protect the interests of the financial intermediary. The employment of such professionals is cost-effective for financial intermediaries because investing funds is their normal business.

In other words, there are economies of scale in contracting and processing information about financial assets, because of the amount of funds managed by financial intermediaries. The lower costs accrue to the benefit of the investor who purchases a financial claim of the financial intermediary and to the issuers of financial assets, who benefit from a lower borrowing cost.

## Providing a Payments Mechanism

While the previous three economic functions may not have been immediately obvious, this last function should be. Most transactions made today are not done with cash. Instead, payments are made using checks, credit cards, debit cards, and electronic transfers of funds. These methods for making payments are provided by certain financial intermediaries.

At one time, non-cash payments were restricted to checks written against non-interest-bearing accounts at commercial banks. Similar check writing privileges were provided later by savings and loan associations and savings banks, and by certain types of investment companies. Payment by credit card was also at one time the exclusive domain of commercial banks, but now other depository institutions offer this service. Debit cards are offered by various financial intermediaries. A debit card differs from a credit card in that, in the latter case, a bill is sent to the credit cardholder periodically (usually once a month) requesting payment for transactions made in the past. In the case of a debit card, funds are immediately withdrawn (that is, debited) from the purchaser's account at the time the transaction takes place.

The ability to make payments without the use of cash is critical for the functioning of a financial market. In short, depository institutions transform assets that cannot be used to make payments into other assets that offer that property.

▶ KEY POINTS THAT YOU SHOULD UNDERSTAND BEFORE PROCEEDING:

1.  The difference between a direct investment and an indirect investment.
2.  How a financial institution intermediates among investors and borrowers in the area of maturity, reduces risk and offers diversification, reduces the costs of contracting and information processing, and provides payment mechanisms.

## OVERVIEW OF ASSET/LIABILITY MANAGEMENT FOR FINANCIAL INSTITUTIONS

In Chapters 4 through 9, we discuss the major financial institutions. To understand the reasons managers of financial institutions invest in particular types of financial assets and the types of investment strategies they employ, it is necessary to have a general understanding of the asset/liability problem faced. In this section, we provide an overview of asset/liability management.

The nature of the liabilities dictates the investment strategy a financial institution will pursue. For example, depository institutions seek to generate income by the spread between the return that they earn on assets and the cost of their funds. That is, they buy money and sell money. They buy money by borrowing from depositors or other sources of funds. They sell money when they lend it to businesses or individuals. In essence, they are spread businesses. Their objective is to sell money for more than it costs to buy money. The cost of the funds and the return on the funds sold is expressed in terms of an interest rate per unit of time. Consequently, the objective of a depository institution is to earn a positive *spread* between the assets it invests in (what it has sold the money for) and the costs of its funds (what is has purchased the money for).

Life insurance companies—and, to a certain extent, property and casualty insurance companies—are in the spread business. Pension funds are not in the spread business in that they do not raise funds themselves in the market. They seek to cover the cost of pension obligations at a minimum cost that is borne by the sponsor of the pension plan. Investment companies face no explicit costs for the funds they acquire and must satisfy no specific liability obligations; one exception is a particular type of investment company that agrees to repurchase shares at any time.

### Nature of Liabilities

By the liabilities of a financial institution we mean the amount and timing of the cash outlays that must be made to satisfy the contractual terms of the obligations issued. The liabilities of any financial institution can be categorized according to four types as shown in Table 2-1. The categorization in the table assumes that the entity that must be paid the obligation will not cancel the financial institution's obligation prior to any actual or projected payout date.

The descriptions of cash outlays as either known or uncertain are undoubtedly broad. When we refer to a cash outlay as being uncertain, we

| TABLE 2-1 | | |
|---|---|---|
| NATURE OF LIABILITIES OF FINANCIAL INSTITUTIONS | | |
| **Liability Type** | **Amount of Cash Outlay** | **Timing of Cash Outlay** |
| Type I | Known | Known |
| Type II | Known | Uncertain |
| Type III | Uncertain | Known |
| Type IV | Uncertain | Uncertain |

do not mean that it cannot be predicted. There are some liabilities where the "law of large numbers" makes it easier to predict the timing and/or amount of cash outlays. This is the work typically done by actuaries, but of course even actuaries cannot predict natural catastrophes such as floods and earthquakes.

As we describe the various financial institutions in later chapters, keep these risk categories in mind. For now, let's illustrate each one.

*Type-I Liabilities.*   Both the amount and the timing of the liabilities are known with certainty. A liability requiring a financial institution to pay $50,000 six months from now would be an example. For example, depository institutions know the amount that they are committed to pay (principal plus interest) on the maturity date of a fixed-rate deposit, assuming that the depositor does not withdraw funds prior to the maturity date.

Type-I liabilities, however, are not limited to depository institutions. A major product sold by life insurance companies is a *guaranteed investment contract*, popularly referred to as a GIC. The obligation of the life insurance company under this contract is that, for a sum of money (called a premium), it will guarantee an interest rate up to some specified maturity date.[1] For example, suppose a life insurance company for a premium of $10 million issues a five-year GIC agreeing to pay 10% compounded annually. The life insurance company knows that it must pay $16.11 million to the GIC policyholder in five years.[2]

*Type-II Liabilities.*   The amount of cash outlay is known, but the timing of the cash outlay is uncertain. The most obvious example of a Type-II liability is a life insurance policy. There are many types of life insurance policies that we shall discuss in Chapter 7, but the most basic type is that, for an annual premium, a life insurance company agrees to make a specified dollar payment to policy beneficiaries upon the death of the insured.

---

[1] A GIC doesn't seem like a product that we would associate with a life insurance company, because the policyholder doesn't have to die in order for someone to be paid. Yet as we shall see when we discuss life insurance companies in Chapter 7, a major group of insurance company financial products are in the pension benefit area. A GIC is one such product.

[2] This amount is determined as follows: $10,000,000 (1.10)^5$.

***Type-III Liabilities.*** With this type of liability, the timing of the cash outlay is known, but the amount is uncertain. An example is where a financial institution has issued an obligation in which the interest rate adjusts periodically according to some interest rate benchmark. Depository institutions, for example, issue accounts called certificates of deposit, which have a stated maturity. The interest rate paid need not be fixed over the life of the deposit but may fluctuate. If a depository institution issues a three-year floating-rate certificate of deposit that adjusts every three months and the interest rate paid is the three-month Treasury bill rate plus one percentage point, the depository institution knows it has a liability that must be paid off in three years, but the dollar amount of the liability is not known. It will depend on three-month Treasury bill rates over the three years.

***Type-IV Liabilities.*** There are numerous insurance products and pension obligations that present uncertainty as to both the amount and the timing of the cash outlay. Probably the most obvious examples are automobile and home insurance policies issued by property and casualty insurance companies. When, and if, a payment will have to be made to the policyholder is uncertain. Whenever damage is done to an insured asset, the amount of the payment that must be made is uncertain.

As we explain in Chapter 9, sponsors of pension plans can agree to various types of pension obligations to the beneficiaries of the plan. There are plans where retirement benefits depend on the participant's income for a specified number of years before retirement and the total number of years the participant worked. This will affect the amount of the cash outlay. The timing of the cash outlay depends on when the employee elects to retire, and whether the employee remains with the sponsoring plan until retirement. Moreover, both the amount and the timing will depend on how the employee elects to have payments made—over only the employee's life or those of the employee and spouse.

## Liquidity Concerns

Because of uncertainty about the timing and/or the amount of the cash outlays, a financial institution must be prepared to have sufficient cash to satisfy its obligations. Also keep in mind that our discussion of liabilities assumes that the entity that holds the obligation against the financial institution may have the right to change the nature of the obligation, perhaps incurring some penalty. For example, in the case of a certificate of deposit, the depositor may request the withdrawal of funds prior to the maturity date. Typically, the deposit-accepting institution will grant this request, but assess an early withdrawal penalty. In the case of certain types of investment companies, shareholders have the right to redeem their shares at any time.

Some life insurance products have a cash-surrender value. This means that, at specified dates, the policyholder can exchange the policy for a lump sum payment. Typically, the lump sum payment will penalize the policyholder for turning in the policy. There are some life insurance products that have a loan value, which means that the policyholder has the right to borrow against the cash value of the policy.

In addition to uncertainty about the timing and amount of the cash outlays, and the potential for the depositor or policyholder to withdraw cash early or borrow against a policy, a financial institution has to be concerned with possible reduction in cash inflows. In the case of a depository institution, this means the inability to obtain deposits. For insurance companies, it means reduced premiums because of the cancellation of policies. For certain types of investment companies, it means not being able to find new buyers for shares.

### Regulations and Taxation

Numerous regulations and tax considerations influence the investment policies that financial institutions pursue. When we discuss the various financial institutions in later chapters, we will highlight the key regulations and tax factors.

▶ KEY POINTS THAT YOU SHOULD UNDERSTAND BEFORE PROCEEDING:

1. What is meant by a financial institution being in the spread business.
2. The two dimensions of the liabilities of a financial institution: amount of the cash outlay and the timing of the cash outlay.
3. Why a financial institution must be prepared to have sufficient cash to satisfy liabilities.

## FINANCIAL INNOVATION

■ ■ ■ ■

### Categorizations of Financial Innovation

Since the 1960s, there has been a surge in significant financial innovations. Observers of financial markets have categorized these innovations in different ways. Here are just three ways suggested to classify these innovations.

The Economic Council of Canada classifies financial innovations into the following three broad categories:[3]

- *market-broadening instruments*, which increase the liquidity of markets and the availability of funds by attracting new investors and offering new opportunities for borrowers
- *risk-management instruments*, which reallocate financial risks to those who are less averse to them, or who have offsetting exposure and thus are presumably better able to shoulder them

---

[3] *Globalization and Canada's Financial Markets* (Ottawa, Canada: Supply and Services Canada, 1989), p. 32.

■ *arbitraging instruments and processes*, which enable investors and borrowers to take advantage of differences in costs and returns between markets, and which reflect differences in the perception of risks, as well as in information, taxation, and regulations.

Another classification system of financial innovations based on more specific functions has been suggested by the Bank for International Settlements: *price-risk-transferring innovations, credit-risk-transferring instruments, liquidity-generating innovations, credit-generating instruments,* and *equity-generating instruments.*[4] Price-risk-transferring innovations are those that provide market participants with more efficient means for dealing with price or exchange rate risk. Reallocating the risk of default is the function of credit-risk-transferring instruments. Liquidity-generating innovations do three things: (1) they increase the liquidity of the market; (2) they allow borrowers to draw upon new sources of funds; and (3) they allow market participants to circumvent capital constraints imposed by regulations. Instruments to increase the amount of debt funds available to borrowers and to increase the capital base of financial and non-financial institutions are the functions of credit-generating and equity-generating innovations, respectively.

Finally, Professor Stephen Ross suggests two classes of financial innovation: (1) new financial products (financial assets and derivative instruments) better suited to the circumstances of the time (for example, to inflation) and to the markets in which they trade, and (2) strategies that primarily use these financial products.[5]

One of the purposes of this book is to explain these financial innovations. For now, let's look at why financial innovation takes place.

## *Motivation for Financial Innovation*

There are two extreme views of financial innovation.[6] There are some who believe that the major impetus for innovation has been the endeavor to circumvent (or "arbitrage") regulations and find loopholes in tax rules.[7] At the other extreme, some hold that the essence of innovation is the introduction of financial instruments that are more efficient for redistributing risks among market participants.

It would appear that many of the innovations that have passed the test of time and have not disappeared have been innovations that provided more efficient mechanisms for redistributing risk. Other innovations may just represent a more efficient way of doing things. Indeed, if we consider the

---

[4] Bank for International Settlements, *Recent Innovations in International Banking* (Basle: BIS, April 1986).

[5] Stephen A. Ross, "Institutional Markets, Financial Marketing, and Financial Innovation," *Journal of Finance* (July 1989), p. 541.

[6] Ian Cooper, "Financial Innovations: New Market Instruments," *Oxford Review of Economic Policy* (November 1986).

[7] Merton H. Miller, "Financial Innovation: The Last Twenty Years and the Next," *Journal of Financial and Quantitative Analysis* (December 1986), pp. 459–471.

ultimate causes of financial innovation,[8] the following emerge as the most important:

1. Increased volatility of interest rates, inflation, equity prices, and exchange rates.
2. Advances in computer and telecommunication technologies.
3. Greater sophistication and educational training among professional market participants.
4. Financial intermediary competition.
5. Incentives to get around existing regulation and tax laws.
6. Changing global patterns of financial wealth.

With increased volatility comes the need for certain market participants to protect themselves against unfavorable consequences. This means new or more efficient ways of risk-sharing in the financial market are needed. Many of the financial products require the use of computers to create and monitor them. To implement trading strategies using these financial products also requires computers, as well as telecommunication networks. Without advances in computer and telecommunication technologies, some innovations would not have been possible. Although financial products and trading strategies created by some market participants may be too complex for other market participants to use, the level of market sophistication, particularly in terms of mathematical understanding, has risen, permitting the acceptance of some complex products and trading strategies.

As you read the chapters on the various sectors of the financial markets that we review in this book, be sure you understand the factors behind any innovations in that market.

▶ KEY POINTS THAT YOU SHOULD UNDERSTAND BEFORE PROCEEDING:

1. The extent of the innovation in many financial markets, securities, and institutions over the last few decades.
2. The causes of innovation, such as the high level of volatility in prices and interest rates, the arrival of technology, the new intensity of competition, and the globalization of markets and institutions.

## ASSET SECURITIZATION AS A FINANCIAL INNOVATION

■ ■ ■ ■

A key financial innovation in the 1980s that will dramatically influence the role of financial intermediaries is the phenomenon of *asset securitization*. The process involves the collection or pooling of loans and the sale of securities backed by those loans. This system is radically different from the traditional system for financing the acquisition of assets, which called for one financial intermediary,

---

[8] Cooper, "Financial Innovations," *op. cit.* See Table 9. We add inflation to the first category described.

such as a depository institution or insurance company, to: (1) originate a loan; (2) retain the loan in its portfolio of assets, thereby accepting the credit risk associated with the loan; (3) service the loan—collect payments and provide tax or other information to the borrower; and (4) obtain funds from the public with which to finance its assets (except for the small amount representing the institution's equity).

Asset securitization means that more than one institution may be involved in lending capital. Consider loans for the purchase of automobiles. A lending scenario can look like this: (1) a commercial bank can originate automobile loans; (2) the commercial bank can issue securities backed by these loans; (3) the commercial bank can obtain credit risk insurance for the pool of loans from a private insurance company; (4) the commercial bank can sell the right to service the loans to another company that specializes in the serving of loans; and (5) the commercial bank can use the services of a securities firm to distribute the securities to individuals and institutional investors.

Besides the original lending bank, an insurance company, another institution that services loans, a securities firm, an individual, and other institutional investors participate. The commercial bank in our example does not have to absorb the credit risk, service the loan, or provide the funding. While we use automobile loans as an example, this system can be applied to mortgage loans, home equity loans, boat loans, credit card loans, credit sales by finance companies and manufacturing firms, senior bank loans, and lease receivables. By far the largest part of the securitized assets market is the mortgage-backed securities market, where the assets collateralizing the securities are mortgage loans. The first public offering of an asset-backed security not backed by mortgage loans was in March 1985 by Sperry Lease Finance Corporation (now Unisys).

Asset securitization has various benefits for issuers, borrowers, and investors as well as far-ranging implications for the U.S. financial system.

### Benefits to Issuers

The most commonly cited benefits of securitization are (1) obtaining a lower cost of funds; (2) using capital more efficiently; (3) managing rapid portfolio growth; (4) enhancing financial performance; and (5) diversifying funding sources.[9]

***Obtaining a Lower Cost of Funds.*** Segregating assets and using them as collateral for a security offering lets lower funding costs be obtained. The cost of funding for a financial intermediary depends on its credit rating. The lower the credit rating, the higher the cost of funding. By using loans as collateral and properly structuring a security, a financial intermediary can obtain a credit

---

[9] William Haley, "Securitizing Automobile Receivables," Chapter 3 in Philip L. Zweig (ed.), *The Asset Securitization Handbook* (Homewood, IL: Dow Jones-Irwin, 1989), p. 75.

rating on the security that is higher than its own credit rating. This will result in a lower cost of funds.

***More Efficient Use of Capital.*** For financial intermediaries that must meet capital guideline requirements, the sale of assets can free up capital. This will become clear when we discuss capital requirements for depository institutions in Chapter 4. Manufacturing corporations or their captive finance companies gain through securitization the opportunity to obtain greater leverage than the credit rating companies might judge acceptable otherwise.

Shifting the credit risk from the originator of the loan to another party reduces the issuer's return together with its risk. At the same time, the issuer may keep or sell the rights to service the loans. Earnings from the business thus come from fee income rather than interest rate spread income.

***Managing Rapid Portfolio Growth.*** As the business of a financial or non-financial entity grows, growth potential will be limited by capital constraints. Selling assets through securitization provides a means for quickly raising capital while keeping the asset, and hence the debt, off the balance sheet, avoiding capital requirements.

***Enhanced Financial Performance.*** When loans are sold via securitization at a yield lower than the interest rate on the loan, the originator realizes the spread. This spread partially reflects the fee for servicing the loans and partially reflects conversion of an illiquid loan into a more liquid security backed by loans and with credit enhancements. This source of spread will of course tend to be eroded by competition, which will tend to reallocate the abnormal spread between final borrowers and final lenders.

***Diversification of Sources.*** Investors who ordinarily could not make mortgage loans, consumer loans, and/or commercial loans can invest in these securities. This provides more sources of capital for both financial and non-financial entities.

## Benefits to Investors

Securitization converts illiquid loans into securities with greater liquidity and reduced credit risk. Credit risk is reduced because (1) it is backed by a diversified pool of loans, and (2) there is credit enhancement. By credit enhancement it is meant a financial device to reduce the credit risk associated with the loans. This permits investors to broaden their universe of investment opportunities. It also tends to improve returns through the reduction of the cost of intermediation.

### Benefits to Borrowers

Because a financial or non-financial entity can securitize a loan it originates, or sell it to some entity that will securitize it, the lender now has a more liquid asset that it can sell if capital is needed. This should reduce the spread between lending rates and safe assets such as Treasury securities. We have seen this in the mortgage market and, to some extent, in the automobile loan market. As the market matures, competition among originators should produce lower lending rate spreads in other loan markets.

### Implications of Securitization for Financial Markets

Securitization has major implications for financial markets as well as the structure of financial intermediaries. Securitization eventually may replace the traditional system of indirect financing. To understand why, let's briefly review the role of financial intermediaries that we discussed earlier in this chapter.

Financial intermediaries act as conduits in bringing savers and borrowers together. They perform this function in several ways. First, certain financial intermediaries are in a better position than individual investors to assess credit risk. After evaluating credit risk, they may agree to grant a loan and hold the loan as an investment. Furthermore, being in a position to distribute their assets over many different borrowers and industries, they achieve risk reduction through diversification. The returns to investors are further made safe by government-guaranteed liabilities (for example, federal guarantee of deposits for depository institutions that we will explain in Chapter 4).

Second, the maturities of loans sought by borrowers may be different from those that investors want. For example, as we shall see in Chapter 4, depository institutions acquire short-term funds and grant loans with longer maturities. This satisfies the objective of investors who may want shorter-term investments and borrowers who want longer-term funds; that is, the institution provides maturity intermediation—although at their risk. Finally, the amount of funds sought by borrowers is typically greater than any one individual investor would be willing to lend. Financial intermediaries make large-denomination loans to borrowers and offer investors investments with smaller denominations. That is, they provide denomination intermediation, transforming very large assets into quite divisible ones.

Securitization provides direct financing between borrowers and investors, short-circuiting the traditional intermediaries. Pooling of assets reinforced by private credit enhancement reduces credit risk to more acceptable levels for investors. Furthermore, redirecting cash flows from the pool of loans on a prioritized basis provides varying maturities acceptable to a wide range of investors. Thus, securitization serves a role similar to maturity intermediation while shifting its risk to the lenders. The availability of securities with smaller denominations than the underlying loans accomplishes denomination intermediation. All of this happens without the need for any government guarantees (although such guarantees may enhance the value of securitized instruments).

The success of securitization indicates that it is a more efficient method for linking borrowers and investors than traditional financing through intermediaries. The true innovations in this market are not really the securities themselves but (1) reduction of risk through pooling of assets and private credit enhancement, and (2) repackaging of the cash flows from assets in a way that relieves the intermediary of reliance on its own assets to finance the credit—that is, that permits off-balance sheet financing.[10]

The process of asset securitization is not unique to the U.S. financial system. The practice is spreading to other countries, fostered by the capital risk guidelines for commercial banks discussed in Chapter 4. For example, securitization of personal loans occurred in France in 1990. The first public asset-backed deal in Canada, issued in May 1991, was for $350 million Canadian backed by automobile loans purchased from Chrysler Credit Canada.

▶ KEY POINTS THAT YOU SHOULD UNDERSTAND BEFORE PROCEEDING:

1. The meaning of securitization and the basic structure of the process of securitizing an asset.
2. How securitizing an asset benefits the issuers through reducing the costs of funding and allowing management of faster growth in portfolios, among other things.
3. How securitizing an asset helps investors, through increasing the opportunities for investment.
4. How securitizing an asset helps borrowers, by raising the available capital and reducing its costs.
5. How the increase in securitization affects financial markets.

SUMMARY

Financial institutions provide various types of financial services. A special group of financial institutions are called financial intermediaries. These entities obtain funds by issuing claims to market participants and use these funds to purchase financial assets. Intermediaries transform funds they acquire into assets that are more attractive to the public. By doing so, financial intermediaries do one or more of the following: (1) provide maturity intermediation; (2) provide risk reduction via diversification at

[10] This is not an entirely new approach, as it underlies such instruments as bankers acceptances (discussed in Chapter 22), mortgage bonds (popular in many foreign countries), and to some extent letters of credit. The current wave of applications, however, goes well beyond past practice in the magnitude and nature of innovative approaches, and it is already spreading to other countries.

lower cost; (3) reduce the cost of contracting and information processing; or (4) provide a payments mechanism.

The nature of their liabilities, as well as regulatory and tax considerations, determines the investment strategy pursued by all financial institutions. The liabilities of all financial institutions will generally fall into one of the four types shown in Table 2-1.

Financial innovation has increased dramatically since the 1960s, particularly in the late 1970s. While financial innovation can be the result of arbitrary regulations and tax rules, innovations that persist after regulations or tax rules have been changed to prevent exploitation are frequently those that have provided a more efficient means for redistributing risk.

Securitization of assets—that is, pooling loans and selling securities backed by the pool of loans—benefits issuers, investors, and borrowers alike. Securitization may be the wave of the future, as it appears to be a more efficient mechanism for bringing borrowers and investors together than traditional financing through financial intermediaries.

## GLOSSARY

**Arbitrage:** The act of taking advantage of a difference in price and/or return of an asset that is traded in more than one market.

**Asset/liability management:** Term for a financial institution's efforts to manage its assets relative to the nature of its liabilities.

**Asset securitization:** The process by which a financial institution pools loans and sells securities backed by those loans.

**Certificate of deposit (or CD):** An interest-earning account, with a specific maturity, at a depository institution.

**Commercial bank:** A financial institution that accepts deposits and may use the proceeds of those deposits to make loans.

**Cost of contracting:** The costs of analyzing and arranging a contract for the performance of certain tasks.

**Debit card:** A payment mechanism that allows for payment of a purchase by an immediate charge against the purchaser's account at the financial institution that sponsors the card.

**Denomination:** The size, in units of money, of a loan or debt security.

**Depository institutions:** Financial institutions that acquire the bulk of their funds by offering their liabilities to the public in the form of deposits.

**Direct investments:** The investments made by financial intermediaries; these assets can be loans or securities.

**Diversification:** Allocating wealth across a significant number of different assets.

**Exchange rate:** The value of one unit of one country's currency in terms of another country's currency.

**Financial institution:** A financial enterprise that may perform one of several financial services such as accepting deposits, brokering securities, managing funds, or underwriting securities.

**Financial intermediary:** Financial enterprise that transforms financial assets, acquired through the market, into a different and more widely preferable type of asset, which becomes the liability of the intermediary.

**Guaranteed investment contract (or GIC):** A product sold by a life insurance company, which obliges the company to guarantee an interest rate, on a specific amount of investment, up to some specified maturity date.

**Indirect investment:** An investment an investor has by holding a claim on a financial intermediary that has made direct investments.

**Investment company:** A financial institution that pools funds and purchases assets on behalf of the investors.

**Liability:** An obligatory payment to a supplier of a good, a service, or funds.

**Maturity intermediation:** The function of a financial intermediary by which it transforms a longer-term asset into a shorter-term one when it gives the borrower a loan for a particular length of time and the investor/depositor a financial asset for a possibly different desired investment horizon.

**Off-balance sheet financing:** Borrowings obtained in which debt does not appear on balance sheet.

**Payment mechanism:** The financial arrangement by which the buyer of a commodity pays the seller with some form of money.

**Portfolio:** A group of financial assets or securities.

**Risk-transfer:** The act of hedging a financial position so as to move some risk to another party.

1. Why is the holding of a claim on a financial intermediary by an investor considered an indirect investment in another entity?

2. The Insightful Management Company sells financial advice to investors. This is the only service provided by the company. Is this company a financial intermediary? Explain why.

3. Explain how a financial intermediary reduces the cost of transacting and information processing.

4. "All financial intermediaries provide the same economic functions. Therefore, the same investment strategy should be used in the management of all financial intermediaries." Indicate whether you agree or disagree with this statement.

5. A bank issues an obligation to depositors in which it agrees to pay 8% guaranteed for one year. With the funds it obtains, the bank can invest in a wide range of financial assets. What is the risk if the bank uses the funds to invest in common stock?

6. Each year, millions of American investors poured billions of dollars into investment companies which use those dollars to buy the common stock of other companies. What did the investment companies offer investors who preferred to invest in the investment companies rather than buying the common stock of these other companies directly?

7. Why does increased volatility in financial markets with respect to the price of financial assets, interest rates, and exchange rates foster financial innovation?

8. In a 1989 study entitled "Globalization and Canada's Financial Markets," a research report prepared for the Economic Council of Canada, the following was reported:

   *An important feature of the increasing significance of some aspects of financial activity is the greater use of financial markets and instruments that intermediate funds directly—a process called "market intermediation," which involves the issuance of, and trading in, securities such as bonds or stocks—as opposed to "financial intermediation," in which the financial institution raises funds by issuing a claim on itself and provides funds in the form of loans.*

   a. Why is asset securitization an example of "market intermediation"?

   b. Identify a benefit from securitization that the capital markets get from securitization. Hint: Until recently, most investors could not cheaply or easily take advantage of good returns from making car loans.

9. In classifying financial innovations, the Bank for International Settlements refers to "liquidity-generating instruments." Two characteristics of liquidity-generating instruments are that they increase the liquidity of the market and they allow borrowers to draw upon new sources of funds. Explain why asset securitization results in liquidity-generating instruments.

# CHAPTER THREE

# The Role
# Of The Government
# In Financial Markets

*After reading this chapter you will understand:*

- the typical justification for governmental regulation of markets.
- the different ways that governments regulate markets, including disclosure regulation, financial activity regulation, financial institution regulation, regulation of foreign firm participation, and regulation of the monetary system.
- the debate about the usefulness of disclosure regulation.
- the role of self-regulatory organizations.
- the various ways that these forms of regulation are implemented in the United States, Japan, Germany, and the United Kingdom.
- the major regulatory agencies in the U.S., Japan, Germany, and the United Kingdom.
- the extent of regulatory reform in the 1980s.
- the causes of reform, including financial crisis, financial innovation, and globalization.

The financial markets play a prominent role in many economies, and governments around the world have long deemed it necessary to regulate certain aspects of these markets. In their regulatory capacities, governments have greatly influenced the development and evolution of financial markets and institutions. It is important to realize that governments, markets, and institutions tend to behave interactively and to affect one another's actions in certain ways. Thus, it is not surprising to find that a market's reactions to regulations often prompt a new response by the government, which can cause the institutions participating in a market to change their behavior further, and so on. A sense of how the government can affect a market and its participants is important to an understanding of the numerous markets and securities to be described in the chapters to come. For that reason, we talk about the regulatory function at this early stage.

Because of differences in culture and history, different countries regulate financial markets and financial institutions in varying ways, emphasizing some forms of regulation more than others. In this chapter, we will discuss regulation in the U.S. and show how regulation in three important financial systems (Japan, Germany, and the United Kingdom) compares with the U.S. approach to regulation. Our purpose is not to provide a detailed account of regulatory structures and rules in any country. Rather, we present a broad view of the goals and types of regulation that governments currently place on their financial systems.

## PURPOSES AND FORMS OF REGULATION

### *Justification for Regulation*

The standard explanation or justification for governmental regulation of a market is that the market, left to itself, will not produce its particular goods or services in an efficient manner and at the lowest possible cost. Of course, efficiency and low-cost production are hallmarks of a perfectly competitive market. Thus, a market unable to produce efficiently must be one that is not competitive at the time, and that will not gain that status by itself in the foreseeable future. Of course, it is also possible that governments may regulate markets that are viewed as competitive currently but unable to sustain competition, and thus low-cost production, over the long run. A version of this justification for regulation is that the government controls a feature of the economy that the market mechanisms of competition and pricing could not manage without help. A short-hand expression economists use to describe the reasons for regulation is "market failure." A market is said to fail if it cannot, by itself, maintain all the requirements for a competitive situation.

Governments in most developed economies have created elaborate systems of regulation for financial markets, in part because the markets themselves are complex and in part because financial markets are so important to the general economies in which they operate. The numerous rules and regulations are designed to serve several purposes, which fall into the following categories:

1. To prevent issuers of securities from defrauding investors by concealing relevant information.
2. To promote competition and fairness in the trading of financial securities.
3. To promote the stability of financial institutions.
4. To restrict the activities of foreign concerns in domestic markets and institutions.
5. To control the level of economic activity.

Corresponding to each of these categories is an important form of regulation. We discuss each form in turn and later explore how these forms of regulations affect the four major financial systems of the world.

## An Introduction to Forms of Regulation

*Disclosure regulation* is the form of regulation that requires issuers of securities to make public a large amount of financial information to actual and potential investors. The standard justification for disclosure rules is that the managers of the issuing firm have more information about the financial health and future of the firm than investors who own or are considering the purchase of the firm's securities. The cause of market failure here, if indeed it occurs, is commonly described as "asymmetric information," which means investors and managers have uneven access to or uneven possession of information. This is referred to as the "agency problem," in the sense that the firm's managers, who act as agents for investors, may act in their own interests to the disadvantage of the investors. The advocates of disclosure rules say that, in the absence of the rules, the investors' comparatively limited knowledge about the firm would allow the agents to engage in such practices.

It is interesting to note that several prominent economists deny the need and justification for disclosure rules. Led by George Benston, they argue that the securities market would, without governmental assistance, get all the information necessary for a fair pricing of new as well as existing securities. In this view, the rules supposedly extracting key data from agent-managers are redundant.[1] One way to look at this argument is to ask what investors would do if a firm trying to sell new shares did not provide all the data investors would want. In that case, investors either would refuse to buy that firm's securities, giving them a zero value, or would discount or underprice the securities. Thus, a firm concealing important information would pay a penalty in the form of reduced proceeds from sale of the new securities. The prospect of this penalty is potentially as much incentive to disclose as the rules of a governmental agency.

*Financial activity regulation* consists of rules about traders of securities and trading on financial markets. A prime example of this form of regulation is the

[1] George J. Benston, "Required Disclosure and the Stock Market: An Evaluation of the Securities Exchange Act of 1934," *American Economic Review* (March 1973), pp. 132-155.

set of rules against trading by insiders who are corporate officers and others in positions to know more about a firm's prospects than the general investing public. Insider trading is another problem posed by asymmetric information, which is of course inconsistent with a competitive market. A second example of this type of regulation would be rules regarding the structure and operations of exchanges where securities are traded. The argument supporting these rules rests on the possibility that members of exchanges may be able, under certain circumstances, to collude and defraud the general investing public.

*Regulation of financial institutions* is that form of governmental monitoring that restricts these institutions' activities in the vital areas of lending, borrowing, and funding. The justification for this form of government regulation is that these financial firms have a special role to play in a modern economy. Financial institutions help households and firms to save; they also facilitate the complex payments among many elements of the economy; and in the case of commercial banks they serve as conduits for the government's monetary policy. Thus, it is often argued that the failure of these financial institutions would disturb the economy in a severe way.

*Regulation of foreign participants* is that form of governmental activity that limits the roles foreign firms can have in domestic markets and their ownership or control of financial institutions.

Authorities use *banking and monetary regulation* to try to control changes in a country's money supply, which is thought to control the level of economic activity. Later chapters will provide a detailed review of this type of governmental regulation. We mention it here briefly in order to provide a comprehensive picture of the government's role in modern financial systems.

▶ KEY POINTS THAT YOU SHOULD UNDERSTAND BEFORE PROCEEDING:

1. The standard explanation for governmental regulation of markets for goods and services.
2. What disclosure is, and the meaning of disclosure regulation.
3. What the term "asymmetric information" means.
4. The reasons why a government might regulate financial activity by certain persons and the behavior of certain financial institutions.

## REGULATION IN THE UNITED STATES

■ ■ ■ ■

The regulatory structure in the United States is largely the result of financial crises that have occurred at various times. Most regulations are the products of the stock market crash of 1929 and the Great Depression in the 1930s. Some of the regulations may make little economic sense in the current financial market, but they can be traced back to some abuse that legislators encountered, or thought they encountered, at one time. Further, with the exception of financial institution regulation, the three other forms of regulation are most often a function of the federal government, with state governments playing a secondary role. For that reason, our discussion of regulation in the U.S. concentrates on the federal government and its agencies. When we discuss certain financial institutions in the U.S., we briefly examine the role of state governments.

The U.S. is firmly committed to disclosure regulation. These regulations are contained in two important federal legislations: the Securities Act of 1933 (or the "Securities Act") and the Securities Exchange Act of 1934 (or the "Exchange Act"). The acts have been amended periodically. The Securities Act deals primarily with the distribution of *new* securities and has two objectives. First it requires that investors be given adequate and accurate disclosure concerning the securities distributed to the public.[2] Second, it prohibits fraudulent acts and practices, misrepresentations, and deceit in the sale of securities. While the Exchange Act covers many regulatory issues, one provision deals with the periodic disclosure provisions designed to provide current material information about publicly traded securities. Thus, while the Securities Act deals with the disclosure requirements for securities when they are first issued, the Exchange Act deals with the periodic disclosure requirements for seasoned securities. The Securities and Exchange Commission (SEC) is empowered with the responsibility for administering the two acts. The SEC was created by the Exchange Act.

None of the disclosure requirements as set forth in the two acts or the activities of the SEC constitute a guarantee, a certification, or an approval of the securities being issued. Moreover, the government's rules do not represent an attempt to prevent the issuance of risky securities. Rather, the government's (and the SEC's) sole motivation in this regard is to supply diligent and intelligent investors with the information needed for a fair evaluation of the securities. This approach to regulation relies heavily upon the "efficient market hypothesis," which broadly posits that publicly available, relevant information about the issuers will lead to a correct pricing of freely traded securities in properly functioning markets.[3] (Chapter 15 will discuss efficient markets in more detail.)

Financial activity regulation is also widely implemented in the U.S. The SEC has the duty of carefully monitoring the trades that corporate officers, directors, or major stockholders ("insiders") make in the securities of their firms. The provisions are set forth in the Exchange Act. To keep the public abreast of these situations, the SEC publishes insiders' trades in its monthly *Official Summary of Securities Transactions and Holdings*.

The organized exchanges, such as the New York Stock Exchange and the American Stock Exchange, also play a role in regulation by setting conditions for listing traded stocks and bonds and by monitoring the relationships of brokers with the public. In this regard, the National Association of Securities Dealers (the NASD) is an important contributor to the regulation of trading. The NASD is a self-regulatory organization (or SRO) whose

---

[2] Nancy H. Wojtas, "Regulation of the Securities Markets: Securities and Exchange Commission," Chapter 7 in Frank J. Fabozzi and Frank G. Zarb (eds.), *Handbook of Financial Markets* (Homewood, IL: Dow Jones-Irwin, 1986), pp. 116–118.

[3] Charles J. Johnson, Jr., *Corporate Finance and the Securities Laws* (Englewood Cliffs, New Jersey: Prentice Hall Law & Business, 1991), p. 43.

members must meet certain standards of conduct in issuing securities and selling them to the public. Other U.S. financial markets have their own SROs, too.

Two agencies share responsibility for the federal regulation of trading in options and futures, which are derivative securities described in detail in Chapters 25 through 30. The Commodity Futures Trading Commission (or CFTC) licenses futures exchanges and monitors trading in them, and it authorizes firms to operate the exchanges and provide services to the public. The CFTC also approves individual futures contracts, which must serve the "economic purpose" of being useful for hedging. Approval is not endorsement of a contract, and investors trade these securities at their own risk. The National Futures Association (NFA) is an SRO which has, since the early 1980s, assisted the CFTC in monitoring trading, preventing fraud, and taking disciplinary action when appropriate. The SEC has responsibility for oversight of most options markets, and it performs many of the functions the CFTC performs with futures markets. The chief SROs of the options markets are the NASD and the various exchanges where options are traded.

The U.S. government has imposed an extensive array of regulations on financial institutions. Although pressure to change the system has been building, and significant change may occur soon, most of these regulations restrict what financial institutions do in the markets and how those institutions manage their liabilities and assets. A major example of these restrictions has been governmental opposition to the creation of national banks with branches in all states and regions. In fact, the U.S. currently has a large and cumbersome set of state and federal regulations that restrict the thousands of comparatively small banks to specific geographical units. The Glass-Steagall Act is another regulation on banks, which limits the freedom of commercial banks in securities markets. Recent troubles in the financial services area, however, highlight the need for institutions to become more competitive and diversified, and the Glass-Steagall wall between the banks and the securities industry is eroding rapidly in the early 1990s.

The Federal Reserve System, an independent agency responsible for the nation's money and banking system, places numerous restrictions on depository institutions. For example, the Fed sets minimum requirements for the amount of equity (or shareholder contributions) that banks must have relative to their assets. The current rules are based on a 1988 agreement (called the Basle Agreement) among the major industrialized countries. In the past, the Fed established a maximum level of interest rates commercial banks could pay, but happily the federal government has discontinued such unproductive rule-making. Another governmental agency, the Office of Thrift Supervision (OTS), monitors the type and amount of loans that savings and loan associations make. (As late as the 1970s, a patchwork of regulatory bodies—the Federal Home Loan Bank Board and the Federal Savings and Loan Insurance Corporation, for example—controlled much S&L activity, but many of their elements are now folded into the structure of the OTS.) More discussion of the regulation of asset and liability management in banks and S&Ls appears in Chapter 4. Other financial institutions, such as insurance companies and pension funds, also must work within complex regulatory systems that are described in Chapters 7 and 9, respectively.

U.S. regulations permit foreign-owned banks to function generally under the same complicated rules that apply to U.S. domestic banks. Several hundred offices of foreign banks operate now in the United States.

Like many countries, the U.S. regulates participation by foreign firms in its domestic financial securities markets. As have most of these countries, however, the United States has been extensively reviewing and changing its policies regarding foreign firms' activities in the financial markets. Some of the changes in the last decade have been particularly worthy of note. In 1984, the federal government abolished the withholding tax on interest payments to nonresident holders of bonds issued by U.S. firms and governmental units. In 1986, the SEC decided to allow certain foreign firms that meet their home country regulations to be active in U.S. markets without having to prove compliance with U.S. rules. In 1987, U.S. markets obtained permission to trade futures based on foreign government bonds, and the SEC decided to allow foreign firms to trade futures based on these bonds. In that same year, the SEC began to permit institutional investors to purchase unregistered shares of foreign firms.

Through the Federal Reserve System, the government controls the money supply. Commercial banks and other depository institutions participate in that process by following rules which the Fed makes.

▶ KEY POINTS THAT YOU SHOULD UNDERSTAND BEFORE PROCEEDING:

1. The main federal acts that set forth the requirements for disclosures: the Securities Act and the Exchange Act.
2. The role of a self-regulatory organization in a market.
3. The scope and implementation of the regulation of financial institutions.
4. The ways in which the U.S. regulates foreign firms and investors.

## REGULATION IN JAPAN

The Japanese Ministry of Finance (MOF) is responsible for the regulation of securities markets in Japan. Statutes and laws give the MOF vast direct power for this purpose. Further, the MOF has substantial indirect power, including its duty to provide "administrative guidance" to financial institutions of all kinds and its authority to audit all securities houses that are members of the Tokyo Stock Exchange.

The Japanese system employs disclosure as a form of regulation, somewhat as the U.S. government does. Through its Securities Bureau, which is empowered by the Securities and Exchange Law and is one of seven bureaus, the MOF seeks to keep securities markets fair and competitive. To this end, the Securities Bureau tries to ensure that investors receive a steady flow of information about issuers.[4]

The Japanese approach differs from the U.S. approach in several notable respects. First, the MOF has a long-standing policy of directing funding in the bond markets to only a small group of large and efficient firms in an industry.[5] Second, the system does discourage certain issuers at certain times from issuing debt securities. The regulating body is the Bond Flotation Committee, a group consisting of over 40 institutions (including large banks and securities firms). Three of the committee's functions are (1) to establish eligibility standards for companies wishing to issue bonds; (2) to monitor the terms and amounts of new issues; and (3) to control the flow of new issues in order to avoid flooding the market.

Financial activity regulation is widely practiced in Japan. By law, the MOF's Securities Bureau supervises and licenses securities companies, and only such firms can deal in the full array of securities. Through its Securities Bureau and the Bank of Japan (BOJ), the MOF punishes insider trading and supervises the activities of dealers in the financial markets.

As in the United States, the Japanese government imposes numerous restrictions on the activities of its financial institutions. Unlike the United States, Japan allows a few large national banks to do business in every part of the country. Although some changes may occur in the near future, Japanese rules currently prohibit commercial banks from full participation in the investment banking or underwriting of securities(that is, the issuance of new securities). However, Japanese banks can invest substantial sums in the common stock of publicly traded firms, while current U.S. law prohibits U.S. banks from doing the same. Interestingly, the Japanese government, for many years, fixed the maximum levels of interest rates on bank deposits. In 1987, it abandoned or modified most of the regulations of that type.

In recent years, Japan has moderated or discontinued many restrictions against participation in financial securities markets by foreign firms and financial institutions.[6] Some foreign banks are now permitted to participate in trust banking, which focuses on investment management and savings. Securities subsidiaries of foreign financial institutions have opened branches, and through the branches, these institutions have become active in some aspects of underwriting. Foreign firms now own seats on the Tokyo Stock Exchange (TSE), and shares of stock of foreign companies are listed there. While numerous official and unwritten rules may remain, it is clear that Japan has achieved meaningful gains in the internationalization and freedom of its financial markets.

---

[4] Noburu Honjo and Lisa J. Turbessi, "Participants in the Japanese Bond Market," Chapter 3 in Frank J. Fabozzi (ed.), *The Japanese Bond Markets* (Chicago: Probus Publishing Company, 1990), p. 56.

[5] Edward William Karp and Akira Koike, "The Japanese Corporate Bond Market," Chapter 11 in *ibid.*, p. 366.

[6] Much of this material is drawn from Issen Sato and E.M. Karnosky, "Historical Development of The Japanese Bond Market," Chapter 2 in Frank J. Fabozzi (ed.), *ibid.*

The MOF, with the assistance of the Bank of Japan, which functions much as the Fed does in the United States, controls the money supply and seeks to influence short-term interest rates. The way the BOJ implements its policy is described in Chapters 5 and 6.

▶ KEY POINTS THAT YOU SHOULD UNDERSTAND BEFORE PROCEEDING:

1. The extensive role of the Japanese Ministry of Finance.
2. How Japanese regulation differs from U.S. regulation.
3. The scope of Japanese regulation of financial institutions, especially commercial banks.
4. Some ways in which Japan has begun to relax its regulation of foreign participants in its markets.
5. The role of the Bank of Japan.

## REGULATION IN GERMANY

The German system uses disclosure regulation to some extent in connection with the issuance of equities. Issuing companies must make public salient facts about the firm in the form of a prospectus. Officials in charge of listing on the exchange where the stock is to be traded must evaluate and approve the prospectus. Further, the firm must make annual and semi-annual reports to investors on its operations and finances.[7] Some officials in the U.S. government insist that, given the vagueness of German accounting rules, the requirements to disclose are actually weak and effectively permit German firms to deceive investors.[8] Whatever the merit of that charge, it does indicate that disclosure may not mean the same thing in the two countries.

The bond market has an interesting structure. A privately owned firm (other than a bank) that wishes to issue a bond must obtain approval of its financial standing and of the bond's collateral. The agency that must give approval is the central bank, or "Bundesbank," which is a largely autonomous unit of the federal government. This cumbersome regulation has led many German firms to rely on banks for debt capital or to issue bonds in the unregulated Eurobond market, with the result that the bond market in Germany is not strong or active.[9]

There are eight German stock exchanges, and the state government where an exchange is located is an important regulator of the exchange. In a manner reminiscent of the American SROs, the government gets assistance from the exchange's board of governors, which is elected by representatives

---

[7] O.W. Breycha, "German Equity Markets," in Jess Lederman and Keith K.H. Parks (editors), *The Global Equity Markets* (Chicago: Probus Publishing Company, 1991), p. 132.

[8] Gregg A. Jarrell, "SEC Crimps Big Board's Future," *Wall Street Journal*, June 19, 1992, p. A15.

[9] Credit Suisse First Boston, *The Deutsche Mark Bond Markets* (Chicago: Probus Publishing Company, 1991), pp. 158-159.

of firms (especially banks) belonging to the exchange. The board authorizes memberships and the securities to be traded and enforces the rules of the exchange.[10] Although Germany has no law against insider trading at this time, industry associations forbid it, and they ensure that insiders sign contractual and binding agreements about not engaging in such trades. Associations monitor these agreements and take disciplinary action if insiders do not adhere to them. In the late 1980s, the government authorized the creation of a futures and options market, which is called the *"Deutsche TerminBörse,"* and enhanced the legal status of those derivative contracts.

German regulation of financial institutions is significantly less stringent than U.S. law and practice. Most German banks are "universal banks," which take part in all types of financial activity, including commercial banking operations and such lines of securities business as underwriting, trading, and investing in shares. For this reason, banks are the largest investors in Germany, and the German secondary markets for bonds and stocks tend to be interbank markets (that is, trading between banks).

Nevertheless, the German government, through the powerful Bundesbank, has a regulatory role with respect to the safety of many of the banks' activities. For that reason, the government endorsed and has begun to implement the Basle Agreement, which requires domestic banks to meet certain standards of capital adequacy.

Germany's regulation of financial activities by foreign firms and investors was quite strict and complex until fairly recently. In the 1980s, foreign firms were given greater freedom to sell their securities in Germany, and more than one-third of the shares listed on the main stock market (in Frankfurt) are foreign stocks. The German government bond market became, because of governmental decisions in 1985, one of the most liberal. The Bundesbank granted permission to domestic subsidiaries of foreign firms to participate fully in some important types of investment banking. In 1988, foreign investors gained permission to buy an important type of federal government bond, called a "Bundes bond" or "Bund" in international financial circles.

The Bundesbank controls the money supply and the availability of credit. Its primary goal is to safeguard the value of the German currency or (which is the same thing) to keep price inflation as close to zero as possible. See Chapters 5 and 6 for more information about the Bundesbank and monetary policy.

▶ KEY POINTS THAT YOU SHOULD UNDERSTAND BEFORE PROCEEDING:

1. The question about Germany's use of disclosure regulation.
2. The scope of German regulation of commercial banks and the meaning of the term "universal banks."
3. The reasons for the small size of the German bond market.

---

[10] O.W. Breycha, *op. cit.*, p. 120.

4.   Some ways in which Germany has begun to relax its regulation of foreign participants in its markets.

5.   The role of the Bundesbank.

## REGULATION IN THE UNITED KINGDOM

In the "Big Bang" of the mid-1980s, which was a sweeping liberalization and restructuring of the securities industry, the British government made a firm commitment to disclosure as a major element in its regulation of securities markets. An important part of that restructuring was the Financial Services Act of 1986.[11] This law imposes a "general duty of disclosure" and applies to any foreign or domestic firm that issues new debt or equity securities, whether or not the securities are to be listed on the London International Stock Exchange. (Listed securities tend to be actively traded issues of well-known firms, while unlisted securities are generally those of new and smaller companies.) The firm must provide investors with an extensive amount of information, including the firm's financial history as well as the method by which the new security is to be marketed to the public. The law mandates penalties for the officers of any firm that either misleads investors or does not take reasonable care to assure the accuracy of its claims. As long as the firm has outstanding issues, it is responsible for disclosing relevant information to the public.

The Financial Services Act assigns responsibility for regulating financial activity to the Department of Trade and Industry (DTI). The DTI delegates much of the task to the Securities and Investment Board (SIB), which is similar in many ways to the U.S. Securities and Exchange Commission. The SIB is the primary agency that authorizes institutions to conduct investment business and monitors their dealings with the public and the adequacy of their funding. In this effort, the SIB gets active support from The Securities Association, which is a powerful self-regulatory organization (or SRO) allied with the Stock Exchange. These various governmental and professional bodies also have responsibility for preventing or punishing "insider trading," which was not well defined in a legal sense, and occurred rather frequently until the Company Securities Act of 1985.

The Bank of England regulates most banking institutions in a way that is similar to the actions of the Federal Reserve Bank in the U.S. In addition to managing the money supply, the Bank of England supervises and sets rules for the capital adequacy of banks, as set forth in the Basle Agreement. Until the "Big Bang" of 1986, banks were not permitted to engage in many activities involving the sale of securities. Since then, however, banks have been allowed to own subsidiaries that are members of the stock exchange, which offer investors many financial services linked to investing.

---

[11] A discussion of the Financial Companies Act may be found in Harriet Creamer, "Issuing Securities in the United Kingdom," *International Financial Law Review* (Special Supplement July 1990), pp. 54–61.

The United Kingdom has been a leader in the process of opening domestic securities markets to participation by foreign firms. Non-British firms may be part of, and even lead, the groups of underwriting firms that sell to the public new issues of debt and equity denominated in pound sterling (the British currency). The shares of numerous foreign companies are listed on London's International Stock Exchange, and subsidiaries of foreign corporations (and banks) may hold memberships on the exchange. The same process of liberalization has affected the U.K.'s banking laws: foreign banks operate in large numbers within Great Britain.

The Bank of England has primary responsibility for managing the U.K.'s money supply. Chapters 5 and 6 provide details on the Bank's activities.

▶ KEY POINTS THAT YOU SHOULD UNDERSTAND BEFORE PROCEEDING:

1. The scope of the deregulation that is called the "Big Bang."
2. The responsibility of the Department of Trade and Industry.
3. The responsibility of the Bank of England.
4. The regulation of activities by foreign and domestic commercial banks in the securities markets.

## REGULATORY REFORM

Regulatory reform is the result of several forces and developments. First, as we noted earlier, financial crisis often prompts significant shifts in the focus and extent of regulation. Several recent examples from the U.S. illustrate the point.

At one time, the maximum interest rate that depository institutions were permitted to pay on certain deposit accounts was set by government regulation. When interest rates in the open market rose above the ceiling imposed by the government, funds inevitably flowed out of depository institutions and were used to purchase securities, that is, to make direct investments. When this process of "disintermediation" threatened the economic well-being of many U.S. banks and S&Ls, the Fed and other regulatory bodies were forced to remove the interest rate ceilings.[12] The U.S. savings and loan crisis is another example. Because many S&Ls encountered difficulties, federal legislation passed in 1989 changed the regulatory structure of these deposit accepting institutions. Finally, the stock market crash of October 1987 produced some shifts in the rules governing the U.S. markets for stock and derivative stock market instruments (stock index futures and stock index options).

A second motivation for regulatory reform in the recent past has been financial innovation, or the development of new financial products. A wide array of new classes of financial assets appeared in the last two decades and

---

[12] This change also hurt the depository institutions by increasing their cost of funds. It is interesting to note that a similar event occurred there. In 1987, the Japanese government abandoned or modified a long-standing and complicated policy of fixing maximum levels of interest rates on bank deposits.

forced the introduction of new regulations on trading these products. Specific products that spurred new regulation in the 1980s include the derivative instruments (options and futures) based on stock market indexes. An example of this process was noted above: the German government extensively revised its laws on futures and options and even authorized the establishment of a German exchange for them. The U.S. government has also found it necessary to devise new rules for the use of these innovative products by regulated financial institutions. An example is the complicated experience that S&Ls had with below-investment grade or "junk" bonds. When these high-yield and risky debt securities emerged as popular and successful investments, S&Ls got permission to invest in them. Congress later (mistakenly) blamed the junk bonds for the problems of many S&Ls and withdrew this permission in 1989.

Globalization of the world's financial markets is the third reason for recent, notable reforms in the regulatory structure of many countries. Naturally, any government's regulations are enforceable only within its borders. If a regulation is too costly, has little economic merit, or simply impedes an otherwise worthwhile financial transaction, market participants can evade it by transacting outside the country. As financial activities move to other nations, many interested parties lose money, and see reason to call for reexamination and reform of the questionable regulation. The German response to the widespread use of futures and options is an example of this phenomenon. Another example is Britain's deregulation of its stock market (or the "Big Bang"), which was, in part, a response to competition from foreign exchanges and trading opportunities.[13]

Another impact of globalization is that it reveals the costs of unwise regulations that prevent financial institutions from competing effectively for business in the world marketplace. Here a good example is regulation of the Japanese financial market. While at one time Japanese banks had sufficient funds to provide funding for non-Japanese multinational companies domiciled in Japan, regulations kept the banks from lending to foreign firms and from capitalizing on clear financial opportunities. The banks protested to the government, which eventually lifted the regulations and permitted them to compete with non-Japanese banks.

An important result of reform has been structural change in the financial institutions being regulated. As noted above, the U.S. regulatory system has separated the activities performed by different financial institutions. (Similar separation was characteristic of the U.K. and Japan.) Today, however, in a change that has global sweep, regulatory reform gradually has permitted financial institutions to offer a wider range of financial services and to become "financial supermarkets." A major focus of current and prospective regulatory reform, in several major industrial countries, is the outdated and unnecessary distinction between commercial banking and investment banking. We discuss

---

[13] Robert A. Schwartz, *Reshaping The Equity Markets* (New York: Harper Business, 1991), p. 69.

this separation of functions, imposed on the U.S. economy in the 1930s, in Chapter 4.

▶ KEY POINTS THAT YOU SHOULD UNDERSTAND BEFORE PROCEEDING:

1. The meaning of "disintermediation."
2. How financial innovation and globalization have given impetus to deregulation and regulatory reform.

SUMMARY

Regulation of the financial system and its various component sectors occurs in almost all countries. A useful way to organize the many instances of regulation is to see it as having four general forms: (1) enforcing the disclosure of relevant information; (2) regulating the level of financial activity through control of the money supply as well as trading in financial markets; (3) restricting the activities of financial institutions and their management of assets and liabilities; and (4) constraining the freedom of foreign investors and securities firms in domestic markets.

We have reviewed the regulatory situation in the United States, Japan, Germany, and the United Kingdom. All these countries currently make extensive use of disclosure regulation as well as the regulation of financial activity and trading in markets. In each case, the government gets some assistance from self-regulatory organizations (or SROs) in the financial community and markets.

Germany restricts the activities of financial institutions less than any other country, but other countries are beginning to allow their banks more latitude in the financial securities markets. All four of these countries, however, have endorsed the Basle Agreement on capital adequacy in banks and are pursuing policies based on that agreement. Finally, while every one of these countries has certain rules about activities by foreign-owned banks and firms in domestic capital markets, the clear and strong trend toward liberalization is steadily reducing the number and scope of those rules.

A significant characteristic of the 1980s has been the extensive and still on-going process of regulatory reform, which has occurred in almost all sectors of the financial system in every country discussed here. This process of reform has been a response to financial crisis, which has revealed flaws in old regulatory arrangements. Reform has also been a consequence of the widespread financial innovation of the last two decades. This innovation has prompted regulators to end old practices and to experiment with new rules. Finally, the irresistible tide of globalization of the financial markets has swept away much of the regulatory apparatus of the major industrial countries. Globalization has brought competition as well as cross-border freedom from onerous and costly regulations. Regulators have abandoned many rules simply because they could not be enforced any more, or because their high cost drove financial activities to other countries.

**Agency problems:** Difficulties that can arise when a firm's managers, who are acting as agents for the firm's owners who are principals, follow their own interests at the owners' expense and to their disadvantage.

**Asymmetric information:** Occurs when the investors in a firm do not have the same access as managers to information relevant to a financial evaluation of the firm.

**Bank of England:** The central bank in the U.K., which plays many key roles in the regulation of banks.

**Bank of Japan (or BOJ):** Japan's central bank and a major regulator of commercial banking.

**Big Bang:** The colloquial term for the radical restructuring and liberalization of the British securities industry and markets in the mid-1980s.

**Bundesbank or Deutsche Bundesbank:** The central bank of Germany and a regulatory authority in the banking industry.

**Bundes bond (or Bund):** A debt security issued by the central German government.

**Commodity Futures Trading Commission (or CFTC):** The U.S. government agency that licenses futures exchanges and monitors trading in them.

**Competitive market:** A market that brings about the efficient production of a good or service at the lowest possible cost.

**Department of Trade and Industry (or DTI):** The U.K.'s government agency responsible for regulation of many markets including financial ones.

**Deutsche Terminbörse:** Futures market in Germany.

**Disclosure regulation:** The regulation that requires issuers of securities to make public a large amount of financial information to actual and potential investors.

**Efficient market hypothesis:** The theory that the public availability of relevant information about the issuers of securities will lead to a correct pricing of those securities if they are freely traded in properly functioning markets.

**Federal Home Loan Bank Board (or FHLBB):** A U.S. agency that once regulated much of the activity of savings and loan associations.

**Federal Reserve System (or Fed):** An independent U.S. government agency responsible for the nation's money and banking system.

**Glass-Steagall Act:** U.S. legislation that regulates and limits the behavior of commercial banks in securities markets.

**Insider trading:** The purchase or sale of a firm's securities by its officers (among others) who are seeking to benefit from their knowledge of non-public information about the firm's financial prospects.

**Interbank market:** A market for funds in which only banks participate.

**London International Stock Exchange:** Great Britain's exchange for trading debt and equity securities.

**Market failure:** The term used by some economists for the inability of a competitive market to remain so without the help of government, or the inability of an uncompetitive market, if not aided by government, to become competitive.

**Ministry of Finance (or MOF):** Japan's powerful regulator of many aspects of the financial system.

**National Association of Securities Dealers (or NASD):** A self-regulatory organization (or SRO), which monitors the relationships among brokers, firms issuing securities, and the investing public.

**National Futures Association (or NFA):** The SRO in the U.S. which has, since the early 1980s, carried out key responsibilities in the futures markets.

**Office of Thrift Supervision (or OTS):** A U.S. government agency that regulates savings and loan associations.

**Organized exchanges:** Structured markets that provide for the trading of selected corporate and governmental securities.

**Securities Act of 1933:** Federal legislation that deals primarily with disclosure requirements for the distribution of new securities.

**Securities Exchange Act of 1934:** Federal legislation that created the Securities and Exchange Commission, and deals with requirements for the periodic disclosure of publicly traded seasoned securities and the regulation of activities in securities markets.

**Securities and Exchange Commission:** A federal regulatory body responsible for administering securities laws in the United States.

**Securities and Investment Board (or SIB):** Great Britain's main governmental monitor of the securities industry.

**Self-Regulatory Organization (or SRO):** A group that, with the sponsorship or authority of a government, monitors the behavior of its members to ensure that they meet certain well-established standards in the conduct of business.

## QUESTIONS

1.  a.  What is the economic rationale for the widespread use of "disclosure regulation"?

    b.  Do you agree with the view that such regulation is redundant because investors can get the information they need through their power to underprice the securities of firms that do not provide all necessary data?

2.  "The Securities and Exchange Commission insures that securities issued in the United States are not risky and therefore are acceptable investments for the general public." Explain why you agree or disagree with this statement.

3.  Why do countries regulate their money supply?

4. What are some key indicators of whether a country is liberalizing its rules on financial activities by foreign-owned banks and companies?

5. Identify two key elements in the United Kingdom's "Big Bang" of the middle 1980s.

6. a. Explain how Germany's regulation of banks' roles in the financial securities industry has differed from regulation in other countries.

   b. Why is it likely that these differences will disappear in the fairly near future?

7. Name some key regulations of trading in common stock that the Securities and Exchange Commission enforces.

8. a. What is an SRO?

   b. Name three SROs.

9. Identify the institutions (and their home countries) labeled by these acronyms:

   a. CFTC; b. DTI; c. SIB; d. BOJ; e. NASD; f. NFA; g. MOF; h. TSE.

10. Identify the central banks that control the money supply and (to some extent) short-term rates in the United States, Germany, Japan, and the United Kingdom.

CHAPTER FOUR

# Depository Institutions: Activities and Characteristics

## LEARNING OBJECTIVES

*After reading this chapter you will understand:*

- the role of depository institutions.
- how a depository institution generates income.
- differences among commercial banks, savings and loan associations, savings banks, and credit unions.
- the asset/liability problem all depository institutions face.
- who regulates commercial banks and thrifts and the types of regulations imposed.
- the funding sources available to commercial banks and thrifts.
- the capital requirements imposed on commercial banks and savings and loan associations.

Depository institutions include commercial banks (or simply banks), savings and loan associations (S&Ls), savings banks, and credit unions. All are financial intermediaries that accept deposits. These deposits represent the liabilities (debt) of the deposit-accepting institution. With the funds raised through deposits and other funding sources, depository institutions both make direct loans to various entities and invest in securities. Their income is derived from two sources: the income generated from the loans they make and the securities they purchase, and fee income.

It is common to refer to S&Ls, savings banks, and credit unions as "thrifts," which are specialized types of depository institutions. Traditionally, thrifts have not been permitted to accept deposits transferable by check (negotiable), or, as they are more popularly known, checking accounts. Instead, they have obtained funds primarily by tapping the savings of households. Since the early 1980s, however, thrifts have been allowed to offer negotiable deposits entirely equivalent to checking accounts, although they bear a different name (NOW accounts, share drafts). By law, the investments that thrifts are permitted to make have been much more limited than those permitted to banks. Recent legislation, however, has expanded the range of investments allowed by thrifts so that they can compete more effectively with banks.

Depository institutions are highly regulated because of the important role that they play in the country's financial system. Demand deposit accounts are the principal means that individuals and business entities use for making payments, and government monetary policy is implemented through the banking system. Because of their important role, depository institutions are afforded special privileges such as access to federal deposit insurance and access to a government entity that provides funds for liquidity or emergency needs. For example, the deposits of most depository institutions are currently insured up to $100,000 per account. We'll give examples of how depository institutions have access to emergency funds later in this chapter.

In this chapter we will look at depository institutions—the nature of their liabilities, where they invest their funds, and how they are regulated. Before we examine the specific institutions, we begin with an overview of the asset/liability problem that a depository institution must manage.

## ASSET/LIABILITY PROBLEM OF DEPOSITORY INSTITUTIONS

The asset/liability problem that depository institutions face is quite simple to explain—although not necessarily easy to solve. A depository institution seeks to earn a positive spread between the assets it invests in (loans and securities) and the cost of its funds (deposits and other sources). The spread is referred to as *spread income* or *margin*. The spread income should allow the institution to meet operating expenses and earn a fair profit on its capital.

In generating spread income a depository institution faces several risks. These include *credit risk*, *regulatory risk*, and *funding* (or *interest rate*) *risk*. Credit risk, also called *default risk*, refers to the risk that a borrower will default on a loan obligation to the depository institution or that the issuer of a security that the depository institution holds will default on its obligation. Regulatory risk is the risk that regulators will change the rules so as to impact the earnings of the institution unfavorably.

### Funding Risk

Funding risk can be explained best by an illustration. Suppose that a depository institution raises $100 million by issuing a deposit account that has a maturity of one year and by agreeing to pay an interest rate of 7%. Ignoring for the time being the fact that the depository institution cannot invest the entire $100 million because of reserve requirements, which we discuss later in this chapter, suppose that $100 million is invested in a U.S. government security that matures in 15 years paying an interest rate of 9%. Because the funds are invested in a U.S. government security, there is no credit risk in this case.

It would seem at first that the depository institution has locked in a spread of 2% (9% minus 7%). This spread can be counted on only for the first year, though, because the spread in future years will depend on the interest rate this depository institution will have to pay depositors in order to raise $100 million after the one-year time deposit matures. If interest rates decline, the spread will increase because the depository institution has locked in the 9% rate. If interest rates rise, however, the spread income will decline. In fact, if this depository institution must pay more than 9% to depositors for the next 14 years, the spread will be negative. That is, it will cost the depository institution more to finance the government securities than it will earn on the funds invested in those securities.

In our example, the depository institution has borrowed short (borrowed for one year) and lent long (invested for 15 years). This policy will benefit from a decline in interest rates but be disadvantaged if interest rates rise. Suppose the institution could have borrowed funds for 15 years at 7% and invested in a U.S. government security maturing in one year earning 9%—borrowed long (15 years) and lent short (one year). A rise in interest rates will benefit the depository institution because it can then reinvest the proceeds from the maturing one-year government security in a new one-year government security offering a higher interest rate. In this case a decline in interest rates will reduce the spread. If interest rates fall below 7%, there will be a negative spread.

All depository institutions face this funding problem. Managers of a depository institution who have particular expectations about the future direction of interest rates will seek to benefit from these expectations. Those who expect interest rates to rise may pursue a policy to borrow funds for a long time horizon (that is, to borrow long) and lend funds for a short time horizon (to lend short). If interest rates are expected to drop, managers may elect to borrow short and lend long.

The problem of pursuing a strategy of positioning a depository institution based on expectations is that considerable adverse financial consequences will result if those expectations are not realized. The evidence on interest rate forecasting suggests that it is a risky business. We doubt if there are managers of depository institutions who have the ability to forecast interest rate moves so consistently that the institution can benefit should the forecast be realized. The goal of management is to lock in a spread as best as possible, not to wager on interest rate movements.

Inherent in any balance sheet of a depository institution is funding risk exposure. Managers must be willing to accept some exposure, but they can take various measures to address the interest rate sensitivity of the institution's liabilities and its assets. A depository institution will have an asset/liability committee that is responsible for monitoring the interest rate risk exposure. There are several asset/liability strategies for controlling interest rate risk. While a discussion of these strategies is beyond the scope of this chapter, we can point out here that development of several financial instruments (such as floating-rate notes, adjustable-rate mortgages, and interest rate swaps) reflects the asset/liability problem that depository institutions seek to solve.

## *Liquidity Concerns*

Besides facing credit risk and funding risk, a depository institution must be prepared to satisfy withdrawals of funds by depositors and to provide loans to customers. There are several ways that a depository institution can accommodate withdrawal and loan demand: (1) attract additional deposits; (2) use existing securities as collateral for borrowing from a federal agency or other financial institution such as an investment bank; (3) raise short-term funds in the money market; or (4) sell securities that it owns.

The first alternative is self-explanatory. The second has to do with the privilege we mentioned earlier. Banks are allowed to borrow at the discount window of the Federal Reserve Banks. The third alternative primarily includes using marketable securities owned as collateral to raise funds in the repurchase agreement market, which we cover in later chapters.

The fourth alternative, selling securities that it owns, requires that the depository institution invest a portion of its funds in securities that are both liquid and have little price risk. By price risk we refer to the prospect that the selling price of the security will be less than its purchase price, resulting in a loss. For example, as we explain in Chapter 10, while a 30-year U.S. government security is a highly liquid security, its price would change dramatically as interest rates rise. A price decline of, say, 25% would not be uncommon in a volatile interest rate environment. A 30-year government bond is therefore highly liquid, but exposes the depository institution to substantial price risk.

In general, as we explain in Chapters 11 and 22, short-term securities entail little price risk. It is therefore short-term, or money market, debt obligations that a depository institution will hold as an investment to satisfy withdrawals and customer loan demand. It does this chiefly by lending federal funds, an investment vehicle that we will discuss later in this chapter. The term to maturity of the securities it holds affects the amount that depository institutions can borrow from some federal agencies because only short-term securities are acceptable collateral.

Securities held for the purpose of satisfying net withdrawals and customer loan demands are sometimes referred to as "secondary reserves."[1] A disadvantage of holding secondary reserves is that securities with short maturities offer a lower yield than securities with a longer maturity in most interest rate environments. The percentage of a depository institution's assets held as secondary reserves will depend both on the institution's ability to raise funds from the other sources and on its management's risk preference for liquidity (safety) versus yield.

Depository institutions hold liquid assets not only for operational purposes, but also because of the regulatory requirements that we discuss below.

▶ KEY POINTS THAT YOU SHOULD UNDERSTAND BEFORE PROCEEDING:

1. That a depository institution needs to earn a positive spread between the return on its assets and the cost of its funds, which it gets through deposits and other sources.
2. The source and impact of a depository institution's credit risk, funding risk, and regulatory risk.
3. The reasons for a depository institution's liquidity concerns and its ways of responding to these concerns.

## COMMERCIAL BANKS

In 1992, there were about 11,900 commercial banks in the United States. A commercial bank can be chartered either by the state (state-chartered banks) or by the federal government (national banks). Of the 11,900 banks, about 65% were state-chartered. All national banks must be members of the Federal Reserve System and must be insured by the Bank Insurance Fund (BIF), which is administered by the Federal Deposit Insurance Corporation (FDIC). While federal depository insurance has existed since the 1930s, and the insurance program is administered by the FDIC, BIF was created early in 1989 by the Financial Institutions Reform, Recovery, and Enforcement Act of 1989 (FIRREA). Coverage is currently $100,000 per account. However, there have been several proposals to restructure deposit insurance coverage, which we will discuss later.

State-chartered banks may elect to join the Federal Reserve System.

---

[1] Roland I. Robinson, *The Management of Bank Funds* (New York: McGraw-Hill, 1962), p. 15. The term secondary reserves is used because primary reserves are the reserves required by the Federal Reserve Board, which we will discuss later. If you looked at the balance sheet of a depository institution, you will not see the term "secondary reserves" on it. A depository institution invests in short-term or money market instruments for reasons other than liquidity and does not report the purpose for which it acquires securities.

Their deposits must be insured by the BIF. A minority of state-chartered banks elect to be members of the Federal Reserve System. In 1992, of the approximately 8,000 state-chartered banks, only about 1,000 are Federal Reserve member banks. In spite of the large number of banks that elect not to be members of the Federal Reserve System, banks that are members hold nearly 70% of all deposits in the U.S. Moreover, with the passage of the Depository Institutions Deregulation and Monetary Control Act of 1980 (DIDMCA), the reserve requirements that we shall discuss below for banks that are members of the Federal Reserve System apply also to state-chartered banks.

The size of banks in the U.S. varies greatly as can be seen from Table 4-1, which shows the distribution for FDIC banks as of December 1989. Shown in the same table are total assets for each asset size. As can be seen, while less than 5% of the banks have total assets in excess of $500 million, these banks hold almost three-quarters of the total assets. The ten largest U.S. bank holding companies as of December 1992, in terms of total assets, are listed in Table 4-2. A bank holding company is a corporation that owns stock in one or more banks.

Table 4-3 shows, as of March 1993, the ten largest banks in the world measured in U.S. dollars and ranked in terms of total assets. Eight of the ten largest banks in the world are Japanese, and two are French. The listing in Table 4-3, however, is misleading because regulations differ across countries. Specifically, U.S. regulations prevent greater degrees of leverage for large banks; Japanese regulation does not apply this brake.

## Bank Services

Commercial banks provide numerous services in our financial system. The services can be broadly classified as follows: (1) individual banking; (2) institu-

| TABLE 4-1 |
|---|

### DISTRIBUTION OF FDIC COMMERCIAL BANKS BY SIZE AS OF DECEMBER 1989

| Asset Size (in Millions) | Number of Banks | % of Banks | Assets (In Billions) | % of Assets |
|---|---|---|---|---|
| Less than $ 5.0 | 153 | 1.2 | $ .5 | < 0.05 |
| $ 5.0 –$9.9 | 619 | 4.9 | 4.8 | 0.1 |
| $ 10.0 –$24.9 | 2,968 | 23.4 | 51.7 | 1.6 |
| $ 25.0 –$49.9 | 3,238 | 25.5 | 117.2 | 3.6 |
| $ 50.0 –$99.9 | 2,744 | 21.6 | 191.3 | 5.8 |
| $100.0 –$499.9 | 2,370 | 18.6 | 463.3 | 14.0 |
| $500.0 or more | 614 | 4.8 | 2,470.4 | 74.9 |

*Source:* The data for this table come from Table No. 802, Selected Financial Institutions— Number and Assets, by Asset Size: 1989, *Statistical Abstract of the United States: 1991* (Department of Commerce, Bureau of the Census).

## TABLE 4-2

TEN LARGEST U.S. BANK HOLDING COMPANIES AS OF APRIL 1993, RANKED BY
TOTAL ASSETS AS OF DECEMBER 1992[a]

| Ranking | Bank | In Millions of U.S. Dollars | |
| | | Total Assets | Tier 1 Capital |
| --- | --- | --- | --- |
| 1 | Citicorp | $213,701 | $10,456 |
| 2 | BankAmerica Corp.[b] | 180,814 | 11,312 |
| 3 | Chemical Banking Corp.[c] | 139,655 | 9,247 |
| 4 | Nations Bank[d] | 119,805 | 7,190 |
| 5 | J.P. Morgan & Co., Inc. | 102,941 | 6,793 |
| 6 | Chase Manhattan Corp. | 95,862 | 6,308 |
| 7 | Bankers Trust New York Corp. | 72,448 | 3,571 |
| 8 | BANC ONE Corp. | 61,331 | 4,908 |
| 9 | Wells Fargo & Co. | 52,537 | 3,289 |
| 10 | PNC Financial Corp. | 51,523 | 3,684 |

*Note:* Tier 1 capital equals funding such as stock, retained earnings, preferred stock, and selected other items.

[a] The rankings reflect these mergers in 1991–92:

[b] After the merger of BankAmerica and Security Pacific.

[c] After the merger of Chemical Banking Corporation and Manufacturers Hanover.

[d] Entity resulting from the merger of NCNB Corporation and C&S/Sovran Corporation.

*Source:* Data provided by Simon G. Davidson of Ferguson & Co., a bank data publishing company in Washington, D.C.

tional banking; and (3) global banking.[2] Of course, different banks are more active in certain of these activities than others. For example, money center banks (defined later) are more active in global banking.

Individual banking encompasses consumer lending, residential mortgage lending, consumer installment loans, credit card financing, automobile and boat financing, brokerage services, student loans, and individual-oriented financial investment services such as personal trust and investment services. Interest and fee income are generated from mortgage lending and credit card financing. Mortgage lending is more popularly referred to as mortgage banking. We'll discuss this activity and how fee income is generated in Chapter 23. Fee income is generated from brokerage services and financial investment services.

Loans to non-financial corporations, financial corporations (such as life insurance companies), and government entities (state and local governments in the U.S. and foreign governments) fall into the category of in-

[2] This classification of activities and their components is adapted from the *1988 Annual Report,* Part Two, of The Chase Manhattan Corporation, p. 92.

| | TABLE 4-3 | | |
|---|---|---|---|

TEN LARGEST BANKS IN THE WORLD AS OF MARCH 1993, RANKED BY TOTAL
ASSETS AS OF MARCH 1992, OR LAST FISCAL YEAR

| | | In Millions of U.S. Dollars | |
|---|---|---|---|
| Rank | Bank Name (Country) | Total Assets | Equity |
| 1 | Dai-Ichi Kangyo Bank (Japan)* | $443,736 | $14,914 |
| 2 | Sumitomo Bank (Japan)* | 424,983 | 16,897 |
| 3 | Sakura Bank (Japan)* | 418,577 | 12,744 |
| 4 | Fuji Bank (Japan)* | 416,122 | 14,674 |
| 5 | Sanwa Bank (Japan)* | 410,001 | 14,516 |
| 6 | Mitsubishi Bank (Japan)* | 388,552 | 13,097 |
| 7 | Crédit Agricole (France) | 307,203 | 15,507 |
| 8 | Norinchukin Bank (Japan)* | 306,498 | 2,050 |
| 9 | Crédit Lyonnais (France) | 306,335 | 8,558 |
| 10 | Industrial Bank of Japan (Japan) | 301,136 | 10,356 |

*Fiscal year-end March 31, 1992. Others are fiscal year-end 1991.
*Source:* Data provided by Jan D. Slee of the EURASTAR Division of Sleigh Corporation, Franklin Lakes, New Jersey

stitutional banking. Also included in this category are commercial real estate financing, leasing activities,[3] and factoring.[4] In the case of leasing, a bank may be involved in leasing equipment either as lessors,[5] as lenders to lessors, or as purchasers of leases. Loans and leasing generate interest income, and other services that banks offer institutional customers generate fee income. These services include management of the assets of private and public pension funds, fiduciary and custodial services, and cash management services such as account maintenance, check clearing, and electronic transfers.

It is in the area of global banking that banks have begun to compete head-to-head with investment banking (or securities) firms. Global banking covers a broad range of activities involving corporate financing and capital market and foreign exchange products and services. Most global banking activities generate fee income rather than interest income.

---

[3] Leasing programs offered by some banks include vendor leasing, direct leasing, and leveraged leasing. For a discussion of these programs and the restrictions imposed on banks with respect to leasing activities, see Peter K. Nevitt, Frank J. Fabozzi, and Edmond J. Seifried, *Equipment Leasing for Commercial Bankers* (Philadelphia, PA: Robert Morris Associates, 1987).

[4] The factoring business involves a bank's purchase of accounts receivable.

[5] This means that the bank buys the equipment and leases it to another party. The bank is the lessor, and the party that uses the leased equipment is the lessee.

Corporate financing involves two components. First is the procuring of funds for a bank's customers. This can go beyond traditional bank loans to involve the underwriting of securities. As we shall explain later, legislation in the form of the Glass-Steagall Act limits bank activities in this area. In assisting customers in obtaining funds, banks also provide bankers acceptances, letters of credit, and other types of guarantees for their customers. That is, if a customer has borrowed funds backed by a letter of credit or other guarantee, its lenders can look to the customer's bank to fulfill the obligation. We'll give further examples in Chapter 22. The second area of corporate financing involves advice on such matters as strategies for obtaining funds, corporate restructuring, divestitures, and acquisitions.

Capital market and foreign exchange products and services involve transactions where the bank may act as a dealer or broker in a service. Some banks, for example, are dealers in U.S. government or other securities. Customers who wish to transact in these securities can do so through the government desk of the bank. Similarly, some banks maintain a foreign exchange operation, where foreign currency is bought and sold. Bank customers in need of foreign exchange can use the services of the bank.

In their role as dealers, banks can generate income in three ways: (1) the bid-ask spread; (2) capital gains on the securities or foreign currency they have transacted in; and (3) in the case of securities, the spread between interest income by holding the security and the cost of funding the purchase of that security.

The financial products that banks have developed to manage risk also yield fee income. These products include interest rate swaps, interest rate agreements, currency swaps, forward contracts, and interest rate options. We discuss interest rate swaps and interest rate agreements in Chapter 29, currency swaps in Chapter 30, forward contracts in Chapter 25, and interest rate options in Chapter 29. Banks can generate either commission income (that is, brokerage fees) or spread income from selling such products.

## Bank Funding

In describing the nature of the banking business, we have focused so far on how banks generate income. Now let's take a look at how a bank raises funds. There are three sources of funds for banks: (1) deposits; (2) non-deposit borrowing; and (3) common stock and retained earnings. Banks are highly leveraged financial institutions, which means that most of their funds come from borrowing—the first two sources we refer to. Included in non-deposit borrowing are borrowing from the Federal Reserve through the discount window facility, borrowing reserves in the federal funds market, and borrowing by the issuance of instruments in the money and bond markets.

Table 4-4 provides a consolidated report of the assets and liabilities of all insured banks and their branches operating in the United States as of March 1992. These numbers illustrate many points made in this section on bank funding and in the previous section on bank services.

| | TABLE 4-4 | |
|---|---|---|

**ASSETS AND LIABILITIES OF INSURED COMMERCIAL BANKS**
**(DOMESTIC AND FOREIGN OFFICES) AS OF MARCH 31, 1992**

| | $ Millions | % of Assets |
|---|---|---|
| *Assets* | | |
| Cash and due from Depository Institutions | 279,923 | 8% |
| Securities | | |
| U.S. Treasuries and Agencies | 542,467 | 16% |
| Municipal Debt | 71,644 | 2% |
| Federal Funds and Repurchase Agreements | 158,381 | 4% |
| Loans | | |
| Loans Secured by Real Estate | 849,611 | 25% |
| Commercial and Industrial Loans | 548,646 | 16% |
| Loans to Individuals | 357,566 | 10% |
| Loans to Foreign Governments and Institutions | 116,389 | 3% |
| All Other Assets | 769,416 | 23% |
| Total Assets | 3,414,120 | 100% |
| *Liabilities* | | |
| Deposits (including Transactions Accounts and Demand Deposits) | 2,659,204 | 78% |
| Federal Funds and Securities Purchased under Resale Agreements | 246,414 | 7% |
| All Other Liabilities | 270,823 | 8% |
| Total Liabilities | 3,176,441 | 93% |
| *Equity Capital* | | |
| Total Equity Capital | 237,669 | 7% |

*Source: Federal Reserve Bulletin*, September 1992

**Deposits.**    There are several types of deposit accounts. Demand deposits (checking accounts) pay no interest and can be withdrawn upon demand. Savings deposits pay interest, typically below market interest rates, do not have a specific maturity, and usually can be withdrawn upon demand.

Time deposits, also called *certificates of deposit*, have a fixed maturity date and pay either a fixed or floating interest rate. Some certificates of deposit that we shall describe in Chapter 22 can be sold in the open market prior to their maturity if the depositor needs funds. Other certificates of deposits cannot be sold. If a depositor elects to withdraw the funds from the bank prior to the maturity date, a withdrawal penalty is imposed. A money market demand account is one that pays interest based on short-term interest rates. The market for short-term debt obligations is called the money market, which is how these deposits get their name. They are designed to compete with money market mutual funds, which we will describe in Chapter 8.

***Reserve Requirements and Borrowing in the Federal Funds Market.***   A bank cannot invest $1 for every $1 it obtains in deposit. All banks must maintain a specified percentage of their deposits in a non-interest-bearing account at one of the 12 Federal Reserve Banks. These specified percentages are called *reserve ratios*, and the dollar amounts based on them that are required to be kept on deposit at a Federal Reserve Bank are called *required reserves*. The reserve ratios, which Chapter 5 also examines, are established by the Federal Reserve Board (the Fed). The reserve ratio differs by type of deposit. The Fed defines two types of deposits: transactions and nontransactions deposits. Demand deposits and what the Fed calls "other checkable deposits" (primarily NOW accounts) are classified as transactions deposits. Savings and time deposits are nontransactions deposits. Reserve ratios are higher for transactions deposits than for nontransactions deposits.

To arrive at its required reserves, a bank does not simply determine its transactions and nontransactions deposits at the close of each business day and then multiply each by the applicable reserve ratio. The determination of a bank's required reserves is more complex. Here we'll give a rough idea of how it is done. First, to compute required reserves, the Federal Reserve has established a two-week period called the deposit computation period. Required reserves are the average amount of each type of deposits held at the close of each business day in the computation period, multiplied by the reserve requirement for each type.

Reserve requirements in each period are to be satisfied by *actual reserves*, which are defined as the average amount of reserves held at the close of business at the Federal Reserve Bank during each day of a two-week reserve maintenance period, beginning on Thursday and ending on Wednesday two weeks later. For transactions deposits, the deposit computation period leads the reserve period by two days. For nontransactions deposits, the deposit computation period is the two-week period four weeks prior to the reserve maintenance period.

If actual reserves exceed required reserves, the difference is referred to as *excess reserves*. Because reserves are placed in non-interest-bearing accounts, there is an opportunity cost associated with excess reserves. At the same time, there are penalties imposed on banks that do not satisfy the reserve requirements. Thus, banks have an incentive to manage their reserves so as to satisfy reserve requirements as precisely as possible.

Banks temporarily short of their required reserves can borrow reserves from banks that have excess reserves. The market where banks can borrow or lend reserves is called the *federal funds market*. The interest rate charged to borrow funds in this market is called the *federal funds rate*.

***Borrowing at the Fed Discount Window.***   The Federal Reserve Bank is the banker's bank—or, to put it another way, the bank of last resort. Banks temporarily short of funds can borrow from the Fed at its discount window. (See Chapter 5 for more discussion of the Fed's use of the discount window.) Collateral is necessary to borrow, but not just any collateral will do. The Fed establishes (and periodically changes) the type of collateral that is eligible. Currently it includes (1) Treasury securities, federal agency securities, and municipal securities, all with a maturity of less than six months, and (2) commercial and industrial loans with 90 days or less to maturity.

The interest rate that the Fed charges to borrow funds at the discount window is called the *discount rate*. The Fed changes this rate periodically in order to implement monetary policy.[6] Bank borrowing at the Fed to meet required reserves is quite limited in amount, despite the fact that the discount rate generally is set below the cost of other sources of short-term funding available to a bank. This is because the Fed views borrowing at the discount window as a privilege to be used to meet short-term liquidity needs, and not a device to increase earnings.

Continual borrowing for long periods and in large amounts is thereby viewed as a sign of a bank's financial weakness or as exploitation of the interest differential for profit. If a bank appears to be going to the Fed to borrow frequently, relative to its previous borrowing pattern, the Fed makes an "informational" call to ask for an explanation for the borrowing. If there is no subsequent improvement in the bank's borrowing pattern, the Fed then makes an "administrative counseling" call in which it tells the bank that it must stop its borrowing practice.

***Other Non-Deposit Borrowing.*** Bank borrowing in the federal funds market and at the discount window of the Fed is short-term. Other non-deposit borrowing can be short-term in the form of issuing obligations in the money market, or intermediate- to long-term in the form of issuing securities in the bond market. An example of the former is the repurchase agreement (or "repo") market. An example of intermediate- or long-term borrowing is floating-rate notes and bonds.

Banks that raise most of their funds from the domestic and international money markets, relying less on depositors for funds, are called *money center banks*. Seven of the ten banks listed in Table 4-2 are money center banks. A regional bank by contrast is one that relies primarily on deposits for funding, and makes less use of the money markets to obtain funds. The largest regional bank is Nations Bank. In recent years, larger regional banks have been merging with other regional banks to form so-called "superregional banks." Nations Bank is the result of a merger between NCNB of Charlotte, North Carolina, and C&S/Sovran of Norfolk, Virginia. With their greater size, these superregional banks can compete in certain domestic and international financial activities that were once the domain of money center banks.

---

[6] While altering the discount rate is a tool to implement monetary policy, along with open market operations and the changing of reserve ratios, today it is not viewed as a primary tool.

## *Regulation*

Because of the special role that commercial banks play in the financial system, banks are regulated and supervised by several federal and state government entities. At the federal level, supervision is undertaken by the Federal Reserve Board, the Office of the Comptroller of the Currency, and the Federal Deposit Insurance Corporation. While much of the legislation defining these activities dates back to the late 1930s, the nature of financial markets and commercial banking has changed in the past 20 years. Consequently, rethinking of regulation is taking place as this chapter is written. Moreover, bank regulation is becoming international in nature.

Here we will review some of the major regulations concerning the activities of commercial banks. The regulations historically cover four areas:

1. Ceilings imposed on the interest rate that can be paid on deposit accounts.
2. Geographical restrictions on branch banking.
3. Permissible activities for commercial banks.
4. Capital requirements for commercial banks.

***Regulation of Interest Rates.*** While regulation of the interest rates that banks can pay has been all but eliminated for accounts other than demand deposits, we discuss the subject because of its historical relevance. Federal regulations prohibit the payment of interest on demand (checking) accounts. Regulation Q at one time imposed a ceiling on the maximum interest rate that could be paid by banks on deposits other than demand accounts.

Until the 1960s, market interest rates stayed below the ceiling (except those on checking deposits), so Regulation Q had virtually no impact on the ability of banks to compete with other financial institutions to obtain funds. As market interest rates rose above the ceiling, and ceilings were extended to all depository institutions after 1966, these institutions found it difficult to compete with other financial institutions—such as the money market funds that we will discuss in Chapter 8—to attract funds. As a result, there was "disintermediation"—funds flowed out of commercial banks and thrift institutions and into the other financial institutions.

To circumvent the ceilings on time deposits and recapture the lost funds, banks developed the negotiable certificate of deposit, which in effect had a higher ceiling, and eventually no ceiling at all. They also opened branches outside the U.S., where no ceilings were imposed on the interest rate they could offer. As all depository institutions found it difficult to compete in the 1970s, federal legislation in the form of the Depository Institutions Deregulation and Monetary Control Act of 1980 gave banks relief. With a few exceptions, the 1980 act phased out the ceilings on interest rates on time deposits and certificates of deposit. The Garn-St. Germain Act of 1982 permitted banks to offer money market accounts, accounts that were similar to those offered by money market funds.

***Geographical Restrictions.*** Each state has the right to set its own rules on intrastate branch banking, which was established by the McFadden Act, passed by Congress in 1926. This rather outdated legislation was intended to prevent large banks from expanding geographically and thereby forcing out or taking over smaller banking entities, possibly threatening competition. There are some states where banks cannot establish branches statewide—so-called unit-banking states. There are also limit branch banking states, which permit some statewide branches, and other states that have virtually no restrictions on statewide branching.

State laws prohibit individual out-of-state banks from establishing a branch in their state. However, all but two states (Hawaii and Montana) have passed laws that allow an out-of-state bank holding company to expand banking operations into the state. Therefore, at this time, interstate bank expansion is only permissible at the holding company level, not the individual bank level. Most states will not permit an out-of-state holding company to establish a new bank in the state. Instead, the out-of-state bank holding company must acquire an existing bank operating in the state.[7]

***Permissible Activities for Commercial Banks.*** The activities of banks and bank holding companies are regulated by the Federal Reserve Board. The Fed was charged with the responsibility of regulating the activities of bank holding companies by the Bank Holding Company Act of 1956, subsequently amended in 1966 and 1970. The act states that the permissible activities of bank holding companies are limited to those that are viewed by the Fed as "closely related to banking."

Early legislation governing bank activities developed against the following background:

1.  Certain commercial bank lending was believed to have reinforced the stock market crash of 1929.
2.  The stock market crash itself led to the breakdown of the banking system.
3.  Transactions between commercial banks and their securities affiliates led to abuses. For example, it was discovered that banks were underwriting securities and then selling those securities to customers whose investment accounts they managed or advised. (We'll discuss the underwriting of securities in Chapter 14.)

Against this background, Congress passed the Banking Act of 1933, which, among other provisions, created the Federal Deposit Insurance Corporation. Four sections of the 1933 act barred commercial bankers from certain investment banking activities—Sections 16, 20, 21, and 32. These four sections are popularly referred to as the Glass-Steagall Act.

---

[7] For a more detailed discussion of interstate banking and current state regulations, see Paul S. Calem, "The Proconsumer Argument for Interstate Branching," *Business Review* (May-June 1993), pp. 15–29.

For banks that are members of the Federal Reserve System, Section 16 provides that:

> *business of dealing in securities and stock by a national bank shall be limited to purchasing and selling such securities and stock without recourse, solely upon the order, and for the account of customers, and in no case for its own account, and the (national bank) shall not underwrite any issue of securities or stock.*

Banks can neither (1) underwrite securities and stock, nor (2) act as dealers in the secondary market for securities and stock, although Section 16 does provide two exceptions. Banks were permitted to underwrite and deal in U.S. government obligations and "general obligations of any state or any political subdivisions thereof." (The latter securities are municipal bonds, which we shall discuss in Chapter 17. The exemption applies to one type of municipal security, general obligation bonds, not another type, revenue bonds.) Section 16 also restricts the activities of banks in connection with corporate securities such as corporate bonds and commercial paper, and securities such as mortgage-backed and asset-backed securities (which we discuss in Chapter 24).

These restrictions were imposed on activities of commercial banks in the United States, not overseas. Commercial banks are not barred from underwriting or dealing in corporate bonds outside the United States, nor are they restricted from aiding in the private placement of corporate securities. More recently developed instruments are not specifically forbidden to commercial banks. A good example is swaps—interest rate and currency swaps, which we discuss in Chapters 29 and 30.

Commercial banks that are members of the Federal Reserve System are prohibited from maintaining a securities firm by Section 20, which states that no member bank shall be affiliated with any organization, association, business trust, or other similar organization engaged principally in the issue, flotation, underwriting, public sale, or distribution at wholesale or retail or through syndicate participation of stocks, bonds, debentures, notes or other securities.

Section 21 prohibits any "person, firm, corporation, association, business trust, or other similar organization" that receives deposits—that is, depository institutions—from engaging in the securities business as defined in Section 16. Section 32 further prevents banks from circumventing the restrictions on securities activities. It does so by prohibiting banks from placing bank employees or board members in positions with securities firms so that they can obtain indirect but effective control.

Subsequent legislation, court rulings, and regulatory decisions have whittled away at the barriers against commercial banks' engagement in investment banking activities. Here is a brief rundown of the significant events. In June 1987, the Fed granted approval to three bank holding companies—Citicorp, Bankers Trust, and J.P. Morgan Guaranty—to underwrite certain securities that were prohibited by the 1933 act: commercial paper, certain municipal revenue bonds, mortgage-backed securities, and asset-backed securities. To do so, the bank holding company must set up a separately capitalized subsidiary to underwrite these securities and must comply with rules established by the Fed regarding limits on market share, income, and revenue. The Comptroller of the Currency ruled subsequently that the 1933 act does permit national banks to underwrite mortgage-backed securities.

Court rulings in the 1980s granted commercial banks opportunities to act as investment advisors and furnish brokerage services. The Supreme Court ruled in 1981 that bank holding companies are allowed to serve as advisors to investment companies. Three years later, the Court ruled that, as long as a bank does not offer investment advice, it could provide discount brokerage services. A Federal Court of Appeals, however, has ruled since that a bank subsidiary could operate a brokerage firm even though it offered investment advice.

The legal distinction between commercial banks and investment banks seems to have been weakened further by a ruling by the Fed in November 1986 that permitted a Japanese bank, Sumitomo Bank Ltd., to invest $500 million in an investment banking firm, Goldman Sachs. While the Fed did impose restrictions to assure that Sumitomo could not exert control over the management of Goldman Sachs' operations, the action set a precedent nonetheless.

Beyond legislation, regulators have placed restrictions of their own on the types of securities that a bank can take a position in for its own investment portfolio. For example, while adjustable-rate mortgages are attractive investments, given the asset/liability problem of depository institutions, permission to invest in such mortgages had to be granted. The most recent example is the Comptroller of the Currency's restrictions on investing in certain mortgage-backed securities.

***Capital Requirements for Commercial Banks.*** The capital structure of banks, like that of all corporations, consists of equity and debt (that is, borrowed funds). Commercial banks, just like the other depository institutions that we discuss in this chapter, and investment banks, which we discuss in Chapter 14, are highly leveraged institutions. That is, the ratio of equity capital to total assets is low, typically less than 8% in the case of banks. This gives rise to regulatory concern about potential insolvency resulting from the low level of capital provided by the owners. An additional concern is that the amount of equity capital is even less adequate because of potential liabilities that do not appear on the bank's balance sheet. These so-called off-balance sheet obligations include commitments such as letters of credit and obligations on customized interest rate agreements (such as swaps, caps, and floors).

Currently there are dual capital adequacy standards. The first set of standards consists of two tests. The first test involves the ratio of "primary capital" to total assets, with primary capital defined as common stock, retained earnings, and undivided profit and reserves established for loan losses. For national banks, this ratio must be at least 5.5%. The second test is based on the ratio of "total capital" to total assets, where total capital is defined as the sum of primary capital and subordinated debt. The minimum ratio is now 6%.

In 1986, the Federal Reserve Board, the Office of the Comptroller of the Currency, and the Federal Deposit Insurance Corporation began to review risk-based capital requirements. In January 1989, the Federal Reserve issued final guidelines to implement risk-based capital requirements, the second set of capital adequacy standards that we referred to above. The guidelines are based on a framework adopted in July 1988 by the Basle Committee on Banking Regulations and Supervisory Practices, which consists of the central banks and supervisory authorities of the G-10 countries.[8]

The principal objectives of the guidelines are as follows. First, regulators in the United States and abroad have sought greater consistency in the evaluation of the capital adequacy of major banks throughout the world. Second, regulators have tried to establish capital adequacy standards that take into consideration the risk profile of the bank. Consider, for example, two banks, A and B, with $1 billion in assets. Suppose that both invest $400 million in identical assets, but the remaining $600 million in different assets. Bank A invests $500 million in U.S. government bonds and $100 million in business loans. Bank B invests $100 million in U.S. government bonds and $500 million in business loans. Obviously, the exposure to default losses is greater for Bank B. While the capital adequacy standards take this greater credit risk into account, they do not recognize liquidity factors or the market price sensitivity to which a bank may be exposed.

The risk-based capital guidelines attempt to recognize credit risk by segmenting and weighting requirements. First, capital is defined as consisting of Tier 1 and Tier 2 capital. Minimum requirements are established for each tier. Tier 1 capital is considered core capital; it consists basically of common stockholders' equity, certain types of preferred stock, and minority interest in consolidated subsidiaries. Tier 2 capital is called supplementary capital; it includes loan-loss reserves, certain types of preferred stock, perpetual debt (debt with no maturity date), hybrid capital instruments and equity contract notes, and subordinated debt.

Second, the guidelines establish a credit risk weight for all assets. The weight depends on the credit risk associated with each asset. There are four credit risk classifications for banks: 0%, 20%, 50%, and 100%, arrived at on no particular scientific basis. Listed below are a few examples of assets that fall into each credit risk classification.[9]

---

[8] Actually the G-10 group includes eleven countries: Belgium, Canada, France, Germany, Italy, Japan, Netherlands, Sweden, Switzerland, United Kingdom, and United States. Luxemburg also accepted the new standards.

[9] There are special rules for determining the amount of capital required for off-balance sheet items. An off-balance sheet item is a position in interest-sensitive contracts and/or foreign exchange-related products that is not reported on the balance sheet.

| Risk Weight | Example of Assets by Credit Risk Classification |
|---|---|
| 0% | U.S. Treasury securities |
| | Mortgage-backed securities issued by the Government National Mortgage Association |
| 20 | Municipal general obligation bonds |
| | Mortgage-backed securities issued by the Federal Home Loan Mortgage Corporation or the Federal National Mortgage Association |
| 50 | Municipal revenue bonds |
| | Residential mortgages |
| 100 | Commercial loans and commercial mortgages |
| | LDC loans |
| | Corporate bonds |
| | Municipal IDA bonds |

The way the credit risk weights work is as follows. The book value of the asset is multiplied by the credit risk weight to determine the amount of core and supplementary capital that the bank will need to support that asset. For example, suppose that the book values of the assets of a bank are as follows:

| Asset | Book Value (in Millions) |
|---|---|
| U.S. Treasury securities | $400 |
| Municipal general obligation bonds | 100 |
| Residential mortgages | 200 |
| Commercial loans | 300 |

The risk-weighted assets are calculated as follows:

| Asset | Book Value (in Millions) | Risk Weight | Product (in Millions) |
|---|---|---|---|
| U.S. Treasury securities | $400 | 0% | $ 0 |
| Municipal general obligation bonds | 100 | 20 | 20 |
| Residential mortgages | 200 | 50 | 100 |
| Commercial loans | 300 | 100 | 300 |
| Risk-weighted assets | | | $420 |

The risk-weighted assets for this bank would be $420 million.

The capital requirement guidelines were phased in between 1990 and 1992. From year-end 1992 and thereafter, the minimum core (Tier 1) capital is 4% of the risk-weighted assets; the minimum total capital (core plus supplementary) capital is 8% of the risk-weighted assets. To see how this works, consider the hypothetical bank we have used to illustrate the calculation of risk-weighted assets. For that bank the risk-weighted assets are $420 million. The minimum core capital is $16.8 million (0.04 times $420 million); the minimum total capital is $33.6 million (0.08 times $420 million).

One implication of the risk-based capital guidelines is that it will encourage banks to sell off their loans in the open market. By doing so, the bank need not maintain capital for the loans (assets) sold off. While the secondary market for individual bank loans has been growing, it has not reached the stage where a bank can efficiently sell large amounts of loans. An alternative is for a bank to pool loans and issue securities that are collateralized by the pool of loans. This is the process of asset securitization, which we discussed in Chapter 2.[10]

## Federal Deposit Insurance

Because of the important economic role played by banks, the U.S. government sought a way to protect them against depositors who, because of what they thought were either real or perceived problems with a bank, would withdraw funds in a disruptive manner. Bank panics occurred frequently in the early 1930s, resulting in the failure of banks that might have survived economic difficulties had it not been for massive withdrawals. The mechanism the U.S. government devised in 1933 to prevent a "run on a bank" was to create federal deposit insurance. The insurance was provided through a new agency, the Federal Deposit Insurance Corporation. A year later, federal deposit insurance was extended to savings and loan associations with the creation of the Federal Savings and Loan Insurance Corporation.

In 1933, federal deposit insurance covered accounts up to $2,500. This amount has been subsequently raised to its current level of $100,000. Prior to FIRREA, the premium that banks paid for this insurance was 0.083% of deposits. Currently it is 0.15% of deposits.

While federal deposit insurance did achieve its objective of preventing a run on banks, it unfortunately created incentives that encourage managers of depository institutions to take on excessive risks. If highly risky investments work out, the benefits accrue to the stockholders and management; if they do not, it is the depositors who are supposed to absorb the losses. Yet, depositors will have little concern about the risks that a depository institution is taking on because their funds are insured by the federal government. From a depositor's perspective, so long as the amount deposited does not exceed the insurance coverage, one depository institution is as good as another.

There have been several proposals to revise federal deposit insurance to overcome the incentive for excessive risk taking while preserving substantial deposit protection.[11] One proposal is to charge an insurance premium based on the riskiness of the bank's assets. The problem with this approach is quantifying the riskiness of assets. A system similar to the risk-based capital guidelines has been suggested. Another proposal is to make depositors discipline the management of depository institutions by either lowering the amount covered by insurance, or limiting the amount that any individual can be insured for, not in one account at one depository institution but in all depository institutions.

---

[10] For a discussion of the development of the market for senior bank loans, see Frank J. Fabozzi and John Carlson (eds.), *The Trading and Securitization of Senior Bank Loans* (Chicago: Probus Publishing, 1992).

[11] For a summary of the various proposals to restructure federal deposit insurance, see Loretta J. Mester, "Curing Our Ailing Deposit-Insurance System," *Business Review*, Federal Reserve Bank of Philadelphia (September-October 1990), pp. 13-24.

Whether depositors have the ability to assess the risks associated with depository institutions and thereby discipline management is questionable.

▶ KEY POINTS THAT YOU SHOULD UNDERSTAND BEFORE PROCEEDING:

1. Bank deposits are insured by government-sponsored insurance programs, and state-chartered banks may elect to join the Federal Reserve System.
2. Banks raise funds from deposits, from issuing debt and equity securities, and from their own earnings.
3. U.S. banks must keep a fraction of their deposits in assets that qualify as reserves.
4. Banks may borrow funds from the Federal Reserve System.
5. Why the government regulates many activities of banks, including their participation in securities markets and their capital structure.

## SAVINGS AND LOAN ASSOCIATIONS

S&Ls represent a fairly old institution. The basic motivation behind creation of S&Ls was provision of funds for financing the purchase of a home. The collateral for the loan would be the home being financed.

S&Ls are either mutually owned or have corporate stock ownership. "Mutually owned" means there is no stock outstanding, so technically the depositors are the owners. To increase the ability of S&Ls to expand the sources of funding available to bolster their capital, legislation facilitated the conversion of mutually owned companies into a corporate stock ownership structure.

Like banks, S&Ls may be chartered under either state or federal statutes. At the federal level, the primary regulator of S&Ls is, at present, the Director of the Office of Thrift Supervision (DOTS), created in 1989 by FIRREA. Prior to the creation of DOTS, the primary regulator was the Federal Home Loan Bank Board (FHLBB). While the FHLBB still exists, its responsibilities have been limited to the credit-facilitating function, that is, making loans (advances) to S&Ls.

Like banks, S&Ls are subject to reserve requirements on deposits established by the Fed. Prior to the passage of FIRREA, federal deposit insurance for S&Ls was provided by the Federal Savings and Loan Insurance Corporation (FSLIC). The Savings Association Insurance Fund (SAIF) has replaced FSLIC. SAIF is administered by the FDIC.

### Assets

Traditionally, the only assets in which S&Ls were allowed to invest have been mortgages, mortgage-backed securities and U.S. government securities. Mortgage loans include fixed-rate mortgages, adjustable-rate mortgages, and other types of mortgage designs. While most mortgage loans are for the purchase of homes, S&Ls do make construction loans. As of April 30, 1992, of the $872 billion of assets held by S&Ls, $525 billion were invested in mortgages and $125 billion in mortgage-related securities.[12]

As the structures of S&L balance sheets and the consequent maturity mismatch led to widespread disaster and insolvency, the Garn-St. Germain Act of 1982 expanded the types of assets in which S&Ls could invest. The acceptable list of investments now includes consumer loans (loans for home improvement, automobiles, education, mobile homes, and credit cards), non-consumer loans (commercial, corporate, business, or agricultural loans), and municipal securities.

While S&Ls had a comparative advantage in originating mortgage loans, they lacked the expertise to make commercial and corporate loans. Rather than make an investment in acquiring those skills, S&Ls took an alternative approach and invested in corporate bonds because these bonds were classified as corporate loans. More specifically, S&Ls became one of the major buyers of non-investment-grade corporate bonds, more popularly referred to as "junk" bonds or "high-yield" bonds. Under FIRREA, S&Ls are no longer permitted to invest new money in junk bonds and must divest themselves of their current holdings by August 1994.

S&Ls invest in short-term assets for operational (liquidity) and regulatory purposes. All S&Ls with federal deposit insurance must satisfy minimum liquidity requirements. These requirements are specified by the FHLBB. Acceptable assets include cash, short-term government agency and corporate securities, certificates of deposit of commercial banks,[13] other money market instruments, and federal funds. In the case of federal funds, the S&L is lending excess reserves to another depository institution that is short of funds.

## *Funding*

Prior to 1981, the bulk of the liabilities of S&Ls consisted of passbook savings accounts and time deposits. The interest rate that could be offered on these deposits was regulated. S&Ls were given favored treatment over banks with respect to the maximum interest rate they could pay depositors. They were permitted to pay an interest rate 0.5% higher, later reduced to 0.25%. With the deregulation of interest rates discussed earlier in this chapter, banks and S&Ls now compete head-to-head for deposits. Deregulation also expanded the types of accounts that may be offered by S&Ls—negotiable order of withdrawal (NOW) accounts and money market deposit accounts (MMDA). NOW accounts are similar to demand deposits. Unlike demand deposits, NOW accounts pay interest.

In the 1980s, S&Ls became more active in raising funds in the money market. For example, they were able to use the repurchase agreement market to raise funds. Some larger S&Ls have issued commercial paper as well as

---

[12] *Federal Reserve Bulletin* (September 1992), p. A26.

[13] The S&L is an investor when it holds the CD of a bank, but the CD represents the liability of the issuing bank.

medium-term notes.[14] They can borrow in the federal funds market and they have access to the Fed's discount window. S&Ls can also borrow from the Federal Home Loan Banks. These borrowings, called *advances*, can be short-term or long-term in maturity, and the interest rate can be fixed or floating.

## Regulation

Federal S&Ls are chartered under the provisions of the Home Owners Loan Act of 1933. Federally chartered S&Ls are now supervised by the Office of Thrift Supervisor. State-chartered banks are supervised by the respective states. A further act in 1933 established the Federal Savings and Loan Insurance Corporation, which at that time insured the deposits of federally chartered S&Ls up to $5,000 and allowed state-chartered S&Ls that could qualify to obtain the same insurance coverage. We discuss some of the important legislation and the players below.

As in bank regulation, S&Ls historically have been regulated with respect to the maximum interest rates on deposit accounts, geographical operations, permissible activities (types of accounts and types of investments), and capital adequacy requirements. In addition, there have been restrictions on the sources of non-deposit funds and liquidity requirements. We mentioned liquidity requirements earlier.[15]

The maximum interest rate that is permitted on deposit accounts has been phased out by the Depository Institutions Deregulation and Monetary Control Act of 1980 (DIDMCA). While this allowed S&Ls to compete with other financial institutions to raise funds, it also raised their funding costs. For reasons to be described later, while banks also faced higher funding costs, their balance sheets were better constituted than those of S&Ls to cope with the higher costs resulting from interest rate deregulation.

Besides phasing in the deregulation of interest rates on deposit accounts, DIDMCA was significant in several other ways. First, it expanded the Fed's control over the money supply by imposing deposit reserve requirements on S&Ls. In return, S&Ls were permitted to offer negotiable order of withdrawal (NOW) accounts.

Subsequent legislation, the Garn-St. Germain Act, not only granted thrifts the right to offer money market demand accounts so that S&Ls could compete with money market funds, but also broadened the types of assets in which S&Ls could invest. While S&Ls were first given permission by the FHLBB in 1979 to originate and invest in adjustable-rate mortgage loans, restrictions on the interest rate and other terms stymied their use. Two years later, the FHLBB removed some major impediments.

Permission to raise funds in the money market and the bond market was granted by the Federal Home Loan Bank Board in 1975 (when it allowed the

---

[14] The medium-term note market is discussed in Chapter 20.
[15] Liquidity requirements are not imposed on banks because the majority of their assets are of less than five years' maturity.

issuance of mortgage pass-through securities by S&Ls) and in 1979 (when it allowed the issuance of commercial paper and Eurodollar issues). FHLBB permission to form finance subsidiaries was granted in 1984. Through these subsidiaries, S&Ls were able to broaden their funding sources by the issuance of mortgage-related securities known as collateralized mortgage obligations.

There are two sets of capital adequacy standards for S&Ls as for banks. For S&Ls there are also two ratio tests based on "core" capital and "tangible" capital. The risk-based capital guidelines are similar to those for banks. Instead of two tiers of capital, however, there are three: Tier 1—tangible capital, Tier 2—core capital, and Tier 3—supplementary capital.

Geographical operations of S&Ls were restricted until 1981, when the FHLBB permitted thrifts to acquire thrifts in other states.

## The S&L Crisis

The story of the growth of the S&L industry since the late 1960s and the ensuing S&L crisis can't be described in one short chapter, but a basic understanding of the downfall of this industry is possible.

Until the early 1980s, S&Ls and all other lenders financed housing through traditional mortgages at interest rates fixed for the life of the loan. The period of the loan was typically long, frequently up to 30 years. Funding for these loans, by regulation, came from deposits having a maturity considerably shorter than the loans. As we explained earlier in this chapter, this is the funding problem of lending long and borrowing short. It is extremely risky—although regulators took a long time to understand it. There is no problem, of course, if interest rates are stable or declining, but if interest rates rise above the interest rate on the mortgage loan, a negative spread will result, which must result eventually in insolvency. Regulators at first endeavored to shield the S&L industry from the need to pay high interest rates without losing deposits by imposing a ceiling on the interest rate that would be paid by S&Ls and by their immediate competitors, the other depository institutions. But the approach did not and could not work.

With the high volatility of interest rates in the 1970s, followed by the historically high level of interest rates in the early 1980s, all depository institutions began to lose funds to competitors exempt from ceilings, such as the newly formed money market funds; this development forced some increase in ceilings. The ceilings in place since the middle of the 1960s did not protect the S&Ls; the institutions began to suffer from diminished profits, and increasingly from operating losses. A large fraction of S&Ls became technically insolvent as rising interest rates eroded asset market values to the point where they fell short of the liabilities.

But regulators, anxious to cover up the debacle of their empire, let them continue to operate, worsening the problem by allowing them to value their mortgage assets at book value. Profitability worsened with deregulation of the maximum interest rate that S&Ls could pay on deposits. While deregulation allowed S&Ls to compete with other financial institutions for funds, it also raised funding costs. Banks were better equipped to cope with rising funding costs because bank portfolios were not dominated by old, fixed-rate mortgages as S&Ls were. A larger portion of bank portfolios consisted of shorter-term assets and other assets whose interest rate reset to market interest rates after short time periods.

The difficulty of borrowing short and lending long was only part of the problem faced by the industry. As the crisis progressed, and the situation of many S&Ls became hopeless, fraudulent management activities were revealed. Many S&Ls facing financial difficulties also pursued strategies that exposed the institution to greater risk, in the hope of recovering if these strategies worked out. What encouraged managers to pursue such high-risk strategies was that depositors had no reason to be concerned with the risks associated with the institution where they kept their funds because the U.S. government, through federal deposit insurance, guaranteed the deposits up to a predetermined amount. Troubled S&Ls could pay existing depositors through attracting new depositors by offering higher interest rates on deposits than financially stronger S&Ls. In turn, to earn a spread on the higher cost of funds, they had to pursue riskier investment policies.

▶ KEY POINTS THAT YOU SHOULD UNDERSTAND BEFORE PROCEEDING:

1. S&Ls may be chartered by state or federal authorities.
2. The majority of assets owned by S&Ls are mortgages and mortgage-backed securities.
3. S&Ls may obtain funding from deposits and issuance of debt and equity securities.
4. The government regulates many aspects of an S&L's activities, including its capital structure.
5. The fundamental causes of the S&L crisis.

## SAVINGS BANKS

Savings banks are institutions similar to, although much older than, S&Ls. They can be either mutually owned (in which case they are called mutual savings banks) or stockholder-owned. While conversion of mutual to corporate structure was made easier by the Garn-St. Germain Act, most savings banks are of the mutual form. Only 16 states in the eastern portion of the U.S. charter savings banks. In 1978, Congress permitted the chartering of federal savings banks.

While the total deposits at savings banks are less than those at S&Ls, savings banks are typically larger institutions. Asset structures of savings banks and S&Ls are similar. The principal assets of savings banks are residential mortgages. Because states have permitted more portfolio diversification than was permitted by federal regulators of S&Ls, savings bank portfolios weathered funding risk far better than S&Ls. Included in savings bank portfolios are corporate bonds, Treasury and government agency securities, municipal securities, common stock, and consumer loans.

The principal source of funds for savings banks is deposits. Typically, the ratio of deposits to total assets is greater for savings banks than for S&Ls. Savings banks offer the same types of deposit accounts as S&Ls. Deposits can be insured by either the Bank Insurance Fund or Savings Association Insurance Fund.

## CREDIT UNIONS

Credit unions are the smallest and the newest of the depository institutions. Credit unions can obtain either a state or federal charter. Their unique aspect is the "common bond" requirement for credit union membership. According to the statutes that regulate federal credit unions, membership in a federal credit union "shall be limited to groups having a common bond of occupation or association, or to groups within a well-defined neighborhood, community, or rural district." They are either cooperatives or mutually owned. There is no corporate stock ownership. The dual purpose of credit unions is therefore to serve their members' saving and borrowing needs.

Technically, because credit unions are owned by their members, member deposits are called *shares*. The distribution paid to members is therefore in the form of dividends, not interest. Since 1970, the shares of all federally chartered credit unions have been insured by the National Credit Union Share Insurance Fund (NCUSIF) for up to $100,000, the same as other depository institutions. State-chartered credit unions may elect to have NCUSIF coverage.

Federal regulations apply to federally chartered credit unions and state-chartered credit unions that have elected to become members of NCUSIF. Most states, however, specify that state-chartered institutions must be subject to the same requirements as federally chartered ones. Effectively, therefore, most credit unions are regulated at the federal level. The principal federal regulatory agency is the National Credit Union Administration (NCUA).

Credit unions obtain their funds primarily from deposits of their members. With deregulation, they can offer a variety of accounts, including share drafts, which are similar to checking accounts but they pay interest. Playing a role similar to the Fed, as the lender of last resort, is the Central Liquidity Facility (CLF) which is administered by NCUA. CLF provides short-term loans to member credit unions with liquidity needs.

Credit union assets consist primarily of small consumer loans to their members. They also provide credit card loans.

## SUMMARY

Depository institutions (commercial banks, savings and loan associations, savings banks, and credit unions) accept various types of deposits. With the funds raised through deposits and other funding sources, they make loans to various entities and invest in securities. The deposits usually are insured by a federal agency. Income is derived from investments (loans and securities) and fee income. Thrifts (savings and loan associations, savings banks, and credit unions) are specialized types of depository institutions. Historically, they have not been authorized to accept demand accounts, but more recently thrifts have been offering some types of deposits equivalent to checking accounts.

A depository institution seeks to earn a positive spread between the assets it invests in and the cost of its funds. In generating spread income, a depository institution faces credit risk and funding or interest rate risk. A depository institution must be prepared to satisfy net withdrawals of funds by depositors and provide loans to customers. A depository institution can accommodate withdrawals or loan demand by attracting additional deposits, using existing securities as collateral for borrowing from a federal agency, raising short-term funds in the money market, or selling securities that it owns.

All national banks must be members of the Federal Reserve System. State-chartered banks may elect to join the Federal Reserve System. The services provided by commercial banks can be broadly classified as individual banking, institutional banking, and global banking.

There are three sources of funds for banks: (1) deposits; (2) nondeposit borrowing; and (3) retained earnings and sale of equity securities. Banks are highly leveraged financial institutions, meaning that most of their funds are obtained from deposits and non-deposit borrowing, which includes borrowing from the Fed through the discount window facility, borrowing reserves in the federal funds market, and borrowing by the issuance of instruments in the money and bond markets.

Banks must maintain reserves at one of the 12 Federal Reserve Banks, according to reserve requirements established by the Fed. Banks temporarily short of their required reserves can borrow reserves in the federal funds market or borrow temporarily from the Fed at its discount window.

There is both federal and state regulation of banks. At the federal level, supervision of banks is the responsibility of the Federal Reserve Board, the Office of the Comptroller of the Currency, and the Federal Deposit Insurance Corporation. Recent legislation has altered the regulatory structure. The major regulations involve geographical restrictions on branch banking, which are administered by the states and therefore vary widely, activities that are permissible for commercial banks, and capital requirements.

Like banks, S&Ls may be chartered under either state or federal statutes. At the federal level, the primary regulator of S&Ls is the Director of the Office of Thrift Supervision. The deposits of S&Ls are subject to reserve requirements established by the Fed. Federal deposit insurance for S&Ls is provided by the Savings Association Insurance Fund.

Much as in the case of bank regulation, S&Ls are regulated with respect to geographical operations, permissible activities, and capital adequacy requirements. S&Ls invest principally in mortgages and mortgage-related securities. Recent deregulation has expanded the types of investments that S&Ls are permitted to make, as well as expanding the types of deposit accounts that may be offered and the available funding sources.

The asset structures of savings banks and S&Ls are similar. As some states have permitted greater portfolio diversification than is permitted by federal regulators of S&Ls, this is reflected in savings bank portfolios. The principal source of funds for savings banks is deposits. Deposits can be federally insured by either the BIF or SAIF.

Credit unions are depository institutions that have a "common bond" requirement for membership. They are owned by their members. Although they can be state- or federally chartered, most credit unions effectively are regulated at the federal level by the National Credit Union Administration. The assets of credit unions consist primarily of small consumer loans to their members and credit card loans.

## GLOSSARY

**Advances:** Funds that savings and loan associations borrow from the Federal Home Loan Banks.

**Bank holding company:** A firm that owns one or more banks, usually by holding all or most of the equity shares of those banks.

**Bank Insurance Fund (or BIF):** Created in 1989 and administered by the Federal Deposit Insurance Corporation, this fund insures deposits of banks.

**Banking Act of 1933:** This law created the Federal Deposit Insurance Corporation and establishes rules on commercial banks' activities in the investment banking area, popularly referred to as the Glass-Steagall Act.

**Basle Committee on Banking Regulations and Supervisory Practices:** An international committee, consisting of the central banks and supervisory authorities of the large industrial and financial economies of the world.

**Capital adequacy standards:** Rules regarding the capital requirements of depository institutions.

**Capital requirements:** Governmental rules about the percentage of a depository institution's funding that must be in the form of equity, or owner-supplied capital.

**Central Liquidity Facility (or CLF):** Managed by the National Credit Union Administration, the CLF provides short-term loans to member credit unions with liquidity needs.

**Charter:** The authorization, by either a federal regulatory agency for national banks or a state agency for state banks, for a financial institution to engage in banking activities.

**Comptroller of the Currency:** A U.S. government agency with responsibility for chartering national banks and monitoring some of their key activities.

**Credit union:** An organization for people with some common bond, which accepts their savings as deposits and lends them money for purchases, mostly of consumer goods.

**Demand deposit:** A checking account that pays no interest and can be withdrawn upon demand.

**Deposit computation period:** The period over which a bank must calculate its actual reserves in order to determine if it has met the required reserve ratio.

**DIDMCA:** Passed by Congress in 1980, the Depository Institutions Deregulation and Monetary Control Act phased out the ceilings on interest rates on time deposits and certificates of deposit.

**Discount rate:** The interest rate that the Fed charges banks to borrow funds for brief periods of time.

**Discount window:** The facility by which banks can borrow short term from the Federal Reserve.

**Disintermediation:** The flow of funds, caused by the discrepancy between regulated and market interest rates, out of the regulated commercial banks and thrift institutions into other, unregulated financial institutions, such as money market mutual funds.

**Excess reserves:** The amount of a bank's reserves that is in excess of its required reserves.

**Federal Deposit Insurance Corporation (or FDIC):** Government agency that acts as an insurance company for deposits in U.S. banks.

**Federal funds:** The short-term loans (also called "fed funds") that banks lend to one another, at the fed funds rate, for the purpose of meeting reserve requirements of the Federal Reserve Board.

**FIRREA:** Passed by Congress in 1989, the Financial Institutions Reform, Recovery, and Enforcement Act that, among other things, created the Office of Thrift Supervision.

**Funding risk:** The risk that a depository institution will misjudge future interest rates and take positions with regard to borrowing and lending that may create a negative spread when rates change.

**Garn-St. Germain Act:** This 1982 legislation permitted banks to offer money market accounts, which are similar to those offered by money market mutual funds, and it increased the types of financial activities that savings and loan associations could engage in.

**Home Owners Loan Act:** The 1933 law that allows the federal government to charter S&Ls.

**Junk bonds:** Corporate debt securities that carry a rather high amount of credit risk or default risk and that offer a high yield commensurate with that risk.

**McFadden Act:** This 1926 legislation had the goal of preventing large banks from expanding geographically and thereby forcing out or taking over smaller banking entities.

**Money center bank:** A bank that raises most of its funds from the domestic and international money markets and that relies very little on deposits or depositors.

**Money market mutual fund:** An investment company that invests only in money market instuments.

**Mortgage:** Loan secured by real estate.

**National Credit Union Administration (or NCUA):** The agency of the federal government that regulates credit unions.

**National Credit Union Share Insurance Fund (or NCUSIF):** A government-sponsored insurance fund for deposits in federally chartered credit unions and state-chartered credit unions that elect to participate.

**NOW (or Negotiable Order of Withdrawal) Account:** A form of a negotiable deposit that is entirely equivalent to a checking account and that savings and loan associations or thrifts have been allowed to offer since the early 1980s.

**Primary capital:** A financial institution's sum of funding provided by common stock, retained earnings, and undivided profit and reserves established for loan losses.

**Regional bank:** A bank that relies primarily on deposits for funding and makes less use of the money markets to obtain funds.

**Regulation Q:** Rule that, at one time, allowed the Fed to impose a ceiling on the maximum interest rate that depository institutions could pay on deposits other than demand accounts.

**Regulatory risk:** The risk that regulators will change the rules so as to impact the earnings of financial institutions unfavorably.

**Reserve requirements:** The percentage of deposits that, by Federal Reserve Board rules, depository institutions must keep in the form of cash or deposits in a Federal Reserve bank.

**Reserves:** The sum of the cash and deposits in the Federal Reserve Bank System that a depository institution holds for the purpose of meeting reserve requirements.

**Risk-based capital guidelines:** Capital requirements for a financial institution that are based on the credit risk of a bank's assets.

**Savings bank:** An early form of the savings and loan association, which appears only in certain geographical areas and that specializes in home mortgages.

**Savings deposit:** An account that pays interest, does not have a specific maturity, and can usually be withdrawn upon demand.

**Secondary reserves:** Short-term or money market securities that a depository institution holds for the purpose of satisfying net withdrawals and customer loan demands.

**Spread income:** A depository institution's margin of profit, which is the difference between the rate earned on assets (loans and securities) and the cost of funds (deposits and other sources).

**Superregional bank:** Large regional banks that compete in certain domestic and international financial activities that were once the domain of money center banks.

**Time deposit:** An interest-paying account that has a fixed maturity date, often called a certificate of deposit.

**Total capital:** A financial institution's sum of primary capital and subordinated debt.

1. Explain the ways in which a depository institution can accommodate withdrawal and loan demand.

2. What is meant by:
   a. Individual banking?
   b. Institutional banking?
   c. Global banking?

3. Explain each of the following:
   a. Reserve ratio.
   b. Required reserves.

4. Explain each of the following types of deposit accounts:
   a. Demand deposit.
   b. Certificate of deposit.
   c. Money market demand account.

5. You and a friend are discussing the savings and loan crisis. She states that "the whole mess started in the early 1980s. When short-term rates skyrocketed, S&Ls got killed—their spread income went from positive to negative. They were borrowing short and lending long."
   a. What does she mean by "borrowing short and lending long"?
   b. Are higher or lower interest rates beneficial to an institution that borrows short and lends long?

6. Alan Greenspan, the Chairman of the Federal Reserve Board, told the U.S. Senate on July 12, 1990:

   *As you know, the Board has long supported repeal of the provisions of the Glass-Steagall Act that separated commercial and investment banking. We still strongly advocate such repeal because we believe that technology and globalization have continued to blur the distinctions among credit markets, and have eroded the franchise value of the classic bank intermediation process. Outdated constraints will only endanger the profitability of banking organizations and their contribution to the American economy.*

     a.   What do you think Mr. Greenspan means when he says that the value of the bank intermediation process has been eroded by technology and globalization?

     b.   What do you think are some of the major benefits and risks of repealing key provisions of the Glass-Steagall Act?

7.   Consider this headline from *The New York Times* of March 26, 1933:

     *Bankers will fight Deposit Guarantees . . . Bad Banking would be encouraged*

     a.   What do you think this means?

     b.   Discuss the pros and cons of deposit insurance by the U.S. government.

8.   The following quotation is from the October 29, 1990 issue of *Corporate Financing Week:*

> *Chase Manhattan Bank is preparing its first asset-backed debt issue, becoming the last major consumer bank to plan to access the growing market, Street asset-backed officials said. . . . Asset-backed offerings enable banks to remove credit card or other loan receivables from their balance sheets, which helps them comply with capital requirements.*

     a.   What capital requirements is this article referring to?

     b.   Explain why asset securitization reduces capital requirements.

9.   Comment on this statement: The risk-based guidelines for commercial banks attempt to gauge the interest rate risk associated with a bank's balance sheet.

10.   a.   What is the primary asset in which savings and loan associations invest?

     b.   Why were banks in a better position than savings and loan associations to weather rising interest rates?

# CHAPTER FIVE

# Central Banks and the Creation of Money

*After reading this chapter you will understand:*

- the structure of the Federal Reserve System and the nature of the Fed's instruments of monetary policy.
- the meaning of required reserves for banks, and the fractional reserve banking system of the U.S.
- the implementation and impact of open market operations and of open market repurchase agreements.
- the role of the Fed's discount rate.
- the different kinds of money and the definitions of key monetary aggregates.
- the money multiplier, and how it generates changes in the monetary aggregates from changes in the banking system's reserves.
- how banks and investors participate, with the Fed, in changing the level of the monetary aggregates.
- how foreign trade and investment influence the Fed's monetary policy.

In most advanced economies, the process by which the supply of money is created is a complex interaction among several economic agents, which perform different functions at different times. The agents are firms and individuals who both save and borrow, depository institutions that accept savings and make loans to firms or individuals or other institutions, and the nation's central bank, which also lends and buys and sells securities. This chapter gives a brief and general description of the complex process of creating the money supply. In so doing, the chapter highlights the role played by U.S. depository institutions and by the financial markets that the process both uses and affects. The chapter also describes the monetary and banking systems of several other major economies.

## THE CENTRAL BANK AND MONEY CREATION IN THE UNITED STATES

### The Central Bank of the United States: The Federal Reserve System

The most important agent in the money supply process is the Federal Reserve System, which is the central bank of the United States and often called just the Federal Reserve or the Fed. Created in 1913, the Fed is the government agency responsible for the management of the U.S. monetary and banking systems. Most large commercial banks in the United States are members of the Federal Reserve System. The Fed is managed by a seven-member Board of Governors, who are appointed by the President and approved by the Congress. These governors have 14-year appointments (with one appointment ending every two years), and one governor is the Board's Chairman. The Chairmanship of the Fed is a highly visible and influential position in the world economy. The Federal Reserve System consists of 12 districts covering the entire country; each district has a Federal Reserve Bank with its own president.

An important feature of the Fed is that, by the terms of the law that created it, neither the legislative nor the executive branch of the federal government should exert control over it. From time to time, critics charge that the Fed guards this autonomy by accommodating either the White House or Congress (or both) far too much. We have noted in Chapters 3 and 4 that the Fed has substantial regulatory power over the nation's depository institutions, especially commercial banks.

It is worth noting here, before we discuss the Fed's tools for monetary management, that financial innovations in the last two decades have made the Fed's task more difficult. The public's increasing acceptance of money market mutual funds has funneled a large amount of money into what are essentially interest-bearing checking accounts. (See Chapter 8 for more information on mutual funds.) Another relevant innovation is the practice of asset securitization, discussed in Chapter 2. Securitization permits commercial banks to change what once were illiquid consumer loans of several varieties into securities. Selling these securities in the financial markets gives the banks a source of funding that is outside the Fed's influence. The many hedging instruments to be analyzed in Section IX of this book have also affected banks' behavior and their relationship with the Fed. In general, that transformation amounts to reduced Fed control of banks and increased difficulty in implementing monetary policy.

### *Instruments of Monetary Policy: How the Fed Influences the Supply of Money*

The Fed has several tools by which it influences, indirectly and to a greater or lesser extent, the amount of money in the economy and the general level of interest rates. These tools are reserve requirements (whose use is somewhat constricted by Congressional mandate), open market operations, open market repurchase agreements, and the discount rate. These instruments represent the key ways that the Fed interacts with commercial banks in the process of creating money. Our discussion of these tools explains the impact of their use on a generally specified money supply. Later, we describe the money supply in more detail.

**Reserve Requirements.** Bank reserves play an important role in the U.S. banking and monetary system and are directly linked to the growth in the money supply. Generally, the higher the growth rate in reserves, the higher the rate of change in the money supply. Later in this chapter, we will discuss this linkage in some detail. At this point, we want to focus on the meaning and function of reserve requirements.

The U.S. has a *fractional reserve banking system*, which means that a bank must hold or "reserve" some portion of the funds that savers deposit in a form approved by the Fed. As a result, a bank may lend to borrowers only a fraction of what it takes in as deposits. The ratio of mandatory reserves to deposits is the *required reserve ratio*. For many years, the Fed had the authority to set this ratio. In the Depository Institutions Deregulation and Monetary Control Act of 1980, Congress assumed much of that responsibility, establishing new rules regarding this ratio to be applied to all depository institutions, including commercial banks, thrifts of various types, and credit unions.

In a key provision of the DIDMCA, Congress adopted a basic ratio of 12% for what are termed checkable or transactional accounts, that is, *demand deposits*, or accounts on which checks may be written often. For nontransactional but short-term deposit accounts—known as *time deposits*—the required reserve ratio is 3%. The 1980 law also authorizes the Fed to change the required reserve ratio on checking accounts to any level between 8% and 14%, and to raise it to 18% under certain conditions. In early 1992, the Fed reduced the ratio to 10% for banks with total checkable accounts at or above $46.8 million. For banks with smaller totals in these accounts, the required reserve ratio is 3%.

A bank must maintain the required reserves as either currency on hand (that is, cash in the bank) or deposits in the Federal Reserve itself. The more important form is the deposit, which serves as an asset for the bank and as a liability of the Fed. A bank has *excess reserves* if its reserves amount to more than the Fed requires. A bank's *total reserves* equal its required reserves plus any excess reserves. A bank whose actual reserves fall short of required levels can borrow excess reserves from other banks (see the next chapter and Chapter 22 for more on the federal funds market), or it can borrow reserves from the Fed itself, which we discuss later in this chapter.

***Open Market Operations.***   The Fed's most powerful instrument is its authority to conduct open market operations, which means that the Fed may buy and sell, in open debt markets, government securities for its own account. These securities may be U.S. Treasury bonds, Treasury bills, or obligations of federal agencies. (We describe these securities in more detail in Chapter 16.) The Fed prefers to use Treasury bills because, in that large and liquid market, it can make its substantial transactions without seriously disrupting the prices or yields of bills. When it buys or sells, the Fed does so at prices and interest rates that prevail in these debt markets. The parties to the Fed's transactions may be commercial banks or other financial agents who are dealers in government securities.

The unit of the Fed that decides on the general issues of changing the rate of growth in the money supply, by open market sales or purchase of securities, is the *Federal Open Market Committee*, or FOMC. The FOMC consists of the Board of Governors, the President of the Federal Reserve Bank of New York, and presidents of some of the other district Fed banks. This committee meets approximately once a month to analyze economic activity and levels of key economic variables. The variables may include short-term interest rates (such as the federal funds rate), the U.S. dollar's rate of exchange with important foreign currencies, commodity prices, and excess reserves, among other things.[1] After this analysis, the committee sets the direction of monetary policy for the near future. The minutes of these meetings are published at a later time.

The implementation of policy, through open market operations, is the responsibility of the *trading desk of the Federal Reserve Bank of New York*. The desk transacts, in large volume, with bigger securities firms or commercial banks that are dealers, or market makers, in Treasury securities. While the desk does not buy and sell for profit, it functions as a rational investor, buying at the lowest prices and selling at the highest prices offered at the time of the transactions.

Fed purchases augment the amount of reserves in the banking system. If the seller is a commercial bank, it alters the composition, but not the total, of its assets by exchanging the securities for reserves at the Fed. If the seller is not a bank, much or all of the check with which the Fed pays will probably be deposited in a bank. The bank receiving the deposit would experience an increase in liabilities (the customer's deposit) and in assets (the growth in its reserve account at the Fed). In either case, the proceeds from selling the

---

[1] D.S. Batten, M.P. Blackwell, I-S. Kim, S.E. Nocera, and Y. Ozeki, *The Conduct of Monetary Policy in the Major Industrial Countries*. Occasional Paper No. 70, International Monetary Fund (Washington: July 1990), p. 24.

securities to the Fed raise the banking system's total reserves. Such an increase in reserves typically leads to an increase in the money supply. Individual banks whose reserves rise will generally make new loans, equal to the new deposit less required reserves, because loans earn interest while reserves do not. New loans represent growth in the money supply.

Conversely, the Fed's sale of Treasury securities reduces the money supply (or its rate of growth), because the funds that security dealers pay for the securities come from either deposits at banks or, if the dealers are banks, from the banks' own accounts. A reduction in deposits reduces reserves and leaves the banks less to lend.

***Open Market Repurchase Agreements.*** The Fed often employs variants of simple open market purchases and sales, and these are called the *repurchase agreement* (or "repo") and the *reverse repo*. The Fed conducts these transactions, which are actually more common than the outright purchases or sales,[2] with large dealers in government securities and, occasionally, with central banks of other countries. In a repurchase agreement, the Fed buys a particular amount of securities from a seller that agrees to repurchase the same number of securities for a higher price at some future time, usually a few weeks. The difference between the original price and the repurchase price is the return to the Fed for letting the dealer have the cash for the life of the agreement and, also, the cost to the dealer of borrowing from the Fed. In a reverse repo (also known as a *matched sale* or a *matched sale-purchase transaction*), the Fed sells securities and makes a commitment to buy them back at a higher price later. The difference in the two prices is the cost to the Fed of the funds and the return to the buyer for lending money.

An example will illustrate some of the points in a Fed repurchase agreement. (A detailed analysis of repos appears in Chapters 16 and 22.) Suppose the Fed wants to increase bank reserves for some reason over a short period of time, and it seeks out a financial institution that has $20 million in Treasury securities but no excess reserves. Suppose further that the institution wants to lend $19 million for seven days to a borrower. After some discussions, the Fed agrees to "buy" the securities from the institution at a price that reflects the current repo rate, and to "sell" them back in seven days, when the institution's borrower pays off that loan. The current annualized rate is 4.3%. The transaction would look like this: the Fed would buy the securities for approximately $19,983,278 and sell them back, seven days later, to the institution at the principal value of $20 million. The difference of nearly $16,722 is the interest the institution pays for the 7-day financing and the return to the Fed for lending that money. And for those seven days, the financial institution and the entire banking system can enjoy an increase in reserves, if, of course, the bank keeps the roughly $20 million in its account at the Fed.

The Fed uses repos and reverse repos to bring about a temporary change in the level of reserves in the system or to respond to some event that the Fed

[2] Alfred Broaddus, "A Primer on the Fed," Chapter 7 in Sumner N. Levine (ed.), *The Financial Analyst's Handbook* (Homewood, IL: Dow Jones-Irwin, 1988), p. 186.

thinks will have a significant but not long-lived effect. A particularly good example of such an event is a large payment by the U.S. Treasury (as in tax refunds or Social Security benefits) that sharply but temporarily raises reserves at the banks. Of course, these temporary changes in the system's reserves alter the banks' ability to make loans and, ultimately, to prompt growth in the money supply for a short period.

***Discount Rate.***    As mentioned in Chapter 4, the Fed makes loans to banks that are members of the System. A bank borrowing from the Fed is said to use the "discount window," and these loans are backed by the bank's collateral. The rate of interest on these loans is the *discount rate*, set at a certain level by the Fed's Board of Governors. As the rate rises, banks are understandably less likely to borrow; a falling rate tends to encourage them to borrow. Proceeds from *discount loans* are also reserves and increase the banks' capacity to make loans. Banks generally do not prefer to gain reserves in this way because the loans cost money as well as invite increased monitoring of the borrowing banks' activities. Accordingly, the flow of this borrowing has a very slight impact on the money banks have and can lend and, therefore, on the supply of money.

There is general agreement that the discount rate is the least effective tool at the Fed's disposal and its use in monetary policy has diminished over time. Today, changes in the discount rate function largely as the Fed's public signals about its intention to change the rate at which the money supply is growing.

## Different Kinds of Money

Until now, we have spoken in general terms about the "money supply." But we can be more precise and identify several different meanings of the word "money" and several different types of money.

First of all, money is that item which serves as a "numeraire," or unit of account—in other words, the unit that is used to measure wealth. In the U.S., the numeraire is the dollar; in France it is the franc, and so on. Second, we call money any instrument that serves as a medium of exchange; that is, anything that is generally accepted in payment for goods, services, and capital transactions. In the United States, the medium of exchange encompasses currency, which is issued by the Treasury or the Fed, and demand deposits, which support payment by means of checks and are held at depository institutions such as commercial banks. The medium of exchange also performs the function of being a store of value, which means that the exchange medium can be used to carry resources over from the present to the future. Obviously, this function is impaired in times of high and unpredictable inflation.[3] Other accounts that

---

[3] The *giro payment*, an alternative to the check, is used in many foreign countries. The giro payment is a direct order to the payer's bank to make a payment to a seller of some good or service. The check, of course, is an order to pay that is drawn on an account at the payer's bank and that the payer gives to the seller.

resemble demand deposits include the NOW account or Negotiable Order of Withdrawal account and share drafts of credit unions.

Other assets that do not function in the role of medium of exchange have many properties in common with the numeraire. These properties include safety, divisibility, and high liquidity, which is the capacity of being transformed into the medium of exchange promptly and at negligible cost. Because of these properties, these assets are good substitutes for money, in particular, as stores of value. The assets of this type include *time deposits* at commercial banks or thrifts: these accounts earn interest over their specified lives, and the investor may not draw on the money in the account for a transaction, without incurring a penalty, until the deposit's maturity date. Other assets that are substitutes for money include balances in money market mutual funds.

## Money and Monetary Aggregates

Monetary policy and the actions of the Federal Reserve System often concentrate on what are called "monetary aggregates." The purpose of the aggregates is to measure the amount of money available to the economy at any time.

The most basic monetary aggregate is the *monetary base*. Also termed "high-powered money," the base is defined as currency in circulation (or coins and Federal Reserve notes held by the public) plus the total reserves in the banking system. It is important to note that reserves make up the bulk of the base, which is under the control of the Fed. Thus, this aggregate is the one that the Fed is most able to influence with its various monetary tools.

The instruments that serve the role of medium of exchange—currency and demand deposits—are included in a monetary aggregate that is sometimes referred to as the narrow measure of the money supply and is labeled $M_1$. Thus, $M_1$ measures the amount of the medium of exchange in the economy.

$M_2$ is a more inclusive aggregate because it takes into account all the instruments that substitute for money in the capacity of storing value. Therefore, $M_2$ is defined as $M_1$ plus all dollars held in time and savings accounts at banks and thrift institutions, plus all dollars invested in retail money market mutual funds, plus some additional accounts such as overnight repurchase agreements. Some analysts also watch developments in two other monetary aggregates, which are labeled $M_3$ and L (for "liquid assets"). These aggregates equal $M_2$ plus certain other financial assets, including long-term time deposits, commercial paper, bankers acceptances, and some Treasury securities.

The ratio of the money supply to the economy's income (as reflected by the Gross National Product or some similar measure) is known as the "velocity of money in circulation." Velocity measures the average amount of transactions carried by a dollar. If the economy's velocity were stable, monetary policy could achieve any desired level of income by simply targeting the aggregate $M_1$. Unfortunately, velocity is not a stable relationship, and in fact, the linkages between the economy's income and the various aggregates vary considerably over time.

Typically, the monetary aggregates move in somewhat similar patterns, rising and falling at roughly the same rates and at roughly the same times. Table

5-1 shows the growth rates for $M_1$, $M_2$, and $M_3$ during the period from 1980 to 1991. However, the differences among the changes in the aggregates are large and frequent enough to suggest that these aggregates are measuring different things. A major question in Fed policymaking (which we discuss below) has revolved around choosing the most appropriate definition of the money supply.

### *The Money Multiplier: The Expansion of the Money Supply*

Our discussion of how the supply of money is created focuses on the linkage between the banking system's reserves and the aggregate $M_1$. The process we describe, the "money multiplier," can be generalized to the other monetary aggregates, but the complexities involved in those processes are not relevant to our task now.

We begin by restating that the creation of the money supply, and changes in it, is a complex interaction of four parties: the Fed, banks, savers, and borrowers. The Fed provides reserves to banks and also requires banks to hold, as reserves, a portion of the deposits that the public holds at the banks. The banks, playing their key role in the "money multiplier," lend the remainder of the deposits (or most of it) to borrowers at an interest rate that exceeds that of demand deposits. For any one bank, the remainder equals deposits less required reserves, which can be expressed as deposits times (1 −

| TABLE | 5 - 1 | | |
|-------|-------|---|---|

ANNUAL RATES OF GROWTH IN MONETARY AGGREGATES,
1980–1991

| Year | $M_1$ | $M_2$ | $M_3$ |
|------|-------|-------|-------|
| 1980 | 6.6% | 9.0% | 10.3% |
| 1981 | 6.3 | 10.0 | 11.4 |
| 1982 | 9.0 | 7.9 | 12.5 |
| 1983 | 9.4 | 11.8 | 10.2 |
| 1984 | 6.3 | 8.1 | 10.2 |
| 1985 | 12.3 | 8.3 | 7.3 |
| 1986 | 16.5 | 9.0 | 8.9 |
| 1987 | 3.6 | 4.3 | 5.2 |
| 1988 | 5.1 | 5.5 | 6.5 |
| 1989 | 0.9 | 5.0 | 3.5 |
| 1990 | 4.0 | 3.3 | 1.4 |
| 1991 | 8.6 | 2.9 | 1.5 |

*Note:* Annual rates are percentage changes of seasonally adjusted money stock measures, from December to December.

*Source:* Various issues, *Federal Reserve Bulletin*, Federal Reserve Board of Governors, Washington, D.C.

required reserve ratio). Clearly, the funds one bank lends to a borrower can become the borrower's deposits in another bank. The borrower's decision to hold wealth as deposits rather than cash also affects the "money multiplier." Then, that second bank must keep a fraction of those new deposits as reserves and can lend out to other borrowers an amount equal to the deposits less required reserves.

We will illustrate this process with an extended example. Suppose the Fed's required reserve ratio is 12%, and deposits at Bank A are $100 million, while those at Bank B are $50 million. Bank A has reserves of $12 million and outstanding loans of $88 million, and Bank B has reserves of $6 million with loans to borrowers of $44 million. For Bank A, the loan amount of $88 million equals either $100 million of deposits less $12 million of reserves, or $100 million times $(1 - 0.12)$. For Bank B, loans of $44 million equal $50 million minus the 12% required reserves of $6 million. Thus, neither Bank A nor Bank B has any *excess reserves* (which equal total less required reserves). The level of reserves in the banking system has led $M_1$ to reach the level of (let us say) $900 billion, which equals $250 billion in currency and $650 billion in demand deposits. For this example, we assume that the amount of currency in the system will not change.

The Fed can increase the reserves by either lending to the banks or by purchasing government securities from the banks or other investors. (We ignore here the Fed's authority to change the required reserve ratio.) In this example, we suppose that the Fed buys $5 million of U.S. Treasury securities from a dealer who deposits the check, which is drawn on the Fed, with Bank A. Bank A's reserve account with the Fed has increased by $5 million and so have its (demand) deposits, its total reserves, and the overall level of $M_1$. But required reserves have risen only by $5 million $\times$ 0.12 or $600,000. This leaves an additional $4.4 million that the bank is free and eager to invest in order to improve its income.

We continue by assuming that a machinery manufacturing firm borrows all of the $4.4 million in a one-year loan, then buys equipment from a company that places all of that money in a checking account (or demand deposit) at another bank, which is Bank B. Bank A must transfer reserves for the amount of the loan to Bank B. The situation regarding Bank A is this: its level of deposits remains unchanged at $105 million; its loans have increased by $4.4 million to $92.4 million; its reserves have fallen by $4.4 million from $17 million to $12.6 million; so, its ratio of reserves to deposits is again the required 12% and it has reached its capacity for making loans. Since Bank A's deposits are unchanged, $M_1$ is also unchanged from its new level of $900.005 billion.

After the transaction, Bank B's deposits have risen by $4.4 million, an increase that raises the amount of $M_1$ by an additional $4.4 million (or $9.4 million altogether, so far) to $900.0094 billion. Bank B has total reserves of $10.4 million and excess reserves equal to 88% of the $4.4 million in new deposits. Thus, Bank B can lend $3.87 million, keeping $528,000 as required reserves. If loans of $3.87 million are made to borrowers who place those loans as deposits with other banks, the process of creating money, in the form of $M_1$, will continue.

Where will the process end and what amount of new money, in the form of new demand deposits, will arise from the new reserves? In other words, what is the "money multiplier"? In this example, the Fed's open market purchase of $5 million of U.S. Treasury securities, along with the banks' incentive to make as many loans as they are permitted to do, has created demand deposits of $9.4 million at the first two banks involved. Still more deposits can be created at other banks. This process will continue as long as other banks use the ever smaller increases in demand deposits to make loans, which become additional demand deposits and excess reserves at still other banks, and so on. Although the process has no set limit in terms of time, there is a maximum number of dollars in new demand deposits that will spring from the new reserves.

This process is a form of a "multiplier series" that can be expressed in an algebraic formula. If we let $\Delta TDD$ be the total demand deposits created, $\Delta R$ be the reserves injected into system by the Fed's purchase of Treasury securities, and REQ be the required reserve ratio, then the total of new deposits generated by the expansion of the initial injection of reserves would equal:

$$\Delta TDD = \Delta R + (1 - REQ) \times \Delta R + (1 - REQ)^2 \times \Delta R + (1 - REQ)^3 \times \Delta R$$
$$+ (1 - REQ)^4 \times \Delta R + \ldots \tag{1}$$

Because there are many potential elements in this series, which can get cumbersome, it is best to use this simple version of it:

$$\Delta TDD = \Delta R / REQ \tag{2}$$

In the example, REQ equals 12% and $\Delta R$ equals $5 million. Hence, new total demand deposits (if banks lend as much as they can and keep no excess reserves) amount to $5 million/0.12, or $41.67 million. The money multiplier is, therefore, 8.33. As a result, total $M_1$ will reach $900.04167 billion dollars when the process is completed, which equals the original $900 billion plus $41.67 million in new deposits. Equation (2) clearly shows that the eventual amount of the new demand deposits is negatively related to the required reserve ratio: as REQ falls, the change in TDD rises; and as REQ increases, the change in TDD declines. Thus, if everything in the example were the same, but REQ were 10% instead of 12%, the new demand deposits would reach $50 million.

Obviously, the process of reducing the money supply works in the opposite way. That is, if the Fed wants to drain reserves from the system and reduce the banks' lending ability, it sells securities. The reduction in reserves, as the public trades deposits for marketable securities, allows banks to make fewer new loans or to renew fewer old ones.

## The Impact of Interest Rates on the Money Supply

A later chapter describes how changes in the money supply affect interest rates. We note here only that interest rates actually influence the change in the money supply. This point emerges from an evaluation of two key assumptions made above.[4] First, banks are assumed to want to make all the loans they can. If, however, banks were to keep some excess reserves, they would make fewer new loans and generate fewer deposits at other banks, which would affect the amount of $M_1$ that the Fed's purchase of securities would generate.

One of the important factors in a bank's decisions about excess reserves is the level of market interest rates. High rates make excess reserves costly, because they represent loans not made and interest not earned. If rates are low, banks may keep some excess reserves. Hence, the level of interest rates positively influences the amount of $M_1$ that any increase in reserves will create. Moreover, interest rates can also positively (but probably only slightly) affect the amount of reserves in the system: high market rates may prompt banks to borrow at the "discount window" in order to make loans, and these borrowed funds are part of reserves.

By the second assumption, borrowers retain none of their loans in cash, but rather deposit all cash flows—proceeds from sold securities, loans, and so on—into checking accounts. In contrast, if borrowers took some of their borrowings in cash, banks would receive fewer deposits and would have fewer reserves from which to make new loans. Accordingly, the public's demand for cash as a portion of its liquid wealth has an impact on the amount of $M_1$ that arises from the Fed's injection of new reserves.

The level of market rates shapes decisions about cash holdings. Many deposit accounts pay interest, so holding cash imposes an opportunity cost. The higher the rate, the greater the cost, and the more money investors will shuttle into deposits. But the rate on deposits is not the only relevant interest rate. The desired amount of deposits, from which transactions can be easily made, also reflects the rates of return from other assets. As those returns rise, investors would hold more in deposit accounts. For these reasons, the level of interest rates positively affects the size of the money multiplier and, hence, the amount of $M_1$ that any increase in reserves will produce.

## The Money Supply Process in An Open Economy

Our discussion so far describes central bank activity in what economists call a *closed economy*. A closed economy is one in which foreign transactors—of either goods or financial assets—play a negligible role. In the modern era, al-

---

[4] Lucas Papademos and Franco Modigliani, "The Supply of Money and the Control of Nominal Income," Chapter 10 in Benjamin M. Friedman and Frank H. Hahn (eds.), *Handbook of Monetary Economics* (Amsterdam: North-Holland (Elsevier), 1990), pp. 428–430.

most every country has an *open economy*, where foreign firms and investors account for a large and increasing share of economic activity. This is especially true of the world's largest economy, that of the United States. Understanding of the money supply process therefore must include the influence of the foreign sector.

Monetarily, the crucial fact of significant foreign participation in the U.S. economy is that foreign central banks, firms, and individuals hold a substantial number of U.S. dollars. They do so for transactional reasons—buying and selling goods and services in the United States—and for investment purposes—treating the dollar as a financial asset. What makes the foreign holdings of dollars important is that the dollar's exchange rate with currencies of most developed countries floats according to demand and supply in the market. (As we explain in Chapter 6, most central banks, including the Fed, try to keep exchange rates within politically acceptable ranges.)

Shifts in the dollar's exchange rates, obviously, affect the prices of domestic and imported goods, the revenues of U.S. companies, and the wealth of all investors in the country. As a result, the Fed accepts the responsibility to maintain some stability in the exchange rates. A major way to discharge this duty is to *intervene in the foreign exchange markets*. (See Chapter 30 for more detail on foreign currency markets.) The Fed intervenes by buying and selling foreign currencies for its own account. (Most central banks of large economies own, or stand ready to own, a large amount of each of the world's major currencies, which are considered *international reserves*.)

If the Fed thinks the dollar is valued too high and a foreign currency is too low, it can purchase some of the foreign currency with its own supply of dollars. A purchase involves increasing the outstanding number of dollars and thereby the monetary base. If the Fed thinks the dollar has too low a value relative to some other currency, it might sell some of its holdings of that currency for dollars. Thus, selling foreign currency entails a reduction in the monetary base. Intervention in the currency market is often a response to a particular international event. Moreover, the intervention usually involves a transaction with other central banks, which consists of an immediate exchange of currencies and an agreement for a future offsetting exchange. Thus, this kind of action allows the Fed to know the terms on which the currency deal will terminate and the time when it will terminate.

Our discussion of the elements of monetary policy in Chapter 6 should make it clear that the dollar's exchange rates with important foreign currencies function as a major goal of monetary policy. That is, in forging and implementing policy, the Fed considers the effect of a change in the money supply on the relative value of the dollar in the foreign exchange market.

Dramatic evidence of the growing importance of international policy coordination on monetary matters occurred in two meetings of central bankers of the large industrial nations in the mid-1980s. In 1985, central bank chairmen and directors of the G-5 countries (the United States, Great Britain, France, Germany, and Japan) met at the Plaza Hotel in New York. There, they agreed to coordinate policies in order to bring down the value of the U.S. dollar and to stabilize international exchange rates and trade. In 1987, at the Louvre Museum in Paris, central bankers from the G-5 and Canada agreed to work together to keep exchange rates at their current levels. These efforts at international cooperation on monetary and exchange issues are generally seen as successful.

▶ KEY POINTS THAT YOU SHOULD UNDERSTAND BEFORE PROCEEDING:

1.  The Federal Reserve System is the central bank of the U.S. and responsible for the conduct of monetary policy.

2.  The instruments of monetary policy, including reserve requirements, open market operations and repurchase agreements, and the discount rate.

3.  The different kinds of money, such as the numeraire, the store of value, and the medium of exchange.

4.  The various monetary aggregates and what they are supposed to convey to policymakers.

5.  The nature of the money multiplier and how it links reserves in the banking system to monetary aggregates.

6.  That interest rates affect the rate at which the money supply changes in response to actions by the Fed.

7.  That the openness of an economy to participation by foreign firms, central banks, and individuals affects monetary management.

## THE CENTRAL BANKS OF OTHER COUNTRIES

We now turn our attention to the monetary and banking systems of three other significant economies in the world: Germany, Japan, and the United Kingdom.

### Germany

Germany's banking system is important for several reasons: (1) Germany is the strongest and largest economy in Europe, whose economic and trade unification will be a key feature of business and finance for years to come; (2) German interest rates are commonly cited benchmarks in many international financial arrangements; and (3) Germany's strategic location near the newly liberated countries of Eastern Europe will permit it to influence the economic development of that potentially rich region.

Established in 1957, the Deutsche Bundesbank is Germany's central bank. It enjoys significant autonomy from the federal government, and is charged with the duty to "regulate the quantity of money in circulation . . . with the aim of safeguarding the currency." The Central Bank Council is the governing board, which includes the bank's president, the vice president, and other officials. Members of this council are nominated by the federal government and appointed by the country's president for terms of eight years. The

Directorate, the unit responsible for operations and for implementing the Council's decisions, includes the president, the vice president, and some other high officers of the bank.[5]

The German banking system requires commercial banks to hold reserves amounting to a certain percentage of their deutsche mark liabilities in demand and short-term time accounts, in the form of non-interest-bearing deposits with the Bundesbank. The Bundesbank has the authority to change the percentages of the required reserve ratio applicable to each type of account, and has changed them from time to time.[6] Changes in required reserve ratios alter the banks' capacity to make loans and, hence, ultimately affect the size of the monetary aggregates. Required reserves are calculated monthly on the basis of average amounts in the various kinds of accounts. Banks whose reserves fall below required levels must pay a high rate of interest on any deficit over that month. Banks that have too few reserves can borrow from banks that have excess reserves: the rate on such interbank borrowing of reserves is the *call money rate*, which can rise to high levels at the end of the month when reserve accounting takes place.

Two other rates are of importance. The *discount rate* is the rate the Bundesbank pays on securities it is willing to buy from banks. The Bundesbank sets a quota or maximum amount of securities it is willing to buy from any commercial bank. The call money rate is usually above the discount rate, which means that banks usually exhaust their discount quota before resorting to the interbank reserves market. The *Lombard rate* is the rate the Bundesbank charges on borrowings by commercial banks through the Lombard facility, which makes short-term loans to banks on the basis of collateral that consists of government securities. Banks make use of the Lombard facility when they encounter shortages of liquidity. The Lombard rate normally lies above the call money rate because the Bundesbank places no limits on the amount of these short-term loans it will make to any bank.

## Japan

For several reasons, knowledge of Japan's money and banking system is valuable. Of course, Japan is a major exporter of many products, particularly consumer goods, and the yen has become a world currency. In recent years, Japan has embarked on a progressive policy of liberalizing and internationalizing its financial markets and securities industry. Further, Japan has a strategic location near the center of the Pacific Rim—one of the world's most dynamic economic regions over the last 20 years.

Following the Bank of Japan Law of 1947, Japan's central bank is the Bank of Japan (BOJ), which is managed by the Governor of the BOJ, who

---

[5] "Central Bank-Government Relations in Major OECD Countries," Joint Economic Committee of the U.S. Congress, 1991, p. 17.

[6] Credit Suisse First Boston. *The Deutsche Mark Bond Markets* (Chicago: Probus Publishing, 1989), p. 262.

heads the decision-making Policy Board. Implementation of monetary policy and open market operations is the responsibility of the Credit and Market Management Department. The Governor and certain other members of the Policy Board are appointed to multi-year terms by the Cabinet with the approval of both houses of the Diet, the Japanese counterpart to the U.S. Congress. The remaining Board members are appointed by the Finance Minister.[7]

Japanese commercial banks are required to keep certain levels of reserves as deposits at the BOJ, which monitors the monthly averages of those levels carefully. Banks that do not have required levels of reserves can borrow from other banks that have excess reserves. Further, Japanese commercial banks can borrow from the BOJ's discount window at the *official discount rate*.

## United Kingdom

Great Britain, or the U.K., is a major financial center both for the world and for the emerging economic entity known as unified Europe. Great Britain's banking system plays an important role in the world economy.

Great Britain's central bank is the Bank of England (BOE), which is managed by its Governor, its Deputy Governor, and four executive directors. Those officials are appointed to renewable five-year terms by the Crown with the advice of the Prime Minister and the Chancellor of the Exchequer. The BOE officials report to the Chancellor, who has ultimate responsibility for monetary policy.[8]

Great Britain's monetary and banking system has three interesting features. The first is that commercial banks are not required to hold reserves in the form of balances or deposits at the BOE. Banks do tend to keep operational balances at the BOE to facilitate the clearing of exchanges of funds and checks. However, these balances are usually small because banks that have deficits in those accounts can borrow from one another in the interbank market or from the BOE itself.

The second feature is the role of the "discount houses." A discount house is a private company that is a dealer in Treasury bills as well as other money market instruments. (The term discount house reflects the fact that a sale or purchase of these short-term instruments occurs at a price below face value.) The houses are members of the London Discount Market Association and serve as intermediaries between the BOE and the commercial banks. Discount houses can borrow directly from the BOE and are the only institutions that are free to buy the BOE's weekly bill offerings. In fact, the houses must buy the entire offering on a prorated basis each week. Banks wishing to buy bills must do so from the houses. The discount houses also serve as intermediaries among the banks, which keep operational balances at the houses, and are active in the interbank market. Banks needing funds typically either draw down

---

[7] "Central Bank-Government Relations in Major OECD Countries," *op. cit.*
[8] *Ibid.*

accounts at discount houses, sell short-term securities to a discount house, or borrow from a discount house. If the discount houses are in need of funds, they either borrow (or much more commonly in recent years) sell securities to the BOE. The rate at which the BOE will deal with the houses and buy securities is called the *central-bank rate* or the *dealing rate.*

The third interesting feature is that the central U.K. government keeps its accounts with the BOE and not with commercial banks. When the government requires funds, the BOE supplies them by buying debt securities with the deposits in the commercial banks' operational BOE accounts. Such an event causes the banks' reserves to fall. When the government runs a surplus, these reserve accounts grow.[9]

▶ KEY POINTS THAT YOU SHOULD UNDERSTAND BEFORE PROCEEDING:

1. All large economies have central banks that are charged with the responsibility for managing monetary affairs and regulating commercial banks.

2. Many central banks lend to commercial banks in their home countries at a rate that reflects, or is designed to implement, the central bank's monetary policy.

3. Many but not all of the world's monetary and banking systems require commercial banks to keep some fraction of their deposits in reserves.

SUMMARY

The Federal Reserve System is the U.S. central bank. Its tools of monetary policy include required reserves, open market operations and repurchases, and discount loans to banks. The Fed supplies reserves to the banking system, which participates, along with investors, in generating the money supply. The chief means of supplying reserves is open market operations: the Fed's purchase of government securities provides reserves, and the Fed's sale of securities reduces reserves. The money supply is composed of various types of money as well as demand and time deposits, which can be grouped into monetary aggregates. The fundamental aggregate is the monetary base, composed of currency plus total reserves in the banking system. $M_1$ equals currency plus all checkable deposits. Other aggregates include various time deposits.

The money multiplier is the process by which changes in bank reserves generate larger changes in the money supply. The banks use the added reserves to buy assets or to make loans; the seller or borrower redeposits these proceeds, which then support additional loans, and so on. The value of the multiplier depends on the required reserve ratio, the pub-

---

[9] Richard Harrington, "The London Financial Markets," in Christopher J. Green and David T. Lewellyn (eds.), *Surveys in Monetary Economics* (Oxford: Basil Blackwell, Ltd., 1991), p. 268.

lic's demand for cash, the banks' willingness to make loans, and the level of interest rates.

The growing international integration of economies requires that the Fed, along with other central banks, consider the impact of its monetary operations on foreign currency exchange rates. Thus, monetary policy must be considered from the standpoint of open economies, not the closed ones of years past.

Germany's central bank is the Deutsche Bundesbank. The Bundesbank sets reserve requirements for commercial banks in that country, makes loans to banks short of reserves, and engages in purchases and sales of certain short-term assets. Changes in the reserves affect the rates of growth in monetary aggregates. Japan's central bank is the Bank of Japan, which has the authority to engage in open market operations and to establish reserve requirements for commercial banks. The Bank of Japan also is a lender of last resort. The Bank of England is Great Britain's central bank, but that country is unusual in that it does not require commercial banks to hold reserves of any level. Banks keep operational reserves and can borrow from the BOE in the event they have too little in that account. Discount houses, which deal in Treasury securities, serve as intermediaries between the Bank of England and the commercial banks. The Bank of England also conducts operations in short-term securities.

GLOSSARY

**Board of Governors of the Federal Reserve:** A group of seven members who are appointed by the President and approved by the Congress for 14-year terms and who are responsible for monetary policy in the U.S.

**Call money rate:** The rate on interbank borrowing of reserves in the German banking system.

**Central-bank rate (or dealing rate):** The rate at which the Bank of England will buy securities from or make loans to the discount houses.

**Chancellor of the Exchequer:** The cabinet minister who has ultimate responsibility for monetary policy in the U.K.

**Discount house:** A private U.K. company that deals in British Treasury bills as well as other money market instruments and that plays an important role in the conduct of British monetary policy.

**Federal Open Market Committee (or FOMC):** The unit of the Fed that decides on the general issues of changing the rate of growth in the money supply by open market sales or purchase of securities.

**Federal Reserve Board Chairman:** The person appointed to be the Chairman of the Fed's Board of Governors.

**Federal Reserve District Bank:** The Federal Reserve Bank in one of the 12 geographical districts.

**Fractional reserve banking system:** One in which a bank must hold or "reserve" some portion of its deposits in a form approved by the central bank, such as the Fed in the U.S.

**G-5 countries:** The five most developed economies and financial systems in the world—the United States, Japan, Great Britain, France, and Germany.

**International reserves:** The amount of currency from large industrial countries that is held by a country's central bank and government.

**L:** An inclusive measure of money and certain liquid assets.

**Lombard rate:** The interest rate the Bundesbank charges on its short-term, collateralized loans to commercial banks that have insufficient liquidity.

**$M_1$:** The monetary aggregate that measures the amount of medium of exchange, defined as the sum of dollars held in the form of currency and demand deposits.

**$M_2$:** The monetary aggregate that measures all forms of money that have the capacity of storing value, defined as $M_1$ plus all dollars held in time and savings accounts at banks and thrift institutions, plus all dollars invested in retail money market mutual funds, plus some additional accounts such as overnight repurchase agreements.

**$M_3$:** The monetary aggregate that equals $M_2$ plus certain other financial assets, including long-term time deposits, commercial paper, bankers acceptances, and some Treasury securities.

**Medium of exchange:** The monetary or financial item that is generally accepted in payment for goods, services, and capital transactions, and that serves as a store of value.

**Monetary aggregate:** A sum of monetary items that helps to measure the amount of money available to the economy at any time.

**Monetary base:** The most basic monetary aggregate, also termed "high-powered money," defined as currency in circulation (or coins and Federal Reserve notes held by the public) plus the total reserves in the banking system.

**Money multiplier:** The linkage between the banking system's reserves and the amount of money, measured by one of the aggregates, in circulation.

**Money supply:** The amount of money in circulation within an economy at any time.

**Numeraire:** The item that serves as a unit of account, which is the unit used to measure wealth.

**Official discount rate:** A major element in BOJ monetary policy, this is the BOJ-set rate at which Japanese commercial banks can borrow from the BOJ's discount window.

**Open economy:** An economy in which foreign firms and investors account for a large share of economic activity, including participation in the financial markets.

**Open market operations:** The Fed's purchase or sale, in open debt markets, of government securities for its own account.

**Repurchase agreement (or repo):** A "matched sale-purchase transaction" which involves a sale coupled with an agreement to repurchase at a set, higher price on a specific future date.

**Required reserve ratio:** The Fed's ratio of mandatory reserves to deposits.

**Total reserves:** The sum of a bank's required reserves and excess reserves.

**Trading Desk of the Federal Reserve Bank of New York:** The unit of the Fed that implements monetary policy by its conduct of open market operations.

**Velocity of money:** The ratio of the money supply to the economy's income (as reflected by the Gross National Product or some similar measure), which indicates the average amount of transactions carried by a unit of money.

**QUESTIONS**

1. Identify the participants in the process by which the money supply changes and monetary policy is implemented.

2. Describe the structure of the Board of Governors of the Federal Reserve System.

3. a. What is meant by the statement that "the U.S. has a fractional reserve banking system"?

   b. How are these items related: total reserves, required reserves, and excess reserves?

4. What is the required reserve ratio, and how has the 1980 Depository Institutions Deregulation and Monetary Control Act constrained the Fed's control over the ratio?

5. In what two forms can a bank hold its required reserves?

6. a. What is an open market purchase by the Fed?

   b. Which unit of the Fed decides on open market policy, and what unit implements that policy?

   c. What is the immediate consequence of an open market purchase?

7. Distinguish between an open market sale and a "matched sale" (which is the same thing as a "matched sale-purchase" or a "reverse repurchase agreement").

8. What is the discount rate, and what type of action by a bank does it apply to?

9. Define the monetary base and $M_2$.

10. Describe the basic features of the "money multiplier."

11. Suppose the Fed were to inject $100 million of reserves into the banking system by an open market purchase of Treasury bills. If the required reserve ratio were 10%, what is the maximum increase in $M_1$ that the new reserves would generate? Describe the decisions by banks and savers that might keep that maximum amount from materializing.

12. You often hear that a change in the money supply might lower interest rates. Explain why it is true that interest rates have an influence over the change in the money supply.

13. Describe the difference between "reserves" in the U.S. and British banking systems.

14. Explain the differences among these three rates in the German banking system: the Lombard rate, the call money rate, and the discount rate.

15. Explain the roles of the dealing rate and the discount houses in the British conduct of monetary policy.

# CHAPTER SIX

# Monetary Policy

*After reading this chapter you will understand:*

- the goals of monetary policy, including price level stability, economic growth, stable interest rates, and stable foreign exchange rates.

- that the operating targets of Fed policy are those monetary and financial variables that are affected by its tools in a predictable way.

- that intermediate targets are economic variables that the Fed can affect indirectly through its work with operating targets.

- that the federal funds rate and bank reserves have often been operating targets of monetary policy.

- that the broad monetary aggregates have sometimes served as intermediate targets, as have certain interest rates.

- the goals and targets of monetary policy in Germany, Japan, and the United Kingdom.

The previous chapter discussed various components of the monetary and banking structure of the United States. In that chapter, we explained how the Fed, in interaction with banks and other units of the economy, creates money and credit. We also explained the tools that the Fed can use to manage the rate of growth in the money supply.

This chapter examines the goals of monetary policy; that is, the conditions in the economy that the Fed seeks to bring about. Although the Fed cannot directly cause these conditions to exist, it can follow policies to target variables that it can influence with its tools. As in the last chapter, we also discuss monetary matters in some other major economies of the world.

## MONETARY POLICY IN THE UNITED STATES

### Goals of Monetary Policy

The Fed, through such tools as open market operations, which change the reserves in the banking system, can prompt the banking system and depositors to implement desired changes in the money supply and in its rates of growth. The Fed manages the money supply in order to achieve certain economic goals. In this section, we identify some of the more commonly cited goals of Fed policy.[1]

*Stability in the price level* is a major goal of the Fed. Price stability gained new respect in the last 20 years as first inflation, then deflation, ravaged entire economies or major sectors such as farm land and commercial real estate. The standard way of measuring inflation is the change in a major price index. Table 6-1 shows the yearly percentage change in the Consumer Price Index

| TABLE 6 - 1 | | | |
|---|---|---|---|
| ANNUAL PERCENTAGE CHANGES IN THE CONSUMER PRICE INDEX FROM 1980–1991 | | | |
| Year | Rate | Year | Rate |
| 1980 | 12.4 | 1986 | 1.1 |
| 1981 | 8.9 | 1987 | 4.4 |
| 1982 | 3.9 | 1988 | 4.4 |
| 1983 | 3.8 | 1989 | 4.6 |
| 1984 | 4.0 | 1990 | 6.1 |
| 1985 | 3.8 | 1991 | 3.1 |

*Source: Federal Reserve Bulletin*, selected issues.

---

[1] Ben Bernanke and Frederic Mishkin, "Guideposts and Signals in the Conduct of Monetary Policy: Lessons from Six Industrialized Countries," presented at the Seventh Annual Conference on Macroeconomics, March 1992.

between 1980 and 1991, and reveals that the high inflation marking the beginning of the 1980s had largely dissipated by the end of that decade. From this experience, policymakers and economists came to appreciate once more that unstable price levels retard economic growth, provoke volatility in interest rates, stimulate consumption, deter savings, and cause capricious redistribution of income and wealth with attendant social disturbances.

Inflation in advanced economies, however, is seldom (if ever) the result of excessive demand due to monetary or fiscal policy. Rather, a more important source of inflation is an economic shock in the supply of a crucial material, such as the oil shocks of the 1970s, which affected almost all countries. Evidence that the inflation at the end of the 1970s was not related to excessive demand for goods and services is that it occurred with high unemployment and gave the world a period of "stagflation," which is a condition of both inflation and recession.

It is important to note that, when confronted with a supply shock, a central bank such as the Fed has two choices. First, the banking authorities can refuse to accommodate the higher price levels that follow the shock by matching them with an increase in the money supply. The results of non-accommodation will initially tend to be higher interest rates and a decline in economic activity. For this reason, central banks and political authorities frequently have opted for the second choice, which is a policy of accommodation and increased growth in the supply of money. Unfortunately, this kind of policy permits the inflation to continue unchecked or possibly to accelerate.

*High employment* (or low unemployment) of the civilian labor force represents a second major goal for the Fed. While politicians often speak of the U.S. government's commitment to promoting "full employment," most people understand that an unemployment rate of zero is not possible. The reason is that "frictional unemployment"—the temporary unemployment of those changing jobs or seeking new or better ones—is both unavoidable and helpful to an economy. It is unavoidable because people do change jobs, and are likely to do so more readily as employment levels rise, and because some workers leave and enter the labor market constantly. Frictional unemployment is helpful because it allows a constant reallocation of labor and leads to increased efficiency in the workforce.

Given that zero unemployment is not a feasible aim, the appropriate goal of the Fed and other governmental policymakers is actually a high level of employment. A practical problem, however, is that economists and policymakers cannot agree on a suitable definition or specification of high employment. It does not help to specify a high level of employment as one that approaches 100% less the level of frictional unemployment, because there is also little agreement on the true rate of frictional unemployment.

For practical purposes, many observers consider that a civilian unemployment rate between 4% and 6% indicates an economy operating at or near a level of high employment. This figure allows for frictional unemployment and the effects of the rapid expansion in the workforce over the last several decades. That expansion occurred because of the entry into the workforce of many women, younger workers, and immigrants into the United States.

| TABLE 6-2 | | | |
|---|---|---|---|
| **ANNUAL RATES OF CIVILIAN UNEMPLOYMENT IN THE U.S. 1980–1991** | | | |
| Year | Rate | Year | Rate |
| 1980 | 7.1 | 1986 | 7.0 |
| 1981 | 7.6 | 1987 | 6.2 |
| 1982 | 9.7 | 1988 | 5.5 |
| 1983 | 9.6 | 1989 | 5.3 |
| 1984 | 7.5 | 1990 | 5.5 |
| 1985 | 7.2 | 1991 | 6.7 |

*Source: Federal Reserve Bulletin*, selected issues.

Table 6-2 provides yearly information on the United States's level of unemployment in the last decade and shows that relatively high employment occurred in the second half of the 1980s.

It is important to realize that high employment is one of the Fed's goals because, in certain circumstances, the Fed's policy can indirectly influence the level of employment. When the economy is operating sluggishly or below capacity, increases in the money supply can bring about economic expansion and employment, because those increases can reduce interest rates, stimulate investment, encourage consumption, and lead to the creation of new jobs. A policy of expansion of the money supply is frequently described as an "easy money policy," because the Fed is said to ease the way for banks to acquire reserves and to extend loans. When the economy's output is close to capacity (given its stock of productive assets and population), however, easy money policies can be disadvantageous, because they may kindle inflation and raise interest rates. Policymakers must often wrestle with the tough question of whether easing monetary policy will create more economic growth or simply ignite inflation.

*Economic growth*, the third goal of the Fed, is the increase in an economy's output of goods and services. Clearly, this goal is closely related to the goal of high employment. As would be expected, there is very little agreement about the exact rate of growth that policymakers should try to achieve. Variously described as "sustainable" or "steady" or "reasonable," the economy's appropriate rate of growth has to be substantial enough to generate high employment in the context of an expanding workforce but low enough to ward off inflation.

Table 6-3 reports the growth rate in the United States over recent years in terms of annual changes in the Gross Domestic Product (or GDP). Note there are three years when growth was negative; in 1982, the growth was significantly negative as GDP fell by more than 2%. On the other hand, growth exceeded a positive 3% in five different years, and it exceeded the high level of 6% in 1984. Interestingly, the period of substantial growth did not usher in unusually high inflation (see Table 6-1).

Once more, economic growth is a Fed goal because its operations may be able to affect the level of growth. As we note in connection with employ-

| TABLE 6-3 | | | |
|---|---|---|---|
| ANNUAL RATES OF GROWTH IN U.S. GROSS DOMESTIC PRODUCT 1980–1991 | | | |
| Year | Rate | Year | Rate |
| 1980 | -0.50 | 1986 | 2.91 |
| 1981 | 1.71 | 1987 | 3.08 |
| 1982 | -2.15 | 1988 | 3.93 |
| 1983 | 3.89 | 1989 | 2.51 |
| 1984 | 6.19 | 1990 | 0.99 |
| 1985 | 3.16 | 1991 | -0.74 |

*Note:* Rates are percentage changes in GDP, in 1987 dollars.
*Source: Economic Report of the President, 1992.*

ment, however, policies expanding the money supply and stimulating growth may be beneficial in some circumstances and detrimental in others, according to the economy's performance relative to its capacity.

The goal of *stabilizing interest rates* is directly related to the goal of growth and to the Fed's responsibility for the health of the nation's financial and banking system. Table 6-4 reports on yearly averages for the rates on Treasury bills (a short-term security) and on Treasury bonds (a long-term asset). The table reveals that interest rate volatility over the early and mid 1980s was especially pronounced. This volatility has been troublesome to financial institutions such as commercial banks and thrift institutions.

Note that the goal is to stabilize rates, not to prevent changes in rates. Obviously, interest rates move up and down with changes in economic conditions. Those movements may provide signals of important economic developments, and it would be making a mistake for the Fed to try to prevent such changes in rates. However, the Fed may help economic conditions by trying to moderate the impact of large moves in rates. Some increases in rates may reflect temporary or reversible developments, and the Fed can appropriately

| TABLE 6-4 | | | | | |
|---|---|---|---|---|---|
| ANNUAL AVERAGE RATES OF INTEREST ON U.S. TREASURY BILLS AND BONDS: 1980–1991 | | | | | |
| Year | Bills | Bonds | Year | Bills | Bonds |
| 1980 | 11.51% | 11.30% | 1986 | 5.97 | 7.80 |
| 1981 | 14.08 | 13.44 | 1987 | 5.82 | 8.59 |
| 1982 | 10.68 | 12.76 | 1988 | 6.68 | 8.96 |
| 1983 | 8.63 | 11.18 | 1989 | 8.12 | 8.45 |
| 1984 | 9.56 | 12.39 | 1990 | 7.51 | 8.61 |
| 1985 | 7.48 | 10.79 | 1991 | 5.42 | 8.14 |

*Source: Federal Reserve Bulletin,* selected issues.

respond to these changes in a way that eliminates or greatly reduces such increases.

*Stability in foreign currency exchange rates* is the final goal that we will discuss. The foreign exchange market has become much more important in recent years, as the economies of the world have become more integrated, and foreign currency exchange rates have begun to affect ever larger segments of the economy. Because exchange rates are clearly dependent in some ways on the monetary policies of the major countries, the Fed has accepted the goal of stabilizing foreign exchange rates.[2]

Table 6-5 indicates how the U.S. dollar's exchange rates with the German mark and the Japanese yen have altered over the past decade. (The table also reveals that the trend in exchange rates since 1986 has been in the direction of a cheaper dollar.) Clearly, exchange rates have been quite unstable in recent years. In fact, the rates have been unstable since the abrupt abandonment, in the early 1970s, of the fixed exchange rate system, known as the "Bretton Woods system," which had been in effect since the end of World War II, or roughly 1945. Of course, some fluctuations in exchange rates arise for economically sound reasons that monetary policy in one country cannot influence or control. A prime example of such a reason is a pronounced difference in the fiscal policies between two countries. In general, an important explanation of unstable rates among most of the world's major currencies has been the failure of the large industrial economies to coordinate their fiscal and monetary policies.

A chief disadvantage of unstable foreign currency exchange rates is that volatility in the prices of currencies inhibits the international trade that offers a host of benefits to all participating countries. Further, both high and low exchange rates for the dollar are considered detrimental to the U.S. economy. High exchange rates (i.e., a "strong" dollar or one with high value in terms of

| TABLE 6-5 | | | | | |
|-----------|---|---|---|---|---|
| ANNUAL AVERAGE RATES OF EXCHANGE OF THE U.S. DOLLAR AND THE DEUTSCHE MARK AND JAPANESE YEN: 1980–1991 | | | | | |
| Year | DM/$ | Yen/$ | Year | DM/$ | Yen/$ |
| 1980 | 1.82 | 225.67 | 1986 | 2.17 | 168.35 |
| 1981 | 2.25 | 220.11 | 1987 | 1.80 | 144.60 |
| 1982 | 2.43 | 249.06 | 1988 | 1.76 | 128.17 |
| 1983 | 2.55 | 237.55 | 1989 | 1.88 | 138.07 |
| 1984 | 2.85 | 237.45 | 1990 | 1.62 | 145.00 |
| 1985 | 2.94 | 238.47 | 1991 | 1.66 | 134.59 |

*Source: Federal Reserve Bulletin*, selected issues.

---

[2] *Ibid.*, p. 11.

foreign currencies) reduce demand for U.S.-made products abroad and stimulate the import of foreign goods; the result is a trade imbalance. A "weak" dollar contributes to inflation, as U.S. buyers pay more for the many goods they do import. For these reasons, the Fed's goal of stability in the currency market often amounts to keeping the value of the dollar, in terms of the major foreign currencies, within some range that is considered politically acceptable and helpful to international trading, especially exporting.

## Trade-offs and Conflicts among Policies

This account of the widely accepted goals of monetary policy reveals a profound problem in the conduct of monetary policy. The goals are numerous, but the Fed's capabilities are limited to the simple menu of (1) trying to raise the rate of growth in the money supply by providing more reserves to banks, and (2) trying to reduce the rate of monetary expansion by reducing the reserves in the banking system. As a result, it is often the case that one of the goals may require a monetary policy that is inconsistent with some other goal. In other words, a monetary policy that furthers progress toward one goal may actually make attaining another either difficult or impossible.

For example, an easy money policy of expanding the money supply (that is, stimulating higher growth rates for one or more monetary aggregates) may appear to promote growth and low interest rates, but it may also raise the prospect of inflation, affect the exchange rate disadvantageously, and increase interest rates. Another example concerns the goal of price stability and the Fed's responsibility for the health of financial institutions. Suppose that, at a time of high inflation, many such institutions have invested according to inflationary expectations and have made many loans to firms dealing in real assets. Suppose, too, that the Fed decides it needs to take steps to curb the current inflation. In such a situation, the tight monetary policy that accomplishes this goal—a policy of reducing the rate of growth in the money supply—actually may imperil the institutions, because the policy might well weaken the financial health of the firms that borrowed from the financial institutions.

Economists frequently describe this problem in this way: the Fed's policy necessarily represents trade-offs among its various goals, which have different levels of relative importance at different times, depending on the state of the economy. Another way of saying this is that the Fed, like any monetary policymaker, has numerous goals but focuses, at any time, on the goal that is most in danger of not being achieved.

## Goals and Types of Targets

A second problem in the implementation of monetary policy is that the Fed has no direct control over the goals that are the final objectives of its policies. The Fed cannot, with any of its monetary tools (open market operations, discount rates, etc.), directly influence such complex economic variables as the prices of goods and services, the unemployment rate, foreign currency exchange rates, and the growth in Gross Domestic Product. We know the Fed can affect the rate of growth in the money supply only by means of its control of reserves in the banking system. And, as we discussed in the previous chapter, the Fed cannot fully determine changes in the money supply. The growth in the money supply depends to a substantial extent on the preferences, actions, and expectations of numerous banks, borrowers, and consumers.

The Fed seeks to achieve its goals through a form of chain reaction, which has the following chronology and structure. The Fed first employs one or more of its tools to affect what are called "operating targets," which are monetary and financial variables whose changes tend to bring about changes in "intermediate targets." Intermediate targets, which may include interest rates or monetary aggregates, are variables that have a reasonably reliable linkage with the variables, such as output or employment, that constitute the Fed's goals or ultimate objectives. Thus, the Fed exerts whatever influence it has on the intermediate targets in an indirect way, by means of its control over the operating targets. Thus, the Fed's power over the variables that make up its goals is quite indirect and dependent upon the linkages among the various targets and goals.

Although economists have argued many years about the identity of appropriate operating and intermediate target variables, there is no dispute about the chief characteristics of a suitable operating or intermediate target.[3] The first characteristic is *linkage:* an operating target must have an expected connection with the intermediate target, which itself must eventually affect the economy in a way that is consistent with the Fed's goals. The second characteristic is *observability:* both operating targets and intermediate targets must be readily and regularly observable economic variables, so that the Fed can monitor its success in influencing their levels or rates of change. The third and final characteristic is *responsiveness:* to function as an operating target, a variable must respond quickly and in an expected way to the Fed's use of one or more of its tools; and an appropriate intermediate target is one that reacts, in an anticipated way and a meaningfully short time, to changes in the operating target.

## Choosing the Operating Target

In some countries, a key foreign currency exchange rate may well function as an operating target. While the Fed has become more conscious of foreign exchange developments in the last ten years or so, it has not adopted the dollar's exchange rate with any currency or group of currencies as an operating target. Rather, the Fed's monetary policy has directly targeted either short-term interest rates or some measure of bank reserves.

An important point about the operating target is that the Fed must choose either a short-term rate or the level of some reserves and cannot choose to tar-

---

[3] A formal treatment of the requirements for targets is available in Benjamin M. Friedman, "Targets and Instruments of Monetary Policy," Chapter 22 in Benjamin M. Friedman and Frank H. Hahn, *Handbook of Monetary Economics* (Amsterdam: North-Holland, 1990).

get both kinds of variables.[4] To understand why the Fed must make a choice, we need to review what the Fed's tools allow it to do. Those tools—whether the secondary ones of discount loans and management of reserve requirements, or the primary tool of open market operations—enable the Fed to change only the level of reserves in the banking system. Obviously, a change in reserves also changes short-term rates, because they are determined in the interbank market for excess reserves. Under most circumstances, the change in reserves is negatively related to the change in interest rates: as the Fed supplies more reserves and banks gain more ability to make more loans and buy other assets, the short-term rates fall; as the Fed withdraws reserves and reduces the banks' lending capacity, the short-term rates rise.

Because of this inverse relationship, it might seem possible for the Fed to view each of these variables as a target and to set each of them at the same time. But, in fact, that is impossible. The reason is that the Fed cannot know or predict the *public's demand for money*, which is the aggregate demand for holding some of its wealth in the form of liquid balances, such as bank deposits. The public's desire to hold money depends on many factors, especially preferences and anticipations about future income and price inflation, among other things, and unexpected changes in those factors may well shift the public's desired holdings in significant ways. Therefore, the Fed cannot be certain how much impact any change in reserves will have on short-term rates. Without knowledge of what the rate will be for a given change in reserves, the Fed cannot simultaneously determine both the rate and the level of reserves.

In choosing its operating target, then, the Fed makes the decision to let the other variable fluctuate in response to changes in the public's demand for money. When an interest rate is the target, the Fed must let the growth in reserves vary as it strives to keep that interest rate at a certain level or to smooth its transition to a new (higher or lower) level. When some aggregate of reserves is the target, the Fed is forced to allow interest rates to change substantially, so that it can try to bring the level of reserves to that dictated by the Fed's policy. Of course, the Fed can change its target from time to time, in order to rein in the variable that has fluctuated while the Fed focused on the other. But, however often the Fed might change targets, it remains a fact that, at any one time, the Fed cannot target both rates and reserves.

### *Choosing the Intermediate Target*

The best known of the intermediate targets is the money supply, measured by one of the more inclusive monetary aggregates that we described in the previous chapter. In the 1970s, many countries began to target the growth rates of one or more aggregates. The policy, at least as publicly stated, was to supply reserves at a pace that would lead to a selected rate of growth in the aggregates. The idea behind this policy was that the goals of central bank

---

[4] William Poole, "Optimal Choice of Monetary Policy Instrument in a Simple Stochastic Macro Model," *Quarterly Journal of Economics* (1970), pp. 197–216.

activity—growth, stable prices, and so on—would be realized if the money supply were to grow at a known and steady rate.

Over time, other intermediate targets have been specified, and they include foreign exchange rates, the level of national output (such as the Gross National Product), and the level of actual or expected inflation.[5] Further, the array of interest rates—including rates available to consumers and investors— may also function as a target variable. We have said that a prime characteristic of a suitable intermediate target is that it is readily observable. Obviously, some of these candidates above do not fit that rule: information on the GNP, for example, is available only on a quarterly basis, while measures of actual or expected inflation may be subject to considerable dispute.[6] For this reason, the most likely intermediate targets are monetary aggregates (measured with more or less frequency and accuracy), key exchange rates, and important short-term interest rates.

## A Review of Recent Federal Reserve Policy

**Targeting the Fed Funds Rate, 1970 to 1979.** During most of the 1970s, the Fed viewed the federal funds rate either largely or exclusively as its operating target. Recall that "fed funds" refers to the excess reserves that commercial banks and other depository institutions keep in the form of deposits in the Federal Reserve System and lend among themselves for short periods of time, especially overnight. The rate on these interbank loans is the fed funds rate, and it is a good indicator of the banking system's supply of loanable funds. When banks have a lot of funds and lending capacity, the rate is low; the rate is high when the banking system has drawn its collective reserves close to the required level. It should be noted that the fed funds rate meets the first requirement listed above for an operating target: the rate is readily observable and continuously available, because the market for fed funds is large and active.

The Fed targets the fed funds rate by its open market operations. As noted above, a requirement of a good operating target is that the Fed can exert substantial control over its level and changes. If the rate were to rise above the level that the Fed thought conducive to economic growth and high employment, the Fed would engage in open market purchases and inject reserves into the banking system. Through the workings of supply and demand, an increase in the reserves of the banking system would normally cause a fall in the fed funds rate, as many banks would have to borrow less to meet their reserve requirements. If the fed funds rate were too low, the Fed would sell securities and bring about a reduction in the growth of the banking system's total supply of reserves. This action would prompt a rise in the fed funds rate. Further, the Fed has also used open market operations in its effort to smooth the transition of the fed funds rate from one level to another, as the rate varies with conditions in the economy.

---

[5] Bernanke and Mishkin, *op. cit.*, p. 41.
[6] Friedman, *op. cit.*, p. 1203.

The rationale for targeting the fed funds rate lies in the belief that changes in the rate can, over some time, affect the level of economic activity. (Recall, that linkage is also a prime requirement of a suitable operating target.) That is, if consumers, investors, and bankers believe that a given change in the fed funds rate is permanent and reflects a shift in Federal Reserve policy, such a change in rates can reverberate through the monetary and banking system, and cause a consequent change in the level of economic activity. Generally speaking, this version of monetary policy is associated with Keynesian economic theory, and it gives the Fed a great deal of discretion in the conduct of monetary policy.

In the Keynesian view, the Fed's decision to reduce the fed funds rate, by increasing the banking system's excess reserves, should have the following consequences. Banks, as the first economic units to be affected, will have more reserves and lower returns from lending in the fed funds market. As a result, the banks will reduce the cost of loans to businesses and consumers and the return (if any) available to investors on short-term deposits. Investors will now be confronted with lower yields on short-term assets, such as Treasury bills and certificates of deposit. Because of these lower yields, investors will reallocate their holdings from short-term to long-term securities, driving their prices up and raising the wealth of investors in financial securities. Declines in the general cost of funding will encourage firms to expand and increase their output. Consumers, seeing lower costs of borrowing, will increase their demand for more expensive purchases.

Overall, according to this view of the economy, a decline in the fed funds rate should lead to a higher level of output and employment in the economy. Obviously, if the Fed chooses to raise the fed funds rate and uses open market sales to reduce the system's excess reserves, the consequent rise in short-term interest rates will restrain the growth in economic activity. In an important sense, then, the array of short-term rates functions as the intermediate target (or one of the intermediate targets) in this view of monetary policy.

A cautionary note is in order here. Economists in the Keynesian tradition believe that declines in targeted rates can cause the sequence of events just described only if the economy is operating at less than full capacity and employment. If the economy is operating at full employment, these actions by the Fed will generally lead only to an increase in prices (that is, inflation) and interest rates.

### A Monetarist Experiment, 1979 to 1982.

One historic consequence of the policy of supplying reserves according to movements in the fed funds rate was that the Fed did not concern itself with the behavior of the level of reserves, or of the monetary base and other monetary aggregates, which expanded in an erratic way. On frequent occasions in this period of the 1970s, interest rates were on a rising path, in part because of the oil-price shock and the consequent inflation. The Fed responded to the rising rates by increasing reserves, as it tried to keep the rates from getting to what it considered a too high level. The expansion in the monetary aggregates was particularly rapid from 1975 to 1978, and that expansion (along with the oil shocks) led to serious inflation and a decline in the dollar's value. In 1979, for example, the rate of inflation was in double-digits (i.e., above 10%), and the dollar's value, in terms of the Deutsche mark, fell almost 30% between 1975 and 1979.

In October of 1979, as a response to inflation, then Chairman of the Fed Paul Volcker announced a new policy. The Fed would henceforth begin to target the banking system's *nonborrowed reserves*, which equal total reserves less those reserves created when banks borrow from the Fed through its discount window. The level of nonborrowed reserves meets the requirements for a good operating target to largely the same extent as the fed funds rate. Moreover, the Fed stated that its purpose in targeting nonborrowed reserves was to control the rate of growth in the money supply, as measured by the monetary aggregates.

This change in policy was widely viewed as a victory for the theory of *monetarism*, which favors a steady, predictable growth in reserves and the monetary base. Monetarists claim that policy that is based on known rules of growth in key monetary aggregates sustains stability in the price level, and that such stability fosters long-run economic growth and employment. Further, monetarists had long criticized the "discretionary" policy whereby the Fed would change the rate of growth in reserves or aggregates in order to achieve short-run adjustments in interest rates or levels of economic activity. Monetarists believe that the "long and variable lags" between the start of a policy and its final impact on the economy make such adjustments unwise and potentially dangerous. This dispute on how best to conduct monetary policy is known as the controversy of "discretion versus rules."

The new Fed policy can be viewed as one where the monetary aggregates became "intermediate targets," and the banking system's quantity of nonborrowed reserves was the "operating target." Through its open market operations, the Fed has considerable control over this operating target. Movements in that target are, in turn, supposed to generate somewhat predictable changes in the levels of the intermediate targets, or monetary aggregates. The money multiplier, which we introduced in the last chapter, is the link between the reserves and the aggregates. Monetarists believe that the money multiplier is basically steady, so that the link between reserves and the monetary aggregates can be identified. Hence, the appropriate policy is to supply reserves (through open market operations) at that steady pace which will lead to a stable and reasonable rate of growth for the monetary aggregates. The changes in interest rates that may result from changes in money demand (which, in the monetarists' view, does not occur often or to a significant extent) should not be allowed to affect the policy on reserves.

Technically speaking, the Fed had claimed throughout most of the 1970s to be targeting certain aggregates, notably $M_1$ and $M_2$, and it had routinely published target ranges and expected growth paths for the aggregates. The Fed's devotion to such a policy was suspect, as the data repeatedly showed the aggregates growing at far faster rates than the Fed said it preferred. When faced with these high growth rates, the Fed often simply adjusted its planned growth path upward. Volcker's 1979 announcement seemed to suggest that the Fed would finally be seriously interested in the growth in aggregates. Indeed, the growth rate in the money supply was far smaller in this time than it had generally been in the 1970s. Also, the new policy stated that the Fed would let interest rates (particularly short-term rates) fluctuate far more freely than they had in the past. In fact, in late 1979 and through the early 1980s, rates of most maturities posted their highest levels in more than a hundred years and displayed a volatility that led to major changes in financial institutions and markets.

***Back to the Fed Funds Rate, 1983 to 1991.*** The Fed did not remain committed to an aggregates policy very long.[7] By 1982, the tight monetary policy had banished the worst of the inflation, which seemed to reach a bottom of about 3% to 4%. Policymakers then faced the prospect of deflation and rising unemployment, which rose to around 10% in 1982. At the end of 1982, the Fed again let the monetary aggregates grow at a rather fast pace. Interest rates fell, employment rose, and economic growth resumed.

In 1983, the Fed adopted a new policy. This time, the Fed identified its operating target as the level of *borrowed reserves*, which are funds that the banks borrow from the Fed through its discount window. It is important to realize that the level of borrowed reserves in the banking system is closely and positively linked to the spread between the fed funds rate and the discount rate (the cost of borrowing at the discount window, which the Fed adjusts infrequently). When the fed funds rate goes up relative to the discount rate, all else being equal, the level of borrowed reserves rises, because banks are more likely to borrow reserves from the Fed rather than from other banks. Thus, targeting borrowed reserves is equivalent to targeting the fed funds rate.

The Fed's policy beginning in 1983 was to keep the growth in borrowed reserves within some specified range. As a result, the Fed supplied reserves through open market purchases when borrowed reserves rose. Thus, the Fed was essentially supplying reserves when the fed funds rate rose. With this policy, the Fed was once more effectively targeting the fed funds rate, while neglecting changes in the monetary aggregates. In 1987, the Fed admitted that fact, and ceased to set targets for growth in $M_1$, substantially widening the acceptable ranges for growth in the larger aggregates, such as $M_2$ and $M_3$. From 1983 to the early 1990s, the Fed's chief operating target has been the level of the fed funds rate. In fact, at the end of 1991, the Fed dramatically lowered short-term rates in a publicly announced effort to stimulate the economy.

***Two Developments in the Mid-1980s.*** In the mid-1980s, however, two developments of note occurred. The first was the need for the Fed, which it publicly acknowledged, to become concerned with the level and stability of the U.S. dollar's foreign currency exchange rate. Table 6-5 reveals the dramatic strength in the value of the U.S. dollar through the early 1980s, which made

---

[7] Franco Modigliani, "The Monetarist Controversy Revisited," *Contemporary Policy Issues* (October 1988), pp. 3–18.

American exports very expensive. In 1985, the Fed implemented an expansionary monetary policy (that is, a policy of expanding aggregates), which drove down the dollar's value. In September of 1985, the United States (with the Fed's support) entered into the Plaza Agreement, which was a plan for international coordination of monetary policies by the United States, Great Britain, France, (West) Germany, and Japan. (The Louvre Accord in 1987 was another effort toward coordination.) The result of these actions was a fast decline in the value of the U.S. dollar (see Table 6-5), which the Fed tried to stabilize in 1987. In a sense, then, the U.S. dollar's exchange rate began to function as a kind of intermediate target for Fed policy.

The second development was the shocking fall in equity prices around the world in October 1987. The Fed's immediate response to the crisis was to provide all necessary liquidity. The fall in prices also brought to the fore the need for stability in the financial markets, and the Fed began to treat that as one of its key objectives.

▶ KEY POINTS THAT YOU SHOULD UNDERSTAND BEFORE PROCEEDING:

1. The Fed has numerous and complex goals related to conditions in the overall economy, which include price stability, high employment, economic growth, and stability in interest rates and the dollar's value in foreign currencies.

2. Policies that might further the attainment of one goal may make another difficult to realize.

3. The Fed is unable to realize its goals directly but must work through operating targets that it can affect and that, in turn, have some predictable influence on intermediate targets and the economy.

4. The Fed's operating targets have included the fed funds rate and various measures of reserves in the banking system; its primary tool has been open market operations.

5. Intermediate targets may include monetary aggregates, interest rates, or foreign currency exchange rates.

6. Keynesians adopt a monetary policy that largely calls for targeting short-term interest rates.

7. Monetarists adopt a monetary policy that largely calls for targeting reserves in order to achieve a steady growth in monetary aggregates.

8. The targets of Fed policy have changed several times in the last 20 years.

## GOALS AND TARGETS OF MONETARY POLICY IN OTHER ECONOMIES

The monetary systems of Germany, Japan, and the United Kingdom have goals that are similar to those of U.S. monetary policy: price stability, growth, and employment, among others. Moreover, these systems have roughly the same set of tools for affecting monetary policy: some form of open market operations, significant control over unborrowed reserves (except in Great Britain, where control is limited and indirect), and loans to banks. However, in the choice of policy targets and in the targeted monetary aggregates, these systems have developed in different ways from that of the United States.

## Germany

For almost 40 years, the goals of German monetary policy have been high employment, minimal inflation, and a stable and export-promoting exchange rate for the Deutsche mark. Since the mid-1970s, the Bundesbank's intermediate target has been a monetary aggregate. The aggregate of importance in the 1970s and most of the 1980s was *central bank money*, which is defined as currency in circulation and required reserves of residents' bank deposits. The Bundesbank set annual targets and ranges for the growth in this aggregate and monitored its success in meeting the targets. In the late 1980s, the Bundesbank grew somewhat concerned about new volatility in central bank money and replaced it with the more stable $M_3$, which equals the simple sum of currency in circulation, demand deposits, and time deposits. The Bundesbank regularly announces target growth paths for this aggregate and follows its value carefully.

The instrument of monetary policy, for many years, was the Bundesbank's lending to commercial banks, either at the discount rate or the Lombard rate (the interest rate the Bundesbank charges commercial banks on short-term loans that the banks make for the purposes of meeting their reserve requirements). In the late 1980s, however, the Bundesbank began to rely much more on influencing bank reserves by open market operations with banks as the other parties. The standard transaction has been a repurchase agreement that is collateralized by government securities, with maturities between four and five weeks.[8] By dealing with just the banks, the Bundesbank is able to exert control over the change in total reserves. Also, the Bundesbank conducts these transactions at a rate (the *repurchase rate*) that reflects its estimate of the money market rate level that will bring about the correct growth in the monetary aggregate.

## Japan

Since the early 1970s, the Bank of Japan (BOJ) has had as its chief monetary goals price stability and high employment, of course, but also exchange rate stability. The methods used to reach these goals have significantly changed over the last 20 years, as the Japanese financial system has undergone fundamental alterations. At the start of the 1970s, the banking system was struc-

---

[8] D.S. Batten, M.P. Blackwell, I.-S. Kim, S.E. Nocera, and Y. Oseki., *The Conduct of Monetary Policy in the Major Industrial Countries*, Occasional Paper #70, International Monetary Fund, Washington, July 1990, p. 12.

tured, regulated, and rather limited. In that time, the BOJ controlled the supply of credit to banks and corporations, and this supply was its primary operating target.

High inflation in 1973 and liberalization of numerous economic policies led the bank to target and manage the growth in two broad monetary aggregates, especially $M_2$ and, later, $M_2$ + the level of large deposits in banks.[9] In effect, these aggregates became intermediate targets, which the BOJ tried to manage through its influence on short-term interest rates. Bernanke and Mishkin report that the BOJ was remarkably successful in managing this growth, and Japan experienced low inflation into the 1980s.[10]

The growth, during the late 1970s and the early 1980s, of some markets in short-term government debt and other money market securities allowed the BOJ to target short-term interest rates. The chosen targets were rates on assets with one to three months until maturity. One rate is the *interbank call rate*, which is the rate on loans of excess reserves among commercial banks. The other is the discount rate, which is the rate on discount securities traded among banks. The BOJ tried to influence these rates by managing the flow of reserves into the banking system. If it wanted rates to rise, the central bank would drain the system of some reserves; if the BOJ wanted rates to fall, it would supply reserves. The BOJ's method of management consisted of both direct loans to banks and a form of open market operations in the money market and the interbank market.[11] (Those open market operations may involve either government bills or debt issues by banks and corporations.[12]) Further changes in the money market and a loss of direct influence on the interbank and discount rates in the late 1980s led the BOJ to begin to target shorter-term rates: those on overnight loans and bills with maturities of less than one month. This shift in targeted rates seems to have coincided with a shift away from the policy of targeting monetary aggregates.

As we noted in the last chapter, the Bank of Japan requires commercial banks to keep certain levels of reserves as deposits at the BOJ, although it has never adopted a policy of targeting bank reserves. Rather, the BOJ will try to adjust reserves in order to achieve the level of short-term rates it deems suitable for its preferred pace of economic growth.

Japanese commercial banks can borrow from the BOJ's discount window at the official discount rate. This rate, set by BOJ policy, is a major signal of its wishes for the future path of interest rates, and changes in the rate have a large impact on the money markets. The reason for that impact is that

[9] *Ibid.*, p. 16.
[10] Bernanke and Mishkin, *op. cit.*, p. 26.
[11] Batten, Blackwell, *et al.*, *op. cit.*, p. 17.
[12] Kumiharu Shigehara, "Japan's Experience with Use of Monetary Policy and the Process of Liberalization," *Bank of Japan Monetary and Economic Studies* 9 (March 1991), p. 11.

a change in the official discount rate is typically supported by and followed by BOJ actions to adjust the system's reserves.

## United Kingdom

The goals of monetary policy, as enunciated and implemented by the Bank of England (or BOE), are stability in the price level and growth in domestic output. From the mid-1970s to the late 1980s, the intermediate targets of policy were growth rates in two monetary aggregates: (1) the broad-based $M_3$, which is currency in circulation plus all bank deposits denominated in pound sterling and held by the private sector of Great Britain with British banks; and (2) the more narrowly defined $M_0$, which equals currency plus British bank deposits with the BOE. The unpredictable relationship between $M_3$ and both output and prices of goods and services has in recent years led the BOE to focus on $M_0$ and to begin considering other variables such as exchange rates (particularly with the German currency or Deutsche mark), interest rates, and inflation in forming its policy. In 1990, Great Britain became part of the European ERM (exchange rate mechanism) and agreed to support a certain exchange rate for the pound sterling with other European currencies. At the time, it appeared that this agreement would serve as a powerful new regulator of the supply of reserves and the growth in money supply.[13] Events in the European currency markets in 1992 have seriously called such hopes into question.

To understand how the BOE carries out its monetary policy, it is necessary to recall some information from the last chapter. As mentioned there, the British monetary and banking system does not require commercial banks to hold reserves, though the banks do tend to keep small operational balances at the BOE. Further, the "discount houses" are intermediaries between the BOE and commercial banks, which keep operational balances at the houses.

The BOE implements its monetary policy by responding to the flow of funds into and out of the reserve accounts that the commercial banks keep at the BOE as well as to the rates of interest on short-term securities. The BOE, in short, tries to maintain a given level of the balances and an appropriate level of interest rates.[14] In the event of a shortage of funds and a decline in reserves, the BOE may do one of two things. First, it may conduct open market operations with the discount houses and buy securities, which reinjects reserves into the banking system. Or, the BOE may choose to force the houses and the banks to borrow reserves. The banks, reluctant to be without liquid reserves, have several methods of rebuilding their accounts: by borrowing from the discount houses, and by selling securities to the discount houses.

The BOE's decision on the rate at which it will either lend to discount houses or buy securities from them is a major policy variable. Known as the

---

[13] *OECD Economic Surveys: United Kingdom, 1990-1991* (Paris: Organization for Economic Cooperation and Development, 1991), p. 36.

[14] Batten, Blackwell, *et al., op. cit.*, p. 21.

dealing rate or central-bank rate, this rate affects a full spectrum of money market and bank interest rates and, indirectly, influences borrowings from commercial banks and the size of deposits in them. Thus, U.K. monetary policy has as an operational target a short-term rate. Management of this rate, by open market operations, is supposed to enable the central bank to control the intermediate target, which is the rate of growth in $M_0$, the U.K. monetary base.

## SUMMARY

The goals of monetary policy include a stable price level, economic growth, high employment, stable interest rates, and predictable and steady currency exchange rates. Unfortunately, monetary policies involve difficult trade-offs, and policies that help achieve one goal may make another less attainable.

Further, the Federal Reserve has no direct control or influence on the complex economic variables that constitute the goals. Hence, it must identify intermediate targets that influence these variables and are, in turn, influenced by operating targets that are variables the Fed can control to a substantial extent. The intermediate targets may be interest rates, monetary aggregates, or possibly exchange rates. The level of bank reserves (borrowed or nonborrowed) and the level of the federal funds rate have served as operating targets from time to time since 1970. The Fed can effectively manage either this rate on interbank loans or the level of various measures of reserves by open market operations that control the flow of reserves to the banking system. However, the Fed cannot target both rates and reserves at the same time: since 1970, the Fed's policy has alternated between targeting rates and targeting reserves.

Germany's central bank, the Deutsche Bundesbank, requires banks to hold reserves in the form of deposits with the Bundesbank. The German monetary policy has the key objectives of economic growth and stability in prices and exchange rates. The policy is implemented through open market operations, which influence bank reserves and short-term rates and, ultimately, the change in key monetary aggregates.

Japan's central bank, the Bank of Japan, seeks primarily to influence short-term rates by lending reserves to banks. The rate at which the BOJ will lend is the official discount rate, a policy variable in the Japanese system. The level of that rate is a major signal to investors about BOJ plans and a serious influence on the direction of short-term interest rates.

The United Kingdom's central bank, the Bank of England, targets short-term interest rates through a bank system where reserves are important for interbank settlements but not required by the authorities. The goal of this targeting is to influence the growth in the monetary base and, through it, the overall economy.

**Borrowed reserves:** The value (for a bank or for the banking system) of loans obtained from the Federal Reserve System through its discount window.

**Central bank money:** The German monetary aggregate, defined as currency in circulation and required reserves of residents' bank deposits, which was a target of monetary policy during the 1970s and most of the 1980s.

**Demand for money:** An individual's or the public's total demand, at any time, for holding wealth in the form of liquid balances, such as currency and deposits at financial intermediaries.

**Discretionary monetary policy:** The view of policy that allows the Fed to change the rate of growth in reserves or aggregates in order to achieve short-run adjustments in interest rates or levels of economic activity.

**Frictional unemployment:** The unavoidable level of unemployment in the civilian workforce that arises because of the temporary unemployment of people changing jobs or those seeking new or better ones.

**Goal of monetary policy:** A condition such as high employment or price level stability that monetary policymakers seek to bring about in the economy.

**Intermediate target:** A financial or economic variable that responds in a reliable way to changes in an operating target, and that has a somewhat predictable impact on the variables constituting the central bank's economic goals.

**Keynesians:** Economists whose view of monetary policy largely focuses on the stimulation of demand by the targeting of short-term interest rates.

**Monetarists:** Economists whose view of monetary policy largely focuses on the need for and benefits of a steady rate of growth in the monetary aggregates.

**Nonborrowed reserves:** The value (computed for a bank or the entire banking system) of total reserves less those reserves created by borrowing from the Fed through its discount window.

**Operating target:** A financial or monetary variable that the central bank can effectively control through the application of its tools of monetary policy.

**Stagflation:** The condition of both inflation and recession with high unemployment.

1. Name three widely accepted goals of monetary policy.
2. What keeps the Fed from being able to achieve its goals in a direct and easy way?
3. Comment on this statement by an official of the Federal Reserve:

> *[the Fed] can control nonborrowed reserves through open market operations (but) it cannot control total reserves, because the level of borrowing at the discount window is determined in the short run by the preferences of depository institutions.*

Quoted from Alfred Broaddus, "A Primer on the Fed," Chapter 7 in Sumner N. Levine (ed.), *The Financial Analyst's Handbook* (Homewood, IL: Dow Jones-Irwin, 1988), p. 194.

4. Why is it impossible for the Fed to target, at the same time, both the fed funds interest rate and the level of reserves in the banking system?

5. Explain the change in the Fed's targets that occurred with the 1979 Volcker announcement about inflation and the new Fed policy.

6. What were the two largely new considerations that influenced the Fed's policymaking in the 1980s?

7. a. Describe the two monetary aggregates which have served as the Bundesbank's intermediate targets in recent years.

   b. What is the Bundesbank's typical method of carrying out open market operations?

8. How does the Bank of England, which does not engage in open market operations directly with commercial banks, supply reserves to the British banking system?

9. The monetary policy of the Bank of Japan changed substantially from 1970 to 1990. A particularly striking change was the BOJ's increased use of open market operations to implement policy. What single development in the Japanese financial system was most responsible for the BOJ's extensive use of open market operations?

CHAPTER SEVEN

# *Insurance Companies*

LEARNING OBJECTIVES

*After reading this chapter you will understand:*

- the nature of the business of insurance companies.
- the differences between the nature of the liabilities of life insurance companies and those of property and casualty insurance companies.
- recent changes in the insurance business, and the factors contributing to those changes.
- the different types of life insurance policies.
- the different types of property and insurance policies.
- the types of assets in which life insurance companies and property and casualty insurance companies invest.
- the regulation of insurance companies.
- some important financial developments in the international insurance industry.

Insurance companies are financial intermediaries that, for a price, will make a payment if a certain event occurs. They function as risk bearers. There are two types of insurance companies: life insurance companies and property and casualty insurance companies.

The principal event that the former insure against is death. Upon the death of a policyholder, a life insurance company agrees to make either a lump sum payment or a series of payments to the beneficiary of the policy. Life insurance protection is not the only financial product sold by these companies; a major portion of the business of life insurance companies is now in the area of providing retirement benefits. In contrast, property and casualty insurance companies insure against a wide variety of occurrences. Two examples are damages to automobiles and homes.

The key distinction between life insurance and property and casualty insurance companies lies in the difficulty of projecting whether a policyholder will be paid off and how much the payment will be. While this is no easy task for either type of insurance company, it is easier for a life insurance company. The amount and timing of claims on property and casualty insurance companies are more difficult to predict because of the randomness of natural catastrophes and the unpredictability of court awards in liability cases. This uncertainty about the timing and amount of cash outlays to satisfy claims has an impact on the investment strategies of property and casualty insurance companies compared to life insurance companies.

While we draw a distinction here between the two types of insurance companies because of the nature of the events they insure against, most large insurance companies do underwrite both life insurance and property and casualty insurance policies.[1] Usually a parent company has a life insurance company subsidiary and a property and casualty insurance company subsidiary.

## LIFE INSURANCE COMPANIES

As of 1991, the total assets of U.S. life insurance companies amounted to $1.52 trillion.[2] The contractual commitment made by a life insurance company is only as good as the issuing company's ability to make the contractual payments. Unlike the liabilities of depository institutions, there is no government entity, state or federal, that steps in to guarantee liabilities of a life insurance company should it fail to satisfy its obligations. Consequently, the pricing terms that life insurance companies offer on policies are related directly to their financial ratings. Most market participants rely on the rating system of A.M. Best, which measures an insurance company's performance in terms of three critical areas: profitability, leverage, and liquidity.

---

[1] Another type of insurance, mortgage insurance, is discussed in Chapter 23.
[2] *Best's Insurance Reports—Life/Health*, 1992, p. vi. Assets are defined as "admitted assets," which means all assets approved by state insurance departments as existing property in the ownership of the company.

## Nature of the Business

The nature of the life insurance business has changed dramatically since the 1970s, largely as a result of high and variable inflation rates and increased domestic and global competitive pressures resulting from financial deregulation throughout the world. Investor sophistication has also increased, forcing life insurance companies to offer more competitive products. For example, consider two common forms of life insurance policies: *term insurance* and *whole life insurance*. Term insurance requires payment of a premium to the insurance company periodically. If the insured does not die by the end of the policy period, the policy has no value. In contrast, whole life insurance has two features: (1) it pays off a stated amount upon the death of the insured, and (2) it accumulates a cash value that the policyholder can call on. The first feature is an insurance protection feature—the same feature that term insurance provides. The second is an investment feature because the policy accumulates value.

Life insurance companies compete with other life insurance companies in providing insurance protection. When it comes to the investment feature, however, life insurance companies compete not only with other life insurance companies but also with other financial institutions that provide investment instruments and with direct investments in securities. The interest rate effectively paid on whole life insurance policies is typically below market interest rates. In fact, a popular saying is "buy term and invest the difference." This means that the policyholder would be better off obtaining insurance protection by purchasing term insurance and investing the cost savings that results from buying term rather than whole life insurance. The underlying principle here is that the policyholder/investor can unbundle the features offered by insurance policies.

As inflation and interest rates escalated in the 1970s, people became more aware of the dangers of nominally fixed contracts relying on nominal rates, and became more sensitive to the rates they were earning on the funds they invested. With persistent and volatile inflation, insurance products such as whole life lost value in real terms and generated uncertainty about the purchasing power of the terminal amount promised by the contract; the product thus became less attractive, consequently reducing the number of policies written. An additional drain on the cash flow of life insurance companies was that the older whole life insurance policies in force permitted the policyholder to borrow from the insurance company against the cash value of the policy at interest rates related to those at which interest was being credited to the policy. These rates soon became considerably less than prevailing rates. Policyholders took advantage of the low borrowing costs and invested the funds borrowed in alternative market instruments.

This cash outflow from life insurance companies is referred to as disintermediation, a process we discussed in Chapter 4 when describing the net outflow of deposit funds from depository institutions. To survive, life insurance companies had to develop new, more attractive products.

## Types of Policies

Policies issued by life insurance companies can be classified as one of four types: (1) pure insurance protection against risk of death; (2) a package consisting of life insurance protection and an investment vehicle; (3) insurance against the risk of life (annuities), primarily designed for pension programs; and (4) pure investment-oriented vehicles (such as guaranteed investment contracts). We have already discussed the prevalent form of pure insurance protection (term policies) and one form of insurance/investment policy (whole life policies). Below we describe other types of insurance/investment policies, annuities, and pure investment-oriented policies.

***Insurance against the Risk of Life.***   Consider a person who retires with a given amount of resources to be spread evenly over her remaining life. Clearly, she faces a problem because the length of life is a random variable, basically unknown to her. A life insurance company, relying on the fact that the average length of life of a (random) group can be estimated rather accurately, can offer the person a fixed annuity as long as she lives, thus relieving her of the risk of outliving her resources. Annuities are one of the oldest types of insurance contracts. At present they are used primarily in connection with a pension fund. In a *single-premium deferred annuity*, the sponsor of a pension plan pays a single premium to the life insurance company, which in turn agrees to make lifelong payments to the employee (the policyholder) when that employee retires.

***Insurance/Investment Policies.***   Two principal policies fall into the insurance/investment category: universal life and variable life. A *universal life policy* pays a dividend that is tied to market interest rates. Insofar as market rates reflect inflation,[3] this protects the insured against real losses from inflation. Because it pays a competitive interest rate, universal life has all but replaced the traditional whole life policy. Essentially, the cash value of a universal life policy builds and is used to buy term insurance. A *variable life insurance contract* provides a death benefit that depends on the market value of the investment at the time of the insured's death. The securities that the premiums are invested in are typically common stock, and hence such policies are referred to as *equity-linked policies*. While the death benefits are variable, there is a guaranteed minimum death benefit that the insurer agrees to pay regardless of the market value of the portfolio.

***Pure Investment-Oriented Policies.***   The policy that falls into the investment-oriented category is the guaranteed investment contract (GIC). These policies typically are purchased by pension plan sponsors as an investment. In a GIC, a life insurance company agrees, for a single premium, to pay a dollar amount at the maturity of the GIC. The dollar amount will be equal to the

---

[3] See the discussion of Fisher's Law in Chapter 11.

premium paid plus accumulated interest. An interest rate guaranteed by the life insurance company is specified in the policy. For example, a $10 million five-year GIC guaranteeing an interest rate of 10% means that, at the end of five years, the life insurance company is guaranteeing a payment of $16,105,100.[4]

The maturity of a GIC can vary from 1 year to 20 years. The interest rate guaranteed depends on market conditions and the rating of the life insurance company. The interest rate will be some spread above the yield offered on U.S. Treasury securities of the same maturity. The lower the rating of the life insurance company, as classified by A.M. Best, the higher the yield it must offer to attract policyholders.

The GIC that we describe above is called a *bullet contract*; it is the most common type. Of other types of GIC policies, we describe just two: the *window contract* and the *floating-rate contract*.[5] In a window contract, instead of accepting a lump sum payment, the life insurance company agrees to accept deposits over some future designated time period, usually between 3 to 12 months. All deposits made are guaranteed the same interest rate.[6] This type of contract is used by a pension sponsor that will make periodic contributions on behalf of employees and wishes to lock in an interest rate. The risk that the life insurance company faces is that, if interest rates decline below the interest rate guaranteed on the window contract, any new deposits must be invested at a lower interest rate than the life insurance company has agreed to pay. Of course, if interest rates rise above the contract rate, the life insurance company will be able to invest the new deposits at a higher rate, thereby increasing its spread income. Nevertheless, to protect against a decline in interest rates, the interest rate offered on window contracts will be below that offered on bullet contracts with the same maturity.

A floating-rate contract is a GIC whose guaranteed interest rate is tied to some predetermined market benchmark such as a specific-maturity Treasury yield. The interest rate will be at some spread to the index. The spread will reflect market conditions and the rating of the life insurance company— the lower the rating, the greater the spread.

It should be emphasized that a GIC is nothing more than the debt obligation of the life insurance company issuing the contract. The word "guarantee" does not mean that there is a guarantor other than the life insurance company. Effectively, a GIC is a zero coupon bond issued by a life insurance company, and, as such, exposes the investor to the same credit risk. The popularity of GICs arises from the favorable accounting treatment accorded these policies. Specifically, the owner of a GIC such as a pension plan sponsor shows the value of a GIC in its portfolio at its purchase price, not at its current mar-

---

[4] Determined as follows: $10,000,000 (1.10)^5 = $16,105,100$.

[5] There are "if" and "but" contracts, participating contracts, bank investment contracts, and pooled GIC funds. For a detailed description of GICs, see Kenneth L. Walker, *Guaranteed Investment Contracts: Risk Analysis and Portfolio Strategies* (Homewood, IL: Dow Jones-Irwin, 1989).

[6] The amount of the deposits may or may not be fixed in advance.

ket value. Thus, a rise in interest rates, which would lower the value of any fixed-rate asset held (as explained in Chapter 10), will not reduce the value of a GIC for financial reporting purposes.

### Investments

Most investments made by life insurance companies are in debt obligations. The distribution of assets of U.S. life insurance companies in 1991 is summarized in Table 7-1.

Life insurance companies are the largest buyers of corporate bonds. They invest not only in publicly traded bonds, but also provide direct commercial loans and invest in private placements, as we will discuss in Chapter 14. Because of the tax advantages granted to life insurance companies, there is no benefit to investment in tax-advantaged securities such as tax-exempt municipal bonds.

As can be seen from Table 7-1, in 1991 bonds plus mortgages constituted almost 68% of total life insurance company assets. A life insurance company's decision to allocate most of its funds to long-term debt obligations is a result of the nature of its liabilities. As most contracts written by life insurance companies are based on some contractually fixed interest rate that will be paid to a policyholder after a long stretch of years, long-term debt obligations are a natural investment vehicle for an insurance company to use to hedge its commitments (or to match maturities). Moreover, there is an incentive to invest in bonds rather than equities because of restrictions on portfolio composition imposed by regulation, which plays an important role for life insurance companies. Regulations require a life insurance company buying equity to report any

### TABLE 7-1

#### DISTRIBUTION OF ASSETS OF U.S. LIFE INSURANCE COMPANIES: 1991

| Asset | Amount (000,000) | Percent |
|---|---|---|
| Government securities | $225,805 | 14.9 |
| Corporate securities | | |
| Bonds | 542,596 | 35.7 |
| Common stock | 56,940 | 3.7 |
| Preferred stock | 10,071 | 0.7 |
| Total corporate securities | 609,607 | 40.1 |
| Mortgages | 256,077 | 16.8 |
| Real estate | 34,949 | 2.3 |
| Policy loans | 61,723 | 4.1 |
| Cash | 5,856 | 0.4 |
| Short-term investments | 40,512 | 2.7 |
| All others | 286,001 | 18.7 |
| Total admitted assets | $1,520,530 | 100.0 |

Source: A.M. Best Company, Best's Insurance Reports—Life/Health, 1992, p. vi.

decline in the value of the equity in the periodic financial statement that must be supplied to regulators. A bond by contrast is carried at acquisition cost; if a bond's market value declines, the reduction in value is not recognized. This accounting rule is under reconsideration by regulators.

## Regulation

Life insurance companies are regulated primarily at the state level as a result of a 1945 federal statute, the McCarran-Ferguson Act. They must also comply with regulations as set forth by the Employee Retirement Income Security Act of 1974 (ERISA) for the portion of their business that deals with pension funds. We'll have more to say about ERISA when we cover pension funds in Chapter 9. Life insurance companies whose stock is publicly traded must comply with the federal regulations set forth by the Securities and Exchange Commission. Our focus here is on state regulation.

Each state establishes its own regulations with respect to (1) the types of securities that are eligible for investment, and (2) the valuation of those securities for regulatory reporting purposes. As for eligible investments, a state will typically restrict the percentage of funds allocated to common stock investments to the lesser of 10% of assets (in some states 20%) or 100% of surplus. (The surplus is the difference between assets and liabilities.) It will also restrict investments in bonds and preferred stock to those of a certain quality rating. A "basket provision" usually permits investments of about 5% of assets in any type of vehicle that is not explicitly prohibited by law.

To insure compliance with its regulations, life insurance companies licensed to do business in a state are required to file an annual statement and supporting documents with the state's insurance department. States also conduct periodic on-site examinations of companies.

The annual statement, referred to as the *convention statement*, shows the assets, liabilities, and surplus of the reporting company. The surplus is closely watched by regulators and A.M. Best because it determines the amount of business that an insurance company can underwrite.

The convention statement must be prepared in accordance with certain accounting principles that are the same for all states. They require that common stock and lower-quality bonds be valued at the lower of cost or market. In contrast, high-quality bonds are carried at acquisition cost. Consequently, if $10 million is invested in a U.S. Treasury security whose market value declines to $7 million because interest rates have increased, the securities continue to be reported at $10 million.

This accounting requirement has two important implications. First, it encourages life insurance companies to allocate only a small portion of their funds to stock and lower quality-rated bonds because a decline in the market value of those assets below cost will reduce the life insurance company's surplus. Second, it may discourage managers of life insurance companies from trying to take advantage of perceived or real opportunities in the bond market. For example, suppose an insurance company that has invested $10 million in a U.S. Treasury security recognizes that it can improve its asset/liability position if it swaps out of these U.S. Treasury securities and into a different U.S. Treasury issue. It would be discouraged to do so if the market value of the U.S. Treasury securities it owns is less than $10 million, because once these securities are sold in order to purchase the new Treasury issue, a loss must be recognized. This would result in a reduction in the life insurance company's surplus. As noted above, these accounting rules are being reconsidered by regulators.

For regulatory reporting purposes, all life insurance companies have general accounts, and most have one or more separate accounts. A separate account is one where the life insurance company reports specific types of insurance contracts. The benefit of separate accounts is that they give the life insurance company greater latitude to match the assets with the specific nature of the liability created by the insurance contracts.

▶ KEY POINTS THAT YOU SHOULD UNDERSTAND BEFORE PROCEEDING:

1. The fact that a life insurance company's ability to make contractual payments depends upon the returns to its investments of the contractholders' premiums.
2. The variety of policies that life insurance companies issue.
3. The kinds of assets that constitute the bulk of life insurance companies' investments.
4. The aspects of life insurance companies regulated by government.

## PROPERTY AND CASUALTY INSURANCE COMPANIES

Property and casualty (P&C) insurance companies provide a broad range of insurance protection against:

1. Loss, damage, or destruction of property.
2. Loss or impairment of income-producing ability.
3. Claims for damages by third parties because of alleged negligence.
4. Loss resulting from injury or death due to occupational accidents.

### Nature of the Business

Property and casualty insurance products can be classified as either "personal lines" or "commercial lines." Personal lines include automobile insurance and homeowner insurance. Commercial lines include product liability insurance, commercial property insurance, and malpractice insurance.

The price that the insured pays for coverage is called a *premium*. The amount of the liability coverage is specified in the policy. The premium is invested until, and if, the insured makes a claim on the entire amount or a fraction of the amount of the policy, and that claim is validated. For some lines of business, the P&C company will know immediately that it has incurred a liability from a policy it has underwritten; when the claim will have to be paid and the amount of the claim may not be known at that time, however.

To illustrate this, suppose that in 1993 an automobile policy is written that provides $1 million liability coverage for Bob Smith. The policy covers him against claims by other parties resulting from an automobile accident. Let's suppose that in 1993 Bob Smith does in fact get into an automobile accident that results in the permanent disability of Karen Lee, the driver of the other car. The P&C company recognizes that it has a liability, but how much will it have to pay Karen Lee? It may be several years before the injured party and the company settle the matter, and a trial may be necessary to determine the monetary damages that the P&C company must pay.

There are some lines of business where a claim is not evident until several years after the policy period. For example, suppose that for the years 1989 through 1990 a P&C company wrote a product liability policy for a toy manufacturing company. It may not be until 1994 that it is discovered that one of the products manufactured by the toy company is defective, causing serious injury to children.

Thus, the costs of the policies underwritten by a P&C company consist of (1) claims for losses that have been incurred and are reported during the year, and (2) actuarially estimated claims on policies written during the year that will not be paid until later years. P&C companies must by law establish *reserves* to satisfy the actuarially estimated claims. Reserves are increased or decreased depending on whether actual claims are above or below those actuarially estimated.

A P&C company's revenue for a year is generated from two sources. First is the premium income for policies written during the year. Second is investment income resulting from the investment of both the reserves established to pay off future claims and the P&C's surplus (assets less liabilities).

The profit of a P&C company is calculated by subtracting from the revenue for the year (as defined in the previous paragraph) each of the following: (1) funds that must be added to reserves for new claims for policies written during the year (called *claim expenses*); (2) funds that must be added to reserves because of underestimates of actuarially projected claims from previous years (called *claim adjustment expenses*); (3) taxes; and (4) administrative and marketing expenses associated with issuing policies. If revenue for the year exceeds (1) through (4), then the surplus of the P&C company is increased; it is decreased if the reverse occurs. Surplus also changes when funds are distributed to shareholders.

As in the case of life insurance companies, surplus is important because it is the surplus that ultimately can be drawn upon to pay policyholders. The growth of the surplus of a P&C company will determine how much future business it can underwrite. The ability of a P&C company to take on risk is measured by the ratio of the annual premium to the capital plus surplus. Usually, this ratio is kept at between two-to-one and three-to-one. Consequently, $2 to $3 in annual premium can be supported for each $1 increase in surplus.

If annual premiums exceed the sum of claim expenses, claim adjustment expenses, and administrative and marketing expenses, the difference is said to be the underwriting profit; an underwriting loss results if claim expenses and claim adjustment expenses exceed annual premiums. A common measure reported by P&C companies is a *combined ratio*,[7] which is calculated by dividing the sum of claim expenses, claim adjustment expenses, and administrative and marketing expenses by annual premiums. A ratio of less than 100% means that a P&C company realized an underwriting profit; a ratio of greater than 100% means that the P&C company realized an operating loss.

Between 1950 and 1973, the overall industry combined ratio exceeded 100% only nine times.[8] That is, in only nine of the 24 years did the industry realize an underwriting loss. Unlike the 1950-1973 period, between 1974 and 1989 the combined ratio was below 100% for only two years. This means that there were only two years when the industry realized an underwriting profit. The industry combined ratio reached a peak (that is, a maximum underwriting loss) of 120% in 1984.

Pricing pressure in the business has come not only from intercompany competition but also from large non-insurance corporations that have established insurance captives in tax havens such as Bermuda or in low-tax states such as Vermont.[9] These insurance captives self-insure the corporation. To reduce their risks, they lay off some of the insurance risks to non-captive insurance companies, a process known as "reinsurance." Additional pressure was put on the P&C industry when the biggest insurance brokerage firm, Marshall & McLennan, created an alternative insurance outlet by pooling the liability risks of large corporations. It has been estimated that these alternative insurance markets have taken away $50 billion in premiums (almost 35% of the market) from traditional P&C companies.[10]

Because of competitive pressure, today there is better coordination between the insurance and investment sides of the business when pricing insurance policies. Firms do this by establishing an asset/liability committee consisting of the actuaries and investment managers. The former measure the liabilities and estimated cash outlay of the P&C company; the latter manage the funds so as to satisfy the projected obligations and earn a return in excess of these obligations.

---

[7] It is called a combined ratio because it depends on two other ratios, an *expense ratio* and a *loss ratio*. The former is the ratio of administrative and marketing expenses to annual premiums. The latter is the ratio of the sum of claim expenses and claim adjustment expenses to annual premiums. The combined ratio is the sum of these two ratios.

[8] Frank D. Campbell, "Asset-Liability Management for Property-Casualty Insurers," Chapter 47 in Frank J. Fabozzi (ed.), *The Handbook of Fixed Income Securities* (Homewood, IL: Business One-Irwin, 1991), p. 1006.

[9] Fredric Dannen, "The Incredible Shrinking Insurance Industry," *Institutional Investor* (January 1990), p. 68.

[10] *Ibid.*, p. 68.

| TABLE 7 - 2 | | |
|---|---|---|

DISTRIBUTION OF ASSETS OF U.S. PROPERTY AND
CASUALTY INSURANCE COMPANIES: 1991

| Asset | Amount ($ billions) | Percent of Total |
|---|---|---|
| Cash and equivalents | 37.5 | 6.5% |
| Equities | 106.8 | 18.6 |
| U.S. Treasury securities | 96.2 | 16.8 |
| Federal Agency securities | 31.0 | 5.4 |
| Municipal bonds | 140.8 | 24.6 |
| Corporate and foreign bonds | 102.0 | 17.8 |
| Mortgages | 7.7 | 1.3 |
| Other | 51.9 | 9.1 |
| Total | 572.8 | 100.0 |

*Note:* These figures are those of the group that the source calls "Other [Than Life] Insurance Companies."

*Source:* Board of Governors of the Federal Reserve System's *Flow of Funds Accounts, Financial Assets and Liabilities*, First Quarter, 1992.

## Investments

The distribution, as of the end of 1991, of the assets held by P&C companies appears in Table 7-2. As the table shows, P&C companies invest more heavily in equities and less so in bonds than life insurance firms do.

## Regulation

As with life insurance companies, P&C companies are regulated at the state level. States regulate P&C companies in several ways. First, they regulate the prices that may be charged for insurance coverage. Competitive pressures, however, have made the need for price regulation less important. In instances where states have imposed prices that insurers feel are uneconomic, companies have withdrawn from offering insurance.

Second, to reduce the likelihood of insolvency, states establish regulations governing eligible investments that P&C companies may make. While life insurance companies are constrained as to eligible assets, P&C companies have greater leeway for investing. For example, a P&C company might be required to invest a minimum in eligible bonds and mortgages. As long as this minimum is satisfied, however, a P&C company is free to allocate its investments any way it pleases among eligible assets in the other asset classes.

▶ KEY POINTS THAT YOU SHOULD UNDERSTAND BEFORE PROCEEDING:

1. That a P&C insurance company's ability to make contractual payments depends upon the returns to its investments of the contractholders' premiums.
2. The many kinds of P&C insurance company policies.

3. The types of assets held by P&C insurance companies, compared to life insurance companies.

4. The aspects of the P&C insurance company business that government regulates.

## FINANCIAL TRENDS IN THE INTERNATIONAL INSURANCE INDUSTRY

■ ■ ■ ■

### Bancassurance

A major development in the international insurance industry has been the disappearance of the traditionally clear line of separation between banks and life insurance companies. In much of the industrialized world, the late 1980s and early 1990s have been times of deregulation of financial institutions and liberalization of the rules governing most of their operations. In such an environment, banks and insurance companies have begun to transform themselves into financial conglomerates that offer the widest possible array of services to individual and institutional investors. A commonly used name for this kind of integrated financial activity is *bancassurance*, and in one form or another, bancassurance has appeared in many industrialized countries, especially Europe.[11] The notable exceptions to this rule have been the United States and Japan, where strict regulations reserving certain lines of business for banks and others for insurance firms have remained generally in force.

Bancassurance can take several forms. The simplest form is *cross-sectoral investing*, whereby banks expand their operations to offer new lines of insurance to customers, or insurance companies introduce some type of deposit and savings accounts to their policyholders. Because governmental regulations still prohibit banking and insurance activities from being carried out at one corporate source, this kind of investing must be effected through linkages among companies. Often, banks conduct this kind of investing through the creation of an insurance subsidiary, and insurance firms follow a similar tactic.

A second form is the *interpenetration of markets*, which may happen because of the merger of a bank and an insurance company.[12] Interpenetration can also occur if a bank or insurance company acquires the majority of (or a significantly large minority of) the equity shares in a firm of the other industry. Interestingly, Europe is the site of many examples of this kind of activity because the European Community regulatory structure, as well as that in most individual European countries, permits banks to hold large equity positions in

---

[11] The term is drawn from "Bancassurance: A Survey of Competition Between Banking and Insurance," which appeared in *Sigma*, a February 1992 publication of the Swiss Reinsurance Company of Zurich, Switzerland.

[12] "Insurance and Other Financial Services: Structural Trends," in *Financial Market Trends*, published by the Organization for Economic Cooperation and Development (February 1992), pp. 31-38.

firms outside the banking or thrift industry. Further, insurance companies are free to hold large, minority positions in the equities of banks.

The third form of bancassurance is a *cooperative arrangement* between a bank and an insurance company whereby each remains independent. Examples include joint ventures and special distribution agreements that call for a bank to market one insurance firm's product line and for the insurance firm to sell the bank's services through its retail outlets.

Several important and global economic forces explain the phenomenon of bancassurance.[13] First, extensive deregulation of the many financial industry sectors has allowed the large financial firms to diversify their product lines. Second, deregulation improved competition and shrank the profit margins of many financial institutions, driving them to seek increased market share and to augment their types of services. Third, with the increased personal savings from the economic boom of the 1980s, investors were looking for higher rates of return on their funds than banks had traditionally paid. Thus, money flowed from the liquid and short-term accounts at banks into other financial institutions. An example is France, where the percentage of individual wealth in bank accounts fell from almost 59% in 1960 to 15% in 1990, while wealth invested in insurance assets rose from 10% to 45% of household financial assets.[14] Finally, the demand for insurance products, particularly life insurance products with investment features, rose dramatically in the last decade. However, insurance buyers were also looking for a wider range of financial services than the firms in this industry were used to providing.

In response to these factors, banks and insurance companies searched for synergistic combinations (that is, combinations of assets that are more valuable than the sum of the individual assets used independently) of financial activities that could cut costs, raise market share, or both. What they developed is a strategy of offering extensive financial services product lines, integrated across insurance and banking products. One place where bancassurance has been quite successful is France: in 1990, 50% of the life insurance policies were sold through banks.[15]

## Cross-Border Activities

Insurance companies are increasingly free of the constraints of international borders and have begun to engage in two major cross-border activities. One of these activities involves mergers or acquisitions of strong equity positions in insurance companies of other countries. For example, the large French insurer *Assurances Générales de France* owns 25% of the shares of Germany's third largest insurance company, *Aachener und Münchener*.[16] In turn, this German firm

---

[13] "Bancassurance: A Survey of Competition Between Banking and Insurance," *op. cit.*, pp. 4-5.

[14] *Ibid.*, p. 7.

[15] *Ibid.*, p.1.

[16] "The French Lay Siege to Fortress Germany," *The Economist* (April 18, 1992), pp. 77-78.

and *Fondiaria,* a large Italian insurer, once jointly held controlling interest in another German insurance company. Other acquisitions of large equity positions appear to be forthcoming.

A second kind of cross-border activity, which is happening in some places now (the U.K. and Germany, for examples) and is likely to accelerate in the future, involves simply branching out from the home country into other countries. That is, an insurance firm in one country can open an office and sell policies in another (subject to the necessary licensing and capital adequacy rules). In Europe, with the approach of market unification, this kind of activity will be common. The European Community has already given explicit support for cross-border selling of insurance through its decision, effective 1995, that any company licensed in one member of the European group of countries will be permitted to write business in any other member country.[17]

In this book, we constantly call attention to the impact of an era of deregulation and globalization of financial activities. Changes in insurance company products and approaches are good examples of that impact on a major financial institution.

### Pension Funds and Insurance Companies

In some countries, insurance companies are active in the pension fund area. For example, in 1988, the British government allowed insurance companies to sell (and manage) pension products.[18] The year before, 1987, the French government had given similar permission to its insurance companies and other financial institutions. In Japan, insurance companies compete for pension fund business with a small number of banks that are called "trust banks." Trust banks, which have branches throughout the country, are long-term financing institutions devoted to savings and investment management. Competition between these banks and insurance firms is rather fierce because the amount of money is so large. Corporate pension funds alone have mounted to a hefty 50 trillion yen in recent years.[19] In the future, more countries may permit insurance firms to enter the pension fund business.

▶ KEY POINTS THAT YOU SHOULD UNDERSTAND BEFORE PROCEEDING:

1. The meaning and implications of the major development in the international insurance industry, which is known as "bancassurance."
2. That some countries permit insurance firms to be active in the area of pension funds and pension management.

[17] Diane Ferriaolo, "Overview of International Insurance," *Best's Review (Property/Casualty)* (May 1992), pp. 11-12.

[18] Ernst & Young Management, *Insurance in the European Community* (New York: Ernst & Young Management, 1990), p.47.

[19] "Forex Fiasco Forces Radical Rethink," *Euromoney* (March 1992), p. 52.

**SUMMARY**

Life insurance companies and property and casualty insurance companies are financial intermediaries that function as risk bearers. While the principal event that life insurance companies insure against is death, since the 1970s a major portion of life insurance company business has been in providing lifetime benefits in the form of retirement policies.

Life insurance policies can be classified as one of four types: (1) pure insurance protection against risk of death (for example, term insurance); (2) a package consisting of insurance protection and an investment vehicle (for example, whole life, universal life, and variable life); (3) insurance against the risk of life (annuities); and (4) a pure investment-oriented vehicle, primarily designed for pension programs (for example, guaranteed investment contracts). Life insurance companies are regulated primarily at the state level; they must also comply with ERISA requirements when they deal in the pension fund area.

Property and casualty insurance companies insure against a wide variety of occurrences. Revenue is generated from two sources: premium income for policies written during the year, and investment income resulting from the investment of both the reserves established to pay off future claims and the P&C's surplus. Today well-managed companies attempt some integration of the insurance and investment sides of the business when pricing insurance policies. P&C companies are regulated at the state level, but are afforded greater latitude than life insurance companies in their investment choices.

Bancassurance, the integration of banking and insurance services, is a major development in the international insurance industry. In many places, banks now offer insurance products, and insurance firms are providing services once associated only with banks. The prime cause of this development is the elimination of regulations segregating the two industries. At this time, the United States and Japan have not experienced bancassurance because their regulations separating banks from insurance firms are still intact and enforced.

**GLOSSARY**

**A.M. Best:** Private firm that rates insurance companies in the areas of profitability, leverage, and liquidity.

**Bancassurance:** The effort of banks and insurance companies to transform themselves into integrated financial conglomerates that offer both banking and insurance products.

**Basket provision:** Feature of regulations on insurance companies that allows a company to invest some small percentage of its assets in any type of vehicle that is not explicitly prohibited by law.

**Bullet-type guaranteed investment contract:** A GIC that guarantees a yearly interest rate over the specified life of the contract.

**Claim expenses:** Funds that property and casualty insurance companies must add to their reserves for new claims for policies written during a year.

**Claim-adjustment expenses:** Funds that property and casualty insurance firms must add to reserves because of underestimates of actuarially projected claims from previous years.

**Combined ratio:** An important measure of a property and casualty firm's financial situation, which is calculated by dividing the sum of claim expenses, claim adjustment expenses, and administrative and marketing expenses by annual premiums.

**Convention statement:** An insurance company's annual statement of its financial situation.

**Floating-rate guaranteed investment contract:** A GIC in which the guaranteed interest rate is tied to some predetermined market benchmark such as a specific-maturity Treasury yield.

**Life insurance company:** Financial intermediary that agrees to make a payment in the event of the death of the person who holds the policy; a life insurance company may also be active in the area of providing retirement benefits.

**Premium on an insurance policy:** The price the policyholder pays for the insurance policy.

**Property and casualty insurance company:** Financial intermediary that insures against a wide variety of losses to personal or commercial property.

**Reinsurance:** The action of one insurance company buying insurance on some of its own policies from a second insurance company independent from the first.

**Reserves of property and casualty insurance company:** Funds available to satisfy the actuarially estimated claims.

**Single-premium deferred annuity:** An arrangement whereby a policyholder pays a single premium to a life insurance company which agrees to make lifelong payments to the policyholder after retirement.

**Surplus:** The difference between an insurance company's assets and liabilities.

**Term insurance:** A form of insurance that has no value if the insured party does not die before the end of the set policy period.

**Underwriting profit or loss:** The difference between a property and casualty firm's annual premiums and the sum of claim expenses, claim adjustment expenses, and administrative and marketing expenses.

**Universal life policy:** An insurance policy that pays a dividend tied to market interest rates.

**Variable contract:** Provides a death benefit that depends on the market value of invested premiums at the time of the insured's death or, if the value of the investments is low, pays a guaranteed minimum amount.

**Whole life insurance:** A form of insurance that pays a stated amount upon the death of the insured, and that accumulates, over time, a cash value that the policyholder can call on.

1. The quotation following is from a survey in *The Economist* on the American insurance industry:

   *Life insurers, like bankers, learnt the hard way about inflation and interest rates a decade ago. Insurance was a fairly straightforward business in the old days. As late as 1979, more than 80% of new premiums were for "whole life" policies with fixed premiums, benefits and surrender values; almost all the rest was "term" insurance which pays out only on death. . . .*

   *That comfortable world had begun to change even before inflation went into double-digits in the late 1970s. Customers realized that the cash values piling up in their insurance companies did not compare favorably with returns on other instruments. Issuers had to offer policies like universal life and variable life and permutations of the two. These gave customers market-related returns, often above a guaranteed minimum, and more flexibility.*

   a. What is meant by whole life, universal life, and variable life insurance policies?

   b. In general, what have been the consequences of life insurance companies having to offer market-related returns?

2. Why are the liabilities and cash outlays of a property and casualty insurance more difficult to predict than for a life insurance company?

3. a. What is a guaranteed investment contract?

   b. What does the term "guarantee" mean? Is it a government entity that guarantees the contract?

   c. What is the risk a life insurance company faces when it issues a GIC in which it has guaranteed a fixed interest rate over the life of the contract?

4. What is the difference between a bullet GIC and a window GIC?

5. a. What is the surplus of an insurance company?

   b. Why is the surplus important?

6. *When medical waste washed up on the beaches of New Jersey and New York in several separate incidents in 1988, the public was disgusted and scared. Many ocean-front resort operators and workers who depend on the allure of the beach for their livelihood were nearly ruined. But the financial losses from that lost summer of 1988 pale in comparison with the economic havoc that improperly handled medical waste can wreak on America's health care providers. . . .*

*To date, no medical facility has been sued for injuries or damages caused by the disposal of medical waste, but given today's consciousness of this issue and the trend in environmental legislation, such litigation is inevitable. Clearly, the eventuality represents both an emerging liability coverage issue and a thorny challenge for the commercial insurance industry.*

Discuss this excerpt from *Best's Review* of June 30, 1990. Your answer should address these issues:

a.  The type of insurance company that would underwrite coverage for medical waste.

b.  Some of the problems that such companies would have in estimating their liabilities to policyholders.

7.  a.  What is meant by the combined ratio of a property and a casualty insurance company?

b.  What does the combined ratio measure?

8.  "There are no restrictions on the assets in which an insurance company can invest." Do you agree with this statement?

9.  Why do life insurance companies prefer to invest in debt obligations?

10.  Why do the pricing terms of an insurance company depend on its rating?

11.  a.  What is meant by "bancassurance"?

b.  What seems to explain its appearance in certain areas and regions?

c.  Why have the United States and Japan not experienced this phenomenon?

# CHAPTER EIGHT

# Investment Companies

*After reading this chapter you will understand:*

- the different types of investment companies: mutual funds, closed-end investment companies, and unit trusts.
- how the share prices of mutual funds and closed-end funds are determined.
- the structure of funds and the costs that they incur.
- how investment companies can differ depending on their investment objectives.
- the economic benefits that investment companies provide, including diversification and reduced costs of investing.
- the meaning of a "regulated investment company."
- how investment companies are regulated with regard to taxes, management, diversification of assets, fees, and advertising.
- the meaning of a family or complex of funds.
- that this industry is highly concentrated, with many of the assets being managed by a relatively few fund families.
- the types of investment companies that exist in selected countries around the world.

Investment companies are financial intermediaries that sell shares to the public and invest the proceeds in a diversified portfolio of securities. Each share sold represents a proportionate interest in the portfolio of securities managed by the investment company on behalf of the companies' shareholders. The type of securities purchased depends on the company's investment objective.

## TYPES OF INVESTMENT COMPANIES

There are three types of investment companies: open-end funds, closed-end funds, and unit trusts.

### Open-End Funds

These funds, more popularly referred to as *mutual funds*, continually stand ready to sell new shares to the public and to redeem their outstanding shares on demand at a price equal to an appropriate share of the value of their portfolio, which is computed daily at the close of the market.

A mutual fund's share price is based on its *net asset value per share*, which is found by subtracting from the market value of the portfolio the mutual fund's liabilities and then dividing by the number of mutual fund shares outstanding. For example, suppose that a mutual fund with 10 million shares outstanding has a portfolio with a market value of $215 million and liabilities of $15 million. The net asset value per share is $20 [($215 million - $15 million) divided by 10 million].

The share price is quoted on a bid-offer basis. The *offer price* is the price at which the mutual fund will sell the shares. It is equal to the net asset value per share plus any sales commission that the mutual fund may charge. The sales commission is referred to as a "load." *Load funds* impose commissions that typically range from 8.5% on small amounts invested to as little as 1% on amounts of $500,000 or over. A mutual fund that does not impose a sales commission is called a *no-load fund*. No-load mutual funds compete directly with load funds and appeal to investors who object to paying a commission (particularly because there is no empirical evidence that suggests that load funds have outperformed no-load funds after accounting for the load charge). The relative attraction of no-load funds has forced many mutual funds to convert to no-load status. (Some funds have adopted a so-called "low-load" strategy, that is, charging a relatively small load of around 3%-3.5%.) For no-load funds, the offer price is the same as the net asset value per share.

The distinction between a no-load fund and a load is easy to spot in the price quotations that appear in the financial sections of newspapers. The quotations will indicate the size of the load if there is one. An example of some quoted bid and offer prices for certain funds will illustrate these points. In 1992, the following prices appeared in newspapers:

| Fund | NAV | Offer Price |
|------|-----|-------------|
| Vanguard Hi-Yield Corporate | 7.55 | NL |
| Safeco Equity | 10.01 | NL |
| Templeton Growth | 15.70 | 16.60 |
| Putnam Tax Exempt | 9.11 | 9.56 |

Here, the term "NL" for the Hi-Yield Corporate Fund of the Vanguard Group and the Equity Fund of the Safeco Group indicates that these are no-load funds. Their initial per share price to the investor equals the per share value of the fund's assets. The per share offer prices of the other two funds exceed their funds' per share Net Asset Values (or NAVs). Thus, the third and fourth funds are load funds. The Templeton fund load is [($16.60 – $15.70)/$15.70], or 5.7%. The Putnam fund load is slightly above 5%.

Even though a fund does not charge a commission for share purchases, it may still charge investors a fee to sell (redeem) shares. Such funds, referred to as *back-end load funds*, may charge a commission of 4% to 6%. Some back-end load funds impose a full commission if the shares are redeemed within a designated time period after purchase, such as one year, reducing the commission the longer the investor holds the shares. The formal name for the back-end load is the *contingent deferred sales charge* or CDSC.

Some mutual funds neither charge an upfront nor a back-end commission but instead take out up to 1.25% of average daily fund assets each year to cover the costs of selling and marketing shares. SEC Rule 12b-1, passed in 1980, allows mutual funds to use such an arrangement for covering selling and marketing costs; such funds are referred to as *12b-1 funds*.

In 1986, the SEC permitted funds to issue two classes of stock with different sales structures. For example, Alliance Mortgage Securities has two classes, Class A and Class B. The former has a 3% front-end load; the latter has a back-end sales charge that depends on the length of time the shares are held.

The number of mutual funds increased fourfold in the 1980s, from 250 in 1980 to more than 3,900 in 1992.[1] The amount of money controlled by funds increased from $240 billion in 1982 to more than $1.5 trillion in 1992. In terms of amount of assets under management, the funds rank behind commercial banks and close to insurance companies, but ahead of thrifts and credit unions.[2] One reason for the growth of the assets invested in mutual funds is the use of mutual funds in certain types of pension funds that we will discuss in the next chapter.

Table 8-1 shows the distribution of mutual fund assets across major categories of assets for 1981 and 1991, revealing the dynamic growth of all aspects of this major financial intermediary.

---

[1] This is the number of mutual funds followed by a leading service, Lipper Analytical Services.

[2] *Mutual Fund Fact Book* (Washington, D.C.: Investment Company Institute, 1992), p. 25.

| TABLE 8 - 1 | | |
|---|---|---|
| DISTRIBUTION OF ASSETS OF OPEN-END STOCK AND BOND FUNDS IN 1981 AND 1991 | | |
| | 1981 (in $ billions) | 1991 (in $ billions) |
| Cash and equivalents | 5.3 | 60.3 |
| Corporate bonds | 7.5 | 84.6 |
| Preferred stock | 0.4 | 8.0 |
| Common stock | 36.7 | 328.1 |
| Municipal bonds | 3.0 | 147.7 |
| U.S. government bonds | 2.2 | 170.1 |
| Other | 0.2 | 8.3 |
| Total | 55.2 | 807.1 |

*Source: Mutual Fund Fact Book* (Washington, D.C.: Investment Company Institute, 1992), p. 93.

### Closed-End Funds

Unlike mutual funds, closed-end funds sell shares like any other corporation but usually do not redeem their shares. Shares of closed-end funds sell on either an organized exchange, such as the New York Stock Exchange, or in the over-the-counter market. Newspapers often list quotations of the prices of these shares under the heading "Publicly Traded Funds." Investors who wish to purchase closed-end funds must pay a brokerage commission at the time of purchase and again at the time of sale.

The price of a share in a closed-end fund is determined by supply and demand, so the price can fall below or rise above the net asset value per share. Shares selling below NAV are said to be "trading at a discount," while shares with prices above NAV are "trading at a premium." Although the divergence of price from NAV is often puzzling, in some cases the premium or discount is easy to understand. A share's price may be below the NAV because the fund has large tax liabilities on capital gains that have swelled the NAV, and investors are pricing the future after-tax distributions of the fund. Another fund's shares may trade at a premium to the NAV because the fund offers relatively cheap access to, and professional management of, stocks in another country where information is not readily available to small investors. In recent years, the "Spain Fund" and the "Korea Fund" have been prominent examples of this situation.[3]

An interesting feature of closed-end funds is that investors bear the substantial cost of underwriting the issuance of the funds' shares.[4] The proceeds

---

[3] The so-called "Country Funds" were popular in the late 1980s and made up a substantial portion of the closed-end funds issued at that time.

[4] Kathleen Weiss, "The Post-Offering Price Performance of Closed-End Funds," *Financial Management* (Autumn 1989), pp. 57-67.

that the managers of the fund have to invest equal the total paid by initial buyers of the shares minus all costs of issuance. These costs, which average around 7.5% of the total amount paid for the issue, normally include selling fees or commissions paid to the retail brokerage firms that distribute them to the public. The high commissions are strong incentives for retail brokers to recommend these shares to their customers who are retail (individual) investors.

Historically, closed-end funds have been far less popular than open-end funds in the U.S. One estimate has it that the amount of dollars in open-end funds is 12 times greater than the amount in closed-end funds.[5] In recent years, however closed-end funds have shown increasing appeal to individual investors. From 1986 to 1991, the number of closed-end funds rose from 69 to 290, and their assets grew from $12 billion to $73 billion.[6] The chief reason for this surge in popularity seems to be the closed-end funds' emphasis on international investment portfolios.

## Unit Trusts

A unit trust is similar to a closed-end fund in that the number of unit certificates is fixed. Unit trusts typically invest in bonds, and they differ in several ways from both mutual funds and closed-end funds that specialize in investing in bonds. First, there is no active trading of the bonds in the portfolio of the unit trust. Once the unit trust is assembled by the sponsor (usually a brokerage firm or bond underwriter) and turned over to a trustee, the trustee holds all the bonds until they are redeemed by the issuer. Usually the only time the trustee can sell an issue in the portfolio is if there is a dramatic decline in the issuer's credit quality. This means that the cost of operating the trust will be considerably less than costs incurred by either a mutual fund or a closed-end fund. Second, unit trusts have a fixed termination date, while mutual funds and closed-end funds do not.[7] Third, unlike the mutual fund and closed-end fund investor, the unit trust investor knows that the portfolio consists of a specific collection of bonds and has no concern that the trustee will alter the portfolio.

All unit trusts charge a sales commission. The initial sales charge for a unit trust is 3.5% to 5.5%. There is often a commission of 3% to sell units, but trusts sponsored by some organizations do not charge a commission when the units are sold. In addition to these costs, there is the spread that an investor indirectly pays. When the brokerage firm or bond underwriting firm assembles the unit trust, the price of each bond to the trust includes the dealer's spread.

---

[5] Peter Donovan, "Closed-End Funds in the United States of America," in Stefano Preda (ed.), *Funds and Portfolio Management Institutions: An International Survey* (Amsterdam: North-Holland, 1991), p. 232.

[6] Securities and Exchange Commission, *Protecting Investors: A Half-Century of Investment Company Regulation* (New York: Commerce Clearing House, Inc., 1992), p. 432.

[7] There are exceptions. Target term closed-end funds have a fixed termination date.

The balance of our discussion in this chapter focuses on open-end (mutual) funds and closed-end funds. We shall refer to both as simply "funds."

▶ KEY POINTS THAT YOU SHOULD UNDERSTAND BEFORE PROCEEDING:

1. The difference between an open-end and a closed-end fund.
2. The meaning of Net Asset Value (NAV) per share.
3. The difference between a load fund and a no-load fund.
4. The meaning of a back-end load fund and of a contingent deferred sales charge.
5. The SEC rule 12b-1 and the type of fund called a 12b-1 fund.
6. The differences between a closed-end fund and a unit trust.

## STRUCTURE OF A FUND

A fund is structured with a board of directors, a financial advisor responsible for managing the portfolio, and a distributing and selling organization. Funds enter into contracts with a financial advisor to manage the fund, typically a company that specializes in the management of funds. The advisor can be a subsidiary of a brokerage firm, an insurance company, an investment management firm, or a bank.

The financial advisor to the fund charges an *advisory fee*. This fee, which is one of the largest costs of administering a fund, is usually equal to 0.4% to 1.5% of the fund's average assets, but the fee may be determined on a sliding scale that declines as the dollar amount of the fund increases. The advisory fee should reflect the difficulty of managing the particular fund.

Funds incur other costs besides the advisory fee. We have already mentioned the costs of selling and marketing in the case of an open-end fund. Beyond these, the fund is charged fees for custodial and accounting services and board of director fees. And, of course, there are transactions costs associated with the implementation of the fund's investment strategy. All cost information on managing and operating a particular fund is publicly available.

▶ KEY POINTS THAT YOU SHOULD UNDERSTAND BEFORE PROCEEDING:

1. The duties of a financial advisor to a fund.
2. The costs that funds incur.

## TYPES OF FUNDS BY INVESTMENT OBJECTIVE

A wide range of funds with different investment objectives is available. The *investment objective* is set forth in the fund's prospectus. Some funds invest exclusively in equities, others in bonds. Even within an asset class, there are funds with different objectives. In the case of funds that invest exclusively in equities, for example, the investment objective of one fund may be to emphasize stable income, another capital gains, or growth, and still another a combination of income and growth. Some limit investments to specific industries so that the fund manager can presumably specialize and achieve better selection and timing. A few funds offer participation in potentially glamorous new research companies by investing in fields such as electronics, oceanography, and telecommunications. There are funds that restrict their investment to small firms and some that invest in foreign stocks. For investors who wish to achieve maximum diversification, the latest development in the mutual fund area is "indexed funds" that hold a portfolio mimicking the composition of a broad index such as the S&P 500.

Funds that specialize in bond investments also have a wide menu of investment goals and strategies. United States government bond funds invest only in U.S. government bonds. There are corporate bond funds, which can have very different investment objectives. Some funds invest only in high-quality corporate bonds, while others invest primarily in low-quality (junk) corporate bonds. Convertible securities funds invest in convertible bonds and convertible preferred stock. Investors interested in mortgage-backed securities can turn to a fund that specializes in those securities.

There is a wide range of funds that invest exclusively in municipal bonds, which are bonds exempt from federal income taxes issued by state and local governments. Some funds specialize in municipal bond issuers within a given state so that investors can take advantage of the exemption of interest income from state and local taxes. Residents of New York State and California, for example, can choose from a dozen or more funds that invest in bonds of issuers within their home state; interest income is then exempt from state taxes.

Money market mutual funds invest in securities with a maturity of one year or less, called money market instruments. There are three types of money market funds. General money market funds invest in taxable money market instruments such as Treasury bills, short-term United States government agency issues, commercial paper, and negotiable certificates of deposit. U.S. government short-term funds invest only in Treasury bills or U.S. government agency securities. The third type of money market mutual fund is the short-term municipal fund.

A balanced fund is one that invests in both stocks and bonds. While there are often limits as to how much a fund manager may allocate to an asset class, there is room to modify the asset mix to take advantage of what the fund manager expects will be the better-performing asset class.

The Investment Company Institute, the national association for the open-end or mutual funds, recognizes all the objectives listed above as well as some others. Table 8-2 provides the Institute's complete list and the public interest in each type of fund, as indicated by the percentage of total assets invested in each type.

| TABLE 8-2 | |
|---|---|
| DISTRIBUTION OF NET ASSETS AMONG ALL OPEN-END FUNDS ACCORDING TO INVESTMENT OBJECTIVES, 1991 | |
| **Objective** | **Percent of All Funds' Net Assets** |
| Aggressive growth | 4.7% |
| Growth | 7.8 |
| Growth and income | 9.6 |
| Precious metals | 2.2 |
| International | 1.4 |
| Global-Equity | 1.3 |
| Income-Equity | 2.2 |
| Option/Income | .1 |
| Flexible portfolio | .7 |
| Balanced | 1.5 |
| Income-Mixed | 1.9 |
| Income-Bond | 2.0 |
| U.S. government income | 7.2 |
| Ginnie Mae | 2.7 |
| Global bond | 2.0 |
| Corporate bond | 1.1 |
| High-Yield bond | 1.9 |
| Municipal bond | 6.6 |
| State municipal bond | 4.9 |
| Money market-tax exempt | 6.7 |
| Money market-taxable | 33.4 |

*Source: Mutual Fund Fact Book* (Washington, D.C.: Investment Company Institute, 1992), pp. 92, 112, and 114.

▶ KEY POINTS THAT YOU SHOULD UNDERSTAND BEFORE PROCEEDING:

1. The meaning of the term "investment objective."
2. The varieties of investment objectives for mutual funds.

## ECONOMIC MOTIVATION FOR FUNDS

Recall from Chapter 2 that financial intermediaries obtain funds by issuing financial claims against themselves and then investing those funds. An investment company is a financial intermediary because it pools the funds of market participants and uses those funds to buy a portfolio of securities. Also recall the special role in the financial markets played by financial intermediaries. They provide at least one of the following four economic functions: (1) maturity intermediation; (2) risk reduction via diversification; (3) lower costs of contracting and information processing; and (4) a payments mechanism. Let's look at which of these economic functions a fund provides.

Consider first maturity intermediation. An investor with a short-term investment horizon wishing to invest in either stocks or debt obligations with a maturity greater than the planned investment horizon faces the risk that the securities may have to be sold at a time when their market value is less than the price paid. This is true even with mutual funds, because the net asset value per share will fluctuate with market conditions. Consequently, maturity intermediation is not an economic function provided by a fund.

Consider next the risk reduction through diversification function. By investing in a fund, an investor can obtain broad-based ownership of a sufficient number of securities either within a sector of the financial market or across market sectors to reduce portfolio risk. (We will be more specific about the type of risk that is reduced in Chapter 13.) While an individual investor may be able to acquire a broad-based portfolio of securities, the degree of diversification will be limited by the amount available to invest. By investing in the investment company, however, the investor can effectively achieve the benefits of diversification at lower cost even if the amount of money available to invest is not large.

Beyond risk reduction via diversification offered by funds, there are reduced costs of contracting and information processing because an investor purchases the services of a presumably skilled financial advisor at less cost than if the investor directly negotiated with such an advisor. The advisory fee is lower because of the larger size of assets managed, as well as the reduced costs of searching for an investment manager and obtaining information about the securities. Also, the costs of transacting in the securities are reduced because a fund has more clout in negotiating transactions costs, and custodial fees and bookkeeping costs are less for a fund than for an individual investor.

Finally, money market funds generally provide payment services by allowing investors to write checks drawn on the fund, although this facility is limited in various ways.

▶ KEY POINTS THAT YOU SHOULD UNDERSTAND BEFORE PROCEEDING:

1. A mutual fund can reduce risk through portfolio diversification.
2. A mutual fund can reduce a variety of costs related to investments and management of portfolios

## REGULATION

All investment companies are regulated at the federal level according to the *Investment Company Act of 1940* and subsequent amendments to that legislation. The securities they issue must be registered with the SEC. Moreover, investment companies must provide periodic financial reports and disclose their investment policies to investors. The act prohibits changes in the nature of an investment company's investment policies without the approval of shareholders. A major goal of the law was to prevent self-dealing and other examples of conflict of interest, such as the imposition of unreasonably high fees. New regulations aimed at potential self-dealing were established in the *Insider Trading*

*and Securities Fraud Enforcement Act of 1988*, which requires mutual fund investment advisors to institute and enforce procedures that reduce the chances of
insider trading.

The most important feature of the Investment Company Act of 1940 has
to do with what the law permits. The law frees any company that qualifies as
a "regulated investment company" from taxation on its gains, either from income or capital appreciation. To qualify as such a company, the fund must distribute to its shareholders 90% of its income each year. (Dividends paid out to
investors, of course, are taxable to the investor.) Further, the fund must follow certain rules about the diversification and liquidity of its investments and
about short-term trading and gains.

The purchases and sales of mutual fund shares must meet the requirements of fair dealing that the SEC and the NASD (National Association of
Securities Dealers), a self-regulatory organization, have established for all securities transactions in the U.S. These rules conform to the guidelines expressed in the Securities Exchange Act of 1934, an early and important piece
of legislation concerning securities and their markets. The SEC extended these
rules, in 1988, to ensure that advertisements and claims by mutual funds would
not be inaccurate or misleading to investors.

Fees charged by mutual funds are, as noted above, subject to regulation.
The foundation of that regulatory power is the government's *de facto* (but not
necessarily justified) role as arbiter of costs of transactions regarding securities in general. For example, the SEC and the NASD have established rules,
as part of the overall guide to fair dealing with customers, about the mark-ups
dealers can charge financial institutions on the sales of financial assets. In the
past, the SEC set a limit of 8.5% on a fund's load but allowed the fund to pass
through certain expenses under the 12b-1 rule. Recently, the SEC has
amended the rule, effective July 1 of 1993, to set a maximum of 8.5% on the
total of all fees, inclusive of front-end and back-end loads as well as expenses
such as advertising.[8]

A recent trend in the regulation of funds and the role of commercial banks
deserves special attention. As we note in several earlier chapters, deregulation
is eroding the once solid wall that separated commercial banks from many securities activities. In the late 1980s, commercial banks responded to the large
drain of investments from their accounts to mutual funds by offering investment accounts that resemble funds in all key respects.[9] Alternatively called
"collective investment funds" or "own-label bank mutual funds," these new investment vehicles led the banks' invasion of the lucrative mutual fund field.
Regulatory agencies within the U.S. appear to accept these actions by the
banks, and the number of dollars in these bank-sponsored mutual funds has
grown to a substantial level. But the game is not over yet, and the precise di-

---

[8] "New Rules May Trim Mutual-Fund Fees," *Wall Street Journal*, July 15, 1992,
pp. C1-C3.
[9] "American Mutual Funds: Arming," *Economist*, May 2, 1991, pp. 92-93.

mensions of the banks' role in this securities business will not be set for some time to come.

At the time of this writing, the SEC has proposed several interesting and possibly revolutionary measures to liberalize the rules for the sale of mutual funds and closed-end funds.[10] The SEC is concerned about two problems. The problem with closed-end funds is that investors in them frequently cannot obtain the NAV for their shares because they trade at a discount in the market. The problem for open-end or mutual funds, which must redeem their shares at NAV at any time, is that regulations oblige them to keep a large percentage of their investments in liquid assets, and these regulations foreclose interesting opportunities to those funds.

In response, the SEC has proposed several new redemption procedures, which may lead to the creation of new types of funds and to the elimination of some existing key distinctions between closed-end and open-end companies. Two proposals are of special importance. First, closed-end funds would periodically (quarterly or semi-annually) redeem a specified number of outstanding shares at NAV. This procedure would keep the share price close to the NAV. Second, investors in open-end funds would no longer be free to redeem shares at NAV on a daily basis, but would have to make their redemptions (which would be unrestricted in amount) only once a quarter or every six months. With this new constraint on redeemability, the funds could invest in the less liquid shares of smaller companies or companies in foreign markets. The response to these proposals has generally been positive, but the chances that these new products will appear soon are hard to determine at this time.

▶ KEY POINTS THAT YOU SHOULD UNDERSTAND BEFORE PROCEEDING:

1. The basic elements of the Investment Company Act of 1940.
2. The scope of government regulation over an investment company's management, operations, and dealing with customers.

## THE CONCEPT OF A FAMILY OF FUNDS

A concept that has revolutionized the fund industry and benefited many investors is what the mutual fund industry calls a "family of funds" or "group of funds" or, less often, a "complex of funds." This term refers to the fact that many management companies offer investors a choice of numerous funds with different investment objectives. In many cases, investors may move their assets from one fund to another within the family, at little or no cost, and with only a phone call to a toll-free number. The same policies regarding load and other costs may apply to all members of the family, but it is possible for a man-

---

[10] Securities and Exchange Commission, *Protecting Investors: A Half-Century of Investment Company Regulation, op. cit.*, pp. 424 and ff.

agement company to have different fee structures for different funds under its control.

The funds in a family usually include choices ranging from money market funds to global funds, and funds devoted to particular industries such as medical technology or gold mining companies. Such famous management companies as Vanguard, T. Rowe Price, and Franklin sponsor and manage varied menus of funds, but the most prominent example of the concept of family of funds is probably Fidelity Investments in Boston. Fidelity manages dozens of funds dedicated to investments in the standard and general categories of government bonds, growth stocks, mortgage-backed securities, municipal bonds, foreign securities, and so on. In addition to these funds, Fidelity also manages a group of "Select Funds." Each of the more than 35 "Fidelity Select" funds concentrates on a single industry; at last count, there was a Fidelity Select fund for each of these sectors in the economy: utilities, brokerage firms, energy companies, firms in the leisure and entertainment sector, electronics, thrifts, food and agriculture, among many others. Clearly, Fidelity provides investors with a wide choice of mutual funds.

Price quotations in the newspapers group the various funds according to families. For example, all the Fidelity funds are listed under the Fidelity or Fidelity Select heading, all the Vanguard funds are listed under that title, and so on. A glance at the financial section of a newspaper will give an idea of just how varied the offerings of a large family of funds can be.

As a final note, we want to point out that the family of funds concept represents this industry's energetic strategy to transform mutual funds into multi-product financial institutions. With this transformation, the industry has shown itself capable of meeting a host of financial needs for households as well as institutional investors. Transformation of the rather myopic mutual fund into the large multi-service family of funds has been a financial innovation of significance, even by the innovation standards of the last two three decades.

▶ KEY POINTS THAT YOU SHOULD UNDERSTAND BEFORE PROCEEDING:

1. The meaning of the term "family of funds."
2. The economic benefits that a family of funds can offer to investors.

## INDUSTRY CONCENTRATION

▪▪▪▪

As we noted earlier, the financial advisor to a fund can be a subsidiary of a brokerage firm, an insurance company, a bank, or an investment management firm. These advisors do not manage one fund but a group or family of funds, as described above. The mutual fund industry is highly concentrated, with the ten largest mutual fund groups managing close to 50% of the market share.

The largest fund group is managed by Fidelity Investments, which was mentioned above. The second largest fund group manager is Merrill Lynch, an investment banking firm. The next three largest fund group managers are the Vanguard Group, Franklin Resources, and Dreyfus, all of whom are investment management firms. These five fund groups together control more than 32% of mutual fund assets.[11]

The fees realized from advising investment companies and selling their shares have attracted the interest of insurance companies and banks. For example, in 1991 Kemper Financial Services, the mutual fund operations division of the Kemper Corporation, an insurance company, generated 60% of the net income of the insurance company.[12]

▶ KEY POINT THAT YOU SHOULD UNDERSTAND BEFORE PROCEEDING:

1.   The extent of concentration in the mutual fund industry.

## MUTUAL FUNDS IN OTHER ECONOMIES

In this section, we discuss mutual funds in three important economies: the United Kingdom, Germany, and Japan. Our discussion focuses on domestic or indigenous funds, which are managed by firms headquartered in the countries. While the globalization and deregulation of financial markets have enabled companies to sell shares in their funds in many countries, we do not discuss the funds that foreign investment management firms may be free to offer to investors in these countries.

### United Kingdom

British mutual funds come largely in one of two forms: the *unit trust* and the *investment trust*. The unit trust is similar to the open-end fund in the United States, and the investment trust is much like the closed-end fund, with shares traded on London's International Stock Exchange. As in the United States, unit trusts grew very popular in Great Britain during the 1980s: assets under management grew almost 900%, the number of accounts rose 250%, and the number of trusts tripled.[13] The appeal of investment trusts has fallen over this same period, although institutional investors continue to make use of them. Reasons for the decline include regulations against marketing the shares and excessive tax rates.[14]

The concept of the funds family has taken root in Great Britain: fewer than 175 management companies sponsor almost 1,300 different unit trusts.[15]

---

[11] Julie Rohrer, "The Mutual Fund Battle Turns Ugly," *Institutional Investor* (September 1992), p. 41.

[12] Ibid., p. 40.

[13] *Handbook of Foreign Markets for Mutual Funds* (Washington, D.C.: Investment Company Institute, 1992), pp. 78 and ff.

[14] Paul Draper, "Closed-End Mutual Funds in Great Britain," in Preda, *Funds and Portfolio Management Institutions: An International Survey, op. cit.,* p. 196.

[15] Brian Chiplin and Mike Wright, "The Situation and the Outlook for Funds and Portfolio Management Institutions in Great Britain," in Preda, *Funds and Portfolio Management Institutions: An International Survey, op. cit.,* p. 37.

In an interesting departure from the experience of the United States, the unit trusts (as of late 1991) have devoted little effort to money market instruments or bonds. Instead, the trusts have invested largely in equities, with about 60% of those being shares of U.K. companies. However, British investors do have some choices regarding the investment objectives of trusts: some trusts are devoted generally to growth, others are dedicated to producing income, while still others focus on foreign markets throughout the world.[16]

The structure of a unit trust involves a managing firm that selects the investments and an independent trustee company that holds the shares and cash on behalf of the trust's unitholders. The trustee company is usually a bank or an insurance company and it performs numerous duties in its role of safeguarding the unitholders' interests. These duties include monitoring the sales and purchases of shares by the management company, distributing payments to unitholders, ensuring that paperwork is properly done, and overseeing the management company's exercise of its powers.[17]

Regulation of the unit trusts is a somewhat complicated matter. In the Financial Services Act of 1986, Parliament empowered the Securities and Investments Board (SIB) to authorize unit trusts and to oversee their management. The Act also directed two self-regulatory organizations (or SROs) to monitor certain activities of the unit trusts. LAUTRO, which stands for "Life Assurance and Unit Trust Regulatory Organization," has the responsibility of overseeing the advertising and marketing of the unit trusts to the public. IMRO, the Investment Management Regulatory Organization, has the task of monitoring the conduct of the managers and trustees of the trusts.[18]

## Germany

German mutual funds take two general forms: public or retail funds and nonpublic funds reserved for institutional buyers. (There are also numerous closed-end funds that focus on real estate and appeal mostly to institutional investors.[19] We do not discuss these.) The institutional funds are called *"Spezialfonds"* and account for almost half the money invested in mutual funds. The retail funds fall into two broad categories: bond funds (*"Retenfonds"*) and equity funds (*"Aktienfonds"*). Of these, the bond funds are by far the more popular, because they attract almost 80% of all the money invested in retail funds.

In the 1980s, mutual funds in Germany experienced significant growth. Total assets in funds grew from 50 billion Deutsche marks in 1981 to more than 260 billion DM in 1991. The number of retail funds grew from 114 in 1982 to 394 by 1992, and the number of *Spezialfonds* increased over that time

---

[16] *Handbook of Foreign Markets for Mutual Funds*, op. cit., pp. 81 and ff.

[17] *Ibid.*, p. 86.

[18] John Kelly, "Open-End Mutual Funds in Great Britain," in Preda, *Funds and Portfolio Management Institutions: An International Survey*, op. cit., p. 140.

[19] Gerhard Gathmann, "Real Estate Investment Funds in Germany," in Preda, *Funds and Portfolio Management Institutions: An International Survey*, op. cit., p. 240.

from 553 to 1,800.[20] It is interesting to note that, while the bond funds invest heavily in short-term debt instruments, money market mutual funds have never become popular. In this respect, the German situation resembles that of Great Britain.

The mutual fund industry is quite concentrated, because relatively few management companies are responsible for offering all these retail and special funds. Actually totaling around 60, these companies have steadily increased the number of funds available to the varied investing public throughout the 1980s. The German banks, which participate in all segments of the securities industry, are very often partners with these managing firms, and occasionally insurance companies are also partners.[21] Most of the sales to the public are made through banks.

As noted, the bond funds are more popular than the equity funds. At the end of 1991, bonds held by the retail funds amounted to almost 70% of assets, while stock accounted for slightly more than 20%. Interestingly, bonds issued by foreign institutions make up more than 40% of bond holdings, while stocks of foreign firms amount to only 20% of total stock holdings. The special funds are reserved for insurance companies, pension funds, and other institutions, but insurance companies are by far the largest investor in these non-public funds.[22]

German mutual funds have a distinctive structure. A management company has a contractual agreement to manage a pool of assets on behalf of investors who own participations in the asset pool. A custodian bank, called a *Depotbank*, and by law necessarily German, supervises the activities of the management firm. The typical investment company is organized as a limited liability company, which is known as *"Gesellschaft mit beschränkter Haftung-GmbH"*. The "GmbH", as it is often called, has a board that also monitors the management of the assets.[23]

Regulation of the mutual funds follows this pattern. The Investment Company Act (known as KAGG for *Gesetz über Kapitalanlagegesellschaten*) requires funds to register and to accept a set of governmental guidelines about the contract between the firm and investors. The Federal Supervisory Agency for Banking (called BAK for *Bundesaufsichtsamt für das Kreditwessen*) must approve the details of implementation of the contract. KAGG selects a bank to serve as custodian to safeguard the investors' interests regarding types and amounts of investments as well as bookkeeping and accounting matters. Marketing by the funds is monitored by BAK because, as noted above, banks are very often partners in the management firms for the funds.[24]

---

[20] *Handbook of Foreign Markets for Mutual Funds, op. cit.*, pp. 62 and ff.
[21] J. Heinrich von Stein, "The Situation and Outlook for Funds and Portfolio Management Institutions in Germany," in Preda, *Funds and Portfolio Management Institutions: An International Survey, op. cit.*, p. 23.
[22] *Handbook of Foreign Markets for Mutual Funds, op. cit.*, p. 64.
[23] *Ibid.*, p. 71.
[24] *Ibid.*, p. 70.

## *Japan*

Individual and institutional Japanese investors have ready access to an investment vehicle similar, in numerous ways, to the United States's mutual fund. This vehicle is the *securities investment trust (shoken toshi shintaku)*. Investors buy share-like "beneficiary certificates" in the trusts, which are regulated along the lines of the 1951 Securities Investment Trust Law, as amended.[25] The tax situation of an investment trust is familiar: the trust's income, if distributed properly, is not taxable to the trust. Partly because of the tax savings and partly because of the wildly appreciating Japanese securities of the 1980s, Japanese investors poured money into these investment trusts from 1986 to 1989. The crash in stock (and real estate) prices, which began in early 1990 and has persisted through the early 1990s, has somewhat cooled interest in the trusts, although they remain a central feature of the Japanese financial picture.

All the trusts are, in practice, open-end funds, because investors can redeem their beneficiary certificates at the trust's net asset value. At the same time, according to a rule of the Ministry of Finance (MOF), investors in most of these trusts are not free to withdraw their money for two years after they first invest it.[26] If an investment trust is an *open type trust*, investors can purchase new certificates, and the size of the trust is not fixed. Open type trusts generally have no specific ending or maturity date. A *unit type* of trust is somewhat similar to a closed-end fund: after it is issued at fixed cost per beneficiary certificate, no new certificates are sold and no new money is raised. The typical unit trust has a specific life, and it generally matures five years after issuing its certificates. At maturity (or redemption), all assets are liquidated and distributed to the owners.[27]

An interesting arrangement, called the "family fund unit-type investment trust," spans the unit type and open type trusts. The family fund allows investors to buy new beneficiary certificates in a grouping of existing and specified unit trusts. The grouping is termed a "parent fund," and the new unit trust that issues the certificates is known as a "baby fund." The baby fund is highly diversified, because it represents a share in each of the unit trusts that have been grouped into the parent fund. The parent fund receives and manages the money or proceeds from the purchases of the certificates in the baby fund. Any parent fund can "give birth" to numerous baby funds over time, a system that channels new money to the parent fund and its component unit trusts.

A securities investment trust is a contractual agreement among four parties: the investor who buys beneficiary certificates; the management company that issues the certificates and decides on the investments of the trust; the securities company that sells the certificates; and the trustee, which is either a commercial bank or a trust bank that manages the assets at the direction of

---

[25] Michael L. Whitener and Eiichi Hiraki, "Managing Money in Japan," *International Financial Law Review, Supplement* (April 1990), pp. 106-111.

[26] "Japan's Staggering Stockmarket," *The Economist* (August 17, 1992), p. 71.

[27] *Securities Markets in Japan 1990* (Tokyo: Japan Securities Research Institute, 1990), p. 164.

the management company.[28] Before issuing a trust's beneficiary certificates, the management company must prepare a prospectus that clearly sets forth the trust's investment objective and all relevant terms of the trust's contract.

The MOF must license a securities firm, or one of its subsidiaries, before it may act as the manager of a securities investment trust. Regulation of the trusts is conducted by the MOF and a self-regulatory organization, the Investment Trust Association. While a very small number of licensed firms are foreign, most are units or subsidiaries of the major Japanese securities companies: Nomura, Nikko, Yamaichi, and Daiwa. Thus, the fund market in Japan, like that of other countries, is highly concentrated in a few domestic firms. Foreign firms sponsoring and managing investment funds may sell their funds (so-called "off-shore" funds) in Japan as long as the firms abide by certain rules. One of those rules, interestingly enough, is that the offshore trust funds must be denominated in a foreign currency. This restriction seems to limit the appeal of foreign trust funds to Japanese investors.[29]

A trust that does not hold any equity shares and is devoted entirely to bonds qualifies as a "bond investment trust." The bond trusts differ by their investment objectives, which range across distinctions between domestic and foreign debt, short-term and long-term bonds, and corporate and government issues. Once a year, each trust distributes all income from its bonds to its investors-beneficiaries.

A trust that invests any portion of its assets in common stocks qualifies as a "stock investment trust." Traditionally, the common stock trust had capital gains or growth as its investment objective. One result of the crash in Japanese stock prices is that a large and increasing number of investors are accepting "income" as the chief investment objective of a trust.[30] The category of open type stock investment trust includes many of the new funds that have appeared in the market. Index funds and select funds, in particular, are grouped with these trusts.

▶ KEY POINTS THAT YOU SHOULD UNDERSTAND BEFORE PROCEEDING:

1. The differences between a unit trust and an investment trust in Great Britain.
2. How trusts are regulated in Great Britain.
3. The differences between public and nonpublic funds in Germany.
4. The regulation of the German public funds.
5. The structure of a securities investment trust in Japan, and the differences between an open type trust and a unit type trust.
6. The structure of a parent fund and baby funds in Japan.

---

[28] Whitener and Hiraki, "Managing Money in Japan," *op. cit.*, p. 106.

[29] *Ibid.*, p. 109.

[30] Anthony Rowley, "A Question of Trusts," *Far Eastern Economic Review* (August 1991), pp. 33-35.

7.  The relative popularity of stock funds and bond funds in the three countries.

**SUMMARY**

Investment companies sell shares to the public and invest the proceeds in a diversified portfolio of securities, with each share representing a proportionate interest in the underlying portfolio of securities. There are three types of investment companies: open-end or mutual funds, closed-end funds, and unit trusts. A wide range of funds with many different investment objectives are available. Securities law requires that a fund clearly set forth its investment objective in its prospectus, and the objective identifies the type or types of assets the fund will purchase and hold.

Mutual funds and closed-end funds provide two crucial economic functions associated with financial intermediaries—risk reduction via diversification and lower costs of contracting and information processing. Money market funds allow shareholders to write checks against their shares, thus providing a payments mechanism, another economic function of financial intermediaries.

Mutual funds are extensively regulated, with most of that regulation occurring at the federal level. The key legislation is the Investment Company Act of 1940. The Insider Trading and Securities Fraud Enforcement Act of 1986 also imposes some constraints on the funds. The most important feature of the legislation in this area, though, is that the funds are exempt from taxation on their gains if the gains are distributed to investors within a relatively short period of time. Even allowing for that special tax-free status, it is necessary to recognize that regulations apply to many features of the funds' administration, including sales fees, asset management, degree of diversification, distributions, and advertising.

An interesting development in recent years has been the consumer-investor's widespread acceptance of the concept of family (or group or complex) of funds. That is, an investment advisory company (such as Fidelity Investments or Vanguard) manages dozens of different funds, which span the spectrum of potential investment objectives, from aggressive growth to balanced income to international diversification. The success of these fund families has led to a considerable concentration of the mutual fund industry in a few large fund groups.

Mutual funds, or their equivalents, have proven popular in countries other than the U.S. Many investors make use of unit trusts in Great Britain, *"fonds"* in Germany, and "securities investment trusts" in Japan. While regulations and certain institutional features may differ from country to country, the basic structure of pooled investments managed by professionals on behalf of investors is common and popular around the globe. Also, the mutual fund industry of many countries tends to be concentrated among a few mutual fund groups, which offer funds covering a wide range of investment objectives. Finally, extensive regulation by governmental authorities is a characteristic of mutual fund activities in many countries.

GLOSSARY

**Advisory fee:** Fee charged by an investment advisory firm for managing the portfolio of an investment company.

**Back-end load fund:** Fund that charges investors a fee to sell (redeem) shares. The formal name for the back-end load is the contingent deferred sales charge or CDSC.

**Closed-end fund:** Fund that manages a pool of investments and that sells shares like any other corporation and usually does not redeem its shares, which trade on either an organized exchange or over the counter.

**Insider Trading and Securities Fraud Enforcement Act of 1988:** Federal law dealing with insider trading, which requires the fund advisors to take precautions against it.

**Investment Company Act of 1940:** A major piece of legislation regarding the operations and regulations of mutual funds and closed-end funds.

**Investment Company Institute:** The national association for open-end or mutual funds.

**Investment objective:** A fund's stated goal, which determines the kinds of assets it invests in.

**Load:** Sales commission that a mutual fund may charge.

**Load funds:** Mutual funds that charge sales commissions.

**Net asset value per share (or NAV):** The ratio of the market value of the portfolio less the mutual fund's liabilities to the number of mutual fund shares outstanding.

**No-load fund:** A mutual fund that charges no sales commission.

**Offshore fund:** A fund managed by a firm in one country but sold to investors in another.

**Open-end (or mutual) funds:** Funds that stand ready to sell new shares to the public and to redeem outstanding shares on demand at a price equal to an appropriate share of their portfolio's value.

**12b-1 fund:** Fund that uses the 1980 SEC Rule 12b-1 to assess investors for selling and marketing costs.

**Unit trust:** In the United States, a pool of money invested in a specific and unchanging group of assets over the planned life of the trust.

QUESTIONS

1. An investment company that has 2 million shares outstanding has total assets of $40 million and total liabilities of $2 million.
   a. What is the net asset value per share?
   b. If this investment company is a no-load fund, how much would an investor have to pay to purchase one share?
   c. Suppose this company charged a sales commission or load of 5%. What would an investor have to pay to buy a share?

2. Suppose the investment company in the previous question is a closed-end investment company. Can you determine how much an investor would have to pay to purchase one share? If so, how? If not, why not?

3. a. What is a back-end load fund?

   b. What is a 12b-1 fund?

4. What is a unit trust, and how does it differ from a mutual fund?

5. What costs are incurred by an investment company?

6. a. What is meant by a money market fund?

   b. Explain three types of money market funds.

7. a. Does an investment company provide maturity intermediation?

   b. What economic functions does an investment company provide?

8. a. What types of regulatory requirements does a "regulated investment company" have to meet?

   b. What is the key advantage to a company of gaining this status?

9. Name three areas of a mutual fund's operations that are subject to governmental regulation.

10. Identify the changes which the SEC proposed in 1992 for redemption of shares in both closed-end and open-end funds.

11. a. What is a "family of funds"?

    b. Why has this concept been so important in the battle between banks and funds for the individual investor's business?

12. a. What is the meaning of the statement that a country's mutual fund industry is highly concentrated?

    b. Is the concentration of the mutual fund industry in the U.S. an unusual phenomenon?

13. What is the difference between a unit trust and an investment trust in Great Britain?

14. Identify the two types of retail funds that are popular among individual investors in Germany.

15. a. What is the major difference, among Japanese securities investment trusts, between a unit type trust and an open type trust?

    b. Explain the differences and similarities between a "family of funds" in the U.S. mutual fund system and the Japanese "family fund" concept that includes a "parent fund" and "baby funds."

# CHAPTER NINE

# Pension Funds

*After reading this chapter, you will understand:*

- what a pension plan sponsor does.
- the different types of pension plans, including defined contribution plans, defined benefit plans, and a recently developed hybrid of the two.
- what a 401(k) plan is.
- what an insured plan is.
- the principal provisions of the Employee Retirement Income Security Act (ERISA) of 1974.
- what the Pension Benefit Guaranty Corporation does.
- who the managers of pension funds are.
- the various financial services provided to pension funds.
- the role of mutual funds in contemporary pension plans.
- how pension plans are managed and regulated in Japan, Germany, and the United Kingdom.
- what endowment funds do.
- the goals of managing money for endowment funds.

Pension funds, which exist in some form in all developed economies, are major institutional investors and participants in the financial markets. Pension funds have become important for several reasons. First, income and wealth have grown steadily over the post-World War II period, leaving households more money for long-term savings. Second, people are living longer, and, can expect more financial needs for longer retirement periods. Third, pensions represent compensation to employees that is free of tax liability until after the workers retire and their income from employment ceases.

This chapter discusses pension plans and pension fund management. An appendix deals briefly with another interesting financial institution, the endowment fund. Common in the United States, the endowment fund is a charitable trust, established in accordance with a network of laws, that supports non-profit institutions such as universities, hospitals, religious institutions, and museums.

## INTRODUCTION TO PENSION PLANS

A pension plan is a fund that is established for the payment of retirement benefits. The entities that establish pension plans—called *plan sponsors*—may be private business entities acting for their employees; federal, state, and local entities on behalf of their employees; unions on behalf of their members; and individuals for themselves.

The total assets of U.S. pension funds have grown rapidly since World War II, almost tripling in the 1980s. By 1989, pension fund total assets were about $2.47 trillion. The top 20 pension funds, as measured by assets as of September 30, 1989, accounted for more than 25% of all pension assets.[1] The assets of corporate-sponsored pension plans in 1992 were about $1.7 trillion, while those of government-sponsored pension plans totaled about $0.9 trillion.[2]

Pension funds are financed by contributions by the employer and/or the employee; in some plans employer contributions are matched in some measure by employees. The great success of private pension plans is somewhat surprising because the system involves investing in an asset—the pension contract—that for the most part has been and is largely illiquid. It cannot be used—not even as collateral—until retirement. The key factor explaining pension fund growth is that the employer's contributions and a specified amount of the employee's contributions, as well as the earnings of the fund's assets, are tax-exempt. In essence a pension is a form of employer remuneration for which the employee is not taxed until funds are withdrawn. Pension funds have also

---

[1] *1990 Money Market Directory.* According to a study of pension funds by Columbia University Law School, the three largest corporate-sponsored pension funds as of September 30, 1989, were AT&T ($42.7 billion), General Motors ($40.9 billion), and IBM ($25.8 billion). The two largest government-sponsored pension funds were California Public Employees ($54.0 billion) and New York State/Local Employees ($44.2 billion). The largest pension fund by far is TIAA/CREF, with total assets as of September 31, 1989, of $81 billion.

[2] Federal Reserve Board, *Flow of Funds Accounts, Financial Assets and Liabilities* (First Quarter 1992).

traditionally served to discourage employees from quitting, as the employee would usually lose at least the accumulation resulting from the employer contribution.

▶ Kᴇʏ ᴘᴏɪɴᴛs ᴛʜᴀᴛ ʏᴏᴜ sʜᴏᴜʟᴅ ᴜɴᴅᴇʀsᴛᴀɴᴅ ʙᴇғᴏʀᴇ ᴘʀᴏᴄᴇᴇᴅɪɴɢ:

1. The role of the sponsor of a pension plan.
2. The importance of tax-exemption to the structure and popularity of pension plans.

## TYPES OF PENSION PLANS

■ ■ ■ ■

There are two basic and widely used types of pension plans: *defined contribution plans* and *defined benefit plans*. A new idea, a hybrid often called a "designer pension," combines features of both these types.

### Defined Contribution Plan

In a defined contribution plan, the plan sponsor is responsible only for making specified contributions into the plan on behalf of qualifying participants. The amount contributed is typically either a percentage of the employee's salary or a percentage of profits. The plan sponsor does not guarantee any certain amount at retirement. The payments that will be made to qualifying participants upon retirement will depend on the growth of the plan assets; that is, payment is determined by the investment performance of the assets in which the pension fund invests. The plan sponsor gives the participants various options as to the investment vehicles in which they may invest. Defined contribution pension plans come in several legal forms: money purchase pension plans, 401(k) plans, and employee stock ownership plans (ESOP).

By far the fastest growing sector of the defined contribution plan is the 401(k). To the firm, this kind of plan offers fewest costs and administrative problems: the employer makes a specified contribution to a specific plan/program, and the employee chooses how it is invested.[3] To the employee, the plan is attractive because it offers some control over how the pension money is managed. In fact, plan sponsors frequently offer participants the opportunity to invest in one of a family of mutual funds. Over half of all defined contribution plans (in public institutions such as state governments as well as private firms) use mutual funds, and the percentage of private corporations following that path is even higher.

Employees in the public and corporate sectors have responded favorably, and almost half of all assets in pensions are now invested in mutual funds, with the bulk of the money placed in funds emphasizing equities and growth.[4] Recent regulations issued by the U.S. Department of Labor require firms to offer their employees a set of distinctive choices, a development that has further

---

[3] "Calling It Quits," *Institutional Investor* (February 1991), p. 125.
[4] "Taking a Fancy to Mutual Funds," *Institutional Investor* (May 1992), p. 119.

encouraged pension plans to opt for the mutual fund approach, because families of mutual funds can readily provide investment vehicles offering different investment objectives.[5]

## Defined Benefit Plan

In a defined benefit plan, the plan sponsor agrees to make specified dollar payments to qualifying employees at retirement (and some payments to beneficiaries in case of death before retirement). The retirement payments are determined by a formula that usually takes into account the length of service of the employee and the employee's earnings. The pension obligations are effectively the debt obligation of the plan sponsor, who assumes the risk of having insufficient funds in the plan to satisfy the contractual payments that must be made to retired employees.

A plan sponsor establishing a defined benefit plan can use the payments made into the fund to purchase an annuity policy from a life insurance company. Defined benefit plans that are guaranteed by life insurance products are called *insured plans;*[6] those that are not are called *non-insured plans*. An insured plan is not necessarily safer than a non-insured plan, as the former depends on the ability of the life insurance company to make the contractual payments.

Whether a private pension plan is insured or non-insured, a federal agency, the *Pension Benefit Guaranty Corporation* or PBGC, which was established in 1974 by the ERISA legislation (see below), insures the vested benefits of participants. Benefits become vested when an employee reaches a certain age and completes enough years of service so that he or she meets the minimum requirements for receiving benefits upon retirement. The payment of benefits is not contingent upon a participant's continuation with the employer or union.

## Hybrid Pension Plans

A survey by *Institutional Investor* reveals that a new phenomenon in pension planning, a hybrid plan, has attracted surprising support.[7] These plans, called "designer pensions," combine features of both basic types of pensions. They first appeared in 1985, and they have been adopted by 8% of companies and public employers in the United States. The appeal of these hybrids is that each of the basic types of plans has flaws: the defined contribution plan causes the employee to bear all the investment risk, while the defined benefit plan is expensive and hard to implement when few workers work for only one company over many years.

---

[5]"The Communication Cloud over 401(k)s," *Institutional Investor* (September 1991), p. 189.

[6]Life insurance companies also manage pension funds without guaranteeing a specified payout. In this case they are acting only as money manager, and the funds they manage are not insured plans.

[7]"Why Designer Pensions Are in Fashion," *Institutional Investor* (June 1992), pp. 123–131.

While hybrids come in many forms, a good example is the "floor-offset plan." In this plan, the employer contributes a certain amount each year to a fund, as in a defined contribution approach. The employer guarantees a certain minimum level of cash benefits, depending on an employee's years of service, as in a defined benefit plan. The employer manages the pension fund and informs the employee periodically of the value of his or her account. If the managed fund does not generate sufficient growth to achieve the preset level of benefits, the employee is obliged to add the amount of the deficit.

## INVESTMENTS

The aggregate asset mix, at the end of 1991, of the 1,000 top pension plans is summarized in Table 9-1. As can be seen, for defined benefit plans, slightly more than 80% is allocated between equities and fixed-income securities. For defined contribution plans, a large proportion of assets are placed in guaranteed investment contracts (GICs), which we discussed in Chapter 7. Qualified pension funds are exempt from federal income taxes. Thus, fund assets can accumulate tax-free. Consequently, pension funds do not invest very much in assets that have the advantage of being largely or completely tax-exempt.

There are no restrictions at the federal level on investing in non-U.S. investments. The sponsors of a fund, however, are free to restrict the allocation of the fund's assets to domestic investments. For example, the state of Okla-

### TABLE 9-1
#### AGGREGATE ASSET MIX FOR TOP 1,000 PENSION FUNDS IN 1991

| *Asset* | *Percent* |
|---|---|
| **Top Defined Benefit Plans** | |
| Equity | 45.7 |
| Fixed income | 35.8 |
| Cash equivalents | 6.2 |
| Real estate equity | 3.9 |
| Mortgages | 1.0 |
| GIC/BIC | 2.3 |
| Annuities | 0.3 |
| Other | 4.8 |
| **Top Defined Contribution Plans** | |
| Company stock | 23.9 |
| Other stock | 17.6 |
| Fixed-income | 11.5 |
| Cash equivalents | 7.7 |
| GIC/BIC | 33.8 |
| Annuities | 0.5 |
| Other | 5.8 |

*Source:* As reported in *Pensions & Investments*, January 20, 1992, p. 30.

homa bans foreign investments for public pension funds. It is not uncommon for union-sponsored pension funds to prohibit non-U.S. investments in their portfolios. A survey of pension fund sponsors conducted by *Institutional Investor* in 1991 found that more than half of the respondents invested in foreign securities of some type. Of those respondents that invested abroad, 96% invested in foreign stocks and 34% foreign bonds.[8]

## REGULATION

Because pension plans are so important for U.S. workers, Congress passed comprehensive legislation in 1974 to regulate pension plans. This legislation, the Employee Retirement Income Security Act of 1974 (ERISA), is fairly technical in its details. For our purposes, it is necessary only to understand its major provisions.

First, ERISA establishes funding standards for the minimum contributions that a plan sponsor must make to the pension plan to satisfy the actuarially projected benefit payments. Prior to enactment of ERISA, many corporate plan sponsors followed a "pay-as-you-go" funding policy. That is, when an employee retired, the corporate plan sponsor took the necessary retirement benefits out of current operations. Under ERISA, such a practice is no longer allowed.

Second, ERISA establishes fiduciary standards for pension fund trustees, managers, or advisors. Specifically, all parties responsible for the management of a pension fund are guided by the judgment of what is called a "prudent man" in seeking to determine which investments are proper. Because a trustee takes care of other people's money, it is necessary to make sure that the trustee takes the role seriously. To fulfill his or her responsibilities, a trustee must use the care of a reasonably prudent person to acquire and use the information that is pertinent to making an investment decision.

Third, ERISA establishes minimum vesting standards. For example, the law specifies that, after five years of employment, a plan participant is entitled to 25% of accrued pension benefits. The percentage of entitlement increases to 100% after ten years.

Finally, ERISA created the PBGC to insure vested benefits. The insurance program is funded from annual premiums that must be paid by pension plans.

Responsibility for administering ERISA is delegated to the Department of Labor and the Internal Revenue Service. To ensure that a pension plan is in compliance with ERISA, periodic reporting and disclosure statements must be filed with these government agencies.

It is important to recognize that ERISA does not require that a corporation establish a pension plan. If a corporation does establish a defined benefit plan, however, it must comply with the numerous and complex regulations set forth in ERISA.

---

[8] "Pensionforum: Over There," *Institutional Investor* (February 1991), p. 70.

▶ KEY POINTS THAT YOU SHOULD UNDERSTAND BEFORE PROCEEDING:

1.  The scope of ERISA legislation.
2.  The meaning of the "prudent man" concept.

## MANAGERS OF PENSION FUNDS

A plan sponsor can do one of the following with the pension assets under its control: (1) use in-house staff to manage all the pension assets itself; (2) distribute the pension assets to one or more money management firms to manage; or (3) combine alternatives (1) and (2). In the case of a contributory pension plan, the plan sponsor typically allows participants to select how to allocate their contributions among funds managed by a fund group.

We have already discussed in Chapter 7 how insurance companies have been involved in the pension business through their issuance of GICs and annuities. Insurance companies also have subsidiaries that manage pension funds. Aetna Life Insurance, for example, managed $48.7 billion in pension assets as of 1991, 36% of the funds representing defined contributions for 1,000 plan sponsors.[9] The trust departments of commercial banks manage funds, as do independent money management firms (that is, firms that are not affiliated with an insurance company or bank). For example, the trust department of Norwest Bank of Minnesota manages about $8.1 billion, of which 30% is defined contributions for 1,300 plan sponsors, while the Harris Trust and Savings Bank manages $11.6 billion of assets, of which 30% is defined contributions for 245 plan sponsors.[10] Fidelity Institutional Retirement Services, an independent money management firm that is a subsidiary of Fidelity Investments, manages $27.5 billion of defined contribution funds for 2,500 pension sponsors.[11]

Foreign entities are not barred from participating in the management of pension funds. In fact, several foreign financial institutions have acquired interests in U.S. money management firms in order to enter the pension fund money management business.

To give some idea of the different types of money managers that pension sponsors might want, we have listed below a few searches for managers completed in 1992:[12]

- the Los Angeles City Employees' Retirement System sought a money manager to invest internationally. The sponsors hired Scudder, Stevens & Clark.
- the U.S. Army NAF Retirement Plan wanted a money manager to invest internationally on an indexed basis and a money manager to invest in stocks of small capitalization U.S. firms. The plan sponsor hired Wells Fargo Nikko for the former and Stong/Corneliuson Capital Management for the latter.

---

[9] "The 1992 Defined Contribution Directory," *Institutional Investor* (June 1992), p. 179.
[10] Ibid.
[11] Ibid.
[12] This information was obtained from several issues of *Money Management Letter*.

- Illinois Teachers' Retirement System wanted to increase its exposure to international bonds. The plan sponsor hired Smith Barney Capital Management and Julius Bear Investment Management for this purpose, giving each $60 million to manage.
- Avon Products wanted a manager for its GIC portfolio and hired Bankers Trust.
- Knight-Ridder sought more diversification of its stock investments and hired four money managers specializing in small capitalization companies, medium-size capitalization companies, and large-capitalization companies. To accomplish this, Knight-Ridder hired four money managers specializing in these areas—Aronson & Fogler, Cadence Capital Management, Southeastern Asset Management, and SunBank Capital Management—allocating a total of $82 million to them.
- Dow Corning Corporation wanted to add options to its defined contribution plan. The plan sponsor hired J.P. Morgan Investment Management to manage its equity options and Wells Fargo Nikko Investment Advisors to manage its S&P 500 index option.[13]
- The District Council of Carpenters in Rhode Island sought to diversify its assets by hiring a money manager to invest in both stocks and bonds (referred to as a "balanced fund"). This plan sponsor hired Bear Stearns Asset Management to manage $10-$15 million of its $60 million of pension assets.

Managers of pension fund money obtain their income from a fee charged to manage the assets. The annual fee can range from 0.75% of assets under management to as little as 0.01% of assets under management. One study found that in 1991, the average effective fee charged by external money managers of public pension funds was 0.31%; for corporate pension funds the average was 0.41%.[14] The fees are lower than advisory fees for mutual funds, in which small investors tend to have small accounts, because of the economies of scale associated with managing large amounts of money for pension funds. Some plan sponsors have been entering into management fee contracts based on performance rather than according to a fixed percentage of assets under management.[15] One study found that 14% of the funds surveyed had entered into performance-based fee contracts with pension sponsors in 1991.[16]

In addition to money managers, there are other advisory services provided to pension plan sponsors. The many ways in which advisors help the plan sponsor include:

[13] We discuss equity options and index options in Chapters 26 to 28.

[14] "Manager Fees Head South, Greenwich Says," *Money Management Letter* (March 30, 1992), p. 1.

[15] See Arjun Divecha and Nick Mencher, "Manager Fees from the Performance Viewpoint," Chapter 9 in Frank J. Fabozzi (ed.), *Pension Fund Investment Management* (Chicago: Probus Publishing, 1990).

[16] "Manager Fees Head South, Greenwich Says," *op. cit.*, p. 23.

- developing plan investment policy and asset allocation among the major asset classes
- providing actuarial advice (liability modeling and forecasting)
- designing benchmarks against which the fund's money managers will be measured
- measuring and monitoring the performance of the fund's money managers
- searching for and recommending money managers to pension plans
- providing specialized research.

Frank Russell Associates, SEI, BARRA, Wilshire, Gifford Fong Associates, Callan, and Rogers, Casey are a few examples of the better-known consultants to pension funds.

▶ KEY POINTS THAT YOU SHOULD UNDERSTAND BEFORE PROCEEDING:

1. Who manages pension fund assets.
2. The types of services advisors provide to pension sponsors.

## EXAMPLES OF PENSION FUNDS

Four different pension fund plans are described to illustrate some of the points discussed above. Two of the plans are sponsored by corporate employers: Exxon and General Motors. The other two are sponsored by public employers: Anchorage (Alaska) Police and Fire Department Retirement Systems and Oakland County (California) Employees' Retirement Plan. In each category, one plan adopts the defined benefit approach, and the other uses both that and the defined contribution method. Each plan employs a large number of investment managers, and, as we discussed above, each manager handles a portion of the total funds in the plan. Tables 9-2 and 9-3 provide the details for these pension funds and their structures.

## PENSION FUNDS IN OTHER COUNTRIES

The U.S. pension fund industry is the largest in the world. In this section we look at pension fund systems in Germany, the United Kingdom, and Japan.

### *Germany*

A distinctive and important feature of German pension funds is that employers may retain and manage assets allegedly dedicated to their employees' pensions. [17] Thus, many companies simply list their contributions to pensions on the liability side of their balance sheets and do not transfer funding into inde-

---

[17] "Ernst Bracker, "Pension Funds in Germany," in Stefano Preda (ed.), *Funds and Portfolio Management Institutions: An International Survey* (Amsterdam: North Holland, 1991), p. 339.

| | | General |
|---|---|---|
| **Name** | **Exxon** | **Motors** |
| Total assets (billions) | $12.4 | $40.2 |
| Defined contributions (billions) | 5.2 | 0.0 |
| Managers:* | Aetna Life | Ameritrust |
| | Sanford C. Bernstein | ANB Inv. Mgmt. |
| | Corporate Property Inv. | Batterymarch F.M. |
| | Equitable Life | BEA Assocs. |
| | Equitable Real Estate | Cypress Cap. Mgmt. |
| | First City, Texas | Fidelity Inv. |
| | Geometry Asset Mgmt. | Frontier Cap. Mgmt. |
| | Grubb & Ellis Realty | G.T. Cap. Mgmt. |
| | Horsley Keogh Assocs. | Invesco MIM |
| | John Hancock Fin. Svs. | Lehman Ark Mgmt. |
| | J.P. Morgan Inv. Mgmt. | Magten Asset Mgmt. |
| | NCNB | Merrill Lynch Asset Mgmt. |
| | Premier Inv. Adv. | Metropolitan Life |
| | Prentiss Properties | Nomura Cap. Mgmt. |
| | Prudential Asset Mgmt. | Providential Inv. |
| | Smith Barney Cap. Mgmt. | Rothschild Int'l Asset |
| | Travelers Co's. | T.A.L. Inv. Counsel |
| | UBS Asset Mgmt. | Union Bank of Switz. |
| | Wells Fargo Nikko | Value Line Asset Mgmt. |
| | Internal Management | Internal Management |

**TABLE 9-2**

EXAMPLES OF LARGE CORPORATE PENSION PLANS: ASSETS AND MANAGERS

* Because of the large number of managers for General Motors, we report only a selected group.
*Source:* "The Largest Corporate Plans," *Institutional Investor* (January 1992), pp. 105 and ff.

pendent accounts. The firms control the funds supposedly earmarked for pensions and, in effect, get long-term and cheap loans from their employees. However, it should be noted that the size of the annual contributions that firms note and claim for pension purposes must conform to some strict actuarial guidelines. Most firms that do not keep these pension reserves within their operating assets and liabilities actually transfer funds, in the necessary amounts, to legally separate but actually captive and in-house management companies known as *"Pensionskassen."*

A recent change in the German regulatory situation came about with the creation of the Pension Guaranty Association. By law, all firms stating or recognizing pension payments to employees must belong to this Association. Further, the law requires each member firm to make a regular premium payment to the Association in order to buy the insurance of the government's backing

| | | |
|---|---|---|
| TABLE 9-3 | | |

EXAMPLES OF LARGE PUBLIC PENSION PLANS: ASSETS AND MANAGERS

| Name | Oakland County | Anchorage Police & Fire |
|---|---|---|
| Total Assets (Millions) | $375 | $234 |
| Defined Contributions (Billions) | 33 | 0 |
| Managers: | Burnham & Co. | Columbia Mgmt. |
| | Fidelity Inv. | Criterion Inv. Mgmt. |
| | Income Res. & Mgmt. | Kennedy Assocs. |
| | Loomis Sayles | Morgan Stanley Asset Mgmt. |
| | MIG Realty Adv. | National Bank of Alaska |
| | NBD Bank | Newbold Asset Mgmt. |
| | Oppenheimer Cap. | Nicholas-Applegate |
| | Putnam Cos. | Trust Co. of the West |
| | Smith Barney Cap. Mgmt. | |

*Source:* "The Largest Public Pension Funds," *Institutional Investor* (January 1992), p. 133ff.

for the firm's pension commitments.[18] In spite of this governmental agency's likely entanglement with failing firms at some future point, German companies now have no restrictions on how they invest pension funds. Among the major industrialized countries, Germany is unique in this regard.[19]

## United Kingdom

A striking feature of British pension funds is their reliance on equity investments: 80% of assets of the funds are invested in stocks, and most of those are British stocks.[20] This fact explains what is called the "institutional dominance" of the London Stock Exchange, which means that large investing institutions rather than small or individual investors are the important participants in the equity market. The investment strategies of the growing pension funds also explain the rapid development of the futures and options markets, because these instruments are necessary for hedging the risk that arises with large commitments to equities.[21]

Pension funds in Great Britian are managed by various kinds of institutions: insurance companies, banks, and the money managers that sponsor the popular unit trusts, which are the British equivalent of mutual funds.

[18] Stephen E. Clark, "When in Rome . . . ," *Institutional Investor* (January 1992), pp. 89-94.
[19] *Ibid.*, p. 92.
[20] *Ibid.*
[21] Peter J. Nowell, "Pension Funds in the UK," in Preda, *op. cit.*, p. 351.

(Chapter 8, dealing with investment companies, explains unit trusts.) More-over, the firms managing pension funds are quite likely to be foreign, and U.S.-based financial companies fully participate in the large U.K. pension fund industry.

Government policy has actively encouraged individuals to increase their savings for retirement. An example of this policy is the Personal Equity Plan (or PEP). The PEP allows substantial savings in equity accounts whose gains from dividends and price appreciation are free of taxation.[22]

The government regulates this industry to a minimal extent. Some people have blamed government indifference for what appears to have been Robert Maxwell's recent and giant theft of the pension fund assets of some of his companies.[23] Another instance of supposed indifference is the fact that the British government does not require a pension fund to have a trustee. Further, the dealings between the firm and the pension fund for employees of the firm can be extensive: the fund can lend to the firm and invest heavily in the firm's stock. Thus, it is clear that U.K. pension fund managers have greater discretion over matters that tend to be closely regulated in other countries, such as the United States. Whether this situation is beneficial or disadvantageous for British employees remains to be seen.

### Japan

The Japanese pension fund industry has many interesting features, but we call attention here to three particularly important ones. The first key feature is the extensive amount of governmental regulation. The Ministry of Finance (MOF) licenses firms that may serve as asset managers. Until recently, the MOF allowed only insurance companies and trust banks to manage pension funds; only in 1992 did the MOF begin to permit foreign firms to operate in this industry.[24] The MOF also sets the guidelines for a manager's allocation of fund across classes of assets.[25] Generally speaking, allocation must follow these rules: at least 50% of a fund should be invested in basically riskless Japanese corporate and government bonds; no more than 30% can be in equities or overseas investments; and a maximum of 20% may be placed in real estate. Rules for the recently licensed foreign managers allow them more latitude on foreign securities.[26]

The second interesting characteristic of Japanese pension funds is the large role played by a firm's *"keiretsu"* (or industrial group) in selecting pension managers. Thus, assignment of funds for management has not normally been conducted on a competitive basis, but rather has reflected a variety of

---

[22] *Ibid.,* p. 354.

[23] Claire Makin, "Eurobonanza? What Eurobonanza?" *Institutional Investor* (April 1992), pp. 51–55.

[24] "Japan: Breakthrough for Foreign Pension Fund Managers," *Institutional Investor* (June 1992), p. 139.

[25] "When in Rome . . . ," *op. cit.,* p. 92.

[26] "Japan: Breakthrough . . . ," *op. cit.,* p. 139.

developed business alliances and affinities. Also, the way of choosing managers has led Japanese pension funds to emphasize performance far less than their counterparts in the United States or Great Britain. In Japan, safety of principal has been the dominant investment objective. (The MOF's investment rules, cited above, show that its chief goal is safety.) The large role played by established business linkages has caused foreign managers considerable difficulty in breaking into the pension fund business in Japan. In fact, foreign managers have enjoyed more success in attracting assignments from the public entities than from the private firms.[27]

The previous two features obviously imply a third aspect that is noteworthy: the Japanese pension fund industry is highly concentrated. The (comparatively) few trust banks and insurance companies handle most accounts and most of the money in the funds. As more firms outside the banking and insurance industries participate actively in this financial sector, this degree of concentration should fall somewhat. Further, an expected new emphasis on performance and growth should loosen the controls that these industry leaders currently have.

▶ KEY POINTS THAT YOU SHOULD UNDERSTAND BEFORE PROCEEDING:

1. The differences in government regulation of pension fund management in the different countries.
2. The various ways in which pension funds are managed by sponsoring firms in the different countries.
3. The differences in the tendency of pension funds to invest in equities in various nations.
4. The kinds of institutions that play an active role in the pension fund industries of the countries.

SUMMARY

A pension plan is a fund that is established by private employers, governments, or unions for the payment of retirement benefits. Pension plans have grown rapidly, largely because of favorable tax treatment. Qualified pension funds are exempt from federal income taxes, as are employer contributions. The two types of pension funds are defined contribution plans and defined benefit plans. In the former plan the sponsor is responsible only for making specified contributions into the plan on behalf of qualifying employees, but does not guarantee any specific amount at retirement. A defined benefit plan sponsor agrees to make specified payments to qualifying employees at retirement. Recently, some hybrid plans blending features of both basic types of plans have appeared.

---

[27] *Ibid.*

There is federal regulation of pension funds, as embodied in the Employee Retirement Income Security Act of 1974 (ERISA). ERISA sets minimum standards for employer contributions, establishes rules of prudent management, and requires vesting in a specified period of time. Also, ERISA provides for insurance of vested benefits.

Pension funds are managed by the plan sponsor and/or by management firms hired by the sponsor. Management fees may reflect the amount of money being managed or the performance of the managers in achieving suitable rates of return for the funds. There are consulting firms that provide assistance in the planning and administration of the funds.

German pension funds are managed largely by the employers, who must belong to an association that provides government-sponsored insurance. In the U.K., many types of financial institutions participate in the management of pension funds, which get little government regulation and tend to favor equities. In Japan, the government regulates pensions to a substantial extent and requires that large portions of funds be committed to fixed-income securities of the government or large and well-regarded corporations.

GLOSSARY

**Defined benefit plan:** Plan whose sponsor agrees to make specified dollar payments to qualifying employees at retirement, according to factors such as the length of service and the earnings of the employee.

**Defined contribution plan:** Plan whose sponsor is responsible only for making specified contributions into the plan on behalf of qualifying participants.

**Employee Retirement Income Security Act of 1974 (or ERISA):** Comprehensive legislation regulating several key features of corporate pension plans and including the "prudent man" statutes and rules.

**Hybrid pension plan:** Plan that combines some features of the defined benefit approach and some aspects of the defined contribution method.

**Insured benefit plan:** Plan whose defined benefits the sponsor insures through an annuity policy with a life insurance company.

**Pension Benefit Guaranty Corporation (or PBGC):** The federal agency established in 1974 by the ERISA legislation to insure the vested benefits of pension plan participants.

**Pension plan:** A fund that is established for the payment of retirement benefits.

**Pension plan sponsor:** The entity that establishes a pension plan for its employees, which may be a private business or a unit of state/local government. Sponsor may also be a union acting on behalf of its members, or individuals acting for themselves.

**Pensionskassen:** German term for legally separate but actually captive and in-house companies that manage pension funds.

**Personal Equity Plan (or PEP):** This policy of the British government encourages individuals to increase their savings for retirement through exemption from taxation of gains from dividends and price appreciation in stock or equity accounts.

## APPENDIX: ENDOWMENT FUNDS

Another group of institutions that have funds to invest in financial markets are endowment funds. These institutions include colleges, private schools, museums, hospitals, and foundations. The investment income generated from the funds invested is used for the operation of the institution. In the case of a college, the investment income is used to meet current operating expenses and such capital expenditures as the construction of new buildings and sports facilities.[28] Many of the organizations that have endowment funds also have a pension plan for their employees. For example, the University of Kentucky has a retirement system for its employees and an endowment fund of $93 million.

Most of the large endowments in the U.S. are independent of any firm or governmental group. Some endowments are company sponsored or linked to certain communities. Still others are termed "operating foundations" because they award most of their gifts to their own units rather than to organizations outside of the foundations. Table 9A-1 lists the ten largest endowment funds, by assets, in the United States as of 1990. All these trusts or foundations are independent, except for the Getty Trust, which is an operating foundation.[29]

As with pension funds, qualified endowment funds are exempt from taxation. The board of trustees of the endowment fund, just like the plan sponsor for a pension fund, specifies the investment objectives and the acceptable investment alternatives. The endowment funds can either be managed in-house or by external money managers. The same organizations that manage money for pension funds manage funds for endowments.

Here are a few examples of hirings by endowment funds in 1992:

- Pomona College in Claremont, California, hired its first international equity manager, The Common Fund, to manage $20 million of its endowment funds.

---

[28] Many colleges have professors who have an "endowed chair." This means that all or a significant part of the funding for the position comes from a financial contribution to the university. Normally, that contribution is a large initial payment, which the university invests in income-earning assets that have little risk of losing value. The interest and/or dividends of those assets provide the annual stipend or support for the chair. The chair normally has a title that includes the name of the person or institution that made the contribution. An appointment to an endowed (or "named") chair is normally an honor and, often, a high honor.

[29] *The Foundation Directory 1992* (New York: The Foundation Center, 1992), p. vi.

| TABLE 9A-1 |
| :---: |

### ASSETS AND GIFTS OF SELECTED LARGE ENDOWMENT FUNDS, 1990

| Fund | Assets (Billions) | Gifts (Millions) |
| :--- | :---: | :---: |
| The Ford Foundation | $5.46 | $227 |
| J.Paul Getty Trust | 4.82 | 227 |
| Lilly Endowment, Inc. | 3.54 | 108 |
| W.K.Kellogg Foundation | 3.51 | 122 |
| John D. and CatherineT. | | |
|   MacArthur Foundation | 3.08 | 116 |
| The Pew Charitable Trusts | 3.08 | 155 |
| The Robert Wood Johnson Foundation | 2.92 | 112 |
| The Rockefeller Foundation | 1.97 | 85 |
| The Andrew W. Mellon Foundation | 1.62 | 75 |
| The Kresge Foundation | 1.22 | 75 |

*Source: The Foundation Directory 1992* (New York: The Foundation Center, 1992), p. viii.

- The Memorial Sloan Kettering Cancer Center in New York hired two equity money managers. Hayez Sarofim was given $45 million to manage and Spears, Benzak, Salomon & Farrell $53 million to manage.
- The Rockefeller Foundation wanted to increase its allocation to international equities. To accomplish this, it hired three money managers: Mercator Asset Management, Arnhold and S. Bleichroeder International, and Acadian Asset Management.

Typically, the managers of endowment funds invest in long-term assets and have the primary goal of safeguarding the principal of the fund. For this reason, endowments tend to favor those equities that offer a steady dividend and comparatively little price volatility. Also, endowment funds often invest in government bonds and corporate bonds of high quality. The second goal, and an important one, is to generate a stream of earnings that allows the endowment to perform its functions of supporting certain operations or institutions.

QUESTIONS

1. a. What is meant by a plan sponsor?
   b. Who are plan sponsors?
2. What is the difference between a defined contribution plan and a defined benefit plan?
3. a. What is a 401(k) plan?
   b. What role can a mutual fund play in this kind of plan?
4. What is meant by an insured pension plan?
5. What is the function of the Pension Benefit Guaranty Corporation?

6. Why are pension funds not interested in tax-advantaged investments?

7. Are U.S. pension funds free to invest in foreign securities?

8. a. What is the major legislation regulating pension funds?

   b. Does this major legislation require that a corporation establish a pension fund?

9. Who manages pension fund assets?

10. What types of services do advisors provide to pension sponsors?

CHAPTER TEN

# Properties and Pricing of Financial Assets

## LEARNING OBJECTIVES

*After reading this chapter you will understand:*

- the many key properties of financial assets: moneyness; divisibility and denomination; reversibility; cash flow and return; term to maturity; convertibility; currency; liquidity; return predictability or risk; complexity; and tax status.

- the components of an asset's discount rate or required rate of return.

- what is meant by a basis point.

- how the discount rate is structured to encompass the components of an asset's risk.

- the principles of valuing complex financial assets.

- the inverse relationship between an asset's price and its discount rate.

- the principles that reveal how the properties of an asset affect its value, either through the discount rate or through its expected cash flow.

- what factors affect the price sensitivity of a financial asset to changes in interest rates.

- what duration means, and how it is related to the price sensitivity of an asset to a change in interest rates.

Financial assets have certain properties that determine or influence their attractiveness to different classes of investors and issuers. This chapter introduces these properties in preparation for a more detailed exposition in later chapters. The chapter also provides the basic principles of the valuation or pricing of financial assets and illustrates how several of the properties of financial assets affect their value. Because the valuation of financial assets requires an understanding of present value, this concept is explained in the appendix.

## PROPERTIES OF FINANCIAL ASSETS

The eleven properties of financial assets are (1) *moneyness*, (2) *divisibility and denomination*, (3) *reversibility*, (4) *cash flow*, (5) *term to maturity*, (6) *convertibility*, (7) *currency*, (8) *liquidity*, (9) *return predictability*, (10) *complexity*, and (11) *tax status*.[1]

### Moneyness

As we discuss in Chapter 5, some financial assets are used as a medium of exchange or in settlement of transactions. These assets are called *money*. In the United States money consists of currency and all forms of deposits that permit check writing. Other assets, although not money, are very close to money in that they can be transformed into money at little cost, delay, or risk. They are referred to as *near money*. In the case of the U.S., these include time and savings deposits and a security issued by the U.S. government called a Treasury bill.[2] Moneyness is clearly a desirable property for investors.

### Divisibility and Denomination

Divisibility relates to the minimum size in which a financial asset can be liquidated and exchanged for money. The smaller the size, the more the financial asset is divisible. A financial asset such as a deposit is typically infinitely divisible (down to the penny), but other financial assets have varying degrees of divisibility depending on their denomination, which is the dollar value of the amount that each unit of the asset will pay at maturity. Thus many bonds come in $1,000 denominations, commercial paper in $25,000 units,[3] and certain types of certificates of deposit in $100,000 and more. In general, divisibility is desirable for investors but not for borrowers.

---

[1] Some of these properties are taken from James Tobin, "Properties of Assets," undated manuscript, Yale University, New Haven.

[2] U.S. Treasury bills are discussed in Chapter 16.

[3] Commercial paper is described in Chapter 20.

### Reversibility

Reversibility refers to the cost of investing in a financial asset and then getting out of it and back into cash again. Consequently, reversibility is also referred to as *turnaround cost* or *round-trip cost*.

A financial asset such as a deposit at a bank is obviously highly reversible because usually there is no charge for adding to or withdrawing from it. Other transactions costs may be unavoidable, but these are small. For financial assets traded in organized markets or with "market makers" (discussed in Chapter 15), the most relevant component of round-trip cost is the so-called *bid–ask spread*, to which might be added commissions and the time and cost, if any, of delivering the asset. The spread charged by a market maker varies sharply from one financial asset to another, reflecting primarily the amount of risk the market maker is assuming by "making" a market.

This market-making risk, which is discussed in more detail in Chapter 15, can be related to two main forces. One is the variability of the price as measured, say, by some measure of dispersion of the relative price over time. The greater the variability, the greater the probability of the market maker incurring a loss in excess of a stated bound between the time of buying and reselling the financial asset. The variability of prices differs widely across financial assets. Treasury bills, for example, have a very stable price, for the reason explained at the end of this chapter, while a speculative stock will exhibit much larger short-run variations.

The second determining factor of the bid–ask spread charged by a market maker is what is commonly referred to as the *thickness of the market*; by this is meant essentially the prevailing rate at which buying and selling orders reach the market maker (that is, the frequency of transactions). A "thin market" is one that has few trades on a regular or continuing basis. Clearly, the greater the frequency of order flows, the shorter the time that the security will have to be held in the market maker's inventory, and hence the smaller the probability of an unfavorable price movement while held.

Thickness too varies from market to market. A three-month U.S. Treasury bill is easily the thickest market in the world. In contrast, trading in stock of small companies is not thick but thin. Because Treasury bills dominate other instruments both in price stability and thickness, their bid–ask spread tends to be the smallest in the market. A low turnaround cost is clearly a desirable property of a financial asset, and as a result thickness itself is a valuable property. This explains the potential advantage of larger over smaller markets (economies of scale), along with a market's tendency to standardize the instruments offered to the public.

### Cash Flow

The return that an investor will realize by holding a financial asset depends on all the cash distributions that the financial asset will pay its owners; this includes dividends on shares and coupon payments on bonds. The return also considers the repayment of principal for a debt security and the expected sale price of a stock. In computing the expected return, non-cash payments, such as stock dividends and options to purchase additional stock, or the distribution of other securities must also be accounted for.

In a world of nonnegligible inflation, it is also important to distinguish between *nominal expected return* and *real expected return*. The expected return that we described above is the nominal expected return. That is, it considers the dollars that are expected to be received, but does not adjust those dollars to take into consideration changes in their purchasing power. The net real expected return is the nominal expected return after adjustment for the loss of purchasing power of the financial asset as a result of anticipated inflation. For example, if the nominal expected return for a one-year investment of $1,000 is 6%, then at the end of one year the investor expects to realize $1,060, consisting of interest of $60 and the repayment of the $1,000 investment. However, if the inflation rate over the same period of time is 4%, then the purchasing power of $1,060 is only $1,019.23 ($1,060 divided by 1.04). Thus, the return in terms of purchasing power, or the real return, is 1.923%. In general, the expected real return can be approximated by subtracting the expected inflation rate from the expected nominal return. In our example, it is approximately 2% (6% minus 4%).

## Term to Maturity

This is the length of the period until the date at which the instrument is scheduled to make its final payment, or the owner is entitled to demand liquidation. Instruments for which the creditor can ask for repayment at any time, such as checking accounts and many savings accounts, are called *demand instruments*. Maturity is an important characteristic of financial assets such as bonds, and can range from one day to a few decades. In the United Kingdom, there is one well-known type of bond that promises to pay a fixed amount per year indefinitely and not to repay the principal at any time; such an instrument is called a *perpetual*, or a *consol*. Many other instruments, including equities, have no maturity and are thus a form of perpetual.

It should be understood that even a financial asset with a stated maturity may terminate before its stated maturity. This may occur for several reasons, including bankruptcy or reorganization, or because of *call provisions* entitling the debtor to repay in advance, usually at some penalty and only after a number of years from the time of issuance. Sometimes the investor may have the privilege of asking for early repayment. This feature is called a *put option*. Some assets have maturities that may be increased or extended at the discretion of the issuer or the investor. For example, the French government issues a six-year *obligation renouvelable du Trésor*, which allows the investor, after the end of the third year, to switch into a new six-year debt. Similar bonds are issued by the British government. All these features regarding maturity are discussed in later chapters.

## Convertibility

As the preceding discussion shows, an important property of some assets is that they are convertible into other assets. In some cases, the conversion takes place within one class of assets, as when a bond is converted into another bond. In other situations, the conversion spans classes. For example, a corporate *convertible bond* is a bond that the bondholder can change into equity shares. Preferred stock (discussed in Chapter 21) may be convertible into common stock. It is important to note that the timing, costs, and conditions for conversion are clearly spelled out in the legal descriptions of the convertible security at the time it is issued.

## Currency

We have noted throughout our discussion that the global financial system has become increasingly integrated. In light of the freely floating and often volatile exchange rates among the major currencies,[4] this fact gives added importance to the currency in which the financial asset will make cash flow payments. Most financial assets are denominated in one currency, such as U.S. dollars or yen or Deutsche marks, and investors must choose them with that feature in mind.

Some issuers, responding to investors' wishes to reduce currency risk, have issued *dual-currency securities*. For example, some Eurobonds[5] pay interest in one currency but principal or redemption value in a second. U.S. dollars and yen are commonly paired in these cases. Further, some Eurobonds carry a currency option that allows the investor to specify that payments of either interest or principal be made in either one of two major currencies.

## Liquidity

This is an important and widely used notion, although there is at present no uniformly accepted definition of liquidity. A useful way to think of liquidity and illiquidity, proposed by Professor James Tobin,[6] is in terms of how much sellers stand to lose if they wish to sell immediately as against engaging in a costly and time-consuming search.

An example of a quite illiquid financial asset is the stock of a small corporation or the bond issued by a small school district. The market for such a security is extremely thin, and one must search for one of a very few suitable buyers. Less suitable buyers, including speculators and market makers, may be located more promptly, but they will have to be enticed to invest in the illiquid financial asset by an appropriate discount in price.

For many other financial assets, liquidity is determined by contractual arrangements. Ordinary deposits, for example, are perfectly liquid because the

---

[4] Exchange rates and the foreign exchange market are the subject of Chapter 30.
[5] Eurobonds are discussed in Chapter 21.
[6] James Tobin, "Properties of Assets," *op. cit.*

bank has a contractual obligation to convert them at par on demand. Financial contracts representing a claim on a private pension fund may be regarded on the other hand as totally illiquid, because these can be cashed only at retirement.

Liquidity may depend not only on the financial asset but also on the quantity one wishes to sell (or buy). While a small quantity may be quite liquid, a large lot may run into illiquidity problems. Note that liquidity is again closely related to whether a market is thick or thin. Thinness always has the effect of increasing the turnaround cost, even of a liquid financial asset. But beyond some point, thinness becomes an obstacle to the formation of a market, and it has a direct effect on the illiquidity of the financial asset.

## Return Predictability

Return predictability is a basic property of financial assets, in that it is a major determinant of their value. Assuming investors are risk-averse, the riskiness of an asset can be equated with the uncertainty or unpredictability of its return. We will see in Chapter 13 how the unpredictability of future returns can be measured and how it is related to the variability of past returns. But whatever measure of volatility is used,[7] it is obvious that volatility varies greatly across financial assets. There are several reasons for this.

First, as illustrated later in this chapter, the value of a financial asset depends on the cash flow expected and on the interest rate used to discount this cash flow. Hence volatility will be a consequence of the uncertainty about future interest rates and future cash flow. Now the future cash flow may be contractual, in which case the sole source of its uncertainty is the reliability of the debtor with regard to fulfilling the obligation. The cash flow may be in the nature of a residual equity claim, as is the case for the payments generated by the equity of a corporation. The cash flows from U.S. government securities are the only cash flows generally regarded as altogether riskless. Corporate debt and corporate stock cash flows are generally riskier than cash flows of U.S. government securities. Corporate equities represent a wide range of risk, from public utilities to highly speculative issues.

As for a change in interest rates, it will in principle affect all prices in the opposite direction, but the effect is much larger in the case of the price of a financial asset with a long maturity than one with a short remaining life, as illustrated later in this chapter. Thus, on this account also, short-term U.S. government securities such as Treasury bills tend to be the safest assets, except for cash (if properly insured). For individual stocks the interest effect is generally swamped by cash flow uncertainty, although movements in interest rates have the characteristic of affecting all stocks in the same direction, while change in expected cash flow is largely dependent on a firm's particular financial situation. In general, uncertainty about returns and future prices can be expected to increase as the investment horizon lengthens.

---

[7] Proxy measures for volatility include the standard deviation of expected returns or the range within which the outcome can be expected to fall with some stated probability.

What has been said so far relates to the predictability of nominal returns, although the relevant measure, of course, is real returns—returns corrected for gains or losses of purchasing power attributable to inflation. Of course, if inflation is absent or small, the determinants of real and nominal uncertainty and risk coincide. But in the presence of highly unpredictable inflation (which usually goes together with high inflation), real returns may be drastically harder to predict than nominal returns.

## Complexity

Some financial assets are complex in the sense that they are actually combinations of two or more simpler assets. To find the true value of such an asset, one must "decompose" it into its component parts and price each separately. The sum of those prices is the value of the complex asset. A good example of a complex asset is the *callable bond*, that is, a bond whose issuer is entitled to repay the debt prior to the maturity date. When investors buy such a bond, they in effect buy a bond and sell to the issuer an option that allows the issuer to redeem the bond at a set price prior to the issue's scheduled maturity. The correct or true price of a callable bond, therefore, is equal to the price of a similar non-callable bond less the value of the issuer's right to retire the bond early.

A complex asset may be viewed as a bundle or package of cash flows and options belonging to either the issuer or the holder, or both. Other examples of a complex asset include convertible bonds, a bond that has payments that can be made in a different currency at the option of the bondholder, and a bond that can be sold back to the issuer at a fixed price (that is, a *putable bond*).

In some cases, the degree of complexity is large: many convertible bonds are also callable, and some bonds give their issuers the right either to extend the asset's maturity or to redeem it early. Also, some Japanese firms have issued bonds that are convertible into Japanese stock (denominated in yen, of course) but that are sold for, and make coupon and principal payments in, another currency, such as U.S. dollars.

## Tax Status

An important feature of any asset is its tax status. Governmental regulations for taxing the income from the ownership or sale of financial assets vary widely, if not wildly. Tax rates differ from year to year, from country to country, and even among municipal units within a country (as with state and local taxes in the United States). Moreover, tax rates may differ from financial asset to financial asset, depending on the type of issuer, the length of time the asset is held, the nature of the owner, and so on. For example, in the United States, pension funds are exempt from income taxes (see Chapter 9 for more detail), and coupon payments on municipal bonds are generally free of taxation by the federal government (see Chapter 17).

► KEY POINTS THAT YOU SHOULD UNDERSTAND BEFORE PROCEEDING:

1.  A financial asset has many properties, and each affects the asset's value in a distinctive and important way.
2.  Some properties are intrinsic to the asset, such as its maturity or promised cash flow.
3.  Other properties are features of the market for the asset, such as the costs of trading the asset.
4.  Still other properties reflect decisions by government about the asset's tax status.
5.  A complex asset is one that provides options for the issuer or the investor, or both, and so represents a combination of simpler assets.

## PRINCIPLES OF PRICING OF FINANCIAL ASSETS

The fundamental principle of finance is that the true or correct price of an asset equals the *present value* of all cash flows that the owner of the asset expects to receive during its life. In general, the correct price for a financial asset can be expressed as follows:

$$P = \frac{CF_1}{(1+r)^1} + \frac{CF_2}{(1+r)^2} + \frac{CF_3}{(1+r)^3} + \ldots + \frac{CF_N}{(1+r)^N}$$

where
$P$ = the price of the financial asset
$CF_t$ = the cash flow in year $t$ ($t = 1, \ldots, N$)
$N$ = maturity of the financial asset
$r$ = appropriate discount rate

### *The Appropriate Discount Rate*

The appropriate discount rate, $r$, is the return that the market or the consensus of investors requires on the asset. A convenient (but approximate) expression for the appropriate discount rate is this:

$$r = RR + IP + DP + MP + LP + EP$$

where
$RR$ = the real rate of interest, which is the reward for not consuming and for lending to other users
$IP$ = the inflation premium, which is the compensation for the expected decline in the purchasing power of the money lent to borrowers
$DP$ = the default risk premium, which is the reward for taking on the risk of default in the case of a loan/bond or the risk of loss of principal for other assets
$MP$ = the maturity premium, which is the compensation for lending money for long periods of time

$LP$ = the liquidity premium, which is the reward for investing in an asset that may not be readily converted to cash at a fair market value

$EP$ = the exchange-rate risk premium, which is the reward for investing in an asset that is not denominated in the investor's home currency.

Obviously, the price of an asset is inversely related to its discount rate: if the discount rate rises, the price falls; and if the rate declines, the price increases.

## Illustration

Let us construct a simple example to illustrate the pricing of a financial asset. We can then use the hypothetical financial asset to illustrate some of the properties explained earlier in this chapter.

Suppose a bond has a maturity of four years and pays annual interest of $50 at the end of each year plus a principal of $1,000 at the conclusion of the fourth year. Since this bond pays $50 per $1,000 of principal, the periodic coupon rate is 5%. This rate is commonly and simply referred to as the *coupon rate*. Thus, using the notation above:

$$N = 4 \quad CF_1 = \$50 \quad CF_2 = \$50 \quad CF_3 = \$50 \quad CF_N = \$1,050$$

Further, assume that the market thinks the real rate is 2.5%, the inflation premium is 3%, the bond's default risk justifies a premium of 2%, the maturity premium is 0.5%, and the liquidity premium is 1%. Since the cash flows are denominated in U.S. dollars, the foreign-exchange rate premium is zero. That is,

$$RR = 2.5\% \quad IP = 3.0\% \quad DP = 2.0\% \quad MP = 0.5\% \quad LP = 1.0\% \quad EP = 0\%$$

Thus, we have this value for the discount rate:

$$r = 2.5\% + 3.0\% + 2.0\% + 0.5\% + 1.0\% + 0\% = 9.0\% \text{ or } 0.09$$

Using the formula for price, the price of this bond is:

$$P = \frac{\$50}{(1.09)^1} + \frac{\$50}{(1.09)^2} + \frac{\$50}{(1.09)^3} + \frac{\$1,050}{(1.09)^4}$$
$$= \$870.41$$

## Price and Asset Properties

We can use this hypothetical financial asset to illustrate the effect of some of the properties of financial assets on price or asset value. First, it should be clear that the price of a financial asset changes as the appropriate discount rate, *r*, changes. More specifically, the price changes in the opposite direction to the change in the appropriate discount rate. An illustration of this principle appears in Table 10-1, which shows the price of our hypothetical financial asset for various discount rates.

Let's look at how reversibility affects an asset's value. Suppose a commission of $35 is imposed by brokers to buy or sell the bond. The price of the four-year bond is then:

$$P = -\$35 + \frac{\$50}{(1.09)^1} + \frac{\$50}{(1.09)^2} + \frac{\$50}{(1.09)^3} + \frac{\$1,050 - \$35}{(1.09)^4}$$

$$= \$810.62$$

Notice that the initial commission of $35 is subtracted on an undiscounted basis because that payment is made at the time of purchase.

Suppose also a government entity imposes a transfer tax of $20 on each transaction. Because this rise in the cost of reversing an investment diminishes its reversibility to some extent, the present value of all cash flows associated with owning the bond now looks like this:

$$P = -\$35 - \$20 + \frac{\$50}{(1.09)^1} + \frac{\$50}{(1.09)^2} + \frac{\$50}{(1.09)^3} + \frac{\$1,050 - \$35 - \$20}{(1.09)^4}$$

$$= \$776.45$$

The change in price is significant and demonstrates why financial markets adjust so sharply (and rapidly) when governments impose restrictions on, or raise the cost of, capital market transactions.

To see how default risk affects the price of an asset, assume that, right

| TABLE 10-1 |
|---|

PRICE OF A FOUR-YEAR BOND
FOR VARIOUS DISCOUNT RATES

CASH FLOW:
$CF_1 = \$50 \quad CF_2 = \$50 \quad CF_3 = \$50 \quad CF_4 = \$1,050$

| Appropriate discount rate (%) | Price ($) |
|---|---|
| 4% | 1,036.30 |
| 5 | 1,000.00 |
| 6 | 965.35 |
| 7 | 932.26 |
| 8 | 900.64 |
| 9 | 870.41 |
| 10 | 841.51 |
| 11 | 813.85 |
| 12 | 787.39 |
| 13 | 762.04 |
| 14 | 737.77 |

before you bought the bond, a news story convinced investors that this bond is less risky than they had thought. So, the default risk premium falls from 2% to 1%, and the appropriate discount rate thus declines from 9% to 8%. Ignoring commissions and transfer fees, Table 10-1 shows that the price would increase from $870.41 to $900.64.

What about liquidity? Suppose immediately after the purchase of this bond, factors in the market for this bond cause its liquidity to decline. An investor buying this asset would plan for such a possibility by raising the liquidity premium. Assume that the liquidity premium increases from 1% to 3%. The appropriate discount rate then increases from 9% to 11%. Ignoring the commission and the transfer fee, Table 10-1 shows that the price would be $813.85. The fall in price, from the original $870.41 to $813.85, shows how important liquidity can be.

Now, let's tackle the notion of complexity by assuming that the bond is convertible into a fixed number of shares of common stock of the company that issued the bond. The price of our four-year bond would then be greater than $870.41 by an amount equal to the value that the market assigns to the right to convert the bond into common stock. For example, suppose we observe that the price of our hypothetical bond with the conversion privilege is $1,000.41. This means that the conversion privilege is valued by the market at $130.

The unresolved question is whether the $130 is a fair value for this conversion privilege. Valuation techniques to determine the fair value of any type of option such as a conversion privilege are available, and we will discuss these techniques in Chapter 27. For now, it is sufficient to understand why a knowledge of how to value an option is important. Because many financial assets have options embedded in them, failure to assess the options properly may lead to the mispricing of financial assets.

Now, let's turn our attention to currency. Suppose that this bond was issued by a German firm and that all payments are in Deutsche marks. The cash flow in U.S. dollars that a U.S. investor will receive is uncertain because the dollar-mark exchange rate will fluctuate over the four years. Suppose that the market assigns an exchange premium of 3%. This means that the appropriate discount rate increases from 9% to 12% and the price would be $787.39 (see Table 10-1). To continue with the effect of currency risk, suppose that immediately after the purchase of this bond the market expects that the exchange rate between the U.S. dollar and the Deutsche mark will become more volatile. The market will adjust for this by increasing the foreign currency risk premium, which, in turn, increases the appropriate discount rate and decreases the price.

It is easy to illustrate the impact of taxes. Suppose that our bond is granted a favorable tax treatment such that the interest and any capital gain from this bond would not be taxed. Suppose that the marginal tax rate on otherwise equivalent taxable bonds is 33.33% and the appropriate discount rate is 9%. This means that the after-tax discount rate would be approximately 6%, as shown below:

$$\text{Pre-tax discount rate} \times (1 - \text{Marginal tax rate})$$
$$0.09 \times (1 - 0.3333) = 6\%$$

Since our hypothetical bond is free of taxes, the appropriate discount rate would be adjusted to compensate for this feature. The discount rate that would be used is 6%, because it is the equivalent of a 9% discount rate and a 33.33% marginal tax rate. From Table 10-1 we see that the price of the bond would be $965.35.

Continuing with the importance of tax features to the price of a financial asset, suppose that immediately after the purchase of this bond, the market comes to expect that the U.S. Congress will raise the marginal tax rate. This expectation would increase the value of the tax-exempt feature by decreasing the discount rate based on the anticipated rise in the marginal tax rate. The opposite would occur if the market came to expect that the U.S. Congress would lower the marginal tax rate.

> ▶ KEY POINTS THAT YOU SHOULD UNDERSTAND BEFORE PROCEEDING:
>
> 1.  An asset's price is the present value of its expected cash flows, discounted at an appropriate rate.
> 2.  The appropriate discount rate for an asset's cash flows depends upon the properties of the assets.
> 3.  The appropriate discount rate can often be approximated as the sum of rewards for the various risks an asset poses to its buyer.
> 4.  The price of an asset moves in the opposite direction of a change in its discount rate.
> 5.  The price of a complex asset is the sum of the prices of its component parts.

## PRICE VOLATILITY OF FINANCIAL ASSETS

As Table 10-1 makes clear, a fundamental principle is that a financial asset's price changes in the opposite direction of the change in the required rate of return. We refer to the required rate of return as the *required yield*. This principle follows from the fact that the price of a financial asset is equal to the present value of its cash flow. An increase (decrease) in the yield required by investors decreases (increases) the present value of the cash flow, and therefore the financial asset's price.

The price sensitivity of a financial asset to a change in the required yield will not be the same for all assets. For example, an increase in the required yield of one percentage point may result in a decline in one asset's price of 20%, but only 3% for another. In this section, we will see how the characteristics of a financial asset and the level of interest rates affect the price responsiveness of a financial asset to a change in the required yield. We also present a measure that can be used to gauge the approximate price sensitivity of a financial asset to changes in the required yield.

It is important to note that the analysis in this section applies fully and directly to bonds and other financial assets that have known expected cash flows and known expected maturities. An analysis of the price sensitivity of other major financial assets, such as preferred stock and common stock (which are perpetuals and have uncertain cash flows), must be postponed to a later chapter.

In our discussion, we will refer to changes in the required yield. It is convenient to measure a change in yield in terms of what market participants refer to as a *basis point* rather than in terms of a percentage change. One basis point is defined as 0.0001, or equivalently, 0.01%. Therefore, 100 basis points is equal to one percentage point, and a yield change from 9% to 10% represents a 100 basis point change in yield. A yield change from 7% to 7.5% is a 50 basis point change, and a yield change from 6% to 8.35% is a 235 basis point change in yield.

## The Effect of Maturity

An asset's maturity is a factor that affects its price sensitivity to a change in yield. In fact, a bond's price sensitivity to a change in the discount rate is positively related to the bond's maturity. Consider the case of two bonds that have the same coupon rate, and the same required yield but different maturities. If the required rate were to change, the price sensitivity of the bond with the longer maturity would be greater than that of the bond with the shorter maturity.

An illustration of this link between maturity and price change appears in Table 10-2, which shows the price of a bond that pays $50 annually and $1,000 at maturity—a 5% coupon rate—for various maturities and discount rates. Table 10-3, which is based on Table 10-2, shows the differences across maturities in a bond's dollar price decline and percentage price decline for an increase in the discount rate of 100 basis points. For example, if the discount rate rises from 9% to 10%, the price of a four-year bond falls from $870.41 to $841.51, which represents a price decline of $28.90 and a percentage price decline of 3.32%. In contrast, a similar rise in the discount rate causes the price of a 20-year bond to fall considerably more, from $634.86 to $574.32, which represents a price decline of $60.54 and a percentage price decline of 9.54%.

| TABLE 10-2 | | | |
|---|---|---|---|

PRICE OF A BOND PAYING $50 ANNUALLY AND $1,000 AT MATURITY FOR
VARIOUS DISCOUNT RATES AND MATURITIES

| Discount rate (%) | Number of years to maturity | | | |
|---|---|---|---|---|
| | 4 | 10 | 15 | 20 |
| 4% | 1,036.30 | 1,081.11 | 1,111.18 | 1,135.90 |
| 5 | 1,000.00 | 1,000.00 | 1,000.00 | 1,000.00 |
| 6 | 965.35 | 926.40 | 902.88 | 885.30 |
| 7 | 932.26 | 859.53 | 817.84 | 788.12 |
| 8 | 900.64 | 798.70 | 743.22 | 705.46 |
| 9 | 870.41 | 743.29 | 677.57 | 634.86 |
| 10 | 841.51 | 692.77 | 619.70 | 574.32 |
| 11 | 813.85 | 646.65 | 568.55 | 522.20 |
| 12 | 787.39 | 604.48 | 523.24 | 477.14 |
| 13 | 762.04 | 565.90 | 483.01 | 438.02 |
| 14 | 737.77 | 530.55 | 447.20 | 403.92 |

| | | TABLE 10-3 | | |

**PRICE DECLINE IF THE DISCOUNT RATE INCREASES 100 BASIS POINTS FOR A BOND PAYING $50 ANNUALLY AND $1,000 AT MATURITY FOR VARIOUS DISCOUNT RATES AND MATURITIES**

*Price Change*

| Discount rate changes from | Number of years to maturity | | | |
| | 4 | 10 | 15 | 20 |
|---|---|---|---|---|
| 4% to 5% | $-36.30 | $-81.11 | $-111.18 | $-135.91 |
| 5% to 6% | -34.65 | -73.60 | - 97.20 | -114.70 |
| 6% to 7% | -33.09 | -66.87 | - 85.04 | - 97.18 |
| 7% to 8% | -31.62 | -60.83 | - 74.62 | - 82.66 |
| 8% to 9% | -30.23 | -55.41 | - 65.65 | - 70.60 |
| 9% to 10% | -28.90 | -50.52 | - 57.87 | - 60.54 |
| 10% to 11% | -27.66 | -46.12 | - 51.15 | - 52.12 |
| 11% to 12% | -26.40 | -42.17 | - 45.13 | - 45.06 |
| 12% to 13% | -25.35 | -38.58 | - 40.23 | - 39.12 |
| 13% to 14% | -24.27 | -35.35 | - 35.81 | - 34.12 |

*Percentage Price Change*

| Discount rate changes from | Number of years to maturity | | | |
| | 4 | 10 | 15 | 20 |
|---|---|---|---|---|
| 4% to 5% | -3.50% | -7.50% | -10.01% | -11.96% |
| 5% to 6% | -3.47 | -7.36 | - 9.71 | -11.47 |
| 6% to 7% | -3.43 | -7.22 | - 9.42 | -10.98 |
| 7% to 8% | -3.39 | -7.08 | - 9.12 | -10.49 |
| 8% to 9% | -3.36 | -6.94 | - 8.83 | -10.01 |
| 9% to 10% | -3.32 | -6.80 | - 8.54 | - 9.54 |
| 10% to 11% | -3.29 | -6.66 | - 8.25 | - 9.08 |
| 11% to 12% | -3.25 | -6.52 | - 7.97 | - 8.63 |
| 12% to 13% | -3.22 | -6.38 | - 7.69 | - 8.20 |
| 13% to 14% | -3.18 | -6.25 | - 7.41 | - 7.79 |

## The Effect of the Coupon Rate

A bond's coupon rate also affects its price sensitivity. More specifically, for two bonds with the same maturity and with the same required yield, the lower the coupon rate, the greater the price responsiveness for a given change in the required yield.

To illustrate this, consider a 5% coupon bond and a 10% coupon bond, each of which has a maturity of 15 years and a principal of $1,000. If the required yield for both bonds is 9%, the price of the 5% coupon bond would be $677.57, and the price of the 10% coupon bond would be $1,080.61. If the required yield increases by 100 basis points, from 9% to 10%, the price of the 5% coupon bond will fall to $619.70, while the price of the 10% coupon bond would fall to $1,000. Thus, the 5% coupon bond's price declines by $57.87 or

8.5% ($57.87/$677.57), while the 10% coupon bond's price declines by $80.61 or by 7.5.% ($80.61/$1,080.61). While the dollar price change is greater for the higher-coupon bond, the percentage price change is less.

In later chapters, we will discuss a special type of bond, one with no coupon rate. This is called a *zero-coupon bond*. The investor who purchases a zero-coupon bond receives no periodic interest payment. Instead, the investor purchases the bond at a price below its principal and receives the principal at the maturity date. The difference between the principal and the price at which the zero-coupon is purchased represents interest earned by the investor over the bond's life. For example, consider a zero-coupon bond with a principal of $1,000 and a maturity of 15 years. If the required yield is 9%, the price of this bond would be $274.54.[8] The difference between the principal of $1,000 and the price of $274.54 is the interest that the investor realizes at the maturity date.

A zero-coupon will have greater price sensitivity than a bond with a coupon rate selling at the same required yield and with the same maturity. For example, consider once again the 15-year zero-coupon bond. If the required yield increases from 9% to 10%, the price of this bond would fall to $239.39, a percentage price decline of 12.8% ($35.15/$274.54). This percentage change is greater than the declines in price for the 15-year maturity 5% coupon and 15-year 10% coupon bonds.

### The Effect of the Level of Yields

Tables 10-2 and 10-3 also bring out another interesting property about asset prices. Notice that, for a given maturity, the dollar price change and the percentage price change is higher for the lower initial discount rates than at the higher initial discount rates. For example, consider the 15-year bond when the discount rate is 5%. The price of the bond falls from $1,000 to $902.88 when the discount rate increases from 5% to 6%, a price decline of $97.20 and a percentage price decline of 9.72%. In contrast, a rise in the discount rate of 100 basis points from 13% to 14% reduces the same bond's price by $35.81 (from $483.01 to $447.20) and by the percentage of 7.41%.

The implication is that the lower the level of yields, the greater the affect a change in interest rates will have on the price of a financial asset.

### Measuring Price Sensitivity to Interest Rate Changes: Duration

From our discussion thus far, we see that three factors affect the price sensitivity of an asset to changes in interest rates: the maturity, the coupon rate, and the level of interest rates. In managing the price sensitivity of a portfolio, mar-

---

[8] The price is the present value of $1,000 15 years from now discounted at 9%.

ket participants seek a measure of the sensitivity of assets to interest rate changes that encompasses all three factors.

A very useful way to approximate an asset's price sensitivity is simply to examine how its price changes if the yield is increased or decreased by a small number of basis points. The following formula can then be used:

$$\frac{\text{Price if yield is decreased} - \text{Price if yield is increased}}{\text{Initial price} \times (\text{Higher yield} - \text{Lower yield})} \times 100$$

By higher yield is meant the yield used to determine the price if the yield is increased; the lower yield is that yield used to determine the price if the yield is decreased.

For example, the price of a 5% coupon bond with a principal of $1,000 and a maturity of 15 years is $677.57. If the yield is increased by 50 basis points, from 9% to 9.5%, the price would be $647.73. If the yield is decreased by 50 basis points, from 9% to 8.5%, the price would be $709.35. Then, we have these values:

> Initial price = $677.57
> Price if yield is increased to 9.5% = $647.73
> Price if yield is decreased to 8.5% = $709.35
> Higher yield = 9.5% or 0.095
> Lower yield = 8.5% or 0.085

The application of the formula given above provides this number:

$$\frac{\$709.35 - \$647.73}{\$677.57 \ (0.095 - 0.085)} \times 100$$

$$= 9.09$$

This measure of price sensitivity is popularly referred to as the bond's *duration*.[9] Table 10-4 shows how the duration is determined for a 5% coupon bond with different maturities, when the interest rate is initially at 9%.

Table 10-5 shows the duration for three coupon bonds with different maturities, under the assumption of different initial yields. As can be seen from this table, the relative magnitude of the duration is consistent with the properties we described earlier. Specifically, (1) for bonds with the same coupon rate and the same yield, the longer the maturity the greater the duration; (2) for bonds with the same maturity and at the same yield, the lower the coupon

---

[9] The term duration was first used in 1938 by Frederick R. Macaulay as a measure of the weighted average time to maturity of a bond (*Some Theoretical Problems Suggested by the Movements of Interest Rates, Bond Yields, and Stock Prices in the United States Since 1865*, New York: National Bureau of Economic Research, 1938). It can be shown that the measure Macaulay developed is related to the price sensitivity of a bond. Unfortunately, too many market participants interpret duration as some measure of average life instead of as a measure of price sensitivity. The formula used above to measure duration approximates the actual duration of a bond and is more useful in the sense that it allows the measuring of the duration for any financial asset, not just a bond.

---

### TABLE 10-4

#### DETERMINATION OF DURATION FOR A 5% COUPON BOND WITH A PRINCIPAL OF $1,000 AND AN INITIAL REQUIRED YIELD OF 9%

| | Number of Years to Maturity | | | |
| --- | --- | --- | --- | --- |
| | 4 | 10 | 15 | 20 |
| price at 9% | 870.41 | 743.29 | 677.57 | 634.86 |
| price at 9.5% | 855.80 | 717.45 | 647.73 | 603.44 |
| price at 8.5% | 885.35 | 770.35 | 709.35 | 668.78 |
| Duration | 3.40 | 7.12 | 9.09 | 10.29 |

$$\text{Duration} = \frac{\text{Price at 8.5\%} - \text{Price at 9.5\%}}{\text{Price at 9\%} \times (0.095 \times 0.085)} \times 100$$

---

rate the greater the duration; and (3) the lower the initial yield, the greater the duration for a given bond. Thus, duration picks up the effect of all three factors: maturity, coupon rate, and initial level of yield.

Duration is related to the price sensitivity as follows:

Approximate percentage change in a financial asset's price =
− Duration × (Yield change in decimal form) × 100

For example, suppose that the required yield on the 5% coupon, 15-year bond increases from 9% to 10% (0.01 in decimal form). Then this bond's duration is 9.09 and:

Approximate percentage change in price = −9.09 × (0.01) × 100 = −9.09%

---

### TABLE 10-5

#### DURATION FOR VARIOUS BONDS BY MATURITY, COUPON RATE, AND YIELD LEVEL

| Coupon | Yield | Number of Years to Maturity | | | |
| --- | --- | --- | --- | --- | --- |
| | | 4 | 10 | 15 | 20 |
| 50 | 5% | 3.55 | 7.73 | 10.39 | 12.48 |
| 50 | 9% | 3.40 | 7.12 | 9.09 | 10.29 |
| 50 | 12% | 3.29 | 6.67 | 8.16 | 8.79 |
| 100 | 5% | 3.36 | 6.93 | 9.15 | 10.95 |
| 100 | 9% | 3.21 | 6.30 | 7.91 | 8.97 |
| 100 | 12% | 3.10 | 5.85 | 7.05 | 7.69 |
| 0 | 5% | 3.81 | 9.53 | 14.30 | 19.08 |
| 0 | 9% | 3.67 | 9.18 | 13.77 | 18.38 |
| 0 | 12% | 3.57 | 8.93 | 13.40 | 17.88 |

We showed earlier that the actual percentage change in price if the required yield increases from 9% to 10% would be a fall of 8.5%. Thus, duration is a close approximation of the percentage price change. The approximation is better for smaller changes in the required yield. For example, if the required yield changes by 20 basis points (.002 in decimal form) from 9% to 9.20% rather than 100 basis points, then based on duration the approximate percentage change in price would be −1.82%. The actual price if the required yield increased by 20 basis points is $665.41, a decline of $12.16 from the price of $677.57 at 9%. The actual percentage price change is therefore −1.79% (−$12.16/$677.57). Duration did an excellent job of approximating the percentage price change in this case.

In general, one can interpret duration as follows: *the approximate percentage change in price for a 100 basis point change in interest rates around the prevailing yield.* Duration does a good job of approximating the price change for a small change in yield on the order of 50 basis points in either direction. The larger the yield change, the poorer the approximation that duration provides.

While we have developed duration in the context of bonds, we want to note that the basic principle applies equally to other financial assets. For example, consider a financial asset whose cash flow is as follows:

| Year | Cash Flow |
|------|-----------|
| 1 | $ 30 |
| 2 | 75 |
| 3 | 120 |
| 4 | 140 |
| 5 | 200 |
| 6 | 250 |
| 7 | 300 |

If the appropriate discount rate is 7%, the present value or price of this asset is $794.31. The duration of the financial asset is 4.59 as the following values show:

Initial price = $794.31
Price if yield is increased by 50 basis points to 7.5% = $776.36
Price if yield is decreased by 50 basis points to 6.5% = $812.82
Higher yield = 7.5% or 0.075
Lower yield = 6.5% or 0.065

Therefore,

$$\frac{\$812.82 - \$776.36}{\$794.31 \ (0.075 - 0.065)} \times 100$$
$$= 4.59$$

▶ KEY POINTS THAT YOU SHOULD UNDERSTAND BEFORE PROCEEDING:

1. Assets have different degrees of price sensitivity to a change in the discount rate or required yield.

2.  Factors that influence an asset's price sensitivity include its maturity, its coupon rate, and the initial level of the required yield.

3.  The longer an asset's maturity, the greater its price sensitivity to a change in the discount rate, other things being constant.

4.  The larger an asset's coupon rate, the lower its price sensitivity to a change in the discount rate, if all else is the same.

5.  The lower the initial discount rate, the greater the price sensitivity of most assets to a change in that rate.

6.  Duration is a measure of price sensitivity that incorporates maturity, coupon, and level of yield; it provides an approximation of the percentage price change for small changes in yield.

## SUMMARY

In this chapter we have introduced some key properties of financial assets: moneyness, divisibility and denomination, reversibility, cash flow, term to maturity, convertibility, currency, liquidity, return predictability or risk, complexity, and tax status. These properties, which determine much of an asset's appeal and value to different classes of investors, are discussed in greater detail in later chapters. Further, we have illustrated how various properties fit into the theory and practice of pricing assets. We presented a number of illustrations of the way to compute the prices of assets. The illustrations rely on the basic financial principle that price is the present value of expected future cash flows and that the discount rate contains rewards for various features of the asset. Many properties, such as risk of default or term to maturity, influence prices through the required rate of return, which is inversely related to price. Other properties, such as reversibility and tax status, may affect the price of an asset through its expected cash flow.

Because it is so important to contemporary finance and to much of the material in this book, we decided that this first chapter on prices was the right place to introduce the concept of "complexity" in financial assets. Many assets contain "rights," which are, in fact, options for issuers or buyers to do something important with the assets. Options are valuable, and they affect the price of the assets that carry them. Later chapters provide extensive and detailed developments of the theme and notion of complexity.

The price of a financial asset will change in the opposite direction of the change in the discount rate or required yield. There are two characteristics of a financial asset that affect its price sensitivity: maturity and coupon rate (in the case of a bond). All other factors constant, the longer the maturity of a financial asset, the greater its price sensitivity to a change in the required yield. All other factors constant, the lower the coupon rate, the greater the price sensitivity to a change in the required yield. The level of interest rates or yields is another factor that affects price sensitivity to interest rate changes: the lower the yield level, the greater the price sensitivity.

Duration is a measure of the approximate price sensitivity of a financial asset to interest rate changes. In general, duration is the approximate percentage price sensitivity of a financial asset to a 100 basis point change in interest rates around some initial level of required yield.

G L O S S A R Y

**Basis point:** A term in the financial markets for one one-hundredth (or one percent) of one percentage point.

**Bid–ask spread:** The element in the cost of buying and selling an asset that arises because of the role played by dealers or "market makers" in purchase and sale.

**Broker's commission:** The fee charged by an intermediary in a transaction of buying or selling a security.

**Call provision:** Entitles the debtor to repay in advance, usually at some penalty and only after a number of years from the time of issuance.

**Complexity:** The property of an asset that represents a combination of two or more simpler assets.

**Convertibility:** Provision of a security's contract that allows the owner to convert it into another security or another type of security.

**Coupon rate:** The percentage of the principal that is a bond's contractual yearly payment, which is the yearly coupon.

**Currency:** The type of nominal monetary unit in which an asset is denominated and its payments are made.

**Default risk premium:** The portion of the required rate of return that compensates the investor for the prospect that the issuer of a security may not make all promised payments.

**Discount rate:** The expected or required return according to which the value of an asset's expected cash flow is determined.

**Divisibility:** The property of an asset that allows it to be divided into small units.

**Duration:** A measure of the percentage change in the price of a bond for a given change in the level of the bond's discount rate.

**Exchange rate premium:** The portion of the required rate of return that compensates an investor for the perceived volatility of the rate of exchange between the home currency and the currency in which an asset's cash flows are denominated.

**Inflation premium:** The portion of the required rate of return that compensates the investor for expected change in the purchasing power of the monetary units in which the cash flows of an asset are denominated.

**Liquidity premium:** The portion of the required rate of return that compensates the investor for the perceived difficulty and cost of selling the asset in the future.

**Market maker:** Also called a "dealer," this institution or individual facilitates trading in an asset by standing ready to buy or sell an asset, holding the asset in inventory, and making a profit on the difference between the two prices.

**Maturity premium:** The portion of the required rate of return that compensates the investor for the price volatility of debt securities of long lives.

**Moneyness:** The property that allows an asset to function as money, which means that it is a medium of exchange and a store of value.

**Nominal return:** The return computed on the basis of nominal monetary units whose possibly different purchasing power is not considered.

**Perpetual:** An asset (also called a "consul") that promises to pay a fixed amount per year indefinitely and not to repay the principal at any time.

**Predictability:** The risk that an asset's value will change over the life of an investment or the uncertainty about the return the asset will generate over that time.

**Present value:** The amount of money that, if invested at a given interest rate, will generate a particular set of future cash flows.

**Put option:** Provision in a loan or debt security that allows the investor to demand early repayment of the security's principal.

**Putable bond:** A bond that the holder can sell back to the issuer at a fixed price.

**Real rate of interest:** The expected or required annual rate of return that rewards the investor for waiting or for time.

**Real return:** The return computed on the basis of nominal monetary units adjusted for differences in purchasing power that may have developed over the life of the investment.

**Reversibility:** The property of the costs of buying and selling an asset that determines how quickly an investor can buy it and turn it back into cash.

**Tax status:** The exposure of gains or payments from an asset to taxation by various governmental units.

**Term to maturity:** Also called "maturity," this is the time remaining in the planned life of a security.

**Thickness:** A term referring to the frequency of transactions in a particular asset.

**Thin market:** Describes a market where an asset is the subject of few trades on a regular or continuing basis.

**Turnaround cost:** Also called the "round-trip cost," this is the total cost of buying and later selling an asset.

**Yield:** The annual percentage return on a debt security.

**Zero-coupon bond:** A bond that makes only one cash payment, and that is the face or par value, which is paid at maturity.

## APPENDIX: REVIEW OF PRESENT VALUE

In the body of this chapter, we explained that the price or value of any financial asset is equal to the present value of the expected cash flow. The purpose of this appendix is to review how the present value of some amount of money to be received in the future is determined.

We begin by looking at how much some amount of money invested today will grow in the future. The formula to determine the future value of an amount invested today and earning some annual interest rate is:

$$\text{Future value} = \text{Amount invested } (1 + \text{Interest rate})^n$$

where $n$ is the number of years that the amount will be invested.

For example, if $142.60 is invested today for five years, and the interest rate that can be earned on that investment is 7%, then the future value is:

$$\text{Future value} = \$142.60 \ (1.07)^5$$
$$= \$200$$

Now we can illustrate how to work the process in reverse; that is, given the future value of an investment, we will illustrate how to determine the amount that must be invested today in order to realize that future value. The amount of money that must be invested today is called the *present value*.

The present value can be determined by solving the future value formula for the amount to be invested:

$$\text{Amount invested} = \frac{\text{Future value}}{(1 + \text{Interest rate})^n}$$

But the amount invested is the present value, so we can rewrite the above formula as

$$\text{Present value} = \frac{\text{Future value}}{(1 + \text{Interest rate})^n}$$

For example, suppose that $200 will be received five years from now and that an investor can earn 7% a year on any amount invested today. The present value is then:

$$\text{Present value} = \frac{\$200}{(1.07)^5}$$
$$= \$142.50$$

If the interest rate that could be earned is 10% rather than 7%, then the present value of $200 is:

$$\text{Present value} = \frac{\$200}{(1.10)^5}$$
$$= \$124.18$$

There are two properties of the present value that should be understood. First, the higher the interest rate that can be earned, the lower the present value. Our examples show this: when the interest rate is 7%, the present value of $200 five years from now is $142.50, but it is $124.18 if the interest rate is 10%. In the present value calculation, the interest rate is called the *discount rate*. The second property is that the farther in the future a cash flow is to be received, the lower is its present value.

Thus far we have calculated the present value of a single cash flow to be received in the future. Most financial assets will generate more than one cash flow in the future. To calculate the present value of any cash flow stream, the present value of each cash flow is calculated and then all the values are summed. In the table below, a cash flow stream is shown in the second column. The present value for each of these cash flows is shown for three discount rates (7%, 10%, and 4%). The present value of $1 shown in the table is equal to:

$$\text{Present value of } \$1 = \frac{\$1}{(1 + \text{Interest rate})^n}$$

The product of the cash flow for any year and the present value of $1 at a given discount rate is the present value of the cash flow for that year. The total present value for the cash flow, for each discount rate, is shown in the last line of the table. As can be seen, the higher the discount rate, the lower the present value.

| Year | Cash Flow | PV of $1 @ 7% | PV of CF | PV of $1@ 10% | PV of CF | PV of $1 @ 4% | PV of CF |
|------|-----------|---------------|----------|---------------|----------|---------------|----------|
| 1 | 30 | 0.9346 | 28.04 | 0.9091 | 27.27 | 0.9615 | 28.85 |
| 2 | 75 | 0.8734 | 65.51 | 0.8264 | 61.98 | 0.9246 | 69.34 |
| 3 | 120 | 0.8163 | 97.96 | 0.7513 | 90.16 | 0.8890 | 106.68 |
| 4 | 140 | 0.7629 | 106.81 | 0.6830 | 95.62 | 0.8548 | 119.67 |
| 5 | 200 | 0.7130 | 142.60 | 0.6209 | 124.18 | 0.8219 | 164.39 |
| 6 | 250 | 0.6663 | 166.59 | 0.5645 | 141.12 | 0.7903 | 197.58 |
| 7 | 300 | 0.6227 | 186.82 | 0.5132 | 153.95 | 0.7599 | 227.98 |
| Total present value | | | 794.31 | | 694.29 | | 914.48 |

**QUESTIONS**

1. Your broker is recommending that you purchase U.S. government bonds. Here is the explanation:

   *Listen, in these times of uncertainty, with many companies going bankrupt, it makes sense to play it safe and purchase long-term government bonds. They're issued by the U.S. government, so they are risk-free.*

   How would you respond to the broker?

2. You just inherited 30,000 shares of a company you have never heard of, ABC Corporation. You call your broker to find out if you have finally struck it rich. After several minutes she comes back on the telephone and says: "I don't have a clue about these shares. It's too bad they are not traded in a financial market. That would make life a lot easier for you." What does she mean by this?

3. Suppose you own a bond that pays $75 yearly in coupon interest and that is likely to be called in two years (because the firm has already announced that it will redeem the issue early). The call price will be $1,050. What is the price of your bond now, in the market, if the appropriate discount rate for this asset is 9%?

4. Your broker has advised you to buy shares of Hungry Boy Fast Foods, which has paid a dividend of $1.00 per year for ten years and will (according to the broker) continue to do so for many years. The broker believes that the stock, which now has a price of $12, will be worth $25 per share in five years. You have good reason to think that the discount rate for this firm's stock is 22% per year, because that rate compensates the buyer for all pertinent risk. Is the stock's present price a good approximation of its true financial value?

5. You have been considering a zero-coupon bond, which pays no interest but will pay a principal of $1,000 at the end of five years. The price of the bond is now $712.99, and its required rate of return is 7.0%. This morning's news contained a surprising development: the government announced that the rate of inflation appears to be 5.5% instead of the 4% that most people had been expecting. (Obviously, most people had thought the real rate of interest was 3%.) What would be the price of the bond, once the market began to absorb this new information about inflation?

6. State the difference in basis points between each of the following:
   a. 5.5% and 6.5%
   b. 7% and 9%
   c. 6.4% and 7.8%
   d. 9.1% and 11.9%

7. a. Does a rise of 100 basis points in the discount rate change the price of a 20-year bond as much as it changes the price of a 4-year bond, assuming that both bonds have the same coupon rate?

   b. Does a rise of 100 basis points in the discount rate change the price of a 4% coupon bond as much as it changes the price of a 10% coupon bond, assuming that both bonds have the same maturity?

   c. Does a rise of 100 basis points in the discount rate change the price of a ten-year bond to the same extent if the discount rate is 4% as it does if the discount rate is 12%?

8. During the early 1980s, interest rates for many long-term bonds were above 14%. In the early 1990s, rates on similar bonds have been far lower. What do you think this dramatic decline in market interest

rates means for the price volatility of bonds in response to a change in interest rates?

9.  a.  What is the cash flow of a 6% coupon bond that pays interest annually, matures in seven years, and has a principal of $1,000?

    b.  Assuming a discount rate of 8%, what is the price of this bond?

    c.  Assuming a discount rate of 8.5%, what is the price of this bond?

    d.  Assuming a discount rate of 7.5%, what is the price of this bond?

    e.  What is the duration of this bond, assuming that the price is the one you calculated in part (b)?

    f.  If the yield changes by 100 basis points, from 8% to 7%, by how much would you approximate the percentage price change to be using your estimate of duration in part (e)?

    g.  What is the actual percentage price change if the yield changes by 100 basis points?

# CHAPTER ELEVEN

# The Level and Structure of Interest Rates

*After reading this chapter you will understand:*

- Fisher's classical approach to explaining the level of the interest rate.

- the role in Fisher's theory of the saver's time preference and the borrowing firm's productivity of capital.

- the meaning of equilibrium and how changes in the demand and supply function affect the equilibrium level of the interest rate.

- the structure of Fisher's Law, which states that the nominal and observable interest rate is composed of two unobservable variables; the real rate of interest and the premium for expected inflation.

- the loanable funds theory, which is an expansion of Fisher's theory.

- the meaning of liquidity preference in Keynes's theory of the determination of interest rates.

- how an increase in the money supply can affect the level of the interest rate through an impact on liquidity, income, and price expectations.

- the features of a bond issue.

- how the yield to maturity of a bond is calculated.
- why the yield on a Treasury security is the base interest rate.
- the different types of bonds.
- what factors affect the yield spread between two bonds.

In this chapter, we deal with two issues. The first is the theory of interest rate determination, and our discussion focuses on the general level of the interest rate in an economy. Second, we explain how interest rates function in the pricing of bonds. That explanation leads to consideration of the many different interest rates that an economy presents a borrower or an investor. We show how the rates are related to one another and to key features of bonds and economic conditions.

## THE THEORY OF INTEREST RATES

An interest rate is the price paid by a "borrower" (or "debtor") to a "lender" (or "creditor") for the use of resources during some interval. The amount of the loan is the *principal*, and the price paid is typically expressed as a percentage of the principal per unit of time (generally, a year). In this section, we present the two most influential theories of the determination of the interest rate: Fisher's theory, which underlies the loanable funds theory, and Keynes's liquidity preference theory.

We focus first on the interest rate that provides the anchor for other rates, namely, the short-term, risk-free, real rate. By the *real rate*, we mean the rate that would prevail in the economy if the average prices for goods and services were expected to remain constant during the loan's life. By the *risk-free rate*, we mean the rate on a loan whose borrower will not default on any obligation. By *short-term*, we mean the rate on a loan that has one year to maturity. All other interest rates differ from this rate according to particular aspects of the loan, such as its maturity or risk of default, or because of the presence of inflation.

### Fisher's Classical Approach

Irving Fisher analyzed the determination of the level of the interest rate in an economy by inquiring why people save (that is, why they do not consume all their resources) and why others borrow.[1] Here, we outline his theory in the context of a very simplified economy. That economy contains only individuals who consume and save with their current income, firms that borrow unconsumed income in loans and invest, a market where savers make loans of resources to borrowers, and projects in which firms invest. The interest rate

---

[1] Irving Fisher, *The Theory of Interest Rates* (New York: Macmillan, 1930).

on loans embodies no premium for default risk because borrowing firms are assumed to meet all obligations. (The prospect of inflation and its impact on the interest rate will be discussed in short order.)

***Decisions on Saving and Borrowing.*** Saving is the choice between current and future consumption of goods and services. Individuals save some of their current income in order to be able to consume more in the future. A chief influence on the saving decision is the individual's *marginal rate of time preference*, which is the willingness to trade some consumption now for more future consumption. Individuals differ in their time preferences. Some people may have a rate of time preference that leads them to forego current consumption for an increase of 10% in their future consumption, while others might save only if their future consumption possibilities rise by 20%.

Another influence on the saving decision is *income*. Generally, higher current income means the person will save more, although people with the same income may have different time preferences. The third variable affecting savings is the *reward for saving*, or the rate of interest on loans that savers make with their unconsumed income. Interest is what borrowers pay for the loans, and it makes greater future consumption possible. As the interest rate rises, each person becomes willing to save more, given that person's rate of time preference.

This description of the savings decision applies to all the people in the economy. The total savings (or the total supply of loans) available at any time is the sum of everybody's savings and a positive function of the interest rate. The relationship between total savings and the interest rate is graphed as the upward sloping supply function, *S*, in Figure 11-1, which relates the amount

## FIGURE 11-1

EQUILIBRIUM IN THE MARKET FOR SAVINGS

of savings/investment on the horizontal axis to the interest rate on the vertical axis.[2]

There can be no reward for savings if there is no demand for borrowed resources, because someone must pay the interest. In our simple economy, firms do all the borrowing, and they borrow from savers in order to invest. Investment means directing resources to assets that will increase the firms' future capacity to produce. An important influence on the borrowing decision is the *gain from investment*, which is the positive difference between the resources used by a process and the total resources it will produce in the future. The gain is not constant, at any one time, across all possible projects and levels of total investment. The reason is that, at any time, only a certain number of projects are available, some offering high gains, others promising moderate gains, and still others yielding low gains. Firms will direct borrowed resources to projects in order of their profitability, starting with the most profitable and proceeding to those with lower gains. The gain from additional projects, as investment increases, is the *marginal productivity of capital*, which is negatively related to the amount of investment. In other words, as the amount of investment grows, additional gains necessarily fall, as more of the less profitable projects are accepted.

The maximum that a firm will invest depends on the *rate of interest*, which is the cost of loans. The firm will invest only as long as the marginal productivity of capital exceeds or equals the rate of interest. In other words, firms will accept only projects whose gain is not less than their cost of financing. Thus, the firm's demand for borrowing is negatively related to the interest rate. If the rate is high, only limited borrowing and investment make sense. At a low rate, more projects offer a profit, and the firm wants to borrow more. This negative relationship exists for each and all firms in the economy. The economy's total demand for borrowed resources (or loans of unconsumed income), as a function of the interest rate, appears as the downward-sloping line labeled $D$ in Figure 11-1.

***Equilibrium in the Market.***   The equilibrium rate of interest is determined by interaction of the supply and demand functions. As a cost of borrowing and a reward for lending, the rate must reach the point where total supply of savings equals total demand for borrowing and investment. Figure 11-1 shows that this equilibrium rate of interest, labeled $i$, occurs at the intersection of the demand and supply curves, $D$ and $S$. The equilibrium level of savings (which is the same as the equilibrium level of borrowing and investment) is given as $SI$. Clearly, Fisher's theory emphasizes that the long-run level of the interest rate and the amount of investment depend on a society's propensity to save and on technological development.

---

[2] For a more extensive analysis of the supply of savings, including the reason why the supply can reach negative levels and the reason why the supply curve can itself turn negative, see Frank J. Fabozzi and Franco Modigliani, *Capital Markets: Institutions and Instruments* (Englewood Cliffs, N.J.: Prentice Hall, 1992), p. 338ff.

Let us now consider the effects of a sudden increase in technological capability, which makes production cheaper. With no change in any other relevant variable, lower production costs mean more gain on investments and a higher marginal productivity of capital. The resulting increase in firms' desired investment and borrowing through loans, at any level of the interest rate, is actually an upward shift in the demand function, as shown in Figure 11-2. That shift (from $D$ to $D^*$) prompts a rise in the equilibrium interest rate, from $i$ to $i^*$, and an increase in equilibrium borrowing and investment from $SI$ to $SI^*$.

Now consider circumstances where individuals suddenly grow more willing to save, which amounts to a fall in the marginal rate of time preference. (All other economic considerations stay the same.) As Figure 11-3 depicts this change, the supply of loans function would shift downward (from $S$ to $S^*$), and savings would be higher at every level of the interest rate. The equilibrium interest rate would also fall, from $i$ to $i^*$. Total investment would rise, from $SI$ to $SI^*$, as firms would get more funds and more projects would be profitable, at any interest rate.

***The Real Rate and the Nominal Rate.***   It is useful here to consider the distinction between the *nominal rate of interest* and the *real rate of interest*. The real rate is the growth in the power to consume over the life of a loan. The nominal rate of interest, by contrast, is the number of monetary units to be paid per unit borrowed, and is, in fact, the observable market rate on a loan. In the absence of inflation, the nominal rate equals the real rate. Because we assume in our discussion that the purchasing power of the monetary units in a loan stays the same over the loan's life, the equilibrium interest rate we have discussed is both the nominal and the real rate of interest.

## FIGURE 11-2

### THE RESULTS OF A SHIFT IN THE DEMAND FOR SAVINGS

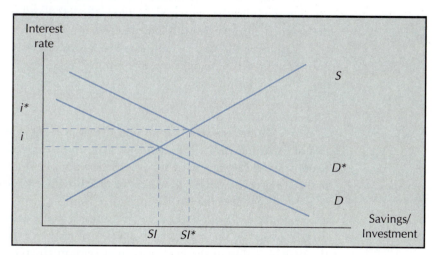

FIGURE 11-3

THE RESULT OF A SHIFT IN THE SUPPLY OF SAVINGS

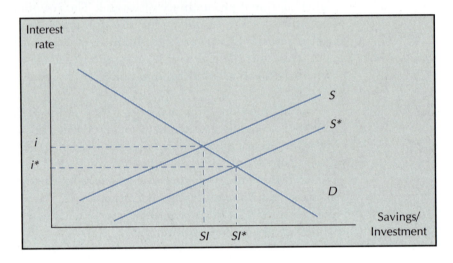

In the presence of inflation, however, the nominal rate is different from, and must exceed, the real rate. The reason is that savers demand a premium above the real rate as compensation for the expected loss in the purchasing power of their interest and principal. The relationship between inflation and interest rates is the well-known *Fisher's Law*, which can be expressed this way:

$$(1 + i) = (1 + r)\times(1 + p), \tag{1}$$

where $i$ is the nominal rate, $r$ is the real rate, and $p$ is the expected percentage change in the price level of goods and services over the loan's life. Equation (1) shows that the nominal rate, $i$, reflects both the real rate and expected inflation. Also, the compensation demanded by savers applies to both the interest payment and the principal, because the left-hand side variable is 100% plus the interest rate, or the full loan plus its interest.

Equation (1) can be simplified to a formula that appeared in Chapter 10 and, in most circumstances, approximates equation (1) closely enough:

$$i = r + p. \tag{2}$$

The only quantities from equation (1) not present in equation (2) are the values of 1, which cancel one another out, and the product of $r$ and $p$, which is usually small enough to be ignored. For example, if the real rate is 3% or 0.03, and the expected inflation rate is 5% or 0.05, their product equals only 0.0015, or 0.15 of 1%. It is important to realize that the expected rate of inflation and the real rate are not observable. With fairly good estimates of expected inflation, $p$, it is possible to get a reasonable estimate of $r$ from the nominal rate, but the precise value of the real rate must remain elusive.

## The Loanable Funds Theory

Fisher's theory is a general one and obviously neglects certain practical matters, such as the power of the government (in concert with depository institutions) to create money and the government's often large demand for borrowed funds, which is frequently immune to the level of the interest rate. Also, Fisher's theory does not consider the possibility that individuals and firms might invest in cash balances. Expanding Fisher's theory to encompass these situations produces *the loanable funds theory of interest rates.*

This theory proposes that the general level of interest rates is determined by the complex interaction of two forces. The first is the total demand for funds by firms, governments, and households (or individuals), which carry out a variety of economic activities with those funds. This demand is negatively related to the interest rate (except for the government's demand, which may frequently not depend on the level of the interest rate). If income and other variables do not change, then an increase in the interest rate will reduce the demand for borrowing on the part of many firms and individuals, as projects become less profitable, and consumption and holding cash grow more costly. The second force affecting the level of the interest rate is the total supply of funds by firms, governments, banks, and individuals. Supply is positively related to the level of interest rates, if all other economic factors remain the same. With rising rates, firms and individuals save and lend more, and banks are more eager to extend more loans. (A rising interest rate probably does not significantly affect the government's supply of savings.)

In an equilibrium situation much like that depicted in Figure 11-1, the intersection of the supply and demand functions sets the interest rate level and the level of loans. In equilibrium, the demand for funds equals the supply of funds. This means that all agents are borrowing what they want, investing to the desired extent, and holding all the money they wish to hold. In other words, equilibrium extends through the money market, the bond market, and the market for investment assets.

As in Fisher's theory, shifts in the demand and supply curves may occur for many reasons: changes in the money supply, government deficits, changed preferences by individuals, new investment opportunities, and so on. These shifts affect the equilibrium level of the interest rate and of investment in predictable ways. Finally, the expectation of inflation can affect the equilibrium rate through the supply of funds curve, as savers demand higher rates (because of inflation) for any level of savings. Note that this analysis has excluded the question of default on loans: the rate discussed is the risk-free rate, either in its real or nominal form.

## The Liquidity Preference Theory

The liquidity preference theory, originally developed by John Maynard Keynes,[3] analyzes the equilibrium level of the interest rate through the in-

---

[3] John Maynard Keynes, *The General Theory of Employment, Interest and Money* (New York: Harcourt, Brace & World, 1936).

teraction of the supply of money and the public's aggregate demand for holding money. Keynes assumed that most people hold wealth in only two forms: "money" and "bonds." For Keynes, money is equivalent to currency and demand deposits, which pay little or no interest but are liquid and may be used for immediate transactions. Bonds represent a broad Keynesian category and include long-term, interest-paying financial assets that are not liquid and that pose some risk because their prices vary inversely with the interest rate level. Bonds may be liabilities of governments or firms. (Default risk is not considered here, and the rate is the risk-free rate, in real or nominal form.)

***Demand, Supply, and Equilibrium.***   The public (consisting of individuals and firms) holds money for several reasons: ease of transactions, precaution against unexpected events, and speculation about possible rises in the interest rate. Although money pays no interest, the demand for money is a negative function of the interest rate. At a low rate, people hold a lot of money because they do not lose much interest by doing so and because the risk of a rise in rates (and a fall in the value of bonds) may be large. With a high interest rate, people desire to hold bonds rather than money, because the cost of liquidity is substantial in terms of lost interest payments and because a decline in the interest rate would lead to gains in the bonds' values. The negative linkage between the interest rate and the demand for money appears as curve $D$ in Figure 11-4, which relates the interest rate to the amount of money in the economy, given the level of income and expected price inflation.

For Keynes, the supply of money is fully under the control of the central bank (which is the Fed in the United States). Moreover, the money supply is not affected by the level of the interest rate. (Recall the discussion in Chapter 5 about the positive link between the interest rate and the growth in the money supply.) Thus, the supply of money appears, in Figure 11-4, as the vertical line,

## FIGURE 11-4

EQUILIBRIUM IN KEYNES'S MARKET FOR MONEY

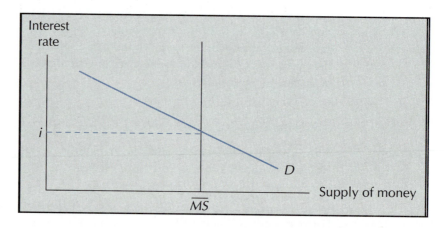

$\overline{MS}$, and the line above the *'MS'* indicates a quantity not varying with the interest rate. Equilibrium in the money market requires, of course, that the total demand for money equals total supply. In Figure 11-4, equilibrium implies an interest rate of *i*. Further, equilibrium in the money market implies the equilibrium of the bond market.

***Shifts in the Rate of Interest.*** The equilibrium rate of interest can change if there is a change in any variable affecting the demand or supply curves. On the demand side, Keynes recognized the importance of two such variables: the level of income and the level of prices for goods and services. A rise in income (with no other variable changing) raises the value of money's liquidity and shifts the demand curve to the right, increasing the equilibrium interest rate. Because people want to hold amounts of "real money," or monetary units of specific purchasing power, a change in expected inflation would also shift the demand curve to the right and raise the level of interest.

The money supply curve can shift, in Keynes's view, only by actions of the central bank. The central bank's power over interest rates arises because of its ability to buy and sell securities (open market operations), which can alter the amount of money available in the economy. Generally, Keynes thought that an increase in the money supply would, by shifting the supply curve to the right, bring about a decline in the equilibrium interest rate. Similarly, he reasoned that a reduction in the money supply would raise rates. As we note in Chapter 6, however, there is now widespread recognition that the question of linkage between the money supply and the level of the interest rate is rather more complex than that.

## Changes in the Money Supply and Interest Rates

In Chapter 6, we provide a general account of how changes in the money supply affect the level of interest rates. Now, we can discuss the matter in more detail, because the Keynesian money demand model that we just developed is a particularly useful framework for analyzing the relationship between the money supply and the level of the interest rate.

A change in the money supply has three different effects upon the level of the interest rate: the "liquidity effect," the "income effect," and the "price expectations effect." These effects do not usually occur in a simultaneous manner but rather tend to be spread out over some time period following the change in the money supply. These effects move rates in different ways and to different extents. One effect may even cancel or overwhelm an earlier effect. The final magnitude and direction of the impact of a change in the money supply depends on the economy's level of output and employment.

***Liquidity Effect.*** This effect represents the initial reaction of the interest rate to a change in the money supply. With an increase in the money supply, the initial reaction should be a fall in the rate. The reason for the fall is that a rise in the money supply represents a shift in the supply curve. For example, let us suppose that (in the United States) the Fed increases the supply of money by buying bonds, raising excess reserves, and allowing banks to offer more loans. With demand unchanging, the increase in the money supply amounts to a rightward shift of the supply and causes a fall in the equilibrium interest rate, from $i$ to $i^*$. Figure 11-5 depicts the rise in the money supply (from $\overline{MS}$ to $\overline{MS}^*$) and the decline in the interest rate from $i$ to $i^*$. (A decrease in the money supply would cause the supply of money function to shift to the left and the liquidity effect of an initial rise in the interest rate.)

***Income Effect.***   It is well known that changes in the money supply affect the economy. A decline in the supply would tend to cause a contraction. An increase in the money supply, generally speaking, is economically expansionary: more loans are available and extended, more people are hired or work longer, and consumers and producers purchase more goods and services. Thus, money supply changes can cause income in the system to vary. Let us focus on an increase in the money supply, which raises income. Because the demand for money is a function of income, a rise in income shifts the demand function and increases the amount of money that the public will want to hold at any level of the interest rate. Figure 11-6 depicts the income effect by indicating that the shift of the demand function to the right, brought on by the increase in the money supply, causes a rise in the equilibrium interest rate.

No empirical data or economic theory can predict whether the income effect of a money supply increase will override its liquidity effect, or if so, after what interval of time. Under most circumstances, the income effect is likely to reverse some of the liquidity effect. But, the relative magnitude of these two effects depends greatly on the state of the economy at the time the money supply changes.

***Price Expectations Effect.***   Although an increase in the money supply is an economically expansionary policy, the resultant increase in income depends

FIGURE   11 - 5

THE LIQUIDITY EFFECT OF AN INCREASE IN THE MONEY SUPPLY

## THE INCOME EFFECT OF A CHANGE IN THE MONEY SUPPLY

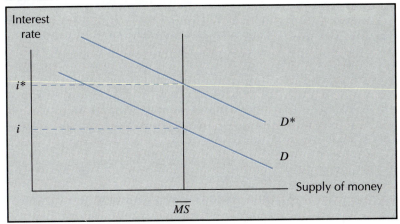

substantially on the amount of slack in the economy at the time of the Fed's action. Chapter 6 addressed this issue: if the economy is operating at less than full strength, an increase in the money supply can stimulate production, employment, and output; if the economy is producing all or almost all of the goods and services it can (given the size of the population and the amount of capital goods), then an increase in the money supply will largely stimulate expectations of a rising level of prices for goods and services. Thus, the price expectations effect usually occurs only if the money supply grows in a time of high output.

Because the price level (and expectations regarding its changes) affects the money demand function, the price expectations effect is an increase in the interest rate. That increase occurs because the demand for money balances shifts upward. This positive effect moves the interest rate in the same direction as the income effect, and in the opposite direction of the liquidity effect. (Of course, in a time of inflation, a reduction in the rate of growth in the money supply might dampen inflationary expectations and shift the demand curve to the left, leading to declines in the interest rate.)

There is no general guide to the relative size of the price expectations effect: it may be great enough to overwhelm the liquidity effect, or it may cancel only part of it. The magnitude of the income effect depends upon how much of the economy's productive capacity it is utilizing when the money supply rises.

▶ KEY POINTS THAT YOU SHOULD UNDERSTAND BEFORE PROCEEDING:

1.  Interest is the price paid for the temporary use of resources, and the amount of a loan is its principal.

2.  Fisher's theory of interest analyzes the equilibrium level of the interest rate as the result of the interaction of savers' willingness to save and borrowers' demand for investment funds.

3.  In Fisher's terms, the interest rate reflects the interaction of the savers' marginal rate of time preference and borrowers' marginal productivity of capital.

4.  Fisher's Law states that the observable nominal rate of interest is composed of two unobservable variables: the real rate of interest and the premium for expected inflation.

5.  The loanable funds theory is an extension of Fisher's theory and proposes that the equilibrium rate of interest reflects the demand and supply of funds, which depend on savers' willingness to save, borrowers' expectations regarding the profitability of investing, and the government's action regarding money supply.

6.  The liquidity preference theory is Keynes's view that the rate of interest is set in the market for money balances.

7.  The demand for money, in this theory, reflects the liquidity of money by comparison with long-term financial instruments and depends on the interest rate, income, and the price level.

8.  Changes in the money supply can affect the level of interest rates through the liquidity effect, the income effect, and the price expectations effect; their relative magnitudes depend upon the level of economic activity at the time of the change in the money supply.

## THE DETERMINANTS OF THE STRUCTURE OF INTEREST RATES

There is not one interest rate in any economy. Rather, there is a structure of interest rates. The interest rate that a borrower will have to pay will depend on a myriad of factors. While we describe these various factors, in the process, we provide an overview of the fixed-income instruments that we examine in much more detail in later chapters. We begin with a basic description of a bond.

### *Features of a Bond*

A bond is an instrument in which the issuer (debtor/borrower) promises to repay to the lender/investor the amount borrowed plus interest over some specified period of time. The *term to maturity* of a bond is the number of years during which the issuer has promised to meet the conditions of the obligation. The *maturity* of a bond refers to the day the debt will cease to exist and the day the issuer will redeem the bond by paying the amount owed. The practice in the bond market, however, is to refer to the "term to maturity" of a bond as simply its "maturity" or "term." As we explain below, there may be provisions that allow either the issuer or bondholder to alter a bond's term to maturity.

The *principal value* (or simply "principal") of a bond is the amount that the issuer agrees to repay the bondholder at the maturity date. This amount is also referred to as the *par value, maturity value, redemption value,* or *face value.*

The *coupon rate* is the interest rate that the issuer agrees to pay each year. The annual amount of the interest payment made to owners during the term of the bond is called the *coupon.* The coupon rate when multiplied by the principal of the bond provides the dollar amount of the coupon. For example, a bond with an 8% coupon rate and a principal of $1,000 will pay annual interest of $80. In the United States and Japan, the usual practice is for the issuer to pay the coupon in two equal semi-annual installments. In contrast, bonds issued in most European bond markets and the Eurobond market make coupon payments only once per year.

## Yield on a Bond

The yield on a bond investment should reflect the coupon interest that will be earned plus either (1) any capital gain that will be realized from holding the bond to maturity, or (2) any capital loss that will be realized from holding the bond to maturity. For example, if a four-year bond with a coupon rate of 5% and a par value of $1,000 is selling for $900.64, the yield should reflect the coupon interest of $50 (5% times $1,000) every year plus the capital gain of $99.36 ($1,000 minus $900.64) when the bond is redeemed at maturity. Moreover, the yield should also reflect the time value of money by considering the timing of the various payments associated with the bond.

The *yield to maturity* is a formal, widely accepted measure of the rate of return on a bond. As typically defined, the yield to maturity of a bond takes into account the coupon interest and any capital gain or loss, if the bond were to be held to maturity. The yield to maturity is defined as the interest rate that makes the present value of the cash flow of a bond equal to the bond's market price. In mathematical notation, the yield to maturity, $y$, is found by solving the following equation for $y$:

$$P = \frac{C}{(1+y)^1} + \frac{C}{(1+y)^2} + \frac{C}{(1+y)^3} + \ldots + \frac{C+M}{(1+y)^n}$$

where
$P$ = market price of bond
$C$ = coupon interest
$M$ = maturity value
$n$ = time to maturity.

The yield to maturity is determined by a trial-and-error process. Even the algorithm in a calculator or computer program, which computes the yield to maturity (or "internal rate of return") in an apparently direct way, uses a trial-and-error process. The steps in that process are as follows:
*Step 1:* Select an interest rate.
*Step 2:* Compute the present value of each cash flow using the interest rate selected in Step 1.

*Step 3:*   Total the present value of the cash flows found in Step 2.

*Step 4:*   Compare the total present value found in Step 3 with the market price of the bond and, if the total present value of the cash flows found in Step 3 is:

- equal to the market price, then the interest rate used in Step 1 is the yield to maturity;
- greater than the market price, then the interest rate is not the yield to maturity. Therefore go back to Step 1 and use a higher interest rate;
- less than the market price, then the interest rate is not the yield to maturity. Therefore go back to Step 1 and use a lower interest rate.

For example, suppose that a four-year bond that pays interest annually has a par value of $1,000, a coupon rate of 5%, and is selling in the market for $900.64. Table 11-1 shows the procedure for calculating the yield to maturity. When a 2% interest rate is tried, the total present value is equal to $1,136.52. As this value is greater than the market price of $900.64, it is not the yield to maturity, and therefore a higher interest rate must be tried. Suppose a 12% interest rate is tried. Now the total present value of $787.39 is smaller than the market price, so a lower interest rate must be tried. When an 8% interest rate is tried, the total present value is equal to the market price, so the yield to maturity is 8%.

Had the market price of this bond been $813.85 rather than $900.64, the yield to maturity would be 11%. Notice that the lower the market price, the higher the yield to maturity.

There are several interesting points about the relationship among the coupon rate, market price, and yield to maturity that can be seen in Table 11-1:

| TABLE 11-1 |
|---|

#### YIELD TO MATURITY OF AN ANNUAL PAY FOUR-YEAR BOND WITH A COUPON RATE OF 5% AND A MARKET PRICE OF $900.64

$C = \$50$   $M = \$1,000$   $P = \$900.64$   $n = 4$

| Interest Rate Tried | Total present value |
|---|---|
| 2 | 1,136.52 |
| 3 | 1,106.57 |
| 4 | 1,036.30 |
| 5 | 1,000.00 |
| 6 | 965.35 |
| 7 | 932.26 |
| 8 | 900.64 |
| 9 | 870.41 |
| 10 | 841.51 |
| 11 | 813.85 |
| 12 | 787.39 |

1. If the market price is equal to the par value, then the yield to maturity is equal to the coupon rate;
2. If the market price is less than the par value, then the yield to maturity is greater than the coupon rate, and;
3. If the market price is greater than the par value, then the yield to maturity is less than the coupon rate.

In our illustration, we assumed that coupon payments are made once per year. As noted earlier, however, the practice in the U.S. bond market is to pay coupon interest every six months. This does not affect the procedure for calculating the yield to maturity; that is, it is still the interest rate that will make the present value of the cash flow equal to the market price. The cash flow, however, is not annual. Instead, the coupon payment is every six months and is equal to one-half the annual coupon payment. The resulting yield to maturity is then a semi-annual yield to maturity. To annualize the semi-annual yield, the *convention* adopted in the bond market is to double the semi-annual yield. The resulting yield to maturity is said to be calculated on a *bond-equivalent yield basis*.

For example, consider an 18-year bond with a coupon rate of 6% and a par value of $1,000. Suppose that the bond pays interest semiannually and is selling for $700.89. The cash flow for this bond is $30 every six-months for 35 six-month periods and $1,030 36 six-month periods from now. That is:

$C = \$30$ $M = \$1,000$ and $n = 36$ (double the number of years to maturity)

Table 11-2 shows the calculation of the yield to maturity for this bond. Notice that the interest rate that makes the total present value equal to the market price of $700.89 is 4.75%. This is the semi-annual yield to maturity. Doubling this semi-annual yield gives 9.5%, which is the yield to maturity on a bond-equivalent yield basis.

### TABLE 11-2
#### YIELD TO MATURITY OF A SEMI-ANNUAL PAY 18-YEAR BOND WITH A COUPON RATE OF 6% AND A MARKET PRICE OF $700.89

$C = \$30$ $M = \$1,000$ $P = \$700.89$ $n = 36$

| Interest rate tried | Total present value |
|---|---|
| 3.25% | $947.40 |
| 3.50 | 898.54 |
| 3.75 | 853.14 |
| 4.00 | 810.92 |
| 4.25 | 771.61 |
| 4.50 | 735.01 |
| 4.75(*) | 700.89 |

(*) Semi-annual yield to maturity. Therefore, the yield to maturity on a bond-equivalent yield basis is 9.5% (2 times 4.75%)

In the discussion to follow, we will refer to the yield to maturity of a bond as simply its yield. The difference between the yield on any two bond issues is called a *yield spread*, or simply *spread*. The spread is typically measured in basis points. For example, if the yield on bond A is 9%, and the yield on bond B is 8.5%, the yield spread is 50 basis points.

## The Base Interest Rate

Now that we have examined the characteristics of a bond and how to measure the yield on a bond, we look at the structure of interest rates. In our discussion, we use the terms interest rate and yield interchangeably.

The securities issued by the United States Department of the Treasury, popularly referred to as "Treasury securities" or simply "Treasuries," are backed by the full faith and credit of the United States government. Consequently, market participants throughout the world view them as having no credit risk. Interest rates on Treasury securities therefore are the benchmark interest rates throughout the U.S. economy, as well as in international capital markets. The fact that the Treasury is the largest single issuer of debt in the world and the large size of any single issue have contributed to making the Treasury market the most active and hence the most liquid market in the world.

There are two categories of U.S. Treasury securities—discount and coupon securities. The fundamental difference between the two types lies in the form of the stream of payments that the holder receives, which in turn is reflected in the prices at which the securities are issued. Coupon securities pay interest every six months, plus principal at maturity. Discount securities pay only a contractually fixed amount at maturity. Treasury securities are typically issued on an auction basis according to regular cycles for securities of specific maturities. Current Treasury practice is to issue all securities with maturities of one year or less as discount securities. These securities are called *Treasury bills*. All securities with maturities of two years or longer are issued as *Treasury coupon securities*.

The most recently auctioned Treasury issues for each maturity are referred to as "on-the-run" or "current coupon" issues. Table 11-3 shows the on-the-run U.S. Treasury yields as of the close of business on August 27, 1992. Issues auctioned prior to the current coupon issues are typically referred to as "off-the-run" issues; they are not as liquid as on-the-run issues. For example, the yield on the off-the-run 10-year and 30-year Treasury as of August 27, 1992 was 6.68% and 7.48%, respectively. This is a higher yield than the corresponding on-the-run Treasury issue. The spread between the off-the-run and on-the-run Treasury 10-year issue is 5 basis points (6.68% minus 6.63%), and the corresponding spread for the 30-year is 6 basis points (7.48% minus 7.42%). This spread reflects the greater liquidity of the on-the-run issues.

The minimum interest rate or *base interest rate* that investors will demand for investing in a non-Treasury security is the yield offered on a comparable maturity for an on-the-run Treasury security. So, for example, if an investor wanted to purchase a ten-year bond, on August 27, 1992, the minimum yield the investor would seek is 6.63%, the on-the-run Treasury yield reported in

| TABLE 11-3 |
|:---:|
| YIELDS FOR ON-THE-RUN TREASURIES ON AUGUST 27, 1992 |

| Maturity | Yield |
|:---:|:---:|
| 3-Mo | 3.22% |
| 6-Mo | 3.33 |
| 1-Yr | 3.47 |
| 2-Yr | 4.22 |
| 3-Yr | 4.74 |
| 5-Yr | 5.65 |
| 7-Yr | 6.18 |
| 10-Yr | 6.63 |
| 20-Yr | 7.02 |
| 30-Yr | 7.42 |

Source: *Weekly Market Update*, Goldman Sachs & Co., Fixed Income Research, August 28, 1992, p. A-1.

Table 11-3. The base interest rate is also referred to as the *benchmark interest rate*.

## The Risk Premium

Market participants talk of interest rates on non-Treasury securities as "trading at a spread" to a particular on-the-run Treasury security. For example, if the yield on a ten-year non-Treasury security is 9% and the yield on a ten-year Treasury security is 8%, the spread is 100 basis points. This spread reflects the additional risks the investor faces by acquiring a security that is not issued by the U.S. government and therefore can be called a *risk premium*. Thus, we can express the interest rate offered on a non-Treasury security as:

base interest rate + spread

or equivalently,

base interest rate + risk premium

The factors that affect the spread include: (1) the type of issuer; (2) the issuer's perceived creditworthiness; (3) the term or maturity of the instrument; (4) provisions that grant either the issuer or the investor the option to do something; (5) the taxability of the interest received by investors; and (6) the expected liquidity of the issue. Notice that these factors are the ones that we discussed in the previous chapter as affecting the price of a security.

***Types of Issuers.*** A key feature of a debt obligation is the nature of the issuer. In addition to the U.S. government, there are agencies of the U.S. government, municipal governments, corporations (domestic and foreign), and foreign governments that issue bonds.

The bond market is classified by the type of issuer, and groups of securities of the various kinds of issuers are referred to as *market sectors*. The spread between the interest rates offered in two sectors of the bond market on obligations with the same maturity is referred to as an *intermarket sector spread*.

Excluding the Treasury market sector, the other market sectors include a wide range of issuers, each with different abilities to satisfy their contractual obligations. For example, within the corporate market sector, issuers are classified as follows: (1) utilities; (2) transportations; (3) industrials; and (4) banks and finance companies. The spread between two issues within a market sector is called an *intramarket sector spread*. For example, for the week of August 27, 1992, the yield on five-year industrial corporate bonds and five-year utility corporate bonds with the same credit rating was 5.85% and 5.79%, respectively.[4] Therefore, the intramarket sector spread was 6 basis points.

***Perceived Creditworthiness of Issuer.***   Default risk or credit risk refers to the risk that the issuer of a bond may be unable to make timely principal or interest payments. Most market participants rely primarily on commercial rating companies to assess the default risk of an issuer. These companies perform credit analyses and express their conclusions by a system of ratings. The five commercial rating companies in the United States are (1) Moody's Investors Service, (2) Standard & Poor's, (3) Duff and Phelps, (4) McCarthy, Crisanti & Maffei, and (5) Fitch Investors Service. The two most widely used systems of credit or *quality* ratings are those of Moody's and Standard & Poor's. In both systems, the term *high grade* means low credit risk, or conversely, high probability of future payments. The highest grade bonds are designated by Moody's by the letters *Aaa*, and by Standard & Poor's by *AAA*. The next highest grade is *Aa* or *AA* and both agencies use *A* for the third grade. The next three grades are designated *Baa* or *BBB*, *Ba* or *BB*, and *B*, respectively. There are also *C* grades.

The spread between Treasury securities and non-Treasuries that are identical in all respects except for quality is referred to as a *quality spread* or *credit spread*. For example, for the week of August 27, 1992, the yield on single-A ten-year industrial bonds was 7.28%, and the corresponding yield for the ten-year on-the-run Treasury was 6.53%.[5] Therefore, the quality spread was 75 basis points.

***Term to Maturity.***   As explained in the previous chapter, the price of a financial asset will fluctuate over its life as yields in the market change. As demonstrated in that chapter, the volatility of a bond's price is dependent on its maturity. More specifically, with all other factors constant, the longer the maturity of a bond, the greater the price volatility resulting from a change in market yields. Generally, bonds with a maturity of between one to five years

---

[4] These yields are estimated from the following publication: *Cross-Sector Weekly*, Lehman Brothers, Fixed Income Research, September 8, 1992, p. 2.

[5] *Cross-Sector Weekly*, ibid., p.2.

are considered "short term"; bonds with a maturity between 5 and 12 years are viewed as "intermediate term," and "long-term" bonds are those with a maturity greater than 12 years. The spread between any two maturity sectors of the market is called a *maturity spread*. The relationship between the yields on comparable securities but different maturities is called the *term structure of interest rates*. This topic is of such importance that we devote the entire next chapter to it.

**Inclusion of Options.**   It is not uncommon for a bond issue to include a provision that gives either the bondholder and/or the issuer an option to take some action against the other party. An option that is included in a bond issue is referred to as an *embedded option*.

The most common type of option in a bond issue is a *call provision*. This provision grants the issuer the right to retire the debt, fully or partially, before the scheduled maturity date. The inclusion of a call feature benefits issuers by allowing them to replace an old bond issue with a lower interest cost issue, should interest rates in the market decline. Effectively, a call provision allows the issuer to alter the maturity of a bond. A call provision is detrimental to the bondholder because the bondholder will be uncertain about maturity and might have to reinvest the proceeds received at a lower interest rate if the bond is called and the bondholder wants to keep his or her funds in issues of similar risk of default.

An issue may also include a provision that allows the bondholder to change the maturity of a bond. An issue with a *put provision* grants the bondholder the right to sell the issue back to the issuer at par value on designated dates. Here, the advantage to the investor is that, if interest rates rise after the issue date and result in a price that is less than the par value, the investor can force the issuer to redeem the bond at par value.

A *convertible bond* is an issue giving the bondholder the right to exchange the bond for a specified number of shares of common stock. This feature allows the bondholder to take advantage of favorable movements in the price of the issuer's common stock.

The presence of these embedded options has an effect on the spread of an issue relative to a Treasury security and the spread relative to otherwise comparable issues that do not have an embedded option. In general, market participants will require a larger spread over a comparable Treasury security for an issue with an embedded option that is favorable to the issuer (e.g. a call option) than for an issue without such an option. In contrast, market participants will require a smaller spread over a comparable Treasury security for an issue with an embedded option that is favorable to the investor (for example, put option and conversion option). In fact, for a bond with an option that is favorable to an investor, the interest rate on an issue may be less than that on a comparable Treasury security!

**Taxability of Interest.**   Unless exempted under the federal income tax code, interest income is taxable at the federal level. In addition to federal income taxes, there may be state and local taxes on interest income.

The federal tax code specifically exempts the interest income from qualified municipal bond issues from taxation at the federal level. Municipal bonds are securities issued by state and local governments and by their creations, such as "authorities" and special districts. The large majority of outstanding municipal bonds are tax-exempt securities. Because of the tax-exempt feature of municipal bonds, the yield on municipal bonds is less than that on Treasuries with the same maturity. Table 11-4 shows this relationship on August 27, 1992, for high-grade, tax-exempt securities. The difference in yield between tax-exempt securities and Treasury securities is typically measured not in basis points but in percentage terms. More specifically, it is measured as the percentage of the yield on a tax-exempt security relative to a comparable Treasury security. This computed percentage is reported in Table 11-4.

The yield on a taxable bond issue after federal income taxes are paid is equal to:

$$\text{after-tax yield} = \text{pre-tax yield} \times (1 - \text{marginal tax rate})$$

For example, suppose a taxable bond issue offers a yield of 9% and is acquired by an investor facing a marginal tax rate of 31%. The after-tax yield would then be:

$$\text{after-tax yield} = 0.09 \times (1 - 0.31) = 0.0621 = 6.21\%$$

Alternatively, we can determine the yield that must be offered on a taxable bond issue to give the same after-tax yield as a tax-exempt issue. This yield is called the *equivalent taxable yield* and is determined as follows:

$$\text{equivalent taxable yield} = \frac{\text{tax-exempt yield}}{(1 - \text{marginal tax rate})}$$

For example, consider an investor facing a 31% marginal tax rate who purchases a tax-exempt issue with a yield of 6.21%. The equivalent taxable yield is then:

## TABLE 11-4

### YIELD ON HIGH-GRADE, TAX-EXEMPT SECURITIES ON AUGUST 27, 1992

| Maturity | Yield | Yield as a percent of Treasury yield |
|----------|-------|--------------------------------------|
| 1-Yr | 3.05% | 87.8% |
| 3-Yr | 4.10 | 86.5 |
| 5-Yr | 4.60 | 81.4 |
| 10-Yr | 5.40 | 81.4 |
| 30-Yr | 6.15 | 82.9 |

Source: *Weekly Market Update*, Goldman Sachs & Co., Fixed Income Research, August 28, 1992, p. A-5.

$$\text{equivalent taxable yield} = \frac{0.0621}{(1 - 0.31)} = 0.09 = 9\%$$

Notice that the higher the marginal tax rate, the higher the equivalent taxable yield. Thus, in our previous example, if the marginal tax rate is 36% rather than 31%, the equivalent taxable yield would be 9.7% rather than 9%, as shown below:

$$\text{equivalent taxable yield} = \frac{0.0621}{(1 - 0.36)} = 0.097 = 9.7\%$$

State and local governments may tax interest income on bond issues that are exempt from federal income taxes. Some municipalities exempt interest income paid on all municipal issues from taxation; others do not. Some states exempt interest income from bonds issued by municipalities within the state but tax the interest income from bonds issued by municipalities outside of the state. The implication is that two municipal securities of the same quality rating and the same maturity may trade at some spread because of different tax policies and, hence, the relative demand for bonds of municipalities in different states. For example, in a high income tax state such as New York, the demand for bonds of municipalities will drive down their yield relative to municipalities in a low income tax state such as Florida.

Municipalities are not permitted to tax the interest income from securities issued by the U.S. Treasury. Thus, part of the spread between Treasury securities and taxable non-Treasury securities of the same maturity reflects the value of the exemption from state and local taxes.

***Expected Liquidity of an Issue.***   Bonds trade with different degrees of liquidity. The greater the expected liquidity with which an issue will trade, the lower the yield that investors would require. As noted earlier, Treasury securities are the most liquid securities in the world. The lower yield offered on Treasury securities relative to non-Treasury securities reflects, to a significant extent, the difference in liquidity. Even within the Treasury market, some differences in liquidity occur, because on-the-run issues have greater liquidity than off-the-run issues.

▶ KEY POINTS THAT YOU SHOULD UNDERSTAND BEFORE PROCEEDING:

1. The on-the-run Treasury security of a given maturity is the base or benchmark interest rate.
2. Non-Treasury securities will trade at a spread (measured in basis points) relative to an on-the-run Treasury security.
3. The factors that affect yield spreads in the bond market are the type of issuer, credit risk, term to maturity, the presence of embedded options, the tax treatment of interest income, and liquidity.
4. The credit risk of an issuer is gauged by ratings assigned by commercial rating companies.

5. Embedded options can either reduce the spread to Treasuries, if the option benefits the bondholder, or increase the spread to Treasuries, if the option benefits the issuer.

6. The interest income from municipal securities is generally exempt from federal income taxation, and as a result municipals offer a lower yield than Treasury securities.

## SUMMARY

Two important theories of the determination of the level of the interest rate are Fisher's theory, adapted to the loanable funds model, and Keynes's liquidity preference theory. Fisher considers the reasons for saving to be the marginal rate of time preference, which is the willingness to forego current consumption for enhanced future consumption, the level of income, and the rate of interest. The demand for borrowing arises because of firms' investment opportunities. The marginal productivity of capital is the gain from additional investment and it is negatively related to the interest rate. The equilibrium rate of interest is determined by the interaction of the demand for and supply of savings. In the presence of inflation, the equilibrium rate is composed of both the real rate of interest and a premium for expected inflation.

Keynes's theory emphasizes the role of liquid balances or money in transaction and states that the interest rate is determined in the money market. Demand for money reflects income and the level of prices for goods and services, and it is negatively related to the level of interest rates. The supply of money, in this theory, is controlled by the central bank, which can, by changing the money supply, affect the rate of interest. In fact, changes in the money supply can have three possibly conflicting effects on the level of the interest rate, depending on the economy's level of output and employment. Those effects are the liquidity effect, the income effect, and the price expectations effect.

The basic features of a bond include the coupon rate, the term to maturity, and the principal or par value. The yield to maturity of a bond is the interest rate that makes the total present value of the bond's cash flow equal to its market price.

In each economy, there is not just one interest rate but a structure of interest rates. The difference between the yield on any two bonds is called the yield spread. The base interest rate is the yield on a Treasury security. The yield spread between a non-Treasury security and a comparable on-the-run Treasury security is called a risk premium. The factors that affect the spread include: (1) the type of issuer (agency, corporation, municipality); (2) the issuer's perceived creditworthiness as measured by the rating system of commercial rating companies; (3) the term or maturity of the instrument; (4) the embedded options in a bond issue (e.g., call, put or conversion provisions); (5) the taxability of interest income at the federal and municipal levels; and (6) the expected liquidity of the issue.

**Base interest rate (also called benchmark interest rate):** The minimum yield sought on an investment as measured by the yield on an on-the-run Treasury issue of the same maturity.

**Bond-equivalent yield:** The convention adopted in the bond market to annualize a semi-annual yield by doubling its value.

**Convertible bond:** A bond issue in which the bondholder has the right to exchange the bond for a specified number of shares of common stock.

**Credit rating (or quality rating):** Rating of an issued bond based on the perceived likelihood of default as assigned by commercial rating companies.

**Embedded option:** An option in a bond issue granted to either the bondholder or the issuer.

**Equivalent taxable yield:** The yield that must be offered on a taxable bond in order to realize a certain tax-exempt yield.

**Fisher's Law:** The theory that the observed nominal rate of interest is composed of the real rate and a premium for expected inflation.

**Fisher's theory of interest:** The classical analysis of the supply and demand for investment funds.

**High-grade bond:** A bond with a quality rating that indicates low credit risk.

**Income effect:** The rise in the interest rate that occurs because an increase in the money supply causes the economy's income to expand and the demand for money to increase.

**Intermarket sector spread:** The spread between the interest rate offered in two sectors of the bond market on issues with the same maturity.

**Intramarket sector spread:** The spread between the yield offered on two bonds in the same sector of the bond market.

**Liquidity effect:** The initial decline in the rate of interest that occurs because of an increase in the money supply.

**Liquidity preference theory of interest:** The theory, propounded by Keynes, that the interest rate is set in the market for money where the demand for money balances interacts with the central bank's supply of liquidity.

**Loanable funds theory of interest:** The theory that the level of the interest rate depends on the supply and demand for funds across the sectors of the economy.

**Marginal productivity of capital:** The additional gain from additional amounts of investment, in Fisher's theory.

**Marginal time preference:** The willingness of someone to trade current consumption for future consumption, in Fisher's theory.

**Market sectors:** The groupings of bond issues according to the type of issuer or other key feature of a bond, such as maturity.

**Maturity:** The day a debt obligation will cease to exist and the day the issuer will redeem the bond by paying the amount owed. The practice in the bond market is to refer to the "term to maturity" of a bond as simply its "maturity" or "term."

**Maturity spread:** The spread between any two maturity sectors of the market.

**Municipal bonds:** Securities issued by state and local governments and by their creations, such as "authorities" and special districts.

**Nominal rate of interest:** The rate of interest measured in terms of the units in the principal and the units paid in interest, without regard to their changes in purchasing power over the loan's life.

**Off-the-run Treasury issue:** A Treasury issue auctioned prior to the current coupon issues.

**On-the-run Treasury issue (also called current coupon issue):** The most recently auctioned Treasury issue for a given maturity.

**Price expectations effect:** The rise in the interest rate that occurs because a rise in the money supply creates expectations of future inflation.

**Principal value (also called principal, par value, maturity value, redemption value, and face value):** The amount that the issuer agrees to repay the bondholder at the maturity date.

**Put provision:** A provision in a bond issue that grants the bondholder the right to sell the issue back to the issuer at par value on designated dates.

**Quality spread (or credit spread):** The spread between Treasury securities and non-Treasuries that are identical in all respects except for creditworthiness or risk of default, as represented by a quality rating.

**Term to maturity:** The number of years during which the issuer has promised to meet the conditions of the obligation.

**Term structure of interest rates:** The relationship between the yields on comparable securities with different maturities.

**Treasury security (also called Treasuries):** Securities issued by the United States Department of the Treasury. There are two categories of U.S. Treasury securities—discount and coupon securities.

**Yield to maturity:** The interest rate that makes the present value of the cash flow of a bond (including its principal) equal to its market price.

**Yield spread (or spread):** The difference between the yields on any two bond issues. The spread is typically measured in basis points.

1. Explain what these terms mean in Fisher's theory of interest rates:
   a.  the marginal rate of time preference;
   b.  the marginal productivity of capital; and
   c.  the equilibrium interest rate.

2. a. How does the loanable funds theory expand Fisher's theory of interest rate determination?

   b. How does a change in the government's deficit affect the equilibrium rate in the loanable funds theory?

3. a. How do the assets, money and bonds, differ in Keynes's liquidity preference theory?

   b. How does a change in income affect the equilibrium level of the interest rate in Keynes's theory?

   c. How does a change in the money supply affect that rate?

4. a. Explain these terms: the liquidity effect; the income effect; and the price expectations effect.

   b. What determines which of these three effects on interest rates an increase in the money supply will have?

5. Consider three bonds, all with a par value of $1,000:

| Bond | Coupon Rate | Market Price |
|------|-------------|--------------|
| A | 8% | $1,100 |
| B | 7% | 900 |
| C | 9% | 1,000 |

   a. What is the yield to maturity of bond C?

   b. Is the yield to maturity of bond A greater than or less than 8%?

   c. Is the yield to maturity of bond B greater than or less than 9%?

6. Consider the following bond: 19 years to maturity, 11% coupon rate, pays interest semi-annually, $1,000 par value. Suppose that the market price of this bond is $1,233.64. Given the information below, determine the yield to maturity for this bond on a bond-equivalent yield basis.

| Interest rate tried | Total present value of cash flow |
|---------------------|----------------------------------|
| 3.00% | $1,562.32 |
| 3.25 | 1,486.96 |
| 3.50 | 1,416.82 |
| 3.75 | 1,351.46 |
| 4.00 | 1,290.52 |
| 4.25 | 1,233.64 |

7. a. Show the cash flows for the two bonds below, each of which has a par value of $1,000 and pays interest semi-annually:

| Bond | Coupon Rate | Years to Maturity | Price |
|------|-------------|-------------------|-------|
| W | 7 | 5 | $884.20 |
| Y | 9 | 4 | 967.70 |

   b. Calculate the yield to maturity for the two bonds.

8. In the May 29, 1992, *Weekly Market Update*, published by Goldman Sachs & Co., the following information was reported in various exhibits for the Treasury market as of the close of business Thursday, May 28, 1992:

| On-the-Run Treasuries | |
|---|---|
| Maturity | Yield |
| 3-Mo | 3.77% |
| 6-Mo | 3.95 |
| 1-Yr | 4.25 |
| 2-Yr | 5.23 |
| 3-Yr | 5.78 |
| 5-Yr | 6.67 |
| 7-Yr | 7.02 |
| 10-Yr | 7.37 |
| 20-Yr | 7.65 |
| 30-Yr | 7.88 |

| Key Off-the-Run Treasuries | |
|---|---|
| Issue | Yield |
| Old 10-Yr | 7.42% |
| Old 30 Yr | 7.90 |

a.   What is the credit risk associated with a Treasury security?

b.   Why is the Treasury yield considered the base interest rate?

c.   What is meant by "on-the-run Treasuries"?

d.   What is meant by "off-the-run Treasuries"?

e.   What are the yield spreads between (i) the off-the-run 10-year Treasury issue and the on-the-run 10-year Treasury issue, and (ii) the off-the-run 30-year Treasury issue and the on-the-run 30-year Treasury issue?

f.   What does the yield spread between the off-the-run Treasury issue and the on-the-run Treasury issue reflect?

9.   In the May 29, 1992, *Weekly Market Update* published by Goldman Sachs & Co., the following information was reported in various exhibits for certain corporate bonds as of the close of business Thursday, May 28, 1992:

| Issuer | Rating | Yield | Spread | Treasury Benchmark |
|---|---|---|---|---|
| General Electric Capital Co. | Triple A | 7.87% | 50 | 10 |
| Mobil Corp. | Double A | 7.77 | 40 | 10 |
| Southern Bell Tel & Teleg | Triple A | 8.60 | 72 | 30 |
| Bell Tel Co Pa | Double A | 8.66 | 78 | 30 |
| AMR Corp | Triple B | 9.43 | 155 | 30 |

a.   What is meant by "rating"?

b.   Which of the five bonds has the greatest credit risk?

c.   What is meant by "spread"?

d.   What is meant by "Treasury benchmark"?

e. Using the information for the Treasury market reported for May 29, 1992, in question 8, explain how each of the spreads reported above was determined.

f. Why does each spread reported above reflect a risk premium?

10. For the corporate bond issues reported in the previous question, answer the following questions:

a. Should a triple A-rated bond issue offer a higher or lower yield than a double A-rated bond issue of the same maturity?

b. What is the spread between the General Electric Capital Co. issue and the Mobil Corp. issue?

c. Is the spread reported in (b) consistent with your answer to (a)?

d. The yield spread between these two bond issues reflects more than just credit risk. What other factors would the spread reflect?

e. The Mobil Corp. issue is not callable. However, the General Electric Capital Co. issue is callable. How does this information help you in understanding the spread between these two issues?

11. For the corporate bond issues reported in question 9, answer the following questions:

a. What is the yield spread between the Southern Bell Telephone and Telegraph bond issue and the Bell Telephone Company (Pennsylvania) bond issue?

b. The Southern Bell Telephone and Telegraph bond issue is not callable but the Bell Telephone Company (Pennsylvania) bond issue is callable. What does the yield spread in (a) reflect?

c. AMR Corp. is the parent company of American Airlines and is therefore classified in the transportation industry. The bond issue cited is not callable. What is the yield spread between AMR Corp. and Southern Bell Telephone and Telegraph bond issue, and what does this spread reflect?

12. In the May 29, 1992, *Weekly Market Update* published by Goldman Sachs & Co., the following information was reported in an exhibit for high-grade, tax-exempt securities as of the close of business Thursday, May 28, 1992:

| Maturity | Yield | Yield as a Percent of Treasury Yield |
|---|---|---|
| 1-Yr | 3.20% | 76.5% |
| 3-Yr | 4.65 | 80.4 |
| 5-Yr | 5.10 | 76.4 |
| 10-Yr | 5.80 | 78.7 |
| 30-Yr | 6.50 | 82.5 |

a. What is meant by a tax-exempt security?

b. What is meant by a "high grade" issue?

c. Why is the yield on a tax-exempt security less than the yield on a Treasury security of the same maturity?

d. What is meant by the equivalent taxable yield?

e. Also reported in the same issue of the Goldman Sachs report is information on "Intra-market Yield Spreads." What is an intra-market yield spread?

13. a. What is meant by an embedded option in a bond?

b. Give three examples of an embedded option that might be included in a bond issue.

c. Does an embedded option increase or decrease the risk premium relative to the base interest rate?

# CHAPTER TWELVE

# The Term Structure of Interest Rates

*After reading this chapter you will understand:*

- what is meant by the term structure of interest rates.
- what the yield curve is.
- the different shapes that the term structure can take.
- what is meant by a spot rate and a spot rate curve.
- how a theoretical spot rate curve can be determined from the Treasury yield curve.
- what is meant by an implicit forward rate and how it can be calculated.
- how long-term rates are related to the current short-term rate and short-term forward rates.
- the different theories about the determinants of the shape of the term structure: pure expectations theory, the liquidity theory, the preferred habitat theory, and the market segmentation theory.
- the risks associated with investing in bonds when interest rates change — price risk and reinvestment risk.

In this chapter, we extend the theories and principles of the last chapter to the relationship between the yield on a bond and its maturity. Since the maturity of a bond is referred to as its "term to maturity" or simply "term," the relationship between yield and maturity is referred to as the *term structure of interest rates*. We also explain the various theories about the determinants of the term structure of interest rates.

## THE YIELD CURVE AND THE TERM STRUCTURE

The graphic that depicts the relationship between the yield on bonds of the same credit quality but different maturities is known as the *yield curve*. Market participants have tended to construct yield curves from observations of prices and yields in the Treasury market. Two reasons account for this tendency. First, Treasury securities are free of default risk, and differences in creditworthiness do not affect yield estimates. Second, as the largest and most active bond market, the Treasury market offers the fewest problems of illiquidity or infrequent trading. Figure 12-1 shows the shape of four hypothetical Treasury yield curves that have been observed from time to time in the United States.

From a practical viewpoint, as we explained in the previous chapter, the Treasury yield curve functions mainly as a benchmark for pricing bonds and

## FIGURE 12-1

FOUR HYPOTHETICAL YIELD CURVES

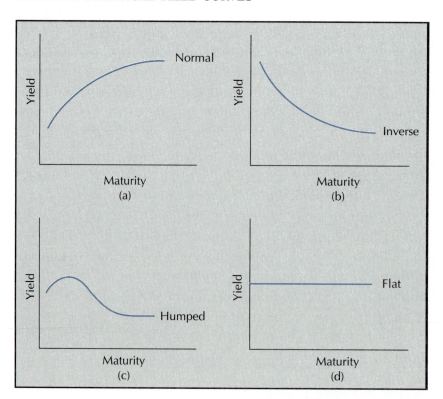

setting yields in many other sectors of the debt market—bank loans, mortgages, corporate debt, and international bonds. More recently market participants have come to realize that the traditionally constructed Treasury yield curve is an unsatisfactory measure of the relation between required yield and maturity. The key reason is that securities with the same maturity may actually provide different yields. As we will explain below, this phenomenon reflects the role and impact of differences in the bonds' coupon rates. Hence, it is necessary to develop more accurate and reliable estimates of the Treasury yield curve. In what follows, we will show the problems posed by traditional approaches to the Treasury yield curve, and offer an innovative and increasingly popular approach to building a yield curve. The approach consists of identifying yields that apply to "zero-coupon" bonds and, therefore, eliminates the problem of non-uniqueness in the yield–maturity relationship.

## Using the Yield Curve to Price a Bond

As we explained in Chapter 10, the price of any financial asset is the present value of its cash flow. However, in our illustrations and our discussion to this point in the book, we have assumed that one interest rate should be used to discount all the cash flows from a financial asset. In the previous chapter, we indicated that the appropriate interest rate is the yield on a Treasury security with the same maturity as the financial asset, plus an appropriate yield premium or spread.

As noted above, however, there is a problem with using the Treasury yield curve to determine the appropriate yield at which to discount the cash flow of a bond. To illustrate this problem, consider the following two hypothetical five-year Treasury bonds, A and B. The difference between these two Treasury bonds is the coupon rate, which is 12% for A and 3% for B. The cash flow for these two bonds per $100 of par value for the ten six-month periods to maturity would be:

| Period | Cash flow for A | Cash flow for B |
|---|---|---|
| 1-9 | $ 6.00 | $ 1.50 |
| 10 | 106.00 | 101.50 |

Because of the different cash flow patterns, it is not appropriate to use the same interest rate to discount all cash flows. Instead, each cash flow should be discounted at a unique interest rate that is appropriate for the time period in which the cash flow will be received. But what should be the interest rate for each period?

The correct way to think about bonds A and B is not as bonds but as packages of cash flows. More specifically, they are packages of zero-coupon instruments. As noted in Chapter 10, a zero-coupon instrument is one that is purchased at an amount below its maturity value and that pays no interest periodically. Instead, the interest is earned at the maturity date when the investor receives the maturity or principal value. Thus, the interest earned is the difference between the maturity value and the price paid. For example, bond A can be viewed as ten zero-coupon instruments: one with a maturity value of

$6 maturing six months from now; a second with a maturity value of $6 maturing one year from now; a third with a maturity value of $6 maturing 1.5 years from now, and so on. The final zero-coupon instrument matures ten six-month periods from now and has a maturity value of $106.

Likewise, bond B can be viewed as ten zero-coupon instruments: one with a maturity value of $1.50 maturing six months from now; one with a maturity value of $1.50 maturing one year from now; one with a maturity value of $1.50 maturing 1.5 years from now, and so on. The final zero-coupon instrument matures ten six-month periods from now and has a maturity value of $101.50. Obviously, in the case of each coupon bond, the value or price of the bond is equal to the total value of its component zero-coupon instruments.

In general, any bond can be viewed as a package of zero-coupon instruments. That is, each zero-coupon instrument in the package has a maturity equal to its coupon payment date or, in the case of the principal, the maturity date. The value of the bond should equal the value of all the component zero-coupon instruments. As we show in the appendix to Chapter 16, if this does not hold, it is possible for a market participant to generate riskless profits. Because no one can pass up riskless and certain profits, the market must drive these two prices to equality, and our discussion here assumes that equality.

To determine the value of each zero-coupon instrument, it is necessary to know the yield on a zero-coupon Treasury with that same maturity. This yield is called the *spot rate*, and the graphical depiction of the relationship between the spot rate and its maturity is called the *spot rate curve*. Because there are very few zero-coupon Treasury issues, it is not possible to construct such a curve solely from observations of market activity. Rather, it is necessary to derive this curve from theoretical considerations of the yields of the actually traded Treasury securities. Such a curve is called a *theoretical spot rate curve*.

### Constructing the Theoretical Spot Rate Curve

In this section, we explain how the theoretical spot rate curve is constructed from the yield curve that is based on the observed yields of Treasury bills and Treasury coupon securities. The process of creating a theoretical spot rate curve in this way is called *bootstrapping*.[1] To explain this process, we'll use the

---

[1] In practice, the Treasury securities that are used to construct the theoretical spot rate curve are the most recently auctioned Treasury securities of a given maturity. Such issues are referred to as the *on-the-run Treasury issues*. As we will explain in Chapter 16, there are actual zero-coupon Treasury securities with a maturity greater than one year that are outstanding in the market. These securities are not issued by the U.S. Treasury but are created by certain market participants from actual coupon Treasury securities. It would seem logical that the observed yield on zero-coupon Treasury securities can be used to construct an actual spot rate curve, but there are problems with this approach. First, the liquidity of these securities is not as great as that of the coupon Treasury market. Second, there are maturity sectors of the zero-coupon Treasury market that attract specific investors who may be willing to trade off yield in exchange for an attractive feature associated with that particular maturity sector, thereby distorting the term structure relationship.

data for the hypothetical price, annualized yield (yield to maturity) and maturity of the 20 Treasury securities shown in Table 12-1.

Throughout the analysis and illustrations to come, it is important to remember that the basic principle underlying bootstrapping is that the value of the Treasury coupon security should be equal to the value of the package of zero-coupon Treasury securities that duplicates the coupon bond's cash flow.

Consider the six-month Treasury bill in Table 12-1. As we explained in the previous chapter, a Treasury bill is a zero-coupon instrument. Therefore, its annualized yield of 8% is equal to the spot rate. Similarly, for the one-year Treasury, the cited yield of 8.3% is the one-year spot rate. Given these two spot rates, we can compute the spot rate for a theoretical 1.5-year zero-coupon Treasury. The price of a theoretical 1.5-year zero-coupon Treasury should equal the present value of the three cash flows from an actual 1.5-year coupon Treasury, where the yield used for discounting is the spot rate corresponding to the cash flow. Using $100 as par, the cash flow for the 1.5-year Treasury with the 8.5% coupon rate is:

| | | |
|---|---|---|
| 0.5 years | 0.085 x $100 x 0.5 | = $ 4.25 |
| 1.0 years | 0.085 x $100 x 0.5 | = $ 4.25 |
| 1.5 years | 0.085 x $100 x 0.5 + 100 | = $ 104.25 |

## TABLE 12-1

MATURITY AND YIELD TO MATURITY FOR 20 HYPOTHETICAL TREASURY SECURITIES

| Maturity (years) | Coupon Rate | Yield to Maturity | Price |
|---|---|---|---|
| 0.50 | 0.0000 | 0.0800 | $ 96.15 |
| 1.00 | 0.0000 | 0.0830 | 92.19 |
| 1.50 | 0.0850 | 0.0890 | 99.45 |
| 2.00 | 0.0900 | 0.0920 | 99.64 |
| 2.50 | 0.1100 | 0.0940 | 103.49 |
| 3.00 | 0.0950 | 0.0970 | 99.49 |
| 3.50 | 0.1000 | 0.1000 | 100.00 |
| 4.00 | 0.1000 | 0.1040 | 98.72 |
| 4.50 | 0.1150 | 0.1060 | 103.16 |
| 5.00 | 0.0875 | 0.1080 | 92.24 |
| 5.50 | 0.1050 | 0.1090 | 98.38 |
| 6.00 | 0.1100 | 0.1120 | 99.14 |
| 6.50 | 0.0850 | 0.1140 | 86.94 |
| 7.00 | 0.0825 | 0.1160 | 84.24 |
| 7.50 | 0.1100 | 0.1180 | 96.09 |
| 8.00 | 0.0650 | 0.1190 | 72.62 |
| 8.50 | 0.0875 | 0.1200 | 82.97 |
| 9.00 | 0.1300 | 0.1220 | 104.30 |
| 9.50 | 0.1150 | 0.1240 | 95.06 |
| 10.00 | 0.1250 | 0.1250 | 100.00 |

The present value of the cash flow is then:

$$\frac{4.25}{(1 + z_1)^1} + \frac{4.25}{(1 + z_2)^2} + \frac{104.25}{(1 + z_3)^3}$$

where   $z_1$ = one-half the annualized six-month theoretical spot rate,
   $z_2$ = one-half the one-year theoretical spot rate, and
   $z_3$ = one-half the 1.5-year theoretical spot rate.

Since the six-month spot rate and one-year spot rate are 8.0% and 8.3%, respectively, we know these facts:

$$z_1 = 0.04 \text{ and } z_2 = 0.0415.$$

We can compute the present value of the 1.5-year coupon Treasury security as:

$$\frac{4.25}{(1.0400)^1} + \frac{4.25}{(1.0415)^2} + \frac{104.25}{(1 + z_3)^3}$$

Since the price of the 1.5-year coupon Treasury security (from Table 12-1) is $99.45, the following relationship between market price and the present value of the cash flow must hold:

$$99.45 = \frac{4.25}{(1.0400)^1} + \frac{4.25}{(1.0415)^2} + \frac{104.25}{(1 + z_3)^3}$$

We can solve for the theoretical 1.5-year spot rate as follows:

$$99.45 = 4.08654 + 3.91805 + \frac{104.25}{(1 + z_3)^3}$$

$$91.44541 = \frac{104.25}{(1 + z_3)^3}$$

$$(1 + z_3)^3 = 1.140024$$

$$z_3 = 0.04465$$

Doubling this yield, we obtain the bond equivalent yield of 0.0893 or 8.93%, which is the theoretical 1.5-year spot rate. That rate is the rate that the market would apply to a 1.5-year zero-coupon Treasury security if, in fact, such a security existed.

Given the theoretical 1.5-year spot rate, we can obtain the theoretical two-year spot rate. The cash flow for the two-year coupon Treasury in Table 12-1 is:

| | | |
|---|---|---|
| 0.5 years | 0.090 x $100 x 0.5 | = $  4.50 |
| 1.0 years | 0.090 x $100 x 0.5 | = $  4.50 |
| 1.5 years | 0.090 x $100 x 0.5 | = $  4.50 |
| 2.0 years | 0.090 x $100 x 0.5 + 100 | = $ 104.50 |

The present value of the cash flow is then:

$$\frac{4.50}{(1+z_1)^1} + \frac{4.50}{(1+z_2)^2} + \frac{4.50}{(1+z_3)^3} + \frac{104.50}{(1+z_4)^4}$$

where $z_4$ = one-half the two-year theoretical spot rate.

Since the six-month spot rate, one-year spot rate, and 1.5-year spot rate are 8.0%, 8.3%, and 8.93%, respectively, then:

$$z_1 = 0.04, z_2 = 0.0415, \text{ and } z_3 = 0.04465$$

Therefore, the present value of the two-year coupon Treasury security is:

$$\frac{4.50}{(1.0400)^1} + \frac{4.50}{(1.0415)^2} + \frac{4.50}{(1.04465)^3} + \frac{104.50}{(1+z_4)^4}$$

Since the price of the two-year coupon Treasury security is $99.64, the following relationship must hold:

$$99.64 = \frac{4.50}{(1.0400)^1} + \frac{4.50}{(1.0415)^2} + \frac{4.50}{(1.04465)^3} + \frac{104.50}{(1+z_4)^4}$$

We can solve for the theoretical two-year spot rate as follows:

$$99.64 = 4.32692 + 4.14853 + 3.94730 + \frac{104.50}{(1+z_4)^4}$$

$$87.21725 = \frac{104.50}{(1+z_4)^4}$$

$$(1+z_4)^4 = 1.198158$$

$$z_4 = 0.046235$$

Doubling this yield, we obtain the theoretical two-year spot rate bond equivalent yield of 9.247%.

One can follow this approach sequentially to derive the theoretical 2.5-year spot rate from the calculated values of $z_1$, $z_2$, $z_3$, $z_4$ (the six-month, one-year, 1.5-year, and two-year rates), and the price and coupon of the bond with a maturity of 2.5 years. Further, one could derive theoretical spot rates for the remaining 15 half-yearly rates. The spot rates thus obtained are shown in Table 12-2. They represent the term structure of interest rates for maturities up to ten years, at the particular time to which the bond price quotations refer.

Column 2 of Table 12-2 reproduces the calculated yield to maturity for the coupon issue listed in Table 12-1. A comparison of this column with the last column giving the yield to maturity of a zero-coupon bond is instructive, for it confirms that bonds of the same maturity may have different yields to maturity. That is, the yield of bonds of the same credit quality does not depend

| TABLE 12-2 | | |
| --- | --- | --- |
| THEORETICAL SPOT RATES | | |
| Maturity (years) | Yield to Maturity | Theoretical Spot Rate |
| 0.50 | 0.0800 | 0.08000 |
| 1.00 | 0.0830 | 0.08300 |
| 1.50 | 0.0890 | 0.08930 |
| 2.00 | 0.0920 | 0.09247 |
| 2.50 | 0.0940 | 0.09468 |
| 3.00 | 0.0970 | 0.09787 |
| 3.50 | 0.1000 | 0.10129 |
| 4.00 | 0.1040 | 0.10592 |
| 4.50 | 0.1060 | 0.10850 |
| 5.00 | 0.1080 | 0.11021 |
| 5.50 | 0.1090 | 0.11175 |
| 6.00 | 0.1120 | 0.11584 |
| 6.50 | 0.1140 | 0.11744 |
| 7.00 | 0.1160 | 0.11991 |
| 7.50 | 0.1180 | 0.12405 |
| 8.00 | 0.1190 | 0.12278 |
| 8.50 | 0.1200 | 0.12546 |
| 9.00 | 0.1220 | 0.13152 |
| 9.50 | 0.1240 | 0.13377 |
| 10.00 | 0.1250 | 0.13623 |

on their maturity alone. While the two columns do not change much at the beginning, they diverge more after the third year, and by the ninth year the zero-coupon yield is nearly 100 basis points higher than that of the same maturity with a coupon of 13% and selling at a premium.

▶ KEY POINTS THAT YOU SHOULD UNDERSTAND BEFORE PROCEEDING:

1.  What the yield curve represents.
2.  Why any financial asset can be viewed as a package of zero-coupon instruments.
3.  What is meant by spot rates and how the theoretical spot rates can be constructed from a Treasury yield curve.

## FORFORWARD RATES

Under certain assumptions, we can also extrapolate additional information from the theoretical Treasury spot rate curve. That information is the market's expectation of future interest rates. The following section will illustrate the process of extrapolating this information about expected future interest rates.

## Determination of the Implicit Six-Month Forward Rate

Suppose that an investor has a one-year investment horizon and is faced with the following two alternatives:

*Alternative 1:* Buy a one-year Treasury bill, or

*Alternative 2:* Buy a six-month Treasury bill and, when it matures in six months, buy another six-month Treasury bill.

The investor will be indifferent between the two alternatives if they produce the same return over the one-year investment horizon. The investor knows the spot rate on the six-month Treasury bill and the one-year Treasury bill, but does not know what yield will be available on a six-month Treasury bill that will be purchased six months from now. The yield on a six-month Treasury bill six months from now is called a *forward rate*. Given the spot rate for the six-month Treasury bill and the one-year bill, the forward rate on a six-month Treasury bill is the rate that will make the investor indifferent between the two alternatives. The value of that rate can be readily determined.

At this point, however, we need to recall several present value and investment relationships. First, if you invested in a one-year Treasury bill, you would receive $100 at the end of one year. The price of the one-year Treasury bill would be:

$$\frac{100}{(1 + z_2)^2}$$

where $z_2$ is one-half the bond-equivalent yield of the theoretical one-year spot rate.

Second, suppose that you purchase a six-month Treasury bill for $X$. At the end of six months, the value of this investment would be:

$$X(1 + z_1)$$

where $z_1$ is one-half the bond-equivalent yield of the theoretical six-month spot rate.

Let $f$ represent one-half the forward rate (expressed as a bond-equivalent yield) on a six-month Treasury bill available six months from now. If you were to renew your investment by purchasing that bill at that time, the future dollars available at the end of one year from the $X$ investment would then be:

$$X(1 + z_1)(1 + f)$$

Third, it is easy to use that formula to find out how many $X$ the investor must invest in order to get $100 one year from now. This can be found as follows:

$$X(1 + z_1)(1 + f) = 100$$

Solving, we get:

$$X = \frac{100}{(1 + z_1)\ (1 + f)}$$

Now, we can return to the investor's choices and analyze what that situation says about forward rates. The investor will be indifferent between the two alternatives presented if the same dollar investment is made, and $100 is received from both alternatives at the end of one year. That is, the investor will be indifferent if:

$$\frac{100}{(1 + z_2)^2} = \frac{100}{(1 + z_1)\ (1 + f)}$$

Solving for $f$, we get:

$$f = \frac{(1 + z_2)^2}{(1 + z_1)} - 1$$

Doubling $f$ gives the bond-equivalent yield for the six-month forward rate six months from now.

We can illustrate the use of this formula with the theoretical spot rates shown in Table 12-2. From that table, we know that:

six-month bill spot rate = 0.080, therefore $z_1$ = 0.0400
one-year bill spot rate   = 0.083, therefore $z_2$ = 0.0415

Substituting into the formula, we have:

$$f = \frac{(1.0415)^2}{1.0400} - 1$$

$$= 0.043$$

Therefore, the forward rate on a six-month Treasury security, quoted on a bond-equivalent basis, is 8.06% (0.043 x 2). Let's confirm our results. The price of a one-year Treasury bill with a $100 maturity value is:

$$\frac{100}{(1.0415)^2} = 92.19$$

If $92.19 is invested for six months at the six-month spot rate of 8%, the amount at the end of six months would be:

$$92.19\ (1.0400) = 95.8776$$

If $95.8776 is reinvested for another six months in a six-month Treasury offering 4.3% for six months (8.6% annually), the amount at the end of one year would be:

$$95.8776 \ (1.043) = 100.$$

Both alternatives will have the same \$100 payoff if the six-month Treasury bill yield six months from now is 4.3% (8.6% on a bond-equivalent basis). This means that, if an investor is guaranteed a 4.3% yield (8.6% bond-equivalent basis) on a six-month Treasury bill six months from now, the investor will be indifferent between the two alternatives.

We used the theoretical spot rates to compute the forward rate. The resulting forward rate is called the *implicit forward rate* or the *implied forward rate*.

## Determination of the Implicit Forward Rate for Any Period

We can take this sort of analysis much further. It is not necessary to limit ourselves to implicit forward rates six months from now. The yield curve can be used to calculate the implicit forward rate for any time in the future for any investment horizon. For example, we can calculate:

- the two-year implicit forward rate five years from now.
- the six-year implicit forward rate ten years from now.
- the seven-year implicit forward rate three years from now.

To demonstrate how to do this, we must introduce some notation. We continue to let $f$ represent the forward rate. But now we must identify two aspects of the forward rate. First, we want to denote when the forward rate begins. Second, we want to denote the length of time of the forward rate (that is, the investment horizon or maturity). To identify these two aspects of the forward rate, we use the notation:

$_nf_t$ = the forward rate, $n$ periods from now, that will be carried by loans with maturities of $t$ periods.

Remember that here each period is equal to six months. The following examples will illustrate this notation. Consider first our earlier example of the six-month forward rate six months from now. In this case, as we are looking at a forward rate six months from now, this is equal to one period from now. Thus, $n$ is 1. Since the length of the forward rate is six months, which means that the forward rate applies to bonds with six months of maturity, then $t$ is equal to 1. Consequently, the six-month forward rate six months from now is denoted by $_1f_1$. The six-month forward rates can then be expressed as follows:

$_2f_1$ = six-month forward rate one year (two periods) from now
$_3f_1$ = six-month forward rate 1.5 years (three periods) from now
$_4f_1$ = six-month forward rate two years (four periods) from now.

For forward rates four years (eight periods) from now, we would have the following:

$_8f_1$ = six-month forward rate four years (eight periods) from now

$_8f_2$ = one-year (two periods) forward rate four years (eight periods) from now

$_8f_3$ = 1.5-year (three periods) forward rate four years (eight periods) from now.

Now let's see how the theoretical Treasury spot rates can be used to calculate the implicit forward rates. Suppose that an investor has a five-year investment horizon and is considering two alternatives:

> *Alternative 1:* Buy a five-year (ten-period) zero-coupon Treasury security,
> or
> *Alternative 2:* Buy a three-year (six-period) zero-coupon Treasury security and, when it matures in three years, buy a two-year zero-coupon Treasury security.

The investor will be indifferent between the two alternatives if they produce the same yield or the same number of dollars per dollar invested over the five-year investment horizon. The investor knows the spot rate on the five-year Treasury security and the three-year Treasury security, but does not know what yield will be available on a two-year Treasury security purchased three years from now. That is, the investor does not know the two-year forward rate three years from now. In terms of our notation, the value of the unknown rate is $_6f_4$.

The price of the five-year zero-coupon Treasury security with a maturity value of $100 would be:

$$\frac{100}{(1 + z_{10})^{10}}$$

where $z_{10}$ is one-half the bond-equivalent yield of the theoretical five-year spot rate.

Suppose that the investor purchases a three-year zero-coupon Treasury security for $P$ dollars. At the end of three years, the value of this investment would be:

$$P (1 + z_6)^6$$

where $z_6$ is one-half the bond-equivalent yield of the theoretical three-year spot rate. Let $_6f_4$ be the semi-annual two-year forward rate three years from now. Then the future dollars available at the end of five years from the P dollars invested is:

$$P (1 + z_6)^6 (1 + {_6f_4})^4$$

Suppose that today we want to know how many dollars (represented by $P$) the investor must invest in order to get $100 five years from now. This can be found as follows:

$$P (1 + z_6)^6 (1 + {_6f_4})^4 = 100$$

Solving we get,

$$P = \frac{100}{(1 + z_6)^6 (1 + {}_6 f_4)^4}$$

The investor will be indifferent between the two alternatives if the same dollar investment is made, and $100 is received at the end of five years from both alternatives. That is, the investor will be indifferent if:

$$\frac{100}{(1 + z_{10})^{10}} = \frac{100}{(1 + z_6)^6 (1 + {}_6 f_4)^4}$$

Solving for ${}_6 f_4$, we get:

$${}_6 f_4 = \left[ \frac{(1 + z_{10})^{10}}{(1 + z_6)^6} \right]^{1/4} - 1$$

Doubling ${}_6 f_4$ gives the bond-equivalent yield for the two-year forward rate three years from now.

To illustrate this formula, we will use the theoretical spot rates shown in Table 12-2. We know that:

three-year spot rate = 0.09787; therefore $z_6$ = 0.048935
five-year spot rate  = 0.11021; therefore $z_{10}$ = 0.055105

Substituting into the formula above, we have:

$${}_6 f_4 = \left[ \frac{(1.055105)^{10}}{(1.048935)^6} \right]^{1/4} - 1$$

$$= \left[ \frac{1.709845}{1.331961} \right]^{1/4} - 1$$

$$= 0.0644$$

The forward rate on a two-year Treasury security three years from now, quoted on a bond-equivalent basis, is 12.88% (0.0644 x 2). Let's confirm our results. The price of a five-year zero-coupon Treasury security with a $100 maturity value is:

$$\frac{100}{(1.055105)^{10}} = 58.48$$

If $58.48 is invested for three years at the three-year spot rate of 9.787%, the amount at the end of six periods would be:

$$58.48 (1.048935)^6 = 77.8931$$

If $77.8931 is reinvested for another two years (four periods) at 6.44% (12.88% annually), the amount at the end of the fifth year is:

$$77.8931 (1.0644)^4 = 100$$

Both alternatives will have the same $100 payoff if the two-year rate on a zero-coupon Treasury security three years from now is 6.44% (12.88% on a bond-equivalent basis).

In general, the formula for the implicit forward rate is:

$$_nf_t = \left[\frac{(1 + z_{n+t})^{n+t}}{(1 + z_n)^n}\right]^{1/t} - 1$$

where $z_n$ is a semi-annual spot rate. Doubling $_nf_t$ gives the implicit forward rate on a bond-equivalent basis.

To illustrate how to apply the formula, consider our earlier example where we sought the six-month forward rate six months from now. That is, we sought $_1f_1$. Since $n$ is equal to 1 and $t$ is equal to 1, the formula becomes:

$$_1f_1 = \left[\frac{(1 + z_{1+1})^{1+1}}{(1 + z_1)^1}\right]^{1/1} - 1$$

or

$$= \left[\frac{(1 + z_2)^2}{(1 + z_1)^1}\right] - 1$$

This agrees with the formula we used earlier to get the six-month forward rate six months from now.

In our previous example, we sought the two-year forward rate three years from now. If we substitute 6 for $n$ and 4 for $t$ in the general formula, we would obtain the same formula we used to compute the forward rate we derived earlier.

### *Relationship Between Spot Rates and Short-Term Forward Rates*

Suppose an investor purchases a five-year zero-coupon Treasury security for $58.48 with a maturity value of $100. The investor could instead buy a six-month Treasury bill and reinvest the proceeds every six months for five years. The number of dollars that will be realized will depend on the six-month forward rates. Suppose that the investor can actually reinvest the proceeds maturing every six months at the implicit six-month forward rates. Let's see how many dollars would accumulate at the end of five years. The implicit six-month forward rates were calculated for the yield curve given in Table 12-2. The semi-annual implicit forward rates using the spot rates shown in that table are:

$$_1f_1 = 0.043000$$
$$_2f_1 = 0.050980$$
$$_3f_1 = 0.051005$$
$$_4f_1 = 0.051770$$
$$_5f_1 = 0.056945$$
$$_6f_1 = 0.060965$$

$$_7f_1 = 0.069310$$
$$_8f_1 = 0.064625$$
$$_9f_1 = 0.062830$$

By investing the $58.48 at the six-month spot rate of 4% (8% on a bond-equivalent basis) and reinvesting at the forward rates given, the number of dollars accumulated at the end of five years would be:

$58.48 (1.04) (1.043) (1.05098) (1.051005) (1.05177) (1.056945)
(1.060965) (1.06931) (1.064625) (1.06283) = $100

Therefore, we see that if the implicit forward rates are realized, the $58.48 investment will produce the same number of dollars as an investment in a five-year zero-coupon Treasury security at the five-year spot rate. From this illustration, we can see that the five-year spot rate is related to the current six-month spot rate and the implicit six-month forward rates.

In general, the relationship between a $t$-period spot rate, the current six-month spot rate, and the implicit six-month forward rates is as follows:

$$z_t = [(1 + z_1) (1 +_1 f_1) (1 +_2 f_1) (1 +_3 f_1) \ldots (1 +_t f_1)]^{1/t} - 1$$

## *Importance of Knowing Forward Rates*

Why should anyone care about forward rates? There are in fact very good reasons for doing so. Foreknowledge of the forward rates implicit in the current long-term rate is relevant in formulating an investment as well as a borrowing policy.

To illustrate, suppose an investor wants to invest for one year (two six-month periods); the current six-month or short rate ($z_1$ or $f_1$) is 7%, and the one-year (two-period) rate ($z_2$) is 6%. Using the formulas we have developed, the investor finds that by buying a two-period security she is effectively making a forward contract to lend six months from now at the rate of 5% for six months. If the investor believes that the second-period rate will turn out to be higher than 5%, it will be to her advantage to lend initially on a one-period contract, then at the end of the first period to reinvest interest and principal in the one-period contract available for the second period.

Similarly, a borrower must choose between a long-term loan with a maturity near the amount of time the money is needed or a series of shorter-term loans. This is a crucial decision, which rests ultimately on the forward rates, because they represent expected costs of renewing the shorter-term loans. In the example above, the borrower would find that a sequence of short-term borrowings would be preferable to a two-period borrowing, if he believes that the second-period market rate will be lower than 5%.

▶ KEY POINTS THAT YOU SHOULD UNDERSTAND BEFORE PROCEEDING:

1. What is meant by an implicit forward rate.
2. How implicit forward rates can be determined from spot rates.

3. How spot rates can be determined from implicit forward rates.

4. Why it is important for market participants to know implicit forward rates.

## DETERMINANTS OF THE SHAPE OF THE TERM STRUCTURE

If we plot the term structure—the yield to maturity, or the spot rate, at successive maturities against maturity—what is it likely to look like? Figure 12-1 shows four shapes that have appeared with some frequency over time. Panel A shows an upward-sloping yield curve; that is, yield rises steadily as maturity increases. This shape is commonly referred to as a "normal" or "positive" yield curve. Panel B shows a downward-sloping or "inverted" yield curve, where yields decline as maturity increases. Panel C shows a "humped" yield curve. Finally, panel D shows a "flat" yield curve.

Two major theories have evolved to account for these observed shapes of the yield curve: the *expectations theory* and the *market segmentation theory*.

There are several forms of the expectations theory—the *pure expectations theory*, the *liquidity theory*, and the *preferred habitat theory*. All share a hypothesis about the behavior of short-term forward rates and also assume that the forward rates in current long-term contracts are closely related to the market's expectations about future short-term rates. These three theories differ, however, on whether other factors also affect forward rates, and how. The pure expectations theory postulates that no systematic factors other than expected future short-term rates affect forward rates; the liquidity theory and the preferred habitat theory assert that there are other factors. Accordingly, the last two forms of the expectations theory are sometimes referred to as *biased expectations theories*.

### The Pure Expectations Theory

According to the pure expectations theory, the forward rates exclusively represent the expected future rates. Thus, the entire term structure at a given time reflects the market's current expectations of the family of future short-term rates. Under this view, a rising term structure, as in Panel A of Figure 12-1, must indicate that the market expects short-term rates to rise throughout the relevant future. Similarly, a flat term structure reflects an expectation that future short-term rates will be mostly constant, while a falling term structure must reflect an expectation that future short rates will decline steadily.

We can illustrate this theory by considering how an expectation of a rising short-term future rate would affect the behavior of various market participants, so as to result in a rising yield curve. Assume an initially flat term structure, and suppose that economic news subsequently leads market participants to expect interest rates to rise.

1. Those market participants interested in a long-term investment would not want to buy long-term bonds because they would expect

the yield structure to rise sooner or later, resulting in a price decline for the bonds and a capital loss on the long-term bonds purchased. Instead, they would want to invest in short-term debt obligations until the rise in yield had occurred, permitting them to reinvest their funds at the higher yield.

2. Speculators expecting rising rates would anticipate a decline in the price of long-term bonds and therefore would want to sell any long-term bonds they own and possibly to "short-sell" some they do not now own.[2] (Should interest rates rise as expected, the price of longer-term bonds will fall. Since the speculator sold these bonds short and can then purchase them at a lower price to cover the short sale, a profit will be earned.) The proceeds received from the selling of long-term debt issues the speculators now hold or the shorting of longer-term bonds will be invested in short-term debt obligations.

3. Borrowers wishing to acquire long-term funds would be pulled toward borrowing now, in the long end of the market, by the expectation that borrowing at a later time would be more expensive.

All these responses would tend either to lower the net demand for, or to increase the supply of, long-maturity bonds, and two responses would increase demand for short-term debt obligations. Clearing of the market would require a rise in long-term yields in relation to short-term yields; that is, these actions by investors, speculators, and borrowers would tilt the term structure upward until it is consistent with expectations of higher future interest rates. By analogous reasoning, an unexpected event leading to the expectation of lower future rates will result in the yield curve sloping down.

Unfortunately, the pure expectations theory suffers from one shortcoming, which, qualitatively, is quite serious. It neglects the risks inherent in investing in bonds and like instruments. If forward rates were perfect predictors of future interest rates, then the future prices of bonds would be known with certainty. The return over any investment period would be certain and independent of the maturity of the instrument initially acquired and of the time at which the investor needed to liquidate the instrument. However, with uncertainty about future interest rates and hence about future prices of bonds, these instruments become risky investments in the sense that the return over some investment horizon is unknown.

Similarly, from a borrower or issuer's perspective, the cost of borrowing for any required period of financing would be certain and independent of the maturity of the instrument initially sold if the rate at which the borrower must refinance debt in the future is known. But with uncertainty about future interest rates, the cost of borrowing is uncertain if the borrower must refinance at some time over the periods that the funds are initially needed for.

---

[2] Short selling means selling a security that is not owned but borrowed. The process for selling stocks short is described in Chapter 15.

In the following section, we examine more closely the sources and types of risk that the pure expectations theory ignores.

***Risks Associated with Bond Investment.***   There are two risks that cause uncertainty about the return over some investment horizon. The first is the uncertainty about the price of the bond at the end of the investment horizon. For example, an investor who plans to invest for five years might consider the following three investment alternatives: (1) invest in a five-year bond and hold it for five years; (2) invest in a 12-year bond and sell it at the end of five years; and (3) invest in a 30-year bond and sell it at the end of five years. The return that will be realized for the second and third alternatives is not known because the price of each long-term bond at the end of five years is not known. In the case of the 12-year bond, the price will depend on the yield on seven-year debt securities five years from now; and the price of the 30-year bond will depend on the yield on 25-year bonds five years from now. Since forward rates implicit in the current term structure for a future 12-year bond and a future 25-year bond are not perfect predictors of the actual future rates, there is uncertainty about the price for both bonds five years from now.

The risk that the price of the bond will be lower than currently expected at the end of the investment horizon is called *price risk*. An important feature of price risk is that it is greater, the longer the maturity of the bond. The reason should be familiar from our discussions in Chapter 10, and it is that the longer the maturity, the greater the price volatility of a bond when yields rise. Thus, investors are exposed to price risk when they invest in a bond that will be sold prior to the bond's maturity date.

The second risk has to do with uncertainty about the rate at which the proceeds from a bond that matures prior to the maturity date can be reinvested until the maturity date. For example, an investor who plans to invest for five years might consider the following three alternative investments: (1) invest in a five-year bond and hold it for five years; (2) invest in a six-month instrument and, when it matures, reinvest the proceeds in six-month instruments over the entire five-year investment horizon; and (3) invest in a two-year bond and, when it matures, reinvest the proceeds in a three-year bond. The risk in the second and third alternatives is that the return over the five-year investment horizon is unknown because rates at which the proceeds can be reinvested until maturity are unknown. This risk is referred to as *reinvestment risk*.

***Interpretations of the Pure Expectations Theory.***   There are several interpretations of the pure expectations theory that have been put forth by economists. These interpretations are not exact equivalents, nor are they consistent with each other, in large part because they offer different treatments of the two risks associated with realizing a return that we have just explained.[3]

---

[3] These formulations are summarized by John Cox, Jonathan Ingersoll, Jr., and Stephen Ross, "A Re-examination of Traditional Hypotheses About the Term Structure of Interest Rates," *Journal of Finance* (September 1981), pp. 769-799.

The broadest interpretation of the pure expectations theory suggests that investors expect the return for any investment horizon to be the same, regardless of the maturity strategy selected.[4] For example, consider an investor who has a five-year investment horizon. According to this theory, it makes no difference if a five-year, 12-year, or 30-year bond is purchased and held for five years because the investor expects the return from all three bonds to be the same over five years. A major criticism of this very broad interpretation of the theory is that, because of price risk associated with investing in bonds with a maturity greater than the investment horizon, the expected returns from these three very different bond investments should differ in significant ways.[5]

A second interpretation, referred to as the *local expectations* form of the pure expectations theory, suggests that the return will be the same over a short-term investment horizon starting today. For example, if an investor has a six-month investment horizon, buying a five-year, 10-year, or 20-year bond will produce the same six-month return. It has been demonstrated that the local expectations formulation, which is narrow in scope, is the only one of the interpretations of the pure expectations theory that can be sustained in equilibrium.[6]

The third and final interpretation of the pure expectations theory suggests that the return that an investor will realize by rolling over short-term bonds to some investment horizon will be the same as holding a zero-coupon bond with a maturity that is the same as that investment horizon. (A zero-coupon bond has no reinvestment risk, so future interest rates over the investment horizon do not affect the return.) This variant is called the *return-to-maturity expectations* interpretation.

For example, let's once again assume that an investor has a five-year investment horizon. By buying a five-year zero-coupon bond and holding it to maturity, the investor's return is the difference between the maturity value and the price of the bond, all divided by the price of the bond. According to return-to-maturity expectations, the same return will be realized by buying a six-month instrument and rolling it over for five years. At this time, the validity of this interpretation is subject to considerable doubt.

## The Liquidity Theory

We have explained that the drawback of the pure expectations theory is that it does not consider the risks associated with investing in bonds. Nonetheless, we have just shown that there is indeed risk in holding a long-term bond for one period, and that risk increases with the bond's maturity because maturity and price volatility are directly related.

Given this uncertainty, and the reasonable consideration that investors typically do not like uncertainty, some economists and financial analysts have

[4] F. Lutz, "The Structure of Interest Rates," *Quarterly Journal of Economics* (1940-41), pp. 36-63.

[5] Cox, Ingersoll and Ross, *op. cit.*, p. 774-775.

[6] *Ibid.*

suggested a different theory. This theory states that investors will hold longer-term maturities if they are offered a long-term rate higher than the average of expected future rates by a risk premium that is positively related to the term to maturity.[7] Put differently, the forward rates should reflect both interest rate expectations and a "liquidity" premium (really a risk premium), and the premium should be higher for longer maturities.

According to this theory, which is called the *liquidity theory of the term structure*, the implicit forward rates will not be an unbiased estimate of the market's expectations of future interest rates because they embody a liquidity premium. Thus, an upward-sloping yield curve may reflect expectations that future interest rates either (1) will rise, or (2) will be flat or even fall, but with a liquidity premium increasing fast enough with maturity so as to produce an upward-sloping yield curve.

## The Preferred Habitat Theory

Another theory, known as the preferred habitat theory, also adopts the view that the term structure reflects the expectation of the future path of interest rates as well as a risk premium. However, the habitat theory rejects the assertion that the risk premium must rise uniformly with maturity.[8] Proponents of the habitat theory say that the latter conclusion could be accepted if all investors intend to liquidate their investment at the first possible date, while all borrowers are eager to borrow long, but that this is an assumption that can be rejected for a number of reasons.

In the first place, it is obvious that many investors wish to carry resources forward for appreciable periods of time—to buy a house, for example, or to provide for retirement. Such investors are concerned with the amount available at the appropriate time, and not the path by which that goal is reached. Hence, risk aversion dictates that they should prefer an instrument with a maturity matching the period for which they wish to invest over shorter-term investment vehicles. If these investors buy a shorter instrument, they will bear reinvestment risk—the risk of a fall in the interest rates available for reinvesting proceeds of the shorter instrument. Investors can avoid that risk only by "locking in" the current long rate, through a long-term contract. Similarly, if they buy an instrument with maturity longer than the time they wish to invest for, they will bear the risk of a loss in the price of the asset (price risk) when liquidating it before its maturity, because of a rise in interest rates. Entirely analogous considerations apply to borrowers; prudence and safety call for borrowing for a maturity by matching the length of time for which funds are required.

[7] John R. Hicks, *Value and Capital* (London: Oxford University Press, 1946), second ed., pp. 141-145.

[8] Franco Modigliani and Richard Sutch, "Innovations in Interest Rate Policy," *American Economic Review* (May 1966), pp. 178-197.

In the second place, a lot of the demand for and supply of securities these days comes from financial intermediaries, which have liabilities with specified maturities, as we explained in Chapters 2, 4, 7, and 9. These institutions seek to match as closely as possible the maturity of their liabilities with the cash flow of a portfolio of assets. In constructing such a portfolio, a financial institution will restrict its investments to certain maturity sectors.

To illustrate this preference for maturity sectors, consider a life insurance company that has issued a five-year guaranteed investment contract.[9] The insurance company will not want to invest in six-month instruments because of the associated reinvestment risk. As another example, assume a thrift has borrowed funds at a fixed rate for one year with the proceeds from the issuance of a one-year certificate of deposit. The thrift is exposed to price (or interest rate) risk if the borrowed funds are invested in a bond with 20 years to maturity. Clearly, then, either of these institutions faces some kind of risk if it invests outside its preferred maturity sector.

The preferred habitat theory asserts that, to the extent that the demand and supply of funds in a given maturity range does not match, some lenders and borrowers will be induced to shift to maturities showing the opposite imbalances. However, they will need to be compensated by an appropriate risk premium whose magnitude will reflect the extent of aversion to either price or reinvestment risk.

Thus, this theory proposes that the shape of the yield curve is determined by both expectations of future interest rates and a risk premium, positive or negative, to induce market participants to shift out of their preferred habitat. Clearly, according to this theory, yield curves sloping up, down, flat, or humped are all possible.

## Market Segmentation Theory

The market segmentation theory also recognizes that investors have preferred habitats dictated by saving and investment flows. This theory also proposes that the major reason for the shape of the yield curve lies in asset/liability management constraints (either regulatory or self-imposed) and/or creditors (borrowers) restricting their lending (financing) to specific maturity sectors.[10] However, the market segmentation theory differs from the preferred habitat theory in that it assumes that neither investors nor borrowers are willing to shift from one maturity sector to another to take advantage of opportunities arising from differences between expectations and forward rates.

Thus, for the segmentation theory, the shape of the yield curve is determined by supply of and demand for securities within each maturity sector. This formulation seems untenable because it presupposes the prevalence of ab-

---

[9] See Chapter 7 for a discussion of guaranteed investment contracts.
[10] This theory was suggested in J.M. Culbertson, "The Term Structure of Interest Rates," *Quarterly Journal of Economics* (November 1957), pp. 489-504.

solute risk aversion, while the evidence does not support that proposition. Thus, market participants must be expected to shift away from their habitat when there are sufficiently large discrepancies between market and expected rates. This potential shifting insures that the differences between market and expected rates will not grow too large, and this consideration leads back to the preferred habitat theory.

▶ KEY POINTS THAT YOU SHOULD UNDERSTAND BEFORE PROCEEDING:

1. The different shapes that have been observed for the yield curve.
2. The common hypothesis about the behavior of short-term forward rates shared by the various forms of the expectations theory.
3. The implications of the shape of the yield curve for future interest rates based on the pure expectations theory.
4. The two types of risks associated with investing in bonds and how these two risks affect the pure expectations theory.
5. How the two biased expectations theories differ from the pure expectations theory.

SUMMARY

The relationship between yield and maturity is referred to as the term structure of interest rates. The graphical depiction of the relationship between the yield on bonds of the same credit quality but different maturities is known as the yield curve. Since the yield on Treasury securities is the base rate off which a non-government bond's yield often is benchmarked, the most commonly constructed yield curve is the Treasury yield curve.

There is a problem with using the Treasury yield curve to determine the one yield at which to discount all the cash payments of any bond. Each cash flow within a bond's total pattern of cash flows should be discounted at a unique interest rate that is applicable to the time period when the cash flow is to be received. Since any bond can be viewed as a package of zero-coupon instruments, its value should equal the value of all the component zero-coupon instruments. The rate on a zero-coupon bond is called the spot rate. The theoretical spot rate curve for Treasury securities can be estimated from the Treasury yield curve using a methodology known as bootstrapping.

Under certain assumptions, the market's expectation of future interest rates can be extrapolated from the theoretical Treasury spot rate curve. The resulting forward rate is called the implicit forward rate. The spot rate is related to the current six-month spot rate and the implicit six-month forward rates. A knowledge of the forward rates implicit in the current long-term rate is relevant in formulating both investment strategies and borrowing policies.

Several theories have been proposed about the determination of the term structure. The pure expectations theory hypothesizes that the one-period forward rates simply represent the market's expectations of future actual rates. Thus, the long-term spot rate would itself be explained fully by the market expectations of future short rates. The term structure might then be rising, falling, or flat, according to whether the market expects rising, falling, or unchanged short-term rates. This formulation fails to recognize the risks associated with investing in bonds—price risk and reinvestment risk—when investors buy bonds whose maturity is different from the time for which they plan to hold the bond.

The fact that there is price risk in investing in long-term bonds, and that it seems to increase with maturity, has given rise to an alternative liquidity theory of the term structure. According to this theory, forward rates are the sum of expected future rates and a risk premium that increases for more and more distant future rates and, hence, rises with the maturity of a bond. This formulation has shortcomings because it presupposes that all lenders want to lend short and all borrowers want to borrow long. If so, long borrowers would have to offer lenders a premium, rising with maturity, to accept the risk of going long. But in reality both lenders and borrowers have quite varied maturity preferences. Each agent can eliminate risk, not by borrowing or lending short, but by lending (or borrowing) for a period coinciding with their preferred habitat. But, at the same time, agents would presumably be willing to depart from their preferred habitat by the inducement of a risk premium.

Accordingly, the third version of the expectations theory—namely, the preferred habitat theory—suggests, like the liquidity theory, that forward rates are the sum of a component reflecting expected future rates and a risk premium. However, the premium will not rise continuously with maturity but will materialize in any maturity neighborhood where supply exceeds demand. A negative premium or discount would be expected if supply exceeds demand.

One final theory explains the shape of the term structure by the concept of market segmentation. In common with the preferred habitat theory, it recognizes that participants in the bond market have maturity preferences. However, it postulates that these preferences are absolute and cannot be overcome by the expectation of a higher return from a different maturity, no matter how large. Each maturity is therefore a separate market, and the interest rate in every such market is determined by the given demand and supply. Thus, the interest rate at any maturity is totally unrelated to expectations of future rates. This formulation is of doubtful use because it implies highly irrational, implausible, and counterfactual behavior.

**Bootstrapping:** A methodology used to construct the theoretical spot rate curve from the yield curve.

**Implicit forward rate (also called implied forward rate):** The rate on an investment beginning at some future date and for some specific length of time. Since it is derived from the yield curve, it is called an implicit forward rate.

**Liquidity theory:** Theory that the term structure reflects expected future rates and a premium that rises with the maturity of issues because their price volatility rises with maturity.

**Preferred habitat theory:** Theory that the term structure reflects expected future rates and a risk premium that depends on the supply-demand situation in maturity sectors and that must be offered to induce market participants to move from their preferred maturity sectors.

**Price risk:** A risk associated with investing in a bond that arises when a bond must be sold before its maturity date at a price that is unknown because the future yield is unknown.

**Pure expectations theory:** Theory that the term structure reflects only expectations of future short-term rates.

**Reinvestment risk:** A risk associated with investing in a bond that arises when proceeds received prior to the planned horizon date must be reinvested at an unknown rate.

**Spot rate:** The yield on a zero-coupon instrument. The term is used interchangeably with zero-coupon rate.

**Spot rate curve:** The graphical depiction of the relationship between the spot rate and its maturity. This curve graphically represents the term structure of interest rates.

**Term structure:** The relationship between yield and maturity.

**Yield curve:** The graphical depiction of the relationship between the yield on bonds of the same credit quality but different maturities.

**Zero-coupon instrument:** Financial debt instrument which is purchased at an amount less than its maturity value and pays no interest periodically.

1.  a.  What is a yield curve?
    b.  Why is the Treasury yield curve the one that is most closely watched by market participants?
2.  What is meant by a spot rate?
3.  Explain why it is inappropriate to use one yield to discount all the cash flows of a financial asset.

4. Explain why a financial asset can be viewed as a package of zero-coupon instruments.

5. Why is it important for lenders and borrowers to have a knowledge of forward rates?

6. How are spot rates related to forward rates?

7. You are a financial consultant. At various times you have heard the following comments on interest rates from one of your clients. How would you respond to each comment?

   a. "The yield curve is upward-sloping today. This suggests that the market consensus is that interest rates are expected to increase in the future."

   b. "I can't make any sense out of today's term structure. For short-term yields (up to three years), the spot rates increase with maturity; for maturities greater than three years but less than eight years, the spot rates decline with maturity; and for maturities greater than eight years the spot rates are virtually the same for each maturity. There is simply no theory that explains a term structure with this shape."

   c. "When I want to determine the market's consensus of future interest rates, I calculate the implicit forward rates."

8. You observe the Treasury yield curve below (all yields are shown on a bond-equivalent basis):

| Year | Yield to Maturity | Spot Rate |
|---|---|---|
| 0.5 | 5.25% | 5.25% |
| 1.0 | 5.50 | 5.50 |
| 1.5 | 5.75 | 5.76 |
| 2.0 | 6.00 | ? |
| 2.5 | 6.25 | ? |
| 3.0 | 6.50 | ? |
| 3.5 | 6.75 | ? |
| 4.0 | 7.00 | ? |
| 4.5 | 7.25 | ? |
| 5.0 | 7.50 | ? |
| 5.5 | 7.75 | 7.97 |
| 6.0 | 8.00 | 8.27 |
| 6.5 | 8.25 | 8.59 |
| 7.0 | 8.50 | 8.92 |
| 7.5 | 8.75 | 9.25 |
| 8.0 | 9.00 | 9.61 |
| 8.5 | 9.25 | 9.97 |
| 9.0 | 9.50 | 10.36 |
| 9.5 | 9.75 | 10.77 |
| 10.0 | 10.00 | 11.20 |

All the securities maturing from 1.5 years on are selling at par. The 0.5-year and 1-year securities are zero-coupon instruments.

a. Calculate the missing spot rates.

b. What should the price of the six-year Treasury security be?

c. What is the implicit six-month forward rate starting in the sixth year?

9. You observe the following Treasury yield curve (all yields are shown on a bond-equivalent basis):

| Year | Yield to Maturity | Spot Rate |
|------|-------------------|-----------|
| 0.5 | 10.00% | 10.00% |
| 1.0 | 9.75 | 9.75 |
| 1.5 | 9.50 | 9.48 |
| 2.0 | 9.25 | 9.22 |
| 2.5 | 9.00 | 8.95 |
| 3.0 | 8.75 | 8.68 |
| 3.5 | 8.50 | 8.41 |
| 4.0 | 8.25 | 8.14 |
| 4.5 | 8.00 | 7.86 |
| 5.0 | 7.75 | 7.58 |
| 5.5 | 7.50 | 7.30 |
| 6.0 | 7.25 | 7.02 |
| 6.5 | 7.00 | 6.74 |
| 7.0 | 6.75 | 6.46 |
| 7.5 | 6.50 | 6.18 |
| 8.0 | 6.25 | 5.90 |
| 8.5 | 6.00 | 5.62 |
| 9.0 | 5.75 | 5.35 |
| 9.5 | 5.50 | ? |
| 10.0 | 5.25 | ? |

All the securities maturing from 1.5 years on are selling at par. The 0.5-year and 1-year securities are zero-coupon instruments.

a. Calculate the missing spot rates.

b. What should the price of the four-year Treasury security be?

10. a. The following is from the February 1991 monthly report published by Blackstone Financial Management:

*On February 1, 1991, the Federal Reserve lowered the discount rate from 6.5% to 6.0% and moved the fed funds target rate from 6.75% to 6.25%. The aggressive easing of monetary policy prompted a significant steepening of the yield curve. Two-year Treasury notes fell 41 basis points to 6.82% while Treasury bonds declined only 16 basis points.*

Explain how the "aggressive easing of monetary policy" resulted in "a steepening of the yield curve."

b. In the March 1991 monthly report, the following appeared:

*The further perception that the Federal Reserve had largely concluded its aggressive easing of monetary policy, along with a sell-off of short and intermediate Trea-*

*suries by Middle Eastern accounts to raise cash to finance war costs, produced a flatter yield curve....*

Explain why the yield curve became flatter as a result of the actions described above.

11.  a.  What is the common hypothesis about the behavior of short-term forward rates shared by the various forms of the expectations theory?

   b.  What are the types of risks associated with investing in bonds, and how do these two risks affect the pure expectations theory?

   c.  Give three interpretations of the pure expectations theory.

12.  a.  What are the two biased expectations theories about the term structure of interest rates?

   b.  What are the underlying hypotheses of these two theories?

13.  a.  What is the market segmentation theory?

   b.  What does this theory have in common with the preferred habitat theory?

   c.  What is the drawback of this theory?

# CHAPTER THIRTEEN

# Risk/Return and Asset Pricing Models

*After reading this chapter you will understand:*

- the fundamental principles of portfolio theory.
- how to calculate the historical single-period investment return for a security or portfolio of securities.
- how to calculate the expected return and variability of expected return of a portfolio.
- the components of a portfolio's total risk: systematic risk and unsystematic risk.
- what the beta of a stock measures.
- why diversification eliminates unsystematic risk.
- the capital asset pricing model, the relevant measure of risk in this model, and the limitations of the model.
- the development of the multifactor capital asset pricing model.
- the empirical difficulties of testing the capital asset pricing model.
- the fundamental principles underlying the arbitrage pricing theory model.
- the empirical difficulties of testing the arbitrage pricing theory model.

Portfolio theory deals with the selection of optimal portfolios by rational risk-averse investors—that is, by investors who attempt to maximize their expected portfolio returns consistent with individually acceptable levels of portfolio risk. Capital markets theory deals with the implications for security prices of the decisions made by these investors—that is, the relationship that should exist between security returns and risk if investors behave in this optimal fashion. Together, portfolio and capital markets theories provide a framework to specify and measure investment risk and to develop relationships between expected security return and risk (and hence between risk and required return on investment).

The purpose of this chapter is to introduce portfolio and capital markets theories. We begin with the basic concepts of portfolio theory and then build upon these concepts to develop the theoretical relationship between the expected return on a security and risk. Because the risk and return relationship indicates how much expected return a security should generate, given its relevant risks, it also tells us how assets should be priced. Hence the risk and return relationship is also referred to as an asset pricing model.

The three asset pricing models that we present in this chapter are those that dominate financial thinking today: the capital asset pricing model, the multifactor capital asset pricing model, and the arbitrage pricing theory model. Our focus is on the key elements underlying portfolio theory and asset pricing theory. We do not attempt to provide a rigorous mathematical presentation of these theories.

## PORTFOLIO THEORY

In designing a portfolio, investors seek to maximize the expected return from their investment, given some level of risk they are willing to accept.[1] Portfolios that satisfy this requirement are called *efficient* (or *optimal*) *portfolios*.[2] To construct an efficient portfolio, it is necessary to understand what is meant by "expected return" and "risk." The latter concept, risk, could mean any one of the many types of risk that we have referred to in earlier chapters in this book. We shall be more specific about its meaning as we proceed in the development of portfolio theory. We begin our exploration of portfolio theory with the concept of investment return.

---

[1] Alternatively stated, investors seek to minimize the risk that they are exposed to, given some target expected return.

[2] The theoretical framework for selecting efficient portfolios was developed in Harry M. Markowitz, "Portfolio Selection," *Journal of Finance* (March 1952), pp. 71-91, and *Portfolio Selection: Efficient Diversification of Investments* (New York: John Wiley & Sons, Inc., 1959).

262 Part Four / Determinants of Assets Prices and Interest Rates

## Investment Return

The return on an investor's portfolio during a given interval is equal to the change in value of the portfolio plus any distributions received from the portfolio, expressed as a fraction of the initial portfolio value. It is important that any capital or income distributions made to the investor be included, or the measure of return will be deficient. Another way to look at return is as the amount (expressed as a fraction of the initial portfolio value) that can be withdrawn at the end of the interval while maintaining the principal intact. The return on the investor's portfolio, designated $R_p$, is given by

$$R_p = \frac{V_1 - V_0 + D_1}{V_0}$$

(1)

where    $V_1$ = the portfolio market value at the end of the interval
$V_0$ = the portfolio market value at the beginning of the interval
$D_1$ = the cash distributions to the investor during the interval.

The calculation assumes that any interest or dividend income received on the portfolio of securities and not distributed to the investor is reinvested in the portfolio (and thus reflected in $V_1$). Further, the calculation assumes that any distributions occur at the end of the interval, or are held in the form of cash until the end of the interval. If the distributions were reinvested prior to the end of the interval, the calculation would have to be modified to consider the gains or losses on the amount reinvested. The formula also assumes no capital inflows during the interval. Otherwise, the calculation would have to be modified to reflect the increased investment base. Capital inflows at the end of the interval (or held in cash until the end), however, can be treated as just the reverse of distributions in the return calculation.

Thus, given the beginning and ending portfolio values, plus any contributions from or distributions to the investor (assumed to occur at the end of an interval), equation (1) lets us compute the investor's return. For example, if the XYZ pension fund had a market value of $100,000 at the end of June, benefit payments of $5,000 made at the end of July, and an end-of-July market value of $103,000, the return for the month would be 8%:

$$R_p = \frac{103,000 - 100,000 + 5,000}{100,000} = 0.08$$

In principle, this sort of calculation of returns could be carried out for any interval of time, say, for one month or ten years. Yet there are several problems with this approach. First, it is apparent that a calculation made over a long period of time, say, more than a few months, would not be very reliable because of the underlying assumption that all cash payments and inflows are made and received at the end of the period. Clearly, if two investments have the same return as calculated from the formula above, but one investment makes a cash payment early and the other late, the one with early payment will be understated. Second, we cannot rely on the formula to compare return on a one-month investment with that on a ten-year return portfolio. For purposes of comparison, the return must be expressed per unit of time — say, per year.

In practice, we handle these two problems by first computing the return over a reasonably short unit of time, perhaps a quarter of a year or less. The return over the relevant horizon, consisting of several unit periods, is computed by averaging the return over the unit intervals.[3]

## Portfolio Risk

The definition of investment risk leads us into less explored territory. Not everyone agrees on how to define risk, let alone measure it. Nevertheless, there are some attributes of risk that are reasonably well accepted.

An investor holding a portfolio of Treasury bills until the maturity date faces no uncertainty about monetary outcome. The value of the portfolio at maturity of the securities will be identical with the predicted value; the investor bears no monetary risk. In the case of a portfolio composed of common stocks, however, it will be impossible to predict the value of the portfolio at any future date. The best an investor can do is to make a best-guess or most-likely estimate, qualified by statements about the range and likelihood of other values. In this case, the investor does bear risk.

One measure of risk is the extent to which possible future portfolio values are likely to diverge from the expected or predicted value. More specifically, risk for most investors is related to the chance that future portfolio values will be less than expected. That is, if the investor's portfolio has a current value of $100,000, and an expected value of $110,000 at the end of the next year, what matters is the probability of values less than $110,000.

Before proceeding to the quantification of risk, it is convenient to shift our attention from the terminal value of the portfolio to the portfolio rate of return, $R_p$, because the increase in portfolio value is related directly to $R_p$.

**Expected Portfolio Return.**   A particularly useful way to quantify the uncertainty about the portfolio return is to specify the probability associated with each of the possible future returns. Assume, for example, that an investor has identified five possible outcomes for the portfolio return during the next year. Associated with each return is a subjectively determined probability, or relative chance of occurrence. The five possible outcomes are:

---

[3] There are three generally used methods of averaging: (1) the arithmetic average return, (2) the time-weighted rate of return (also referred to as the geometric rate of return), and (3) the dollar-weighted return. The averaging yields a measure of return per unit of time period. The measure can be converted to an annual or other period yield by standard procedures. For an explanation of these three methods of averaging, see Franco Modigliani and Gerald A. Pogue, "Risk, Return, and CAPM: Concepts and Evidence," Chapter 37 in Sumner N. Levine (ed.), *The Financial Analysts Handbook* (Homewood, IL: Dow Jones-Irwin, 1988).

| Outcome | Possible Return | Subjective Probability |
|---------|-----------------|------------------------|
| 1 | 50% | 0.1 |
| 2 | 30 | 0.2 |
| 3 | 10 | 0.4 |
| 4 | -10 | 0.2 |
| 5 | -30 | 0.1 |

Note that the probabilities sum to 1 so that the actual portfolio return is confined to one of the five possible values. Given this probability distribution, we can measure the expected return and risk for the portfolio.

The expected return is simply the weighted average of possible outcomes, where the weights are the relative chances of occurrence. In general, the expected return on the portfolio, denoted $E(R_p)$, is given by

$$E(R_p) = P_1 R_1 + P_2 R_2 + \ldots + R_n P_n,$$

or

$$E(R_p) = \sum_{j=1}^{n} P_j R_j \qquad (2)$$

where the $R_j$s are the possible returns, the $P_j$s the associated probabilities, and $n$ is the number of possible outcomes.

The expected return of the portfolio in our illustration is:

$$E(R_p) = 0.1(50.0) + 0.2(30.0) + 0.4(10.0) + 0.2(-10.0) + 0.1(-30.0)$$
$$= 10\%$$

***Variability of Expected Return.*** If risk is defined as the chance of achieving returns lower than expected, it would seem logical to measure risk by the dispersion of the possible returns below the expected value. Risk measures based on below-the-mean variability are difficult to work with, however, and moreover are unnecessary as long as the distribution of future return is reasonably symmetric about the expected value. Figure 13-1 shows three probability distributions: the first symmetric, the second skewed to the left, and the third skewed to the right. For a symmetrical distribution, the dispersion of returns on one side of the expected return is the same as the dispersion on the other side of the expected return.

Empirical studies of realized rates of return on diversified common stock portfolios show that skewness is not a significant problem.[4] If future distributions are shaped like historical distributions, it makes little difference whether we measure variability of returns on one or both sides of the expected return. If the probability distribution is symmetric, measures of the total variability of return will be twice as large as measures of the portfolio's variability below the

---

[4] For example, see Marshall E. Blume, "Portfolio Theory: A Step Toward its Practical Application," *Journal of Business* (April 1970), pp. 152–173.

FIGURE 13-1

POSSIBLE SHAPES FOR PROBABILITY DISTRIBUTIONS

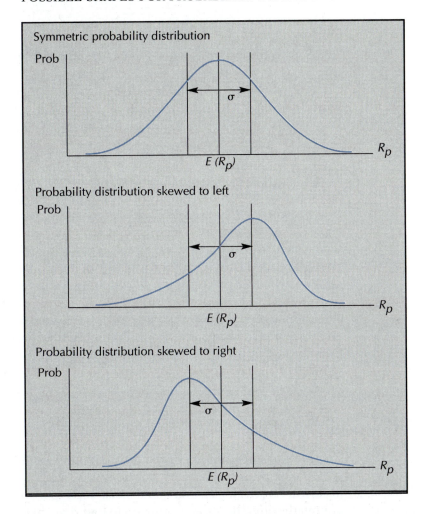

expected return. Thus, if total variability is used as a risk surrogate, the risk ranking for a group of portfolios will be the same as when variability below the expected return is used. It is for this reason that total variability of returns has been used so widely as a surrogate for risk.

It now remains to choose a specific measure of total variability of returns. The most commonly used measures are the *variance* and *standard deviation* of returns.

The variance of return is a weighted sum of the squared deviations from the expected return. Squaring the deviations ensures that deviations above and below the expected value contribute equally to the measure of variability regardless of sign. The variance for the portfolio, designated $\sigma_p^2$, is given by

$$\sigma_p^2 = P_1[R_1 - E(R_p)]^2 + P_2[R_2 - E(R_p)]^2$$
$$+ \ldots + P_n[R_n - E(R_p)]^2$$

or

$$\sigma_p^{\,2} = \sum_{j=1}^{n} P_j [R_j - \mathrm{E}(R_p)]^2 \qquad (3)$$

In the previous example, the variance for the portfolio is

$$\sigma p^2 = 0.1\,(50.0 - 10.0)^2 + 0.2(30.0 - 10.0)^2$$
$$+ 0.4(10.0 - 10.0)^2 + 0.2(-10.0 - 10.0)^2$$
$$+ 0.1(-30.0 - 10.0)^2$$
$$= 480\% \text{ squared.}$$

The standard deviation ($\sigma_p$) is defined as the square root of the variance. It is equal to 22% in our example. The larger the variance or standard deviation, the greater the possible dispersion of future realized values around the expected value, and the larger the investor's uncertainty. As a rule of thumb for symmetric distributions, it is often suggested that roughly two-thirds of the possible returns will lie within one standard deviation on either side of the expected value, and that 95% will be within two standard deviations of the expected value.

A final remark before leaving portfolio risk measures. We have assumed implicitly that investors are *risk-averse*; that is, they seek to minimize risk for a given level of return. This assumption appears to be valid for most investors in most situations. The entire theory of portfolio selection and capital asset pricing rests on the assumption that investors on the average are risk-averse.

## Diversification

Empirically, a comparison of the distribution of historical returns for a large portfolio of randomly selected stocks (say, 50 stocks) with the distribution of historical returns for an individual stock in the portfolio has indicated a curious relationship. It is not uncommon to find that (1) the standard deviation of return for the individual stocks in the portfolio is considerably larger than that of the portfolio, and (2) the average return of an individual stock is less than the portfolio return. Is the market so imperfect that it tends to reward substantially higher risk with lower stock return?

Not so. The answer lies in the fact that not all of an individual stock's risk is relevant. Much of the *total risk* (which equals standard deviation of return) is diversifiable. That is, if an investment in an individual stock is combined with other securities, a portion of the variation in its returns could be smoothed or canceled by complementary variation in the other securities. The same portfolio diversification effect accounts for the low standard deviation of return for a large stock portfolio. In fact, the portfolio standard deviation is lower than that of the typical security in the portfolio. Much of the total risk of the component securities has been eliminated by diversification. As long as much of the total risk can be eliminated simply by holding a stock in a portfolio, there is no economic requirement for the anticipated return to be in line with the total risk. Instead, we should expect realized returns to be related to that portion of security risk that cannot be eliminated by portfolio combination — so-called *systematic risk*. (We will have more to say on risk/return relationships later in this chapter.)

Diversification results from combining securities whose returns are less than perfectly correlated in order to reduce portfolio risk. The portfolio return is simply a weighted average of the individual security returns, no matter the number of securities in the portfolio. Therefore, diversification will not systematically affect the portfolio return, but it will reduce the variability (standard deviation) of return. In general, the less the correlation among security returns, the greater the impact of diversification on reducing variability. This is true no matter how risky the securities of the portfolio are when considered in isolation.

Theoretically, if we could find sufficient securities with uncorrelated returns, we could eliminate portfolio risk completely. Unfortunately, this situation is not typical in real financial markets, where returns are positively correlated to a considerable degree because they tend to respond to the same set of influences (for example, to business cycles and interest rates). Thus, while portfolio risk can be reduced substantially by diversification, it cannot be eliminated entirely.

This has been demonstrated very clearly by Wayne Wagner and Sheila Lau, who measured the standard deviations of randomly selected portfolios including various numbers of New York Stock Exchange securities.[5] Their study shows that the average return and the standard deviation for portfolios from the average return is unrelated to the number of issues in the portfolio. Yet the standard deviation of return declines as the number of holdings increases. On the average, Wagner and Lau find that approximately 40% of the risk of an individual common stock is eliminated by forming randomly selected portfolios of 20 stocks. They also find (1) additional diversification yields rapidly diminishing reduction in risk, with the improvement only slight when the number of securities held is increased beyond, say, ten, and (2) a rapid decline in total portfolio risk as the portfolios were expanded from one to ten securities.

Another key finding of the Wagner-Lau study was that the return on a diversified portfolio follows the market very closely. The degree of association is measured by the correlation coefficient of each portfolio with an unweighted index of NYSE stocks. Two securities with perfectly correlated patterns will have a correlation coefficient of 1.0. Conversely, if the return patterns are perfectly negatively correlated, the correlation coefficient will equal $-1.0$. Two securities with uncorrelated (that is, statistically unrelated) returns will have a correlation coefficient of zero. The 20-security portfolio in the Wagner-Lau

---

[5] Wayne H. Wagner and Sheila Lau, "The Effect of Diversification on Risk," *Financial Analysts Journal* (November-December 1971), pp. 2-7.

study had a correlation of 0.89 with the market. The implication is that the risk remaining in the 20-stock portfolio is predominantly a reflection of uncertainty about the performance of the stock market in general.

These results of the Wagner–Lau study show that, while some risks can be eliminated through diversification, others cannot. Thus, we are led to distinguish between a security's *unsystematic risk*, which can be washed away by mixing the security with other securities in a diversified portfolio, and its *systematic risk*, which cannot be eliminated by diversification. As the Wagner-Lau study shows, total portfolio risk declines as the number of holdings increases. Increasing diversification gradually tends to eliminate the unsystematic risk, leaving only systematic, i.e., market-related risk. The remaining variability results from the fact that the return on nearly every security depends to some degree on the overall performance of the market. This is illustrated in Figure 13-2. Consequently, the return on a well-diversified portfolio is highly correlated with the market, and its variability or uncertainty is basically the uncertainty of the market as a whole. Investors are exposed to market uncertainty no matter how many stocks they hold.

## The Risk of Individual Securities

From the empirical evidence we have cited, we can conclude that the systematic risk of an individual security is that portion of its total risk (which, again, is the same as standard deviation of return) that cannot be eliminated by combining it with other securities in a well-diversified portfolio. We now need a

### FIGURE 13-2

SYSTEMATIC AND UNSYSTEMATIC RISK

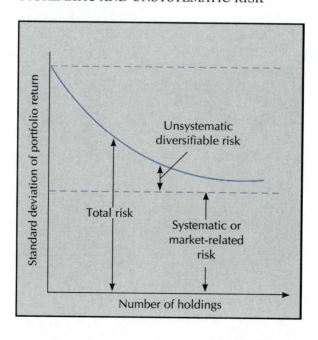

way of quantifying the systematic risk of a security and relating the systematic risk of a portfolio to that of its component securities. This can be accomplished by dividing a security's return into two parts: one perfectly correlated with and proportionate to the market return, and a second independent from (uncorrelated with) the market. The first component of return is usually referred to as *systematic*, the second as *unsystematic*. Thus, we have

$$\text{Security return} = \text{Systematic return} + \text{Unsystematic return} \qquad (4)$$

As the systematic return is proportional to the market return, it can be expressed as the symbol *beta* (or $\beta$) times the market return, $R_m$. The proportionality factor of beta is a market sensitivity index, indicating how sensitive the security return is to changes in the market level. (How to estimate beta for a security or portfolio is discussed later.) The unsystematic return, which is independent of market returns, is usually represented by the symbol *epsilon* ($\epsilon'$). Thus, the security return, $R$, may be expressed

$$R = \beta R_m + \epsilon' \qquad (5)$$

For example, if a security has a $\beta$ factor of 2.0, then a 10% market return will generate a 20% systematic return for the stock. The security return for the period would be the 20% plus the unsystematic component.

The unsystematic component in equation (5) depends on factors that are unique or specific to the company that issued the security, such as labor difficulties, unexpectedly high or low sales, managerial issues, and so on. Thus, the unsystematic component is not linked to the overall market or economic system. It is important to note that a security's return variability that is due to this unsystematic component is diversifiable precisely because that variability represents events or situations that are specific (or unique) to the firm that issued the security. If a portfolio contains many securities issued by many companies, then events that are specific to any firm and affect that firm's returns can readily be offset by contrary or opposite developments that are unique to other firms and that influence their returns in different ways.

The security returns model given by equation (5) is usually written in such a way that the average value of the residual term, $\epsilon'$, is zero. This is accomplished by adding a factor, *alpha* ($\alpha$), to the model to represent the average value of the unsystematic returns over time. That is, we set $\epsilon' = \alpha + \epsilon$ so that

$$R = \alpha + \beta R_m + \epsilon \qquad (6)$$

where the average $\epsilon$ over time should tend to zero. The reason the average value of the term is zero is that the term represents the eventual impact of unexpected events that are particular to the firm. If those events are random and unpredictable, their overall impact should be zero.

The model for security returns given by equation (6) is usually referred to as the *market model.*[6] Graphically, the model can be depicted as a line fitted to a plot of security returns against rates of return on the market index. This kind of line-fitting is shown for a hypothetical security in Figure 13-3.

The beta factor can be thought of as the slope of the line. It gives the expected increase in security return for a 1% increase in market return. In Figure 13-3, the security has a beta of 1.0. Thus, a 10% market return will result, on the average, in a 10% security return.

The alpha factor is represented by the intercept of the line on the vertical security return axis. It is equal to the average value over time of the unsystematic returns ($\epsilon'$) on the stock. For most stocks, the alpha factor tends to be small and unstable.

Using this definition of security return given by the market model, the specification of systematic and unsystematic risk is simply the standard deviations of the two return components.

The systematic risk of a security is equal to $\beta$ times the standard deviation of the market return:

$$\text{Systematic risk} = \beta\sigma_m \qquad (7)$$

The unsystematic risk equals the standard deviation of the residual return factor $\epsilon$, or

$$\text{Unsystematic risk} = \sigma_\epsilon \qquad (8)$$

## FIGURE  1 3 - 3

THE MARKET MODEL FOR SECURITY RETURNS

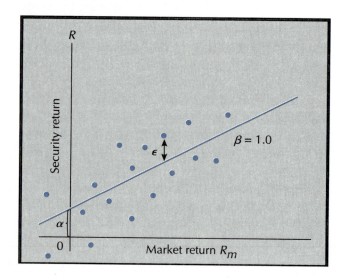

---

[6] It is also referred to as the *single-index market model* and the *characteristic line.*

Given measures of individual-security systematic risk, we can now compute the systematic risk of the portfolio. It is equal to the beta factor for the portfolio, $\beta_p$, times the risk of the market index, $\sigma_m$:

$$\text{Portfolio systematic risk} = \beta_p \sigma_m \qquad (9)$$

The portfolio beta factor in turn can be shown to be simply an average of the individual security betas, weighted by the proportion of each security in the portfolio, or

$$\beta_p = X_1\beta_1 + X_2\beta_2 + \ldots + X_n\beta_n$$

or more concisely as

$$\beta_p = \sum_{i=1}^{n} X_i\beta_i \qquad (10)$$

where $\quad X_i =$ the proportion of portfolio market value represented by security $i$

$n =$ the number of securities.

Thus, the systematic risk of a portfolio is simply the market value-weighted average of the systematic risk of the individual securities. It follows that the $\beta$ for a portfolio consisting of all stocks is 1. If a stock's $\beta$ exceeds 1, it is above the average; if its beta is below 1, it is below the average. If the portfolio is composed of an equal dollar investment in each stock, the $\beta_p$ is simply an unweighted average of the component security betas.

The unsystematic risk of the portfolio is also a function of the unsystematic security risks, but the form is more complex. The important point is that, with increasing diversification, this risk approaches zero.

To summarize these results, first, roughly 40% to 50% of total security risk can be eliminated by diversification. Second, the remaining systematic risk is equal to the security $\beta$ times market risk. Third, portfolio systematic risk is a weighted average of security systematic risks.

The implications of these results are substantial. First, we would expect realized rates of return over substantial periods of time to be related to the systematic as opposed to the total risk of securities. As the unsystematic risk is relatively easily eliminated, we should not expect the market to offer investors a "risk premium" for bearing such risk. Second, because security systematic risk is equal to the security beta times $\sigma_m$ (which is common to all securities), beta is useful as a *relative* risk measure. The $\beta$ gives the systematic risk of a security (or portfolio) relative to the risk of the market index. Thus, it is often convenient to speak of systematic risk in relative terms; that is, in terms of beta rather than beta times $\sigma_m$.

### Estimating Beta

The beta of a security or portfolio can be estimated only using statistical analysis. More specifically, we use regression analysis on historical data to estimate the market model given by equation (6). The estimated slope for the market model is the estimate of beta. A series of returns is computed according to equation (1) over some time interval for some broad market index (such as the S&P 500 stock market index) and for the stock (or portfolio). For example, monthly returns can be calculated for the past five years; thus, there would be 60 return observations for both the market index and the stock or portfolio. Or, weekly returns can be calculated for the past year.

There is nothing in portfolio theory that indicates whether weekly, monthly, or even daily returns should be used. Nor does theory indicate any specific number of observations, except that statistical methodology entails that more observations will give a more reliable measure of beta.[7] Our purpose here is not to provide an explanation of the mechanics of calculating beta but to point out the practical problems in obtaining beta. (There are many statistical issues also, but we do not focus on these.)

There will be a difference in the calculated beta depending on: (1) the length of time over which a return is calculated (e.g., daily, weekly, monthly); (2) the number of observations used (e.g., three years of monthly returns or five years of monthly returns); (3) the specific time period used (January 1, 1985, to December 31, 1989, for example, or January 1, 1983, to December 31, 1987); and (4) the market index selected (for instance, the S&P 500 stock market index or an index consisting of all stocks traded on exchanges weighted by their relative market value). Moreover, there is the question of the stability of beta over different time intervals—that is, does the beta of a stock or portfolio remain relatively unchanged over time, or does it change?

A very interesting question has to do with the economic determinants of the beta of a stock. The risk characteristics of a company should be reflected in its beta. Several empirical studies have attempted to identify these macroeconomic and microeconomic factors.

▶ KEY POINTS THAT YOU SHOULD UNDERSTAND BEFORE PROCEEDING:

1. Risk-aversion means that investors want to minimize risk for any given level of expected return, or want to maximize return, for any given level of risk.
2. Risk is the likelihood that an actual return will deviate from the expected return.
3. Investors hold diversified portfolios rather than individual securities because portfolios eliminate some of the risk of most securities.

---

[7] This assumes that the economic determinants that affect the beta of a stock do not change over the measurement period.

4. The relevant risk of any individual security is not total variability in returns but rather systematic variability, which is that portion of total variability that cannot be eliminated by combining it with other securities in a diversified portfolio.

5. The market model is the hypothesis that a security's return may be attributed to two forces, the returns on securities in general or the market, and events related to the firm itself.

6. The index of the sensitivity of a security's returns to movement in the market is the security's beta, which can be estimated with regression techniques from historical data.

## THE CAPITAL ASSET PRICING MODEL

We have now developed two measures of risk: one is a measure of total risk (standard deviation), the other a relative index of systematic or nondiversifiable risk (beta). The beta measure would appear to be the more relevant for the pricing of securities. Returns expected by investors logically should be related to systematic as opposed to total risk. Securities with higher systematic risk should have higher expected returns.

The question of interest now is the form of the relationship between risk and return. In this section we describe a relationship called the *capital asset pricing model* (or CAPM), which is based on elementary logic and simple economic principles.[8] The basic postulate underlying this finance theory is that assets with the same systematic risk should have the same expected rate of return; that is, the prices of assets in the capital markets should adjust until equivalent risk assets have identical expected returns. This principle is called the "law of one price."

To see the implications of this postulate, consider an investor who holds a risky portfolio that has the same risk as the market portfolio (beta equal to 1.0).[9] What return should she expect? Logically, she should expect the same return as that of the market portfolio. Consider another investor who holds a riskless portfolio, or one with a beta equal to zero. In this case, the investor should expect to earn the rate of return on riskless assets, such as Treasury bills. In other words, the investor who takes no risk earns only the riskless rate of return.

Now, consider the case of an investor who holds a mixture of these two portfolios. Assume he invests a proportion $X$ of his money in the risky portfolio and the rest, or $(1 - X)$, in the riskless portfolio. What systematic risk

[8] CAPM theory was developed by William F. Sharpe, "Capital Asset Prices: A Theory of Market Equilibrium Under Conditions of Risk," *Journal of Finance* (September 1964), pp. 425-442.
[9] We use the term portfolio in a general sense, including the case where the investor holds only one security. Because portfolio return and (systematic) risk are simply weighted averages of security values, risk/return relationships that hold for securities must also be true for portfolios, and vice versa.

does he bear, and what return should he expect? The risk of the composite portfolio is easily computed. Recall that the beta of a portfolio is simply a weighted average of the component security betas, where the weights are the portfolio proportions. Thus, the portfolio beta, $\beta_p$, is a weighted average of the beta of the market portfolio and that of the riskless portfolio. The market beta is 1.0, and the beta of the risk-free asset is 0. Thus,

$$\beta_p = (1 - X) \times 0 + X \times 1$$
$$= X. \tag{11}$$

Thus, $\beta_p$ is equal to the fraction of the money invested in the risky portfolio. If 100% or less of the investor's funds are invested in the risky portfolio, the portfolio beta will be between 0 and 1. If the investor borrows at the risk-free rate and invests the proceeds in the risky portfolio, so that $X$ is larger than 1 and $(1 - X)$ is negative, the portfolio beta will be greater than 1.

The expected return of the composite portfolio is also a weighted average of the expected returns on the two portfolios; that is,

$$E(R_p) = (1 - X) \times R_f + X \times E(R_m) \tag{12}$$

where $E(R_p)$ and $E(R_m)$ are the expected returns on the portfolio and the market index, and $R_f$ is the risk-free rate. Now, from equation (11) we know that $X$ is equal to $\beta_p$. Substituting into equation (12), we have

$$E(R_p) = (1 - \beta_p) \times R_f + \beta_p \times E(R_m),$$

or

$$E(R_p) = R_f + \beta_p [E(R_m) - R_f]. \tag{13}$$

Equation (13) is the capital asset pricing model. This extremely important theoretical result says that the expected return on a portfolio should exceed the riskless rate of return by an amount that is proportional to the portfolio beta. That is, the relationship between expected return and risk should be linear.

The CAPM model is often stated in risk premium form. Risk premiums or excess returns are obtained by subtracting the risk-free rate from the rate of return. The expected portfolio and market risk premiums—designated $E(r_p)$ and $E(r_m)$, respectively—are given by

$$E(r_p) = E(R_p) - R_f, \text{ and}$$
$$E(r_m) = E(R_m) - R_f.$$

Substituting these risk premiums into equation (13), we obtain

$$E(r_p) = \beta_p E(r_m). \tag{14}$$

In this form, the CAPM states that the expected risk premium for the investor's portfolio is equal to its beta value times the expected market risk premium. Or, equivalently stated, the expected risk premium should be equal to the *quantity of risk* (as measured by beta) and the *market price of risk* (as measured by the expected market risk premium).

We can illustrate the model by assuming that the short-term (risk-free) interest rate is 6% and the expected return on the market is 10%. The expected risk premium for holding the market portfolio is simply the difference between the 10% and the short-term interest rate of 6%, or 4%. Investors who hold the market portfolio expect to earn 10%, which is 4% greater than they could earn on a short-term market instrument for certain. In order to satisfy equation (13), the expected return on securities or portfolios with different levels of risk must be as follows:

| Beta | Expected Return |
|------|-----------------|
| 0.0  | 6%              |
| 0.5  | 8               |
| 1.0  | 10              |
| 1.5  | 12              |
| 2.0  | 14              |

The predictions of the model are inherently sensible. For safe investments ($\beta = 0$), the model predicts that investors would expect to earn the risk-free rate of interest. For a risky investment, ($\beta > 0$), investors would expect a rate of excess return proportional to the market sensitivity (or $\beta$) of the investment. Thus, stocks with lower-than-average market sensitivities would offer expected returns less than the expected market return. Stocks with above-average values of beta would offer expected returns in excess of the market.

## Underlying Assumptions

In our development of the CAPM, we have implicitly made a number of assumptions that are required if the model is to be established on a rigorous basis. These assumptions involve investor behavior and conditions in the capital markets. The assumptions following are sufficient to allow a single derivation of the model.

1.  The market is made up of risk-averse investors who measure risk in terms of standard deviation of portfolio return. This assumption provides a basis for the use of risk measures such as beta.

2.  All investors have a common time horizon for investment decision-making (for example, one month, one year, and so on). This assumption allows us to measure investor expectations over some common interval, thus making comparisons meaningful.

3.  All investors are assumed to have the same expectations about future security returns and risks. The only reason why they choose different portfolios is differences in systematic risk and in risk preferences. Without this assumption, the analysis would become much more complicated.

4.  Capital markets are perfect in the sense that all assets are completely divisible, there are no transactions costs or differential taxes, and

borrowing and lending rates are equal to each other and the same for all investors. Without these conditions, there would exist frictional barriers to the equilibrium conditions on which the model is based.

While these assumptions are sufficient to derive the model, it is not clear that all are necessary in this exact form. It may well be that several of the assumptions can be relaxed substantially without major change in the form of the model. A good deal of research has been conducted toward this end.

### Tests of the Capital Asset Pricing Model

The CAPM is indeed a simple and elegant model, but these qualities do not in and of themselves guarantee that it will be useful in explaining observed risk/return patterns. Here we briefly review the empirical literature on attempts to verify the model.

The major difficulty in testing the CAPM is that the model is stated in terms of investors' expectations and not in terms of realized returns. To test the CAPM, it is necessary to convert the theoretical CAPM given by equation (14) into a form that can be tested empirically. We will not go through this exercise here, but will simply provide a general statement of the model that is typically tested.[10] Nor will we delve into the statistical problems associated with testing the CAPM, although we will discuss later an important theoretical issue that raises serious questions about the testability of the CAPM and therefore the empirical findings of researchers.

The empirical analogue of equation (14) asserts that, over the period of time analyzed, (1) there is a linear relationship between the average risk premium return on the market and the average risk premium return on a stock or portfolio, and its slope is $\beta$, and (2) the linear relationship should pass through the origin. Moreover, according to the CAPM, beta is a complete relative measure of a stock's risk. Consequently, various alternative risk measures that might be proposed, the most common being the standard deviation of return, should not be significant contributors to the explanation of a stock's return. Recall that the standard deviation measures a stock's total risk and includes both systematic and unsystematic components.

The CAPM theoretically applies to both individual securities and portfolios. Therefore, the empirical tests can be based on either. However, there are statistical problems associated with estimating the magnitude of the risk/return trade-off using individual securities. By grouping securities into portfolios, we can eliminate most of the statistical problems encountered for

---

[10] The interested reader can find the procedure for developing the empirical model tested in Franco Modigliani and Gerald A. Pogue, "Introduction to Risk and Return: Concepts and Evidence: Part II," *Financial Analysts Journal* (May-June 1974), pp. 69-86.

individual stocks and thereby get a much clearer view of the relationship between return and systematic risk.

The major results of the empirical tests conducted in the early 1970s are summarized below:[11]

1.  The evidence shows a significant positive relationship between realized returns and systematic risk as measured by beta. The average market risk premium estimated is usually less than that predicted by the CAPM, however.

2.  The relationship between risk and return appears to be linear. The studies give no evidence of significant curvature in the risk/return relationship.

3.  Tests that attempt to discriminate between the effects of systematic and unsystematic risk do not yield definitive results. Both kinds of risk appear to be positively related to security returns, but there is substantial support for the proposition that the relationship between return and unsystematic risk is at least partly spurious—that is, partly a reflection of statistical problems rather than the true nature of capital markets.

Obviously, we cannot claim that the CAPM is absolutely right. On the other hand, the early empirical tests do support the view that beta is a useful relative risk measure and that high-beta stocks tend to be priced so as to yield correspondingly high rates of return.

In 1977, however, Richard Roll wrote a paper criticizing the previously published tests of the CAPM.[12] Roll argued that while the CAPM is testable in principle, no correct test of the theory had yet been presented. He also argued that there was practically no possibility that a correct test would ever be accomplished in the future.

The reasoning behind Roll's assertions is based on his observation that there is only one potentially testable hypothesis associated with the CAPM, namely, that the true market portfolio is mean-variance efficient. (This means that the market portfolio must have minimum risk for its level of return.) Fur-

---

[11] Some of the earlier studies are: Nancy Jacob, "The Measurement of Systematic Risk for Securities and Portfolios: Some Empirical Results," *Journal of Financial and Quantitative Analysis* (March 1971), pp. 815-834; Merton H. Miller and Myron S. Scholes, "Rates of Returns in Relation to Risk: A Reexamination of Recent Findings," and Fischer Black, Michael C. Jensen, and Myron S. Scholes, "The Capital Asset Pricing Model: Some Empirical Evidence," in Michael C. Jensen (ed.), *Studies in the Theory of Capital Markets* (New York: Praeger Books, 1972); Marshall E. Blume and Irwin Friend, "A New Look at the Capital Asset Pricing Model," *Journal of Finance* (March 1973), pp. 19–33; and Eugene F. Fama and James D. MacBeth, "Risk, Return and Equilibrium: Empirical Tests," Working Paper No. 7237, University of Chicago, Graduate School of Business, August 1972.

[12] Richard Roll, "A Critique of the Asset Pricing Theory: Part I. On the Past and Potential Testability of the Theory," *Journal of Financial Economics* (March 1977), pp. 129–176.

thermore, because the true market portfolio must contain all worldwide assets, the value of most of which cannot be observed (for example, human capital), the hypothesis is in all probability untestable.

Since 1977, there have been a number of studies that purport either to support or reject the CAPM. These tests have attempted to examine implications of the CAPM other than the linearity of the risk/return relation as the basis of their methodology. Unfortunately, none provides a definitive test, and most are subject to substantial criticism, suffering from the same problem of identifying the "true" market portfolio.

▶ KEY POINTS THAT YOU SHOULD UNDERSTAND BEFORE PROCEEDING:

1. The Capital Asset Pricing Model (or CAPM) hypothesizes that assets with the same level of systematic risk should experience the same level of returns.

2. The level of returns expected from any asset (which may be an individual security or a portfolio of securities) is a linear function of the risk-free rate, the asset's beta, and the returns expected on the market portfolio of risky assets.

3. Some reservations about the CAPM are inevitable because it makes many assumptions about investors' behavior and the structure of the market where assets are traded.

4. A major criticism of the CAPM is that it is basically untestable because the true or relevant market portfolio is an unobservable or unattainable portfolio diversified across all risky assets in the world.

## THE MULTIFACTOR CAPM

■ ■ ■ ■

The CAPM described above assumes that the only risk that an investor is concerned with is uncertainty about the future price of a security. Investors, however, usually are concerned with other risks that will affect their ability to consume goods and services in the future. Three examples would be the risks associated with future labor income, the future relative prices of consumer goods, and future investment opportunities.

Recognizing these other risks that investors face, Robert Merton has extended the CAPM to describe consumers deriving their optimal lifetime consumption when they face these "extra-market" sources of risk.[13] These extra-market sources of risk are also referred to as "factors," so the model derived by Merton is called a *multifactor CAPM* and is given below in risk-premium form:

$$E(r_p) = B_{pm} E(r_m) + B_{pF1} E(r_{F1}) + B_{pF2} E(r_{F2}) + \ldots + B_{pFK} E(r_{FK}) \qquad (15)$$

---

[13] Robert C. Merton, "An Intertemporal Capital Asset Pricing Model," *Econometrica* (September 1973), pp. 867-888.

where $\quad K$ = number of factors or extra-market sources of risk

$\qquad B_{pFk}$ = the sensitivity of the portfolio to the $k$-th factor

$\qquad E(r_{Fk})$ = the expected return of factor $k$ minus the risk-free rate.

The total extra-market sources of risk are equal to

$$B_{pF1}\,E(r_{F1}) + B_{pF2}\,E(r_{F2}) + \ldots + B_{pFK}\,E(r_{FK}) \qquad (16)$$

Equation (15) says that investors want to be compensated for the risk associated with each source of extra-market risk, in addition to market risk. Note that, if there are no extra-market sources of risk, equation (15) reduces to the CAPM as given by equation (14). In the case of the CAPM, investors hedge the uncertainty associated with future security prices through diversification by holding the market portfolio, which can be thought of as a mutual fund that invests in all securities based on their relative capitalizations. In the multifactor CAPM, besides investing in the market portfolio, investors will also allocate funds to something equivalent to a mutual fund that hedges a particular extra-market risk. While not all investors are concerned with the same sources of extra-market risk, those that are concerned with a specific extra-market risk will basically hedge them in the same way.

As individual securities are nothing more than portfolios consisting of only one security, equation (15) must hold for each security, $i$. That is,

$$E(r_i) = B_{im}\,E(r_m) + B_{iF1}\,E(r_{F1}) + B_{iF2}\,E(r_{F2}) + \ldots + B_{iFK}\,E(r_{FK}) \qquad (17)$$

From an empirical perspective, it may be difficult to identify the relevant extra-market risks. Moreover, it is difficult to distinguish the multifactor CAPM empirically from the next risk and return model described.

▶ KEY POINTS THAT YOU SHOULD UNDERSTAND BEFORE PROCEEDING:

1.  The multifactor CAPM posits that extra-market factors influence expected returns on securities or portfolios.
2.  This approach entails that a security's return has a beta-like sensitivity to each factor.

## ARBITRAGE PRICING THEORY MODEL

An alternative model to the CAPM and the multifactor CAPM was developed by Stephen Ross in 1976.[14] This model is based purely on arbitrage arguments, and hence is called the *Arbitrage Pricing Theory* (APT) model. It postulates that a security's expected return is influenced by a variety of factors, as opposed to just the single market index of the CAPM.

The APT model assumes that there are several factors that determine the rate of return on a security, not just one as in the case of the CAPM. To un-

---

[14] Stephen A. Ross, "The Arbitrage Theory of Capital Asset Pricing," *Journal of Economic Theory* (December 1976), pp. 343–362.

derstand this, look back at equation (5), which states that the return on a security is dependent on its market sensitivity index and an unsystematic return. The APT in contrast states that the return on a security is linearly related to $H$ "factors." The APT does not specify what these factors are, but it is assumed that the relationship between security returns and the factors is linear.

For now, to illustrate the APT model, let's assume a simple world with a portfolio consisting of three securities in the presence of two factors. The notation is as follows:

$\tilde{R}_i$ = the random rate of return on security $i$ ($i$ = 1,2,3)
$E(R_i)$ = the expected return on security $i$ ($i$ = 1,2,3)
$\tilde{F}_h$ = the $h$-th factor that is common to the returns of all three assets ($h$ = 1,2)
$\beta_{ih}$ = the sensitivity of the $i$-th security to the $h$-th factor
$\tilde{e}_i$ = the unsystematic return for security $i$ ($i$ = 1,2,3)

The APT model asserts that the random rate of return on security $i$ is given by the relationship:

$$\tilde{R}_i = E(R_i) + \beta_{i1}\tilde{F}_1 + \beta_{i2}\tilde{F}_2 + \tilde{e}_i \qquad (18)$$

For equilibrium to exist among these three assets, an arbitrage condition must be satisfied: using no additional funds (wealth) and without increasing risk, it should not be possible, on average, to create a portfolio to increase return. In essence, this condition states that there is no "money machine" available in the market. Ross has shown that the following risk and return relationship, in risk premium form, will result for each security $i$:

$$E(r_i) = \beta_{iF1}\, E(r_{F1}) + \beta_{iF2}\, E(r_{F2}) \qquad (19)$$

where $\quad r_i$ = the excess return of security $i$ over the risk-free rate
$\beta_{iFj}$ = the sensitivity of security $i$ to the $j$th factor
$r_{Fj}$ = the excess return of the $j$th systematic factor over the risk-free rate, which can be thought of as the price (or risk premium) for the $j$th systematic risk.

Equation (19) can be generalized to the case where there are $H$ factors as follows:

$$E(r_i) = \beta_{iF1}\, E(r_{F1}) + \beta_{iF2}\, E(r_{F2}) + \ldots + \beta_{iFH}\, E(r_{FH}) \qquad (20)$$

Equation (20) is the APT model. It states that investors want to be compensated for all the factors that systematically affect the return of a security. The compensation is the sum of the product of the quantity of systematic risk accepted for factor $i$, which is measured by the beta of the security with respect to the factor, and how the financial market prices that factor's risk, which is measured by the difference between the expected return for the factor and the risk-free rate. As in the case of the two other risk and return models described earlier, an investor is not compensated for accepting unsystematic risk.

Contrast equation (20) with the CAPM. If there is only one factor, equation (20) reduces to equation (14), and the one factor would be market risk. The CAPM is therefore a special case of the APT model. Now, contrast equation (20) with the multifactor CAPM given by equation (15). They look similar. Both say that investors are compensated for accepting all systematic risk and no unsystematic risk. The multifactor CAPM states that one of these systematic risks is market risk, while the APT model does not.

Supporters of the APT model argue that it has several major advantages over the CAPM or the multifactor CAPM. First, it makes less restrictive assumptions about investor preferences toward risk and return. The CAPM theory assumes investors trade off between risk and return solely on the basis of the expected returns and standard deviations of prospective investments. The APT, on the other hand, simply requires that some rather unobtrusive bounds be placed on potential investor utility functions. Second, no assumptions are made about the distribution of security returns. Finally, as the APT does not rely on identifying the true market index, the theory is potentially testable.

## Empirical Evidence

To date, attempts to test the APT model empirically in the stock market have been inconclusive. Indeed, because of inability to find a set of factors that consistently explain security returns, some question whether the APT is testable at all. The APT gives no direction as to the choice of the factors themselves or even how many factors might be required. Thus, the APT replaces the problem of the market portfolio in the CAPM with uncertainty over the choice and measurement of the underlying factors.

One study by Nai-fu Chen, Richard Roll, and Stephen Ross suggests four plausible economic factors:[15]

1. Unanticipated changes in industrial production.
2. Unanticipated changes in the spread between the yield on low-grade and high-grade bonds.
3. Unanticipated changes in interest rates and the shape of the yield curve.
4. Unanticipated changes in inflation.

It is interesting to note that a brochure recently published by the Roll and Ross Asset Management Corporation expands that list to five factors, some similar to the previous group and some new.[16] The factors whose unexpected changes are said to have systematic impact on stock returns are these:

1. The business cycle, as measured by the Index of Industrial Production.
2. Interest rates, as given by the yields on long-term government bonds.

---

[15] Nai-fu Chen, Richard Roll, and Stephen A. Ross, "Economic Forces and the Stock Market: Testing the APT and Alternative Asset Pricing Theories," *Journal of Business* (July 1980), pp. 383–403.

[16] Roll and Ross Asset Management Corporation, *APT: Balancing Risk and Return* (undated), p. 14.

3. Investor confidence, as proxied by the spread between yields on high-grade and yields on low-grade bonds that are similar with regard to call provisions, maturity, and other features.

4. Short-term inflation, as measured by month-to-month changes in the Consumer Price Index.

5. Inflationary expectations, as represented in the changes in the short-term risk-free interest rate.

As this brochure points out, some stocks are responsive to some factors, while other stocks are closely linked to different factors. Portfolio building involves identifying the pertinent factors and finding the price/risk reward for them. In its consideration of differing sensitivities to various systematic variables, the APT departs significantly from the CAPM.

▶ KEY POINTS THAT YOU SHOULD UNDERSTAND BEFORE PROCEEDING:

1. The Arbitrage Pricing Theory (or APT) model postulates that a security's return is a function of several factors and the security's sensitivity to changes in each of them.

2. If a security's market price were to deviate from the level justified by these factors and the security's price-sensitivity to them, investors would engage in arbitrage and drive the market price to an appropriate level.

3. An appealing feature of the APT model is that it makes few assumptions about investors and the structure of the market.

SUMMARY

This chapter explains the principles of portfolio theory, a theory that deals with the construction of optimal portfolios by rational risk-averse investors, and its implications for the returns on different assets, and hence security prices. One way to evaluate the risk of a portfolio is by estimating the extent to which future portfolio values are likely to deviate from expected portfolio return. This is measured by the variance of the portfolio's return and is called the total portfolio risk. Total portfolio risk can be decomposed into two types of risk: systematic risk and unsystematic risk.

*Systematic risk*, also called *market risk*, is the risk that affects all securities. The beta of any security or portfolio is the relative systematic risk of the asset and is measured statistically (using historical return data) by the slope of the regression between the asset's and the market's returns. The regression line estimated is called the market model. Unsystematic risk is the risk that is unique to a company, and it can be eliminated by diversifying the portfolio. Thus, systematic risk and unsystematic risk are referred to as nondiversifiable and diversifiable risk, respectively.

The capital asset pricing model is an economic theory that attempts to provide a relationship between risk and return, or, equivalently, it is a model for the pricing of risky securities. The CAPM asserts that the only relevant risk that investors will require compensation for assuming is systematic risk, because that risk cannot be eliminated by diversification. Basically, CAPM says that the expected return of a security or a portfolio is equal to the rate on a risk-free security plus a risk premium. The risk premium in the CAPM is proportional to the security or the portfolio beta. More specifically, the risk premium is the product of the quantity of risk and the market price of risk, measured by beta, and the difference between the expected market return and risk-free rate, respectively.

The CAPM assumes that investors are concerned with only one risk: the risk having to do with the future price of a security. However, there are other risks, such as the capacity of investors to consume goods and services in the future. The multifactor CAPM assumes investors face such extra-market sources of risk called factors. The expected return in the multifactor CAPM is the market risk, as in the case of the basic CAPM, plus a package of risk premiums. Each risk premium is the product of the beta of the security or portfolio with respect to the particular factor and the difference between the expected return for the factor and the risk-free rate.

The Arbitrage Pricing Theory model is developed purely on arbitrage arguments. It postulates that the expected return on a security or a portfolio is influenced by several factors. Proponents of the APT model cite its use of less restrictive assumptions as a feature that makes it more appealing than the CAPM or the multifactor CAPM. Moreover, testing the APT model does not require identification of the "true" market portfolio. It does, however, require empirical determination of the factors because they are not specified by the theory. Consequently, the APT model replaces the problem of identifying the market portfolio in the CAPM with the problem of choosing and measuring the underlying factors.

All things considered, the CAPM, the multifactor CAPM, and the APT model all provide interesting conceptual insights into the issues of the pricing of risk and portfolio selection in securities markets. None can be said to dominate the others in terms of theoretical content or the simplicity of empirical testing. Only the future will decide which has the best claim to the ultimate truth. Indeed, on this question, all three pricing theories will probably make valuable contributions to development of the next generation of equilibrium models.

**GLOSSARY**

**Alpha:** A statistical measure of the typical unsystematic change in the price of a stock.

**Arbitrage pricing theory (or APT) model:** The theory that a security's expected return is influenced by a variety of factors, rather than just by the movement in the value of the overall market for securities.

**Beta:** A statistical index of the sensitivity of an asset's price changes to changes in the value of the overall market or of assets in general.

**Capital asset pricing model (or CAPM):** Theory that hypothesizes that the expected return on a well-diversified portfolio should (in a linear relationship) equal the riskless rate of return plus an amount that is proportional to the portfolio beta.

**Capital gain:** A gain arising from an increase in the market value of an investment.

**Correlation:** A statistical measure of the extent to which two variables move around their respective means.

**Diversifiable risk:** That variability in an asset's returns that, when it is grouped with other assets in a portfolio, will be reduced or offset by variation in the returns of other members of the portfolio. This term is another name for unsystematic risk (see below).

**Efficient (or optimal) portfolio:** A portfolio that offers the highest expected return for any given level of risk.

**Expected return:** The central tendency or mean of a probability distribution of returns.

**Extra-market source of risk:** A cause of the variability in the returns of securities that is independent of both movements in the general market value of securities and developments particular to the situations of the firms that issued the securities.

**Market model:** The mathematical expression of the hypothesis that the returns on a stock reflect only two forces, the overall market for securities and developments particular to the firm that issued the stock.

**Market-related risk:** The variability in an asset's returns that reflects changes in the average or typical value of assets. Also, another term for systematic risk.

**Probability distribution:** A listing, through a table or a mathematical formula, of the possible values of a random variable and the likelihood that each value will occur.

**Skewness:** The characteristic of a probability distribution that creates a greater likelihood of values on one side of the mean than on the other.

**Standard deviation:** The square root of a distribution's variance.

**Symmetric distribution:** A probability distribution in which the probability for values above the mean is the same as for those below the mean.

**Systematic risk:** The variability in an asset's return that derives from its relationship to the general market for securities and that cannot be eliminated by inclusion of the asset in a portfolio.

**Total risk:** The standard deviation (or variance) of returns to an asset or portfolio of assets.

**Unsystematic risk:** The portion of the variability in a security's returns that reflects only the situations unique or specific to the firm that issued the security. This concept is the same as diversifiable risk (see above).

**Variance of a probability distribution:** The mean of the squared deviation of the differences between possible values and the distribution's mean.

**QUESTIONS**

1. A friend has asked you to help him figure out a statement he received from his broker. It seems that, at the start of last year, your friend paid $900 for a bond, and sold it at the end of the year for $890. During the year, he received a single coupon payment of $110. The statement claims that his return (not including commissions and taxes) is 11.11% for the year. Is this claim correct?

2. Suppose the probability distribution for the one-period return of some asset is as follows:

| Return | Probability |
|--------|-------------|
| 0.20 | 0.10 |
| 0.15 | 0.20 |
| 0.10 | 0.30 |
| 0.03 | 0.25 |
| -0.06 | 0.15 |

   a. What is this asset's expected one-period return?

   b. What is this asset's variance and standard deviation for the one-period return?

3. "A portfolio's expected return and variance of return are simply the weighted average of the individual asset expected returns and variances." Do you agree with this statement?

4. In the January 25, 1991, issue of *The Value Line Investment Survey*, you note the following:

| Company | Beta ($\beta$) |
|---------|----------------|
| IBM | 0.95 |
| Bally Manufacturing | 1.40 |
| Cigna Corp. | 1.00 |
| British Telecom | 0.60 |

   a. How do you interpret these betas?

   b. Is it reasonable to assume that the expected return on British Telecom is less than that on IBM shares?

   c. "Given that Cigna Corporation has a $\beta$ of 1.00, one can mimic the performance of the stock market as a whole by buying only these shares." Do you agree with this statement?

5. Assume the following:

$$\text{Expected market return} = 15\%$$
$$\text{Risk-free rate} = 7\%$$

   If a security's beta is 1.3, what is its expected return according to the CAPM?

6. Professor Harry Markowitz, corecipient of the 1990 Nobel Prize in Economics, wrote the following:

   *A portfolio with sixty different railway securities, for example, would not be as well diversified as the same size portfolio with some railroad, some public utility, mining, various sort of manufacturing, etc.*

Why is this true?

7. Following is an excerpt from an article, "Risk and Reward," in *The Economist* of October 20, 1990:

> *Next question: is the CAPM supported by the facts? That is controversial, to put it mildly. It is a tribute to Mr. Sharpe [cowinner of the 1990 Nobel Prize in Economics] that his work, which dates from the early 1960s, is still argued over so heatedly. Attention has lately turned away from beta to more complicated ways of carving up risk. But the significance of CAPM for financial economics would be hard to exaggerate.*

   a. Summarize Roll's argument on the problems inherent in empirically verifying the CAPM.

   b. What are some of the other "more complicated ways of carving up risk"?

8. a. What are the difficulties in practice of applying the arbitrage pricing theory model?

   b. Does Roll's criticism also apply to this pricing model?

   c. "In the CAPM investors should be compensated for accepting systematic risk; for the APT model, investors are rewarded for accepting both systematic risk and unsystematic risk." Do you agree with this statement?

CHAPTER FOURTEEN

# Primary Markets and the Underwriting of Securities

## LEARNING OBJECTIVES

*After reading this chapter you will understand:*

- the role investment bankers play in the distribution of newly issued securities.
- the risk associated with the underwriting of a security.
- the different types of underwriting arrangements.
- the types of entities that are involved in investment banking.
- how the SEC regulates the distribution of newly issued securities.
- what a registration statement is.
- the impact of the SEC Rule 415 ("shelf registration").
- what is a bought deal underwriting for a bond issue, and why it is used.
- what a competitive bidding underwriting is.
- what a rights offering for the sale of common stock is.
- the advantages and disadvantages from an issuer's perspective of a private placement.
- the reason for Rule 144A and its potential impact on the private placement market.

As we explain in Chapter 1, financial markets can be categorized as those dealing with financial claims that are newly issued, called the *primary market*, and those for exchanging financial claims previously issued, called the *secondary market*, or the market for seasoned securities. In this chapter we focus on the primary market for securities; the next chapter covers the secondary market.

The primary market involves the distribution to investors of newly issued securities by central governments, its agencies, municipal governments, and corporations.[1] The participants in the marketplace that work with issuers to distribute newly issued securities are called *investment bankers*. The activity of investment banking is undertaken by basically two types of firms: securities houses and commercial banks. In this chapter, we explain the various ways that investment banking firms are involved in the issuance of new securities, the regulation of the primary market, and the private placement market.

## THE TRADITIONAL PROCESS FOR ISSUING NEW SECURITIES

The traditional process in the United States for issuing new securities involves investment bankers performing one or more of the following three functions: (1) advising the issuer on the terms and the timing of the offering, (2) buying the securities from the issuer, and (3) distributing the issue to the public.[2] The advisor role may require investment bankers to design a security structure that is more palatable to investors than a particular traditional instrument. For example, the high interest rates in the United States in the late 1970s and early 1980s increased the cost of borrowing for issuers of even the highest quality rating. To reduce the cost of borrowing for their clients, investment bankers designed securities with characteristics that were more attractive to investors but not onerous to issuers. They also designed security structures for low-quality bond issues, so-called high-yield or junk bond structures. We'll give several examples of these financial innovations in later chapters.

In the sale of new securities, investment bankers need not undertake the second function—buying the securities from the issuer. An investment banker may merely act as an advisor and/or distributor of the new security. The function of buying the securities from the issuer is called *underwriting*. When an investment banking firm buys the securities from the issuer and accepts the risk of selling the securities to investors at a lower price, it is referred to as an *underwriter*. When the investment banking firm agrees to buy the securities from the issuer at a set price, the underwriting arrangement is referred to as a *firm commitment*. In contrast, in a *best efforts* arrangement, the investment banking

---

[1] This also includes the offering of securities of government-owned companies to private investors. This process is referred to as *privatization*. An example in the U.S. is the initial public offering of the U.S. government-owned railroad company Conrail in March of 1987. Non-U.S. examples include Great Britain's British Telecom, Chile's Pacifica, and France's Paribas.

[2] When an investment banking firm commits its own funds on a long-term basis by either taking an equity interest or creditor position in companies, this activity is referred to as *merchant banking*.

firm agrees only to use its expertise to sell the securities—it does not buy the entire issue from the issuer.

The fee earned from underwriting a security is the difference between the price paid to the issuer and the price at which the investment bank reoffers the security to the public. This difference is called the *gross spread*, or the *underwriter discount*. There are numerous factors that affect the size of the gross spread.[3] Typical gross spreads for common stock offerings, *initial public offerings* (IPOs), and bond offerings are shown in Table 14-1. IPOs are typically common stock offerings issued by companies that had not previously issued common stock to the public. Because of the risk associated with pricing and then selling IPOs to investors, the gross spread is higher.

## TABLE 14-1

### TYPICAL GROSS SPREADS BY OFFERING SIZE: STOCKS AND BONDS

| Common Stock Offering* | | Initial Public Offering | |
|---|---|---|---|
| Size (in Millions) | Gross Spread | Size (in Millions) | Gross Spread |
| $ 10 | 6.0-8.0% | $ 5 | 8.0-10.0% |
| 15 | 5.0-7.5 | 10 | 7.5- 9.0 |
| 20 | 5.0-7.0 | 15 | 7.0-8.0 |
| 30 | 3.5-5.0 | 20 | 6.5-7.0 |
| 50 | 2.0-5.0 | 30 | 5.5-7.0 |
| 100 | 2.0-4.5 | 50 | 5.0-7.0 |
| 150 | 2.0-4.0 | 200 | 2.0-4.0 |

### Fixed Income Offering**

| Size (in Millions) | Gross Spread |
|---|---|
| $ 20 | 1.3% |
| 25 | 1.2 |
| 30 | 1.0 |
| 50 | 0.7 |
| 100 | 0.7 |
| 150 | 0.7 |
| 200 | 0.7 |

* For industrial companies not utilities.

**Typical offering of A-rated corporate debt with ten years to maturity.

*Source:* Adapted from Figures 1, 2, and 3 of G. Clyde Buck, "Spreads and Fees in Investment Banking," Chapter 5 in Robert Lawrence Kuhn (ed.), *The Library of Investment Banking*, Volume II (Homewood, IL: Dow Jones-Irwin, 1990).

---

[3] For a discussion of these factors, see G. Clyde Buck, "Spreads and Fees in Investment Banking," Chapter 5 in Robert Lawrence Kuhn (ed.), *The Library of Investment Banking*, Volume II (Homewood, IL: Dow Jones-Irwin, 1990), pp. 146–147.

The typical underwritten transaction involves so much risk of capital loss that a single investment banking firm undertaking it alone would be exposed to the danger of losing a significant portion of its capital. To share this risk, an investment banking firm forms a *syndicate* of firms to underwrite the issue. The gross spread is then divided among the lead underwriter(s) and the other firms in the underwriting syndicate. The lead underwriter manages the deal (or "runs the books" for the deal). In many cases, there may be more than one lead underwriter, so that the lead underwriters are said to "co-lead" or "co-manage" the deal.

To realize the gross spread, the entire securities issue must be sold to the public at the planned reoffering price. This usually requires a great deal of marketing muscle. Investment banking firms have an investor client base (retail and institutional) to which they attempt to sell the securities. To increase the potential investor base, the lead underwriter will put together a *selling group*. This group includes the underwriting syndicate plus other firms that are not in the syndicate. Members of the selling group can buy the security at a concession price—a price less than the reoffering price. The gross spread is thereby divided among the lead underwriter, members of the underwriting syndicate, and members of the selling group.

A successful underwriting of a security requires that the underwriter have a strong sales force. The sales force provides feedback on advance interest in the security, and the traders (also called market makers) provide input in pricing the security as well. (Traders are discussed in Chapter 15.) It would be a mistake to think that once the securities are all sold the investment banking firm's ties with the deal are ended. In the case of bonds, those who bought the securities will look to the investment banking firm to make a market in the issue. This means that the investment banking firm must be willing to take a principal position in secondary market transactions.

▶ KEY POINTS THAT YOU SHOULD UNDERSTAND BEFORE PROCEEDING:

1. There are three functions performed by investment bankers in the offering of new securities.

2. Depending on the type of underwriting agreement, the underwriting function may expose the investment banking firm to the risk of selling the securities to the public at a price less than the price paid to the issuer.

3. The gross spread earned by the underwriter depends on numerous factors.

4. Because of the risks associated with the underwriting of securities, an underwriting syndicate and a selling group are typically formed.

## INVESTMENT BANKERS

■ ■ ■ ■

Investment banking is performed by two groups: commercial banks, which we discussed in Chapter 4, and securities houses. As we explained in our discussion of commercial banks, the Glass-Steagall Act restricts the types of securities that commercial banks in the United States may underwrite. No restrictions are placed on investment banking activity of commercial banks outside the United States.

Securities houses are firms that not only distribute newly issued securities but also are involved in the secondary market as market makers and brokers. Just as in the United States, the securities laws and banking regulations of each country will specify the entities that are permitted to underwrite securities. Japanese securities law, for example, places even greater restrictions on the underwriting activities of commercial banks than in the United States. In countries such as Germany, there is no separation of commercial banking and investment banking activities. Banks in Germany are referred to as *universal banks* because they are involved in both activities. The underwriting of new securities is primarily done by commercial banks in Germany.

A country will also regulate the activities of foreign firms in its financial market. For example, a country may not permit a foreign commercial bank or securities house to participate in the primary market for a government and/or corporate security. The liberalization of financial markets in recent years has opened up investment banking activities to foreign entities.

A popular classification of U.S. securities firms involved in the underwriting of securities is as follows: bulge-bracket firms, major bracket firms, submajor bracket firms, and regional firms. *Bulge-bracket firms* are viewed as the premier investment banking firms because of their size, reputation, presence in key markets, and customer base. Included in this exclusive group are First Boston Corporation; Goldman Sachs & Co.; Merrill Lynch; Morgan Stanley, Salomon Brothers Inc. and Lehman Brothers (formerly Shearson Lehman Hutton). Large investment banking firms that do not have the same status as the bulge-bracket firms but nevertheless provide full-line services are called *major bracket firms*. Included in this group are Bear Stearns & Co.; Smith Barney, Harris Upham; Kidder Peabody; Paine Webber; Donaldson, Lukfin & Jenrette; Dean Witter; and Prudential Securities. *Submajor bracket firms* are frequently New York-based firms that cater to smaller issuing companies. Firms located outside New York and that serve regional issuers (corporate and local governments) are classified as *regional firms*.

In Japan, the major securities houses—popularly referred to as the Big Four—are Nomura, Daiwa, Yamaichi, and Nikko. These firms are actively involved in the underwriting of securities issued in the United States and the Euromarket, as well as in Japan.

▶ KEY POINTS THAT YOU SHOULD UNDERSTAND BEFORE PROCEEDING:

1. The two groups that underwrite securities are investment banking firms and commercial banks. Banks' activities in the U.S. are restricted by the Glass-Steagall Act.

2. Investment banking firms in the United States can be classified as either bulge-bracket, major bracket, submajor bracket, or regional firms.

3.  There are four major firms that dominate investment banking in Japan.

## REGULATION OF THE PRIMARY MARKET

■ ■ ■ ■   Underwriting activities are regulated by the Securities and Exchange Commission (SEC). The Securities Act of 1933 governs the issuance of securities. The act requires that a registration statement be filed with the SEC by the issuer of a security. The type of information contained in the registration statement is the nature of the business of the issuer, key provisions or features of the security, the nature of the investment risks associated with the security, and the background of management.[4] Financial statements must be included in the registration statement and they must be certified by an independent public accountant.[5]

The registration is actually divided into two parts. Part I is the *prospectus*. It is this part that is typically distributed to the public as an offering of the securities. Part II contains supplemental information, which is not distributed to the public as part of the offering but is available from the SEC upon request.

The act provides for penalties in the form of fines and/or imprisonment if the information provided is inaccurate or material information is omitted. Moreover, investors who purchase the security are entitled to sue the issuer to recover damages if they incur a loss as a result of the misleading information. The underwriter may also be sued if it can be demonstrated that the underwriter did not conduct a reasonable investigation of the information reported by the issuer. One of the most important duties of an underwriter is to perform *due diligence*. The following quotation comes from a court decision that explains the obligation of an underwriter to perform due diligence:

> *An underwriter by participating in an offering constructively represents that statements made in the registration materials are complete and accurate. The investing public properly relies upon the underwriter to check the accuracy of the statements and the soundness of the offer; when the underwriter does not speak out, the investor reasonably assumes that there are no undisclosed material deficiencies. The representations in the registration statement are those of the underwriter as much as they are those of the issuer.*[6]

The filing of a registration statement with the SEC does not mean that the security can be offered to the public. The registration statement must be reviewed and approved by the SEC's Division of Corporate Finance before a public offering can be made. Typically, the staff of this division will find a problem with the registration statement. The staff then sends a "letter of comments" or "deficiency letter" to the issuer explaining the problem it has encountered.

---

[4] SEC Regulation S-K and the Industry Guidelines (SEC Securities Act Release No. 6384, March 3, 1982) specify the information that must be included in the registration statement.

[5] SEC Regulation S-X specifies the financial statements that must be disclosed.

[6] Chris-Craft Industries, Inc. *v.* Piper Aircraft Corp, 1973.

The issuer must remedy any problem by filing an amendment to the registration statement. If the staff is satisfied, the SEC will issue an order declaring that the registration statement is "effective," and the underwriter can solicit sales. The approval of the SEC, however, does not mean that the securities have investment merit or are properly priced or that the information is accurate. It merely means that the appropriate information appears to have been disclosed.

The time interval between the initial filing of the registration statement and the time the registration statement becomes effective is referred to as the *waiting period*. During the waiting period, the SEC does allow the underwriters to distribute a preliminary prospectus. Because the prospectus has not become effective, its cover page states this in red ink and, as a result, the preliminary prospectus is commonly called a *red herring*. During the waiting period, the underwriter cannot sell the security, nor may it accept written offers from investors to buy the security.

In 1982 the SEC approved Rule 415, which permits certain issuers to file a single registration document indicating that they intend to sell a certain amount of a certain class of securities at one or more times within the next two years.[7] Rule 415 is popularly referred to as the *shelf registration rule* because the securities can be viewed as sitting on a "shelf," and can be taken off that shelf and sold to the public without obtaining additional SEC approval. In essence, the filing of a single registration document allows the issuer to come to market quickly because the sale of the security has been preapproved by the SEC. Prior to establishment of Rule 415, there was a lengthy period required before a security could be sold to the public. As a result, in a fast-moving market, issuers could not come to market quickly with an offering to take advantage of what they perceived to be attractive financing opportunities. For example, if a corporation felt that interest rates were low and wanted to issue a bond, it had to file a registration statement and could not issue the bond until the registration statement became effective. The corporation was then taking the chance that during the waiting period interest rates would rise, making the bond offering more costly.

▶ KEY POINTS THAT YOU SHOULD UNDERSTAND BEFORE PROCEEDING:

1. The SEC regulates underwriting activities.
2. An issuer must file a registration statement, one part of which is the prospectus.
3. The underwriter must exercise due diligence to assure that there are no misstatements or omissions of fact in the registration statement or prospectus.

---

[7] The issuer qualifies for Rule 415 registration if the securities are investment grade securities and/or the securities of companies that have historically filed registration statements and whose securities comply with minimum flotation requirements.

4.  SEC Rule 415 (the shelf registration rule) gives greater flexibility to certain issuers by permitting them to file a single registration document for the offering of certain securities at one or more times within the next two years.

## VARIATIONS IN THE UNDERWRITING PROCESS

■ ■ ■ ■

Not all deals are underwritten using the traditional syndicate process we have described. Variations in the United States, the Euromarkets, and foreign markets include the "bought deal" for the underwriting of bonds, the auction process for both stocks and bonds, and a rights offering for underwriting common stock.

### Bought Deal

The bought deal was introduced in the Eurobond market in 1981 when Credit Suisse First Boston purchased from General Motors Acceptance Corporation a $100 million issue without lining up an underwriting syndicate prior to the purchase. Thus, Credit Suisse First Boston did not use the traditional syndication process to diversify the capital risk exposure associated with an underwriting that we described earlier.

The mechanics of a bought deal are as follows. The lead manager or a group of managers offers a potential issuer of debt securities a firm bid to purchase a specified amount of the securities with a certain interest (coupon) rate and maturity. The issuer is given a day or so (maybe even only a few hours) to accept or reject the bid. If the bid is accepted, the underwriting firm has bought the deal. It can, in turn, sell the securities to other investment banking firms for distribution to their clients and/or distribute the securities to its clients. Typically, the underwriting firm that buys the deal will have presold most of the issue to its institutional clients.

The bought deal appears to have found its way into the United States in mid-1985 when Merrill Lynch underwrote a bond issue for which it was the only underwriter. The gross spread on the bond, a $50 million issue of Norwest Financial, was 0.268%. This is far less than the 0.7% gross spread indicated in Table 14-1. Merrill Lynch offered a portion of the securities to investors and the balance to other investment banking firms.

There are several reasons why some underwriting firms find the bought deal attractive. While Rule 415 gives certain issuers timing flexibility to take advantage of "windows" of opportunities in the global marketplace, it requires that underwriting firms be prepared to respond on short notice to commit funds to a deal. This fact favors the bought deal because it gives the underwriting firm very little time to line up a syndicate. A consequence of accepting bought deals, however, is that underwriting firms need to expand their capital so that they can commit greater amounts of funds to such deals.

The risk of capital loss in a bought deal may not be as great as it first appears. There are some deals that are so straightforward that a large underwriting firm may have enough institutional investor interest to keep the risks of distributing the issue at the reoffering price quite small. Moreover, in the case of bonds, hedging strategies using the interest rate risk control tools that we discuss in Chapters 25 and 26 can reduce or eliminate the risk of realizing a loss of selling the bonds at a price below the reoffering price.

## Auction Process

Another variation for underwriting securities is the auction process. In this method, the issuer announces the terms of the issue, and interested parties submit bids for the entire issue. The auction form is mandated for certain securities of regulated public utilities and many municipal debt obligations. It is more commonly referred to as a "competitive bidding underwriting." For example, suppose that a public utility wishes to issue $100 million of bonds. Various underwriters will form syndicates and bid on the issue. The syndicate that bids the lowest yield (i.e., the lowest cost to the issuer) wins the entire $100 million bond issue and then reoffers it to the public.

In a variant of the process, the bidders indicate the price they are willing to pay and the amount they are willing to buy. The security is then allocated to bidders from the highest bid price (lowest yield in the case of a bond) to the lower ones (higher yield in the case of a bond) until the entire issue is allocated. For example, suppose that an issuer is offering $500 million of a bond issue, and nine bidders submit the following yield bids:

| Bidder | Amount (in Millions) | Bid |
|--------|----------------------|-------|
| A | $150 | 5.1% |
| B | 110 | 5.2 |
| C | 90 | 5.2 |
| D | 100 | 5.3 |
| E | 75 | 5.4 |
| F | 25 | 5.4 |
| G | 80 | 5.5 |
| H | 70 | 5.6 |
| I | 85 | 5.7 |

The first four bidders above—A, B, C, and D—will be allocated the amount for which they bid because they submitted the lowest yield bids. In total, they will receive $450 million of the $500 million to be issued. That leaves $50 million to be allocated to the next lowest bidders. Both E and F submitted the next lowest yield bid, 5.4%. In total, they bid for $100 million. Since the total they bid for exceeds the remaining $50 million, they will receive an amount proportionate to the amount for which they bid. Specifically, E will be allocated three-quarters ($75 million divided by $100 million) of the $50 million or $37.5 million, and F will be allocated one-quarter ($25 million divided by $100 million) of the $50 million or $12.5 million.

The next question is the actual yield that all of the six winning bidders— A, B, C, D, E, and F—will have to pay for the amount of the issue allocated to them. One way in which a competitive bidding can occur is all bidders pay the highest winning yield bid (or, equivalently, the lowest winning price). In our example, all bidders would buy the amount allocated to them at 5.4%. This type of auction is referred to as a *Dutch auction*. Another way is for each bidder to pay whatever it bid. As we explain in Chapter 16, this is the procedure used in the issuance of U.S. Treasury securities.

Using an auction allows corporate issuers to place newly issued debt obligations directly with institutional investors rather than follow the indirect path of using an underwriting firm. One step in this direction is the service provided by CapitaLink Securities, which links issuers directly to institutional investors. In 1989, CapitaLink was successful in offering a new corporate bond issue directly to institutional investors through its computerized auction system.[8] At the end of 1990, 125 major institutions and 16 prospective issuers had joined the service.[9] In February 1988, Great Northern Nekoosa used this service to place $75 million in publicly registered bonds directly with Metropolitan Life Insurance Company.[10]

Investment bankers' response to the practice of direct purchase of publicly registered securities is that, as intermediaries, they add value by searching their institutional client base, which increases the likelihood that the issuer will incur the lowest cost, after adjusting for the underwriting fees. By dealing with just a few institutional investors, investment bankers argue, issuers cannot be sure of obtaining funds at the lowest cost. In addition, investment bankers say that they often play another important role: they make a secondary market in the securities they issue. This market improves the perceived liquidity of the issue and, as a result, reduces the cost to issuers. The question whether investment bankers can obtain lower cost funding (after accounting for underwriting fees) to issuers, by comparison to the cost of funding from a direct offering, is an interesting empirical question.

## Preemptive Rights Offering

A corporation can issue new common stock directly to existing shareholders via a *preemptive rights offering*. A preemptive right grants existing shareholders the right to buy some proportion of the new shares issued at a price below market value. The price at which the new shares can be purchased is called the *subscription price*. A rights offering insures that current shareholders may maintain their proportionate equity interest in the corporation. In the United States, the practice of issuing common stock via a preemptive rights offering is uncommon. In other countries it is much more common; in some countries, it is the only means by which a new offering of common stock may be sold.

For the shares sold via a preemptive rights offering, the underwriting services of an investment banker are not needed. However, the issuing corporation may use the services of an investment banker for the distribution of

---

[8] Beth Selby, "End-Running the Underwriters," *Institutional Investor* (June 1989), p. 27.

[9] Chris Welles and Monica Roman, "The Future of Wall Street," *Business Week* (November 5, 1990), p. 122.

[10] Beth Selby, "End-Running the Street," *Institutional Investor* (June 1989), p. 181.

common stock that is not subscribed to. A *standby underwriting arrangement* will be used in such instances. This arrangement calls for the underwriter to buy the unsubscribed shares. The issuing corporation pays a standby fee to the investment banking firm.

To demonstrate how a rights offering works, the effect on the economic wealth of shareholders, and how the terms set forth in a rights offering affects whether or not the issuer will need an underwriter, we will use an illustration. Suppose that the market price of the stock of FMF Corporation is $20 per share and that there are 30,000 shares outstanding. Thus, the capitalization of this firm is $600,000. Suppose that the management of FMF corporation is considering a rights offering in connection with the issuance of 10,000 new shares. Each current shareholder would receive 1 right for every 3 shares owned. The terms of the rights offering are as follows: for 3 rights and $17 (the subscription price) a new share can be acquired. The subscription price must always be less than the market price or the rights will not be exercised. However, as we will see, the amount of the discount (that is, the difference between the market price and subscription price) is relevant. In our illustration, the subscription price is 15% ($3/20) below the market price.[11]

In addition to the number of rights and the subscription price, there are two other elements of a rights offering that are important. First is the choice to transfer the rights. This is done by selling the right in the open market. This is critical since, as we will see, the right has a value and that value can be captured by selling the right. The second element is the time when the right expires (that is, when it can no longer be used to acquire the stock). Typically, the time period before a right expires is short.

Table 14-2 shows the impact of the rights offering on the position of an initial shareholder. The share price declines from $20 to $19.25. The difference between the price before the rights offering and after the rights offering expressed as a percentage of the original price is called the *dilution effect of the rights issue*. In the present case, the dilution effect is $0.75/$20, or 3.75%. The dilution is larger, the larger the ratio of old and new shares, and the larger the discount.[12]

The last section of Table 14-2 shows the net gain or loss to the initial shareholder. The result of row 10 in the table is important because it shows that the rights offering as such will not affect the sum of the value of the share ex rights plus the value of the rights he receives, no matter how much the di-

---

[11] Note that the same results can be achieved by issuing one right per share but requiring 3 rights plus the subscription price for a new share (except for rounding off problems and implications for the value of one right discussed below).

[12] Specifically:

$$\text{dilution effect} = \frac{\text{discount\%}}{1 + (\text{ratio of old to new shares})}$$

In our illustration the discount is 15% and the ratio of old to new shares is 30,000/10,000 or 3, so the dilution effect is 15%/4, or 3.75%.

| TABLE 14-2 |
|:---:|

### ANALYSIS OF RIGHTS OFFERING ON THE MARKET PRICE OF FMF CORPORATION

#### I. Before rights issue

| | |
|---|---|
| 1. Capitalization | $600,000 |
| 2. Number of shares | 30,000 |
| 3. Share price (rights on) | $20.00 |

#### II. After issuance of shares via rights offering

| | |
|---|---|
| 4. Number of shares | 40,000 (= 30,000 + 10,000) |
| 5. Capitalization | $770,000 (= $600,000 + 10,000 × $17) |
| 6. Share price (ex-rights) | $19.25 (= $770,000 / 40,000) |
| 7. Value of one right | $2.25 (= $19.25 – $17) |

#### III. Net gain or loss to initial stockholder

| | |
|---|---|
| 8. Loss per share due to dilution | $0.75 (= 3.75% × $20) |
| 9. Gain per share from selling or exercising rights | $0.75 (= $2.25 / 3) |
| 10. Net gain or loss | $0 |

lution or the initial discount offered. This is because a larger dilution is exactly compensated by the increase in the value of the rights.

However, this does not mean that the size of the discount and dilution is irrelevant for the welfare of the stockholders. On the contrary, the value of one right will, in general, not be constant during the period over which the rights may be exercised. In our example, it is $2.25 on the day the rights begin trading and are exercisable. However, for any successive day between this day and the last day that the rights may be exercised the value of the rights will tend to be equal to the difference between the market price of the stock at that date and the subscription price. This is because in a perfect market, with no transaction costs, any difference can be arbitraged (risklessly), forcing the stock and the right to be priced consistently. Thus, suppose that just after the rights issuance the price of the stock is at $19.25 as expected, but at the same time the price of a right is underpriced selling at only $1.50. Then one can arbitrage by buying the "cheap" rights, exercising them by paying the subscription price of $17, and receiving shares at the cost of $18.50, which can be simultaneously sold at $19.25, for a gain of $0.75 per share. This arbitrage activity will drive the price of the shares and the rights to be priced consistently so as to not allow any arbitrage profit.

In reality, however, there are transaction costs in this arbitrage transaction, including at least the double commission and other costs. Therefore, the price of the right may remain somewhat lower than the difference between the market price of the shares and the subscription price.

This has two implications. First, if the market price of the stock were to fall by more than the initial value of the rights, then the rights would become worthless and remain worthless as long as the market price remained below that critical level. From the point of view of the issuing company, this would mean that some rights would fail to be exercised and therefore the firm would be unable to raise the amount of financing it intended to. For this reason it has been suggested that the firm should rely on the services of an investment banker who would commit to buy any unsold shares at the subscription price.

The risk of a rights offering failing will depend on the value of the right relative to the volatility of the stock price. But the value of the right (given the shares to be issued) depends on the discount chosen in designing the issue. Now suppose that the subscription is to occur within one month and the monthly price volatility (as measured by the standard deviation) can be estimated. Then, by the choice of an appropriately high discount and resulting value of the right, the issuer can make the probability of failure as small as desired (at least if there are no other constraints on the discount which we discuss below). Therefore, we conclude that in general the rights offering can be so designed that the services of an investment banker are not needed, which can reduce substantially the cost of the issue to shareholders.[13]

There is another consideration which suggests the desirability of designing the rights offering with a relatively high discount. We have already seen that the value of the right will be unfavorably affected by transaction costs. In addition, these costs will reduce the net amount received by a stockholder who decides to sell his rights rather than exercise them. For both reasons it is desirable to keep transaction costs low. Since transaction cost per dollar transacted increases the smaller the share price, this means that it is desirable to design the offering so that the right has a large unit value, which means a relatively high discount.

There is potential disadvantage, however, to designing a rights offering with a high discount. Some stockholders fail to either exercise or sell their rights. This may occur because they did not receive notice of the rights offering and its terms or because, for some reason, they simply elected not to act. Stockholders who fail to act will suffer a net loss per share equal to the value of the right per share times the number of shares held (or equivalently equal to the dilution times the value of the holdings, which dilution is no longer compensated for from the proceeds from the sale of the rights) and this increases with the value of the rights. On the other hand, it can be argued that when the rights have greater value, stockholders are less likely to fail to make use of their opportunity, though, admittedly, there seems to be no empirical evidence on this point. In any event, it seems safe to conclude that there is a strong case for

---

[13] The value of the rights is also affected by the choice described in footnote 11. Clearly, the value of one right is three times larger if a shareholder is given 1 right per three shares than if the shareholder is given one right per share but requires three shares to buy one unit of the stock. In other words, the value of rights are enhanced by giving one right to each $1/y$ shares than one right per share and requiring $1/y$ rights to buy one new share.

a design that makes the value of the rights substantial but that the greater the value the more it behooves the board of directors to make efforts to ensure that stockholders are apprised of the economic value of their rights. Without going into further detail, we merely note here that the proportion of stockholders that are "hard to locate" will differ from one circumstance to the other. There are a variety of ways for reaching hard to locate stockholders, and they have differential costs, making the problem of choice among alternatives a nontrivial one.

Note, finally, that when there is no banker acting as the residual buyer, and there is the probability that at least some of the stockholders will fail to either exercise or sell their rights, there is a risk that some of the stock will remain unsold. This danger can be eliminated by giving the stock to those who will exercise the right—the privilege of over-subscribing (that is, of buying additional shares at the subscription price) in proportion to their purchases. If there are then some non-exercised rights, they are allocated to the over-subscribers. There are various possible criteria for this allocation. One reasonable gauge may be to allocate what is available first to the stockholders of record before the issue, ensuring that at least a portion of the losses to the non-exercisers will remain within the stockholder family. Because one over-subscription is worth as much as one right, there is a substantial possibility that the abundance of over-subscription will absorb the entire number of shares not exercised during the primary offering. (Warning: Over-subscription could cause the rights to be overpriced!)

▶ KEY POINTS THAT YOU SHOULD UNDERSTAND BEFORE PROCEEDING:

1. There are variations in the traditional underwriting process.
2. In a bought deal, a lead manager or a group of managers offers a potential issuer of debt securities a firm bid to purchase a specified amount of a security.
3. An offering of a new security can be made by means of an auction process.
4. A corporation can offer existing shareholders new shares in a preemptive rights offering, and using a standby underwriting arrangement, the corporation can have an investment banking firm agree to distribute any shares not subscribed to.

## PRIVATE PLACEMENT OF SECURITIES

In addition to underwriting securities for distribution to the public, securities may be placed with a limited number of institutional investors such as insurance companies, investment companies, and pension funds. *Private placement*, as this process is known, differs from the "public" offering of securities that we have described so far. The size of the private placement market is estimated to be $200 billion.[14]

---

[14] John W. Milligan, "Two Cheers for 144A," *Institutional Investor* (July 1990), p. 117.

Public and private offerings of securities differ in terms of the regulatory requirements that the issuer must satisfy. The Securities Act of 1933 and the Securities Exchange Act of 1934 require that all securities offered to the general public must be registered with the SEC, unless there is a specific exemption.

The Securities Acts allow three exemptions from federal registration. First, intrastate offerings—that is, securities sold only within a state—are exempt. Second, there is a small-offering exemption (Regulation A). Specifically, if the offering is for $1 million or less, the securities need not be registered. Finally, Section 4(2) of the 1933 Act exempts from registration "transactions by an issuer not involving any public offering." At the same time, the 1933 Act does not provide specific guidelines to identify what is a private offering or placement.

In 1982, the SEC adopted Regulation D, which sets forth the guidelines that determine if an issue is qualified for exemption from registration. The guidelines require that, in general, the securities cannot be offered through any form of general advertising or general solicitation that would prevail for public offerings. Most importantly, the guidelines restrict the sale of securities to "sophisticated" investors. Such "accredited" investors are defined as those who (1) have the capability to evaluate (or who can afford to employ an advisor to evaluate) the risk and return characteristics of the securities, and (2) have the resources to bear the economic risks.[15]

The exemption of an offering does not mean that the issuer need not disclose information to potential investors. In fact, the issuer must still furnish the same information deemed material by the SEC. The issuer supplies this information in a private placement memorandum, as opposed to a prospectus for a public offering. The distinction between the private placement memorandum and the prospectus is that the former does not include information deemed by the SEC "non-material," if such information is required in a prospectus. Moreover, unlike a prospectus, the private placement memorandum is not subject to SEC review.

Investment banking firms assist in the private placement of securities in several ways. They work with the issuer and potential investors on the design and pricing of the security. Often it has been in the private placement market that investment bankers first design new security structures. Field testing of many of the innovative securities that we describe in this book occurred in the private placement market.

The investment bankers may be involved with lining up the investors as well as designing the issue. Or, if the issuer has already identified the investors, the investment banker may serve only in an advisory capacity. An investment

---

[15] Under the current law, an accredited investor is one who satisfies either a net worth test (at least $1 million excluding automobiles, home, and home furnishings) or an annual income test (at least $200,000 for a single individual, $300,000 for a couple for the last two years, with expectations of such income to continue for the current year).

302 *Part Five / Organization and Structure of Markets*

banker can also participate in the transaction on a best efforts underwriting arrangement.

### *Rule 144A*

One restriction originally imposed on buyers of privately placed securities is that they were not free to resell the securities for two years after acquisition. Thus, these issues long lacked liquidity for that time period, and buyers of privately placed securities expected a return that compensated them for this lack of liquidity.

In April 1990, however, SEC Rule 144A became effective. This rule eliminates the two-year holding period by permitting large institutions to trade securities acquired in a private placement among themselves without having to register these securities with the SEC. Rule 144A defines a large institution as one holding at least $100 million of the security.

Rule 144A has had a significant impact on the growth of the private placement market. It has encouraged non-U.S. corporations to issue securities in the U.S. private placement market for two reasons. First, the rule attracted new large institutional investors into the market who had been unwilling previously to buy private placements because of the requirement to hold the securities for two years. Such an increase in the number of institutional investors prompted non-U.S. entities to use this market. Second, foreign entities have been unwilling to raise funds in the U.S. prior to establishment of Rule 144A because they had to register their securities and furnish the necessary disclosure set forth by U.S. securities laws. Private placement requires less disclosure. Rule 144A also has improved liquidity, reducing the cost of raising funds.

▶ KEY POINTS THAT YOU SHOULD UNDERSTAND BEFORE PROCEEDING:

1.  A private placement is the distribution of shares to a limited number of institutional investors rather than through a public offering.
2.  The SEC specifies the conditions that must be satisfied to qualify for a private placement.
3.  Investment bankers will typically work with issuers in the design of a security for a private placement and line up the potential investors.
4.  SEC Rule 144A improves the liquidity of securities acquired by certain institutional investors in a private placement.

**SUMMARY**

The primary market involves the distribution to investors of newly issued securities. Investment bankers perform one or more of three functions: (1) advising the issuer on the terms and the timing of the offering, (2) buying the securities from the issuer, and (3) distributing the issue to investors. The second function is referred to as the underwriting function. Investment banking activities are performed by commercial banks and securities houses.

The SEC is responsible for regulating the issuance of new securities, with the major provisions set forth in the Securities Act of 1933. The act requires that the issuer file a registration statement for approval by the SEC. Rule 415, the shelf registration rule, permits certain issuers to file a single registration document indicating that they intend to sell a certain amount of a certain class of securities at one or more times within the next two years.

Variations in the underwriting process include the bought deal for the underwriting of bonds, the auction process for both stocks and bonds, and a rights offering coupled with a standby arrangement for underwriting common stock.

A private placement is different from the public offering of securities in terms of the regulatory requirements that must be satisfied by the issuer. If an issue qualifies as a private placement, it is exempt from the more complex registration requirements imposed on public offerings. Rule 144A will contribute to the growth of the private placement market by improving the liquidity of securities issued in this market.

GLOSSARY

**Best efforts underwriting:** An underwriting arrangement in which an investment banking firm agrees only to use its expertise to sell the securities and does not buy the entire issue from the issuer.

**Bought deal:** An underwriting arrangement whereby an investment banking firm or group of firms offers to buy an entire issue from the issuer.

**Bulge-bracket firms:** Investment banking firms that because of their size, reputation, presence in key markets, and customer base are viewed as the premier firms.

**Competitive bidding underwriting:** An underwriting arrangement in which the issuer announces the terms of the issue, and interested parties submit bids for the entire issue.

**Due diligence:** Duty of an underwriter to assure that there are no misstatements or omissions of fact in the registration statement or prospectus.

**Dutch auction:** An auction process for a new offering of securities in which bidders indicate the amount they are willing to buy and winning bidders agree to pay the lowest accepted bid price (or equivalently, the highest accepted bid yield).

**Firm commitment underwriting:** An underwriting arrangement whereby an investment banking firm agrees to buy the securities from the issuer at a set price.

**Gross spread (or underwriter discount):** The difference between the price at which a security is reoffered to the public and the price paid by the underwriter to the issuer.

**Initial public offering (or IPO):** The common stock offerings issued by firms that have not previously sold common shares to the public.

**Investment bankers:** Market participants who work with issuers to distribute newly issued securities.

**Major bracket firms:** Large investment banking firms that do not have the same status as bulge-bracket firms but nevertheless provide full-line services.

**Preemptive rights offering:** The offering of common stock by a corporation to existing shareholders at a price below market value.

**Primary market:** The financial market where financial claims that are newly issued are sold.

**Private placement:** The sale of new securities directly to one or a few investors rather than through public offering.

**Prospectus:** A part of the registration statement that is filed with the SEC by an issuer of a security and distributed to the public.

**Red herring:** The preliminary prospectus filed with the SEC by the issuer of a security.

**Regional firms:** Investment banking firms located outside New York that serve regional issuers.

**Registration statement:** Statement filed with the SEC for the purpose of disclosing pertinent information about a security and the issuer.

**Rule 144A:** SEC rule permitting large institutions to trade securities acquired in a private placement among themselves without having to register these securities with the SEC.

**Selling group:** Syndicate formed to distribute (sell) a new issue.

**Shelf registration (or SEC Rule 415):** The rule allowing firms to sell securities on a continuous basis by filing a single registration document.

**Standby fee:** Fee paid to an underwriter in a standby underwriting arrangement.

**Standby underwriting arrangement:** An underwriting arrangement calling for the underwriter to buy a firm's unsubscribed shares, which are those that cannot be distributed by the issuer.

**Submajor bracket firms:.** Frequently New York-based investment banking firms that cater to smaller security-issuing entities.

**Underwriting:** An investment banking function in which securities are purchased from the issuer for resale to the public.

**Underwriting syndicate:.** Group of investment banking firms formed to underwrite an issue.

**Waiting period:** The time interval between the initial filing of the registration statement and the time the registration statement becomes effective.

1. a. What are the three ways in which an investment banking firm may be involved in the issuance of a new security?
   b. What is meant by the underwriting function?

2. What is the difference between a firm commitment underwriting arrangement and a best efforts arrangement?

3. a. What is meant by a bought deal?
   b. Why do bought deals expose investment banking firms to greater capital risk than traditional underwriting?

4. A foreign government is issuing a bond on a competitive bidding basis. We will denote the local currency of the foreign government as LC. The government has indicated that it will issue LC 1 billion of an issue. The following yield bids and the corresponding amounts were submitted:

| Bidder | Amount (in LC Millions) | Bid |
|---|---|---|
| A | 100 | 7.4% |
| B | 200 | 7.5 |
| C | 50 | 7.5 |
| D | 250 | 7.5 |

| Bidder | Amount (in LC Millions) | Bid |
|---|---|---|
| E | 200 | 7.6% |
| F | 100 | 7.6 |
| G | 50 | 7.7 |
| H | 50 | 7.7 |
| I | 100 | 7.8 |
| J | 125 | 7.9 |
| K | 140 | 7.9 |
| L | 100 | 8.0 |
| M | 90 | 8.1 |

   a. Who are the winning bidders?
   b. How much of the security will be allocated to each winning bidder?
   c. If this auction is a Dutch auction, at what yield will each winning bidder pay the amount it will be awarded?

5. a. What is a preemptive right?
   b. What is a preemptive rights offering?
   c. Is a preemptive rights offering common in the United States?

6. a. What is meant by a bulge-bracket firm?
   b. Name three U.S. bulge-bracket firms.
   c. Name the Big Four Japanese firms.
   d. Who are the typical underwriters in Germany, securities houses or commercial banks?

7. a. What is a registration statement?
   b. What is meant by the waiting period?

8. An underwriter is responsible for performing due diligence before offering a security to investors. What does due diligence mean?

9. The following statements come from the December 24, 1990, issue of *Corporate Financing Week:*

   > *As in the public market, growth in the private placement market was slowed this year by a rise in interest rates that pushed many issuers to the sidelines, by the Mideast crisis and by a flight to quality by investors. . . . Foreign private placements saw a marked increase due to Rule 144A.*

   a. What are the key distinctions between a private placement and a public offering?

   b. What is Rule 144A?

   c. Why do you think Rule 144A has increased foreign private placements?

# CHAPTER FIFTEEN

# *Secondary Markets*

*After reading this chapter you will understand:*

- the definition of a secondary market.
- the need for secondary markets for financial assets.
- the various trading locations for securities.
- the difference between a continuous and a call market.
- the requirements of a perfect market.
- frictions that cause actual financial markets to differ from a perfect market.
- why brokers are necessary.
- the role of a dealer as a market maker and the costs associated with market making.
- what is meant by the operational efficiency of a market.
- what is meant by the pricing efficiency of a market.
- the implications of pricing efficiency.
- the different forms of pricing efficiency.
- the implications of pricing efficiency for market participants.

In Chapter 1, we described the various functions of financial markets. We note in that chapter that financial markets can be divided into primary and secondary markets. It is in the secondary market where already issued financial assets are traded. The key distinction between a primary market (as described in the last chapter) and a secondary market is that, in the secondary market, the issuer of the asset does not receive funds from the buyer. Rather, the existing issue changes hands in the secondary market, and funds flow from the buyer of the asset to the seller.

In this chapter, we will explain the various features of secondary markets. These features are common to the trading of any type of financial instrument. We take a closer look at individual markets in later chapters.

## FUNCTION OF SECONDARY MARKETS

It is worthwhile to review once again the function of secondary markets. It is in the secondary market where an issuer of securities, whether the issuer is a corporation or a governmental unit, may be provided with regular information about the value of the asset. The periodic trading of the asset reveals to the issuer the consensus price that the asset commands in an open market. Thus, firms can discover what value investors attach to their stocks, and firms or non-corporate issuers can observe the prices of their bonds and the implied interest rates investors expect and demand from them. Such information helps issuers assess how well they are using the funds acquired from earlier primary market activities, and it also indicates how receptive investors would be to new offerings. The other service that a secondary market offers issuers is the opportunity for the original buyer of an asset to reverse the investment by selling it for cash. Unless investors are confident that they can shift from one financial asset to another as they may feel necessary, they would naturally be reluctant to buy any financial asset. Such reluctance would harm potential issuers in one of two ways: either issuers would be unable to sell new securities at all, or they would have to pay a high rate of return, as investors would increase the discount rate in compensation for expected illiquidity in the securities.

Investors in financial assets receive several benefits from a secondary market. Such a market obviously offers them liquidity for their assets as well as information about the assets' fair or consensus values. Further, secondary markets bring together many interested parties and thereby reduce the costs of searching for likely buyers and sellers of assets. Moreover, by accommodating many trades, secondary markets keep the cost of transactions low. By keeping the costs of both searching and transacting low, secondary markets encourage investors to purchase financial assets.

▶ KEY POINTS THAT YOU SHOULD UNDERSTAND BEFORE PROCEEDING:

1.  Secondary markets help the issuer of securities to track their values and required returns.
2.  Secondary markets benefit investors by providing liquidity.

## TRADING LOCATIONS

One indication of the usefulness of secondary markets is that they exist throughout the world. Here, we give just a few examples of these markets.

In the United States, secondary trading of common stock occurs in a number of trading locations. Many shares are traded on major national stock exchanges and regional stock exchanges, which are organized and somewhat regulated markets in specific geographical locations. Additional significant trading in stock takes place on the so-called "over-the-counter" or OTC market, which is a geographically dispersed group of traders linked to one another via telecommunication systems. Some bonds are traded on exchanges, but most trading in bonds in the United States and throughout the world occurs in the OTC market.

The London International Stock Exchange (ISE) is basically an over-the-counter market whose members are in various places but communicate directly with one another through sophisticated electronic and computer facilities. Assets traded on the ISE include stocks of domestic and international firms as well as a wide array of bonds and options. Germany has eight organized stock exchanges, the most important of which is the Frankfurt Stock Exchange, which handles over half of the turnover on listed shares and also trades in bonds and currencies. The Paris *Bourse*, another organized exchange located in a specific place, is France's main secondary market for stocks, bonds, and some derivative securities. Japan has eight exchanges. The largest is the Tokyo Stock Exchange where trading in stocks, bonds, and futures takes place. The second largest is the Osaka Stock Exchange. The Stock Exchange of Hong Kong Limited (SEHK) is an organized secondary market for shares and bonds in that major Southeast Asian city.

▶ KEY POINTS THAT YOU SHOULD UNDERSTAND BEFORE PROCEEDING:

1.  What an organized exchange is.
2.  A large volume of trading may also occur on a market with no fixed location and with geographically dispersed traders.

## MARKET STRUCTURES

Many secondary markets are *continuous*, which means that prices are determined continuously throughout the trading day as buyers and sellers submit orders. For example, given the order flow at 10:00 a.m., the market clearing price of a stock on some organized stock exchange may be $70; at 11:00 a.m. of the same trading day, the market clearing price of the same stock, but with different order flows, may be $70.75. Thus, in a continuous market, prices may vary with the pattern of orders reaching the market and not because of any change in the basic situation of supply and demand. We will return to this point later.

A contrasting market structure is the *call market*, in which orders are batched or grouped together for simultaneous execution at the same price. That is, at certain times in the trading day (or possibly more than once in a day), a market maker holds an auction for a stock. The auction may be oral or written. In either case, the auction will determine or "fix" the market- clearing price at a particular time of the trading day. (This use of the word "fix" is traditional, and not pejorative or suggestive of illegal activity. For example, the *Financial Times* reports on the activities of the London gold bullion market, which is a call market, and records prices set at the "morning fix" and the "afternoon fix." These fixes take place at the two call auctions which are held daily.) Until the mid 1980s, the Paris *Bourse* was a call market, with auctions for large stocks being oral and auctions for smaller issues being written. It has since become a continuous market, and trading takes place *"en continu."*

Currently, some markets are mixed, using elements of the continuous and the call frameworks. For example, the New York Stock Exchange begins trading (at 9:30 a.m.) with a call auction. With opening prices set in that manner, trading proceeds in a continuous way until closing. The Tokyo Stock Exchange also begins trading in large stocks with an auction. Exchanges in Germany and Switzerland still use the call market system to a significant extent.

▶ KEY POINTS THAT YOU SHOULD UNDERSTAND BEFORE PROCEEDING:

1. The basic features of the call method of trading.
2. What a continuous market is.
3. Some markets conduct the day's initial trades with a call method and most other trades in a continuous way.

## PERFECT MARKETS

In order to explain the characteristics of secondary markets, we first describe a "perfect market" for a financial asset. Then we can show how common occurrences in real markets keep them from being theoretically perfect.

In general, a perfect market results when the number of buyers and sellers is sufficiently large, and all participants are small enough relative to the market so that no individual market agent can influence the commodity's price. Consequently, all buyers and sellers are price takers, and the market price is determined where there is equality of supply and demand. This condition is more likely to be satisfied if the commodity traded is fairly homogeneous (for example, corn or wheat). But there is more to a perfect market than market agents being price takers. It is also required that there be no transactions costs or impediments that interfere with the supply and demand of the commodity. Economists refer to these various costs and impediments as "frictions." The costs associated with frictions generally result in buyers paying more than in the absence of frictions and/or sellers receiving less.

In the case of financial markets, frictions would include:

- commissions charged by brokers
- bid-ask spreads charged by dealers
- order handling and clearance charges
- taxes (notably on capital gains) and government-imposed transfer fees
- costs of acquiring information about the financial asset
- trading restrictions, such as exchange-imposed restrictions on the size of a position in the financial asset that a buyer or seller may take
- restrictions on market makers
- halts to trading that may be imposed by regulators where the financial asset is traded.

An investor who expects that the price of a security will increase can benefit from buying that security. However, suppose that an investor expects that the price of a security will decline and wants to benefit should the price actually decline. What can the investor do? The investor may be able to sell the security without owning it. How can this happen? There are various institutional arrangements that allow an investor to borrow securities so that the borrowed security can be delivered to satisfy the sale. We describe this for the stock market in Chapter 18.

This practice of selling securities that are not owned at the time of sale is referred to as *selling short*. The security is purchased subsequently by the investor and returned to the party that lent it. In this way, the investor covers her short position. A profit will be realized if the purchase price is less than the price at which the issuer sold short the security.

The ability of investors to sell short is an important mechanism in financial markets. In the absence of an effective short-selling mechanism, security prices will tend to be biased toward the view of more optimistic investors, causing a market to depart from the standards of a perfect price-setting situation.

▶ KEY POINTS THAT YOU SHOULD UNDERSTAND BEFORE PROCEEDING:

1. A market can be perfect, in a theoretical sense, only if it meets many conditions regarding number of participants, flow of information, freedom from regulation, and freedom from costs that hinder trading.
2. Market imperfections are called frictions.
3. A perfect market must also permit short selling, which is the sale of borrowed securities.

## ROLE OF BROKERS AND DEALERS IN REAL MARKETS

Common occurrences in real markets keep them from being theoretically perfect. Because of these occurrences, brokers and dealers are necessary to the smooth functioning of a secondary market.

### Brokers

One way in which a real market might not meet all the exacting standards of a theoretically perfect market is that many investors may not be present at all times in the marketplace. Further, a typical investor may not be skilled in the art of the deal or completely informed about every facet of trading in the asset. Clearly, most investors in even smoothly functioning markets need professional assistance. Investors need someone to receive and keep track of their orders for buying or selling, to find other parties wishing to sell or buy, to negotiate for good prices, to serve as a focal point for trading, and to execute the orders. The broker performs all these functions. Obviously, these functions are more important for the complicated trades, such as the small or large trades, than for simple transactions or those of typical size.

A broker is an entity that acts on behalf of an investor who wishes to execute orders. In economic and legal terms, a broker is said to be an "agent" of the investor. It is important to realize that the brokerage activity does not require the broker to buy and sell or hold in inventory the financial asset that is the subject of the trade. (Such activity is termed "taking a position" in the asset, and it is the role of the dealer, another important financial market participant discussed below.) Rather, the broker receives, transmits, and executes investors' orders with other investors. The broker receives an explicit commission for these services, and the commission is a "transactions cost" of the securities markets. If the broker also provides other services, such as research or record-keeping or advising, investors may pay additional charges.

### Dealers as Market Makers

A real market might also differ from the perfect market because of the possibly frequent event of a temporary imbalance in the number of buy and sell orders that investors may place for any security at any one time. Such unmatched or unbalanced flow causes two problems. One is that the security's price may change abruptly, even if there has been no shift in either supply or demand for the security. Another problem is that buyers may have to pay higher than market-clearing prices (or sellers accept lower ones) if they want to make their trade immediately.

An example can illustrate these points. Suppose that the consensus price for ABC security is $50, which was determined in several recent trades. Now, suppose that a flow of buy orders from investors who suddenly have cash arrives in the market, but there is no accompanying supply of sell orders. This temporary imbalance could be sufficient to push the price of ABC security to, say, $55. Thus, the price has changed sharply even though there has been no change in any fundamental financial aspect of the issuer. Buyers who want to buy immediately must pay $55 rather than $50, and this difference can be viewed as the price of "immediacy." By immediacy, we mean that buyers and sellers do not want to wait for the arrival of sufficient orders on the other side of the trade, which would bring the price closer to the level of recent transactions.

The fact of imbalances explains the need for the dealer or market maker, who stands ready and willing to buy a financial asset for its own account (to add to an inventory of the financial asset) or sell from its own account (to reduce the inventory of the financial asset). At a given time, dealers are willing to buy a financial asset at a price (the bid price) that is less than what they are willing to sell the same financial asset for (the ask price).

In the 1960s, two economists, George Stigler[1] and Harold Demsetz,[2] analyzed the role of dealers in securities markets. They viewed dealers as the suppliers of immediacy—the ability to trade promptly—to the market. The bid-ask spread can be viewed in turn as the price charged by dealers for supplying immediacy together with short-run price stability (continuity or smoothness) in the presence of short-term order imbalances. There are two other roles that dealers play: providing reliable price information to market participants, and, in certain market structures, providing the services of an auctioneer in bringing order and fairness to a market.[3]

The price stabilization role follows from our earlier example of what may happen to the price of a particular transaction in the absence of any intervention when there is a temporary imbalance of orders. By taking the opposite side of a trade when there are no other orders, the dealer prevents the price from materially diverging from the price at which a recent trade was consummated.

Investors are concerned not only with immediacy, but also with being able to trade at prices that are reasonable, given prevailing conditions in the market. While dealers do not know with certainty the true price of a security, they do have a privileged position in some market structures with respect not just to the flow of market orders but also to "limit" orders, which are special orders that can be executed only if the market price of the asset changes in a specified way. (See Chapter 18 for more on limit orders.) For example, the dealers of the organized markets, called "specialists" and discussed in Chapter 18, have just such a privileged position from which they get special information about the flow of market orders.

Finally, the dealer acts as an auctioneer in some market structures, thereby providing order and fairness in the operations of the market. For example, as we will explain in Chapter 18, the market maker on organized stock exchanges in the United States performs this function by organizing trading to make sure that the exchange rules for the priority of trading are followed. The role of a market maker in a call market structure is that of an auctioneer. The market maker does not take a position in the traded asset, as a dealer does in a continuous market.

---

[1] George Stigler, "Public Regulation of Securities Markets," *Journal of Business* (April 1964), pp. 117–134.

[2] Harold Demsetz, "The Cost of Transacting," *Quarterly Journal of Economics* (October 1968), pp. 35–36.

[3] For a more detailed discussion, see Chapter 1 in Robert A. Schwartz, *Equity Markets: Structure, Trading, and Performance* (New York: Harper & Row Publishers, 1988), pp. 389–397.

What factors determine the price dealers should charge for the services they provide? Or equivalently, what factors determine the *bid-ask spread*? One of the most important is the order processing costs incurred by dealers. The costs of equipment necessary to do business and a dealer's administrative and operations staff are examples. The lower these costs, the narrower the bid-ask spread. With the reduced cost of computing and better-trained personnel, these costs have declined since the 1960s.

Dealers also have to be compensated for bearing risk. A *dealer's position* may involve carrying inventory of a security (a *long position*) or selling a security that is not in inventory (a *short position*). There are three types of risks associated with maintaining a long or short position in a given security. First, there is the uncertainty about the future price of the security. A dealer who has a net long position in the security is concerned that the price will decline in the future; a dealer who is in a net short position is concerned that the price will rise.

The second type of risk has to do with the expected time it will take the dealer to unwind a position and its uncertainty. And this, in turn, depends primarily on the thickness of the market for the security. Finally, while a dealer may have access to better information about order flows than the general public, there are some trades where the dealer takes the risk of trading with someone who has better information.[4] This results in the better-informed trader obtaining a better price at the expense of the dealer. Consequently, a dealer in establishing the bid-ask spread for a trade will assess whether the trader might have better information.[5]

▶ KEY POINTS THAT YOU SHOULD UNDERSTAND BEFORE PROCEEDING:

1. The relationship between a broker and an investor.
2. How a dealer makes a profit when making a market.
3. The benefits that a market derives from the actions of dealers.

## MARKET EFFICIENCY

The term "efficient" capital market has been used in several contexts to describe the operating characteristics of a capital market. There is a distinction, however, between an *operationally* (or *internally*) *efficient market* and a *pricing* (or *externally*) *efficient capital market*.[6]

[4] Walter Bagehot, "The Only Game in Town," *Financial Analysts Journal* (March-April 1971), pp. 12–14, 22.

[5] Some trades that we will discuss in Chapter 18 can be viewed as "informationless trades." This means that the dealer knows or believes that a trade is being requested to accomplish an investment objective that is not motivated by the potential future price movement of the security.

[6] Richard R. West, "Two Kinds of Market Efficiency," *Financial Analysts Journal* (November-December 1975), pp. 30–34.

## Operational Efficiency

In an operationally efficient market, investors can obtain transaction services as cheaply as possible, given the costs associated with furnishing those services. For example, in national equity markets throughout the world the degree of operational efficiency varies. At one time, brokerage commissions in the United States were fixed, and the brokerage industry charged high fees and functioned poorly. But that began to change in May 1975, as the American exchanges adopted a system of competitive and negotiated commissions. Non-U.S. markets have been moving toward more competitive brokerage fees. France, for example, adopted a system of negotiated commissions for large trades in 1985. In its "Big Bang" of 1986, the London Stock Exchange abolished fixed commissions. Although some Japanese political and business leaders are trying to bring about a change, brokerage commissions in Japan remain fixed as of early 1992, with levels depending upon the stock's price and the number of shares involved in the trade.

Commissions are only part of the cost of transacting, as we note above. The other part is the dealer spread, which we discuss fully in Chapter 18. Bid-ask spreads for bonds vary by type of bond. For example, the bid-ask spread on U.S. Treasury securities is much smaller than for other bonds. Even with the U.S. Treasury securities market, certain issues have a narrower bid-ask spread than other issues.

## Pricing Efficiency

Pricing efficiency refers to a market where prices at all times fully reflect all available information that is relevant to the valuation of securities. That is, relevant information about the security is quickly impounded into the price of securities.

A price-efficient market has implications for the investment strategy that investors may wish to pursue. Throughout this book, we refer to various active strategies employed by investors. In an *active strategy*, investors seek to capitalize on what they perceive to be the mispricing of a security or securities. In a market that is price-efficient, active strategies will not consistently generate a return after taking into consideration transactions costs and the risks associated with a strategy other than simply buying and holding securities. This has led investors in certain markets that empirical evidence suggests are price-efficient to pursue a strategy of *indexing*, which simply seeks to match the performance of some financial index. We look at the pricing efficiency of the stock market in Chapter 18. It is in this market where the greatest amount of empirical evidence exists.

► KEY POINTS THAT YOU SHOULD UNDERSTAND BEFORE PROCEEDING:

1. What makes a market operationally or internally efficient.
2. The key characteristic of a market that has pricing or external efficiency.

**SUMMARY**

A secondary market in financial assets is one where existing or outstanding assets are traded among investors. A secondary market serves several needs of the firm or governmental unit that issues securities in the primary market. The secondary market provides the issuer with regular information about the value of its outstanding stocks or bonds, and it encourages investors to buy securities from issuers because it offers them an ongoing opportunity for liquidating their investments in securities.

Investors also get services from the secondary market: the market supplies them with liquidity and prices for the assets they are holding or want to buy; and the market brings interested investors together, thereby reducing the costs of searching for other parties and of making trades.

Secondary markets for financial securities exist around the world. Such markets may be continuous, where trading and price determination go on throughout the day as orders to buy and sell reach the market. Some markets are call markets: prices are determined by executions of batched or grouped orders to buy and sell at a specific time (or times) within the trading day. Some secondary markets combine features of call and continuous trading.

Even the most developed and smoothly functioning secondary market falls short of being "perfect" in the economically theoretical meaning of the term. Actual markets tend to have numerous "frictions" that affect prices and investors' behavior. Some key frictions are transactions costs, which include commissions, fees, and execution costs.

Because of imperfections in actual markets, investors need the services of two types of market participants: dealers and brokers. Brokers aid investors by collecting and transmitting orders to the market, by bringing willing buyers and sellers together, by negotiating prices, and by executing orders. The fee for these services is the broker's commission.

Dealers perform three functions in markets: (1) they provide the opportunity for investors to trade immediately rather than waiting for the arrival of sufficient orders on the other side of the trade ("immediacy"), and they do this while maintaining short-run price stability ("continuity"); (2) they offer price information to market participants; and (3) in certain market structures, dealers serve as auctioneers in bringing order and fairness to a market. Dealers buy for their own account and maintain inventories of assets, and their profits come from selling assets at higher prices than the prices at which they purchased them.

A market is operationally efficient if it offers investors reasonably priced services related to buying and selling. A market is price-efficient if at all times prices fully reflect all available information that is relevant to the valuation of securities. In such a market, active strategies pursued will not consistently produce superior returns after adjusting for risk and transactions costs.

**Active investment strategy:** A strategy of regular buying and selling assets that is based on the belief that they are mispriced by and in the market where they are traded.

**Auctioneer:** A market participant who facilitates trades by seeking bids from buyers and sellers that establish the market-clearing amount to be traded and the price that makes amount demanded equal amount offered.

**Bid-ask spread:** This difference between the price at which a dealer is willing to buy an asset (the bid price) and the price at which the dealer is ready to sell the asset (the ask price) is the dealer's profit.

**Broker:** An agent of an investor who executes, for a commission or fee, the investor's order to buy or sell assets.

**Call market:** A secondary market where orders to buy and sell securities are batched or grouped together for simultaneous execution at the same price and at certain times in the day.

**Continuous market:** A secondary market where prices are determined continuously throughout the trading day as buyers and sellers submit orders.

**Dealer:** Participant in a market who takes a position in an asset, keeps an inventory of it, and is ready to buy or sell to other participants.

**Dealer's position:** The amount of an asset a dealer is holding in inventory.

**Fix:** A colloquial term, used in certain U.K. markets, for the determination of the market-clearing price in a call market system.

**Frictions:** Economic term for features of a market, or its environment, that keep the price it sets from being the fair market price.

**Immediacy:** Term for a market's ability to provide an investor with a quick execution of a trade order, whether it is to buy or to sell, at a fair market price.

**Indexing:** A passive investment strategy that involves buying stocks according to the composition of an index in order to generate the level of returns that the index achieves.

**Limit order:** An order to buy or sell a security that may be executed only when the market price of the security changes in a specific way.

**Operational or internal efficiency:** The characteristic of a market that allows investors to obtain buying and selling services at the lowest possible prices.

**Over-the-counter (or OTC) market:** A largely unregulated market whereby geographically dispersed traders, who are linked to one another via telecommunication systems and computers, trade in securities.

**Passive investment strategy:** Strategy of buying and holding assets for long periods of time because of the belief that the assets are fairly priced at any one point in the market.

**Perfect market:** Term from economic theory for the kind of market that has specific characteristics of trading and price-setting and that is free of the frictions that keep a fair market price from being set in trading.

**Pricing or external efficiency:** The characteristic of a market in which the trading price reflects all relevant information about the value of the asset being traded.

**Short sale:** The sale of an asset that the seller has borrowed and must repay to the lender.

**Stock exchange:** An organized and somewhat regulated secondary market, where trading in stock occurs in a specific geographical location.

## QUESTIONS

1. Consider two transactions. The Norwegian government sells bonds in the U.S. The buyer of one of those bonds is an insurance company, which, after holding the bond for a year, sells it to a mutual fund. Which of these transactions occurs in the primary market and which in the secondary market? Does the Norwegian government get any proceeds from the sale between the insurance company and the mutual fund?

2. Recently, Japan's four largest brokerage firms (Yamaichi Securities Co., Nomura Securities Co., Daiwa Securities Co., and Nikko Securities Co.) formally asked their government to lift bans that restrict their freedom to invest in stocks. One of those bans prevents a brokerage firm from trading for its own account (that is, buying and selling for itself rather than for clients) during certain times of the trading day. The other ban restricts a brokerage firm from participating in more than 30% of the trading of any one stock within a month. Consider these restrictions in terms of the role of dealers in financial markets and the requirements for operational and price efficiency in a market. Do you think that lifting the restrictions would help the Tokyo Stock Exchange to be more efficient with regard to price and operations?

3. The residential real estate market boasts many brokers but very few dealers. What explains this situation?

4. Some years ago, legislators in a state claimed that speculation on land was driving prices to too high a level. They proposed to pass a law that would require the buyer of any piece of land in the state to hold the land for at least three years before he or she could resell it.

   a. Analyze this proposal in terms of perfect markets and possible frictions that have been described in this chapter.

      b.   If that proposal had passed, do you think land prices would have risen or fallen?

5.   What is meant by the statement that "dealers offer both immediacy and price continuity to investors"?

6.   In 1990, a trader on the Paris *Bourse* once claimed to one of the authors of this book that "now, we are just like New York; everything is continuous." Do you think that the *Bourse*'s change from a call market to a continuous market, which took place in the 1980s, could have improved either price or operational efficiency in that market enough to warrant this assertion?

7.   In most stock market environments, brokerage commissions are fixed. Outline the problems such a situation can create.

CHAPTER SIXTEEN

# Treasury and Agency Securities Markets

## LEARNING OBJECTIVES

*After reading this chapter you will understand:*

- the importance of the Treasury market.
- the different types of securities issued by the Treasury.
- the operation of the primary market for Treasury securities.
- the role of government dealers and government brokers.
- the secondary market for Treasury securities.
- the changes taking place in the regulatory structure of the market.
- how Treasury securities are quoted in the secondary market.
- how government dealers use the repurchase agreement market.
- the zero-coupon Treasury securities market.
- the difference between federally sponsored agency securities and federally related institutions.
- functions of the federally sponsored agencies that issue securities.

Treasury securities are issued by the United States Department of the Treasury and are backed by the full faith and credit of the United States government. Consequently, market participants view them as having no credit risk. Interest rates on Treasury securities are the benchmark interest rates throughout the U.S. economy as well as in international capital markets. In Chapter 11, we briefly described this important role played by Treasury securities. In this chapter, we discuss the Treasury securities market and the market for U.S. agency securities.

## TREASURY SECURITIES

Two factors account for the prominent role of U.S. Treasury securities: volume (in terms of dollars outstanding) and liquidity. The Department of the Treasury is the largest single issuer of debt in the world, with Treasury securities accounting for $1.9 trillion (represented by over 180 different Treasury note and bond issues and 30 Treasury bill issues). The large volume of total debt and the large size of any single issue have contributed to making the Treasury market the most active and hence the most liquid market in the world. The spread between bid and ask prices is considerably narrower than in other sectors of the bond market, and most issues can be traded easily. Many issues in the corporate and municipal markets are illiquid by contrast, and cannot be traded readily.

Treasury securities are available in book-entry form at the Federal Reserve Bank. This means that the investor receives only a receipt as evidence of ownership instead of an engraved certificate. An advantage of book-entry is ease in transferring ownership of the security.

Interest income from Treasury securities is subject to federal income taxes but is exempt from state and local income taxes.

### *Types of Treasury Securities*

There are two categories of government securities—*discount* and *coupon securities*. The fundamental difference between the two types lies in the form of the stream of payments that the holder receives, which is reflected in turn in the prices at which the securities are issued. Coupon securities pay interest every six months, plus principal at maturity. Discount securities pay only a contractually fixed amount at maturity, called maturity value or face value. Discount instruments are issued below maturity value, and return to the investor the difference between issue price and maturity value.

Current Treasury practice is to issue all securities with maturities of one year or less as discount securities. These securities are called *Treasury bills*. All securities with maturities of two years or longer are issued as coupon securities. Treasury coupon securities issued with original maturities between two and ten years are called *Treasury notes*; those with original maturities greater than ten years are called *Treasury bonds*. While there is therefore a distinction between Treasury notes and bonds, in this chapter we refer to both as simply Treasury bonds.

## The Primary Market

Treasury securities typically are issued on an auction basis with regular cycles for securities of specific maturities. Treasury bills with three and six months to maturity are auctioned every Monday, and one-year Treasury bills are auctioned on the third week of every month. The Treasury regularly issues coupon securities with maturities of two, three, five, seven, 10, and 30 years. Two- and 5-year notes are auctioned each month. At the beginning of the second month of each calendar quarter (February, May, August, and November), the Treasury conducts its regular refunding operations. At this time, it auctions 3-year, 10-year, and 30-year Treasury securities. The Treasury announces on the Wednesday of the month preceding: (1) the amount that will be auctioned; (2) what portion of that amount is to replace maturing Treasury debt; (3) what portion of that amount is to raise new funds; and (4) the estimated cash needs for the balance of the quarter and how the Treasury plans to obtain the funds. During the second half of each calendar quarter, the Treasury conducts its "mini-refunding" and issues 7-year Treasury notes.

The auction for Treasury securities is conducted on a competitive bid basis. Competitive bids must be submitted on a yield basis. Noncompetitive tenders may also be submitted for up to a $1 million face amount. Such tenders are based only on quantity, not yield. The price paid by noncompetitive bidders is the average price of the competitive bids.

The auction results are determined by first deducting the total noncompetitive tenders and nonpublic purchases (such as purchases by the Federal Reserve itself) from the total securities being auctioned. The remainder is the amount to be awarded to the competitive bidders. The lowest-yield (that is, highest price) bidders are awarded securities at their bid price. Successively higher-yielding bidders are awarded securities at their bid price until the total amount offered (less noncompetitive tenders) is awarded. The highest yield accepted by the Treasury is referred to as the "stop yield," and bidders at that price are awarded a percentage of their total tender offer. The difference between the average yield of all the bids accepted by the Treasury and the stop is called the "tail."

Table 16-1 shows the results of the auction for 7-year Treasury notes which was held on April 8, 1992. The amount auctioned was $9.754 billion. Competitive bidders were awarded $9.28 billion and noncompetitive bidders $0.474 billion. The average yield was 7.11%, and the high yield (that is, the stop yield) was 7.14%. Thus, the tail is 0.03 (7.14 minus 7.11). Each bidder at the stop yield was awarded 62% of the amount for which it bid. For example, if a financial institution bid for $100 million at 7.14%, it would be awarded $62 million. Bidders higher in yield than 7.14% "missed" or were "shut out."

Any firm can deal in government securities, but in implementing its open market operations, the Federal Reserve will deal directly only with dealers that it designates as primary dealers. Primary dealers include large commercial banks and investment banking firms, both domestic and foreign. Table 16-2 lists the primary government dealers as of January 1992.

Until 1991, primary dealers and large commercial banks that were not

| TABLE 16-1 | |
| :---: | :---: |
| RESULTS OF AUCTION OF 7-YEAR NOTES, APRIL 8, 1992 | |
| Applications | $18,794,398,000 |
| Accepted Bids | 9,754,610,000 |
| Accepted at Low Price | 62% |
| Accepted Noncompetitively | 474,000,000 |
| Average Price (Rate) | 99.402 (7.11%) |
| High Price (Rate) | 99.510 (7.09%) |
| Low Price (Rate) | 99.239 (7.14%) |
| Interest Rate | 7.00% |

\* Notes are dated April 15, 1992, and mature April 15, 1999.

primary dealers would submit bids for their own account and for their customers. Others who wished to participate in the auction process could submit competitive bids only for their own account, not their customers. Consequently, a broker-dealer in government securities that was not a primary dealer could not submit a competitive bid on behalf of its customers. Moreover, unlike primary dealers, nonprimary dealers had to make large cash deposits or provide guarantees to assure that they could fulfill their obligation to purchase the securities for which they bid.

Well publicized violations of the auction process by Salomon Brothers in the summer of 1991 forced Treasury officials to scrutinize the activities of primary dealers more closely and also to reconsider the procedure by which Treasury securities are auctioned.[1] Specifically, the Treasury announced that it would allow qualified broker-dealers to bid for their customers at Treasury auctions. If a qualified broker-dealer establishes a payment link with the Federal Reserve system, no deposit or guaranty would be required. Moreover, the auction would no longer be handled by the submission of hand-delivered sealed bids to the Federal Reserve. The new auction process will be a computerized auction system which can be electronically accessed by qualified broker-dealers.

## The Secondary Market

The secondary market for Treasury securities is an over-the-counter market where a group of U.S. government securities dealers offer continuous bid and ask prices on specific outstanding Treasuries.[2] The secondary market is the

---

[1] Salomon Brothers admitted that it repeatedly violated a restriction that limited the amount that any one firm could purchase at the Treasury auction. The firm also admitted that it submitted unauthorized bids for some of its customers.

[2] Some trading of Treasury coupon securities does occur on the New York Stock Exchange, but the volume of these exchange-traded transactions is very small when compared to over-the-counter transactions.

## TABLE 16-2

### PRIMARY GOVERNMENT SECURITIES DEALERS

Bank of America NT & SA
Barclays de Zoete Wedd Securities Inc.
Bear, Stearns & Co., Inc.
BT Securities Corporation
Carroll McEntee & McGinley Incorporated
Chase Securities, Inc.
Chemical Securities, Inc.
Citicorp Securities Markets, Inc.
CRT Government Securities, Ltd.
Daiwa Securities America Inc.
Dean Witter Reynolds Inc.
Deutsche Bank Government Securities, Inc.
Dillon, Read & Co. Inc.
Discount Corporation of New York
Donaldson, Lufkin & Jenrette Securities Corporation
The First Boston Corporation
First Chicago Capital Markets, Inc.
Fuji Securities Inc.
Goldman, Sachs & Co.
Greenwich Capital Markets, Inc.
Harris Government Securities Inc.
Kidder, Peabody & Co., Incorporated
Aubrey G. Lanston & Co., Inc.
Lehman Government Securities, Inc.
Merrill Lynch Government Securities Inc.
J.P. Morgan Securities, Inc.
Morgan Stanley & Co. Incorporated
The Nikko Securities Co. International, Inc.
Nomura Securities International, Inc.
Paine Webber Incorporated
Prudential Securities, Inc.
Salomon Brothers Inc.
Sanwa-BGK Securities Co., L.P.
Smith Barney, Harris Upham & Co., Inc.
SBC Government Securities Inc.
UBS Securities Inc.
S.G. Warburg & Co., Inc.
Yamaichi International (America), Inc.

*Source:* Market Reports Division, Federal Reserve Bank of New York, January 3, 1992.

most liquid financial market in the world. Daily average trading volume for all Treasury securities by primary dealers for the week of January 22, 1992, was about $164.869 billion, with the distribution among Treasury securities as follows:[3]

| | |
|---|---|
| Treasury bills | $ 33.157 billion |
| Coupon securities maturing in | |
| under 3.5 years | 50.068 |
| 3.5 years to under 7.5 years | 44.285 |
| 7.5 years to under 15 years | 18.857 |
| 15 years and over | 18.502 |

As we explained in Chapter 11, the most recently auctioned Treasury issues for each maturity are referred to as "on-the-run" or "current coupon" issues. Issues auctioned prior to the current coupon issues typically are referred to as "off-the-run" issues; they are not as liquid as on-the-run issues. That is, the bid–ask spread is larger for off-the-run issues relative to on-the-run issues.

Dealer profits are generated from one or more of three sources: (1) the bid–ask spread; (2) appreciation in the securities held in inventory or depreciation in the securities sold short; and (3) the difference between the interest earned on the securities held in inventory and the cost of financing that inventory. The last source of profits is referred to as *carry*. Dealers obtain funds to finance inventory position using the repo market, which we describe later in this chapter.

Another component of the Treasury secondary market is the "when-issued market," or "wi market," where Treasury securities are traded prior to the time they are issued by the Treasury. When-issued trading for both Treasury bills and Treasury coupon issues extends from the day the auction is announced until the issue day. All deliveries on when-issued trades occur on the issue day of the Treasury security traded.

***Government Brokers***. Treasury dealers trade with the investing public and with other dealer firms. When they trade with each other, it is through intermediaries known as *government brokers*. Dealers leave firm bids and offers with brokers who display the highest bid and lowest offer in a computer network tied to each trading desk and displayed on a monitor. The dealer responding to a bid or offer by "hitting" or "taking" pays a commission to the broker. The size and prices of these transactions are visible to all dealers at once.

Treasury dealers use brokers because of the speed and efficiency with which trades can be accomplished. Brokers never trade for their own account, and they keep the names of the dealers involved in trades confidential. Four

---

[3] This figure represents immediate transactions of purchases and sales in the market as reported to the Federal Reserve Bank of New York on January 22, 1992. Immediate transactions are those scheduled for delivery in five days or less. The figure excludes all transactions under purchase and reverse repurchase agreements. (These transactions are described in the appendix to this chapter.)

major brokers handle about 50% of the daily trading volume. They include RMJ Securities Corp.; Garban Ltd.; Cantor, Fitzgerald Securities Corp.; and Chapdelaine & Company Government Securities, Inc. These four firms service the primary government dealers and a dozen or so other large government dealers aspiring to be primary dealers.

The quotes provided on the government dealer screens represent prices in the "inside" or "interdealer" market, and the primary dealers have resisted attempts to allow the general public to have access to them. In 1989, when one government dealer offered to disseminate quotes to some large institutional investors, pressure from the primary dealers persuaded the broker to withdraw its offer. However, pressure from the General Accounting Office and Congress in 1991 has forced government brokers to disseminate some information to nonprimary dealers.

***Bid and Offer Quotes on Treasury Bills.*** The convention for quoting bids and offers is different for Treasury bills and Treasury coupon securities. Bids and offers on Treasury bills are quoted in a special way. Unlike bonds that pay coupon interest, Treasury bill values are quoted on a *bank discount basis*, not on a price basis. The yield on a bank discount basis is computed as follows:

$$Y = \frac{D}{F} \times \frac{360}{t}$$

where  $Y$ = annualized yield on a bank discount basis (expressed as a decimal)
$D$ = dollar discount, which is equal to the difference between the face value and the price
$F$ = face value
$t$ = number of days remaining to maturity.

As an example, a Treasury bill with 100 days to maturity, a face value of $100,000, and selling for $97,569 would be quoted at 8.75% on a bank discount basis:

$$D = \$100,000 - \$97,569$$
$$= \$2,431$$

Therefore:

$$Y = \frac{\$2,431}{\$100,000} \times \frac{360}{100}$$

$$= 8.75\%$$

Given the yield on a bank discount basis, the price of a Treasury bill is found by first solving the formula for $Y$ for the dollar discount as follows:

$$D = Y \times F \times t/360$$

The price is then:

$$Price = F - D$$

For the 100-day Treasury bill with a face value of $100,000, if the yield on a bank discount basis is quoted as 8.75%, $D$ is equal to:

$$D = 0.0875 \times \$100,000 \times 100/360$$
$$= \$2,431$$

Therefore:

$$Price = \$100,000 - \$2,431$$
$$= \$97,569$$

The quoted yield on a bank discount basis is not a meaningful measure of the return from holding a Treasury bill for two reasons. First, the measure is based on a face value investment rather than on the actual dollar amount invested. Second, the yield is annualized according to a 360-day rather than 365-day year, making it difficult to compare Treasury bill yields with Treasury notes and bonds, which pay interest on a 365-day basis. Despite its shortcomings as a measure of return, this is the method dealers have adopted to quote Treasury bills.

***Bid and Offer Quotes on Treasury Coupon Securities.*** Treasury coupon securities are quoted differently from Treasury bills. They trade on a dollar price basis in price units of 1/32 of 1% of par (par is taken to be $100). For example, a quote of 92-14 refers to a price of 92 and 14/32. If a Treasury coupon security has a $100,000 par value, then a change in price of 1% equates to $1,000, and 1/32 equates to $31.25. A plus sign following the number of 32nds means that a 64th is added to the price. For example, 92-14+ refers to a price of 92 and 29/64, or 92.453125% of par value.

On quote sheets and screens, the price quote is followed by some "yield to maturity" measure, a calculation we explained in Chapter 11.

***Regulation of the Secondary Market.*** As we will explain in Chapter 18, in the stock market Congressional and SEC actions have resulted in movement toward a consolidated tape for reporting trades on exchanges and the over-the-counter market, with a composite quotation system for the collection and display of bid and ask quotations. In the Treasury market, however, despite the fact that trading activity is concentrated in the over-the-counter market, and that daily trading volume exceeds $100 billion, reporting of trades does not exist. Nor is there a display of bid and ask quotations that provides reliable price quotes at which the general public can transact. Such quotations do exist, as we explained earlier, in the interdealer market on government broker screens. While nonprimary dealers can subscribe to the government broker screens, the information that they can obtain on these screens is limited. In particular, the government dealers that permit access to their screens provide information on only the best bid and offer quotation but not the size of the transaction.

Moreover, the rules for the sale of U.S. government securities have been exempt from most SEC provisions and rules.[4] Thus, government broker-dealers are not required to disclose the bid–ask spread on the Treasury securities that they buy from or sell to customers. There are guidelines established by the National Association of Security Dealers for reasonable bid–ask spreads, but lack of disclosure to customers makes it difficult for customers to monitor the pricing practice of a broker-dealer. At the time of this writing, Congress is considering passage of the Government Securities Act of 1992, which would regulate the pricing practices of broker-dealers who sell Treasury securities and would increase reporting requirements to allow closer monitoring of the Treasury market.

***Dealer Use of the Repurchase Agreement Market.***   Suppose a government securities dealer has purchased $10 million of a particular Treasury security. Where does the dealer obtain the funds to finance that position? Of course, the dealer can use its own funds or borrow from a bank. Typically, however, the dealer uses the repurchase agreement or "repo" market to obtain financing. In the repo market the dealer can use the $10 million of Treasury security purchased as collateral for a loan. The term of the loan and the interest rate that the dealer agrees to pay (called the "repo rate") are specified. When the term of the loan is one day, it is called an *overnight repo*; a loan for more than one day is called a *term repo*.

The transaction is referred to as a repurchase agreement because it calls for the sale of the security and its repurchase at a future date. Both the sale price and the purchase price are specified in the agreement. The difference between the purchase (repurchase) price and the sale price is the dollar interest cost of the loan.

Now, let's return to the dealer who needs to finance $10 million of a Treasury security. Suppose that the dealer plans to hold the bonds overnight. Suppose also that a customer of the dealer has excess funds of $10 million. (The customer might be a municipality with tax receipts that it has just collected, and no immediate need to disburse the funds.) The dealer would agree to deliver ("sell") $10 million of the Treasury security to the customer for an amount determined by the repo rate and buy ("repurchase") the same Treasury security from the customer for $10 million the next day. Suppose that the overnight repo rate is 6.5%. Then, as will be explained below, the dealer would agree to deliver the Treasury securities for $9,998,194 and repurchase the same securities for $10 million the next day. The $1,806 difference between the "sale" price of $9,998,194 and the repurchase price of $10 million is the dollar inter-

---

[4] Broker-dealers who sell government securities are always subject to the general fraud provisions of the Securities Act of 1933.

est on the financing. From the customer's perspective, the agreement is called a *reverse repo*.

The advantage to the dealer of using the repo market for borrowing on a short-term basis is that the rate is less than the cost of bank financing. From the customer's perspective, the repo market offers an attractive yield on a short-term secured transaction that is highly liquid.

While the example illustrates financing a dealer's long position in the repo market, dealers can also use the market to cover a short position. For example, suppose a government dealer sold $10 million of Treasury securities two weeks ago and must now cover the position—that is, deliver the securities. The dealer can do a reverse repo (agree to buy the securities and sell them back). Of course, the dealer eventually would have to buy the Treasury security in the market in order to cover its short position.

There is a good deal of Wall Street jargon describing repo transactions. To understand it, remember that one party is lending money and accepting the security as collateral for the loan;[5] the other party is borrowing money and giving collateral to borrow money. When someone lends securities in order to receive cash (that is, to borrow money), that party is said to be "reversing out" securities. A party that lends money with the security as collateral is said to be "reversing in" securities. The expressions "to repo securities" and "to do repo" are also used. The former means that someone is going to finance securities using the security as collateral; the latter means that the party is going to invest in a repo. Finally, the expressions "selling collateral" and "buying collateral" are used to describe a party financing a security with a repo on the one hand, and lending on the basis of collateral, on the other.

It is important to note that both parties to the transaction are exposed to credit risk. The failure of a few small government securities dealer firms involved in repo transactions in the 1980s has made market participants more cautious about the creditworthiness of the counterparty to a repo. Repos are now more carefully structured to reduce credit risk exposure.[6]

There is no one repo rate; rates vary from transaction to transaction depending on factors such as the term of the repo and the availability of collateral. The more difficult it is to obtain the collateral, the lower the repo rate. To understand why this is so, remember that the borrower (or equivalently the seller of the collateral) has a security that is a *hot* or *special issue*. The party that needs the collateral will be willing to lend funds at a lower repo rate in order to obtain the collateral.

While the factors given above determine the repo rate on a particular transaction, the federal funds rate determines the general level of repo rates. The repo rate will be slightly below the federal funds rate because a repo in-

---

[5] The collateral in a repo is not limited to government securities. Money market instruments, federal agency securities, and mortgage-backed securities are also used.

[6] For a description of the procedures used to reduce credit risk, see Oskar H. Rogg, "Repurchase Agreements," Chapter 12 in Frank J. Fabozzi (ed.), *The Handbook of Fixed Income Securities* (Homewood, IL: Business One-Irwin, 1991).

volves collateralized borrowing, while a federal funds transaction is unsecured borrowing.

Because it is used by dealer firms (investment banking firms and money center banks acting as dealers) to finance positions and cover short positions, the repo market has evolved into one of the largest sectors of the money market. Financial and non-financial firms participate in the market as both sellers and buyers, depending on the circumstances they face. Thrifts and commercial banks are typically net sellers of collateral (that is, net borrowers of funds); money market funds, bank trust departments, municipalities, and corporations are typically net buyers of collateral (that is, providers of funds).

While a dealer firm uses the repo market as the primary means for financing its inventory and covering short positions, it will also use the repo market to run a matched book where it takes on repos and reverse repos with the same maturity. The firm will do so to capture the spread at which it enters into the repo and reverse repo agreements. For example, suppose that a dealer firm enters into a term repo of ten days with a money market fund and a reverse repo rate with a thrift for ten days in which the collateral is identical. This means that the dealer firm is borrowing funds from the money market fund and lending money to the thrift. If the rate on the repo is 7.5% and the rate on the reverse repo is 7.55%, the dealer firm is borrowing at 7.5% and lending at 7.55%, locking in a spread of 0.05% (five basis points).

***A Note on Terminology in the Repo Market.***   As noted in Chapter 5, the Federal Reserve conducts open market operations by the outright purchase or sale of government securities or, more often, by repurchase agreements. In these agreements, the Fed either purchases or sells collateral. By buying collateral (that is, lending funds), the Fed injects money into the financial markets, thereby exerting downward pressure on short-term interest rates. When the Fed buys collateral for its own account, this is called a *system repo*. The Fed also buys collateral on behalf of foreign central banks in repo transactions that are referred to as *customer repos*. It is primarily through system repos that the Fed attempts to influence short-term rates. By selling securities for its own account, the Fed drains money from the financial markets, thereby exerting upward pressure on short-term interest rates. This transaction is called a *matched sale*.

Note the language that is used to describe the transactions of the Fed in the repo market. When the Fed lends funds based on collateral, we call it a system or customer repo, not a reverse repo. Borrowing funds using collateral is called a matched sale, not a repo. The jargon is confusing, which is why we used the terms of "buying collateral" and "selling collateral" to describe what parties in the repo market are doing.

## Stripped Treasury Securities

The Treasury does not issue zero-coupon notes or bonds. In August 1982, however, both Merrill Lynch and Salomon Brothers created synthetic zero-coupon Treasury receipts. Merrill Lynch marketed its Treasury receipts as "Treasury

Income Growth Receipts" (TIGRs); Salomon Brothers marketed its as "Certificates of Accrual on Treasury Securities" (CATS). The procedure was to purchase Treasury bonds and deposit them in a bank custody account. The firms then issued (that is, sold) receipts representing an ownership interest in each coupon payment on the underlying Treasury bond in the account and a receipt for ownership of the underlying Treasury bond's maturity value. This process of separating each coupon payment, as well as the principal (called the "corpus"), and selling securities against them is referred to as "coupon stripping." Although the receipts created from the coupon stripping process are not issued by the U.S. Treasury, the underlying bond deposited in the bank custody account is a debt obligation of the U.S. Treasury, so the cash flow from the underlying security is certain.

To illustrate the process, suppose $100 million of a Treasury bond with a 20-year maturity and a coupon rate of 10% is purchased to create zero-coupon Treasury securities. The cash flow from this Treasury bond is 40 semi-annual payments of $5 million each ($100 million times 0.10 divided by two) and the repayment of principal (corpus) of $100 million 20 years from now. This Treasury bond is deposited in a bank custody account. Receipts are then issued, each with a different single payment claim on the bank custody account. As there are 41 different payments to be made by the Treasury, a receipt representing a single payment claim on each payment is issued, which is effectively a zero-coupon bond. The amount of the maturity value for a receipt on a particular payment, whether coupon or corpus, depends on the amount of the payment to be made by the Treasury on the underlying Treasury bond. In our example, 40 coupon receipts each have a maturity value of $5 million, and one receipt, the corpus, has a maturity value of $100 million. The maturity dates for the receipts coincide with the corresponding payment dates by the Treasury.

Other investment banking firms followed suit by creating their own receipts.[7] They all are referred to as "trademark zero-coupon Treasury securities," because they are associated with particular firms.[8] Receipts of one firm were rarely traded by competing dealers, so the secondary market was not liquid for any one trademark. Moreover, the investor was exposed to the risk—as small as it may be—that the custodian bank may go bankrupt.

To broaden the market and improve liquidity of these receipts, a group of primary dealers in the government market agreed to issue "generic receipts" that would not be directly associated with any of the participating dealers. These generic receipts are referred to as "Treasury Receipts" (TRs). Rather than representing a share of the trust as the trademarks do, TRs represent ownership of a Treasury security. A common problem with both trademark

---

[7] Lehman Brothers offered "Lehman Investment Opportunities Notes" (LIONs); E.F. Hutton offered "Treasury Bond Receipts" (TBRs); and Dean Witter Reynolds offered "Easy Growth Treasury Receipts" (ETRs). There were also GATORs, COUGARs, and—you'll like this one—DOGS (Dibs on Government Securities).

[8] They are also called "animal products" for obvious reasons.

and generic receipts was that settlement required physical delivery, which is often cumbersome and inefficient.

In February 1985, the Treasury announced its Separate Trading of Registered Interest and Principal of Securities (STRIPS) program to facilitate the stripping of designated Treasury securities. Specifically, all new Treasury bonds and all new Treasury notes with maturities of ten years and longer are eligible. The zero-coupon Treasury securities created under the STRIPS program are direct obligations of the U.S. government. Moreover, the securities clear through the Federal Reserve's book-entry system.[9] Creation of the STRIPS program ended the origination of trademarks and generic receipts.

In Chapter 12, we explained that the price of a Treasury security should be equal to the present value of its cash flow, where each cash flow is discounted at its theoretical spot rate. What we did not identify, however, are the market mechanisms that force the price of the Treasury security to this theoretical value. It has been the stripping of Treasury securities that assures that the market price will be equal to the theoretical price. If the market price of a Treasury security is less than its theoretical price, this would allow a market participant to strip the Treasury security and sell the resulting zero-coupon instruments for more than the cost of buying the Treasury security. This action is illustrated in the appendix of this chapter.

▶ KEY POINTS THAT YOU SHOULD UNDERSTAND BEFORE PROCEEDING:

1. U.S. Treasury securities play a prominent role in global financial markets because they do not have credit risk.
2. Treasury securities are issued on an auction basis with regular cycles for securities of specific maturities.
3. In the secondary market, the most actively traded Treasury securities are the on-the-run issues, and government brokers are used as intermediaries for trading among primary dealers.
4. Securities dealers use the repo market to finance their position in Treasury securities.
5. Stripped Treasury securities are zero-coupon instruments that, while not issued by the U.S. government, are backed by Treasury securities from which they are created.

## FEDERAL AGENCY SECURITIES

■ ■ ■ ■

The federal agency securities market can be divided into two sectors—the *federally sponsored agency securities market* and the *federally related institution securities market*. Federally sponsored agencies, also *called government-sponsored entities*,

---

[9] In 1987, the Treasury permitted the conversion of stripped coupons into book-entry form under its Coupons Under Book-Entry Safekeeping (CUBES) program.

are privately owned, publicly chartered entities. They were created by Congress to reduce the cost of capital for certain borrowing sectors of the economy deemed to be important enough to warrant assistance. The entities in these privileged sectors include farmers, homeowners, and students. Federally sponsored agencies issue securities directly in the marketplace. The market for these securities, while smaller than that of Treasury securities, has in recent years become an active and important sector of the bond market.

Federally related institutions are arms of the federal government and generally do not issue securities directly in the marketplace (although they did prior to 1973). Instead, they obtain all or part of their financing by borrowing from the Federal Financing Bank, an entity created in 1973. The relatively small size of these issues made the borrowing cost for individual issues significantly greater than that of Treasury securities. Creation of the Federal Financing Bank was intended to consolidate and reduce the borrowing cost of federally related institutions.

Federally related institutions include the Export-Import Bank of the United States, the Commodity Credit Corporation, the Federal Housing Administration, the General Services Administration, the Government National Mortgage Association, the Maritime Administration, the Private Export Funding Corporation, the Rural Electrification Administration, the Rural Telephone Bank, the Small Business Administration, the Tennessee Valley Authority, and the Washington Metropolitan Area Transit Authority. All federally related institutions are exempt from SEC registration. With the exception of securities of the Private Export Funding Corporation and the Tennessee Valley Authority, the securities are backed by the full faith and credit of the United States government. As of October 1991, the outstanding amount of federally related institution debt was $42.6 billion.[10]

## Federally Sponsored Agency Securities

There are eight federally sponsored agencies. The Federal Farm Credit Bank System is responsible for the credit market in the agricultural sector of the economy. The Farm Credit Financial Assistance Corporation was created in 1987 to address problems in the existing Farm Credit System. Three federally sponsored agencies—Federal Home Loan Bank, Federal Home Loan Mortgage Corporation, and Federal National Mortgage Association—are responsible for providing credit to the mortgage and housing sectors. The Student Loan Marketing Association provides funds to support higher education. The Financing Corporation was created in 1987 to recapitalize the Federal Savings and Loan Insurance Corporation. Because of continuing difficulties in the savings and loan association industry, the Resolution Trust Corporation was created in 1989 to liquidate or bail out insolvent institutions.

The federally sponsored agencies issue two types of securities: discount notes and bonds. Discount notes are short-term obligations, with maturities

---

[10] *Federal Reserve Bulletin* (March 1992), p. A31.

ranging from overnight to 360 days. Bonds are sold with maturities greater than two years. At the end of 1991, these agencies had a total outstanding debt of almost $400 billion.[11]

With the exception of the securities issued by the Farm Credit Financial Assistance Corporation, federal agency securities are not backed by the full faith and credit of the U.S. government, as is the case with Treasury securities. Consequently, investors purchasing a federally sponsored agency security are exposed to some potential credit risk. The yield spread between these securities and Treasury securities of comparable maturity reflects differences in perceived credit risk and liquidity. The spread attributable to credit risk reflects financial problems faced by the issuing federally sponsored agency and the likelihood that the federal government will allow the agency to default on its outstanding obligations.

The price quotation convention for federally sponsored agency securities is the same as that for Treasury securities. That is, the bid and ask price quotations are expressed as a percentage of par plus fractional 32nds of a point. There are some issues of federally sponsored agencies that trade with almost the same liquidity as Treasury securities. Other issues that are supported only by a few dealers trade much like off-the-run corporate bonds.

We describe six of the eight federally sponsored agencies briefly here. The two agencies not discussed here—Federal Home Loan Mortgage Corporation and Federal National Mortgage Association—are covered in Chapter 24.

***Federal Farm Credit Bank System.***   The purpose of the Federal Farm Credit Bank System (FFCBS) is to facilitate adequate, dependable credit and related services to the agricultural sector of the economy. The Farm Credit System consists of three entities: the Federal Land Banks, Federal Intermediate Credit Banks, and Banks for Cooperatives. Before 1979, each entity issued securities in its own name. Starting in 1979, they began to issue debt on a consolidated basis as "joint and several obligations" of the FFCBS. All financing for the FFCBS is arranged through the Federal Farm Credit Banks Funding Corporation, which issues consolidated obligations through a selling group consisting of approximately 150 members. For discount notes, the selling group consists of only four dealers.

***Farm Credit Financial Assistance Corporation.***   In the 1980s, the FFCBS faced financial difficulties because of defaults on loans made to farmers. The defaults were caused largely by high interest rates in the late 1970s and early 1980s and by depressed prices on agricultural products. To recapitalize the Federal Farm Credit Bank System, Congress created the Farm Credit Financial Assistance Corporation (FACO) in 1987. This federally sponsored agency is authorized to issue debt to assist the FFCBS. FACO bonds, unlike the debt of other federally sponsored government agencies, are backed by the Treasury.

---

[11] *Ibid.*

***Federal Home Loan Bank System.***   The Federal Home Loan Bank System (FHLBS) consists of the 12 district Federal Home Loan Banks (which are instrumentalities of the U.S. government) and their member banks. An independent federal agency, the Federal Home Loan Bank Board was originally responsible for regulating all federally chartered savings and loan associations and savings banks, as well as state-chartered institutions insured by the Federal Savings and Loan Insurance Corporation. These responsibilities have been curtailed since 1989. The major source of debt funding for the Federal Home Loan Banks is the issuance of consolidated debt obligations, which are joint and several obligations of the 12 Federal Home Loan Banks.

***Financing Corporation.***   The deposits of savings and loans were once insured by the Federal Savings and Loan Insurance Corporation (FSLIC), overseen by the Federal Home Loan Bank Board. When difficulties encountered in the savings and loan industry raised concerns about FSLIC's ability to meet its responsibility to insure deposits, Congress passed the Competitive Equality and Banking Act in 1987. This legislation included provisions to recapitalize FSLIC and establish a new federally sponsored agency, the Financing Corporation (FICO), to issue debt in order to raise funds.

FICO is capitalized by the non-voting stock purchased by the 12 regional Federal Home Loan Banks. FICO issued its first bonds on September 30, 1987 — a 30-year noncallable $500 million issue. The issue was priced 90 basis points over the 30-year Treasury security at the time. The principal of these bonds is backed by zero-coupon Treasury securities. The legislation permits FICO to issue up to $10.825 billion but not more than $3.75 billion in any one year. FICO is legislated to be dismantled in 2026, or after all securities have matured, whichever comes sooner.

***Resolution Trust Corporation.***   The 1987 legislation that created FICO did not go far enough to resolve the problems facing the beleaguered savings and loan industry. In 1989, Congress passed more comprehensive legislation, the Financial Institutions Reform, Recovery and Enforcement Act (FIRREA). This legislation has three key elements. First, it transfers supervision of savings and loans to the Office of Thrift Supervision. Second, it shifts the FSLIC insurance function to a Savings Association Insurance Fund (SAIF), placed under the supervision of the Federal Deposit Insurance Corporation. Third, it establishes the Resolution Trust Corporation (RTC) as a federally sponsored agency charged with the responsibility of liquidating or bailing out insolvent savings and loan institutions. RTC is to obtain its funding from the Resolution Funding Corporation (REFCORP), which is authorized to issue up to $40 billion of long-term bonds. The principal of this debt is backed by zero-coupon Treasury bonds. REFCORP has issued both 30-year and 40-year bonds.[12]

---

[12] The 40-year bonds represent the first offering of such a government or government agency bond since the Treasury issued 40-year bonds in the 1950s. The auction for the $5 billion, 40-year bond offering in January 1990 was not a successful undertaking.

*Student Loan Marketing Association.* Popularly known as "Sallie Mae," the Student Loan Marketing Association provides liquidity for private lenders participating in the Federal Guaranteed Student Loan Program, the Health Education Assistance Loan Program, and the PLUS loan program (a program that provides loans to the parents of undergraduate students). Sallie Mae is permitted to purchase and offer investors participation in student loans. Sallie Mae issues unsecured debt obligations in the form of discount notes. In January of 1982, Sallie Mae first issued floating-rate securities based on the bond-equivalent yield on 91-day Treasury bills. Sallie Mae also has long-term fixed-rate securities and zero-coupon bonds outstanding.

### Future Regulation of Federally Sponsored Agencies

The U.S. bailout of the savings and loan industry raised increasing concerns in Congress over the potential cost of bailing out federally sponsored agencies. The Financial Institutions Reform, Recovery and Enforcement Act of 1989 mandated the General Accounting Office (GAO) and the Secretary of the Treasury to study the issues and prepare reports for Congress. Specifically, both the GAO and the Treasury were to investigate whether each federally sponsored agency maintained appropriate capital levels, given the risks associated with their activities. The Treasury was also charged with assessment of the impact of the activities of federally sponsored agencies on federal borrowing.

The Treasury interim report recommends that a federally sponsored agency be required to maintain a triple-A credit rating from two nationally recognized rating companies.[13] The rating must be achieved in the absence of government sponsorship (that is, as a stand-alone private entity). Failure to obtain such a credit rating would result in the loss of sponsorship by the federal government. The GAO interim report puts forth two possible forms of regulation. One is the same as that recommended by the Treasury. The alternative is to require federally sponsored agencies to maintain a specified level of risk-weighted capital similar to the risk-weighted capital requirements for commercial banks discussed in Chapter 4. At the time of this writing, Congress has not settled upon the form of regulation, if any, to implement.

► KEY POINTS THAT YOU SHOULD UNDERSTAND BEFORE PROCEEDING:

1. Federal agencies securities fall into two categories: federally related institutions securities and federally sponsored securities.
2. Federally related institutions are generally backed by the full faith and credit of the U.S. government.

---

[13] We discussed credit ratings in Chapter 11.

3. Federally sponsored agencies (also called government-sponsored entities) are privately owned, publicly chartered entities that, unlike federally related institutions, do issue securities directly in the marketplace.

4. In general, the securities issued by federally sponsored agencies are not backed by the full faith and credit of the U.S. government.

5. Congress is currently considering proposals to regulate federally sponsored agencies.

## SUMMARY

The U.S. Treasury market is closely watched by all participants in the financial markets because interest rates on Treasury securities are the benchmark interest rates throughout the world. The Treasury issues three types of securities: bills, notes, and bonds. Treasury bills have a maturity of one year or less, are sold at a discount from par, and do not make periodic interest payments. Treasury notes and bonds are coupon securities.

Treasury securities are issued on a competitive bid auction basis, according to a regular auction cycle. The auction process relies on the participation of the primary government securities dealers, with which the Federal Reserve deals directly. The auction process has been revised to allow greater participation by eligible nonprimary dealers.

The secondary market for Treasury securities is an over-the-counter market, where dealers trade with the general investing public and with other dealers. In the secondary market, Treasury bills are quoted on a bank discount basis; Treasury coupon securities are quoted on a price basis. Government brokers are used by primary dealers to trade among themselves. Pressure has been placed on primary dealers to provide greater access to prices of Treasury securities.

Treasury dealers finance their position in the repo market. They also use the repo market to cover short positions.

While the Treasury does not issue zero-coupon Treasury securities, government dealers have created these instruments synthetically by a process called coupon stripping. Zero-coupon Treasury securities include trademarks, Treasury receipts, and STRIPS. Creation of the first two types of zero-coupon Treasury securities has ceased; STRIPS now dominate the market.

Federally sponsored agency securities and federally related institution securities comprise the federal agency securities market. The former are privately owned, publicly chartered entities created to reduce the cost of borrowing for certain sectors of the economy. Federally related institutions are arms of the federal government whose debt is guaranteed by the U.S. government. While federally sponsored agencies issue their own securities, federally related institutions obtain all or part of their financing by borrowing from the Federal Financing Bank.

## COUPON STRIPPING AND THE THEORETICAL
## PRICING OF TREASURY SECURITIES

■ ■ ■ ■

Financial theory tells us that the theoretical price of a Treasury security should be equal to the present value of the cash flow, where each cash flow is discounted at the appropriate theoretical spot rate. We reviewed this theory in Chapter 12. What we did not do in that chapter, however, is demonstrate what economic force will assure that the actual market price of a Treasury security will not depart significantly from its theoretical price. We could not explain that in Chapter 12 because we had not yet introduced stripped Treasury securities. Given our discussion of these instruments in this chapter, we can now demonstrate the economic force that will move the actual price of Treasury security toward its theoretical price.

To demonstrate this, we will use the 20 hypothetical Treasury securities given in Table 12-1 in Chapter 12 (page 237). The longest maturity bond given in that table is the ten-year, 12.5% coupon bond selling at par and therefore with a yield to maturity of 12.5%. Suppose that a government dealer buys the issue at par and strips it, expecting to sell the zero-coupon Treasury securities at the yields to maturity indicated in Table 12-1 for the corresponding maturity.

Table 16A-1 shows the price that would be received for each zero-coupon Treasury security created. The price for each is just the present value of the cash flow from the stripped Treasury discounted at the yield to maturity corresponding to the maturity of the security (from Table 12-1). The total proceeds received from selling the zero-coupon Treasury securities created would be $104.1880 per $100 of par value of the Treasury issue purchased by the dealer. This would result in an arbitrage profit of $4.1880 per $100 of the ten-year, 12.5% coupon Treasury security purchased.

To understand why the government dealer has the opportunity to realize this profit, look at the third column of Table 16A-1, which shows how much the government dealer paid for each cash flow by buying the entire package of cash flows (that is, by buying the bond). For example, consider the $6.25 coupon payment in four years. By buying the ten-year Treasury bond priced to yield 12.5% (6.25% semiannual) for that coupon payment, or, equivalently, $3.8481. Under the assumptions of this illustration, however, investors were willing to accept a lower yield to maturity, 10.4% (5.2% semi-annual), to purchase a zero-coupon Treasury security with four years to maturity. Thus, investors were willing to pay $4.1663. On this one coupon payment, the government dealer realizes a profit equal to the difference between $4.1663 and $3.8481 (or $0.3182). From all the cash flows, the total profit is $4.1880. In this instance, coupon stripping shows that the sum of the parts is greater than the whole.

Suppose that, instead of the observed yield to maturity from Table 12-1, the yields that investors want are the same as the theoretical spot rates that are

| | | **TABLE 16A-1** | | |
|---|---|---|---|---|
| | | ILLUSTRATION OF ARBITRAGE PROFIT FROM COUPON STRIPPING | | |
| Maturity | Cash Flow | Present Value at 12.5% | Yield to Maturity | Present Value at Yield to Maturity |
| 0.50 | 6.25 | 5.8824 | 0.0800 | 6.0096 |
| 1.00 | 6.25 | 5.5363 | 0.0830 | 5.7618 |
| 1.50 | 6.25 | 5.2107 | 0.0890 | 5.4847 |
| 2.00 | 6.25 | 4.9042 | 0.0920 | 5.2210 |
| 2.50 | 6.25 | 4.6157 | 0.0940 | 4.9676 |
| 3.00 | 6.25 | 4.3442 | 0.0970 | 4.7040 |
| 3.50 | 6.25 | 4.0886 | 0.1000 | 4.4418 |
| 4.00 | 6.25 | 3.8481 | 0.1040 | 4.1663 |
| 4.50 | 6.25 | 3.6218 | 0.1060 | 3.9267 |
| 5.00 | 6.25 | 3.4087 | 0.1080 | 3.6938 |
| 5.50 | 6.25 | 3.2082 | 0.1090 | 3.4863 |
| 6.00 | 6.25 | 3.0195 | 0.1120 | 3.2502 |
| 6.50 | 6.25 | 2.8419 | 0.1140 | 3.0402 |
| 7.00 | 6.25 | 2.6747 | 0.1160 | 2.8384 |
| 7.50 | 6.25 | 2.5174 | 0.1180 | 2.6451 |
| 8.00 | 6.25 | 2.3693 | 0.1190 | 2.4789 |
| 8.50 | 6.25 | 2.2299 | 0.1200 | 2.3210 |
| 9.00 | 6.25 | 2.0987 | 0.1220 | 2.1528 |
| 9.50 | 6.25 | 1.9753 | 0.1240 | 1.9930 |
| 10.00 | 106.25 | 31.6046 | 0.1250 | 31.6046 |
| Total | | 100.0000 | | 104.1880 |

shown in Table 12-2. If we use these spot rates to discount the cash flows, the total proceeds from the sale of the zero-coupon Treasury securities would be equal to $100, making coupon stripping uneconomical.

In our illustration of coupon stripping, the price of the Treasury security is less than its theoretical price. Suppose instead that the Treasury security is greater than its theoretical price. In such cases, investors can purchase in the market a package of zero-coupon Treasury securities such that the cash flow of the package of securities replicates the cash flow of the mispriced coupon Treasury security. By doing so, the investor will realize a yield higher than the yield on the coupon Treasury security. For example, suppose that the market price of the ten-year Treasury security we used in our illustration (Table 16A-1) is $106. By buying the 20 zero-coupon bonds shown in Table 16A-1 with a maturity value identical to the cash flow shown in the second column, the investor is effectively purchasing a ten-year Treasury coupon security at a cost of $104.1880 instead of $106.

It is the process of coupon stripping and reconstituting that will prevent the market price of a coupon Treasury security from departing significantly from its theoretical value based on the spot rates.

**Cost of carry (or simply carry):** The difference between the interest earned on the securities held in inventory by a dealer firm and the cost of financing that inventory.

**Federally related institutions:** Entities that are arms of the federal government.

**Federally sponsored agencies (also called government-sponsored entities):** Privately owned, publicly chartered entities that are created by Congress to reduce the cost of capital for certain borrowing sectors of the economy deemed to be important enough to warrant assistance.

**Government brokers:** Brokers used by primary dealers trading Treasury securities with each other.

**Hot issue (also called special issue):** Refers to a security (collateral) that is in short supply for a repurchase agreement.

**Overnight repo:** A repurchase agreement with a maturity of one day.

**Primary dealers:** Securities firms and commercial banks that the Federal Reserve will deal with in implementing its open market operations.

**Repurchase agreement:** Transaction calling for the sale of a security and its repurchase at a future date. Both the sale price and the purchase price are specified in the agreement, the difference between the two prices being the dollar interest cost of the loan.

**Stop yield:** In a Treasury securities auction, the highest yield accepted by the Treasury.

**Stripped Treasury security:** A zero-coupon instrument created by stripping a Treasury security.

**STRIPS:** A zero-coupon instrument created from stripping a Treasury security and created as part of the Treasury's Stripped Trading of Registered Interest and Principal Securities program.

**Tail:** The difference between the average yield of all the bids accepted by the Treasury at an auction and the stop yield.

**Term repo:** A repurchase agreement with a maturity of more than one day.

**Trademark zero-coupon Treasury securities:** A zero-coupon instrument created by a particular government dealer firm by stripping a Treasury security. The resulting instrument is associated with that firm (e.g., TIGRs and CATs).

**Treasury bills:** Treasury securities with maturities of one year or less. Current Treasury practice is to issue these securities as discount securities.

**Treasury bonds:** Treasury coupon securities issued with original maturities greater than ten years.

**Treasury coupon securities:** Treasuries that make periodic coupon interest payments. Current Treasury practice is to issue all securities with maturities of two years or longer as coupon securities.

**Treasury discount securities:** Treasury securities that pay only a contractually fixed amount at maturity and no periodic coupon payments. Current Treasury practice is to issue Treasury bills as discount securities.

**Treasury notes:** Treasury coupon securities issued with original maturities between two and ten years.

**Treasury Receipt (or TR):** A zero-coupon instrument created by a group of primary government dealers by stripping a Treasury security. The resulting instrument is not directly associated with any of the participating dealers.

**When issued (or wi) market:** The market where Treasury securities are traded prior to the time they are issued by the Treasury.

**Yield on a bank discount basis:** Convention used in the Treasury market to quote the yield on Treasury bills.

**QUESTIONS**

1. Why do government dealers use government brokers?
2. Suppose that the price of a Treasury bill with 90 days to maturity and a $1 million face value is $980,000. What is the yield on a bank discount basis?
3. The bid and ask yields for a Treasury bill maturing on January 16, 1992, are quoted by a dealer as 5.91% and 5.89%, respectively. Shouldn't the bid yield be less than the ask yield, because the bid yield indicates how much the dealer is willing to pay, and the ask yield is what the dealer is willing to sell the Treasury bill for?
4. Calculate the dollar price for the following Treasury coupon securities:

|  | Price Quoted | Par |
|---|---|---|
| a. | 95-4 | $ 100,000 |
| b. | 87-16 | 1,000,000 |
| c. | 102-10 | 10,000,000 |
| d. | 116-30 | 10,000 |
| e. | 102-4+ | 100,000 |

5. The following is from the March 1991 monthly report published by Blackstone Financial Management:

   *The Treasury also brought $34.5 billion in new securities to the market in February as part of the normal quarterly refunding. . . . The auctions went slightly better than expected given the significant size and the uncertainties surrounding the duration of the war. The 3-year was issued at a 6.98% average yield, the 10-year at a 7.85% average yield, and the 30-year at a 7.98% average yield. All bids were accepted at the average yield or better (that is, with no tail), indicating ample demand for the securities.*

   a. What is meant by the average yield and the "tail"?

b. Why does the absence of a tail indicate ample demand for the Treasuries auctioned?

6. a. What is the difference between a STRIP, a trademark Treasury zero-coupon security, and a Treasury receipt?

   b. What is the most common type of Treasury zero-coupon security?

7. a. How can a repurchase agreement be used by a dealer firm to finance a long position in a Treasury security?

   b. One party in a repo transaction is said to "buy collateral," the other party to "sell collateral." Why?

   c. When there is a shortage of a specific security for a repo transaction, will the repo rate increase or decrease?

8. Which rate should be higher: the overnight repo rate, or the overnight federal funds rate? Why?

9. What is the difference between a federally sponsored agency security and a federally related institution?

10. Are federally sponsored agency securities backed by the full faith and credit of the U.S. government?

11. What economic mechanism forces the actual market price of a Treasury security toward its theoretical price?.

# CHAPTER SEVENTEEN

# Municipal Securities Markets

*After reading this chapter you will understand:*

- who buys municipal securities and why the securities are attractive investments to these buyers.
- the types of municipal securities and why they are issued.
- the risks unique to investment in municipal securities.
- the primary and secondary markets for municipal securities.
- the yield relationship between municipal securities and taxable bonds.
- the yield relationships among municipal securities within the municipal market.
- the degree of regulation of the municipal securities market.

In this chapter, we discuss municipal securities and the market in which they trade. Municipal bonds are securities issued by state and local governments and by their creations, such as "authorities" and special districts. There are both tax-exempt and taxable municipal bonds. Interest on tax-exempt municipal securities is exempt from federal income taxation. The large majority of outstanding municipal bonds are tax-exempt securities, so the municipal securities market is also referred to as the "tax-exempt securities market." Because of the tax-exempt feature of municipal bonds, the yield on municipal bonds is less than that on Treasuries with the same maturity.

Municipal securities are issued for various purposes. Short-term notes typically are sold in anticipation of the receipt of funds from taxes or proceeds from the sale of a bond issue, for example. The proceeds from the sale of short-term notes permit the issuing municipality to cover seasonal and temporary imbalances between outlays for expenditures and tax inflows. Municipalities issue long-term bonds as the principal means for financing both (1) long-term capital projects such as the construction of schools, bridges, roads, and airports, and (2) long-term budget deficits that arise from current operations.

As the single most important advantage of municipal securities to investors is the exemption of interest income from federal taxation, the investor groups that have purchased these securities are those that benefit the most from this exemption. The three categories of investors dominating the municipal securities market are households (retail investors), commercial banks, and property and casualty insurance companies. Individual investors may purchase municipal securities directly or through investment companies.

## TYPES AND FEATURES OF MUNICIPAL SECURITIES

There are basically two different types of municipal bond security structures: general obligation bonds and revenue bonds. There are also securities that share characteristics of both general obligation and revenue bonds.

### General Obligation Bonds

General obligation bonds (often called "GOs") are debt instruments issued by states, counties, special districts, cities, towns, and school districts. Usually, a general obligation bond is secured by the issuer's unlimited taxing power. However, some GOs are backed by taxes that are limited as to revenue sources and maximum property-tax millage amounts.[1] Such bonds are known as *limited-tax general obligation bonds*. For smaller governmental entities such as school districts and towns, the only available unlimited taxing power is on property. For larger general obligation bond issuers such as states and big cities, tax revenue sources are more diverse and may include corporate and individual income taxes, sales taxes, and property taxes. The security pledges for these

---

[1] Tax rates are assessed according to a millage, where one mill is equal to 0.001. So, if a municipality has a millage rate of 5 mills, and a property has an assessed value of $80,000, the tax would be 0.005 times $80,000, or $400.

larger issuers, such as states, are sometimes referred to as being *full faith and credit obligations*.

Additionally, certain general obligation bonds are secured not only by the issuer's general taxing powers to create revenues accumulated in a general fund, but also by certain identified fees, grants, and special charges, which provide additional revenues from outside the general fund. Such bonds are known as "double-barreled in security" because of the dual nature of the revenue sources.

## Revenue Bonds

The second basic type of security structure is found in a revenue bond. Such bonds are issued for either project or enterprise financings where the bond issuers pledge to the bondholders the revenues generated by the operating projects financed. A feasibility study is performed before the endeavor is undertaken to determine whether it will be self-supporting.

In 1970, only 33.5%, or $5.96 billion of the total amount of municipal bonds issued in that year, were revenue bonds; in 1989, 65.6%, or $68.58 billion, of all municipals issued were revenue bonds.[2]

Following are examples of revenue bonds: airport revenue bonds, college and university revenue bonds, hospital revenue bonds, single-family mortgage revenue bonds, multifamily revenue bonds, public power revenue bonds, resource recovery revenue bonds, seaport revenue bonds, sports complex and convention center revenue bonds, student loan revenue bonds, toll road and gas tax revenue bonds, and water revenue bonds.

Table 17-1 shows the amounts of the major kinds of municipal debt that have been issued in the last few years.

## Hybrid and Special Bond Securities

Some municipal bonds that have the basic characteristics of general obligation bonds and revenue bonds have more issue-specific structures as well. Examples are *insured bonds* and *refunded bonds*.

Insured bonds are backed by insurance policies written by commercial insurance companies, as well as by the credit of the municipal issuer. Municipal bond insurance is a contractual commitment by an insurance company to pay the bondholder any bond principal and/or coupon interest that is due on a stated maturity date but that has not been paid by the bond issuer. Once issued, this municipal bond insurance usually extends for the term of the bond issue, and it cannot be cancelled by the insurance company.

Municipal bond insurance has been available since 1971. By 1990, approximately 25% of all new municipal issues were insured. Some of the largest and financially strongest insurance companies in the U.S. have been partici-

---

[2] These data are derived from the *Merrill Lynch Fixed Income Strategy Report*, First Quarter 1990, p. 22.

| TABLE 17-1 | | | | | |
|---|---|---|---|---|---|

NEW SECURITIES ISSUED BY TAX-EXEMPT STATE AND
LOCAL GOVERNMENTS, 1987-1991, IN $ BILLIONS

|  | *1987* | *1988* | *1989* | *1990* | *1991* |
|---|---|---|---|---|---|
| All Issues | 95.0 | 114.5 | 113.7 | 120.3 | 154.4 |
| Gn. Obligation | 29.6 | 30.3 | 35.8 | 39.6 | 55.1 |
| Revenue | 65.4 | 84.2 | 77.9 | 81.3 | 99.3 |
| Type of Issuer | | | | | |
| State | 8.4 | 8.8 | 11.8 | 15.2 | 24.9 |
| Special Unit | 61.7 | 74.4 | 71.1 | 72.2 | 80.6 |
| City, County | 24.9 | 31.2 | 30.1 | 32.5 | 48.9 |
| Use of New Capital | | | | | |
| Education | 9.2 | 15.0 | 15.1 | 17.0 | 21.1 |
| Transportation | 3.6 | 6.8 | 6.9 | 11.7 | 13.4 |
| Utilities | 7.3 | 8.5 | 11.4 | 11.7 | 21.0 |
| Other | 33.7 | 49.2 | 50.6 | 63.3 | 64.3 |

Note: All numbers are rounded values.
*Source: Federal Reserve Bulletin*, selected issues.

pants in this industry, as have smaller *monoline* (single-line) insurance companies. The monoline companies that are major municipal bond insurers as of
1990 include: AMBAC Indemnity Corporation, Capital Guaranty Insurance
Company, Financial Guaranty Insurance Corporation, and Municipal Bond
Investors Assurance. In general, although insured municipal bonds sell at
yields lower than they would without the insurance, they tend to have yields
substantially higher than triple-A-rated noninsured municipal bonds.

Refunded bonds (also called "prerefunded bonds") are bonds that originally may have been issued as general obligation or revenue bonds but are
now secured by an "escrow fund" consisting entirely of direct U.S. government obligations that are sufficient for paying the bondholders. There are three
reasons why a municipal issuer may refund an issue by creating an escrow
fund. First, many refunded issues were originally issued as revenue bonds with
covenants restricting certain activities of the issuer. The municipality may wish
to eliminate these restrictions. The creation of an escrow fund to pay the bondholders legally eliminates the restrictive covenants. Second, some issues are
refunded in order to alter the maturity schedule of the obligation. Finally, when
interest rates have declined after a municipal security has been issued, there
is a tax arbitrage opportunity available to the issuer by paying existing bondholders a lower interest rate and using the proceeds to create a portfolio of
U.S. government securities paying a higher interest rate.[3]

---

[3] Since the interest rate that a municipality must pay on borrowed funds is less than the
interest rate paid by the U.S. government, in the absence of any restrictions in the tax code, a
municipal issuer can realize a tax arbitrage. This can be done by issuing a bond and immediately investing the proceeds in a U.S. government security. Tax rules may prevent such

Most refunded bonds are structured to be called at the first call date, which is the first time that the call provision allows the issuer to retire the debt. When the issuer's objective is to eliminate restrictive bond covenants, refunded bonds are structured to meet the maturity schedule of the original bond issue. Because refunded bonds are collateralized by U.S. government obligations, they are among the safest of all municipal obligations if the escrow is properly structured.[4]

## Municipal Notes

Municipal securities issued for periods up to three years are considered to be short-term in nature. These include *tax anticipation notes* (TANs), *revenue anticipation notes* (RANs), *grant anticipation notes* (GANs), and *bond anticipation notes* (BANs).

TANs, RANs, GANs, and BANs are temporary borrowings by states, local governments, and special jurisdictions. Usually, notes are issued for a period of 12 months, although it is not uncommon for notes to be issued for periods as short as three months and for as long as three years. TANs and RANs (also known as TRANs) are issued in anticipation of the collection of taxes or other expected revenues. The purpose of these borrowings is to even out irregular flows into the treasuries of the issuing entity. BANs are issued in anticipation of the sale of long-term bonds.

## Redemption Features

Municipal bonds are issued with one of two debt retirement structures or a combination of both. Either a bond has a *serial maturity structure* or a *term maturity structure*. A serial maturity structure requires a portion of the debt obligation to be retired each year. A term maturity structure provides for the debt obligation to be repaid at the end of the bond's planned life. Usually, term bonds have maturities ranging from 20 to 40 years. Such bonds often have sinking fund provisions that call for partial and systematic retirement of the debt on a set schedule that begins five or ten years before the time of maturity. Another provision that permits the early redemption of a term bond is the call privilege, which allows the issuer, under certain and well specified circumstances, to pay off the debt prior to the scheduled maturity. Sinking fund and call provisions are noted features of corporate debt and will be discussed further in Chapter 21.

---

arbitage in some cases. Should a municipal issuer violate the tax arbitrage rules, the issue will be ruled to be taxable. If subsequent to the issuance of a bond, however, interest rates decline so that the issuer will find it advantageous to call the bond, the establishment of the escrow fund will not violate the tax arbitrage rules.

[4] For a further discussion of refunded bonds, see Chapter 5 in Sylvan G. Feldstein and Frank J. Fabozzi, *Dow Jones-Irwin Guide to Municipal Bonds* (Homewood, IL: Dow Jones-Irwin, 1987).

▶ KEY POINTS THAT YOU SHOULD UNDERSTAND BEFORE PROCEEDING:

1.  There are two types of municipal securities: general obligation bonds and revenue bonds.

2.  A general obligation bond is secured by the issuer's unlimited taxing power.

3.  A revenue bond is issued for either project or enterprise financings where the bond issuer pledges the revenues generated by the project that is financed to the bondholders.

4.  Municipal notes are issued for periods up to three years and represent temporary borrowings by states, local governments, and special jurisdictions.

5.  The debt retirement structure for a municipal bond can be either a serial maturity structure or a term maturity structure.

## CREDIT RATINGS

■ ■ ■ ■

While municipal bonds have long been considered second in safety only to U.S. Treasury securities, today there are new concerns about the credit risks of many municipal bonds.[5]

The first concern came out of the New York City billion-dollar financial crisis in 1975. On February 25, 1975, the state of New York's Urban Development Corporation defaulted on a $100 million note issue that was the obligation of New York City. Many market participants had been convinced that the state of New York would not allow the issue to default. Although New York City was able later to obtain a $140 million revolving credit from banks to cure the default, lenders became concerned that the city would face difficulties in repaying its accumulated debt, which stood at $14 billion on March 31, 1975.[6] This financial crisis sent a loud and clear warning to market participants: despite supposedly ironclad protection for the bondholder, when issuers such as large cities have severe financial difficulties, the financial stakes of public employee unions, vendors, and community groups may be dominant forces in balancing budgets. This reality was reinforced by the federal bankruptcy law taking effect in October 1979, which makes it easier for the issuer of a municipal security to go into bankruptcy.

The second reason for concern about the credit risk of municipal securities is the proliferation in this market of innovative financing techniques to secure new bond issues. In addition to the established general obligation bonds

---

[5] For a history of defaults of municipal bonds, see Chapter 2 in Feldstein and Fabozzi, *The Dow Jones-Irwin Guide to Municipal Bonds*.

[6] Securities and Exchange Commission Staff Report on *Transactions in Securities of the City of New York* (Washington, D.C.: U.S. Government Printing Office, 1977), p. 2. The reasons for the New York City financial crisis are documented in Donna E. Shalala and Carol Bellamy, "A State Saves a City: The New York Case," *Duke Law Journal* (January 1976), pp. 1119-1126.

and revenue bonds, there are now more innovative, and legally untested, security mechanisms that do not require voters' approval of new debt. What distinguishes these newer bonds from the more traditional general obligation and revenue bonds is that there is no history of court decisions or other case law that firmly establishes the rights of the bondholders and the obligations of the issuers. It is not possible to determine in advance the probable legal outcome if the newer financing mechanisms were to be challenged in court. The importance of this uncertainty is illustrated most dramatically by the bonds of the Washington Public Power Supply System (WPPSS) where bondholder rights to certain revenues were not upheld by the highest court in the state of Washington.

Many institutional investors in the municipal bond market rely on their own in-house municipal credit analysts for determining the creditworthiness of a municipal issue; other investors rely on commercial credit ratings. The two leading commercial rating companies are Moody's and Standard & Poor's. The assigned rating system is essentially the same as that used for corporate bonds that we discussed in Chapter 11.

To evaluate general obligation bonds, the commercial rating companies assess information in four basic categories. The first category includes information on the issuer's debt structure and overall debt burden. The second category relates to the issuer's ability and political discipline to maintain sound budgetary policy. The focus of attention here usually is on the issuer's general operating funds and whether it has maintained at least balanced budgets over three to five years. The third category involves determining the specific local taxes and intergovernmental revenues available to the issuer, as well as obtaining historical information both on tax collection rates, which are important when looking at property tax levies, and on the dependence of local budgets on specific revenue sources. The fourth and last category of information necessary to the credit analysis is an assessment of the issuer's overall socioeconomic environment. The determinations that have to be made here include trends of local employment distribution and composition, population growth, real estate property valuation, and personal income, among other economic factors.

While there are numerous security structures for revenue bonds, the underlying principle in rating is whether the project being financed will generate sufficient cash flow to satisfy the obligations due bondholders.

▶ KEY POINTS THAT YOU SHOULD UNDERSTAND BEFORE PROCEEDING:

1. The investor in a municipal security is exposed to credit risk.
2. Commercial rating companies evaluate the credit risk associated with municipal securities and express the results of their analysis in the form of rating categories.
3. The factors used to determine a rating for a general obligation bond are different from those used for a revenue bond.

## TAX RISKS ASSOCIATED WITH INVESTING
## IN MUNICIPAL SECURITIES

■ ■ ■ ■

There are two types of tax risk to which tax-exempt municipal securities buyers are exposed. The first is the risk that the federal income tax rate will be reduced. The higher the marginal tax rate, the more valuable the tax exemption feature. As the marginal tax rate declines, the price of a tax-exempt municipal security will decline.

The second type of tax risk is that a municipal bond issued as a tax-exempt issue may be eventually declared by the Internal Revenue Service to be taxable. This could happen because many municipal revenue bonds have elaborate security structures that could be subject to future adverse Congressional action and IRS interpretation. A loss of the tax exemption feature will cause the municipal bond to decline in value in order to provide a yield comparable to similar taxable bonds. An example of this risk is the following situation: in June of 1980, the Battery Park City Authority sold $97.315 million in notes, which at the time of issuance seemed to be exempt from federal income taxation. In November of 1980, however, the IRS held that interest on these notes was not exempt. The legal question was not settled until September 1981, when the Authority and the IRS signed a formal agreement resolving the matter so as to make the interest on the notes tax-exempt.

▶ Key points that you should understand before proceeding:

1. A tax risk associated with investing in municipal bonds is that the highest marginal tax rate will be reduced, resulting in a decline in the value of municipal bonds.
2. Another tax risk associated with investing in municipal bonds is that a tax-exempt issue may be eventually declared by the Internal Revenue Service to be taxable.

## THE PRIMARY MARKET

■ ■ ■ ■

A substantial number of municipal obligations are brought to market each week. A state or local government can market its new issue by offering bonds publicly to the investing community or by placing them privately with a small group of investors. When a public offering is selected, the issue usually is underwritten by investment bankers and/or municipal bond departments of commercial banks. Public offerings may be marketed by either competitive bidding or direct negotiations with underwriters. In a competitive process, the bidder submitting the highest bid price for the security gets the right to market the debt to investors.[7]

Most states mandate that general obligation issues be marketed through competitive bidding, but generally this is not necessary for revenue bonds.

---

[7] See Chapter 14 for more information about underwriting.

Usually, state and local governments require a competitive sale to be announced in a recognized financial publication, such as *The Bond Buyer*, which is a trade publication for the municipal bond industry. *The Bond Buyer* also provides information on upcoming competitive sales and most negotiated sales, as well as the results of previous weeks. However the debt is marketed, the municipal unit prepares an *official statement* describing its financial situation and the terms of the issue. These terms include the call and sinking fund provisions mentioned above.

## THE SECONDARY MARKET

Municipal bonds are traded in the over-the-counter market supported by hundreds of municipal bond dealers across the country. Markets for the debts of smaller issuers (referred to as "local credits") are maintained by regional brokerage firms, local banks, and by some of the larger Wall Street firms. Markets for the bonds of bigger issuers (referred to as "general names") are supported by the larger brokerage firms and banks, many of whom have investment banking relationships with these issuers.

There are brokers who serve as intermediaries in the sale of large blocks of municipal bonds among dealers and large institutional investors. In addition to these brokers and the daily offerings sent out over *The Bond Buyer's* "munifacts" teletype system, many dealers advertise their municipal bond offering for the retail market in what is known as *The Blue List*. This is a 100-plus-page booklet published every weekday by Standard & Poor's Corporation, which gives municipal securities offerings and prices.

Dealer spreads depend on several factors. For the retail investor, the spread can range from as low as one-quarter of one point ($12.50 per $5,000 par value) on large blocks of actively traded bonds to four points ($200 per $5,000 of par value) for odd lot sales of an inactive issue. For institutional investors, the dealer spread rarely exceeds one-half of one point ($25 per $5,000 of par value).

## REGULATION OF THE MUNICIPAL SECURITIES MARKET[8]

Congress has specifically exempted municipal securities from both the registration requirements of the Securities Act of 1933 and the periodic reporting requirements of the Securities Exchange Act of 1934. Antifraud provisions apply nevertheless to offerings of, or dealings in, municipal securities.

The reasons for the exemption afforded municipal securities appear to relate to (1) a desire for harmonious and cooperative relations among the various levels of government in the United States; (2) the absence of recurrent abuses in transactions involving municipal securities; (3) the greater level of

---

[8] Parts of this section are drawn from Thomas F. Mitchell, "Disclosure and the Municipal Bond Industry," Chapter 40, and Nancy H. Wojtas, "The SEC and Investor Safeguards," Chapter 42 in Frank J. Fabozzi, Sylvan G. Feldstein, Irving M. Pollack, and Frank Zarb (eds.), *The Municipal Bond Handbook: Volume I* (Homewood, IL: Dow Jones-Irwin, 1983).

sophistication of investors in this segment of the securities markets (the market was long dominated by institutional investors); and (4) the fact that there had been few defaults by municipal issuers. Consequently, between the enactment of federal securities acts in the early 1930s and the early 1970s, the municipal securities market was relatively free from federal regulation.

In the early 1970s, however, circumstances changed. As incomes rose, individual investors began to participate in the municipal securities market to a much greater extent, and public concern over selling practices was expressed with greater frequency. Moreover, the financial problems of some municipal issuers, notably New York City, made market participants aware that municipal issuers have the potential to experience severe financial difficulties approaching bankruptcy levels.

Congress passed the Securities Act Amendment of 1975 to broaden federal regulation in the market for municipal debt. This legislation brought brokers and dealers in the municipal securities market, including banks that underwrite and trade municipal securities, under the regulatory umbrella of the Securities Exchange Act of 1934. The legislation mandated also that the SEC establish a 15-member Municipal Securities Rulemaking Board (MSRB) as an independent, self-regulatory agency whose primary responsibility is to develop rules governing the activities of banks, brokers, and dealers in municipal securities. Rules adopted by the MSRB must be approved by the SEC. The MSRB has no enforcement or inspection authority. That authority is vested with the SEC, the National Association of Securities Dealers, and certain regulatory banking agencies such as the Federal Reserve Bank.

The Securities Act Amendment of 1975 does not require municipal issuers to comply with the registration requirement of the 1933 act or the periodic reporting requirement of the 1934 act, despite several legislative proposals to mandate such financial disclosure. Even in the absence of federal legislation dealing with the regulation of financial disclosure, however, underwriters began insisting upon greater disclosure as it became apparent that the SEC was exercising stricter application of the antifraud provisions. Moreover, underwriters recognized the need for improved disclosure to sell municipal securities to an investing public that had become much more concerned about the credit risk of municipal issuers.

On June 28, 1989, the SEC formally approved the first bond disclosure rule, effective January 1, 1990. While the disclosure rule has several exemptions, in general it applies to new issue municipal securities offerings of $1 million or more.

| SUMMARY | Municipal securities are issued by state and local governments and their authorities, with the interest on most issues being exempt from federal income taxes. The primary investors in these securities are households (which includes mutual funds), commercial banks, and property and casualty insurance companies. |

The two basic security structures are general obligation bonds and revenue bonds. The former are secured by the issuer's general taxing power. Revenue bonds are used to finance specific projects, and a municipality's ability to satisfy such a bond's obligations depends on revenues from those projects. Hybrid securities have certain characteristics of both general obligation and revenue bonds, and some hybrid securities have unique structures.

Municipal notes are issued for shorter periods (one to three years) than municipal bonds. Municipal bonds may be retired with a serial maturity structure, a term maturity structure, or a combination of both. Investing in municipal securities exposes investors to credit risk and tax risk.

**GLOSSARY**

**Anticipation note:** Debt with a maturity between three months and three years, which municipalities sell in anticipation of some future inflow, from taxes or revenues among other sources.

**General obligation bonds:** Debt instruments issued by states, counties, special districts, cities, towns, and school districts, and usually secured by the issuer's unlimited taxing power.

**Insured bonds:** Municipal bonds backed by insurance policies written by commercial insurance companies, as well as by the credit of the municipal issuer.

**Refunded bonds (or "prerefunded bonds"):** Municipal bonds that originally may have been issued as general obligation or revenue bonds but that are now secured by an "escrow fund" consisting entirely of direct U.S. government obligations that are sufficient for paying the bondholders.

**Revenue bonds:** Municipal bonds issued for either project or enterprise financings where the bond issuers pledge the revenues generated by the project to the bondholders.

**Serial maturity structure:** A bond issue's requirement that a portion of the debt obligation be retired each year.

**Term maturity structure:** A bond issue's provision that requires the debt to be fully repaid at the end of the bond's planned life.

**QUESTIONS**

1. a. Who are the three major investors in municipal securities?
   b. What aspect of their situation and what feature of these bonds attract these investors to this market?
2. If it is expected that Congress will change the tax law so as to increase marginal tax rates, what do you think will happen to the price of municipal bonds?

3.  a.  What is the major difference between a general obligation bond and a revenue bond?

    b.  What conditions make a bond a full faith and credit obligation of a municipal government?

4.  a.  Why are more municipal bonds insured today than in 1970?

    b.  In your view, would the typical AAA- or AA-rated municipal bond be insured?

5.  a.  What is a refunded or prerefunded bond?

    b.  Identify two reasons why an issuing municipality would want to prerefund an outstanding bond.

6.  Explain these two provisions of a bond issue: the call provision and the sinking fund provision.

7.  What is the meaning of each of these acronyms: TAN, RAN, GAN, and BAN?

8.  For years, observers and analysts of the debt market believed that municipal securities were free of any risk of default. Why do most people now believe that municipal debt can carry a substantial amount of credit or default risk?

9.  Because many people know that interest payments on municipal debt generally are exempt from taxation by the federal government, they would undoubtedly be surprised by the term "tax risk of investing in municipal bonds." Can you explain this term, and state why an astute investor should always be aware of this risk when buying municipal bonds?

CHAPTER EIGHTEEN

# Common Stock Markets

## LEARNING OBJECTIVES

*After reading this chapter you will understand:*

- the reasons why the stock market has undergone significant structural changes since the 1960s.
- the various trading locations for stocks.
- trading mechanisms such as the types of orders, short-selling, and margin transactions.
- the key structural difference between a stock exchange and an over-the-counter market.
- the key elements of the proposed national market system.
- trading arrangements to accommodate institutional traders such as block trades and program trades.
- what the upstairs market is and its role in institutional trading.
- the role played by stock market indicators and how those indicators are constructed.
- the various stock market indicators of interest to market participants.
- evidence on the pricing efficiency of the stock market.
- the implications of pricing efficiency for a common stock strategy.

Our focus in this chapter is on the secondary market for common stock in the United States. It is in the stock market that investors express their opinions about the economic prospect of a company through the trades they make. The aggregate of these trades gives the market consensus opinion about the price of the stock. This market has undergone significant changes since the 1960s, reflecting primarily the three interacting factors we described in Chapter 1, which have led to globalization of markets: (1) the institutionalization of the stock market as a result of a shift away from traditional small investors to large institutional investors; (2) changes in government regulation of the market; and (3) innovation, largely due to advances in computer technology.

The institutionalization of this market has had important implications for the design of trading systems because the demands made by institutional investors are different from those made by traditional small investors. We describe in this chapter the arrangements that have evolved to accommodate institutional investors in the secondary market for common stocks. We also review evidence on how efficiently common stocks are priced and the implications of efficiency for investment strategies.

## CHARACTERISTICS OF COMMON STOCK

Equity securities represent an ownership interest in a corporation. Holders of equity securities are entitled to the earnings of the corporation when those earnings are distributed in the form of dividends; they are also entitled to a pro rata share of the remaining equity in case of liquidation. Holders of equity securities also have voting rights.

There are two types of equity securities: *preferred stock* and *common stock*. The key distinction between the two forms of equity securities is the degree to which their holders may participate in any distribution of earnings and capital and the priority given to each class in the distribution of earnings. Typically, preferred stockholders are entitled to a fixed dividend, which they receive before common stockholders may receive any dividends. We refer therefore to preferred stock as a "senior" corporate security, in the sense that preferred stock interests are senior to the interests of common stockholders. We postpone an explanation of preferred stock to Chapter 21 where we discuss the market for senior corporate securities.

An important measure of the performance of the management of a corporation is its *net income*. Net income alone, however, is a misleading measure because it does not relate income to the number of shares outstanding. For example, suppose that the net income after taxes of company A last year is $6 million and that of company B $4 million. Does that mean that the common shareholders of company A are better off than those of company B? Not necessarily. Suppose there are 2 million shares of company A's common stock outstanding but only 1 million shares of company B's outstanding. The amount earned for each share of company A is $3 ($6 million divided by 2 million shares), but the amount earned for each share of company B is greater, $4 ($4 million divided by 1 million shares).

The amount earned for each share of common stock outstanding is called *earnings per share*. The formula for calculating the earnings per share of a company is

$$\text{Earnings per share} = \frac{\text{Net income after taxes} - \text{Preferred stock dividends}}{\text{Number of shares of common stock outstanding}}$$

The amount of dividends distributed to preferred stockholders is subtracted from net income after taxes in the numerator of the formula because that amount does not accrue to the benefit of common stockholders.

The price of a stock will trade in the market at some multiple above its earnings per share. This multiple is called the *price–earnings ratio;* it reflects investors' anticipations about the future economic prospects of the corporation. For example, if the price of company A is $15 per share, then its price-earnings ratio is 5 ($15 divided by the earnings per share of $3).

▶ KEY POINTS THAT YOU SHOULD UNDERSTAND BEFORE PROCEEDING:

1.  The rights of an owner of a common share of stock.
2.  The rights of an owner of a share of preferred stock.
3.  The meaning of earnings per share and the price-earnings ratio.

## TRADING LOCATIONS

In the United States, secondary trading of common stock occurs in a number of trading locations: on major national stock exchanges and regional stock exchanges, and in the over-the-counter (OTC) market. In addition to these trading locations, independently operated electronic trading systems are being developed.

### Stock Exchanges

Stock exchanges are formal organizations, approved and regulated by the Securities and Exchange Commission (SEC), that are made up of members that use the facilities to exchange certain common stocks. Stocks that are traded on an exchange are said to be *listed stocks*. To be listed, a company must apply and satisfy requirements established by the exchange where listing is sought. Listing of a common stock on more than one exchange has been permitted.

To have the right to trade securities on the floor of the exchange, firms or individuals must buy a "seat" on the exchange; that is, they must become a member of the exchange. The cost of a seat is market-determined. A member firm may trade for its own account or on behalf of a customer. In the latter case it is acting as broker.

Each stock is traded at a specific location, called a *post*, on the trading floor. Firms that are members of an exchange and that are brokers trade stock on behalf of their customers. The market maker role on an exchange is performed by a specialist. A member firm may be designated as a specialist for the common stock of more than one company, but only one specialist is designated for the common stock of a given company. An important difference between exchanges and the OTC market is the market structure design with respect to a single market maker or multiple market makers. This is a critical institutional difference underlying some controversy associated with secondary trading on an exchange versus over-the-counter, which we discuss later in this chapter.

The two major national stock exchanges are the New York Stock Exchange (NYSE), popularly referred to as the "Big Board," and the American Stock Exchange (ASE or AMEX). The NYSE is the largest exchange in the U.S. As of June 1991, about 2,300 companies were listed, with a total common stock market value of approximately $3.2 trillion. The NYSE's Rule 390, applicable only to that exchange, requires permission from the exchange for a member firm to execute a transaction in an NYSE-listed stock off the exchange.[1] In recent years the NYSE has faced considerable competition for certain types of orders from regional exchanges and the London Stock Exchange.

The AMEX is the second largest exchange. At the end of 1990, there were 1,063 AMEX issues listed with a total market value of $102 billion. There are five regional stock exchanges: Midwest, Pacific, Philadelphia, Boston, and Cincinnati. On these exchanges there are two kinds of stocks listed: (1) stocks of companies that could not qualify for listing (or do not wish to list) on one of the major national exchanges, and (2) stocks that are also listed on one of the major national exchanges. The latter are called "dually listed stocks." The motivation for dual listing is that a local brokerage firm that purchases a membership on a regional exchange can trade these stocks without having to purchase a considerably more expensive membership on the major national stock exchange where the stock is also listed. A local brokerage firm, of course, could use the services of a member of a major national stock exchange to execute an order, if it were willing to give up part of its commission. The regional stock exchanges themselves compete with the NYSE for the execution of smaller trades such as those for 5,000 shares or less. Major national brokerage firms have in recent years routed such orders to regional exchanges because of the lower cost they charge for executing orders.

At one time stock exchanges fixed minimum commissions on transactions, according to the value and the volume of shares involved. The fixed commission structure did not allow the commission rate to decline as the number of shares in the order increased, thereby ignoring the economies of scale in executing transactions. For example, brokers incur lower total costs in executing an order of 10,000 shares of one stock for one investor than in executing 100 orders for the same stock from 100 investors. The institutional investors that had come to dominate trading activity required larger order size, yet did not reap the benefits of the economies of scale in order execution that brokers did. Pressure from institutional investors led the SEC in May 1975 to elimi-

---

[1] Certain stocks listed on the NYSE are exempt from this rule.

nate fixed commission rates, and commissions are now fully negotiable between investors and their brokers.

## Over-the-Counter Market

The over-the-counter (OTC) market is the market for unlisted stocks. The National Association of Securities Dealers (NASD), a private organization, represents and regulates the dealers in the OTC market under the supervision of the SEC. The National Association of Securities Dealers Automated Quotation (NASDAQ) system is an electronic quotation system that provides price quotations to market participants on the more actively traded issues in the OTC market. As of the end of 1990, there were about 3,800 common stocks included in the NASDAQ system with a total market value of $229 billion.

A stock may be both listed on an exchange and traded in the OTC market. The *third market* refers to the trading of such listed stocks in the OTC market.[2] Dealers in this market are not members of an exchange, and therefore never charged the fixed minimum commissions once set by the exchange. The third market grew as institutional investors used it in the early 1960s to avoid fixed minimum commissions.

## Independent Electronic Trading Systems

It is not always necessary for two parties to a transaction to use the services of a broker or a dealer to execute a trade. The direct trading of stocks between two transactors without the use of a broker is called the *fourth market*. This market grew for the same reasons as the third market: the excessively high minimum commissions established by the exchanges. Its growth was limited initially by the availability of information on other institutions that wanted to trade.

Today, systems have been developed that allow institutional investors to "cross" trades—that is, match buyers and sellers—via computer. The two major systems that handle large institution-to-institution trades are INSTINET and POSIT. The latter started in late 1980 and currently has 80 institutional money managers. POSIT, which stands for Portfolio System for Institutional Investors, is a trading system developed by BARRA and Jefferies & Co.[3]

## Trading Mechanics

Below we describe the key features involved in trading stocks. Later in the chapter, we discuss trading arrangements (block trades and program trades)

---

[2] The "first market" refers to the trading of listed stocks executed on the floor of the exchange. The "second market" refers to the execution of unlisted stock trades in the over-the-counter market.

[3] POSIT is more than a simple order-matching system but rather matches the purchase and sale of portfolios in such a way so as to optimize the liquidity of the system.

that developed specifically for coping with the trading needs of institutional investors.

***Types of Orders and Trading Priority Rules.*** When an investor wants to buy or sell a share of common stock, the price and conditions under which the order is to be executed must be communicated to a broker. The simplest type of order is the *market order*, an order to be executed at the best price available in the market. If the stock is listed and traded on an organized exchange, the best price is assured by the exchange rule that when more than one order on the same side of the buy/sell transaction reaches the market at the same time, the order with the best price is given priority. Thus, buyers offering a higher price are given priority over those offering a lower price; sellers asking a lower price are given priority over those asking a higher price.

Another priority rule of exchange trading is needed to handle receipt of more than one order at the same price. Most often, the priority in executing such orders is based on the time of arrival of the order—first orders in are the first orders executed—although there may be a rule that gives higher priority to certain types of market participants over other types of market participants who are seeking to transact at the same price. For example, on exchanges, orders can be classified as either "public orders" or orders of those member firms dealing for their own account (both nonspecialists and specialists). Exchange rules require that public orders be given priority over orders of member firms dealing for their own account.

The danger of a market order is that an adverse move may take place between the time the investor places the order and the time the order is executed. To avoid this danger, the investor can place a *limit order* that designates a price threshold for the execution of the trade. A *buy limit* order indicates that the stock may be purchased only at the designated price or lower. A *sell limit* order indicates that the stock may be sold at the designated price or higher. The danger of a limit order is that there is no guarantee that it will be executed at all; the designated price may simply not be obtainable. A limit order that is not executable at the time it reaches the market is recorded in a *limit order book*.

The limit order is a conditional order: it is executed only if the limit price or a better price can be obtained. Another type of conditional order is the *stop order*, which specifies that the order is not to be executed until the market moves to a designated price, at which time it becomes a market order. A *buy stop order* specifies that the order is not to be executed until the market rises to a designated price—that is, until it trades at or above, or is bid at or above, the designated price. A *sell stop order* specifies that the order is not to be executed until the market price falls below a designated price—that is, until it trades at or below, or is offered at or below, the designated price. A stop order is useful when an investor cannot watch the market constantly. Profits can be preserved or losses minimized on a stock position by allowing market movements to trigger a trade. In a sell (buy) stop order, the designated price is lower (higher) than the current market price of the stock. In a sell (buy) limit order, the designated price is higher (lower) than the current market price of the stock.

There are two dangers associated with stop orders. Stock prices sometimes exhibit abrupt price changes, so the direction of a change in a stock price may be quite temporary, resulting in the premature trading of a stock. Also, once the designated price is reached, the stop order becomes a market order and is subject to the uncertainty of the execution price noted earlier for market orders.

A *stop-limit order*, a hybrid of a stop order and a limit order, is a stop order that designates a price limit. In contrast to the stop order, which becomes a market order if the stop is reached, the stop-limit order becomes a limit order if the stop is reached. The stop-limit order can be used to cushion the market impact of a stop order. The investor may limit the possible execution price after the activation of the stop. As with a limit order, the limit price may never be reached after the order is activated, which therefore defeats one purpose of the stop order—to protect a profit or limit a loss.

An investor may also enter a "market if touched order." This order becomes a market order if a designated price is reached. A market if touched order to buy becomes a market order if the market falls to a given price, while a stop order to buy becomes a market order if the market rises to a given price. Similarly, a market if touched order to sell becomes a market order if the market rises to a specified price, while the stop order to sell becomes a market order if the market falls to a given price. We can think of the stop order as an order designed to get out of an existing position at an acceptable price (without specifying the exact price), and the market if touched order as an order designed to get into a position at an acceptable price (also without specifying the exact price).

Orders may be placed to buy or sell at the open or the close of trading for the day. An opening order indicates a trade to be executed only in the opening range for the day, and a closing order indicates a trade is to be executed only within the closing range for the day.

An investor may enter orders that contain order cancellation provisions. A "fill or kill" order must be executed as soon as it reaches the trading floor or it is immediately cancelled. Orders may designate the time period for which the order is effective—a day, week, or month, or perhaps by a given time within the day. An *open order*, or "good till cancelled" order, is good until the investor specifically terminates the order.

Orders are also classified by their size. One round lot is typically 100 shares of a stock. An *odd lot* is defined as less than a round lot. For example, an order of 75 shares of Digital Equipment Corporation (DEC) is an odd lot order. An order of 350 shares of DEC includes an odd lot portion of 50 shares. A *block trade* is defined on the NYSE as an order of 10,000 shares of a given stock or a total market value of $200,000 or more.

***Automated Order Routing.*** Both the major national stock exchanges and the regional stock exchanges have systems for routing orders of a specified size (that are submitted by brokers) through a computer directly to the specialists' posts where the orders can be executed. On the NYSE, this system is called the *SuperDOT* (Super Designated Order Turnaround) system. SuperDOT handled an average of 180,000 orders per day in 1992. The AMEX's Post Execution Reporting system allows orders up to 2,000 shares to be routed directly to specialists. The regional stock exchanges have computerized systems for routing small orders to specialists. The Small Order Execution system of the NASDAQ routes and executes orders up to 1,000 shares of a given stock.

## Short-Selling

As we explained in Chapter 15, short selling involves the sale of a security not owned by the investor at the time of sale. The investor can arrange to have her broker borrow the stock from someone else, and the borrowed stock is delivered to implement the sale. To "cover" her short position, the investor must subsequently purchase the stock and return it to the party that lent the stock.

Let us look at an example of how this is done in the stock market. Suppose Ms. Stokes believes that Wilson Steel common stock is overpriced at $20 per share and wants to be in a position to benefit if her assessment is correct. Ms. Stokes calls her broker, Mr. Yats, indicating that she wants to sell 100 shares of Wilson Steel. Mr. Yats will do two things: (1) sell 100 shares of Wilson Steel on behalf of Ms. Stokes, and (2) arrange to borrow 100 shares of that stock to deliver to the buyer. Suppose that Mr. Yats is able to sell the stock for $20 per share and borrows the stock from Mr. Jordan. The shares borrowed from Mr. Jordan will be delivered to the buyer of the 100 shares. The proceeds from the sale (ignoring commissions) will be $2,000. However, the proceeds do not go to Ms. Stokes because she has not given her broker the 100 shares. Thus, Ms. Stokes is said to be "short 100 shares."

Now, let's suppose one week later the price of Wilson Steel stock declines to $15 per share. Ms. Stokes may instruct her broker to buy 100 shares of Wilson Steel. The cost of buying the shares (once again ignoring commissions) is $1,500. The shares purchased are then delivered to Mr. Jordan, who lent 100 shares to Ms. Stokes. At this point, Ms. Stokes has sold 100 shares and bought 100 shares. So, she no longer has any obligation to her broker or to Mr. Jordan — she has covered her short position. She is entitled to the funds in her account that were generated by the selling and buying activity. She sold the stock for $2,000 and bought it for $1,500. Thus, she realizes a profit before commissions of $500. From this amount, commissions are subtracted.

Two more costs will reduce the profit further. First, a fee will be charged by the lender of the stock. Second, if there are any dividends paid by Wilson Steel while the stock is borrowed, Ms. Stokes must compensate Mr. Jordan for the dividends he would have been entitled to.

If, instead of falling, the price of Wilson Steel stock rises, Ms. Stokes will realize a loss when she is forced to cover her short position. For example, if the price rises to $27, Ms. Stokes will lose $700, to which must be added commissions and the cost of borrowing the stock (and possibly dividends).

Exchanges impose restrictions as to when a short sale may be executed; these so-called *tick-test rules* are intended to prevent investors from destabilizing the price of a stock when the market price is falling. A short sale can be made only when either (1) the sale price of the particular stock is higher than the last trade price (referred to as an uptick trade), or (2) if there is no change in the last trade price of the particular stock (referred to as a zero uptick), the previous trade price must be higher than the trade price that preceded it. For example, if Ms. Stokes wanted to short Wilson Steel at a price of $20, and the two previous trade prices were $20 1/8 and then $20, she could not do so at this time because of the uptick trade rule. If the previous trade prices were $19 7/8, $19 7/8, and then $20, she could short the stock at $20 because of the uptick trade rule. Suppose that the sequence of the last three trades is: $19 7/8, $20, and $20. Ms. Stokes could short the stock at $20 because of the zero uptick rule.

## Margin Transactions

Investors can borrow cash to buy securities and use the securities themselves as collateral. For example, suppose Mr. Boxer has $10,000 to invest and is considering buying Wilson Steel, which is currently selling for $20 per share. With his $10,000, Mr. Boxer can buy 500 shares. Suppose his broker can arrange for him to borrow an additional $10,000 so that Mr. Boxer can buy an additional 500 shares. Thus, with a $20,000 investment, he can purchase a total of 1,000 shares. The 1,000 shares will be used as collateral for the $10,000 borrowed, and Mr. Boxer will have to pay interest on the amount borrowed.

A transaction in which an investor borrows to buy shares using the shares themselves as collateral is called *buying on margin*. By borrowing funds, an investor creates financial leverage. Note that Mr. Boxer, for a $10,000 investment, realizes the consequences associated with a price change of 1,000 shares rather than 500 shares. He will benefit if the price rises but be worse off if the price falls (compared to borrowing no funds).

To illustrate, let's look at what happens if the price subsequently changes. If the price of Wilson Steel rises to $29 per share, ignoring commissions and the cost of borrowing, Mr. Boxer will realize a profit of $9 per share on 1,000 shares, or $9,000. Had Mr. Boxer not borrowed $10,000 to buy the additional 500 shares, his profit would be only $4,500. Suppose, instead, the price of Wilson Steel stock decreases to $13 per share. Then, by borrowing to buy 500 additional shares, he lost $7 per share on 1,000 shares instead of $7 per share on just 500 shares.

The funds borrowed to buy the additional stock will be provided by the broker, and the broker gets the money from a bank. The interest rate that banks charge brokers for such purposes is named the *call money rate* (also labeled the *broker loan rate*). The broker charges the borrowing investor the call money rate plus a service charge.

The broker is not free to lend as much as it wishes to the investor to buy securities. The Securities Exchange Act of 1934 prohibits brokers from lending more than a specified percentage of the market value of the securities. The *initial margin requirement* is the proportion of the total market value of the securities that the investor must pay for in cash. The 1934 act gives the Board of Governors of the Federal Reserve (the Fed) the responsibility to set initial margin requirements, which it does under Regulations T and U. The Fed changes margin requirements as an instrument of economic policy. The initial margin requirement has been below 40%; it is 50% as of this writing. Initial margin requirements vary for stocks and bonds.

The Fed also establishes a maintenance margin requirement. This is the minimum proportion of (1) the equity in the investor's margin account to (2) the total market value. If the investor's margin account falls below the minimum maintenance margin, the investor is required to put up additional cash. The investor receives a margin call from the broker specifying the additional cash to be put into the investor's margin account. If the investor fails to put up the additional cash, the broker has the authority to sell the securities for the investor's account.

## Transaction Costs

Transactions costs are more than merely brokerage commissions. Transactions costs consist of commissions, fees, and execution costs. Commissions are fees paid to brokers to trade securities. Since May 1975 commissions have been fully negotiable. According to a survey by Greenwich Associates, the trend of average commissions in cents per share has declined from $0.136 in 1977 to $0.089 in 1989.[4] In addition to commissions, there may be various fees that an investor must pay. These include custodial fees and transfer fees. Custodial fees are the fees charged by an institution that holds securities in safekeeping for an investor.

Execution costs represent the difference between the execution price of a stock and the price that would have existed in the absence of the trade. Execution costs can be further decomposed into *market* (or *price*) *impact* and *market timing costs*. Market impact cost is the result of the bid–ask spread and a price concession demanded by dealers in the stock to mitigate their risk that an investor's demand for the stock is motivated by information that the investor may have that is not embodied in the stock's price. Market timing cost arises when an adverse price movement of the stock during the time of the transaction can be attributed in part to other activity in the stock and is not the result of a particular transaction. Execution costs then are related to both the demand for liquidity and the trading activity on the trade date. Unlike commissions, these costs are not easily measured but they can nevertheless be a major component of the cost of trading in a stock.

## Role of Dealers in Exchange and OTC Markets

In Chapter 15, we explain the role of dealers in secondary markets. There is an important structural difference between exchanges and the OTC market with respect to the activities of dealers. On the exchanges there is only one market maker or dealer per stock, and the dealer is known as the *specialist*. The

---

[4] "Getting Down to Business," Greenwich Associates, Greenwich, CT, 1990.

specialist keeps the limit order book. Designation of who will be a specialist for a stock is determined by the exchange, taking numerous factors into account. Because capital is necessary to perform as a market maker, one requirement for becoming a specialist is satisfaction of the minimum capital requirement. Specialists realize a profit only from those trades in which they are involved.

As there is only one specialist for a given stock, there is no competition from other market makers on the exchange. Does this mean that the specialist has a monopolistic position? Not necessarily, because specialists do face competition from several sources. The existence of public limit orders affects the bid–ask spread. There are brokers in the crowd who have public orders that compete with specialists. In the case of multiple-listed stocks, there is competition from specialists on other exchanges where the stock is listed. For stocks that are exempt from Rule 390 (restricting member firms to execute trades on the exchange), there is competition from dealers in the OTC market (discussed below). Finally, as we discuss later in this chapter, when a block trade is involved, specialists compete with the "upstairs market."

In the OTC market, there may be more than one dealer for a stock. For example, at the time of this writing, there are more than 50 dealers for MCI Corporation. The number of dealers depends on the volume of trading in a stock. If a stock is not actively traded, there may be no need for more than one or two dealers. As trading activity increases in a stock, there are no barriers preventing more entities from becoming dealers in that stock, other than satisfaction of capital requirements. Competition from more dealers—or the threat of new dealers—forces bid–ask spreads to more competitive levels. Moreover, the capital-raising ability of more than one dealer is believed to be more beneficial to markets than that of a single specialist performing the role of a market maker.

Arguments based on the greater competition and greater potential capital have been put forth by those citing the advantages of the OTC market. The exchanges, however, insist that the commitment of the dealers to provide a market for shares in the OTC market is not the same obligation as that of the specialist on the exchange. On the NYSE, for example, Rule 104 sets forth the specialist's obligation to maintain fair and orderly markets. Failure to fulfill this obligation results in a loss of specialist status. A dealer in the OTC market is under no such obligation to continue its market making activity during volatile and uncertain market conditions.

## The National Market System

In the 1960s and early 1970s, U.S. secondary markets for stocks became increasingly fragmented. By a "fragmented market," we mean one in which some orders for a given stock are handled differently from other orders. An example is a stock that can be bought on several exchanges as well as in the over-the-counter market. An order to buy IBM stock, for example, could be executed on one of the exchanges where IBM is listed (i.e., on the specialist system) or in the third market using the multiple-dealer system. Thus, the treatment of the order differs, depending upon where it is ultimately executed.

The concern of public policy makers has been that investors were not receiving the best execution. That is, transactions were not necessarily being executed by a broker on behalf of a customer at the most favorable price available. Another concern with the increased fragmentation of the secondary market for stocks was the growing number of completed transactions in listed stocks that were not reported to the public. This happened because transactions in the third market and on the regional exchanges were not immediately disclosed on the major national exchange ticker tapes where the stock was listed.

As a result of these concerns, Congress enacted the Securities Act of 1975. The most important provision of this legislation for us here is Section 11A(a) (2), which amended the Securities Exchange Act of 1934 and directed the SEC to "facilitate the establishment of a national market system for securities." The SEC, in its efforts to implement a national market system (NMS), targeted six elements, described as follows by Posner:

1. A system for public reporting of completed transactions on a consolidated basis (consolidated tape).
2. A composite system for the collection and display of bid and asked quotations (composite quotation system).
3. Systems for transmitting from one market to another both orders to buy and sell securities and reports of completed transactions (market linkage systems).
4. Elimination of restrictions on the ability of exchange members to effect over-the-counter transactions in listed securities (off-board trading rules).
5. Nationwide protection of limit price orders against inferior execution in another market.
6. Rules defining the securities that are qualified to be traded in the NMS.[5]

These six elements required either changes in technology or legislative initiative. A consolidated tape, a composite quotation system, a market linkage system, and a system for nationwide protection of limit price orders are examples of the former; elimination of off-board trading rules and specification of securities to be included in a national market system are examples of the latter.

Overall, the general issue that the SEC faced was how to design the national market system. Should it be structured as an electronic linkage of

---

[5] N. S. Posner, "Restructuring the Stock Markets: A Critical Look at the SEC's National Market System," *New York University Law Review* (November-December 1981), p. 916.

existing exchange floors? Or should it be an electronic trading system that was not tied to any existing exchange? After experimentation with several pilot programs, the SEC developed a set of arrangements for listed stocks. The Intermarket Trading System (ITS), whose operations began in April 1978, is an electronic system that displays the quotes posted on all the exchanges where a stock is listed, as well as in the OTC market, and provides for intermarket executions. The Consolidated Quotation System is a display system providing data on trades of listed stocks in different market centers.

▶ KEY POINTS THAT YOU SHOULD UNDERSTAND BEFORE PROCEEDING:

1. The differences between organized exchanges and the OTC market.
2. The role and duties of a specialist on an organized exchange.
3. The variety of conditional orders that an investor may place.
4. The structure of a short sale and the costs associated with a short sale.
5. The structure of a margin transaction or a margined purchase of stock, and the role of the broker in that transaction.
6. The role of a dealer on the OTC market.
7. The role of the specialist on the organized exchanges.
8. The meaning and structure of the National Market System.

## TRADING ARRANGEMENTS FOR INSTITUTIONAL INVESTORS

Evidence of institutionalization of the stock market can be seen from the ownership distribution of stocks and the share of trading by individuals (referred to as "retail" trading) and institutions (pension funds, insurance companies, investment companies, bank trusts, and endowment funds). In 1949, institutional ownership of New York Stock Exchange-listed stocks was 13%; in recent years, it has been almost 50%. Moreover, over 80% of the volume of trading on the NYSE is done by institutional investors.[6] This, of course, does not mean that individuals' ownership of stocks has diminished. Instead, institutions trade on behalf of individuals, who hold stock through the instruments of mutual funds, pension funds, and so forth.

With the increase in trading by institutional investors, trading arrangements more suitable to these investors had to be developed. This has resulted in the evolution of special arrangements for the execution of certain types of orders commonly sought by institutional investors: (1) orders requiring the execution of a trade of a large number of shares of a given stock, and (2) orders requiring the execution of trades in a large number of different stocks at as near the same time as possible. The former types of trades are called *block*

---

[6] Securities Industry Association, *Trends* (March 16, 1989).

*trades*; the latter are called *program trades*. An example of a block trade would be a mutual fund that seeks to buy 15,000 shares of IBM stock. An example of a program trade is a pension fund that seeks to buy shares of 200 "names" (by "names" we mean companies) at the end of a trading day.

The institutional arrangement that has evolved to accommodate these two types of institutional trades is the development of a network of trading desks of the major securities firms and institutional investors that communicate with each other by means of electronic display systems and telephones. This network is referred to as the *upstairs market*. Participants in the upstairs market play a key role by (1) providing liquidity to the market so that such institutional trades can be executed, and by (2) arbitrage activities that help to integrate the fragmented stock market.

### Block Trades

Block trades are defined as trades of 10,000 shares or more of a given stock, or trades of shares with a market value of $200,000 or more. In 1961, there were about nine block trades per day, which accounted for about 3% of trading volume; in recent years, by contrast, there have been about 3,000 block trades per day, accounting for almost half the trading volume.[7]

Because the execution of large numbers of block orders places strains on the specialist system, special procedures have been developed to handle them. An institutional customer contacts its salesperson at a brokerage firm, indicating that it wishes to place a block order. The salesperson then gives the order to the brokerage firm's block execution department. Notice that the salesperson does not submit the order to be executed to the exchange where the stock might be traded or, in the case of an unlisted stock, try to execute the order on the NASDAQ system. The sales traders in the block execution department then contact other institutions in the hope of finding one or more institutions that would be willing to take the other side of the order. That is, they use the upstairs market in their search to fill the block trade order. If this can be accomplished, the execution of the order is completed.

If, on the other hand, the sales traders cannot find enough institutions to take the entire block (for example, if the block trade order is for 40,000 shares of IBM, but only 25,000 can be crossed with other institutions), then the balance of the block trade order is given to the firm's market maker. The market maker must then make a decision as to how to handle the balance of the block trade order. There are two choices: (1) the brokerage firm can take a position in the stock and buy the shares for its own account, or (2) the unfilled order can be executed by using the services of competing market makers. Remember that in the former case the brokerage firm is committing its own capital.

[7] U.S. Congress, Office of Technology Assessment, "Electronic Bulls & Bears: U.S. Securities Markets & Information Technology," OTA-CIT-469 (Washington, DC: U.S. Government Printing Office, September 1990), p. 8.

## *Program Trades*

Program trades involve the buying and/or selling of a large number of names simultaneously. Such trades are also called basket trades, because effectively a "basket" of stocks is being traded. Some obvious examples of why an institutional investor may want to use a program trade are deployment into the stock market of new cash, implementation of a decision to move funds invested from the bond market to the stock market (or vice versa), and rebalancing the composition of a stock portfolio because of a change in investment strategy.

Still other reasons that an institutional investor may have a need to execute a program trade will become apparent later in this chapter, when we discuss an investment strategy called indexing. Another use, which we explain when we discuss stock index futures contracts in Chapter 28, is to arbitrage any price discrepancies between the stock market and the stock index futures market. This strategy is called *index arbitrage*. Unfortunately, the popular press tends to use the terms "program trading" and "index arbitrage" interchangeably, which is incorrect. One is an investment strategy (index arbitrage), and the other is an institutional trading arrangement (program trading), even though it is true that a program trade will be employed to implement an index arbitrage. Another confusion is worth noting: because computers are used to execute a program trade, the popular press wrongly characterizes program trading as "computerized trading."

There are several commission arrangements available to an institution for a program trade, and each arrangement has numerous variants. Considerations in selecting one (besides commission costs) are the risk of failing to realize the best execution price, and the risk that the brokerage firms to be solicited about executing the program trade will use their knowledge of the program trade to benefit from the anticipated price movement that might result—in other words, that they will "frontrun" the transaction.

A program trade executed on an *agency basis* involves the selection of a brokerage firm solely on the basis of commission bids (cents per share) submitted by various brokerage firms. The brokerage firm selected uses its best efforts as an agent of the institution to obtain the best price. The disadvantage of the agency basis arrangement for a program trade is that, while commissions may be the lowest, the execution price may not be the best because of market impact costs and the potential frontrunning by the brokerage firms that were solicited to submit a commission bid.

In an *agency incentive arrangement*, a benchmark portfolio value is established for the group of stocks in the program trade. The price for each name in the program trade is determined as either the price at the end of the previous day or the average price of the previous day. If the brokerage firm can execute the trade on the next trading day such that a better-than-benchmark portfolio value results—a higher value in the case of a program trade involving selling, or a lower value in the case of a program trade involving buying—then the brokerage firm receives the specified commission plus some predetermined additional compensation.

What if the brokerage firm does not achieve the benchmark portfolio value? Here is where the variants come into play. One arrangement may call for the brokerage firm to receive just an agreed-upon commission. Other arrangements may involve sharing the risk of not realizing the benchmark portfolio value with the brokerage firm. That is, if the brokerage firm falls short of the benchmark portfolio value, it must absorb a portion of the shortfall. In these risk-sharing arrangements, the brokerage firm is risking its own capital. The greater the risk-sharing the brokerage firm must accept, the higher the commission it will charge.

One problem that remains is the possibility of frontrunning. If brokerage firms know that an institution will execute a program trade with the prices as determined the previous day, they can take advantage of the knowledge. To minimize the possibility of frontrunning, institutions use other types of program trade arrangements. They call for brokerage firms to receive, not specific names and quantities, but only enough information about key portfolio parameters to allow several brokerage firms to bid on the entire portfolio. When the winning bidder has been selected, it gets the details of the portfolio. This procedure, however, increases the risk to the brokerage firm of successfully executing the program trade, although the brokerage firm can use stock index futures (described in Chapter 28) to protect itself if the characteristics of the portfolio in the program trade are similar to the general market.

Brokerage firms can execute the trade in the upstairs market or send orders electronically to exchange floors or the NASDAQ system through the automated order routing systems such as the NYSE SuperDOT System.

▶ KEY POINTS THAT YOU SHOULD UNDERSTAND BEFORE PROCEEDING:

1. Because of the dominance of institutional investors, trading arrangements have developed to accommodate their trading needs.
2. The two trading accommodations for institutional trading are block trading and program trading.
3. There are several commission arrangements for program trading.

## STOCK MARKET INDICATORS

Stock market indicators have come to perform a variety of functions, from serving as benchmarks for evaluating the performance of professional money managers to answering the question "How did the market do today?". Thus, stock market indicators (indexes or averages) have become a part of everyday life. Even though many of the stock market indicators are used interchangeably, it is important to realize that each indicator applies to, and measures, a different facet of the "stock market."

The most commonly quoted stock market indicator is the Dow Jones Industrial Average (DJIA). Other stock market indicators cited in the financial press are the Standard & Poor's 500 Composite (S&P 500), the New York Stock Exchange Composite Index (NYSE Composite), the American Stock

Exchange Market Value Index (AMEX), the NASDAQ Composite Index, and the Value Line Composite Average (VLCA). There are a myriad of other stock market indicators such as the Wilshire stock indexes and the Russell stock indexes, which are followed primarily by institutional money managers.

In general, market indicators rise and fall in fairly similar patterns. There are, however, important differences in the magnitude of these moves. These differences arise because the various indicators represent different universes of stocks, employ different weighting schemes for individual stocks in their universes, and also compute average values in different ways.

Stock market indicators can be classified into three groups: (1) those produced by stock exchanges based on all stocks traded on the exchanges; (2) those produced by organizations that subjectively select the stocks to be included in indexes; and (3) those where stock selection is based on an objective measure, such as the market capitalization of the company. (By "market capitalization," we mean the total market value of the firm's common stock, which equals the number of outstanding shares times the price per share of the stock on the market. Thus, market capitalization is a measure of size.) The first group includes the New York Stock Exchange Composite Index and the American Stock Exchange Market Value Index, which reflect the market value of all stocks traded on the respective exchange. While it is not an exchange, the NASDAQ Composite Index falls into this category because the index represents all stocks tracked by the NASDAQ system.

The three most popular stock market indicators in the second group are the Dow Jones Industrial Average, the Standard & Poor's 500, and the Value Line Composite Average. The DJIA is constructed from 30 of the largest blue-chip industrial companies traded on the NYSE. The companies included in the average are those selected by Dow Jones & Company, publisher of *The Wall Street Journal*. The S&P 500 represents stocks chosen from the two major national stock exchanges and the over-the-counter market. The stocks in the index at any given time are determined by a committee of Standard & Poor's Corporation, which may occasionally add or delete individual stocks or the stocks of entire industry groups. The aim of the committee is to capture present overall stock market conditions as reflected in a very broad range of economic indicators. The VLCA, produced by Arnold Bernhard & Co., covers a broad range of widely held and actively traded NYSE, AMEX, and OTC issues selected by Value Line.

In the third group we have the Wilshire Indexes produced by Wilshire Associates (Santa Monica, California) and Russell Indexes produced by the Frank Russell Company (Tacoma, Washington), a consultant to pension funds and other institutional investors. The criterion for inclusion in each of these indexes is solely a firm's market capitalization.

▶ KEY POINTS THAT YOU SHOULD UNDERSTAND BEFORE PROCEEDING:

1. What a market index is and what it is supposed to convey.
2. The key differences in sample size and selection among the popular indexes.

## PRICING EFFICIENCY OF THE STOCK MARKET

As explained in Chapter 15, a price-efficient market is one in which security prices at all times fully reflect all available information that is relevant to their valuation. When a market is price-efficient, investment strategies pursued to outperform a broad-based stock market index will not consistently produce superior returns after adjusting for (1) risk, and (2) transactions costs.

Numerous studies have examined the pricing efficiency of the stock market. While it is not our intent in this chapter to provide a comprehensive review of these studies, we can summarize their basic findings and their implications for investment strategies.

### Forms of Efficiency

There are three different forms of pricing efficiency: (1) weak form; (2) semistrong form; and (3) strong form.[8] The distinctions among these forms lie in the relevant information that is believed to be taken into consideration in the price of the security at all times. *Weak form efficiency* means that the price of the security reflects the past price and trading history of the security. *Semistrong form efficiency* means that the price of the security fully reflects all public information (which, of course, includes but is not limited to, historical price and trading patterns). *Strong form efficiency* exists in a market where the price of a security reflects all information, whether it is publicly available or known only to insiders such as the firm's managers or directors.

The preponderance of empirical evidence supports the claim that the common stock market is efficient in the weak form. The evidence emerges from sophisticated tests that explore whether historical price movements can be used to project future prices in such a way as to produce returns above what one would expect from market movements and the risk class of the security. Such returns are known as *positive abnormal returns*. The implications are that investors who follow a strategy of selecting stocks solely on the basis of price patterns or trading volume—such investors are referred to as *technical analysts* or *chartists*—should not expect to do better than the market. In fact, they may fare worse because of higher transactions costs associated with frequent buying and selling of stocks.

Evidence on whether the stock market is price-efficient in the semistrong way is mixed. Some studies support the proposition of efficiency when they suggest that investors who select stocks on the basis of *fundamental security analysis*—which consists of analyzing financial statements, the quality of management, and the economic environment of a company—will not outperform the market. This result is certainly reasonable: there are so many analysts using the same approach, with the same publicly available data, that the price of the stock remains in line with all the relevant factors that determine

---

[8] Eugene F. Fama, "Efficient Capital Markets: A Review of Theory and Empirical Work," *Journal of Finance* (May 1970), pp. 383-417.

value. On the other hand, a sizable number of other studies have produced evidence indicating that there have been instances and patterns of pricing inefficiency in the stock market over long periods of time. Economists and financial analysts often label these examples of inefficient pricing as *anomalies in the market*, that is, phenomena that cannot be easily explained.

Empirical tests of strong form pricing efficiency fall into two groups: (1) studies of the performance of professional money managers, and (2) studies of the activities of "insiders" (individuals who are either company directors, major officers, or major stockholders). Studying the performance of professional money managers to test the strong form of pricing efficiency has been based on the belief that professional managers have access to better information than the general public. Whether this is true is moot, because the empirical evidence suggests professional managers have not been able to outperform the market consistently. In contrast, evidence based on the activities of insiders has generally revealed that this group often achieves higher returns than the stock market. Of course, insiders could not get those high abnormal returns if the stock prices fully reflected all relevant information about the values of the firms. Thus, the empirical evidence on insider trading argues against the notion that the market is efficient in the strong form sense.

## *Implications for Investing in Common Stock*

Common stock investment strategies can be classified into two general categories: active strategies and passive strategies. *Active strategies* are those that attempt to outperform the market by one or more of the following: timing the selection of transactions, such as in the case of technical analysis, identifying undervalued or overvalued stocks using fundamental security analysis, or selecting stocks according to one of the market anomalies. Obviously, the decision to pursue an active strategy must be based on the belief that there is some type of gain from such costly efforts; but gains are possible only if pricing inefficiencies exist. The particular strategy chosen depends on why the investor believes this is the case.

Investors who believe that the market prices stocks efficiently should accept the implication that attempts to outperform the market cannot be systematically successful, except by luck. This implication does not mean that investors should shun the stock market, but rather that they should pursue a *passive strategy*, which is one that does not attempt to outperform the market. Is there an optimal investment strategy for someone who holds this belief in the pricing efficiency of the stock market? Indeed there is. Its theoretical basis is the modern portfolio theory and capital market theory that we discussed in Chapter 13. According to modern portfolio theory, the "market" portfolio offers the highest level of return per unit of risk in a market that is price-efficient. A portfolio of financial assets with characteristics similar to those of a portfolio consisting of the entire market—the market portfolio—will capture the pricing efficiency of the market.

But how can such a passive strategy be implemented? More specifically, what is meant by a "market" portfolio, and how should that portfolio be constructed? In theory, the market portfolio consists of all financial assets, not just common stock. The reason is that investors compare all investment opportunities, not just stock, when committing their capital. Thus, our principles of investing must be based on capital market theory, not just stock market theory. When the theory is applied to the stock market, the market portfolio has been defined as consisting of a large universe of common stocks. But how much of each common stock should be purchased when constructing the market portfolio? Theory states that the chosen portfolio should be an appropriate fraction of the market portfolio; hence the weighting of each stock in the market portfolio should be based on its relative market capitalization. Thus, if the aggregate market capitalization of all stocks included in the market portfolio is $T and the market capitalization of one of these stocks is $A, then the fraction of this stock that should be held in the market portfolio is $A/$T.

The passive strategy that we have just described is called *indexing*. As pension fund sponsors have increasingly come in the 1980s to believe that money managers are unable to outperform the stock market, the amount of funds managed using an indexing strategy has grown substantially. Index funds, however, still account for a relatively small fraction of institutional stock investments.

▶ KEY POINTS THAT YOU SHOULD UNDERSTAND BEFORE PROCEEDING:

1. The relevant information that is believed to be discounted in the price of a stock at all times for the three forms of pricing efficiency (weak form, semistrong form, and strong form).
2. The implications of the weak form of pricing efficiency for chartists or technical analysts.
3. The implications of the semi-strong form of pricing efficiency for fundamental security analysts.
4. The general conclusion about pricing efficiency that empirical research into U.S. markets tends to support.
5. Why the price efficiency of a market influences the decision as to whether an investor will pursue an active strategy or passive strategy.

SUMMARY

Common stock represents an ownership interest in a corporation. In the United States, secondary trading of common stock occurs in one or more of the following trading locations: two major national stock exchanges (the NYSE and AMEX), five regional stock exchanges, and the OTC market (NASDAQ system). Independent electronic trading systems such as INSTINET and POSIT permit institution-to-institution trading without the use of a broker.

The secondary market has undergone significant changes since the 1960s. The major participants are now institutional investors rather than small (retail) investors. Elimination of fixed commissions and the government's mandate to develop a national market system to reduce the fragmentation of the stock market have fostered increased competition among market makers on the exchanges and in the over-the-counter-market. Advances in computer technology have ushered in developments for linking the various market locations and systems for institution-to-institution direct trading.

An important structural difference between exchanges and the OTC market is that on exchanges there is only one market maker or dealer per stock, the specialist, while there is no restriction on the number of dealers per stock in the OTC market.

To accommodate the trading needs of institutional investors who tend to place orders of larger sizes and with a large number of names, special arrangements have evolved. Block trades are trades of 10,000 shares or more of a given stock or trades with a market value of $200,000 or more. Program trades, or basket trades, involve the buying and/or selling of a large number of names simultaneously. The institutional arrangement that has evolved to accommodate these needs is the upstairs market, which is a network of trading desks of the major investment banking firms and institutional investors that communicate with each other by means of electronic display systems and telephones.

Stock market indicators can be classified into three groups: (1) those produced by stock exchanges and that include all stocks traded on the exchange; (2) those in which a committee subjectively selects the stocks to be included in the index; and (3) those in which the stocks selected are based solely on stocks' market capitalizations.

There are three forms of pricing efficiency according to what is hypothesized to be the relevant information set that is believed to be embodied in the price of a stock at all times: (1) weak form, (2) semi-strong form, and (3) strong form. Most of the empirical evidence appears to suggest that markets are efficient in the weak form. The evidence on the semi-strong form is mixed, as pockets of inefficiency have been observed. Empirical tests of strong form pricing efficiency have also produced conflicting results.

Active investment strategies, consisting of efforts to time purchases and select stocks, are pursued by investors who believe that securities are mispriced enough that it is possible to capitalize on strategies that are designed to exploit the perceived inefficiency. The optimal strategy to pursue when the stock market is perceived to be price-efficient is indexing, because it allows the investor to capture the efficiency of the market.

**GLOSSARY**

**Abnormal returns:** That portion of a security's returns that is above (positive) or below (negative) what one would expect from market movements and the risk class of the security.

**Anomalies in the market:** Examples of inefficient pricing of securities.

**Automated order routing:** A computerized system for routing buy and sell orders of certain sizes for quick execution.

**Big Board:** Common term for the New York Stock Exchange.

**Block trades:** Trades of 10,000 shares or more of a given stock, or trades of shares with a market value of $200,000 or more.

**Call money rate:** Also known as the "broker loan rate," this is the interest rate banks charge brokers for the funding of loans to investors who buy on margin.

**Capitalization (or market capitalization):** The total market value of a firm's common stock, which equals the number of outstanding shares times the price per share of the stock on the market.

**Chartist:** See technical analyst, below.

**Computerized trading:** Common but misleading term for program trades.

**Consolidated Quotation System:** An electronic display system providing data on trades of listed stocks in different market centers.

**Dually listed stock:** A stock traded both on a national exchange and on a regional exchange.

**Earnings per share (or EPS):** The amount earned for each share of common stock outstanding. It is found by dividing the net income after taxes after subtracting preferred stock dividend payments by the number of shares of common stock outstanding.

**Execution costs:** The difference between the execution price of a stock and the price that would have existed in the absence of the trade. It includes market (or price) impact and market timing costs.

**Fill or kill order:** An order to buy or sell shares that must be executed immediately or be cancelled.

**Forms of pricing efficiency:** Known as the weak form, the semi-strong form, and strong form, these relate to the various types of information believed to be impounded or embedded in the prices of publicly traded securities.

**Fourth market:** Term for the direct trading of stocks between two transactors without the use of a broker.

**Frontrun:** The action of a brokerage firm, which knows of an institutional investor's plans to execute a program trade, to take positions that will benefit from the price movement that might result from the program trade.

**Fundamental security analysis:** Analysis of key financial and economic variables that is designed to reveal mispriced securities.

**Index arbitrage:** An investment strategy involving derivative securities, which is based on a stock market index and shares of stocks that make up the indexes.

**Initial margin requirement:** The percentage of the total market value of a security that an investor must put up in cash when buying a security on margin.

**Intermarket Trading System (ITS):** An electronic system that is part of the National Market System and that displays the quotes posted on all the exchanges where a stock is listed, as well as in the OTC market, and provides for intermarket executions.

**Limit order book:** The listing of those orders (to buy or sell shares) that a specialist may not execute unless the stock's price is at a specified level.

**Listed stock:** A stock eligible for trading on an organized exchange.

**Maintenance margin requirement:** The minimum percentage of the equity in the investor's margin account to the total market value. If the investor's margin account falls below the minimum maintenance margin, the investor is required to put up additional cash.

**Margin buying:** Purchasing stock with money borrowed (at some rate of interest) from the brokerage firm handling the order, with the stock serving as collateral for the loan.

**Market if touched order:** An order to buy or sell shares that becomes a market order if the stock's price reaches a specified level.

**Market impact cost:** A form of execution cost resulting from the bid–ask spread and a price concession demanded by dealers in the stock to mitigate their risk that an investor's demand for the stock is motivated by information that the investor may have that is not embodied in the stock's price.

**Market index (or indicator):** A measure, based on the prices and often number of outstanding shares of a selected number of stocks, that is supposed to convey information about the relative value of shares traded on a market.

**Market order:** An order to buy or sell shares immediately at the best available price.

**Market timing cost:** A form of execution cost that arises when an adverse price movement of the stock during the time of the transaction can be attributed in part to other activity in the stock and is not the result of a particular transaction.

**National Association of Securities Dealers Automated Quotation (or NASDAQ) System:** An electronic system that provides price quotations to market participants about the more actively traded OTC stocks.

**Odd lot:** Anything less than a round lot of a stock.

**Open order:** Also known as "good till cancelled," this type of order to buy or sell shares remains in effect until the broker is notified otherwise.

**Post on an exchange:** The location for the trading of a particular stock or number of stocks.

**Post Execution Reporting System:** The American Stock Exchange's automated routing system.

**Preferred stock:** A form of equity that has priority over common stock in dividends and distributions in the event of liquidation.

**Price-earnings (or P/E) ratio:** The ratio of the price per share of stock to the earnings per share.

**Program (or "basket") trade:** The computer-assisted and simultaneous sale (or purchase) of shares in a large number of different stocks.

**Public order:** An order to buy or sell shares of an exchange-listed stock that a member firm is executing for one of its customers.

**Round lot:** Typically, 100 shares of a stock.

**Rule 390:** The NYSE rule that requires the exchange's permission for a member firm to execute a transaction of an NYSE-listed stock off the exchange.

**Seat on an exchange:** Term for membership in an organized exchange.

**Small Order Execution System:** The NASDAQ system of automating routing of orders.

**Specialist:** The person designated and approved by an organized exchange to function as a market maker in a stock.

**Stop order:** An order to buy or sell a set number of shares of stock that is conditional on the level of the stock's price and becomes a market order when and if the price reaches a specific level.

**SuperDOT:** The NYSE's automated routing system; DOT stands for Designated Order Turnaround.

**Technical analyst:** Also called a "chartist," this investor follows a strategy of selecting stocks solely on the basis of price patterns or trading volume.

**Third market:** Term for the trading of shares of listed stocks on the OTC market.

**Tick-test rules:** Rules about stock price movements that determine whether short sale orders can be executed.

**Trading priority rules:** Rules about the sequence in which exchange specialists must execute stock orders.

**Upstairs market:** The informal but extensive arrangements, employing electronic communications systems, that institutional investors and securities firms have developed to accommodate their typically large trades.

QUESTIONS

1.  This quotation is from an interview with William Donaldson, Chairman of the New York Stock Exchange, that appeared in *The New York Times* of January 30, 1990:

    *Sure it's possible to beat the market. . . . By investing for the long term with an individual selection of stocks, it's quite possible to beat the market. . . .*

    *My concern is that by simply buying an index, investors are not channeling their capital into the best investments, and that has long-term negative implications for the cost of capital in this country. The risk of indexing and treating all companies the same is to give in to a very mediocre goal.*

    a.  What can you infer about Donaldson's views on pricing efficiency from his comment?
    b.  Assuming he is correct, why do you think so few professional stock pickers have been able to "beat the market"?

2.  This quotation is from the same interview with William Donaldson:

    *There's a need to understand the advantages of an auction market versus a dealer market. The auction market allows a buyer and a seller to get together and agree on a price and the dealer is not involved at all. That's opposed to a dealer market where the house is on both sides of the trade and the dealer makes the spread rather than having the spread shared by the buyer and the seller. One of the things we're coming to the forefront on now is the whole idea of what makes a good market. I think the best market is where you have the maximum number of people coming together in a single location and bidding against each other. . . . That is far superior to what we are getting now, which is a fractionalization of the market. Traders on machines, trades in the closet, trades in many areas where buyers and sellers don't have the opportunity to meet.*

    Discuss Donaldson's opinion. In your answer be sure to address the pros and cons of the different trading locations and practices addressed in the chapter.

3.  Following is a quotation from "The Taxonomy of Trading Strategies" by Wayne H. Wagner that appears in *Trading Strategies and Execution Costs,* published by The Institute of Chartered Financial Analysts in 1988. (The publication is the product of a conference held in New York City on December 3, 1987.)

    *The NYSE is not the only operating market; there are ancillary markets that provide trading facilities beyond what is available on the Exchange floor. This suggests that some needs are not well served by the process as it occurs on the Exchange. Examples of how the NYSE is augmented by other trading facilities include the supporting specialists (particularly on the regional exchange); the upstairs brokers . . . the third market, the fourth market, and crossing networks; and the informal floor accommodations. All of these structures are intended to accommodate trading. Without these facilities, the NYSE as it exists today probably could not exist. . . .*

    a.  What is meant by: (i) the upstairs brokers, (ii) the third market, (iii) the fourth market, and (iv) crossing networks?
    b.  How would you complete the last sentence in the quotation by Wagner?

4. Why should an investor who believes that the market is efficient pursue an indexing strategy?

5. a. What is a program trade?

   b. What are the various types of commission arrangements for executing a program trade and the advantages and disadvantages of each?

6. What is meant by the term "institutionalization of the market"?

7. Why is earnings per share a better measure of a firm's performance than net income after taxes?

8. Identify two key differences between an organized exchange such as the New York Stock Exchange and the over-the-counter market.

9. Explain these terms: (a) market order; (b) good till cancelled order; (c) public order; (d) stop loss order; (e) buy limit order; (f) block trade; and (g) closing order.

10. Identify and explain each of the following: (a) National Market System; (b) SuperDOT System; and (c) NASDAQ.

11. Explain the mechanics and some key rules of a short sale.

12. What role does the broker loan rate play in a margin purchase?

13. Many participants and analysts of the stock market are called "chartists" or "technical analysts." What does the theory that the market is weak form efficient say about these investors' chances of beating the market?

# CHAPTER NINETEEN

# Non-U.S. Common Stock Markets

## LEARNING OBJECTIVES

*After reading this chapter you will understand:*

- how the stock markets of the world compare in terms of the value of the securities traded on them and their costs of trading.

- why some stocks are listed on several exchanges around the world.

- that investors want to diversify their portfolios across the markets of the world because prices in different national markets tend to rise and fall at somewhat different times.

- that some stock markets enjoy extensive freedom for self-management, while others experience substantial control by governments, and still others are dominated by commercial banks.

- that most exchanges allow prices of actively traded stocks to be set continuously during the day as buy and sell orders reach the market.

- that some exchanges determine opening prices or prices of inactively traded shares through a call auction procedure, which batches orders for simultaneous execution.

- that computerization has caused most markets to become competitive dealer markets.

- that the specialist system used in the United States appears only in a few other markets of the world.
- the key features of trading on the major national stock markets.
- the structure of national and international stock market indexes in the world.
- the role and importance of the Euroequity markets.
- what an International Depository Receipt is.
- what an American Depository Receipt is, and how it differs from an American Depository Share.

It is increasingly important for students of finance to understand how the non-U.S. national stock markets and the Euroequities market function, perform, and are managed. Our discussion of the U.S. stock market explained that the market, which was once dominated by retail investors, is now dominated by financial institutions. This change has occurred in other industrialized countries as well. A key characteristic of financial institutions is that they have been more willing than retail investors to transfer funds across national borders to improve portfolio diversification and/or exploit perceived mispricing of securities in foreign countries. In recent times, too, corporations have become more willing to raise equity funds outside of their home country. Also, governments have come to rely on equity markets outside their home country to raise capital for enterprises that were once owned and operated by the government. These developments make the world's equity markets more important to one another and to students of finance and economics.

## NATIONAL STOCK MARKETS

Table 19-1 provides a comparative analysis of the size, in U.S. dollars, of the equity markets of the world. The stock markets of the United States and Japan are the largest in the world. Because the markets are measured in U.S. dollars, the relative size of the U.S. and Japanese market varies as the value of the yen changes against the dollar; U.S. share increases when the yen depreciates and decreases when the yen appreciates. The third largest market, but trailing considerably behind the United States and Japan, is the U.K. market.

Trading activity by major national stock markets is shown in Table 19-2. Effective transactions costs (commissions and taxes) are higher in stock markets outside the United States, as can be seen in Table 19-3. Deregulation in many countries, however, is reducing the gap between transactions costs in stock markets outside the United States.

### *Multiple Listings on National Markets*

Stocks of some firms are listed for trading on stock exchanges in other countries as well as on the exchange in their own country. Some stocks of very large firms are listed on stock exchanges in several countries. Table 19-4 shows the

| TABLE 19-1 |
|---|

ESTIMATED TOTAL MARKET VALUE OF NATIONAL
STOCK MARKETS INCLUDED IN MORGAN STANLEY
CAPITAL INTERNATIONAL INDICES AS OF DECEMBER
31, 1992 (IN BILLIONS OF U.S. DOLLARS)

| Area and Country | Estimated Market Value |
|---|---|
| Austria | $    22.5 |
| Belgium | 63.3 |
| Denmark | 32.2 |
| Finland | 11.9 |
| France | 333.0 |
| Germany | 325.7 |
| Italy | 124.4 |
| Netherlands | 129.8 |
| Norway | 18.0 |
| Spain | 95.1 |
| Sweden | 87.2 |
| Switzerland | 195.2 |
| United Kingdom | 914.9 |
| Europe | $2,353.1 |
| Australia | 133.2 |
| Hong Kong | 161.9 |
| Japan | 2,331.5 |
| New Zealand | 15.8 |
| Singapore/Malaysia | 74.7 |
| EAFE | $5,070.1 |
| Canada | 219.7 |
| South African Gold Mines | 7.4 |
| United States | 4,022.8 |
| "World" | $9,320.1 |

*Source: Morgan Stanley Capital International Perspective,* Quarterly
Issue 1, 1993, p. 5.

number of stocks of firms from foreign countries that are listed on national exchanges. Multiple listing of stocks is clearly an increasingly common phenomenon.

The readiness of an exchange to list and trade the shares of a foreign company varies across countries and exchanges. Foreign firms that seek listing for their shares on U.S. exchanges face some costs. In other countries, regulations on the listing and trading of stock of a foreign company are not particularly stringent or costly. In the United Kingdom, for example, the rules on the issuance and trading of foreign companies' shares are basically the same as those for issuing domestic firms' stock.[1]

---

[1] Harriet Creamer, "Issuing Securities in the United Kingdom," *International Financial Law Review*, Special Supplement (July 1990), pp. 54–61.

| TABLE 19-2 | | | |
|---|---|---|---|
| **TURNOVER ON MAJOR STOCK EXCHANGES IN (1992)** | | | |
| Country | Exchange | Total Value of Turnover (billions of U.S. Dollars) | Percent of Total |
| United States | NYSE | 1,765.5 | 51.9 |
| Japan | Tokyo 1st Section | 465.6 | 13.7 |
| Germany | All Exchanges | 428.6 | 12.6 |
| United Kingdom | London | 221.3 | 6.5 |
| France | Paris | 124.5 | 3.7 |
| Canada | All Exchanges | 78.2 | 2.3 |
| Hong Kong | All Exchanges | 75.6 | 2.2 |
| Australia | All Exchanges | 45.5 | 1.3 |
| Netherlands | Amsterdam | 44.5 | 1.3 |
| Spain | Main Exchanges | 42.5 | 1.2 |
| Italy | Milano | 26.4 | 0.8 |
| Sweden | Stockholm | 21.5 | 0.6 |
| Denmark | Copenhagen | 18.9 | 0.6 |
| Singapore | Singapore | 17.2 | 0.5 |
| Norway | Oslo | 10.1 | 0.3 |
| Belgium | Brussels | 6.2 | 0.2 |
| Austria | Vienna | 4.9 | 0.1 |
| New Zealand | All Exchanges | 3.3 | 0.1 |
| Finland | Helsinki | 2.8 | 0.1 |
| Total Major Stock Markets | | 3,402.3 | 100.0 |

The annual figures for turnover values in U.S. dollars are calculated by converting monthly values at month-end exchange rates.

*Source: Morgan Stanley Capital International Perspective*, Monthly Issue 3, 1993, p. 14.

The reasons firms want their shares to be listed on several markets are straightforward. Firms seek to diversify their sources of capital across national boundaries and to increase the total amount of available funds for new issues. Also, firms believe that an internationally varied ownership diminishes the prospect of takeover by other domestic concerns. Finally, there is some reason to believe that firms may expect foreign listing to boost its name and sales of its products.[2] Recent research tends to support these views of multiple listing: firms whose shares are listed on exchanges in different countries tend to be quite large, in terms of assets, and to have a relatively substantial amount of foreign sales revenue.[3]

An important question is whether a share traded in different markets has different prices in those markets. The answer is no, because investors can buy

---

[2] Bruno Solnik, *International Investments*, Second Edition, (Reading, MA: Addison-Wesley, 1991), pp. 112–113.

[3] Shahrokh M. Saudagran, "An Empirical Study of Selected Factors Influencing the Decision to List on Foreign Stock Exchanges," *Journal of International Business Studies* (Spring 1988), pp. 101–127.

| TABLE 19-3 | | | |
|---|---|---|---|

**EFFECTIVE TRANSACTIONS COSTS IN NATIONAL STOCK MARKETS***

| Country | Buy | Sell | Average |
|---|---|---|---|
| Australia | 0.80% | 0.80% | 0.80% |
| Belgium | 0.70 | 0.70 | 0.70 |
| Canada | 0.60 | 0.60 | 0.60 |
| France | 0.58 | 0.58 | 0.58 |
| Germany | 0.58 | 0.58 | 0.58 |
| Hong Kong | 1.07 | 1.07 | 1.07 |
| Italy | 0.72 | 0.72 | 0.72 |
| Japan | 0.45 | 1.00 | 0.73 |
| Netherlands | 0.40 | 0.40 | 0.40 |
| Singapore | 1.20 | 1.00 | 1.10 |
| Spain | 1.00 | 1.00 | 1.00 |
| Sweden | 1.36 | 1.36 | 1.36 |
| Switzerland | 0.55 | 0.55 | 0.55 |
| United Kingdom | 0.75 | 0.25 | 0.50 |
| United States | 0.20 | 0.20 | 0.20 |

*Transaction size assumed to be $500,000.

*Source:* Gary P. Brinson and Richard C. Carr, "International Equities and Bonds," Chapter 19 in Frank J. Fabozzi (ed.), *Portfolio and Investment Management: State-of-the-Art Research, Analysis and Strategies* (Chicago: Probus Publishing, 1989), Table 12, p. 437.

or sell the shares in any of the markets, and they would *arbitrage* any meaningful differences in prices. (Arbitrage means exploiting different prices for the same item in different markets.) That is, if the price of a stock were significantly lower in country X than in country Y, investors would buy as many shares as they could in country X and sell them in Y. Investors would do this until the pressure they were putting on prices in both markets would drive the prices together. A falling gap in prices means that profit would shrink. Investors would stop the arbitraging when profits (the price difference) equaled the costs of the transactions. Therefore, when the various costs of transactions, including commissions and taxes and costs of exchanging currencies, are fully acknowledged, the price of any share tends to be the same across the different markets where it is traded.

## *Global Diversification: Correlation of World Equity Markets*

Numerous studies have documented the potential portfolio diversification benefits associated with global investing.[4] That is, the inclusion of securities

[4] For a review of these studies, see Bruno Solnik, *op. cit.*, Chapter 2.

## TABLE 19-4

### LISTINGS OF FOREIGN STOCKS ON NATIONAL EXCHANGES

| Stock Exchange | Total Number of Stocks | Number of Foreign Stocks |
|---|---|---|
| Australian Stock Exchange | 1,185 | 33 |
| Vienna Stock Exchange (Austria) | 142 | 45 |
| Rio de Janeiro Stock Exchange (Brazil) | 812 | 0 |
| Montreal Stock Exchange (Canada) | 667 | 21 |
| Toronto Stock Exchange (Canada) | 1,193 | 54 |
| Paris Bourse (France) | 1,105 | 231 |
| Frankfurt Stock Exchange (Germany) | 743 | 354 |
| Stock Exchange of Hong Kong | 299 | 15 |
| Bombay Stock Exchange (India) | 2,447 | 0 |
| Tokyo Stock Exchange (Japan) | 1,752 | 125 |
| Istanbul Stock Exchange (Turkey) | 110 | 0 |
| International Stock Exchange (United Kingdom) | 2,559 | 563 |
| American Stock Exchange (United States) | 859 | 70 |
| NASDAQ Stock Market (United States) | 4,132 | 256 |
| New York Stock Exchange (United States) | 1,769 | 96 |

*Source: Institutional Investor*, International Edition, April 1991, pp. 195–202

from other countries can increase a portfolio's expected return without increasing its risk, which is variability in returns (as we described in Chapter 13 in more detail). Similarly, including securities from other countries may reduce the portfolio's risk with no fall in its expected return. The basis of these benefits from diversification is that international capital markets are less than perfectly correlated. Correlation is a statistical measurement of similarity in upward and downward movement in two variables, such as rates of return on groups of stock from two different countries. Stock markets that are not highly correlated move in a somewhat independent way from one another.

This degree of independence is not really surprising: the different countries tend to have different experiences in such important areas as taxation, monetary management, banking policies, political stability and goals, population growth, and so on. Because the largest influences on stock prices are domestic or local events and policies, the prices of groups of stocks from different areas tend to move up or down at somewhat different times and to somewhat different extents. This pattern of dissimilar security price changes allows investors to diversify a certain amount of risk and creates the benefits of international or global investing.

Table 19-5 provides evidence regarding the degree of dissimilarity in the movement of stock prices on selected national stock exchanges. The table presents correlation coefficients for the monthly changes in the stock indexes of ten countries, which measure the overall or general level of share prices on the exchanges in those countries, for the period from 1969 to 1992. (Stock price indexes for markets of the world are discussed in a later section of this chapter.)

To interpret the table, it is necessary to remember only a few points about the correlation coefficient. First, correlation has a maximum value of 1.00, which occurs if two variables always move in the same way, and a minimum value of −1.00, which occurs if two variables always move in exactly the opposite directions. Second, anything has a correlation of 1.00 with itself, which simply means that it moves in exactly the same way that it moves. For example, Australia's index moves just as Australia's index does, and the correlation of Australia with Australia is therefore given as 1.00. Third, a positive correlation that is less than 1.00 means that the two variables move, generally, in the same direction. For example, Germany's stock market has a correlation coefficient of 0.61 with France's market, which implies that these markets

### TABLE 19-5

MONTHLY CORRELATION COEFFICIENTS FOR STOCK PRICE INDEXES FROM SELECTED NATIONAL MARKETS: DECEMBER 1969–DECEMBER 1992. MONTHLY INDEX PRICES WITHOUT DIVIDENDS CALCULATED IN U.S. DOLLARS

| | 1 | 2 | 3 | 4 | 5 | 6 | 7 | 8 | 9 | 10 |
|---|---|---|---|---|---|---|---|---|---|---|
| 1. Australia | 1.00 | | | | | | | | | |
| 2. Belgium | .33 | 1.00 | | | | | | | | |
| 3. France | .37 | .67 | 1.00 | | | | | | | |
| 4. Germany | .29 | .65 | .61 | 1.00 | | | | | | |
| 5. Italy | .24 | .43 | .45 | .40 | 1.00 | | | | | |
| 6. Japan | .25 | .45 | .40 | .41 | .38 | 1.00 | | | | |
| 7. Netherlands | .41 | .67 | .61 | .68 | .37 | .44 | 1.00 | | | |
| 8. Spain | .33 | .41 | .40 | .39 | .37 | .41 | .39 | 1.00 | | |
| 9. U.S. | .49 | .43 | .44 | .36 | .23 | .28 | .57 | .28 | 1.00 | |
| 10. U.K. | .47 | .53 | .54 | .43 | .37 | .38 | .64 | .35 | .51 | 1.00 |

*Source:* Morgan Stanley Capital International.

move in the same way much of the time. Fourth, the correlation coefficient of any two variables, such as Germany's market and France's, is the same as the coefficient of France's market and Germany's. So, the table reports that coefficient only once in the column for France. As a result, the table of coefficients is diagonal and only half-filled.

The table reveals some interesting points. First, these markets are quite different from one another, and the correlations of their returns tend to be substantially less than unity. The highest coefficient is 0.67, for France and Belgium, and many values are below 0.50. Thus, investors can diversify by spreading their portfolio across these various markets.

The second notable point of Table 19-5 is that geography and political alliances do influence the correlations. Thus, stock prices in Germany and Japan move less similarly (coefficient equals 0.40) than do the prices in Germany and France (correlation of 0.61) or the prices in France and Belgium (correlation of 0.67). Investors seeking diversification must choose carefully from among the various markets.

And, finally, it is interesting that all the correlations are positive and well above 0.00, a value which implies complete independence of action. The positive values mean that the world's asset prices are, like their economies, somewhat integrated. Thus, the benefit of international diversification has limits. In other words, the markets of the world are members of a somewhat loosely connected system of economies, and allocating funds among the various economies provides some, but not complete, reduction of variability in returns on securities.

## Ownership and Control of National Stock Markets

A convenient and informative way of outlining key comparisons among some of the larger and more established national stock markets is to analyze traditional patterns of ownership and control of the exchanges.[5] One group of markets has enjoyed great freedom. In Chapter 3, we pointed out that, while stock exchanges in the United States are regulated by the SEC, they are privately owned and competitive entities. The exchanges decide upon the number of memberships, the rules for acquiring membership, and the criteria for listed securities. The exchanges and related Self-Regulatory Organizations (SROs) supervise the activities of members, and commissions are fully negotiable. Further, the various exchanges are actually in competition with one another, and market participants are free to conduct private trades without funneling them through an exchange. For these reasons, it can be said that the U.S. equity markets are in fact private markets, which basically regulate themselves but comply with some governmental regulations.

Market structures that have similar ownership and management traditions exist in Japan, the United Kingdom, Canada, Hong Kong, and Australia.

---

[5] Categorizing markets by ownership and management is a concept suggested by Bruno Solnik, *op. cit.*, p. 106.

These exchanges are privately owned and self-regulating, with the government largely playing the role of monitor. Competition among exchanges occurs in some of these countries. Japan, for example, has eight major exchanges, but more than 98% of the trades occur on the Tokyo Stock Exchange, the Osaka Exchange, and the Nagoya Exchange. Canada has large exchanges in both Montreal and Toronto. In contrast, the United Kingdom has one dominant exchange, the International Stock Exchange in London, and it represents a consolidation of regional exchanges that occurred almost 40 years ago. The Stock Exchange of Hong Kong similarly represents a unification of four previously separate, small exchanges.[6] In many countries where exchanges are privately owned, deregulation has resulted in either fully or partially negotiable commissions. Currently, Japan is the most important exception to this rule.

The rules for membership and listing securities represent another important feature of the exchanges: in Great Britain, Canada, Hong Kong, and Australia, the exchanges determine which securities will be listed and the criteria that firms must meet for membership. Japan handles this matter somewhat differently: the Ministry of Finance (MOF) must approve all listed securities;[7] and while the exchange has set a limit on the number of members, only financial firms licensed by the MOF can become members.

A second group of national markets includes those where the stock exchange has traditionally been a public or quasi-public institution. In these countries, the government has exercised considerable control over the exchange's operations and activities. For example, the government has selected brokers (mostly individuals, but occasionally limited partnerships) and given them a monopoly over the bulk of stock transactions. Often, too, the government has fixed commission rates or has given its approval to fixed rates. Typically, the government has required that all transactions go through the exchange and that a broker get a fee, even if a buyer and a seller conclude a private deal without the assistance of a broker.

Most countries whose stock markets were owned and operated in this fashion are European and include France, Belgium, Spain, and Italy. However, the 1980s—a time of extensive liberalization, innovation, and computerization in the international securities industries—brought about several significant changes in these markets. In recent years, the governments mandated that individual brokers be replaced by corporations with limited liability, public shareholders, and authority to conduct both brokerage and dealer functions. Shares in these firms can be owned by foreign firms as well as by banks in the home country. In France and Belgium, a brokerage firm is a *Société de Bourse*; in Italy, it is a *Societá di Intermediazione Mobiliare*; and in Spain, brokerage firms are *Sociedades de Valores*.

---

[6] Kie Ann Wong, "The Hong Kong Stock Market," in Richard Yan-Ki Ho *et al.* (eds.), *The Hong Kong Financial System* (Hong Kong: Oxford University Press, 1991), pp. 222–223.

[7] Stuart Allen and Selina O'Connor (eds.), *The Guide to World Equity Markets 1992* (London: Euromoney Publications PLC, 1992), p. 288.

Despite this change, government agencies exercise extensive supervisory authority over the exchanges. For example, membership on an exchange may still require government approval or licensing[8] and government agencies set minimum capital requirements as insurance against insolvency.[9] In several of these countries, negotiable fees are replacing fixed commissions at varying speeds. In another significant change, computerized trading systems, frequently modeled on the Toronto Stock Exchange's Computer Assisted Trading System (or CATS), are now integral features of these markets. In some countries (such as France), off-exchange trading among dealers is permitted for large blocks of stock, while in Spain and Italy all trading must be handled by a licensed securities firm on the exchange.

The last group of national markets includes those countries in which the majority of exchange trading is done through banks. We described in Chapter 3 how, in Germany, the universal banks dominate securities transactions. This type of structure also appears in Switzerland, Austria, and (in modified form) in Sweden. The domination by the banks reflects regulatory or government policy. In Germany, only banks can act as brokers on behalf of the public throughout the eight competing exchanges in the country.[10] On the Zurich Stock Exchange (ZSE), which is the largest of three different exchanges, only 27 banks (known as the "Ring Banks") have licenses to trade in securities.[11] It is interesting to note that over-the-counter trading, which has a volume at least as large as the ZSE, is open to anyone who can get a securities license from any of the Swiss cantons, which are subfederal jurisdictions in the country. About 240 dealers operate in that market.[12]

It would be a mistake to leave this account of banker-dominated exchanges without mentioning the fact that several national exchanges display a less than friendly attitude toward banks' participation on exchanges. Hong Kong's exchange prohibits banks from membership,[13] and both Japan and the United States impose many (but possibly weakening) restrictions on banking activity in the securities industry. (See Chapter 4 for more discussion about the U.S.'s Glass-Steagall Act and recent developments on that front.)

Two other features of these national situations are worthy of note. The markets of Austria and Germany also have brokers (the word for broker is *"Makler"*), some of whom are officially appointed and some of whom are independent (the *"Freie Makler"*). The brokers tend to perform tasks related to smaller and less actively traded stocks whose prices are set in call auctions

---

[8] Government approval is still needed in France. See Roger D. Huang and Hans R. Stoll, *Major World Equity Markets: Current Structure and Prospects for Change* (New York: New York University Salomon Center Monograph in Finance and Economics, 1991), p. 30.

[9] Allen and O'Connor, *op. cit.*, p. 266.

[10] Huang and Stoll, *op. cit.*, p. 44.

[11] George Sellerberg, "Swiss Equity Market," in Jess Lederman and Keith K.H. Park (eds.), *The Global Equity Markets* (Chicago: Probus Publishing Company, 1991), p. 165.

[12] Allen and O'Connor, *op. cit.*, p. 444.

[13] Wong, "The Hong Kong Stock Market," *op. cit.*, p. 224.

rather than in the continuous trading that occurs with the shares of the larger firms. Also, Germany and Switzerland, which have several exchanges, allow the regulation of the various exchanges to be conducted by agencies that are not part of the federal government: in Germany the states (or *"Länder"*), in Switzerland the cantons. Local pride and interest thus accentuate all normal competitive tendencies in the markets.

## Trading Procedures and Computerization

In Chapter 15, we explained the difference between continuous and call markets. In the former, prices are determined continuously throughout the trading day as buyers and sellers submit orders. In a call market, orders are batched for simultaneous execution at the same price and at a particular time (or times) during the day. We also noted that some markets (such as the New York Stock Exchange in the United States) that are largely continuous in nature will set opening prices with a call auction procedure based on bids submitted over night, when the market is closed.

Equity markets in Canada, Japan, Hong Kong, and most of Europe employ the method of continuous trading. The Tokyo Stock Exchange is an example of an exchange that has continuous trading but that opens trading with a call market auction. The auction method is the *Itayosa* method: essentially, it involves the grouping of orders to buy and sell the stock and identifying the representative price as a central price that will bring about a trade or batch of trades. After the opening, the market uses the *Zaraba* auction method, which arranges individual trades that match the lowest sale price to the highest buy price. The markets of Germany, Belgium, and Austria still use call-based trading for the stocks of smaller companies.

The widespread adoption of computerized and electronic technology has brought many changes to the world's equity markets. Continuous markets that adopted the new technology saw a substantial rise in their volumes of trading. Further, the technology has increased the amount of information that dealers and brokers can get, which has contributed to the efficiency of the trading on the exchanges.[14] Some outstanding successes of computer technology in stock exchanges include the following: Toronto Stock Exchange's CATS, which means Computer Assisted Trading System; the London Stock Market's "Stock Exchange Automatic Quotation System" (called "SEAQ"); and the Tokyo Stock Exchange's CORES, which means Computerized Order Routing and Execution System and which handles all but the largest stocks (the "First Section") because they are traded on the trading floor.

One of the most interesting consequences of computerized trading is the conversion of traditional call markets to continuous markets.[15] France is a good

---

[14] Huang and Stoll, *op. cit.*, p. 44.

[15] For a discussion of how this is being done and the advantages of this approach, see Chapter 10 of Robert A. Schwartz, *Reshaping the Equity Markets: A Guide for the 1990s* (New York: HarperBusiness, 1991).

example of this change. Once a rather large call market, the Paris Bourse adopted the Toronto Stock Exchange's CATS in the mid 1980s. The French renamed the system CAC, for *"Cotation Assistée–Continu."* CAC or CATS is a fully automated electronic trading system that enables traders to work from computer screens without being physically present on a trading floor (except for unusual or possibly very large orders). Spain, Belgium, Italy, and Sweden are other examples of markets where the implementation of computerized trading (often, some version of CATS) has spurred the advance of continuous market structures (except possibly for the initial trades of the day).[16]

### *Dealers in Major Markets* [17]

A continuous stock market can actually take two forms, according to how the dealer's function is carried out. One form has been adopted by the organized U.S. stock exchanges, such as the New York and American exchanges. The exchange designates a specialist for specific shares who is the sole market maker or dealer for those shares. The second form is the competitive dealer system like the one found in the U.S.'s over-the-counter or NASDAQ market. Here, several dealers may be market makers for any stock, and the dealers do not have a special authorization from the exchange to play this role.

The specialist system is rarely used outside the United States. The Amsterdam Stock Exchange gives certain firms the specialist's status and duties; a firm of this type is called a *hoekman*. Changes in this system, however, seem to be forthcoming. Market makers on the Toronto Stock Exchange are similar to specialists. Limited in number and selected by the exchange, these registered traders use stabilizing trades for their own accounts to create orderly price changes in stocks that the exchange has assigned to them. Also, these traders are obligated to post bid and ask prices all through the day and to keep their bid–ask spreads rather small.

Aside from these exceptions, all continuous markets in the world employ some version of the competitive dealer mechanism. London's International Stock Exchange is a good example of a full-scale commitment to this approach. On the ISE, any well capitalized firm that abides by certain regulations can enter the competition as a dealer on any security. Market makers publish firm bid–ask quotes for their stocks in standardized lots. There are more than ten dealers for the majority of the large and actively traded shares.

The Tokyo Stock Exchange employs a variant of the competitive dealer system. A broker, called a *saitori*, functions as an intermediary between the dealers and the brokers who are members of the exchange. The saitoris cannot buy or sell for their own accounts, but rather arrange transactions among dealers. Saitoris also conduct the auctions during the trading day and match

---

[16] "European Equity Markets," a Supplement to the January 1992 issue of *Euromoney*, p. 48.

[17] Schwartz, *op. cit.*, contains more information on large markets around the world.

buy and sell orders submitted by the brokers on behalf of their own accounts or those of their clients.

Roger Huang and Hans Stoll make an interesting distinction between "a continuous dealer market" and "a continuous auction market."[18] The difference has to do with whether dealers have information about the array of special or "limit" orders that investors have placed with the market. As discussed in Chapter 18, limit orders are buy or sell orders which are triggered when a stock's price reaches a certain market level. On London's International Stock Exchange, only the broker or dealer that accepts a limit order from the customer knows of that order, because the computerized trading system does not record or reveal the existence of the order. The dealer that has the order implements the trade when the dealer's own price for the stock reaches the designated level. In the view of Huang and Stoll, this is a continuous dealer market, while the Paris Bourse might be considered a continuous auction market. Of course, the Bourse is a competitive dealer market, but the point is that dealers operate differently on the two exchanges.

The Bourse's computerized trading system displays all limit orders in effect at any time. This "computerized central book of limit orders" allows any dealer to execute trades against those orders even if the orders were taken by another dealer. In effect, then, the computer system is allowing dealers to match buy and sell orders across the entire array of participants in the market. The action of the dealer in matching buy and sell orders is a type of auction. It should be noted that the Bourse's computerized trading system is like that of the Toronto Stock Exchange. The auction is a specific task of the Tokyo Stock Exchange's saitori member who is responsible for keeping track of limit orders. This function is often referred to as "keeping the limit book," and the saitori makes the book available to all members of the exchange through the exchange's computer system.

The final point we want to consider here has to do with the execution of "block trades," which are trades of large numbers of shares and typically represent investment activities of large institutional investors. The size of block trades calls for special procedures, such as the "upstairs market" in the U.S. system, which uses negotiation among institutions in order to bypass the specialist of the organized exchanges as well as the dealers of the OTC market. (See Chapter 18 for more on block trades.)

Dealers in London tend to take larger positions—they commit more of their capital than do American dealers.[19] Also, the London SEAQ system does not quote the full size of an offered block trade, thus protecting block traders from a disclosure of their needs to potential parties on the other side of the trades. For these reasons, while block trading in London also uses negotiation among institutions, the trades go through the computerized trading system in the normal manner. Because the CATS system of Toronto and Paris provides, as noted above, more information about bids than does London's SEAQ, it

---

[18] Huang and Stoll, *op. cit.*, p. 49.

[19] *Ibid.*

discloses more about block trades than those initiating the trades generally want to disclose. Thus, block traders do not find Paris and Toronto well suited to block trades, and large institutional trades have flowed toward New York and London. In response, the Paris Bourse is experimenting with more off-exchange trading of large orders.

### Stock Market Indexes

There are many indexes of stock prices that chart and measure the performance of foreign stock markets. In every country where stock trading takes place, there is at least one index that measures general share price movements. If a country has more than one stock exchange, each exchange usually has its own index. Also, news organizations and financial advisory services create indexes. In the United States, examples of the exchange indexes are the NYSE Composite Index and the AMEX Composite Index, while examples of the indexes constructed by non-exchange firms include Standard & Poor's 500 Common Stock Index and the Dow Jones Industrial Average.

In Japan, there are two major indexes. The Tokyo Stock Exchange produces the *Tokyo Stock Price Index* or TOPIX. This is a composite index, which is based on all the shares in the Tokyo market's First Section, a designation reserved for the established and large companies whose shares are the most actively traded and widely held. A financial information firm, Nihon Keizai Shimbun, Inc., calculates and publishes the *Nikkei 225 Stock Average*. This average is based on 225 of the largest companies in the First Section.

The United Kingdom's London Stock Exchange is covered by several widely followed indexes. The *Financial Times Industrial Ordinary Index* is based on the prices of shares of 30 leading companies and is known as the "FT 30." A broader index is the *Financial Times–Stock Exchange 100*, commonly referred to as the "FTSE 100" (and pronounced "Footsie 100"). This index is based on the shares of the largest 100 U.K. firms, whose market value makes up a majority of the market value of all U.K. equities.[20] Indexes for different sectors, and a composite index across sectors, are produced by the *Financial Times* and the Institute for Actuaries. These "FT-A" indexes are very broadly based, with the composite including over 700 shares.

The primary German stock index is the *DAX*, which stands for the "*Deutscher Aktienindex,*" produced by the Frankfurt Stock Exchange. (The German name for this exchange is the "*Frankfurter Wertpapierbörse.*" Some financial services regularly refer to the exchange by its initials, FWB.) The DAX is based on the 30 most actively traded shares listed on the Frankfurt exchange. The *FAZ Index* is another popular German index. Compiled by the *Frankfurter Allgemeine Zeitung*, which is a daily newspaper, the FAZ Index is computed from the share prices of the 100 largest companies listed on the Frankfurt exchange. In France, a national association of stockbrokers and the Paris Bourse

---

[20] Carolyn Moses, "U.K. Equity Market," in Lederman and Park (eds.), *The Global Equity Markets*, p. 105.

produce an index based on the shares of 40 large and prominent firms traded on the exchange. The index is known as the *CAC 40 Index*, after the name of the Bourse's electronic trading system. Given the increasing economic integration of Europe, the CAC 40, like the FTSE 100 and possibly the DAX, may well be a reliable indicator of the overall performance of European stocks and markets. Other widely followed national stock indexes include the *Hang Seng Index* produced by the Stock Exchange of Hong Kong, the *TSE 300 Composite* of the Toronto Stock Exchange, and the *Swiss Performance Index* or SPI, which applies to almost 400 firms and is published by the stock exchanges in that country.

To meet the increased interest in global equity investing, financial institutions have crafted several respected international equity indexes. The international equity index followed most by U.S. pension funds is the *Morgan Stanley Capital International Europe, Australia, Far East Index* or EAFE Index. This index, started by Capital International in 1968 and acquired by Morgan Stanley in 1986, covers more than 2,000 companies in 21 countries. Relatively new international equity indexes include: *The Financial Times World Index* (a joint product of the Institute of Actuaries in the U.K., Goldman Sachs & Co., and Wood MacKenzie & Co.), the *Salomon Brothers–Russell Global Equity Index* (a joint product of Salomon Brothers Inc. and Frank Russell, Inc.), and the *Global Index* (a joint product of First Boston Corporation and London-based *Euromoney* magazine).

▶ <u>KEY POINTS THAT YOU SHOULD UNDERSTAND BEFORE PROCEEDING</u>:

1. Why large international firms have their stocks listed on several national exchanges.
2. What the level of correlation between national market indexes says about the benefits from diversifying investments across those countries.
3. How and why exchanges can differ in significant respects among different countries.
4. The role of dealers in national stock exchanges.
5. The names of the market indexes for the important national stock exchanges.

## EUROEQUITY ISSUES

*Euroequity issues* are those issued simultaneously in several national markets by an international syndicate. The first modern Euroequity offering was in 1983 by Bell Canada. The offering, $43 million, was managed by the United Bank of Switzerland. By 1986, issuance of Euroequities was between $8 and $10 billion.[21] This growth was fuelled by rising stock prices throughout the world, by

---

[21] P.L. Gilibert, B. Lygum, and F. Wurtz, "The International Capital Market in 1986," *Cahiers BEI/EIB Papers*, European Investment Bank, Luxembourg, March 1987.

the desire of investors to diversify their portfolios internationally and the desire of corporations to expand their sources of equity funding, and by governments seeking international investors for the entities that they had privatized. The market crash of October 1987 slowed the growth of this market. While in 1987 issuance of Euroequities was about $15 to $18 billion (privatization offerings representing about half of this amount), it declined to about $8 billion in 1988 (with only a small amount resulting from privatization offerings). In 1989, Euroequities issuance rebounded to approximately $15 billion.[22]

An increasing number of U.S. firms have equity offerings that include a Euroequity tranche. (In the international financial vocabulary, the word "tranche," which is French for slice or segment or cut, means a distinctive portion of the issue of a financial security. In this context, the word means that some of the newly issued equity shares were reserved for sale in Euromarkets.) Similarly, more European firms are offering equity securities with a U.S. tranche. For example, in 1990, 84 issues were offered by European firms with U.S. tranches having a market value of $3.85 billion compared to the first three quarters of 1991 in which 154 equity offerings with a total market value of $7.09 billion were made. [23]

Corporations have not limited their equity offerings to just their domestic equity market and a foreign market of another country. Instead, the offerings have been more global in nature. For example, the initial public offering (IPO) of British Telecommunications (the United Kingdom's government-owned telephone company) in 1984 was offered simultaneously in the United Kingdom, the United States, Japan, and Canada. As a more recent example, the Dutch Aircraft manufacturer Fokker expected to raise Dfls 500 million in equity during the first half of 1992. Seven tranches were planned: the United States, the United Kingdom, Germany, Switzerland, Canada, Benelux, and the rest of the world.[24]

Innovation occurs in the Euroequities markets not in terms of new equity structures but in the development of an efficient international channel for distributing equities. This development can probably be traced back to 1984 and 1985 when issues of three non-U.S. corporations, Nestlé, British Telecom, and Eselte, utilized the international market to raise equity. The depth and breadth of the market can be illustrated by Nestlé, which was able to use the

---

[22] These statistics come from the following two reports: Bjorn Lygum, Jacques Girard, Danield Ottolenghi, Pier-Luigi Gilibert, and Alfred Steinherr, "International Capital Markets in 1988," *Cahier BEI/EIB Papers*, Luxembourg, European Investment Bank, March 1989, p. 38; and I. Drummond, P.L. Gilibert, B. Lygum, and E. Peree, "International Markets in 1989," *Cahier BEI/EIB Papers*, Luxembourg, European Investment Bank, March 1990, p. 23. Unfortunately, good data are not available for the Euroequities market. In the annual market surveys of the staff of the European Investment Bank, the Euroequities issuance data for a given year are reported inconsistently from one annual report to the next.

[23] As reported in Janine Schultz, "International Equity Tranches to Shed Weak Sister Image," *Corporate Financing Week*, Special Supplement, November 25, 1991, pp. 1 and 8.

[24] *International Financial Review*, Issue 902 (November 2, 1991), p. 39.

international market to raise more than $400 million in equity funds three separate times in 1985.[25]

The size of the Euroequities market, however, is still considerably smaller than that of the Eurobond market discussed in Chapter 21.

▶ KEY POINTS THAT YOU SHOULD UNDERSTAND BEFORE PROCEEDING:

1. What a Euroequity issue is.
2. Why the Euroequity is a popular way to raise capital.

## INTERNATIONAL DEPOSITORY RECEIPTS

When a corporation issues equity outside its domestic market, and the equity issue is subsequently traded in the foreign market, it is typically in the form of an *International Depository Receipt* (IDR). IDRs are issued by banks as evidence of ownership of the underlying stock of a foreign corporation that the bank holds in trust. Each IDR may represent ownership of one or more shares of common stock of a corporation. The advantage of the IDR structure is that the corporation does not have to comply with all the regulatory issuing requirements of the foreign country where the stock is to be traded. IDRs are typically sponsored by the issuing corporation. That is, the issuing corporation will work with a bank to offer its common stock in a foreign country via the sale of IDRs.

As an example, consider the United States version of the IDR, the *American Depository Receipt* (ADR). It was the success of the ADR structure that in fact resulted in the rise of IDRs throughout the world. ADRs are denominated in U.S. dollars and pay dividends in U.S. dollars. The holder of an ADR does not have voting or preemptive rights.

ADRs can be created in one of two ways. First, one or more banks or brokerage firms can assemble a large block of the shares of a foreign corporation and issue ADRs without the participation of the foreign corporation. More typically, ADRs are sponsored by the foreign corporation that seeks to have its stock traded in the United States. In these instances, there is only one depository bank that issues the ADRs. A sponsored ADR is commonly referred to as an *American Depository Share* (ADS). Periodic financial reports are provided in English to the holder of an ADS. ADSs can either be traded on one of the two major organized exchanges (the New York Stock Exchange and the American Stock Exchange) or traded in the over-the-counter market. The nonsponsored ADR is typically traded in the over-the-counter market.

In the British Telecom IPO we cited earlier, the offerings in the United States and Canada were in the form of an ADR (or ADS, because the ADR was sponsored by British Telecom) listed on the New York Stock Exchange and the Toronto Stock Exchange. Each ADR represented ten shares of British Telecom.

---

[25] Julian Walmsley, *The New Financial Instruments* (New York: John Wiley & Sons, 1988), p. 328.

Here are two more recent examples. In 1991, Orbital Engine Corporation, an Australian corporation, made an IPO in the United States via an ADR to raise U.S. $87 million. The offering was underwritten by a syndicate led by Merrill Lynch, SG Warburg, and Kidder Peabody. Orbital Engine's ADR will be listed on the New York Stock Exchange.[26] The ADSs of Kia Motors, Korea's second largest automobile manufacturer, issued in the United States in November 1991 were privately placed rather than publicly offered.[27]

These are but two examples of the offerings in 1991, a year that saw a substantial increase in ADSs issued in the United States In 1990, only $104 million of ADSs were issued in the United States For the first 11 months of 1991, the amount of ADSs issued jumped to $3.47 billion.[28]

▶ KEY POINTS THAT YOU SHOULD UNDERSTAND BEFORE PROCEEDING:

1. What an International Depository Receipt (IDR) is.
2. How the IDR is a response to often stringent governmental regulation about the issuance of foreign shares.
3. What an American Depository Receipt (ADR) and an American Depository Share (ADS) are.

SUMMARY

In terms of the value of listed shares, the United States and Japanese stock markets are the two largest stock markets in the world, followed by the U.K. stock market. Effective transactions costs (commissions and taxes) are lower for trades in the United States than in any other stock market of the world, although the gap has been closing as a result of deregulation in many countries.

Stocks of large corporations may be listed in more than one country. Firms are in favor of multiple listings, because they boost company images and, among other things, allow access to funding in many major financial centers.

The prices of stocks on markets around the world do not move together in an exact way, because the economic systems in which those markets are located have dissimilar environments in terms of taxation, industrial growth, political stability, monetary policy, and so on. Low levels of comovement of stock prices offer investors a benefit from diversifying their holdings across the markets of countries. That is, investors who allocate some of their portfolio to shares from other countries can reduce the portfolio's risk with no fall in expected return or raise the portfolio's expected return with no increase in risk. This benefit of international diversification has led many investors to allocate some of their wealth to foreign markets and shares of foreign firms.

---

[26] *International Financial Review*, Issue 902, November 2, 1991, p. 36.

[27] Ibid., p. 35. The issue was privately placed under Rule 144A, as discussed in Chapter 14.

[28] *Corporate Financing Week*, Special Supplement, December 23, 1991, p. 6.

It is possible to group the stock market structures throughout the world into three categories. The first includes private markets that are basically self-regulated. Markets in the United States, England, Hong Kong, Canada, Japan, and Australia fit this description. Second, some markets are public institutions where government plays a traditionally active role in licensing brokers and directing operations of some key exchange activities. Exchanges in France, Spain, Italy, and Belgium fall into this category. The third category contains stock markets where the majority of trading is done through banks. Key markets in Germany and Switzerland, as well as the Austrian market, are members of this group.

A stock market may be a continuous market or a call market. Many markets use call auction procedures to set an opening price and then allow prices to be determined on a continuous basis. Most former call markets have, with the advent of computerization, become continuous markets. Computerization has had great success across the world, from Toyko to Toronto to London, and many markets have adopted computerized trading systems.

Only a few markets of the world use the specialist system. Most markets employ some form of the competitive dealer system, which lets market makers actively take positions in any stock or stocks they choose. Computerization has been quite consistent with the competitive dealer system.

Every market in the world has an index, which is a measure of the general movement in the prices of shares on the market. Some indexes are produced by exchanges and some by financial news services. The largest markets have well known and widely followed indexes: the TOPIX and the Nikkei 225 in Japan, the FTSE 100 in the U.K., the DAX and FAZ indexes of Germany, and the CAC 40 in France. Popular international equity price indexes are based on several markets; a good example is the Morgan Stanley EAFE Index, which covers Europe, Australia, and the Far East.

The Euroequities market includes stocks issued simultaneously in several national markets by an international syndicate. An International Depository Receipt (IDR) is a bank-issued title to shares of stock traded in a foreign country. IDRs help issuers to reach investors in countries where regulations regarding the trading and listing of foreign securities may be burdensome or costly.

An American Depository Receipt (ADR) is the right to a foreign share (or set of shares) that a U.S. citizen can purchase. ADRs are sponsored by banks and brokerage firms. An American Depository Share (ADS) is an ADR sponsored by the foreign corporation seeking to attract U.S. investors without listing the stock on a U.S. market.

**American Depository Receipt (or ADR):** A tradable right, which U.S. citizens can buy, to ownership of a specific number of a foreign company's shares, which are held in trust by a U.S. financial institution that issues the ADR.

**American Depository Share (or ADS):** An ADR that is sponsored by the foreign company to whose shares the ADR represents an ownership claim.

**Bourse:** The stock exchange in Paris.

**CAC:** The acronym for *"Cotation Assistée en Continu,"* which is the computerized trading system on the Paris Bourse.

**CAC 40 Index:** A stock price index based on 40 large stocks traded on the Paris Bourse.

**Computer Assisted Trading System (or CATS):** Computerized stock trading system, developed on the Toronto Stock Exchange, and now used in several countries.

**Computerized Order Routing and Execution System (or CORES):** The Tokyo Stock Exchange's computerized trading system.

**DAX:** The acronym for the *"Deutscher Aktienindex,"* a stock index for the Frankfurt Stock Exchange.

**EAFE Index:** The term for the Morgan Stanley Capital International Europe, Australia, Far East Index, which covers over 20 countries.

**Euroequity issue:** An issue of stock offered to investors in different countries at the same time.

**FAZ Index:** A stock market index based on the share prices for the 100 largest firms listed on the Frankfurt Stock Exchange, which is compiled by the newspaper *Frankfurter Allgemeine Zeitung.*

**Financial Times Industrial Ordinary Index (or FT 30):** An index based on the prices of shares of 30 leading companies, which is compiled by the newspaper *Financial Times.*

**Financial Times–Stock Exchange 100 (or FTSE 100):** An index based on the shares of the largest 100 U.K. firms.

**Financial Times World Index:** An international stock market index.

**First Section:** The term for the stocks of the largest companies traded on the Tokyo Stock Exchange.

**Frankfurter Wertpapierbörse (or FWB):** The Frankfurt Stock Exchange.

**Global Index:** An international stock market index that is a joint product of First Boston Corporation and London-based Euromoney.

**Hang Seng Index:** The stock index of the Hong Kong Stock Exchange.

**Hoekman:** A specialist on the Amsterdam Stock Exchange.

**International Depository Receipt (or IDR):** A tradable right to ownership of a specific number of a foreign company's shares, which is issued by a financial institution holding the shares in trust.

**Itayosa and Zaraba:** Two auction methods used on the Tokyo Stock Exchange.

**Makler:** A broker in Austria or Germany.

**Multiple listing:** The listing of a stock on an exchange in its home country and on an exchange in at least one other country.

**Nikkei 225 Stock Average:** A market index based on 225 of the largest companies on the Tokyo Stock Exchange.

**Ring banks:** The small number of banks licensed to trade securities on the Zurich Stock Exchange.

**Saitori:** A broker on the Tokyo Stock Exchange.

**Sociedades de Valores:** Term for Spanish brokerage firms.

**Societá di Intermediazione Mobilaire:** A brokerage firm in Italy.

**Société de Bourse:** A brokerage firm in France or Belgium.

**Stock Exchange Automatic Quotation System (or SEAQ):** The London International Stock Exchange's computerized trading system.

**Swiss Performance Index (or SPI):** The stock market index based on almost 400 firms drawn from the Swiss stock exchanges.

**TOPIX:** The Tokyo Stock Price Index, which is based on prices for the stocks of the established, large, and widely held companies.

**Tranche:** A financial term meaning a specific portion of the issue of a financial security.

**TSE 300 Composite:** The stock market index for the Toronto Stock Exchange.

**Turnover:** Common term for the volume of trading in a particular stock or in a market.

**QUESTIONS**

1. In recent years, the Japanese stock market has sometimes been ranked as the largest and sometimes as second in size to the market in the United States. What accounts for this fairly frequent change in the size rankings of the two markets?

2. Some stocks are listed on several exchanges around the world. Give three reasons why a firm might want its stock to be listed on an exchange in the firm's home country as well as on exchanges in other countries.

3. Suppose the stock of company UNA is selling for $10/share in New York and for $10.75/share (after adjustment for the dollar/pound exchange rate) on London's ISE.

   a. Would you buy 1,000 shares in New York and sell them in London if the total cost of both transactions and all related fees were $375?

    b.  What is the lowest dollar price on the ISE that would make this arbitrage unprofitable?

4.  Provide a general explanation why stocks of Dutch companies in Holland might sustain a significant decline over the same time period that brings about a sharp increase in the value of shares of a typical Australian company, which are traded in Australia.

5.  a.  What is the correlation coefficient and how does a low value (say, +0.30) of correlation between stocks in two countries offer investors an interesting investment opportunity?

    b.  Why, if the correlation coefficient were +0.95, would the same kind of opportunity not exist?

    c.  Claudia Barelli and Roberto Moro-Visconti, in their working paper titled, "The Link Between Volatility and Correlation in International Stock Markets," report that share price volatility, especially sharp falls as in times of market "crashes," actually encourages investors to increase the international diversification of their holdings because they want to protect themselves against severe market declines. Comment on whether you find this analysis intuitively appealing.

6.  Explain how rules of structure and ownership help to group the world's stock markets into three broad categories.

7.  a.  Identify the types of trades for which many markets use the call auction method.

    b.  Why do markets tend to favor continuous methods for the pricing of actively traded stocks?

    c.  Can you name and distinguish the two methods of auction used by the Tokyo Stock Exchange?

8.  Identify the meaning of these acronyms: CORES, SEAQ, CATS, and CAC.

9.  a.  What does the term "First Section" mean on the Tokyo Stock Exchange?

    b.  What are the key differences between the two major Japanese stock market indexes, the TOPIX and the Nikkei 225?

10.  a.  Which markets in the world use some form of the specialist system that is favored by the organized U.S. exchanges?

    b.  What system do most markets use instead of the specialist arrangement?

11.  Often, a news report will survey the day's trading in Europe with a statement like this: "The Footsie 100 rose 1.5% today, while the DAX dropped 0.25% and the CAC 40 finished unchanged." What are the formal names of the indexes referred to, and to which country do they apply?

12. a. Do you think that the prominent stock price indexes for European exchanges, which focus on the shares of large companies, always convey an accurate impression of what is happening to the values of the new and small companies of Europe?

    b. Is it possible that the smaller firms sometimes (maybe often) experience different rates of growth in sales, earnings, and so on?

13. a. What is the key feature of a Euroequity Issue?

    b. What is the most important innovation that Euroequities have achieved?

    c. What does it mean that a U.S. firm's new stock offering might contain a Euroequity "tranche"?

14. a. What is an IDR?

    b. How does an IDR facilitate issuance of a domestic firm's securities in a foreign country?

15. What is the major difference between an ADR and an American Depository Share?

# CHAPTER TWENTY

# Markets for Corporate Senior Instruments: I

*After reading this chapter you will understand:*

- the various financing alternatives available to corporations.
- the importance of credit ratings.
- what commercial paper is.
- the types of commercial paper: directly placed paper and dealer paper.
- the differences between the U.S. commercial paper market and the Eurocommercial paper market.
- what a medium-term note is.
- what a note issuance facility and a Euronote are.
- what a syndicated loan is.
- the two different ways a syndicated loan can be sold: assignment and participation.
- the basic terms of a loan agreement.
- what a lease financing transaction is.
- the difference between a single investor lease and a leveraged lease.

Corporate senior instruments are financial obligations of a corporation that have priority over its common stock in the case of bankruptcy. They include debt obligations and preferred stock.

The market for corporate debt obligations can be classified into five sectors: (1) commercial paper market; (2) medium-term note market; (3) Euronote market; (4) bank loan market; and (5) bond market. In this chapter, we look at the first four sectors, while in the next chapter we cover the corporate bond market, as well as another market for long-term funding, the preferred stock market. Unlike our discussion of common stock, in which we focused first on the U.S. equity market and then the non-U.S. equity market, here we discuss both the United States and Euromarkets in which corporations can borrow funds.

Securities such as commercial paper, Euronotes, medium-term notes, and bonds represent alternatives to bank loans for companies needing to raise funds. The issuance of securities in the international market has increased substantially since the 1980s, in stark contrast to the bank borrowing trend. This phenomenon of borrower preference for issuing securities over borrowing directly from banks is referred to as the *securitization* of capital markets. The term "securitization" is actually used in two ways. It is in the broader sense that we use it here. In the more narrow sense, the term securitization, more specifically, asset securitization, is used to describe the process of pooling loans and issuing securities backed by these loans. We described asset securitization in Chapter 2.

## CREDIT RISK AND THE ROLE OF RATING COMPANIES

Unlike Treasury securities, corporate debt obligations expose the investor to credit risk. This is the risk that the issuer will default on its obligation to the lender. At any given time, the yield offered in the market for a corporate debt instrument varies according to investors' expectations about the issuer's likely ability to satisfy its obligations. The greater the perceived credit risk, the greater the yield investors will demand. As we explained in Chapter 11, the difference between the yield on two issues that are identical in all respects except for quality is referred to as a "quality spread" or "credit spread."

We explained credit risk first in our discussion of municipal securities Professional money managers analyze an issuer's financial information and the specifications of the debt instrument itself in order to estimate the ability of the issuer to live up to its future contractual obligations. This activity is known as *credit analysis*.

Some large institutional investors have their own credit analysis department but most individual and institutional investors do not conduct such analytical studies. Instead, they rely primarily on commercial rating companies that perform credit analysis and express their conclusions by a system of ratings. As we explained in Chapter 11, there are five commercial rating companies in the United States. The two most widely used systems of credit or quality ratings are those of Moody's and Standard & Poor's.

The credit rating companies play a key role in the functioning of debt markets. Investors take great comfort in knowing that the rating companies monitor the creditworthiness of issuers and keep the investing public informed of their findings. One would expect that other countries would have organizations that provide a similar function. This has not been the case. Only in recent years have credit rating companies appeared in other countries. For example, in Japan it was not until 1977 that a formal corporate bond rating system was introduced. The original system for rating corporate bonds that was introduced in Japan in 1959 was based solely on the size of the issue.[1]

▶ KEY POINTS THAT YOU SHOULD UNDERSTAND BEFORE PROCEEDING:

1. Corporate debt obligations expose an investor to credit risk.
2. Credit risk is typically measured by the credit or quality ratings assigned by nationally recognized commercial rating companies.
3. Commercial rating companies play a key role in the functioning of debt markets in the United States, and their role in other countries is increasing.

## COMMERCIAL PAPER

Commercial paper is a short-term unsecured promissory note issued in the open market that represents the obligation of the issuing corporation. The issuance of commercial paper is an alternative to bank borrowing for large corporations (nonfinancial and financial) with strong credit ratings.

While the original purpose of commercial paper was to provide short-term funds for seasonal and working capital needs, companies have used this instrument for other purposes in recent years. It has been used quite often for "bridge financing." For example, suppose that a corporation needs long-term funds to build a plant or acquire equipment. Rather than raising long-term funds immediately, the corporation may elect to postpone the offering until more favorable capital market conditions prevail. The funds raised by issuing commercial paper are used until longer-term securities are sold. Interestingly, commercial paper has sometimes been used as bridge financing to finance corporate takeovers.[2]

In the United States, the maturity of commercial paper is typically less than 270 days, with the most common maturity range 30 to 50 days or less.[3] There are reasons for this pattern of maturities. First, as explained in Chapter 3, the Securities Act of 1933 requires that securities be registered with the SEC. Special provisions in the 1933 act exempt commercial paper from reg-

---

[1] Edward W. Karp and Akira Koike, "The Japanese Corporate Bond Market," Chapter 11 in Frank J. Fabozzi (ed.), *The Japanese Bond Markets* (Chicago: Probus Publishing, 1990), p. 377.

[2] Commercial paper also has been used as an integral part of an interest rate swap transaction. We discuss these transactions in Chapter 29.

[3] *Money Market Instruments* (New York: Merrill Lynch Money Markets Inc., 1989), p. 16.

istration so long as the maturity does not exceed 270 days. Hence, to avoid the costs associated with registering issues with the SEC, firms rarely issue commercial paper with maturities exceeding 270 days. Another consideration in determining the maturity is whether the commercial paper would be eligible collateral for a bank borrowing from the Federal Reserve Bank's discount window. In order to be eligible, the maturity of the paper may not exceed 90 days. Since eligible paper trades at a lower cost than paper that is not eligible, firms prefer to issue paper whose maturity does not exceed 90 days.

To pay off holders of maturing paper, issuers generally use the proceeds obtained by selling new commercial paper. This process is often described as "rolling over" short-term paper. The risk that the investor in commercial paper faces is that the issuer will be unable to sell new paper at maturity. As a safeguard against this "rollover risk," commercial paper is typically backed by unused bank credit lines. The commitment fee the bank charges for providing a credit line increases the effective cost of issuing commercial paper.

The U.S. commercial paper market has grown from $124 billion in December 1980 to almost $540 billion in April 1992.[4] Since 1988, the size of the commercial paper market has exceeded that of the Treasury bill market. Investors in commercial paper are institutional investors. Money market mutual funds purchase roughly one-third of all the commercial paper issued. Pension funds, commercial bank trust departments, state and local governments, and nonfinancial corporations seeking short-term investments purchase the balance. The minimum round-lot transaction is $100,000, though some issuers will sell commercial paper in denominations of $25,000.

There is very little secondary trading of commercial paper. Typically, an investor in commercial paper is an entity that plans to hold it until maturity. This is understandable because an investor can purchase commercial paper in a direct transaction with the issuer, which will sell paper with the specific maturity the investor desires.

## *Issuers of Commercial Paper*

As of 1988, there were 1,350 corporate entities issuing commercial paper in the United States.[5] Corporate issuers of commercial paper can be divided into financial companies and nonfinancial companies. Of the $537 billion of commercial paper outstanding as of April 1992, $398 billion had been issued by financial companies.

There are three types of financial companies: *captive finance companies, bank-related finance companies,* and *independent finance companies*. Captive finance companies are subsidiaries of equipment manufacturing companies. Their primary purpose is to secure financing for the customers of the parent company. For example, the three major U.S. automobile manufacturers have captive fi-

---

[4] *Federal Reserve Bulletin*, Board of Governors of the Federal Reserve (November 1992), p. A23.

[5] *Handbook of Securities of the United States Government and Agencies* (NY: First Boston Corporation, 1988), p. 140.

nance companies: General Motors Acceptance Corporation (GMAC), Ford Credit, and Chrysler Financial. GMAC is by the far the largest issuer of commercial paper in the United States. Further, a bank holding company may have a subsidiary that is a finance company, which provides loans to enable individuals and businesses to acquire a wide range of products. Independent finance companies are those that are not subsidiaries of equipment manufacturing firms or bank holding companies.

While the issuers of commercial paper typically have high credit ratings, smaller and less well-known companies with lower credit ratings have been able to issue paper in recent years. They have been able to do so by means of credit support from a firm with a high credit rating (such paper is called *credit-supported commercial paper*) or by collateralizing the issue with high-quality assets (such paper is called *asset-backed commercial paper*). An example of credit-supported commercial paper is one supported by a "letter of credit." The terms of a letter of credit specify that the bank issuing the letter guarantees that the bank will pay off the paper when it comes due, if the issuer fails to do so. The bank will charge a fee for the letter of credit. From the issuer's perspective, the fee enables it to enter the commercial paper market and thereby obtain funding at a lower cost than that of bank borrowing. Commercial paper issued with this credit enhancement is referred to as *LOC paper*. The credit enhancement may also take the form of a surety bond from an insurance company.[6]

Both domestic and foreign corporations issue commercial paper in the United States. Commercial paper issued by foreign entities is called *Yankee commercial paper*.

### Credit Ratings

Rating companies such as Moody's, Standard & Poor's, Duff & Phelps, Fitch Investors Service, and McCarthy, Crisanti & Maffei assign ratings to commercial paper. These ratings are shown in Table 20-1.

### Directly Placed versus Dealer-Placed Paper

Commercial paper is classified as either *direct paper* or *dealer-placed paper*. Direct paper is sold by the issuing firm directly to investors without the help of an agent or an intermediary. A large majority of the issuers of direct paper are financial companies. These entities require continuous funds in order to provide loans to customers. As a result, they find it cost-effective to establish a sales force to sell their commercial paper directly to investors.

Dealer-placed commercial paper requires the services of an agent to sell an issuer's paper. The agent distributes the paper on a "best efforts" underwriting basis. (For more on "best efforts" underwriting, see Chapter 14.) His-

---

[6] A surety bond is a policy written by an insurance company to protect another party against loss or violation of a contract.

| TABLE 20-1 | | | | |
|---|---|---|---|---|
| COMMERCIAL PAPER RATINGS | | | | |
| Rating company | | | | |
| Moody's | S&P | Duff & Phelps | Fitch | McCarthy, Crisanti & Maffei |
| Prime-1 (P-1) | A-1/A-1+ | Duff-1 (D-1) | F-1 | MCM 1 |
| Prime-2 (P-2) | A-2 | Duff-2 (D-2) | F-2 | MCM 2 |
| Prime-3 (P-3) | A-3 | Duff-3 (D-3) | F-3 | MCM 3 |
| Prime-4 (P-4) | | | | MCM 4 |
| | | | | MCM 5 |
| | | | | MCM 6 |

Note: The ranking is from highest to lowest credit rating assigned.

torically, the dealer paper market was dominated by securities houses because commercial banks were prohibited from underwriting commercial paper by the Glass-Steagall Act. In June 1987, however, the Fed granted subsidiaries of bank holding companies permission to underwrite commercial paper. While securities houses still dominate the dealer market, commercial banks are making inroads.[7] This seems natural because, for the most part, the funds being raised in the commercial paper market represent those previously raised through short-term bank loans. Banks are seeking to generate underwriting fees associated with commercial paper underwriting in order to recoup part of the interest income lost from borrowers that have come to favor commercial paper issuance rather than short-term bank borrowing.

### Non-U.S. Commercial Paper Markets

Other countries have developed their own commercial paper markets. For example, in November 1987, the Japanese Ministry of Finance (MOF) approved the issuance of commercial paper by Japanese corporations in its domestic market. A few months later, the MOF approved the issuance of yen-denominated commercial paper in Japan by non-Japanese entities. Such paper is referred to as *Samurai commercial paper*.

*Eurocommercial paper* is issued and placed outside the jurisdiction of the currency of denomination. There are several differences between U.S. commercial paper and Eurocommercial paper with respect to the characteristics of the paper and the structure of the market. First, commercial paper issued in the United States usually has a maturity of less than 270 days, with the most common maturity range 30 to 50 days or less. The maturity of Eurocommercial paper can be considerably longer. Second, while an issuer in the United

[7] At the end of 1989, the four largest commercial paper dealers were Merrill Lynch, Goldman Sachs, Shearson Lehman Hutton, and First Boston. The three largest commercial banks that underwrite commercial paper are Bankers Trust, Citicorp, and Morgan Guaranty.

States must have unused bank credit lines, it is possible to issue commercial paper without such backing in the Eurocommercial paper market. Third, while in the United States commercial paper can be directly placed or dealer-placed, Eurocommercial paper is almost always dealer-placed. The fourth distinction is that numerous dealers participate in the Eurocommercial paper market, while only a few dealers dominate the market in the United States. Finally, because of the longer maturity of Eurocommercial paper, that paper is traded more often in the secondary market than U.S. commercial paper. Investors in commercial paper in the United States typically buy and hold to maturity, and the secondary market is thin and illiquid.

▶ KEY POINTS THAT YOU SHOULD UNDERSTAND BEFORE PROCEEDING:

1. Commercial paper is a short-term unsecured promissory note that is issued in the open market and that represents the obligation of the issuing corporation. It is an alternative to bank borrowing for large corporations.
2. By using credit support, smaller and less well-known companies with lower credit ratings have been able to issue paper.
3. Commercial paper is rated by private rating companies.
4. Commercial paper can be directly placed by the issuer or issued by using the services of an agent or intermediary.
5. Other countries have developed their own commercial paper markets, and there is a Eurocommercial paper market.

## MEDIUM-TERM NOTES

A medium-term note is another vehicle by which corporations can raise funds. The unique characteristic of medium-term notes is that they are continuously offered to investors over a period of time by an agent of the issuer. Investors can select issues from a variety of maturity bands: nine months to one year, more than one year to 18 months, more than 18 months to two years—up to 30 years. Medium-term notes are registered with the Securities and Exchange Commission under Rule 415 (the shelf registration rule).[8] Registering under Rule 415 gives the issuer the maximum flexibility for issuing securities on a continuous basis.

Issuers in the market include finance companies, bank or bank holding companies, industrial companies, thrifts, utilities, and sovereign or government agencies. As of December 1989, finance companies offered the largest number of programs, followed by bank or bank holding companies and then industrials.[9] Typically, an issuer of medium-term notes is one with a high quality rating. The system used by commercial rating companies to rate medium-

---

[8] The shelf registration rule is explained in Chapter 14.

[9] The source of this information is "Medium-Term Note Issuer Profile: 1982-1989," in *Money Market Instruments, op. cit.*

term notes is the same as that used for corporate bonds and described in Chapter 11. While at one time restricted to highly rated issuers, the medium-term note market has been opened up to lower-rated issuers that now use credit enhancements such as letters of credit or guarantees or collateralize the issue with high-quality assets.

Investment companies are the largest institutional investors in medium-term notes, followed by banks and bank trust departments, and then insurance companies.[10]

The medium-term note was pioneered by Merrill Lynch in 1981 to cover the funding gap between commercial paper and long-term bonds. The first medium-term note issuer was Ford Motor Credit Company. By 1983, GMAC and Chrysler Financial had used Merrill Lynch as an agent to issue medium-term notes. The subsequent growth of the domestic medium-term note market and its importance as a funding source can be seen by comparing it to the amount of domestic public debt issued.[11]

In 1982, the first full year medium-term notes were offered, a total of $3.8 billion was offered. This amount was only about 10% of the $36.8 billion of domestic public debt issued that year. In sharp contrast, by 1989 the amount of domestic medium-term notes issued exceeded the issuance of domestic public debt: $118.4 billion versus $108.7 billion. In that year, 24.1% or $28.5 billion of the medium-term notes issued had maturities from 9 months to 2 years; 50.1% or $59.3 billion had maturities between two years and five years. Thus, in 1989 alone, $87.8 billion (74.2%) of the medium-term notes issued had maturities between 9 months and 5 years.[12] As of December 31, 1989, the amount of medium-term notes outstanding was $339 billion. Of this amount, $261 billion was underwritten by Merrill Lynch.[13]

*Euro medium-term notes* are those issued in the Euromarket. The market began in 1987 and, by 1991, issuance volume was $19.8 billion. Euro medium-term notes are issued by sovereign issuers (that is, governments and government agencies), corporations, and financial institutions. The last two entities are now the major issuers, accounting for about two-thirds of issuance volume in 1991.[14] Euro medium-term notes have been issued in a variety of currencies. Borrowers from 19 countries have issued Euro medium-term notes. U.S. borrowers raised $3.1 billion in 1991, while the European Community raised $7.7 billion. In 1991, Euro medium-term notes were issued in 14 currencies,

---

[10] *Money Market Instruments, op. cit.*

[11] This includes nonconvertible, dollar-denominated debt, excluding junk bonds, mortgage-backed securities and asset-backed securities. The information was obtained from IDD Information Services.

[12] This is reported in "Maturity Distribution of Primary MTN Sales by Merrill Lynch," *Money Market Instruments, op. cit.*

[13] This information is taken from "A History of Leadership," in *Money Market Instruments, op. cit.*

[14] *Eurobonds and Euro Medium-Term Notes: 1991 Review* (New York: Salomon Brothers Inc., 1992), pp. 11–12.

with the major currency being the U.S. dollar, which accounted for $9.4 billion of the $19.8 billion.

Most Euro medium-term notes have been issued in the private placement market. Moody's rated most of the Euro medium-term notes issued in 1991, and about 70% received one of the top two ratings.[15]

▶ KEY POINTS THAT YOU SHOULD UNDERSTAND BEFORE PROCEEDING:

1. A unique characteristic of medium-term notes is that they are continuously offered to investors over a period of time by an agent of the issuer.
2. Investors can select issues from several maturity bands.
3. The system used by commercial rating companies to rate medium-term notes issued by corporations is the same as that used for corporate bonds.
4. Euro medium-term notes are those issued in the Euromarket.

## EURONOTES

A corporation that seeks short-term funding can issue short-term securities. A corporation can use a commercial paper program to issue securities through an agent to investors. The risk that the corporation faces is that when the paper becomes due and the corporation requires additional short-term financing, market conditions may be such that the corporation cannot sell its new paper.

To eliminate this risk, the *note issuance facility* was developed. A note issuance facility is a contract between a borrower and a group of banks (a syndicate) in which the banks assure that the borrower can issue short-term notes (usually with a maturity of three to six months) over a designated future time period. These notes are called *Euronotes*. The bank syndicate assures that the borrower can raise short-term funds by agreeing either to extend credit to the borrower or to buy the Euronotes issued by the borrower, if they cannot be sold at a predetermined minimum price. The length of the agreement is typically five to seven years. The bank syndicate receives a fee for its commitment.

The bank syndicate is said to have underwritten the agreement because it has committed funds to the issuer should the issuer not be able to issue the Euronotes.[16] Thus, note issuance facilities are referred to as *underwritten* or *committed note issuance facilities*. In contrast, commercial paper programs and medium-term note programs are referred to as *uncommitted* or *nonunderwritten note issuance facilities*, as the agent only sells the securities on a best efforts basis and does not commit to provide funds to the issuer.

---

[15] *Ibid.*, p.14.

[16] There are variants of the note issuance facility. For example, a *transferable underwritten facility* allows the banks that have underwritten the facility to transfer their commitments to another counterparty. A *multiple component facility* allows the borrower to raise funds in a variety of forms other than Euronotes.

The first note issuance facility was created in 1981. The market grew steadily to reach $34 billion by 1985. Its use has declined subsequently for two reasons. First, capital requirements have been imposed on banks that under-write a note issuance facility. Second, those multinational corporations that had strong credit ratings felt that this back-up facility was unnecessary and just increased the cost of raising short-term funds because of the commitment fee that had to be paid. Consequently, rather than using note issuance facili-ties, multinational corporations have relied more on the Eurocommercial pa-per market to raise short-term funds.

▶ KEY POINTS THAT YOU SHOULD UNDERSTAND BEFORE PROCEEDING:

1.  The risk faced by a corporation that uses a commercial paper pro-gram to borrow short term is that, when the paper matures, market conditions may be such that the corporation cannot sell new paper.
2.  The note issuance facility was developed to reduce this risk.
3.  The securities issued by means of a note issuance facility are Eu-ronotes.

## BANK LOANS

■ ■ ■ ■

As an alternative to the issuance of securities, a corporation can raise funds by borrowing from a bank.[17] There are five sourcing alternatives for a corpora-tion: (1) a domestic bank in the corporation's home country; (2) a subsidiary of a foreign bank that is established in the corporation's home country; (3) a foreign bank domiciled in a country where the corporation does business; (4) a subsidiary of a domestic bank that has been established in a country where the corporation does business; or (5) an offshore or Eurobank. Loans made by offshore banks are referred to as *Eurocurrency loans*.[18]

### Syndicated Bank Loans

A *syndicated bank loan* is one in which a group (or syndicate) of banks provides funds to the borrower. The need for a group of banks arises because the amount sought by a borrower may be too large for any one bank to be exposed to the credit risk of that borrower. Therefore, the syndicated bank loan market is used by borrowers who seek to raise a large amount of funds in the loan mar-ket rather than through the issuance of securities.

These bank loans are called "senior bank loans" because they have a pri-ority position over subordinated lenders (bondholders) with respect to re-payment of interest and principal. The interest rate on a syndicated bank loan

---

[17] Bank debt is widely used as the senior financing for a leveraged buyout, acquisition, or recapitalization. These are collectively referred to as "highly leveraged transactions" or "HLTs."

[18] A loan can be denominated in a variety of currencies. Loans denominated in U.S. dol-lars are called *Eurodollar loans.* Similarly there are *Euroyen loans* and *Eurodeutschemark* loans.

is a rate that *floats*, which means that the loan rate is based on some reference rate. The loan rate is periodically reset at the reference rate plus a spread. The reference rate is typically the London Interbank Offered Rate (LIBOR), although it could be the prime rate (that is, the rate that a bank charges its most creditworthy customers) or the rate on certificates of deposits. The term of the loan is fixed. A syndicated loan is typically structured so that it is amortized according to a predetermined schedule, and repayment of principal begins after a specified number of years (typically not longer than five or six years). Structures in which no repayment of the principal is made until the maturity date can be arranged. Such loan structures are referred to as *bullet loans*.

A syndicated loan is arranged by either a bank or a securities house. The arranger then lines up the syndicate. Each bank in the syndicate provides the funds for which it has committed. The banks in the syndicate have the right to sell their parts of the loan subsequently to other banks.

Syndicated loans are distributed by two methods—assignment or participation. Each method has its relative advantages and disadvantages, with the method of assignment the more desirable of the two.

The holder of a loan who is interested in selling a portion can do so by passing the interest in the loan by the *method of assignment*. In this procedure, the seller transfers all rights completely to the holder of the assignment, now called the *assignee*. The assignee is said to have *privity of contract* with the borrower. Because of the clear path between the borrower and assignee, assignment is the more desirable choice of transfer and ownership.

A *participation* involves a holder of a loan "participating out" a portion of the holding in that particular loan. The holder of the participation does not become a party to the loan agreement, and has a relationship not with the borrower but with the seller of the participation. Unlike an assignment, a participation does not confer privity of contract on the holder of the participation, although the holder of the participation has the right to vote on certain legal matters concerning amendments to the loan agreement. These matters include changes regarding maturity, interest rate, and issues concerning the loan collateral. Because syndicated loans can be sold in this manner, they have become marketable.

In response to the large amount of bank loans issued in the 1980s and their strong credit protection, some commercial banks and securities houses have shown a willingness to commit capital and resources to facilitate trading as broker-dealers. Also, these senior bank loans have been securitized through the same innovations discussed in Chapter 2 for the securitization of mortgage loans.[19] Further development of the senior bank loan market will no doubt eventually erode the once important distinction between a security and a loan: a security has long been seen as a marketable financial asset, while a loan has not been marketable. Interestingly, the trading of these loans is not limited to

---

[19] For a discussion of the trading and securitization of senior bank loans, see John H. Carlson and Frank J. Fabozzi (eds.), *The Trading and Securitization of Senior Bank Loans* (Chicago: Probus Publishing, 1992).

*performing loans*, which are loans whose borrowers are fulfilling contractual commitments. There is also a market in the trading of nonperforming loans — loans in which the borrowers have defaulted.

### Lease Financing

The market for lease financing is a segment of the larger market for equipment financing. Any type of equipment that can be purchased with borrowed funds can also be leased. Our interest here is in the leasing of equipment that can be classified as a "big-ticket item" (that is, equipment costing more than $5 million). Included in this group are commercial aircraft, large ships, large quantities of production equipment, and energy facilities. A special type of leasing arrangement, known as a *leveraged lease,* is used in financing such equipment.

Leasing works as follows. The potential equipment user, called the *lessee*, first selects the equipment and the dealer or manufacturer from whom the equipment will be purchased. The lessee negotiates such aspects of the transaction as the purchase price, specifications, warranties, and delivery date. When the lessee accepts the terms of the deal, another party, such as a bank or finance company, buys the equipment from the dealer or manufacturer and leases it to the lessee. This party is called the *lessor*. The lease is so arranged that the lessor realizes the tax benefits associated with the ownership of the leased equipment.

Basically, leasing is a vehicle by which tax benefits can be transferred from the user of the equipment (the lessee), who may not have the capacity to take advantage of the tax benefits associated with equipment ownership (such as depreciation and any tax credits), to another entity who can utilize them (the lessor). In exchange for these tax benefits, a lessor provides lower-cost financing to the lessee than the lessee could get by purchasing the equipment with borrowed funds. Such leases are referred to as *tax-oriented leases*.

There are two possible ways for the lessor to finance the purchase of the equipment. One way is to provide all the financing from its own funds and therefore be at risk for 100% of the funds used to purchase the equipment. Such leasing arrangements are referred to as *single-investor* or *direct leases*. Essentially, such leases are two-party agreements (the lessee and the lessor). The second way is for the lessor to use only a portion of its own funds to purchase the equipment, and to borrow the balance from a bank or group of banks. This type of leasing arrangement is called a *leveraged lease*. There are three parties to a leveraged lease agreement: the lessee, the lessor, and the lender. The leveraged lease arrangement allows the lessor to realize all the tax benefits from owning the equipment and the tax benefits from borrowing funds — deductible interest payments — while putting up only a portion of its own funds to purchase the equipment. Because of this, leveraged leasing is commonly used in financing big-ticket items.

In a leveraged lease transaction, it is necessary for a party to arrange for the equity and the debt portions of the funding involved. The same party can arrange both. The equity portion is typically provided by one or more institutional investors. The debt portion is arranged with a bank. Since leveraged lease transactions are for large-ticket items, the bank debt is typically arranged as a syndicated bank loan.

The financing of aircraft is normally accomplished through leveraged lease financing. For example, between May and October 1991, Japanese banks arranged $1 billion in leveraged lease financing for airlines throughout the world.[20] One large Japanese bank, Mitsubishi Trust, arranged for a total of almost $250 million of equity and debt financing for British Airways to acquire four aircraft. Mitsubishi Trust also arranged for the equity financing in purchases by Quantas.[21]

▶ KEY POINTS THAT YOU SHOULD UNDERSTAND BEFORE PROCEEDING:

1. Bank loans are an alternative to the issuance of securities.
2. A syndicated bank loan is one in which a group of banks provides funds to the borrower, with the reference rate on the loan typically the London Interbank Offered Rate.
3. Senior loans can be distributed by either assignment or participation.
4. Any type of equipment that can be purchased with borrowed funds can also be leased.
5. A tax-oriented lease effectively allows the lessee to obtain a financing at less cost than by bank borrowing.

SUMMARY

Corporate senior instruments include debt obligations and preferred stock. Holders of these obligations have priority over holders of a corporation's common stock in the case of bankruptcy. In this chapter we discussed four sectors of this market: the commercial paper market, the medium-term note market, the Euronote market, and the bank loan market.

Investors typically do not perform their own analysis of the issuer's creditworthiness. Instead, they rely on a system of credit rating developed by commercial rating companies. The five companies in the United States that rate corporate debt in terms of the likelihood of default are (1) Moody's Investors Service, (2) Standard & Poor's, (3) Duff and Phelps, (4) McCarthy, Crisanti & Maffei, and (5) Fitch Investors Service.

Commercial paper is a short-term unsecured promissory note issued in the open market that represents the obligation of the issuing entity. Generally, commercial paper maturity is less than 90 days. Financial and non-financial corporations issue commercial paper, with the majority issued by the former. Direct paper is sold by the issuing firm directly to investors without using an agent as an intermediary; for dealer-placed commercial paper, the issuer uses the services of an agent to sell its paper. Commer-

---

[20] *International Financial Review*, Issue 902 (November 2, 1991), p. 12.

[21] *Ibid.*, p. 11.

cial paper markets have been developed in other countries. Eurocommercial paper is paper issued and placed outside the jurisdiction of the currency of denomination.

Medium-term notes are corporate debt obligations offered on a continuous basis. The maturities range from 9 months to 30 years and have provided a financing alternative with maturities between those of commercial paper and long-term bonds.

A note issuance facility is a contract between a borrower and a group of banks in which the banks assure that the borrower can issue short-term Euronotes over a designated future time period. The bank syndicate assures that the borrower can raise short-term funds by agreeing either to extend credit to the borrower or buy the Euronotes issued by the borrower that cannot be sold at a predetermined minimum price. The use of the note issuance facility has declined in popularity.

Bank loans represent an alternative to the issuance of securities. A syndicated bank loan is one in which a group of banks provides funds to the borrower. Senior bank loans have become marketable; they are now more actively traded and have been securitized.

Leasing is a form of bank borrowing. Basically, leasing is a vehicle by which tax benefits can be transferred from the user of the equipment (the lessee), who may not have the capacity to utilize the tax benefits associated with equipment ownership, to another entity who can utilize them. A single-investor lease is a two-party agreement involving the lessee and the lessor. In a leveraged lease, the lessor uses only a portion of its own funds to purchase the equipment and borrows the balance from a bank or group of banks.

## GLOSSARY

**Bullet loan.** A loan structured such that no repayment of the principal is made until the maturity date.

**Captive finance companies:** Finance companies that are subsidiaries of equipment manufacturing companies.

**Commercial paper:** A short-term unsecured promissory note issued in the open market that represents the obligation of the issuing corporation.

**Dealer-placed paper:** Commercial paper in which the issuer uses the services of an agent to sell its paper.

**Direct lease:** A lease in which the lessor acquires the equipment without borrowing funds.

**Direct paper:** Commercial paper sold by the issuing firm directly to investors without the help of an agent or an intermediary.

**Eurocommercial paper:** Commercial paper issued and placed outside the jurisdiction of the currency of denomination.

**Eurocurrency loans:** Loans made by offshore banks.

**Euro medium-term notes:** Medium-term notes issued in the Euromarket.

**Euronotes:** Securities issued under a note issuance facility.

**Floating rate:** An interest rate whose value is based on some reference rate and is periodically reset.

**Lessee:** The party to a lease agreement that uses but does not own the equipment being leased.

**Lessor:** The party to a lease agreement that owns but does not use the equipment being leased.

**Leveraged lease:** A type of leasing arrangement whereby the lessor provides only a portion of the funds to finance the cost of the leased asset, and the balance is borrowed from a third party.

**LOC paper:** Commercial paper supported by a letter of credit from a bank.

**Medium-term note:** Debt obligations that are continuously offered to investors over a period of time by an agent of the issuer.

**Note issuance facility:** A contract between a borrower and a group of banks (a syndicate) in which the banks assure that the borrower can issue short-term notes (called Euronotes) over a designated future time period.

**Performing loan:** A loan whose borrower has fulfilled all obligations to date.

**Samurai commercial paper:** Yen-denominated commercial paper sold in Japan by non-Japanese entities.

**Senior bank loan:** A bank loan that has a priority position over subordinated lenders (bondholders) with respect to repayment of interest and principal.

**Single-investor (or direct) lease:** A lease in which all of the financing of the leased asset is provided by the lessor from its own funds.

**Syndicated bank loan:** A bank loan provided by a group of banks.

**Tax-oriented leases:** A lease in which in exchange for tax benefits, a lessor provides lower-cost financing to the lessee than the lessee could get by purchasing the equipment with borrowed funds.

**Yankee commercial paper:** Commercial paper issued in the United States by foreign entities.

**QUESTIONS**

1. a. What role do rating companies play in financial markets?
   b. What are the two major companies that assign ratings to debt obligations?
2. What is meant by a "quality spread"?
3. a. Why is commercial paper an alternative to short-term bank borrowing for a corporation?
   b. What is the difference between directly placed paper and dealer-placed paper?

   c.  What does the yield spread between commercial paper and Treasury bills of the same maturity reflect?

4.  a.  What is Eurocommercial paper?

   b.  How does it differ from U.S. commercial paper?

5.  a.  What is a medium-term note?

   b.  What determines the yield that will be offered on a medium-term note?

   c.  What is a Euro medium-term note?

6.  a.  Why was the note issuance facility developed?

   b.  What is a Euronote?

   c.  Why has there been decreased use in the note issuance facility market by borrowers?

7.  a.  What is a syndicated bank loan?

   b.  What is the reference rate typically used for a syndicated bank loan?

   c.  What is the difference between an amortized bank loan and a bullet bank loan?

8.  Explain the two ways in which a bank can sell its position in a syndicated loan.

9.  a.  For a lease financing transaction, who is the lessee and the lessor?

   b.  Who is entitled to the tax benefits, and what are those tax benefits?

   c.  If a manufacturing corporation has no taxable income, is it likely to buy equipment or lease equipment? Why?

10.  What is the difference between a single-investor lease and a leveraged lease?

# CHAPTER TWENTY-ONE

# Corporate Senior Instruments: II

*After reading this chapter you will understand:*

- the key provisions of a corporate bond issue.
- the risks associated with investing in corporate bonds.
- what a callable bond is.
- bonds with special features and why they are issued.
- the "high-yield" or "junk" bond sector of the corporate bond market.
- the purpose for which junk bond issuers use bond proceeds.
- the different type of bond structures used in the junk bond market.
- the Eurobond market and the different types of bond structures issued.
- the difference between preferred stock, corporate debt, and common stock.
- the difference between the various types of preferred stock: fixed-rate, adjustable-rate, and auction and remarketed preferred stock.
- the basic provisions in the Bankruptcy Reform Act of 1978.

- the difference between a liquidation and a reorganization.
- the principle of absolute priority in a bankruptcy.

In this chapter, we continue coverage of corporate senior instruments, focusing on corporate bonds and preferred stock. Preferred stock is classified as a senior instrument in that holders of these securities have priority over common stockholders in the case of bankruptcy. We conclude this chapter with a discussion of corporate bankruptcy.

## CORPORATE BONDS

The corporate bond market is an important part of the U.S. financial system. According to the Federal Reserve's estimates, the amount of outstanding corporate bonds in March 1992 was almost $1.7 trillion.[1] Table 21-1 shows the levels of newly issued corporate debt in the last five years.

Corporate bonds are classified by the type of issuer. The four general classifications used by bond information services are: (1) utilities; (2) transportations; (3) industrials; and (4) banks and finance companies. Finer breakdowns are often made to create more homogeneous groupings. For example,

| TABLE 21-1 | | | | | |
| --- | --- | --- | --- | --- | --- |
| NEW BOND ISSUES BY U.S. CORPORATIONS: 1987 TO 1991 ($ BILLIONS) | | | | | |
| | 1987 | 1988 | 1989 | 1990 | 1991 |
| Total: | | | | | |
|   Publicly Placed | 209.3 | 202.0 | 180.8 | 189.6 | 287.0 |
|   Privately Placed | n.a. | 127.7 | 117.4 | 87.0 | 74.9 |
|   Sold Abroad | 24.3 | 23.1 | 22.9 | 23.1 | 28.0 |
| By Industry; | | | | | |
| Manufacturing/ | | | | | |
|   Commercial | 65.1 | 133.1 | 126.7 | 93.1 | 123.3 |
| Transportation | 2.0 | 10.3 | 10.0 | 12.7 | 13.6 |
| Utilities | 17.4 | 20.8 | 18.7 | 17.5 | 24.0 |
| Communication | 5.8 | 5.6 | 8.5 | 6.6 | 9.3 |
| Real Estate/ | | | | | |
|   Financial | 143.2 | 183.3 | 158.1 | 169.3 | 219.6 |

*Note:* n.a. means not available. Figures are rounded values computed from numbers in the *Federal Reserve Bulletin*, selected issues.

---

[1] Board of Governors of the Federal Reserve System, *Flow of Funds Accounts, Financial Assets and Liabilities* (First Quarter 1992), p. 44.

utilities are subdivided into electric power companies, gas distribution companies, water companies, and communication companies. Transportations are further divided into airlines, railroads, and trucking companies. Industrials are the catchall class, and the most heterogeneous of the groupings with respect to investment characteristics. Industrials include all kinds of manufacturing, merchandising, and service companies.

In recent years, industrials have raised the largest amount in the corporate bond market, followed by financial institutions and then utilities.[2] The largest investor group is life insurance companies, which own about 30% of corporate bonds, followed by pension funds, public and private, which own about 24%.[3]

## Basic Features of a Corporate Bond Issue

The essential features of a corporate bond are relatively simple. The corporate issuer promises to pay a specified percentage of par value (known as the coupon payments) on designated dates, and to repay par or principal value of the bond at maturity. Failure to pay either principal or interest when due constitutes legal default, and court proceedings can be instituted to enforce the contract. Bondholders, as creditors, have a prior legal claim over common and preferred stockholders as to both income and assets of the corporation for the principal and interest due them.

The promises of corporate bond issuers and the rights of investors who buy them are set forth in great detail in contracts called *bond indentures*. If bondholders were handed the complete indenture, they would have trouble understanding its language, and even greater difficulty in determining at a particular time whether the corporate issuer were keeping all its promises. These problems are solved for the most part by bringing in a corporate trustee as a third party to the contract. The indenture is made out to the corporate trustee as a representative of the interests of bondholders; that is, the trustee acts in a fiduciary capacity for investors who own the bond issue. A corporate trustee is a bond or trust company with a corporate trust department and officers who are experts in performing the functions of a trustee.

A bond's indenture clearly outlines three important aspects: its maturity, its security, and its provisions for retirement.

**Maturity of Bonds.**   Most corporate bonds are *term bonds*; that is, they run for a term of years, then become due and payable. Term bonds are often referred to as "bullet-maturity," or, simply, "bullet" bonds. Any amount of the liability

---

[2] *Moody's Bond Survey*, selected, year-end issues.

[3] Estimated from various issues of *Flow Accounts, Financial Assets and Liabilities*, Board of Governors of the Federal Reserve System.

that has not been paid off prior to maturity must be paid off at that time. The bond's term may be long or short. Generally, obligations due less than 10 years from the date of issue are called *notes*.[4]

Most corporate borrowings take the form of *bonds* due in 20 to 30 years. Term bonds may be retired by payment at final maturity or retired prior to maturity if provided for in the indenture. Some corporate bond issues are so arranged that specified principal amounts become due on specified dates prior to maturity. Such issues are called *serial bonds*. Equipment trust certificates (discussed later) are structured as serial bonds.

***Security for Bonds.*** Either real property (using a mortgage) or personal property may be pledged to offer security beyond that of the general credit standing of the issuer. A *mortgage bond* grants the bondholders a lien against the pledged assets. A *lien* is a legal right to sell mortgaged property to satisfy unpaid obligations to bondholders. In practice, foreclosure and sale of mortgaged property is unusual. If a default occurs, there is usually a financial reorganization of the issuer when provision is made for settlement of the debt to bondholders. The mortgage lien is important, though, because it gives the mortgage bondholders a very strong bargaining position relative to other creditors in determining the terms of a reorganization.

Some companies do not own fixed assets or other real property, and so have nothing on which they can give a mortgage lien to secure bondholders. Instead, these firms own securities of other companies and, thus, are *holding companies*. The firms whose shares are owned are *subsidiaries*. To satisfy the desire of bondholders for security, the holding companies pledge stocks, notes, bonds or whatever other kind of financial instruments they own. These assets are termed *collateral* (or personal property), and bonds secured by such assets are called *collateral trust bonds*.

Many years ago the railway companies developed a way of financing the purchase of cars and locomotives, called *rolling stock*, that enabled them to borrow at just about the lowest rates in the corporate bond market. Railway rolling stock has for a long time been regarded by investors as excellent security for debt. The equipment is sufficiently standardized that it can be used by one railway as well as another. And of course it can readily be moved from the tracks of one railroad to those of another. Therefore, there is generally a good market for lease or sale of cars and locomotives. The railroads have taken advantage of these characteristics of rolling stock by developing a legal arrangement for giving investors a legal claim on it that is different from, and generally superior to, a mortgage lien.

The legal arrangement in this situation is one that vests legal title to railway equipment in a trustee. When a railway company orders some cars and

[4] From our discussion of the various debt instruments in the previous chapter, it can be seen that the word "notes" is used to describe a variety of instruments—medium-term notes and Euronotes. The use of the term "notes" here is as a market convention distinguishing notes and bonds on the basis of the number of years to maturity at the time the security is issued.

locomotives from a manufacturer, the manufacturer transfers legal title to the equipment to a trustee. The trustee, in turn, leases the equipment to the railroad, and at the same time sells *equipment trust certificates* to obtain the funds to pay the manufacturer. The trustee collects lease payments from the railroad and uses these receipts to pay interest and principal on the certificates. The principal is therefore paid off on specified dates, a provision that makes a certificate different from a term bond.

The general idea of the equipment trust arrangement has also been used by companies engaged in providing other kinds of transportation. For example, trucking companies finance the purchase of huge fleets of trucks in the same manner; airlines use this kind of financing to purchase transport planes; and international oil companies use this financing method to buy huge tankers.

A *debenture bond* is not secured by a specific pledge of property, but that does not mean that this type of bond has no claim on property of issuers or on their earnings. Debenture bondholders have the claim of general creditors on all assets of the issuer not pledged specifically to secure other debt. Also, holders of debentures even have a claim on pledged assets to the extent that these assets have value greater than necessary to satisfy secured creditors. A *subordinated debenture bond* is an issue that ranks after secured debt, after debenture bonds, and often after some general creditors in its claim on assets and earnings.

The type of corporate security issued determines the cost to the issuer. For a given corporation, mortgage bonds will cost less than debenture bonds; debenture bonds will cost less than subordinated debenture bonds.

A *guaranteed bond* is an obligation guaranteed by another entity. The safety of a guaranteed bond depends upon the financial capability of the guarantor to satisfy the terms of the guarantee, as well as the financial capability of the issuer. The terms of the guarantee may call for the guarantor to guarantee the payment of interest and/or repayment of the principal.

It is important to recognize that a superior legal status will not prevent bondholders from suffering financial loss when the issuer's ability to generate cash flow adequate to pay its obligations is seriously eroded.

***Provisions for Paying Off Bonds.*** Most corporate issues have a call provision allowing the issuer an option to buy back all or part of the issue prior to maturity. Some issues carry a sinking fund provision, which specifies that the issuer must retire a predetermined amount of the issue periodically.[5]

An important question in negotiating the terms of a new bond issue is whether the issuer shall have the right to redeem the *entire amount* of bonds outstanding on a date before maturity. Issuers generally want this right because they recognize that at some time in the future the general level of interest rates may fall sufficiently below the issue's coupon rate, so that redeeming

---

[5] For a more detailed explanation of corporate call provisions, see Richard S. Wilson and Frank J. Fabozzi, *The New Corporate Bond Market* (Chicago: Probus Publishing, 1990).

the issue and replacing it with another issue carrying a lower coupon rate would be attractive. For reasons discussed later in this chapter, this right represents a disadvantage to the bondholder.

The usual practice is a provision that denies the issuer the right to redeem bonds during the first five to ten years following the date of issue with proceeds received from the sale of lower-cost debt obligations that have an equal or superior rank to the debt to be redeemed. This type of redemption is called *refunding*. While most long-term issues have these refunding restrictions, they may be immediately callable, in whole or in part, if the source of funds is something other than money raised with debt of a lower interest. Under such a provision, acceptable sources include cash flow from operations, proceeds from a common stock sale, or funds from the sale of property.

Investors often confuse refunding protection with call protection. Call protection is much more comprehensive because it prohibits the early redemption of the bonds *for any reason*. Refunding restrictions, by contrast, provide protection only against the one type of redemption mentioned above.

As a rule, corporate bonds are callable at a premium above par. Generally, the amount of the premium declines as the bond approaches maturity and often reaches zero after a number of years following issuance. The initial amount of the premium may be as much as one year's coupon interest, or as little as the coupon interest for one-half of a year.

If the issuer has the choice to retire all or part of an issue prior to maturity, the buyer of the bond takes the chance that the issue will be called away at a disadvantageous time. This risk is referred to as *call risk*, or *timing risk*. There are two disadvantages of call provisions from the investor's perspective. First, as explained in Chapter 10, a decline in interest rates in the economy will increase the price of a debt instrument, although in the case of a callable bond, the price increase is somewhat limited. If and when interest rates decline far enough below the coupon rate to make call an immediate or prospective danger, the market value of the callable bond will not rise as much as that of noncallable issues that are similar in all other respects. Second, when a bond issue is called as a result of a decline in interest rates, the investor must reinvest the proceeds received at a lower interest rate (unless the investor chooses debt of greater risk).

Corporate bond indentures may require the issuer to retire a specified portion of an issue each year. This *sinking fund* provision for the repayment of the debt may be designed to liquidate all of a bond issue by the maturity date, or it may call for the liquidation of only a part of the total by the end of the term. If only a part of the outstanding bond is paid before retirement, the remainder is called a *balloon maturity*. The purpose of the sinking fund provision is to reduce credit risk. Generally, the issuer may satisfy the sinking fund requirement by either (1) making a cash payment of the face amount of the bonds to be retired to the corporate trustee, who then calls the bonds for redemption using a lottery, or (2) delivering to the trustee bonds with a total face value equal to the amount that must be retired from bonds purchased in the open market.

## *Bonds with Special Features*

Prior to the 1970s, securities issued in the U.S. bond market had a simple structure. They had a fixed coupon rate and a fixed maturity date. The only option available to the issuer was the right to call all or part of the issue prior to the stated maturity date. The historically high interest rates that prevailed in the United States in the late 1970s and early 1980s, and the volatile interest rates since the 1970s, prompted introduction of new structures or the increased use of existing structures with special features that made issues more attractive to both borrowers and investors. Various bond structures are reviewed below.

***Convertible and Exchangeable Bonds.***   The conversion provision in a corporate bond issue grants the bondholder the right to convert the bond to a predetermined number of shares of common stock of the issuer. A *convertible bond* is therefore a corporate bond with a call option to buy the common stock of the issuer. An *exchangeable bond* grants the bondholder the right to exchange the bonds for the common stock of a firm *other* than the issuer of the bond. For example, Ford Motor Credit exchangeable bonds are exchangeable for the common stock of its parent company, Ford Motor Company.

***Issues of Debt with Warrants.***   Warrants may be attached as part of a bond issue. A *warrant* grants the holder the right to purchase a designated security at a specified price from the issuer of the bond. A warrant is simply a call option. It may permit the holder to purchase the common stock of the issuer of the debt or the common stock of a firm other than the issuer's. Or, the warrant may grant the holder the right to purchase a debt obligation of the issuer. Generally, warrants can be detached from the bond and sold separately. Typically, in exercising the warrant, an investor may choose either to pay cash or to offer the debt, to be valued at par, that was part of the offering. A major difference between warrants and either convertible or exchangeable bonds is that an investor exercising the option provided by the latter must turn the bond in to the issuer.

***Putable Bonds.***   A putable bond grants the bondholder the right to sell the issue back to the issuer at par value on designated dates. The advantage to the bondholder is that if interest rates rise after the issue date, thereby reducing the market value of the bond, the bondholder can sell the bond back to the issuer for par.

***Zero-Coupon Bonds.***   Zero-coupon bonds are, just as the name implies, bonds without coupon payments or a stated interest rate. We discussed zero-coupon bonds in Chapter 16, where we covered stripped Treasury securities. In the Treasury market, the U.S. government does not issue zero-coupon bonds. Dealers strip issues and create these bonds from the cash flow of a coupon Treasury bond. Corporations, however, can and do issue zero-coupon bonds. The first such public offering was in the spring of 1981. The attractiveness of a zero-coupon bond from the investor's perspective is that the investor who holds the bond to the maturity date will realize a predetermined return on the bond, unlike a coupon bond where the actual return realized, if the bond is held to maturity, depends on the rate at which coupon payments can be reinvested.

*Floating-Rate Securities.* The coupon interest on floating-rate securities is reset periodically to follow changes in the level of some predetermined benchmark rate. For example, the coupon rate may be reset every six months to a rate equal to a spread of 100 basis points over the six-month Treasury bill rate.

Floating-rate securities are attractive to some institutional investors because they allow them to buy an asset with an income stream that closely matches the floating nature of the income of some of their liabilities. Certain floating-rate instruments are viewed by some investors as a passive substitute for short-term investments, particularly that part of a short-term portfolio that is more or less consistently maintained at certain minimum levels. Thus, floating-rate securities save on the costs of constantly rolling over short-term securities as they reach maturity.

Why do corporations issue floating-rate securities? Closer matching of their income flows from variable-rate assets with floating-rate liabilities is of major importance, especially with lenders such as banks, thrifts, and finance companies. Issuers can fix or lock in a spread between the cost of borrowed funds and the rate at which those funds are lent out. Another reason might be to avoid uncertainties associated with what could be an unreceptive market at some future date. The issuer can tap a new source for intermediate- to long-term funds at short-term rates, thereby making fewer trips to the marketplace and avoiding related issuance costs.

Also, in the presence of inflation, a floating-rate security (rolled over, if needed) may have a lower interest cost than a fixed-rate, long-term security. The reason is that, with inflation, the long rate may incorporate a substantial premium against the uncertainty of future inflation and interest rates. Finally, as we note in our Chapter 29 discussion of the innovative world of swaps, an issuer may find that it can issue a floating-rate security and convert its payments into a fixed-rate stream through an interest rate swap agreement. An issuer will elect this approach if the cost of issuing a floating-rate security and then using an interest rate swap will result in a lower cost than simply issuing a fixed-rate security.

There may be other features in a floating-rate issue. For example, many floating-rate issues include a put option. Some issues are exchangeable either automatically at a certain date (often five years after issuance) or at the option of the issuer into fixed-rate securities. A few issues are convertible into the common stock of the issuer. Some floating-rate issues have a ceiling or maximum interest rate for the coupon rate; some have a floor or minimum interest rate for the coupon rate.

## Quality Ratings

As we stated in the previous chapter, market participants typically do not perform their own credit analysis of a debt obligation. Instead, they rely primarily on commercial rating companies that perform credit analysis and express their conclusions by a system of ratings. The two most widely used systems of bond (and medium-term note) ratings are those of Moody's and Standard & Poor's. In both systems, the term *high grade* means low credit risk, or, conversely, high probability of promised, future payments. Moody's designates the highest grade bonds by the letters *Aaa*; Standard & Poor's uses *AAA*. The next highest-grade is *Aa* or *AA*; for the third grade, both agencies use *A*. The next three grades are designated *Baa* or *BBB*, *Ba* or *BB*, and *B*, respectively. There are also *C* grades. Standard & Poor's also uses plus and minus signs to provide a narrower credit quality breakdown within each class. Moody's uses 1, 2, or 3 to provide this further refinement of the ratings.

Bonds rated triple-A (AAA or Aaa) are said to be *prime*; double-A (AA or Aa) are of *high quality*; single-A issues are *upper medium grade*; and triple-B bonds are of *medium grade*. These four categories make up the *investment grade*. Lower-rated bonds are said to have speculative elements or to be *distinctly speculative*. They are also known as *high-yield* or *junk bonds*. We'll have more to say about this market sector in the next part of this chapter.

There has been a dramatic decline in the number of new issues rated Aaa, from a high of 42.6% in 1977 to only 11.89% in 1988. A similar trend has occurred in bonds in the two highest rating categories (Aaa and Aa): in each year prior to 1982, a little more than half the issues merited one of these ratings; but in 1988, only about 25% of the new issues were rated that high. In contrast, the proportion of issues rated Ba and lower increased dramatically over that same interval.

Occasionally, the ability of an issuer to make interest and principal payments is seriously and unexpectedly changed by (1) a natural or industrial accident or some regulatory change, or (2) a takeover or corporate restructuring. These risks are referred to generically as *event risk*. Two examples of the first type of event risk are (a) a change in the accounting treatment of loan losses for commercial banks, and (b) the cancellation of nuclear plants by public utilities.

An example of the second type of event risk is the takeover in 1988 of RJR Nabisco for $25 billion through a financing technique known as a *leveraged buyout* (LBO). The new company took on a substantial amount of debt to finance the acquisition of the firm.[6] In the case of RJR Nabisco, the debt and equity after the leverage buyout were $29.9 and $1.2 billion, respectively. Because of the need to service a larger amount of debt, the company's quality rating was reduced. RJR Nabisco's quality rating as assigned by Moody's

---

[6] For a discussion of event risk associated with takeovers, see N.R. Vijayarghavan and Randy Snook, "Takeover Event Risk and Corporate Bond Portfolio Management," in Frank J. Fabozzi (ed.) *Advances and Innovations in Bond and Mortgage Markets* (Chicago: Probus Publishing, 1989).

dropped from A1 to B3. As a result, investors demanded a higher credit spread because of this new capital structure with a greater proportion of debt. The yield spread to a benchmark Treasury rate increased from about 100 basis points to 350 basis points.

## High-Yield Sector

*High-yield bonds*, commonly called *junk bonds*, are issues whose quality rating is designated as noninvestment-grade. Bond issues in this sector of the market were either rated investment-grade at the time of issuance but have subsequently been downgraded to noninvestment-grade, or they received a noninvestment-grade rating at the time of issuance. Bonds in the former category are commonly referred to as "fallen angels." By the end of 1990, the high-yield market was estimated to total around $240 billion, which amounts to roughly 20% of the total corporate bond market.

Prior to development of the high-yield market, U.S. corporations that could not issue securities in the public debt market would borrow from commercial banks on a short-term basis. In recent years, however, financing by these firms has shifted from commercial banks to the public market. John Paulus, Chief Economist at Morgan Stanley, has estimated that the majority of the high yield bonds issued are simply a replacement for bank borrowing.[7]

Corporate bond issuers use the proceeds from a bond sale for a variety of reasons. These include expansion of facilities, working capital, refinancing of outstanding debt, and financing takeovers (mergers and acquisitions). In the case of noninvestment-grade bonds, it is the use of proceeds to finance takeovers (particularly hostile takeovers) that has stirred controversy over the excessive use of debt by U.S. corporations.[8]

Issuers of high-yield bonds favor certain special bond structures. In a leveraged buyout or recapitalization, the heavy interest payment burden the corporation must make places severe cash flow constraints on the firm. To reduce this burden, firms involved in LBOs and recapitalizations have issued *deferred coupon structures* that permit the issuer to avoid using cash to make interest payments for a period of three to seven years. There are three types of deferred coupon structures: (1) deferred-interest bonds, (2) step-up bonds, and (3) payment-in-kind bonds.

*Deferred-interest bonds* are the most common type of deferred coupon structure. These bonds sell at a deep discount and do not pay interest for an initial period, typically from three to seven years. *Step-up bonds* do pay coupon interest, but the coupon rate is low for an initial period, and then increases ("steps up") to a higher level in later years. Finally, *payment-in-kind (PIK) bonds* give the issuer an option either to pay cash at a coupon payment date or to give the bondholder a similar bond. That similar bond is one with the same coupon rate

---

[7] This is from a November 1986 speech presented to a conference sponsored by the *Citizens for a Sound Economy*.

[8] A hostile takeover is one in which the acquired firm management resists the merger or acquisition.

and a par value equal to the amount of the coupon payment that would have been paid. The period during which the issuer has this choice varies from five to ten years.

## Secondary Market

There are really two secondary corporate bond markets: the exchange market (New York Stock Exchange and American Stock Exchange) and the over-the-counter (OTC) market. Almost all trading volume takes place in the OTC market, which is the market used by institutional investors and professional money managers.

The secondary market for corporate bonds has two problems, which we first discussed in Chapter 16 in our account of the secondary Treasury market. One problem is that there is too little public reporting of completed transactions in corporate bonds. The other is that it is difficult for many investors to get information on reliable bid and ask prices at which investors can trade corporate bonds.

The liquidity of corporate bonds varies from issue to issue. The bonds of large firms, usually sold to the public in large amounts, can have a high degree of liquidity. However, the issues of smaller, less well-known firms may be quite illiquid.

## Eurobond Market

The Eurobond sector of the global bond market includes bonds with several distinguishing features: (1) they are underwritten by an international syndicate; (2) at issuance they are offered simultaneously to investors in a number of countries; (3) they are issued outside the jurisdiction of any single country; and (4) they are in unregistered form. Although Eurobonds are typically listed on a national stock exchange (the most common are the Luxembourg, London, or Zurich exchanges), the bulk of all trading is in the over-the-counter market. Firms list these bonds purely to circumvent restrictions imposed on some institutional investors that are prohibited from purchasing securities not listed on an exchange. Some of the stronger issuers privately place their debt with international institutional investors.

Borrowers in the Eurobond market include nonfinancial corporations, banks, sovereign governments, entities whose debt is guaranteed by a sovereign government, provinces, municipalities, cities, and supranational entities such as the World Bank. In 1991, the major issuer group was nonfinancial corporations, followed by banks. Of the $258 billion issued in the Eurobond market in 1991, nonfinancial corporations issued about $98 billion of Eurobonds (or 38%), and banks issued about $52 billion (or 20%).[9]

Traditionally, the main currency used in Eurobond offerings has been the U.S. dollar, although the share of Eurobond offerings denominated in U.S.

---

[9] *Eurobonds and Euro Medium-Term Notes: 1991 Review,* Salomon Brothers Inc., p. 3.

dollars has been declining. In 1991, 30% of the $258 billion issued was de-nominated in U.S. dollars, followed by the Japanese yen (14%), the European Currency Unit (12%),[10] and the U.K.'s pound sterling.[11] In total, Eurobonds were issued in 21 currencies during 1991. In that year, there were issuers from 36 different countries, and U.S. borrowers raised $19.85 billion in this market. Borrowers from Western Europe and Japan raised $94.16 and $59.48 billion, respectively.[12]

The Eurobond market has been characterized by new and innovative bond structures to accommodate particular needs of issuers and investors throughout the world. Some issues, of course, are the "plain vanilla," fixed-rate coupon bonds, referred to as *Euro straights*. Because they are issued on an unsecured basis, they are usually the debt of high-quality entities.

Coupon payments on Eurobonds are made annually, rather than semi-annually. There are also zero-coupon bond issues, deferred-coupon issues, and step-up issues. Some of the innovative issues in this market are *dual-currency issues:* they pay coupon interest in one currency but the principal in a different currency. For example, the coupon interest payments can be made in Swiss francs, while the principal may be paid in U.S. dollars.

Some Eurobonds are convertible or exchangeable, and bonds with attached warrants represent a large part of the market. Most warrants on Eurobonds are detachable from the bond with which they originally came to market. That is, the bondholder may detach the warrant from the bond and sell it separately.

The warrants on Eurobonds are varied: some are equity warrants, others are debt warrants, and still others may be currency warrants. An equity warrant permits the warrant owner to buy the common stock of the issuer at a specified price. A debt warrant entitles the warrant owner to buy additional bonds from the issuer at the same price and yield as the host bond. The debt warrant owner will benefit if interest rates decline because the warrant allows the owner to purchase a bond with a higher coupon than the same issuer would offer. A currency warrant permits the warrant owner to exchange one currency for another at a set price (that is, a fixed exchange rate). This feature protects the bondholder against a depreciation of the foreign currency in which the bond's cash flows are denominated. Finally, we also note that some warrants are gold warrants and allow the warrant holder to purchase gold from the bond issuer at a prespecified price.

Eurobonds make use of a wide variety of floating-rate structures. Almost all the floating-rate notes are denominated in U.S. dollars, and non-U.S. banks are the major issuers of these bonds. The coupon rate on a Eurodollar floating-rate note is some stated margin over the London Interbank Offered Rate (LIBOR), the bid on LIBOR (referred to as LIBID), or the arithmetic average of LIBOR and LIBID (referred to as LIMEAN). Many floating-rate is-

---

[10] The European Currency Unit, or ECU, is discussed in Chapter 30.

[11] *Ibid.*, p. 1.

[12] *Ibid.*, p. 4.

sues have either a minimum rate (or floor) that the coupon rate cannot fall below or a maximum rate (or cap) that the coupon rate cannot exceed. An issue that has both a floor and a cap is said to be "collared." Some floating-rate issues grant the borrower the right to convert the floating coupon rate into a fixed coupon rate at some time. Some issues, referred to as *drop-lock bonds*, automatically convert the floating coupon rate into a fixed coupon rate under certain circumstances.

▶ KEY POINTS YOU SHOULD UNDERSTAND BEFORE PROCEEDING:

1. The bond indenture sets forth the obligations of the issuer and the rights of the bondholders.
2. Either real property or personal property may be pledged to offer security beyond that of the general credit standing of the issuer.
3. Bonds typically carry provisions that allow for the principal to be repaid prior to the stated maturity date, with the most common provision being the right of the issuer to call the issue. This is an advantage to the issuer and a disadvantage to the bondholder.
4. There are a wide variety of bond structures with special features that make issues more attractive to both borrowers and investors.
5. In addition to credit risk, corporate bond investors are exposed to event risk.
6. High-yield bonds are issues whose quality rating is designated as noninvestment-grade, and there are several unique bond structures in this sector of the market.
7. The Eurobond market has been characterized by new and innovative bond structures to accommodate particular needs of issuers and investors throughout the world.

## PREFERRED STOCK

Preferred stock is a class of stock, not a debt instrument, but it shares characteristics of both common stock and debt. Like the holder of common stock, the preferred stockholder is entitled to dividends. Unlike those on common stock, however, preferred dividends are a specified percentage of par or face value.[13] The percentage is called the dividend rate; it need not be fixed, but may float over the life of the issue.

Failure to make preferred stock dividend payments cannot force the issuer into bankruptcy. Should the issuer not make the preferred stock dividend payment, usually paid quarterly, one of two things can happen, depending on

[13] Almost all preferred stock limits the securityholder to the specified amount. Historically, there have been issues entitling the preferred stockholder to participate in earnings distribution beyond the specified amount (based on some formula). Preferred stock with this feature is referred to as participating preferred stock.

the terms of the issue. First, the dividend payment can accrue until it is fully paid. Preferred stock with this feature is called *cumulative preferred stock*. If a dividend payment is missed and the securityholder must forgo the payment, the preferred stock is said to be *noncumulative preferred stock*. Second, the failure to make dividend payments may result in the imposition of certain restrictions on management. For example, if dividend payments are in arrears, preferred stockholders might be granted voting rights.

Preferred stock differs from debt in a major way: the current tax code for corporations treats payments made to preferred stockholders as a distribution of earnings and not as tax-deductible expenses, which is how the tax code views interest payments. While this difference in tax status raises the after-tax cost of funds for a corporation issuing preferred stock rather than borrowing, another factor in the tax code reduces the cost differential. A provision in the tax code exempts 70% of qualified dividends from federal income taxation, if the recipient is a qualified corporation.

For example, if Corporation A owns the preferred stock of Corporation B, then only $30 of each $100 that A receives in dividends from B will be taxed at A's marginal tax rate. The purpose of this provision is to mitigate the effect of the double taxation of corporate earnings. There are two implications of this tax treatment of preferred stock dividends. First, the major buyers of preferred stock are corporations seeking tax-advantaged investments. Second, the cost of preferred stock issuance is lower than it would be in the absence of the tax provision, because the tax benefits are passed through to the issuer by the willingness of buyers to accept a lower dividend rate.

Preferred stock, particularly cumulative preferred stock, has some important similarities with debt: (1) the issuer promises fixed cash payments to preferred stockholders, and (2) preferred stockholders have priority over common stockholders with respect to dividend payments and the distribution of assets in the case of bankruptcy. (The position of noncumulative preferred stock is considerably weaker.) It is because of this second feature that preferred stock is called a senior corporate instrument—it is senior to common stock. Note, however, that preferred stock is classified as equity on corporate balance sheets.

Almost all preferred stock has a sinking fund provision, and some preferred stock is convertible into common stock. Preferred stock may be issued without a maturity date. This is called *perpetual preferred stock*.

As noted above, the estimated size of the domestic corporate bond market in 1991 was about $1.7 trillion. In contrast, as of 1988 the 1,370 preferred stock issues outstanding had a par value of only $57 billion.[14] The Federal Reserve Board estimates that only $45 billion in publicly placed preferred stock came to the market from 1989 to 1992 (June).[15] Clearly, the preferred stock

[14] Richard S. Wilson, "Nonconvertible Preferred Stock," Chapter 16 in *The Handbook of Fixed Income Securities* (Homewood, IL: Business One Irwin, 1991).

[15] Board of Governors of the Federal Reserve System, *Federal Reserve Bulletin*, selected issues.

market is not much larger than $125 billion, and so is a relatively small part of the financial system.

Historically, utilities have been the major issuers of preferred stock, accounting for more than half of each year's issuance. Since 1985, major issuers have become financially oriented companies—finance companies, banks, thrifts, and insurance companies. In 1985 and 1987, for example, only 10% of preferred stock issued was utility stock.

The same five commercial companies that assign ratings to corporate bond issues also rate preferred stock issues.

There are three types of preferred stock: (1) fixed-rate preferred stock, (2) adjustable-rate preferred stock, and (3) auction and remarketed preferred stock. Before 1982, all publicly issued preferred stock was fixed-rate preferred stock. In May of 1982, the first adjustable-rate preferred stock issue was sold in the public market.[16]

## Adjustable-Rate Preferred Stock

The dividend rate on an adjustable-rate preferred stock (ARPS) is fixed quarterly and based on a predetermined spread from the highest of three points on the Treasury yield curve.[17] The predetermined spread is called the *dividend reset spread*. The motivation for linking the dividend rate to the highest of the three points on the Treasury yield curve is to provide the investor with protection against unfavorable shifts in the yield curve.

Most ARPS are perpetual, with a floor and ceiling imposed on the dividend rate of most issues. Because most ARPS are not putable, they can trade below par if, after issuance, the spread demanded by the market to reflect the issuer's credit risk is greater than the dividend reset spread.

The major issuers of ARPS have been bank holding companies. There are two reasons bank holding companies have become major issuers of ARPS. First, floating-rate obligations provide a better liability match, given the floating-rate nature of bank assets. Second, bank holding companies are seeking to strengthen their capital positions, and regulators permit bank holding companies to count perpetual preferred stock as part of their primary capital. Issuing ARPS provides not only a better asset/liability match, but also permits bank holding companies to improve primary capital without having to issue common stock.

---

[16] Private placement of ARPS occurred as early as 1978–illustrating how an innovation is first developed in this market. For historical background on the development of the ARPS market, see Richard S. Wilson, "Adjustable Rate Preferred Stocks," Chapter 3 in Frank J. Fabozzi (ed.), *Floating Rate Instruments: Characteristics, Valuation and Portfolio Strategies* (Chicago: Probus Publishing, 1986).

[17] The Treasury yield curve is described in Chapter 12. The three points on the yield curve (called the benchmark rate) to which the dividend reset spread is either added or subtracted are the highest of: (1) the three-month Treasury bill rate; (2) the two-year constant maturity rate; or (3) a 10-year or 30-year constant maturity rate. The Treasury constant maturity rate is reported in the Federal Reserve Report H.15(519). It is based on the closing market bid yields on actively traded Treasury securities.

## Auction and Remarketed Preferred Stock

The popularity of ARPS declined when instruments began to trade below their par value—because the dividend reset rate is determined at the time of issuance, not by market forces. In 1984, a new type of preferred stock, *auction preferred stock* (APS), was designed to overcome this problem, particularly for corporate treasurers who sought tax-advantaged short-term instruments to invest excess funds.[18] The dividend rate on APS is set periodically, as with ARPS, but it is established through an auction process.[19] Participants in the auction consist of current holders and potential buyers. The dividend rate that participants are willing to accept reflects current market conditions.

In the case of *remarketed preferred stock* (RP), the dividend rate is determined periodically by a remarketing agent who resets the dividend rate so that any preferred stock can be tendered at par and be resold (remarketed) at the original offering price. An investor has the choice of dividend resets every seven days or every 49 days.

Since 1985, APS and RP have become the dominant type of preferred stock issued.

► KEY POINTS YOU SHOULD UNDERSTAND BEFORE PROCEEDING:

1. Preferred stock is a class of stock in which the dividend rate is typically a fixed percentage of par or face value.

2. Payments made to preferred stockholders are treated as a distribution of earnings and therefore are not tax-deductible to the issuing corporation.

3. Because the tax code exempts 70% of qualified dividends from federal income taxation if the recipient is a qualified corporation, the major buyers of preferred stock are corporations seeking tax-advantaged investments; these investors are willing to accept a lower dividend rate.

4. Preferred stock has some important similarities with debt.

5. There are various types of preferred stock: fixed-rate, adjustable-rate, auction, and remarketed.

## BANKRUPTCY AND CREDITOR RIGHTS

■ ■ ■ ■

In this chapter and the previous one, we refer to "senior" corporate securities. By senior, we mean that the holder of the security has priority over the equity owners in the case of bankruptcy of a corporation. And, as we explained in this chapter, there are creditors who have priority over other creditors. In this

---

[18] Each investment bank developed its own trademark name for APS. The instrument developed by Shearson Lehman/American Express was called Money Market Preferred (MMP). Salomon Brothers called it Dutch Auction Rate Transferable Securities (DARTS).

[19] The auction process is described in Richard S. Wilson, "Money Market Preferred Stock," Chapter 4 in Frank J. Fabozzi (ed.), *Floating Rate Instruments, op. cit.*, pp. 85-88.

section, we provide an overview of the bankruptcy process and then look at what actually happens to creditors in bankruptcies.

The law governing bankruptcy in the United States is the Bankruptcy Reform Act of 1978.[20] One purpose of the act is to set forth the rules for a corporation to be liquidated or reorganized. *Liquidation* means that all the assets of the corporation will be distributed to holders of claims on the corporation, and no corporate entity will survive. In a *reorganization*, a new corporate entity will result. Some holders of claims on the bankrupt corporation will receive cash in exchange for their claims; others may receive new securities in the corporation that results from the reorganization; and still others may receive a combination of both cash and new securities in the resulting corporation.

Another purpose of the bankruptcy act is to give a corporation time to decide whether to reorganize or to liquidate, and then provide the necessary time to formulate a plan to accomplish either a reorganization or liquidation. This is achieved because a bankruptcy filing allows the corporation protection from creditors who seek to collect their claims.[21] A company that files for protection under the bankruptcy act generally becomes a "debtor-in-possession," and continues to operate its business under the supervision of the court.

The bankruptcy act has 15 chapters, each covering a particular type of bankruptcy. Of particular interest to us are two of the chapters, Chapter 7 and Chapter 11. Chapter 7 deals with the liquidation of a company; Chapter 11 covers reorganization.

When a company is liquidated, creditors receive distributions based on the "absolute priority rule" to the extent assets are available. The absolute priority rule is the principle that senior creditors are paid in full before junior creditors are paid anything. For secured creditors and unsecured creditors, the absolute priority rule guarantees their seniority to equity holders.

In liquidations, the absolute priority rule generally holds, but in reorganizations under Chapter 11, it is often violated. Studies of actual reorganizations under Chapter 11 have found that the violation of absolute priority is the rule rather than the exception.[22]

There are several reasons that have been suggested as to why, in a reorganization, the distribution made to claimholders will diverge from that re-

---

[20] For a discussion of the Bankruptcy Reform Act of 1978 and a nontechnical description of its principal features, see Jane Tripp Howe, "Investing in Chapter 11 and Other Distressed Companies," Chapter 20 in Frank J. Fabozzi (ed.), *The Handbook of Fixed Income Securities, op. cit.*

[21] The petition for bankruptcy can be filed either by the company itself, in which case it is called a *voluntary bankruptcy*, or be filed by its creditors, in which case it is called an involuntary bankruptcy.

[22] See: Julian R. Franks and Walter N. Torous, "An Empirical Investigation of U.S. Firms in Reorganization," *Journal of Finance*, (July 1989), pp. 747-769; Lawrence A. Weiss, "Bankruptcy Resolution: Direct Costs and Violation of Priority of Claims," *Journal of Financial Economics* (1990), pp. 285-314; and Frank J. Fabozzi, Jane Tripp Howe, Takashi Makabe, and Toshihide Sudo, "Recent Evidence on the Distribution Patterns in Chapter 11 Reorganizations," *Journal of Fixed Income* (Spring 1993), pp. 6-23

quired by the absolute priority principle.[23] One reason commonly cited has to do with the negotiation process that takes place among the various classes of claimholders in a reorganization. In a reorganization, a committee representing the various claimholders is appointed with the purpose of formulating a plan of reorganization. To be accepted, a plan of reorganization must be approved by at least two-thirds of the amount and a majority of the number of claims voting, and at least two-thirds of the outstanding shares of each class of interests. Consequently, a long-lasting bargaining process is expected. The longer the negotiation process among the parties, the more likely the company is to be operated in a manner that is not in the best interest of the creditors and, as a result, the smaller the amount to be distributed to all parties. Since all impaired classes including equityholders generally must approve the plan of reorganization, creditors often convince equityholders to accept the plan by offering to distribute some value to them.

Consequently, while investors in the debt of a corporation may feel that they have priority over the equity owners and priority over other classes of debtors, the actual outcome of a bankruptcy may be far different from what the terms of the debt agreement state.

▶ KEY POINTS YOU SHOULD UNDERSTAND BEFORE PROCEEDING:

1. The Bankruptcy Reform Act of 1978 is the law governing bankruptcy in the United States.
2. Chapter 7 of the act deals with the liquidation of a company, and Chapter 11 deals with the reorganization of a company.
3. When a company is liquidated, creditors receive distributions based on the "absolute priority rule" to the extent assets are available.
4. In liquidations, the absolute priority rule generally holds, but in reorganizations under Chapter 11, it is often violated.

**SUMMARY**

Corporate bonds are debt obligating a corporation to pay periodic interest with full repayment at maturity. The promises of the corporate bond issuer and the rights of the investors are set forth in the bond indenture. Provisions to be specified include call and sinking fund provisions.

Security for bonds may be real or personal property. Debenture bonds are not secured by a specific pledge of property. Subordinated debenture bonds are issues that rank after secured debt, after debenture bonds, and often after some general creditors in their claim on assets and earnings.

Special corporate bond features include convertible and exchangeable bonds, units of debt with warrants, putable bonds, zero-coupon bonds, and floating-rate securities. Junk bonds or high-yield bonds are is-

---

[23] For a discussion of these reasons, see Fabozzi, *et. al.* "Recent Evidence on the Distribution Patterns in Chapter 11 Reorganizations," *op. cit.*

sues with quality ratings below triple-B. Recent years have seen the introduction of several complex bond structures in the junk bond area, particularly bonds issued for LBO financing and recapitalizations producing higher levels of debt to equity. These include deferred-coupon bonds (deferred-interest bonds, step-up bonds, and payment-in-kind bonds) and extendable reset bonds.

Many innovative bond structures have been introduced in the Eurobond market such as dual-currency issues and various types of convertible bonds and bonds with warrants. A warrant permits its owner to enter into another financial transaction with the issuer if the owner will benefit as a result of exercising. The floating-rate sector of the Eurobond market is dominated by U.S. dollar-denominated issues.

Preferred stock as a class of stock has characteristics of both common stock and debt. Because a special provision in the tax code allows taxation of only a portion of dividends when they are received by a corporation, the major buyers of preferred stock are corporations. There are three types of preferred stock besides the traditional fixed-rate preferred stock: adjustable-rate preferred stock, auction preferred stock, and remarketed preferred stock.

The Bankruptcy Reform Act of 1978 governs the bankruptcy process in the United States. Chapter 7 of the bankruptcy act deals with the liquidation of a company. Chapter 11 deals with the reorganization of a company. Creditors receive distributions based on the absolute priority rule to the extent assets are available. This means that senior creditors are paid in full before junior creditors are paid anything. Generally, this rule holds in the case of liquidations. In contrast, the absolute priority rule is typically violated in a reorganization.

## GLOSSARY

**Absolute priority rule:** In a bankruptcy, the principle that senior creditors are paid in full before junior creditors are paid anything.

**Adjustable-rate preferred stock (ARPS):** Preferred stock for which the dividend rate is adjusted quarterly on the basis of a predetermined spread from the highest of three points on the Treasury yield curve.

**Auction preferred stock (APS):** Preferred stock where the dividend rate is set periodically through an auction process.

**Bankruptcy Reform Act of 1978:** The law governing bankruptcy in the United States.

**Bond indenture:** In a corporate bond agreement, the contract that specifies the obligations of the issuer and the rights of bondholders.

**Bullet bond (or bullet-maturity bond):** A bond where no principal payments are made until the maturity date.

**Call risk (or timing risk):** The disadvantages associated with the early retirement of a bond issue.

**Chapter 7:** Chapter of the Bankruptcy Reform Act of 1978 dealing with the liquidation of a company.

**Chapter 11:** Chapter of the Bankruptcy Reform Act of 1978 dealing with the reorganization of a company.

**Collateral trust bond:** A bond secured by stocks, notes, bonds, or other kinds of financial instruments.

**Convertible bond:** A bond that grants the bondholder the right to convert the bond into the common stock of the issuer.

**Cumulative preferred stock:** Preferred stock in which the dividend payment accrues until it is fully paid.

**Debenture bond:** A bond not secured by a specific pledge of property, but giving the bondholders the claim of general creditors on all assets of the issuer not pledged specifically to secure other debt.

**Debtor-in-possession:** A company that files for protection under the bankruptcy act and continues to operate its business under the supervision of the court.

**Deferred coupon structure:** A high-yield bond structure that permits the issuer to avoid using cash to make interest payments for a period of typically three to seven years.

**Deferred-interest bond:** A form of deferred coupon structure in which the issue sells at a deep discount and the issuer does not pay interest for an initial period.

**Dual-currency issue:** A Eurobond in which the issuer pays coupon interest in one currency but retires the principal in a different currency.

**Equipment trust certificate:** A form of borrowing secured by property such that title to the property is held in trust until the debt obligation is paid off.

**Euro straight bond:** A bond that is a "plain vanilla," fixed-rate coupon Eurobond.

**Eurobond:** In general, a bond that is underwritten by an international syndicate, is offered simultaneously to investors in a number of countries, and is issued outside the jurisdiction of any single country.

**Exchangeable bond:** A bond that grants the bondholder the right to exchange the bonds for the common stock of a firm other than the issuer of the bond.

**Fallen angel:** A bond rated investment-grade at the time of issuance but subsequently downgraded to noninvestment-grade.

**Floating-rate security:** A debt obligation in which the coupon interest is adjusted periodically on the basis of some predetermined benchmark.

**Guaranteed bond:** A bond whose obligation is guaranteed by another entity.

**High-yield bond (also called junk bond):** A bond whose quality rating is designated as noninvestment-grade.

**Investment grade:** The term for bonds rated in the highest four quality categories of Moody's or Standard & Poor's systems.

**Leveraged buyout (or LBO):** The acquisition of a company by another that uses a substantial amount of debt to finance the acquisition.

**Mortgage bond:** A bond in which the issuer has granted the bondholders a lien against pledged assets.

**Noncumulative preferred stock:** Preferred stock in which the dividend payment, if missed, is forgone by the stockholder.

**Payment-in-kind (PIK) bond:** A form of deferred coupon structure that gives the issuer an option to pay cash at a coupon payment date or to give the bondholder a similar bond.

**Perpetual preferred stock:** Preferred stock that does not have a maturity date.

**Preferred stock:** A class of stock in which the stockholder is entitled to dividends but, unlike dividends on common stock, dividends are a specified percentage of par or face value.

**Putable bond:** A bond that grants the bondholder the right to sell the issue back to the issuer at par value on designated dates.

**Refunding provision:** A provision that denies the issuer the right to redeem bonds during some period of time after issuance with proceeds received from issuing lower-cost debt obligations ranking equal to or superior to the debt to be redeemed.

**Remarketed preferred stock:** Preferred stock whose dividend rate is determined periodically by a remarketing agent who resets the dividend rate so that any preferred stock can be tendered at par and be resold (remarketed) at the original offering price.

**Serial bond:** A bond issue in which specified principal amounts become due on specified dates.

**Sinking fund provision:** A provision that requires the issuer to retire a specified portion of an issue each year.

**Step-up bond:** A form of deferred coupon structure in which the coupon rate is low for an initial period and then increases to a higher coupon rate thereafter.

**Subordinated debenture bond:** A bond in which the bondholders rank after secured debt, after debenture bonds, and often after some general creditors in their claim on assets and earnings.

**Warrant:** A contract that grants the holder the right to purchase a designated security at a specified price.

1.  a.  What are the disadvantages of investing in a callable bond?
    b.  What is the advantage to the issuer of issuing a callable bond?
    c.  What is the difference between a noncallable bond and a nonrefundable bond?

2.  a.  What is a sinking fund requirement in a bond issue?
    b.  "A sinking fund provision in a bond issue benefits the investor." Do you agree with this statement?

3.  What is a:
    a.  serial bond?
    b.  mortgage bond?
    c.  equipment trust certificate?
    d.  collateral bond?

4.  What is the difference between a convertible bond and an exchangeable bond?

5.  Do you agree or disagree with this statement: "Zero-coupon corporate bonds are created in the same way as in the Treasury market—by stripping coupon bonds"?

6.  a.  What is event risk?
    b.  Give two examples of event risk.

7.  a.  What is a Eurobond?
    b.  How often is the coupon payment on a Eurobond made?
    c.  Name the two currencies most often used to denominate Eurobonds.

8.  What is a dual-currency bond?

9.  a.  Why are corporate treasurers the main buyers of preferred stock?
    b.  What was the reason for the popularity of auction and remarketed preferred stock?

10. a.  What is the difference between a liquidation and a reorganization?
    b.  What is the difference between a Chapter 7 and a Chapter 11 bankruptcy filing?
    c.  What is meant by a "debtor-in-possession"?

11. a.  What is meant by the principle of "absolute priority"?
    b.  Comment on this statement: "An investor who purchases the mortgage bonds of a corporation knows that, should the corporation become bankrupt, mortgage bondholders will be paid in full before the common stockholders receive any proceeds."

# CHAPTER TWENTY-TWO

# The Markets for Bank Obligations

## LEARNING OBJECTIVES

*After reading this chapter you will understand:*

- a categorization of banks that is useful for understanding the supply of bank obligations.
- what a negotiable certificate of deposit or CD is, and the different types of certificates of deposit.
- what a Euro CD is and how it differs from a Yankee CD.
- what determines a CD's yield or rate of interest.
- what federal funds are, and how banks use them to meet Federal Reserve requirements.
- what the effective fed funds rate is.
- the size of the fed funds market and the role brokers play in it.
- what a bankers acceptance or BA is, and how it is created.
- what the BA's credit risk is, and what an eligible BA is.

Commercial banks are special types of corporations. We described their activities and how they raise funds to finance these activities in Chapter 4. Banks will raise equity in the same manner that we described in Chapter 14. Larger banks will also raise funds using the various debt markets described in the previous two chapters. In this chapter, we describe three other debt obligations: large-denomination certificates of deposit, federal funds, and bankers acceptances. All these instruments trade in what is collectively known as the *money market*, the market for short-term debt instruments. Typically, money market instruments have a maturity of one year or less. While our discussion focuses on commercial banks, other depository institutions may also issue the same types of obligations.

## TYPES OF BANKS OPERATING IN THE UNITED STATES

Banks in the United States can be classified into four groups. First are the *money center banks* — banks that raise most of their funds from the domestic and international money markets and rely less on depositors for funds. The second group is *regional banks*, which rely primarily on deposits for funding and make less use of the money markets to obtain funds. *Japanese banks* are the third group of banks. Japanese banks are classified as one of the following: city banks, local banks, long-term credit banks, trust banks, and mutual banks.[1] City banks are the most powerful depository institutions in Japan, with 13 city banks holding approximately 20% of all deposits in Japan. The fourth group of banks are *Yankee banks*. These are foreign banks with U.S. branches. Included in this group are non-Japanese branches of foreign banks, such as Credit Lyonnais and Deutsche Bank.

## LARGE-DENOMINATION NEGOTIABLE CDS

A certificate of deposit (CD) is a financial asset issued by a bank or thrift that indicates a specified sum of money has been deposited at the issuing depository institution. CDs are issued by banks and thrifts to raise funds for financing their business activities. A CD bears a maturity date and a specified interest rate, and can be issued in any denomination. CDs issued by banks are insured by the Federal Deposit Insurance Corporation but only for amounts up to $100,000. There is no limit on the maximum maturity, but by Federal Reserve regulations CDs cannot have a maturity of less than seven days.

A CD may be *nonnegotiable* or *negotiable*. In the former case, the initial depositor must wait until the maturity date of the CD to obtain the funds. If the depositor chooses to withdraw funds prior to the maturity date, an early withdrawal penalty is imposed. In contrast, a negotiable CD allows the initial depositor (or any subsequent owner of the CD) to sell the CD in the open market prior to the maturity date.

Negotiable CDs were introduced in the early sixties. At that time the in-

---

[1] For a discussion of these different institutions, see Chapters 4 and 5.

terest rate banks could pay on various types of deposits was subject to ceilings administered by the Federal Reserve (except for demand deposits defined as deposits of less than one month that by law could pay no interest). For complex historical reasons, these ceiling rates started very low, rose with maturity, and remained below market rates up to some fairly long maturity. Before introduction of the negotiable CD, those with money to invest for, say, one month had no incentive to deposit it with a bank, for they would get a below-market rate unless they were prepared to tie up their capital for a much longer period of time. When negotiable CDs came along, they could buy a three-month or longer negotiable CD yielding a market interest rate, and recoup all or more than the investment (depending on market conditions) by selling it in the market.

This innovation was critical in helping banks to increase the amount of funds raised in the money market, a position that had languished in the earlier postwar period. It also motivated competition among banks, ushering in a new era. There are now two types of negotiable CDs. The first is the large-denomination CD, usually issued in denominations of $1 million or more. These are the negotiable CDs whose history we described above.

In 1982, Merrill Lynch entered the retail CD business by opening up a primary and secondary market in small-denomination (less than $100,000) CDs. While it made the CDs of its numerous banking and savings institution clients available to retail customers, Merrill Lynch also began to give these customers the negotiability enjoyed by institutional investors by standing ready to buy back the CDs prior to maturity. Today, several retail-oriented brokerage firms offer CDs that are salable in a secondary market. These are the second type of negotiable CD. Our focus in this chapter, though, is on the large-denomination negotiable CD, and we refer to them simply as CDs throughout the chapter.

The largest group of CD investors is investment companies, and money market funds make up the bulk of them. Far behind are banks and bank trust departments, followed by municipal entities and corporations. One indication of the size of the market available to these investors is the Federal Reserve Board's data series for "Time Deposits in amounts of $100,000 or more." In the mid 1980s, the value of these deposits was near $400 billion. Although recently down to a level of $170 billion, these deposits/securities still represent a meaningful part of the money market and the obligations of the banking system of the United States.

## CD Issuers

CDs can be classified into four types, according to the issuing institution. First are CDs issued by domestic banks. Second are CDs that are denominated in U.S. dollars but are issued outside the U.S. These CDs are called *Eurodollar CDs*, or *Euro CDs*. A third type of CD is the *Yankee CD*, which is a CD denominated in U.S. dollars and issued by a foreign bank with a branch in the United States. Finally, *thrift CDs* are those issued by savings and loan associations and savings banks.

Money center banks and large regional banks are the primary issuers of domestic CDs. Most CDs are issued with a maturity of less than one year. Those issued with a maturity greater than one year are called *term CDs*.

Unlike Treasury bills, commercial paper, and bankers acceptances, yields on domestic CDs are quoted on an interest-bearing basis. CDs with a maturity of one year or less pay interest at maturity. For purposes of calculating interest, a year is treated as having 360 days. Term CDs issued in the U.S. normally pay interest semiannually, again with a year taken as 360 days.

A *floating-rate CD* (FRCD) is one whose interest rate changes periodically in accordance with a predetermined formula that indicates the spread (or margin) above some index at which the rate will reset periodically. There are FRCDs that reset the coupon daily, weekly, monthly, quarterly, or semiannually. Typically FRCDs have maturities from 18 months to 5 years.

Euro CDs are U.S. dollar-denominated CDs issued primarily in London by U.S., Canadian, European, and Japanese banks. Branches of large U.S. banks once were the major issuers of Euro CDs. In 1982, of the $93 billion Euro CDs issued, $50 billion were issued by branches of U.S. banks.[2] Since 1982, however, the share of Euro CDs issued by branches of U.S. banks has declined, and Japanese banks have become the major issuers of Euro CDs.

## Yields on CDs

The yields posted on CDs vary depending on three factors: (1) the credit rating of the issuing bank; (2) the maturity of the CD; and (3) the supply and demand for CDs. With respect to the third factor, banks and thrifts issue CDs as part of their liability management strategy, so the supply of CDs will be driven by the demand for bank loans and the cost of alternative sources of capital to fund these loans. Moreover, bank loan demand will depend on the cost of alternative funding sources such as commercial paper. When loan demand is weak, CD rates decline. When demand is strong, the rates rise. The effect of maturity depends on the shape of the yield curve, a topic we covered in Chapter 12.

Credit risk has become more of an issue. At one time domestic CDs issued by money center banks traded on a *no-name basis*. Recent financial crises in the banking industry, however, have caused investors to take a closer look at issuing banks. *Prime CDs* (those issued by high-rated domestic banks) trade at a lower yield than *nonprime CDs* (those issued by lower-rated domestic banks). Because of the unfamiliarity investors have with foreign banks, generally Yankee CDs trade at a higher yield than domestic CDs.

Euro CDs offer a higher yield than domestic CDs. There are three reasons for this. First, there are reserve requirements imposed by the Federal

---

[2] As reported in *Quarterly Bulletin* published by the Bank of England.

Reserve on CDs issued by U.S. banks in the United States that do not apply to issuers of Euro CDs. The reserve requirement effectively raises the cost of funds to the issuing bank because it cannot invest all the proceeds it receives from the issuance of a CD, and the amount that must be kept as reserves will not earn a return for the bank. Because it will earn less on funds raised by selling domestic CDs, the domestic issuing bank will pay less on its domestic CD than a Euro CD. Second, the bank issuing the CD must pay an insurance premium to the FDIC, which again raises the cost of funds. Finally, Euro CDs are dollar obligations that are payable by an entity operating under a foreign jurisdiction, exposing the holders to a risk (referred to as sovereign risk) that their claim may not be enforced by the foreign jurisdiction. As a result, a portion of the spread between the yield offered on Euro CDs and domestic CDs reflects what can be termed a sovereign risk premium. This premium varies with the degree of confidence in the international banking system.

CD yields are higher than yields on Treasury securities of the same maturity. The spread is due mainly to the credit risk that a CD investor is exposed to and the fact that CDs offer less liquidity. The spread due to credit risk will vary with both economic conditions and confidence in the banking system, increasing when there is a "flight to quality" (which means investors shift their funds in significant amounts to debt of high quality or little risk), or when there is a crisis in the banking system. Table 22-1 compares CD yields and Treasuries.

At one time, there were more than 30 dealers who made markets in CDs. The presence of that many dealers provided good liquidity to the market. Today, fewer dealers are interested in making markets in CDs, and the market can be characterized as an illiquid one.

| TABLE 22-1 | | | | | |
|---|---|---|---|---|---|
| AVERAGE YIELDS ON CDs AND TREASURY BILLS: 1987 – 1991 | | | | | |
| Year | 1987 | 1988 | 1989 | 1990 | 1991 |
| T-Bills | | | | | |
| 3-Month | 5.78 | 6.67 | 8.03 | 7.50 | 5.38 |
| 6-Month | 6.03 | 6.91 | 7.92 | 7.56 | 5.44 |
| CDs | | | | | |
| 3-Month | 6.87 | 7.73 | 9.08 | 8.15 | 5.83 |
| 6-Month | 7.01 | 7.91 | 9.09 | 8.17 | 5.91 |
| Euro CDs | | | | | |
| 3-Month | 7.06 | 7.85 | 9.16 | 8.16 | 5.86 |

*Note:* Yields on CDs are computed to reflect their interest-earning character; T-Bills are discount securities. Euro CD rate is that of Eurodollar deposit.

*Source: Federal Reserve Bulletin,* selected issues.

► KEY POINTS YOU SHOULD UNDERSTAND BEFORE PROCEEDING:

1. A negotiable CD allows the initial depositor (or any subsequent owner of the CD) to sell the CD in the open market prior to the maturity date.

2. CDs can be classified into four types, based on the issuing entity: domestic CD, Eurodollar CD, Yankee CD, and thrift CD.

3. The yield offered on a CD depends on the credit rating of the issuing bank, the maturity of the CD, and the supply and demand for CDs.

4. CD yields are higher than yields on Treasury securities of the same maturity.

## FEDERAL FUNDS

The rate determined in the federal funds market is the major factor that influences the rates paid on all the other money market instruments described in this chapter. As we explained in Chapter 4, depository institutions (commercial banks and thrifts) are required to maintain reserves. The reserves are deposits at their district Federal Reserve Bank, which are called *federal funds*. The level of the reserves that a bank must maintain is based on its average daily deposits over the previous 14 days. Of all depository institutions, commercial banks are by far the largest holders of federal funds.

No interest is earned on federal funds. Consequently, a depository institution that maintains federal funds in excess of the amount required incurs an opportunity cost—the loss of interest income that could be earned on the excess reserves. At the same time, there are depository institutions whose federal funds are less than the amount required. Typically, smaller banks have excess reserves, while money center banks find themselves short of reserves and must make up the shortfall. Banks maintain federal funds desks whose managers are responsible for the bank's federal funds position.

Most transactions involving fed funds last for only one night: that is, a bank with insufficient reserves that borrows excess reserves from another financial institution will typically do so for the period of one full day. Because these loans last for such a short time, fed funds is often referred to as "overnight money."

One way that banks with less than the required reserves can bring reserves to the required level is to enter into a repurchase agreement (or "repo," as described in Chapter 16) with a nonbank customer. The repo, which consists of the sale of a security and an agreement by the bank to repurchase it later, will provide funds for a short period of time, after which the bank buys back the security, as previously agreed. An alternative to the repo is for the bank to borrow federal funds from a bank that has excess reserves. The market in which federal funds are bought (borrowed) by banks that need these funds and sold (lent) by banks that have excess federal funds is called the federal funds market. The equilibrium interest rate, which is determined by the supply and demand for federal funds, is the federal funds rate.

### Federal Funds Rate

The federal funds rate and the repo rate are tied together because both are a means for a bank to borrow. The federal funds rate is higher because the lending of federal funds is done on an unsecured basis; this differs from the repo, where the lender has a security as collateral. The spread between the two rates varies depending on market conditions; typically the spread is around 25 basis points.

The rate most often cited for the fed funds market is known as the *effective fed funds rate*. The *Federal Reserve Bulletin* defines "the daily effective rate" as "a weighted average of rates on trades through N.Y. brokers." This weighting process, which takes the size of transactions into account, can be illustrated in an example. Suppose only two transactions took place on September 1, one for $50 million at 3.375% and another for $150 million at 3.625%. The simple arithmetic average of this day's rates would be (3.375% + 3.625%)/2 or 3.5%. By contrast, the transactions-weighted average for that day is (50/200)(3.375%) + (150/200)(3.625%), or 3.5625%. The weighted average exceeds the arithmetic average because the larger transaction occurred at the higher interest rate. Table 22-2 provides some recent fed funds rates.

As we explained in Chapter 6, the fed funds rate is frequently a significant operating target of the Federal Reserve Board's monetary policy. Through its open market operations that lower or raise the level of excess reserves in the banking system, the Fed will often change the fed funds rate as part of its effort to change the rate of activity in the country's economy. For this reason, the fed funds rate often shows a high level of volatility over short periods of time. Although this rate does generally tend to move in the direction of other money market rates, the fed funds rate often is the first of these rates to change, and frequently it changes more substantially than the other money market rates.

| TABLE 22-2 | | | | |
|---|---|---|---|---|
| AVERAGE YIELDS ON FED FUNDS: 1987 – 1991 | | | | |
| Year | 1987 | 1988 | 1989 | 1990 | 1991 |
| Fed Funds | 6.66 | 7.57 | 9.21 | 8.10 | 5.69 |

*Note:* The Fed Funds rate is the "effective rate" — see text. Yields are annualized figures.
*Source: Federal Reserve Bulletin*, selected issues.

## Market For Federal Funds

While the term of most federal funds transactions is overnight, there are longer-term transactions that range from one week to six months. Trading typically takes place directly between the buyer and seller—usually between a large bank and one of its correspondent banks. Some federal funds transactions require the use of a broker. The broker stays in constant touch with likely buyers and sellers of funds and arranges deals between them for a commission. Brokers provide another service to this market in (normally) unsecured loans because they often can give lenders credit analyses of borrowers if the lenders have not done business with them previously.[3]

Although the fed funds market is known to be very large, no precise numbers for the volume of activity are available. A good indicator of the level of trading in this market is a somewhat complicated Federal Reserve Board data series for all chartered banks in the U.S. That series records the end-of-month values of the sum of "federal funds, repurchase agreements (RPs), and other borrowing from nonbanks and net balances due to related foreign offices." In the *Federal Reserve Bulletin* of March 1992, the figure for this sum, as of December 1991, is $283 billion. A high percentage of that amount is due to fed funds. One estimate is that the daily level of fed funds averages around $130 billion a day.[4] The magnitude of these numbers provides one reason why this market and this borrowing arrangement are so important.

▶ KEY POINTS YOU SHOULD UNDERSTAND BEFORE PROCEEDING:

1. The rate determined in the federal funds market is the major factor that influences the rate paid on all other private money market instruments.

2. Commercial banks are by far the largest holders of federal funds, with most transactions involving fed funds lasting for only one night.

3. Borrowing in the federal funds market is an alternative to borrowing in the repo market.

4. The federal funds rate is higher than the repo rate because the lending of federal funds is done on an unsecured basis.

5. The effective fed funds rate is the rate most often cited for the fed funds market.

---

[3] Marvin Goodfriend, "Federal Funds," in *Instruments of the Money Market*, Federal Reserve Bank of Richmond, 1993.

[4] *Ibid.*

## BANKERS ACCEPTANCES

Simply put, a bankers acceptance is a vehicle created to facilitate commercial trade transactions. The instrument is called a bankers acceptance because a bank accepts the ultimate responsibility to repay a loan to its holder. The use of bankers acceptances to finance a commercial transaction is referred to as "acceptance financing."

The transactions in which bankers acceptances are created include (1) the importing of goods into the United States; (2) the exporting of goods from the United States to foreign entities; (3) the storing and shipping of goods between two foreign countries where neither the importer nor the exporter is a U.S. firm;[5] and (4) the storing and shipping of goods between two entities in the United States.

As of April 1992, the dollar amount of bankers acceptances outstanding was $39 billion.[6] Of this amount, $12 billion was created in transactions involving the importing of goods into the U.S. and $9 billion in the exporting of goods from the United States. The balance, $18 billion, mostly covers transactions involving the storing and shipping of goods between two foreign countries. Little use is made of acceptance financing by two parties within the United States. Unlike the commercial paper market, the bankers acceptance market has been shrinking since 1984, when it reached a peak of $78 billion.

Bankers acceptances are sold on a discounted basis just as Treasury bills and commercial paper. (See Chapter 16 for a discussion of discount securities.) The major investors in bankers acceptances are money market mutual funds and municipal entities.

### *Illustration of the Creation of a Bankers Acceptance*

The best way to explain the creation of a bankers acceptance is by an illustration.

Several entities are involved in our transaction:

- Car Imports Corporation of America ("Car Imports"), a firm in New Jersey that sells automobiles
- Germany Fast Autos Inc. ("GFA"), a manufacturer of automobiles in Germany
- First Hoboken Bank ("Hoboken Bank"), a commercial bank in Hoboken, New Jersey
- West Berlin National Bank ("Berlin Bank"), a bank in Germany
- High-Caliber Money Market Fund, a mutual fund in the United States that invests in money market instruments.

---

[5] Bankers acceptances created from these transactions are called third country acceptances.

[6] Board of Governors of the Federal Reserve System, *Federal Reserve Bulletin* (August 1992).

Car Imports and GFA are considering a commercial transaction. Car Imports wants to import 15 cars manufactured by GFA. GFA is concerned with the ability of Car Imports to make payment on the 15 cars when they are received.

Acceptance financing is suggested as a means for facilitating the transaction. Car Imports offers $300,000 for the 15 cars. The terms of the sale stipulate payment to be made to GFA 60 days after it ships the 15 cars to Car Imports. GFA determines whether it is willing to accept the $300,000. In considering the offering price, GFA must calculate the present value of the $300,000, because it will not be receiving payment until 60 days after shipment. Suppose that GFA agrees to these terms.

Car Imports arranges with its bank, Hoboken Bank, to issue a letter of credit. The letter of credit indicates that Hoboken Bank will make good on the payment of $300,000 that Car Imports must make to GFA 60 days after shipment. The letter of credit, or time draft, will be sent by Hoboken Bank to GFA's bank, Berlin Bank. Upon receipt of the letter of credit, Berlin Bank will notify GFA, which will then ship the 15 cars. After the cars are shipped, GFA presents the shipping documents to Berlin Bank and receives the present value of $300,000. GFA is now out of the picture.

Berlin Bank presents the time draft and the shipping documents to Hoboken Bank. The latter will then stamp "accepted" on the time draft. By doing so, Hoboken Bank has created a bankers acceptance. This means that Hoboken Bank agrees to pay the holder of the bankers acceptance $300,000 at the maturity date. Car Imports will receive the shipping documents so that it can procure the 15 cars once it signs a note or some other type of financing arrangement with Hoboken Bank.

At this point, the holder of the bankers acceptance is the Berlin Bank. It has two choices. It can continue to hold the bankers acceptance as an investment in its loan portfolio, or it can request that Hoboken Bank make a payment of the present value of $300,000. Let's assume that Berlin Bank requests payment of the present value of $300,000.

Now the holder of the bankers acceptance is Hoboken Bank. It has two choices: retain the bankers acceptance as an investment as part of its loan portfolio, or sell it to an investor. Suppose that Hoboken Bank chooses the latter, and that High-Caliber Money Market Fund is seeking a high-quality investment with the same maturity as that of the bankers acceptance. Hoboken Bank sells the bankers acceptance to the money market fund at the present value of $300,000. Rather than sell the instrument directly to an investor, Hoboken Bank could sell it to a dealer, who would then resell it to an investor such as a money market fund. In either case, at the maturity date, the money market fund presents the bankers acceptance to Hoboken Bank, receiving $300,000, which the bank in turn recovers from Car Imports.

## Accepting Banks

All four groups of banks that we described earlier in this chapter create bankers acceptances (that is, are accepting banks). The major money center banks that issue bankers acceptances are Bankers Trust, Bank of America, Chase Manhattan, Citibank, and Morgan Guaranty. They maintain their own sales forces to sell bankers acceptances rather than using the services of a dealer.

The larger regional banks such as Harris Trust and Pittsburgh National Bank are accepting banks. They will maintain their own sales forces to sell the bankers acceptances they create but will use dealers to unload those they cannot sell. Japanese city banks are now the major issuers of bankers acceptances. In April 1988, for example, there was approximately $32 billion of Japanese bankers acceptances outstanding, close to half of the total at that time.[7] Because they do not have the sales force to distribute the bankers acceptances they create directly to investors, Japanese accepting banks use the services of dealers.

The amount of bankers acceptances issued by Yankee banks is small. For example, First Boston Corporation estimates that in April 1988 the amount of foreign bankers acceptances outstanding (Japanese and Yankee) was $35 billion, and Japanese bankers acceptances outstanding represented $32 billion of that amount. Therefore, Yankee bankers acceptances outstanding totaled only $3 billion.

***Eligible Bankers Acceptance***.   An accepting bank that has decided to retain a bankers acceptance in its portfolio may be able to use it as collateral for a loan at the discount window of the Federal Reserve. The reason we say "may" is that, to be used as collateral, bankers acceptances must meet certain eligibility requirements established by the Federal Reserve. One requirement for eligibility is maturity, which with a few exceptions cannot exceed six months. While the other requirements for eligibility are too detailed to review here, the basic principle is simple.[8] The bankers acceptance should be financing a self-liquidating commercial transaction.

Eligibility is also important because the Federal Reserve imposes a reserve requirement on funds raised via bankers acceptances that are ineligible. Bankers acceptances sold by an accepting bank are potential liabilities of the bank, but no reserve requirements are imposed for eligible bankers acceptances. Consequently, most bankers acceptances satisfy the various eligibility criteria. Finally, the Federal Reserve also imposes a limit on the amount of eligible bankers acceptances that may be issued by a bank.[9]

***Rates Banks Charge on Acceptances***.   To calculate the rate to be charged the customer for issuing a bankers acceptance, the bank determines the rate for which it can sell its bankers acceptance in the open market. To this rate it adds

---

[7] *Handbook of Securities of the United States Government and Agencies* (New York: First Boston Corporation, 1988), p. 130. The largest issuer of Japanese bankers acceptances is Dai-Ichi Kangyo Bank.

[8] The eligibility requirements are described in Jean M. Hahr and William C. Melton, "Bankers' Acceptances," *Quarterly Review*, Federal Reserve Bank of New York, Summer 1981.

[9] It may not exceed 150% of a bank's capital and surplus.

a commission. It is here that competition from Japanese banks has significantly affected the bankers acceptance business. Japanese banks have been willing to accept lower commissions than U.S. banks. For a high-credit-rated customer, for example, a U.S. commercial bank may charge 25 to 30 basis points, while a Japanese bank may charge ten to 15 basis points.[10] In the case of ineligible bankers acceptances, a bank will add an amount to offset the cost of the reserve requirements imposed.

### Dealers

We mentioned that banks may sell their bankers acceptances directly to investors, or may sell all or part to dealers. When the bankers acceptance market was growing in the early 1980s, there were over 25 dealers. By 1989, the decline in the amount of bankers acceptances issued drove many one-time major dealers such as Salomon Brothers out of the business. Today, the major dealer is Merrill Lynch. Lehman Brothers is another dealer in bankers acceptances. The other key dealers are commercial banks such as Bankers Trust and Morgan Guaranty.

### Credit Risk

Investing in bankers acceptances exposes the investor to credit risk. This is the risk that neither the borrower nor the accepting bank will be able to pay the principal due at the maturity date. The market interest rates that acceptances offer investors reflect this risk, because BAs have higher yields than risk-free Treasury bills. Table 22-3 exhibits some recent rates. As detailed in Chapter 10, a yield may also include a premium for relative illiquidity. The BA yield has such a premium because its secondary market is far less developed than that of the T-bill. Hence, the spread between BA rates and T-bill rates in

| TABLE 22-3 | | | | | |
|---|---|---|---|---|---|
| AVERAGE YIELDS ON BANKERS ACCEPTANCES AND TREASURY BILLS: 1987 – 1991 | | | | | |
| Year | 1987 | 1988 | 1989 | 1990 | 1991 |
| T-Bills | | | | | |
| 3-Month | 5.78 | 6.67 | 8.03 | 7.50 | 5.38 |
| 6-Month | 6.03 | 6.91 | 7.92 | 7.56 | 5.44 |
| BAs | | | | | |
| 3-Month | 6.75 | 7.56 | 8.87 | 7.93 | 5.70 |
| 6-Month | 6.78 | 7.60 | 8.67 | 7.80 | 5.67 |

*Source: Federal Reserve Bulletin*, selected issues.

---

[10] Marcia Stigum, *The Money Market* (Homewood, IL: Dow Jones-Irwin, 1990), p. 1007.

the table represents a combined reward to investors for bearing the higher risk and relative illiquidity of the acceptance. As the table reveals, that spread is not constant over time. The change in the spread reveals shifting investor valuation of the risk and illiquidity differences between the assets.

▶ **KEY POINTS YOU SHOULD UNDERSTAND BEFORE PROCEEDING:**

1.  A bankers acceptance is a vehicle created to facilitate commercial trade transactions wherein a bank accepts the ultimate responsibility to repay a loan to its holder.
2.  Banks creating banker acceptances are money center banks, regional banks, Japanese banks, and Yankee banks.
3.  Eligible bankers acceptance held in a bank's portfolio may be used as collateral for a loan at the discount window of the Federal Reserve.
4.  A bank may sell its bankers acceptances directly to investors, or may sell all or part to dealers.
5.  The investor in a bankers acceptance is exposed to credit risk.

**SUMMARY**

Commercial banks raise funds in the same equity and debt markets that we described in earlier chapters of the book. In addition, they can issue special debt obligations: large-denomination CDs, federal funds, and bankers acceptances.

Certificates of deposit are issued by banks and thrifts to raise funds for financing their business activities. Unlike other bank deposits, these are negotiable in the secondary market. CDs can be classified into four types: domestic CDs, Eurodollar CDs (or Euro CDs), Yankee CDs, and thrift CDs. Japanese banks have become major issuers of Euro CDs. Unlike Treasury bills, commercial paper, and bankers acceptances, yields on domestic CDs are quoted on an interest-bearing basis. A floating-rate CD is one whose coupon interest rate changes periodically in accordance with a predetermined formula.

The federal funds market is the market where depository institutions borrow (buy) and sell (lend) excess reserves held in the form of deposits in a Federal Reserve bank. The federal funds rate, which is the rate at which all money market interest rates are anchored, is determined in this market. The federal funds rate is higher than the repo rate because borrowing done in the federal funds market is unsecured borrowing. The fed funds rate is often a target of the Fed's monetary policy, so it can exhibit a considerable amount of volatility or change in level over time.

A bankers acceptance is a vehicle created to facilitate commercial trade transactions, particularly international transactions. The name, bankers acceptance, arises because a bank accepts the responsibility to repay a loan to the holder of the vehicle created in a commercial transaction in case the debtor fails to perform. Bankers acceptances are sold on a discounted basis as are Treasury bills and commercial paper.

## GLOSSARY

**Acceptance financing:** The use of a bankers acceptance to finance a commercial transaction.

**Accepting bank:** A bank that creates a bankers acceptance.

**Bankers acceptance:** A vehicle created to facilitate commercial trade transactions.

**Certificate of deposit (CD):** A financial asset issued by a bank or thrift that indicates a specified sum of money has been deposited at the issuing depository institution.

**Effective fed funds rate:** The rate most often cited for the fed funds market.

**Eurodollar certificate of deposit:** A CD that is denominated in U.S. dollars but is issued outside the United States.

**Floating-rate certificate of deposit:** A CD whose interest rate changes periodically in accordance with a predetermined formula that indicates the spread above some index at which the rate will reset periodically.

**Japanese banks:** These banks include Japanese city banks, local banks, long-term credit banks, trust banks, and mutual banks.

**Money center bank:** A bank that raises most of its funds from the domestic and international money markets and relies less on depositors for funds.

**Negotiable certificate of deposit:** A CD that allows the initial depositor (or any subsequent owner of the CD) to sell the CD in the open market prior to the maturity date.

**Nonprime CD:** A CD issued by lower-rated domestic banks.

**Prime CD:** A CD issued by high-rated domestic banks.

**Regional bank:** A bank that relies primarily on deposits for its funding and makes less use of the money markets to obtain funds.

**Term certificate of deposit:** A CD issued with a maturity greater than one year.

**Thrift certificate of deposit:** A CD issued by savings and loan associations and savings banks.

**Yankee bank:** A foreign bank that has a U.S. branch.

**Yankee certificate of deposit:** A CD denominated in U.S. dollars and issued by a foreign bank with a branch in the United States.

## QUESTIONS

1. Explain the difference between a domestic U.S. bank and a Yankee Bank.

2. Explain what a negotiable certificate of deposit is.

3. What are the four types of negotiable CDs?

4. a. What is the chief reason that the yield on a six-month CD exceeds that on a six-month Treasury bill?

b.  Explain why a Euro CD should offer a higher yield than a domestic CD issued by the same bank for the same time to maturity.

5.  Explain how federal funds are related to the reserve requirements that the Federal Reserve places on commercial banks.

6.  How does a repurchase agreement that a bank might enter into with a securities dealer regarding a U.S. Treasury bill substitute for the borrowing of federal funds from another bank?

7.  Why are fed funds called "overnight money"?

8.  Explain whether the rate on an overnight repurchase agreement can be higher than the rate on overnight federal funds.

9.  What is the chief reason that the fed funds rate is an unusually volatile short-term interest rate?

10.  What are the four transactions whose financing can lead to the creation of bankers acceptances?

11.  Why is a bank that creates a BA called an "accepting bank"?

12.  Why is the "eligibility" of a bankers acceptance important?

13.  How does a bank determine the rate it will charge its customer for issuing a bankers acceptance?

CHAPTER TWENTY-THREE

# The Mortgage Market

## LEARNING OBJECTIVES

*After reading this chapter you will understand:*

- what a mortgage is.
- who the major originators of mortgages are.
- the mortgage origination process.
- the risks associated with the mortgage origination process.
- what the servicing of a mortgage involves.
- the fixed-rate, level-payment, fully amortized mortgage instrument (or traditional mortgage), and its cash flow characteristics.
- deficiencies of the traditional mortgage: mismatch and tilt problems.
- alternative mortgage instruments, their cash flow characteristics, and how they correct for the deficiencies of the traditional mortgage instrument.
- risks associated with investing in mortgages.
- the significance of prepayment risk.

The mortgage market is a collection of markets, which includes a primary (or origination) market, and a secondary market where mortgages trade. We look in this chapter at the market participants (mortgage originators and investors) and the risks they face. We also review the various types of mortgage instruments. We discuss the development of the current secondary mortgage market in the next chapter, when we explain the securitization of mortgage loans. We postpone the discussion because development of the secondary market is tied to development of the market for instruments backed by mortgage loans (that is, mortgage-backed securities).

## WHAT IS A MORTGAGE?

By definition, a mortgage is a pledge of property to secure payment of a debt. Typically, property refers to real estate, which is often in the form of a house; the debt is the loan given to the buyer of the house by a lender. Thus, a mortgage might be a pledge of a house to secure payment of a loan. If a homeowner (the *mortgagor*) fails to pay the lender (the *mortgagee*), the lender has the right to foreclose the loan and seize the property in order to ensure that it is repaid.

When the loan is based solely on the credit of the borrower and on the collateral for the mortgage, the mortgage is said to be a *conventional mortgage*. The lender also may take out mortgage insurance to provide a guarantee for the fulfillment of the borrower's obligations. There are three forms of mortgage insurance guaranteed by the U.S. government if the borrower can qualify: Federal Housing Administration (FHA), Veterans Administration (VA), and Farmers Home Administration (FmHA) insurance. There are also private mortgage insurers such as Mortgage Guaranty Insurance Company (owned by Northwestern Mutual) and PMI Mortgage Insurance Company (owned by Sears, Roebuck). The cost of mortgage insurance is paid to the guarantor by the mortgage originator but passed along to the borrower in the form of higher mortgage payments.

The types of real estate properties that can be mortgaged are divided into two broad categories: residential and nonresidential properties. The former category includes houses, condominiums, cooperatives, and apartments. Residential real estate can be subdivided into single-family (one- to four-family) structures and multifamily structures (apartment buildings in which more than four families reside). Nonresidential property includes commercial and farm properties.

## MORTGAGE ORIGINATION

The original lender is called the *mortgage originator*. The principal originators of residential mortgage loans are thrifts, commercial banks, and mortgage bankers. Other private mortgage originators are life insurance companies and, to a much lesser extent, pension funds. Table 23-1 shows residential mortgage originations by type of institution originating the loan.

Mortgage originators may generate income from mortgage activity in one or more ways. First, they typically charge an *origination fee*. This fee is expressed

## TABLE 23-1

TOTAL RESIDENTIAL MORTGAGE LOAN ORIGINATIONS, 1984–1990 ($ MILLIONS)

| | Thrifts | Commercial Banks | Mortgage Bankers | Life Insurance Companies | Pension Funds | Federal Credit Agencies | State & Local Credit Agencies | Total |
|---|---|---|---|---|---|---|---|---|
| 1984 | 124,085 | 45,406 | 48,032 | 2,292 | 32 | 5,630 | 5,804 | 231,281 |
| 1985 | 133,236 | 61,529 | 66,042 | 4,078 | 98 | 5,154 | 4,870 | 275,007 |
| 1986 | 229,950 | 115,789 | 138,800 | 7,537 | 123 | 4,415 | 8,308 | 504,922 |
| 1987 | 231,383 | 132,851 | 112,502 | 6,756 | 50 | 4,010 | 7,811 | 495,363 |
| 1988 | 209,422 | 108,783 | 89,833 | 7,063 | 166 | 4,013 | 2,444 | 421,724 |
| 1989 | 171,145 | 130,862 | 70,049 | 4,229 | 153 | 3,888 | 2,745 | 383,171 |
| 1990 | 147,509 | 160,325 | 166,689 | 2,778 | 122 | 4,539 | 2,796 | 484,758 |

*Note:* Residential mortgage loans include loans for the following types of property: conventional one-to-four family, conventional multifamily, FHA/VA one-to-four family, and FHA multifamily. Original source is the U.S. Department of Housing and Urban Development, Survey of Mortgage Lending Activity. Mortgage origination data beginning with the first quarter of 1990 are not comparable to previous data because of a change in HUD's survey methodology, the effect of which is to capture greater origination activity by mortgage bankers.

*Source: Secondary Mortgage Markets* (Summer 1991) by permission of Freddie Mac. All rights reserved.

in terms of points, where each point represents 1% of the borrowed funds. For example, an origination fee of two points on a $100,000 mortgage loan is $2,000. Originators also may charge application fees and certain processing fees. The second source of revenue is the profit that might be generated from selling a mortgage at a higher price than it originally cost. This profit is called *secondary market profit.* If mortgage rates rise, an originator will realize a loss when the mortgages are sold in the secondary market.

While technically the sources of revenue attributable to the origination function are origination fees and secondary marketing profits, there are two other potential sources. First, mortgage originators may service the mortgages they originate, for which they obtain a *servicing fee.* Servicing of the mortgage involves collecting monthly payments from mortgagors and forwarding proceeds to owners of the loan, sending payment notices to mortgagors, reminding mortgagors when payments are overdue, maintaining records of mortgage balances, furnishing tax information to mortgagors, administering an escrow account for real estate taxes and insurance purposes, and, if necessary, initiating foreclosure proceedings. The servicing fee is a fixed percentage of the outstanding mortgage balance, typically 50 basis points to 100 basis points per year. The mortgage originator may sell the servicing of the mortgage to another party who would then receive the servicing fee. Second, the mortgage originator may hold the mortgage in its investment portfolio.

Historically, regulatory and tax considerations have encouraged thrifts to invest in mortgages, and, until quite recently, they tried to keep mortgages in their portfolios. Lately, however, both because they have become more conscious of the problem of mismatching maturities (their liabilities being short-term and mortgage loans being long-term), and because the tax benefits have been reduced by the 1986 tax act, banks and thrifts have tended to sell a good portion of what they originate and to become increasingly dependent on the fees generated from originating and servicing mortgages.

*Mortgage banking* refers to the activity of originating mortgages. As explained above, banks and thrifts undertake mortgage banking. However, there are companies not associated with a bank or thrift that are involved in mortgage banking. These mortgage bankers, unlike banks and thrifts, typically do not invest in the mortgages that they originate. Instead, they derive their income from the origination fees. Commercial banks derive their income from all three sources, but there are no regulatory benefits to them from investing in mortgages or mortgage-backed securities.

## The Mortgage Origination Process

Someone who wants to borrow funds to purchase a home will apply for a loan from a mortgage originator. The potential homeowner completes an application form, which provides financial information about the applicant, and pays an application fee; then the mortgage originator performs a credit evaluation of the applicant. The two primary factors in determining whether the funds will be lent are the (1) *payment-to-income* (PTI) ratio, and (2) the *loan-to-value* (LTV) ratio. The first is the ratio of monthly payments to monthly income, which measures the ability of the applicant to make monthly payments (both mortgage and real estate tax payments). The lower this ratio, the greater the likelihood that the applicant will be able to meet the required payments.

The difference between the purchase price of the property and the amount borrowed is the borrower's down payment. The LTV is the ratio of the amount of the loan to the market (or appraised) value of the property. The lower this ratio, the greater the protection for the lender if the applicant defaults on the payments and the lender must repossess and sell the property. For example, if an applicant wants to borrow $150,000 on property with an appraised value of $200,000, the LTV is 75%. Suppose the applicant subsequently defaults on the mortgage. The lender can then repossess the property and sell it to recover the amount owed. But the amount that will be received by the lender depends on the market value of the property. In our example, even if conditions in the housing market are weak, the lender will still be able to recover the proceeds lent, if the value of the property declines by $50,000. Suppose, instead, that the applicant wanted to borrow $180,000 for the same property. The LTV would then be 90%. If the lender had to sell the property because the applicant defaults, there is less protection for the lender.

If the lender decides to lend the funds, it sends a *commitment letter* to the applicant. This letter commits the lender to provide funds to the applicant. The length of time of the commitment varies between 30 and 60 days. At the time of the commitment letter, the lender will require that the applicant pay a commitment fee. It is important to understand that the commitment letter obligates the lender—not the applicant—to perform. The commitment fee that the applicant pays is lost if the applicant decides not to purchase the property or uses an alternative source of funds to purchase the property. Thus, the commitment letter states that, for a fee, the applicant has the right but not the obligation to require the lender to provide funds at a certain interest rate and on certain terms.

At the time the application is submitted, the mortgage originator will give the applicant a choice among various types of mortgages. Basically, the choice is between a *fixed-rate mortgage* or an *adjustable-rate mortgage*. In the case of a fixed-rate mortgage, the lender typically gives the applicant a choice as to when the interest rate on the mortgage will be determined. The three choices may be: (1) at the time the loan application is submitted; (2) at the time a commitment letter is issued to the borrower; or (3) at the closing date (the date that the property is purchased).

These choices granted the applicant—the right to decide whether to close on the property and the right to select when to set the interest rate—expose the mortgage originator to certain risks, which the originator will protect itself against.

Mortgage originators can either (1) hold the mortgage in their portfolio; (2) sell the mortgage to an investor that wishes to hold the mortgage in its portfolio or that will place the mortgage in a pool of mortgages to be used as collateral for the issuance of a security; or (3) use the mortgage themselves as collateral for the issuance of a security. When a mortgage is used as collateral for the issuance of a security, the mortgage is said to be *securitized*. We discussed the process of securitizing loans in Chapter 4. In the next chapter, we will discuss the securitization of mortgage loans.

When a mortgage originator intends to sell the mortgage, it will obtain a commitment from the potential investor (buyer). Two federally sponsored agencies and several private companies buy mortgages. As these agencies and private companies pool these mortgages and sell them to investors, they are called *conduits*.

Two agencies, the Federal Home Loan Mortgage Corporation and the Federal National Mortgage Association, purchase only *conforming mortgages*—that is, a mortgage loan that meets the agency underwriting standards to be included in a pool of mortgages underlying a security that they guarantee. Three underwriting standards established by these agencies in order to qualify as a conforming mortgage are (1) a maximum PTI; (2) a maximum LTV; and (3) a maximum loan amount. If an applicant does not satisfy the underwriting standards, the mortgage is called a *nonconforming mortgage*.[1] The mortgages acquired by the agency may be held as a portfolio investment or securitized.

Examples of private conduits are Citimae, Inc. (a subsidiary of Citicorp), Bear Stearns Mortgage Capital Corporation, Residential Funding Corpora-

---

[1] Loans that exceed the maximum loan amount and therefore do not qualify as conforming mortgages are called jumbo loans.

tion (a subsidiary of General Motors Acceptance Corporation), FBS Mortgage Corporation (a subsidiary of First Boston), and Sears Mortgage Securities Corporation. Both conforming and nonconforming mortgages are purchased.

Nonconforming mortgages do not necessarily have greater credit risk. For example, an individual with an annual income of $500,000 may apply for a mortgage loan of $200,000 on real estate that she wants to purchase for $1 million. This would be a nonconforming mortgage because the amount of the mortgage exceeds the limit currently established for a conforming mortgage, yet the individual's income can easily accommodate the monthly mortgage payments. Moreover, the lender's risk exposure is minimal, as it has lent $200,000 backed by collateral of $1 million.

The mortgage rate that the originator will set on the loan will depend on the mortgage rate required by the investor who plans to purchase the mortgage. At any time, there are different mortgage rates for delivery at different future times (30 days, 60 days, or 90 days).

## The Risks Associated with Mortgage Origination

The loan applications being processed and the commitments made by a mortgage originator together are called its *pipeline*. *Pipeline risk* refers to the risks associated with originating mortgages. This risk has two components: *price risk* and *fallout risk*.

Price risk refers to the adverse effects on the value of the pipeline if mortgage rates rise. If mortgage rates rise, and the mortgage originator has made commitments at a lower mortgage rate, it will either have to sell the mortgages when they close at a value below the funds lent to homeowners, or retain the mortgages as a portfolio investment earning a below-market mortgage rate. The mortgage originator faces the same risk for mortgage applications in the pipeline where the applicant has elected to fix the rate at the time the application is submitted.

Fallout risk is the risk that applicants or those who were issued commitment letters will not close (complete the transaction by purchasing the property with funds borrowed from the mortgage originator). The chief reason that potential borrowers may cancel their commitment or withdraw their mortgage application is that mortgage rates have declined sufficiently so that it is economic to seek an alternative source of funds. Fallout risk is the result of the mortgage originator giving the potential borrower the right but not the obligation to close (that is, the right to cancel the agreement). There are reasons other than a decline in mortgage rates that may cause a potential borrower to fall out of the pipeline. There may be an unfavorable property inspection report, or the purchase could have been predicated on a change in employment that does not occur.

Mortgage originators have several alternatives to protect themselves against pipeline risk. To protect against price risk, the originator could get a commitment from the agency or the private conduit to whom the mortgage originator plans to sell the mortgage.[2] This sort of commitment is effectively a forward contract, a contract that we will describe in Chapter 25. The mortgage originator agrees to deliver a mortgage at a future date, and another party (either one of the agencies or a private conduit) agrees to buy the mortgage at that time at a predetermined price (or mortgage rate).

Consider what happens, however, if mortgage rates decline, and potential borrowers elect to cancel the agreement. The mortgage originator has agreed to deliver a mortgage with a specified mortgage rate. If the potential borrower does not close, and the mortgage originator has made a commitment to deliver the mortgage to an agency or private conduit, the mortgage originator cannot back out of the transaction. As a result, the mortgage originator will realize a loss—it must deliver a mortgage at a higher mortgage rate in a lower mortgage rate environment. This is fallout risk.

Mortgage originators can protect themselves against fallout risk by entering into an agreement with an agency or private conduit for optional rather than mandatory delivery of the mortgage. In such an agreement, the mortgage originator is effectively buying an option that gives it the right, but not the obligation, to deliver a mortgage. The agency or private conduit has sold that option to the mortgage originator and therefore charges a fee for allowing optional delivery.

▶ <u>KEY POINTS THAT YOU SHOULD UNDERSTAND BEFORE PROCEEDING</u>:

1. The mortgage originator is the original lender of mortgage funds, and the activity of originating mortgages is called mortgage banking.
2. The principal originators of residential mortgage loans are thrifts, commercial banks, and mortgage bankers.
3. Mortgage originators may generate income from origination fees, secondary market profit, servicing fees, and investment income from holding the mortgages.
4. The two primary factors in determining whether funds will be lent to a mortgage loan applicant are the payment-to-income ratio and the loan-to-value ratio.
5. Two federally sponsored agencies and several private companies buy mortgages for purposes of pooling them and selling them to investors.
6. Pipeline risk is the risk associated with mortgage origination; it is made up of price risk and fallout risk.

---

[2] This commitment that the mortgage originator obtains to protect itself should not be confused with the commitment that the mortgage originator gives to the potential borrower.

## TYPES OF MORTGAGE DESIGNS

■ ■ ■ ■

Between the mid-1930s and the early 1970s, only one type of mortgage loan was available in the United States: the fixed-rate, level-payment, fully amortized mortgage. The deficiencies of this mortgage design, commonly referred to as the *traditional mortgage*, led to the introduction of new mortgage designs.

### Fixed-Rate, Level-Payment, Fully Amortized Mortgages

The basic idea behind the design of the traditional mortgage is that the borrower pays interest and repays principal in equal installments over an agreed-upon period of time, called the maturity or term of the mortgage. Thus at the end of the term, the loan has been fully amortized—there is no mortgage balance remaining. The interest rate is generally above the risk-free rate because of servicing costs, default risk that is present despite the collateral, and some further risks discussed below. The frequency of payment is typically monthly, and the prevailing term of the mortgage is 15 to 30 years.

***Cash Flow Characteristics of the Traditional Mortgage.*** Each monthly mortgage payment for a level-payment fixed-rate mortgage is due on the first of each month and consists of:

1.  Interest of 1/12th of the fixed annual interest rate times the amount of the outstanding mortgage balance at the beginning of the previous month, and
2.  A repayment of a portion of the outstanding mortgage balance (principal).

The difference between the monthly mortgage payment and the portion of the payment that represents interest equals the amount that is applied to reduce the outstanding mortgage balance. The monthly mortgage payment is designed so that after the last scheduled monthly payment of the loan is made, the amount of the outstanding mortgage balance is zero (that is, the mortgage is fully repaid).

As an illustration of a level-payment fixed-rate mortgage, consider a 30-year (360-month), $100,000 mortgage with a 9.5% mortgage rate. The monthly mortgage payment would be $840.85. Table 23-2 shows for selected months how each monthly mortgage payment is divided between interest and repayment of principal. At the beginning of Month 1, the mortgage balance is $100,000, the amount of the original loan. The mortgage payment for Month 1 includes interest on the $100,000 borrowed for the month. As the interest rate is 9.5%, the monthly interest rate is 0.0079167 (0.095 divided by 12). Interest for Month 1 is therefore $791.67 ($100,000 times 0.0079167). The $49.18 difference between the monthly mortgage payment of $840.85 and the interest of $791.67 is the portion of the monthly mortgage payment that represents repayment of principal. This $49.18 in Month 1 reduces the mortgage balance.

## TABLE 23-2

### AMORTIZATION SCHEDULE FOR A LEVEL-PAYMENT, FIXED-RATE MORTGAGE

MORTGAGE LOAN: $100,000
MORTGAGE RATE: 9.5%
MONTHLY PAYMENT: $840.85
TERM OF LOAN: 30 YEARS (360 MONTHS)

| Month | Beginning Mortgage Balance | Monthly Mortgage Payment | Interest for Month | Principal Repayment | Ending Mortgage Balance |
|---|---|---|---|---|---|
| 1 | $100,000.00 | $840.85 | $791.67 | $49.19 | $99,950.81 |
| 2 | 99,950.81 | 840.85 | 791.28 | 49.58 | 99,901.24 |
| 3 | 99,901.24 | 840.85 | 790.88 | 49.97 | 99,851,27 |
| 4 | 99,851.27 | 840.85 | 790.49 | 50.37 | 99,800.90 |
| 5 | 99,800.90 | 840.85 | 790.09 | 50.76 | 99,750.14 |
| 6 | 99,750.14 | 840.85 | 789.69 | 51.17 | 99,698.97 |
| 7 | 99,698.97 | 840.85 | 789.28 | 51.57 | 99,647.40 |
| 8 | 99,647.40 | 840.85 | 788.88 | 51.98 | 99,596.42 |
| 9 | 99,595.42 | 840.85 | 788.45 | 52.39 | 99,543.03 |
| 10 | 99,543.03 | 840.85 | 788.05 | 52.81 | 99,490.23 |
| . . . | . . . | . . . | . . . | . . . | . . . |
| . . . | . . . | . . . | . . . | . . . | . . . |
| . . . | . . . | . . . | . . . | . . . | . . . |
| 98 | 99,862.54 | 840.85 | 735.16 | 105.69 | 92,756.85 |
| 99 | 92,756.85 | 840.85 | 734.33 | 106.53 | 92,650.32 |
| 100 | 92,640.32 | 840.85 | 733.48 | 107.37 | 92,542.95 |
| 101 | 92,542.95 | 840.85 | 732.63 | 108.22 | 92,434.72 |
| 102 | 92,434.72 | 840.85 | 731.77 | 109.08 | 92,325.64 |
| 103 | 92,325.64 | 840.85 | 730.91 | 109.94 | 92,215.70 |
| 104 | 92,215.70 | 840.85 | 730.04 | 110.81 | 92,104.89 |
| 105 | 92,104.89 | 840.85 | 729.16 | 111.69 | 91,993.20 |
| 106 | 91,993.20 | 840.85 | 728.28 | 112.57 | 91,880.62 |
| . . . | . . . | . . . | . . . | . . . | . . . |
| . . . | . . . | . . . | . . . | . . . | . . . |
| . . . | . . . | . . . | . . . | . . . | . . . |
| 209 | 74,177.40 | 840.85 | 587.24 | 253.62 | 73,923.78 |
| 210 | 73,923.78 | 840.85 | 585.23 | 255.62 | 73,668.16 |
| 211 | 73,668.16 | 840.85 | 583.21 | 257.65 | 73,410.51 |
| 212 | 73,410.51 | 840.85 | 581.17 | 259.69 | 73,150.82 |
| . . . | . . . | . . . | . . . | . . . | . . . |
| . . . | . . . | . . . | . . . | . . . | . . . |
| . . . | . . . | . . . | . . . | . . . | . . . |
| 354 | 5,703.93 | 840.85 | 45.16 | 795.70 | 4,908.23 |
| 355 | 4,908.23 | 840.85 | 38.86 | 802.00 | 4,106.24 |
| 356 | 4,106.24 | 840.85 | 35.21 | 808.35 | 3,297.89 |
| 357 | 3,297.89 | 840.85 | 26.11 | 814.75 | 2,483.14 |
| 358 | 2,483.14 | 840.85 | 19.66 | 821.20 | 1,661.95 |
| 359 | 1,661.95 | 840.85 | 13.16 | 827.70 | 834.25 |
| 360 | 834.25 | 840.85 | 6.60 | 834.26 | 0.00 |

The mortgage balance at the end of Month 1 (beginning of Month 2) is then $99,950.81 ($100,000 minus $49.19).[3] The interest for the second monthly mortgage payment is $791.28, which equals the monthly interest rate (0.0079167) times the mortgage balance at the beginning of Month 2 ($99,950.81). The difference between the $840.85 monthly mortgage payment and the $791.28 interest is $49.57, representing the amount of the mortgage balance paid off with that monthly mortgage payment. Notice that the last monthly mortgage payment is sufficient to pay off the remaining mortgage balance. When a loan repayment schedule is structured in this way, so that the payments made by the borrower will completely pay off the interest and principal, the loan is said to be self-amortizing. Table 23-2 is referred to as an amortization schedule.

As Table 23-2 clearly shows, the portion of the monthly mortgage payment applied to interest declines each month, and the portion applied to reducing the mortgage balance increases. The reason for this is that, as the mortgage balance is reduced with each monthly mortgage payment, the interest on the mortgage balance declines. Because the monthly mortgage payment is fixed, a larger part of the monthly payment is applied to reduce the principal in each subsequent month.

***Deficiencies of the Traditional Mortgage.*** There are problems with the traditional mortgage design. In the presence of high and variable inflation, this mortgage design suffers from two basic and serious shortcomings: the *mismatch problem* and the *tilt problem.*

Savings and loan associations have faced the mismatch problem during most of the post-World War II period, because mortgages—a very long-term asset—have been financed largely by depository institutions that obtain their funds through deposits that are primarily, if not entirely, of a short-term nature. These institutions have engaged inevitably in a highly speculative activity: borrowing short and lending very long. That is, there is a mismatch of the maturity of the assets (mortgages) and the liabilities raised to fund those assets. Speculation of this sort will prove a losing proposition if interest rates rise, as is bound to happen in the presence of significant inflation. The institution may be earning the contractual rate, but to attract the deposits needed to finance the loan, it will have to pay the current higher market rate. Considering that the intermediation margin or spread is modest—some 100 to 200 basis points—it will not take much inflation or rise in interest rates before an institution runs into a loss.

Another way to describe the mismatch problem is in terms of the balance sheet rather than the income statement. The difference between lending and borrowing rates will cause the lending institution to become technically insolvent, in the sense that the market value of its assets will be insufficient to cover its liabilities. The reason for this is that the institution's liabilities are related to the face value of its mortgage assets, but the market value of these assets

---

[3] Because Table 23-2 is computer generated, rounding results in slightly different values in the table.

will be below the face value of the mortgage loan. For these reasons, both losses and technical insolvencies have occurred on a large scale since the late 1960s, especially in the 1970s and early 1980s.

One obvious way to resolve this problem is for the institution that primarily finances fixed-rate mortgages to lengthen its liabilities through term deposits or analogous instruments. Actually, this has been done in recent years, but only to a modest extent. In fact, it is doubtful that this approach could go very far in meeting the problem, for what has made S&Ls so popular is unquestionably the highly liquid, riskless nature of their deposits. If they were allowed to finance mortgages only by long-term deposits, we might expect a substantial decline in the volume of funds available to them for mortgage financing. A second alternative is to design a different sort of mortgage.

The tilt problem refers to what happens to the real burden of mortgage payments over the life of the mortgage as a result of inflation. If the general price level rises, the real value of the mortgage payments will decline over time. If a homeowner's real income rises over time, this coupled with a decline in the real value of the mortgage payments will mean that the burden of the mortgage payments will decline over time. Thus, the mortgage obligation represents a greater burden in real terms for the homeowner in the initial years. In other words, the real burden is "tilted" to the initial years. This discourages people purchasing a home in their early earning years. The tilt problem is behind the development of other types of mortgage instruments.

## Adjustable-Rate Mortgages

One way to resolve the mismatch problem is to redesign the traditional mortgage so as to produce an asset whose return would match the short-term market rates, thus better matching the cost of the liabilities. One instrument that satisfies these requirements, and that has won considerable popularity, is the so-called *adjustable-rate mortgage*.

***Characteristics of the Adjustable-Rate Mortgage.*** The adjustable-rate mortgage (ARM) calls for resetting the interest rate periodically, in accordance with some appropriately chosen index reflecting short-term market rates. This mortgage represents an approach applied to many other instruments, such as bank loans, especially in the Eurodollar market. By using a short-term rate as the index, S&Ls are able to improve the matching of their returns to their cost of funds. An instrument earning the market rate could be expected to remain close to par whether interest rates rise or fall, thus avoiding the problems of technical insolvency that have plagued the S&Ls relying on the traditional mortgage. Note also that, with high and variable rates of inflation, an adjustable-rate, in principle, reduces risk for the borrower—reduced inflation generally is accompanied by a fall in interest rates, which will benefit borrowers with an adjustable-rate contract.

The adjustable-rate contracts currently popular in the U.S. call for resetting the interest rate either every month, six months, year, two years, or three years. The interest rate at the reset date is equal to a benchmark index plus a spread. The spread is between 100 and 200 basis points.

The two most popular indexes are the one-year Treasury rate and the 11th District Cost of Funds. The latter index is a calculation based on the monthly weighted average interest cost for liabilities of thrifts in the 11th Federal Home Loan Bank Board District.[4] This district includes the states of California, Arizona, and Nevada.

ARMs have been popular with lenders because they shift interest rate risk from the lender to the borrower. To be sure, the risk resulting from falling rates tends to be shifted from the borrower to the lender, but then this risk is born by the lenders anyway, at least in part, because of the borrower's prepayment option. Thrifts accordingly prefer to hold ARMs in their portfolios rather than fixed-rate mortgages such as the traditional mortgage, because ARMs provide a better matching with their liabilities. As liabilities are closely tied to the calculated cost of funds index, thrifts prefer ARMs benchmarked to the 11th District Cost of Funds.

The basic ARM is one that resets periodically and has no other terms that affect the monthly mortgage payment.[5] Typically, the mortgage rate is affected by other terms. These include: (1) periodic caps, and (2) lifetime rate caps and floors. Periodic caps limit the amount that the interest rate may increase or decrease at the reset date. The periodic rate cap is expressed in percentage points. Most ARMs have an upper limit on the mortgage rate that can be charged over the life of the loan. This lifetime loan cap is expressed in terms of the initial rate; the most common lifetime cap is 5% to 6%. For example, if the initial mortgage rate is 7% and the lifetime cap is 5%, the maximum interest rate that the lender can charge over the life of the loan is 12%. Many ARMs also have a lower limit (floor) on the interest rate that can be charged over the life of the loan.

***Balloon/Reset Mortgages.*** Another type of adjustable-rate mortgages is: the *balloon/reset mortgage*. The primary difference between a balloon/reset mortgage design and the basic ARM is that the mortgage rate is reset less frequently.

While new to the U.S. mortgage market, the balloon/reset mortgage has long been used in Canada, where it is referred to as a *rollover mortgage*. In this mortgage design, the borrower is given long-term financing by the lender but at specified future dates the contract rate is renegotiated. Thus, the lender is providing long-term funds for what is effectively a short-term borrowing, how short depending on the frequency of the renegotiation period. Effectively, it is a short-term balloon loan in which the lender agrees to provide financing for the remainder of the term of the mortgage. The balloon payment is the original amount borrowed less the amount amortized.

---

[4] The cost of funds is calculated by first computing the monthly interest expenses for all thrifts included in the 11th District. The interest expenses are summed and then divided by the average of the beginning and ending monthly balance.

[5] There are ARMs that can be converted into fixed-rate mortgages called *convertible ARMs*.

The Federal Home Loan Bank Board attempted to introduce this mortgage design in January 1980, when it proposed a prototype rollover mortgage design. The prototype called for the contract rate to be renegotiated every three to five years (with the specific time period determined at the time the mortgage is originated), with a maximum contract rate change of 50 basis points for each year in the renegotiation period (for example, 150 basis points if renegotiated every three years and 250 basis points if every five years), and the lender guaranteeing to provide new financing. There were several proposals as to how the new contract rate should be determined.

While the rollover mortgage was hailed as an important step in alleviating the mismatch problem that thrifts face, it did not catch on until 1990. Now called *balloon/reset mortgages*, or simply *balloon mortgages*, these mortgages are the focal points of purchase programs of two government-sponsored entities, Fannie Mae and Freddie Mac. Freddie Mac's 30-year balloon/resets, for example, can have either a renegotiation period of five years ("30-due-in-5" FRMs) or seven years ("30-due-in-7" FRMs). If certain conditions are met, Freddie Mac guarantees the extension of the loan. The contract rate set by Freddie Mac is based on its 30-year, single-family, fixed-rate 60-day delivery mortgage rate. If the borrower elects to extend the mortgage, a $250 processing fee is charged.

***Assessment of Adjustable-Rate Mortgages.***   On the whole, the adjustable-rate mortgage and its variants have the merit of providing a manageable solution to the problem of the mismatch of maturities. To borrowers, these mortgages reduce the risk associated with uncertain inflation. Unfortunately, the merits of the ARM have been significantly impaired by arbitrary and misguided regulatory rules, particularly interest rate caps. These caps, meant to protect the borrower, might make sense if rates were set unilaterally by the lender, but they do not make sense when they are tied to an objective market rate, or to the cost of funds to the lending institution. Furthermore, we know that an increase in nominal rates tends to occur when there is an appreciable rise in inflation, in which case the borrower, in general, can afford to pay the higher interest rate while it lasts.

The main effect of caps is to increase the risk of inflation to intermediary lenders who have no way of putting a cap on the rate they have to pay. Nor is a lower cap adequate compensation, because borrowers have the right to repay. Of course, some of the expected loss will tend to be recouped by a higher spread, and thus finally unloaded on some borrowers; even so, it would be best to leave the matter of caps to private bargaining.

Unfortunately, regulators have still not grasped these simple principles. Nor have they understood that in many cases the consumer generally pays for "consumer protection" in the form of higher rates or other less favorable terms. Finally, the adjustable-rate mortgage is not a satisfactory answer to inflation-swollen interest rates because it does not address the tilt problem. And the tilt problem remains in effect because, in these mortgages, the payments are still based on a nominal rather than a real interest rate.

## Other Mortgage Designs

The traditional mortgage was designed so that the borrower would repay the debt in constant nominal installments. This form of repayment would seem highly desirable from the debtor's point of view, so long as inflation is zero or small, because a level nominal repayment rate in that case implies a level real rate of repayment. But when there is significant inflation, the traditional mortgage turns into a malfunctioning, very undesirable vehicle for home financing. The reason is not, as frequently supposed, that inflation increases interest rates. To be sure, with a 10% rate of inflation we would expect nominal interest rates to rise by roughly 10 percentage points—say, from 5% to 15%. But this rise does not, per se, make the lender any better off or the borrower any worse off, as the increase is offset by inflation losses and gains, leaving the real rate largely unchanged. The higher interest rate is, by and large, compensated for by the erosion of the principal in terms of purchasing power. (In nominal terms, the higher rate is offset by the rise in the value of the property.)

Rather, the reason for the unsatisfactory performance of the traditional mortgage lies in the "tilt" effect: with 10% steady inflation, if the nominal payment is level, then the real payment will decrease at 10% per year. By the twentieth year, it will be down to some 15% of the initial installment payment. If the creditor is to receive the same real amount as in the absence of inflation, the gradual erosion of the repayments in terms of purchasing power will have to be made up by sufficiently high initial real (and hence nominal) payments. Indeed, with the interest rate rising from 5% to 15%, the first payment on a long-term mortgage will rise roughly threefold.

The nature of the distortion or tilt in the real payment path is illustrated in Figure 23-1 for different rates of inflation. Notice that, for an 8% rate of inflation, the path starts at more than twice the no-inflation level, to terminate at well below half. The high initial payment caused by inflation has the effect of foreclosing home ownership to large segments of the population, or forcing buyers to scale down their demands. Indeed, not many people would be able to pay a multiple of what they were paying in the preinflation period for the same home. This is especially true in the case of young people who have little asset accumulation.

The first thing to note about this problem is that it is not addressed by the adjustable-rate mortgage. That mortgage uses throughout a nominal interest rate comparable to the fixed-rate mortgage. In particular, the critical early payment will be roughly as high as with a traditional mortgage. Actually, one can show that the adjustable rate is, in some ways, even worse for borrowers than the traditional mortgage. It starts with a rate as high as the traditional mortgage independently of inflation, and will make a substantial jump every time the interest rate is adjusted and the payment shifts from one nominal level to another—even though the rate of payment is level as long as the interest rate does not change.

Can the tilt problem be remedied? It is clear that in principle a solution must involve reducing the interest rate used in the early payments and recouping later. Three mortgage designs (with many variants) have been offered

FIGURE 23-1

NATURE OF TILT PROBLEM: REAL VALUE OF
MONTHLY PAYMENTS
*Source:* D. Tucker, "The Variable-Rate Graduated Payment
Mortgage," *Real Estate Review* (Spring 1975), p. 72.

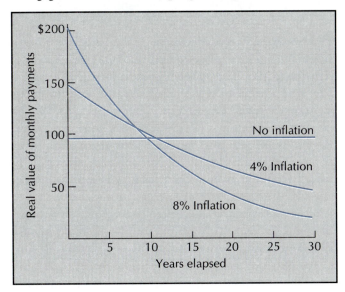

to solve the tilt problem: the *graduated-payment mortgage*, the *price-level-adjusted mortgage*, and the *dual-rate mortgage*.

***Graduated-Payment Mortgage.*** A graduated-payment mortgage (GPM) is one whose nominal monthly payment grows at a constant rate during a portion of the life of the contract, thereafter leveling off. The mortgage rate is fixed for the life of the loan, despite the fact that the monthly mortgage payment gradually increases. The terms of a GPM plan include (1) the mortgage rate; (2) the term of the mortgage; (3) the number of years over which the monthly mortgage payment will increase (and when the level payments will begin); and (4) the annual percent increase in the mortgage payments. The most popular 30-year GPM plan that qualifies for FHA insurance calls for monthly payments that increase by 7.5% for five years, then at the beginning of the sixth year remain constant for the remaining 25 years. The monthly mortgage payments under this GPM program for a $100,000, 30-year, 10% mortgage would be: (1) $667.04 per month in the first year; (2) $717.06 per month in the second year; (3) $770.84 in the third year; (4) $828.66 in the fourth year; (5) $890.80 in the fifth year; and (6) $957.62 for the remaining term of the mortgage, beginning with the sixth year.

Because this mortgage design involves a fixed rate over the life of the loan, while the rate of inflation may be highly variable over the same period, the GPM is not likely to succeed in assuring the debtor anything approaching a level real repayment stream. Thus, it does not solve the tilt problem. It should be apparent that it cannot solve the mismatching problem. These shortcomings have probably contributed to the decreasing popularity of GPMs in recent years. In fact, the only two basic mortgage designs that can provide a more or less foolproof solution to both problems are the price-level-adjusted mortgage and the dual-rate mortgage.

***Price-Level-Adjusted Mortgage.***    This mortgage design is similar to the traditional mortgage except that monthly payments are designed to be level in purchasing power terms rather than in nominal terms, and that the fixed rate is the "real" rather than the nominal rate.[6] To compute the monthly payment under a price-level-adjusted mortgage (PLAM), the terms of the contract must be specified, namely: (1) the real interest rate; (2) the term of the loan; and (3) the index to be used to measure the price level, usually the Consumer Price Index (CPI). On the basis of an ordinary mortgage table, the annual payment and the unpaid balance at the end of each year, corresponding to the stipulated real interest and maturity, can then be computed. These figures represent payments and balances in real terms. To compute the payments actually due in each year, we simply multiply the real payment by an inflation correction factor equal to the ratio of the stipulated index in the last year to the value of the index in the initial year. Similarly, to compute the actual debt, we multiply the real debt by the inflation correction factor.[7]

The PLAM is not a new concept; it has been used for decades in many countries with high inflation, where the housing industries could not possibly have survived with the traditional mortgage. These include Finland right after World War II, many South American countries, and Israel. Somewhat surprisingly, it has not been used to any significant extent in the United States. This is largely explained because no innovation in home financing has been possible without some sanction of government regulators, and regulators have been unimaginative, and rather disinclined toward real indexation of any type. Critical in this respect has been HUD's lack of approval for FHA insurance. Quite recently, however, HUD seems poised to change this attitude and to issue regulations to standardize these mortgages. PLAM may soon be making its debut in the United States.

***Dual-Rate Mortgage.***    Also referred to as the *inflation-proof mortgage*, the dual-rate mortgage (DRM) is similar in spirit and objective to the PLAM: payments start low—at current mortgage rates of around 10%, payments would start around 30% to 40% below those required by the traditional mortgage or by the ARM. They then rise smoothly at the rate of inflation, if any, achieving, like the PLAM, annual payments approximately level in terms of purchasing

---

[6] The real rate, it will be recalled from Chapter 11, is the interest rate that one could expect to prevail if there were no inflation in the economy.

[7] For a discussion of the PLAM, see Susan E. Woodward and David A. Crowe, "A Power-Packed Mortgage," *Secondary Mortgage Markets* (Fall 1988), pp. 2–7.

power. Finally, by construction, the debt is fully amortized by the end of the contract.

The DRM differs from the PLAM in that the amount owed by the borrower is computed on the basis of a floating short-term rate. This has several important consequences. First, just as in the case of other instruments where a fluctuating rate is indexed to short-term market rates, the market value of the instrument is not subject to interest rate risk but should instead remain close to par, except of course for credit risk. Second, there is little danger of prepayment risk, i.e., of the borrower taking the option to repay when rates fall, for the DRM rate would automatically fall. And finally, this mortgage can be financed through the existing institution of short-term nominal deposits.

A DRM requires specification of three parameters. The first is the "payment" rate. This is a "real" rate of interest fixed for the life of the loan, much as with a PLAM. The purpose of this rate is not to establish how much the debtor will pay, but rather how the amount will be paid—to make possible a desirable and affordable distribution of payments over the life of the instrument. The second parameter is the "effective" or "debiting" rate, a short-term rate that, as in the ARM, determines how much the borrower effectively pays (or is debited for) and how much the creditor earns. This debiting rate changes periodically, say, once a year, on the basis of an agreed-upon reference short-term rate (for example, the one-year Treasury bill). And the third parameter is the life of the mortgage, just as for any other fully amortized mortgage contract.

So far, the DRM has had rather limited application in the United States, largely because it has not yet received FHA approval for insurance. The DRM has had some application abroad and should have a future also in the United States after the PLAM has been introduced. There are a number of variants of the DRM that improve the working of the instrument in some directions, at the cost of reduced effectiveness in other directions.[8]

▶ KEY POINTS THAT YOU SHOULD UNDERSTAND BEFORE PROCEEDING:

1. The fixed-rate, level-payment mortgage (or traditional mortgage) is the most common type of mortgage design in the United States.
2. In the presence of high and variable inflation, the traditional mortgage design suffers from two basic and serious shortcomings: the mismatch problem and the tilt problem.
3. An adjustable-rate mortgage is a mortgage design whose rate resets periodically in accordance with some appropriately chosen index reflecting short-term market rates and overcomes the mismatch problem but not the tilt problem.
4. To overcome the tilt problem, several mortgage designs that take into account inflation have been developed or proposed.

[8] For a further discussion, of the DRM, its variants, and the difference between the PLAM and DRI, see Chapter 7 of Frank J. Fabozzi and Franco Modigliani, *Mortgage and Mortgage-Backed Securities Markets* (Boston: Harvard Business School Press, 1992).

## INVESTMENT RISKS

The principal investors in mortgage loans include thrifts and commercial banks. Pension funds and life insurance companies also invest in these loans, but their ownership is small compared to that of the banks and thrifts.

Investors face four main risks by investing in mortgage loans: (1) credit risk; (2) liquidity risk; (3) price risk; and (4) prepayment risk.

### Credit Risk

Credit risk is the risk that the homeowner/borrower will default. For FHA-, VA-, and FmHA-insured mortgages, this risk is minimal. For privately insured mortgages, the risk can be gauged by the credit rating of the private insurance company that has insured the mortgage. For conventional mortgages, the credit risk depends on the borrower. The LTV provides a useful measure of the risk of loss of principal in case of default. When LTV is high, default is more likely because the borrower has little equity in the property.

### Liquidity Risk

While there is a secondary market for mortgage loans, which we discuss in the next chapter, the fact is that bid–ask spreads are large compared to other debt instruments. That is, mortgage loans tend to be rather illiquid because they are large and indivisible.

### Price Risk

As explained in Chapter 10, the price of a fixed-income instrument will move in an opposite direction from market interest rates. Thus, a rise in interest rates will decrease the price of a mortgage loan.

### Prepayments and Cash Flow Uncertainty

Our illustration of the cash flow from a level-payment fixed-rate mortgage assumes that the homeowner does not pay off any portion of the mortgage balance prior to the scheduled due date. But homeowners do pay off all or part of their mortgage balances prior to the maturity date. Payments made in excess of the scheduled principal repayments are called *prepayments*.

Prepayments occur for one of several reasons. First, homeowners prepay the entire mortgage when they sell their house for any number of reasons that require moving. Second, the borrower has the right to pay off all or part of the mortgage balance at any time. Effectively, those who invest in mortgages grant the borrower an option to prepay the mortgage, and the debtor will have an incentive to do so as the interest rate in the mortgage market falls below the mortgage rate that the borrower is paying. Third, if homeowners cannot meet their mortgage obligations, the property is repossessed and sold, with the proceeds from the sale used to pay the lender in the case of a conventional mortgage. For an insured mortgage, the insurer will pay off the mortgage balance. Finally, if property is destroyed by fire, or another insured catastrophe occurs, the insurance proceeds are used to pay off the mortgage.

The effect of the prepayment right is that the cash flow from a mortgage is not known with certainty. This is true not only for level-payment fixed-rate mortgages but also for all the mortgages we discussed in this chapter.

▶ KEY POINTS THAT YOU SHOULD UNDERSTAND BEFORE PROCEEDING:

1. There are four main risks associated with investing in mortgages: credit risk, liquidity risk, price risk, and prepayment risk.
2. Credit risk can be reduced if the mortgage is insured by a government agency or a private insurance company.
3. Mortgages are not liquid assets—they tend to have a large bid–ask spread.
4. Because of prepayments, the investor is uncertain about the cash flows that will be realized from investing in a mortgage.

SUMMARY

The major originators of mortgage loans are thrifts, banks, and mortgage bankers. The risks associated with originating mortgages (pipeline risk) include price risk and fallout risk.

The traditional type of mortgage, characterized by a fixed-rate, level (nominal) payment, and full amortization, performed well in the first years of the postwar period, becoming the dominant vehicle for house financing. But this design showed drawbacks in the presence of high and variable inflation. First, traditional mortgages were financed mainly by depository institutions with very short-term funds, even though a mortgage is a very long-term instrument; this mismatch of maturities proved catastrophic when short-term rates rose sharply, leading to widespread insolvency of S&Ls, the major lenders. Second, in the presence of inflation-driven high interest rates, mortgage repayment in real terms is no longer level, but instead starts high and ends low, shutting off many would-be borrowers.

Two remedies in use in the United States are the adjustable-rate mortgage (ARM) and the graduated-payment mortgage (GPM). The first addresses the mismatch problem, and the second (imperfectly) the tilt problem; neither addresses both. Two other solutions, the price-level-adjusted mortgage (PLAM) and the dual-rate mortgage (DRM), fairly effectively address both problems, but neither of these instruments has yet been adopted on a large scale in the United States.

There is uncertainty associated with investing in any of these mortgages; because of prepayments, the cash flow is not known with certainty. This uncertainty is called prepayment risk. Investors in mortgages also face marketability risk and price risk, and may be exposed to credit risk.

**Adjustable-rate mortgage:** A mortgage design calling for the mortgage rate to reset periodically in accordance with some appropriately chosen index that reflects short-term market rates.

**Balloon/reset mortgage:** A mortgage design in which the borrower is given long-term financing by the lender but at a specified date, which is considerably shorter than the maturity date, the loan is paid off and the lender agrees to provide financing for the remainder of the term of the mortgage at a new mortgage rate.

**Commitment letter:** An agreement that the lender sends to a mortgage loan applicant that commits the lender to provide funds to the applicant.

**Conduits:** Entities that pool mortgages and sell interests in these pools to investors.

**Conforming mortgage:** A mortgage loan that meets the underwriting standards allowing an agency to include it in a pool of mortgages that is collateral for a mortgage pass-through security.

**Conventional mortgage:** A mortgage loan based solely on the credit of the borrower and on the collateral for the mortgage.

**Dual-rate mortgage (also called inflation-proof mortgage):** A mortgage design in which the mortgage payments are lower than for a traditional mortgage but then rise smoothly at the rate of inflation, if any, achieving mortgage payments approximately level in terms of purchasing power.

**Fallout risk:** In mortgage lending, the risk that applicants or those issued commitment letters by a mortgage originator will not close (complete the transaction by purchasing the property with funds borrowed from the mortgage originator).

**Graduated-payment mortgage:** A mortgage design in which the mortgage rate is fixed over the life of the mortgage, and the monthly mortgage payment grows at a constant rate during a portion of the life of the contract, thereafter leveling off.

**Lifetime cap:** A limit placed on the maximum and minimum mortgage rate that can be set on an adjustable-rate mortgage over the life of the loan.

**Loan-to-value ratio:** The ratio of the amount of the loan to the market (or appraised) value of the property.

**Mismatch problem:** The mismatching of the maturity of assets and liabilities of an institution.

**Mortgage banking:** The activity of originating mortgages.

**Mortgage loan (or simply mortgage):** A loan in which there is a pledge of property to secure payment of a debt.

**Mortgage market:** A collection of markets, which includes a primary market, or origination market, and a secondary market where mortgages trade.

**Mortgage originator:** In a mortgage loan transaction, this is the original lender.

**Mortgage servicing:** Activities including collecting monthly payments from mortgagors and forwarding proceeds to owners of the loan, sending payment notices to mortgagors, reminding mortgagors when payments are overdue, maintaining records of mortgage balances, furnishing tax information to mortgagors, administering an escrow account for real estate taxes and insurance purposes, and, if necessary, initiating foreclosure proceedings.

**Mortgagee:** The lender/investor in a mortgage loan.

**Mortgagor:** The borrower in a mortgage loan.

**Nonconforming mortgage:** A mortgage that does not meet the underwriting standards for inclusion in a pool that is collateral for a mortgage pass-through security issued or guaranteed by an agency.

**Origination fee:** A fee, expressed in points, that a mortgage originator charges the borrower for originating a loan.

**Payment-to-income ratio:** The ratio of monthly payments to monthly income, which is a measure of the ability of a mortgage applicant to make monthly payments (both mortgage and real estate tax payments).

**Periodic cap:** A restriction in an adjustable-rate mortgage as to the amount that the mortgage rate may increase or decrease at the reset date.

**Pipeline risk:** In mortgage lending, the risk associated with originating mortgages.

**Prepayment:** A payment made in excess of the monthly mortgage payment.

**Price-level-adjusted mortgage:** Similar to the traditional mortgage except that monthly payments are designed to be level in purchasing power rather than in nominal terms, and that the fixed rate is the "real" rate rather than the nominal rate.

**Tilt problem:** The fact that, in real or inflation-adjusted terms, the early payments on a mortgage can be, and often are, larger and more burdensome to a borrower than the later payments.

QUESTIONS

1. What are the sources of revenue arising from mortgage origination?
2. What are the risks associated with the mortgage origination process?
3. What are the two primary factors in determining whether funds will be lent to an applicant for a mortgage loan?
4. What can mortgage originators do with a loan after originating it?

5. Explain why in a fixed-rate, level-payment mortgage the amount of the mortgage payment applied to interest declines over time, while the amount applied to the repayment of principal increases.

6. Consider the following fixed-rate, level-payment mortgage:

   maturity = 360 months
   amount borrowed = $100,000
   annual mortgage rate = 10%
   monthly mortgage payment = $877.57

   a. Construct an amortization schedule for the first ten months.

   b. What will the mortgage balance be at the end of the 360th month?

7. Why is the interest rate on a mortgage loan not necessarily the same as the interest rate that the investor receives?

8. a. Why is the cash flow of a mortgage unknown?

   b. In what sense has the investor in a mortgage granted the borrower (homeowner) a call option?

9. a. What features of an adjustable-rate mortgage will affect its cash flow?

   b. What are the two categories of benchmark indexes used in adjustable-rate mortgages?

10. What is the motivation for the design of price-level-adjusted mortgages and dual-rate mortgages?

# CHAPTER TWENTY-FOUR

# Mortgage-Backed Securities Market

*After reading this chapter you will understand:*

- the development of the current mortgage market, and the role of public and private conduits.
- the agency pass-through market.
- the conventional pass-through market.
- the investment characteristics of mortgage pass-through securities.
- the importance of prepayments.
- why a collateralized mortgage obligation is created.
- the different types of collateralized mortgage obligation structures.
- the investment characteristics of stripped mortgage-backed securities.

Our focus in this chapter is on the market for securities created from mortgage loans. The basic mortgage-backed security is the mortgage pass-through security. From this security, derivative mortgage-backed securities are created: collateralized mortgage obligations and stripped mortgage-backed securities. We begin by describing how the process of securitizing mortgages resulted in the strong secondary mortgage market that exists today.

## DEVELOPMENT OF THE SECONDARY MORTGAGE MARKET

The driving force in the development of a strong secondary mortgage market was a financial innovation that involves the packaging (or "pooling") of mortgages and the issuance of securities collateralized by these mortgages. As we explained in Chapter 2, this system, called *asset securitization*, is radically different from the traditional system for financing the acquisition of assets, which calls for one financial intermediary, such as a commercial bank, thrift, or insurance company, to: (1) originate a loan; (2) retain the loan in its portfolio of assets, thereby accepting the credit risk associated with the loan; (3) service the loan (that is, collect payments and provide tax or other information to the borrower); and (4) obtain funds from the public with which to finance its assets (except for the small amount representing the institution's equity).

With asset securitization more than one institution may be involved in lending capital. In the case of mortgage activities, a lending scenario can look like this: (1) a thrift or commercial bank can originate a mortgage loan; (2) the thrift or commercial bank can sell its mortgages to an investment banking firm that creates a security backed by the pool of mortgages; (3) the investment banker can obtain credit risk insurance for the pool of mortgages from a private insurance company; (4) the investment banker can sell the right to service the loans to another thrift or a company specializing in serving mortgages; and (5) the investment banking firm can sell the securities to individuals and institutional investors. Besides the original bank or thrift, participants include an investment bank, an insurance company, another thrift, an individual, and other institutional investors. The bank or thrift in this case does not have to absorb the credit risk, service the mortgage, or provide the funding.

### *Foundations of the Mortgage Market*

The foundations for the secondary mortgage market can be traced back to the Great Depression and the legislation that followed. Congress's response to the Depression and its effects on financial markets was to establish several public purpose agencies. The Federal Reserve provided increased liquidity for commercial banks through the Federal Reserve discount window. Liquidity for thrifts was provided by the creation of the Federal Home Loan Banks (FHLBs), which were granted the right to borrow from the Treasury.

Another creation of Congress, the Federal Housing Administration (FHA), addressed the problems presented by the mortgages used at that time.

It is this government agency that developed and promoted the fixed-rate level-payment, fully amortized mortgage. The FHA also reduced credit risk for investors by offering insurance against mortgage defaults. Not all mortgages could be insured, however—the mortgage applicant had to satisfy FHA underwriting standards, which made the FHA the first to standardize mortgage terms. While we may take this for granted today, standardization is the basis for the development of a secondary mortgage market. In 1944, the Veterans Administration began insuring qualified mortgages.

But who was going to invest in these mortgages? Thrifts could do so, especially with the inducement provided by several tax and regulatory advantages. But the investment would be illiquid in the absence of a market where mortgages are traded. Congress thought of that, too. It created another government-sponsored agency, the Federal National Mortgage Association (FNMA). This agency, popularly known as "Fannie Mae," was charged with the responsibility to create a liquid secondary market for FHA- and VA-insured mortgages, which it tried to accomplish by buying mortgages. Fannie Mae needed a funding source in case it faced a liquidity squeeze. Congress provided this by giving Fannie Mae a credit line with the Treasury.

Despite the creation of Fannie Mae, the secondary mortgage market did not develop to any significant extent. During periods of tight money, Fannie Mae could do little to mitigate the housing crisis. In 1968, Congress divided Fannie Mae into two organizations: (1) the current Fannie Mae, and (2) the Government National Mortgage Association (popularly known as "Ginnie Mae"). Ginnie Mae's function is to use the "full faith and credit of the U.S. government" to support the FHA and VA mortgage market. Two years later, in 1970, Congress authorized Fannie Mae to purchase conventional mortgage loans (that is, those not insured by the FHA or VA) and created the Federal Home Loan Mortgage Corporation (popularly known as "Freddie Mac") to provide support for FHA/VA insured mortgages and conventional mortgages.

## Securitization of the Mortgages

Ginnie Mae accomplished its objective by guaranteeing securities issued by private entities who pooled mortgages together and then used these mortgages as collateral for the security sold. Freddie Mac and Fannie Mae purchased mortgages, pooled these mortgages, and issued securities using the pool of mortgages as collateral. The securities created are called *mortgage pass-through securities*. They are purchased by many types of investors (domestic and foreign) who had previously shunned investment in the mortgage market.

In the 1980s, private issuers of mortgage pass-through securities who did not use the backing of the three agencies but instead some form of private credit enhancement began issuing pass-through securities backed by conventional family mortgages and commercial real estate mortgages.

▶ KEY POINTS THAT YOU SHOULD UNDERSTAND BEFORE PROCEEDING:

1. The securitization of a mortgage loan to create mortgage pass-through securities was the key factor in the development of a strong secondary mortgage market.
2. Securitization of mortgage loans is one form of asset securitization.
3. Three government agencies were created to promote the secondary mortgage market: Ginnie Mae, Fannie Mae, and Freddie Mac.

## MORTGAGE PASS-THROUGH SECURITIES

■ ■ ■ ■

As we noted in the previous chapter, investing in mortgages exposes the investor to default risk, price risk, liquidity risk, and prepayment risk. A more efficient investment technique is to invest in a *mortgage pass-through security*. This is a security created when one or more holders of mortgages form a collection (pool) of mortgages and sell shares or participation certificates in the pool. A pool may consist of several thousand mortgages or only a few. The first mortgage pass-through security was created in 1968. Risk-averse investors prefer investing in a pool to investing in a single mortgage, partly because a mortgage pass-through security is considerably more liquid than an individual mortgage.

When a mortgage is included in a pool of mortgages that is used as collateral for a mortgage pass-through security, the mortgage is said to be *securitized*. More than one-third of mortgages for one- to four-family houses have been securitized. Only 22% of conventional mortgages have been securitized, but 85% of FHA/VA insured mortgages have been. Only 7% of multi-family unit mortgages have found their way into a mortgage pool backing a mortgage pass-through security.

### *Cash Flow Characteristics*

The cash flow of a mortgage pass-through security depends on the cash flow of the underlying mortgages. As we explained in the previous chapter, the cash flow consists of monthly mortgage payments representing interest, the scheduled repayment of principal, and any prepayments.

Payments are made to securityholders each month. The amounts and the timing of the cash flow from the pool of mortgages and the cash flow passed through to investors, however, are not identical. The monthly cash flow for a pass-through security is less than the monthly cash flow of the underlying mortgages by an amount equal to servicing and other fees. The other fees are those charged by the issuer or guarantor of the pass-through security for guaranteeing the issue (discussed later).[1]

---

[1] Actually, the servicer pays the guarantee fee to the issuer or guarantor.

The timing of the cash flow is also different. The monthly mortgage payment is due from each mortgagor on the first day of each month, but there is a delay in passing through the corresponding monthly cash flow to the securityholders. The length of the delay varies by the type of pass-through security.

Figure 24-1 illustrates the process of creating a mortgage pass-through security.

FIGURE 24-1

ILLUSTRATION OF CREATION OF A MORTGAGE PASS-THROUGH SECURITY

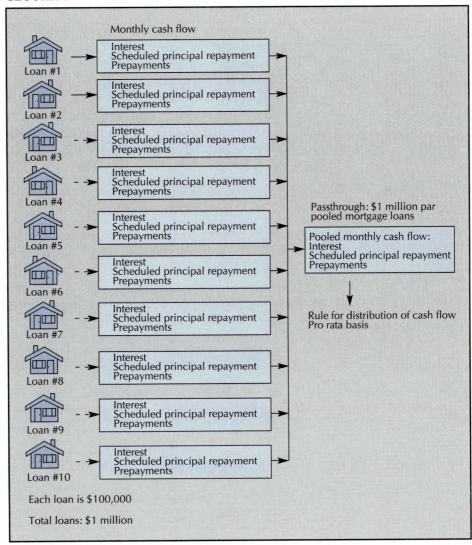

### Issuers of Mortgage Pass-Through Securities

The three major types of pass-through securities are guaranteed by the agencies created by Congress to increase the supply of capital to the residential mortgage market and to provide support for an active secondary market: Government National Mortgage Association ("Ginnie Mae"), Federal Home Loan Mortgage Corporation ("Freddie Mac"), and Federal National Mortgage Association ("Fannie Mae").

While Fannie Mae and Freddie Mac are commonly referred to as "agencies" of the U.S. government, in fact both are corporate instrumentalities of the government. Their stock trades on the New York Stock Exchange; therefore they are effectively quasi-private corporations. They do not receive a government subsidy or appropriation, and are taxed like any other corporation. Fannie Mae and Freddie Mac are more appropriately referred to as *federally sponsored agencies* or *government-sponsored entities*. Their guarantee does not carry the full faith and credit of the U.S. government. Ginnie Mae, by contrast, is a federally related institution because it is part of the Department of Housing and Urban Development. Its guarantee therefore carries the full faith and credit of the U.S. government.

The securities associated with these three entities are known as *agency pass-through securities*. About 98% of all pass-through securities are agency pass-through securities. The balance of mortgage pass-through securities are privately issued. These securities are called *conventional mortgage pass-through securities*. While the major portion of pass-through issues have residential mortgages as their collateral, pass-throughs collateralized by mortgages on commercial property also have been issued.

### Agency Pass-Through Securities

Table 24-1 shows the total amount of pass-throughs issued or guaranteed by the three agencies, while Table 24-2 shows the origination of pass-throughs by agency from 1984 to 1991.

There is substantial trading activity in agency mortgage-backed securities. According to the Market Reports Division of the Federal Reserve Bank of New York, for the week ended May 15, 1991, daily average primary dealer

TABLE 24-1

OUTSTANDING PASS-THROUGHS BY AGENCY:
SEPTEMBER 1, 1991

| Agency | Outstanding (Millions of Dollars) |
|---|---|
| Ginnie Mae | 418,421 |
| Freddie Mac | 341,132 |
| Fannie Mae | 331,089 |
| Total | 1,090,642 |

*Source:* Board of Governors, Federal Reserve System.

| | TABLE 24-2 | | | | |
|---|---|---|---|---|---|

ORIGINATION OF PASS-THROUGHS BY AGENCY: 1984-
1991
(MILLIONS OF DOLLARS)

| Year | Ginnie Mae | Freddie Mac | Fannie Mae | Private Firms | Total |
|---|---|---|---|---|---|
| 1984 | 28,097 | 18,684 | 13,546 | 6,273 | 66,600 |
| 1985 | 45,980 | 38,829 | 23,649 | 6,916 | 115,374 |
| 1986 | 101,433 | 100,198 | 60,566 | 13,163 | 275,360 |
| 1987 | 94,929 | 75,018 | 63,229 | 18,576 | 251,764 |
| 1988 | 55,248 | 39,777 | 54,878 | 20,699 | 170,667 |
| 1989 | 57,190 | 73,518 | 69,764 | 12,010 | 212,715 |
| 1990 | 64,651 | 73,815 | 96,695 | 14,341 | 249,502 |
| 1991 | 62,752 | 92,479 | 112,903 | 21,794 | 289,928 |

*Source:* Adapted from *Secondary Mortgage Markets*, Selected issues, by
permission of Freddie Mac. All rights reserved.

transactions of agency mortgage-backed securities totaled about $12.4 billion,
$5.7 being transactions between primary dealers and brokers, and $6.7 billion
being transactions between primary dealers and customers. For U.S. government
securities over the same week, the corresponding daily average primary
dealer transactions totaled $136.9 billion ($83.7 billion and $53.2 billion, respectively).
While the amount of secondary market transactions of agency
mortgage-backed securities is large, it is still small in comparison to trading in
U.S. government securities.

***Government National Mortgage Association.*** Ginnie Mae's mortgage-backed
securities represent the largest proportion of mortgage pass-through securities
outstanding. They are guaranteed by the full faith and credit of the United
States government with respect to timely payment of both interest and principal.
That is, the interest and principal will be paid when due even if mortgagors
fail to make their monthly mortgage payment.

While Ginnie Mae provides the guarantee, it is not the issuer. Pass-through
securities are issued by lenders it approves, such as thrifts, commercial
banks, and mortgage bankers. These lenders receive approval only if the
underlying mortgages satisfy the underwriting standards established by Ginnie
Mae. When it guarantees securities issued by approved lenders, Ginnie
Mae permits these lenders to convert illiquid individual mortgages into liquid
securities backed by the U.S. government. In the process, Ginnie Mae accomplishes
its goal to supply funds to the residential mortgage market and provide
an active secondary market. For the guarantee, Ginnie Mae receives a
fee, called the *guaranteeing fee*.

The security guaranteed by Ginnie Mae is called a *mortgage-backed security*
(MBS). These securities are sold in minimum denominations of $25,000

and in increments of $5,000 thereafter. The first MBS was issued in 1968. Only mortgages insured or guaranteed by either the Federal Housing Administration, the Veterans Administration, or the Farmers Home Administration can be included in a mortgage pool guaranteed by Ginnie Mae.

***Federal Home Loan Mortgage Corporation.***   The second largest category of agency pass-through securities contains those issued by the Federal Home Loan Mortgage Corporation (FHLMC). The security issued by Freddie Mac is called a *participation certificate* (PC). The first PCs were issued in 1971.

Most of the pools of mortgages underlying Freddie Mac participation certificates consist of conventional mortgages, although participation certificates with underlying pools consisting of FHA-insured and VA-guaranteed mortgages have been issued. While there are participation certificates that guarantee the timely payment of both interest and principal, most Freddie Mac participation certificates guarantee only the timely payment of interest. The scheduled principal is passed through as it is collected, with Freddie Mac guaranteeing only that the scheduled payment will be made no later than one year after it is due. A Freddie Mac guarantee is not a guarantee by the U.S. government. Most market participants, though, view Freddie Mac participation certificates as similar in creditworthiness to Ginnie Mae pass-throughs, which are fully guaranteed by the U.S. government.

Freddie Mac has two programs from which it creates PCs: the Cash Program and the Guarantor/Swap Program. The underlying loans for both programs are conventional mortgages (i.e., mortgages not backed by a government agency). Conventional Regular PCs are issued under the Cash Program. In this program, the mortgages that back the PC include individual conventional one- to four-family mortgage loans that Freddie Mac purchases from mortgage originators, pools, and sells. Under the Conventional Guarantor/Swap Program, Freddie Mac allows originators to swap pooled mortgages for PCs in those same pools. For example, a thrift may have $50 million of mortgages. It can swap these mortgages for a Freddie Mac PC whose underlying mortgage pool is the $50 million mortgage pool the thrift swapped for the PC.

Both programs provide capital to the residential mortgage market and foster a secondary mortgage market. The Guarantor/Swap Program was designed specifically to provide liquidity to the troubled thrift industry. It allows thrifts to swap mortgages trading below par (because mortgage rates are lower than the current mortgage rate) without recognizing an accounting loss for financial reporting purposes. The PC that the thrift gets in exchange for the mortgage pool can then be either (1) held as an investment; (2) used as collateral for either short-term or long-term borrowing; or (3) sold. The Guarantor/Swap program has been a huge success and is one of the reasons for the significant growth of the amount of PCs issued.

In the fall of 1990, Freddie Mac introduced its Gold PC, which it issues in both its Cash Program and Guarantor/Swap Program. The Gold PC is the only type of pass-through it will issue in the future. Gold PCs are guaranteed with respect to timely payment of both interest and principal.

***Federal National Mortgage Association.*** While it was created by Congress in 1938, the Federal National Mortgage Association (FNMA), in its current form, is the newest player in the agency pass-through securities market. Fannie Mae was charged by Congress with promoting a secondary market for conventional and FHA/VA single- and multi-family mortgages. To meet that obligation, since 1972 it has purchased these mortgages and held them as investments. It was not until 1981 that Fannie Mae pooled these mortgages and issued its first mortgage pass-through securities, called *mortgage-backed securities* (MBS). These pass-throughs are guaranteed with respect to the timely payment of both interest and principal. Like Freddie Mac participation certificates, Fannie Mae mortgage-backed securities are not obligations of the U.S. government. Fannie Mae also has a swap program similar to that of Freddie Mac. It provides liquidity to mortgage originators such as thrifts.

## Conventional Pass-Through Securities

The mortgages that the agencies could purchase or guarantee in securitized form are restricted to those that meet their underwriting standards related to the maximum size of the loan and the maximum ratio of the amount of the loan to the market value of the mortgaged property. Such mortgages are called *conforming mortgages*. A mortgage that fails to satisfy the underwriting standard is called a *nonconforming mortgage*. Mortgage loans that are greater than the maximum permissible loan size are referred to as *jumbo loans*. While Congress has periodically increased the maximum amount of the loan that may be included in pass-throughs guaranteed by the three agencies, the loan size is still often below the typical average cost of a home in certain geographical areas.

The agencies cannot affect the liquidity of nonconforming mortgages such as jumbo mortgages. The importance of the nonconforming mortgage market can be seen by the size of the jumbo loan market, estimated at $500 billion. In 1988, jumbos constituted about 25% (or $91 billion) of newly originated mortgages.[2] This sector of the mortgage market has had to be securitized by the private sector, without government guarantee.

Privately issued—that is, *conventional* or *private label*—pass-throughs were first issued in 1977 by the Bank of America, but faced many impediments to widespread acceptance. The government wanted to see the private sector market develop, not only to improve its liquidity, but also because it was concerned about the huge potential liability of the U.S. government, should the agencies have to make good on their guarantee in the event of massive homeowner defaults. One of the objectives of the Presidential Commission on Housing, established in mid-1981, was to recommend a number of private sector alternatives.

---

[2] Robert Gerber, "Introduction to the Private Label Pass-Through Market," in Frank J. Fabozzi (ed.), *The Handbook of Mortgage-Backed Securities* 3d ed. (Chicago: Probus Publishing, 1992).

The Commission's report in April 1982 recommended the privatization of Fannie Mae and Freddie Mac and the development of private sector alternatives to the two government-sponsored entities. The Commission identified three major problems to be solved before an efficient private sector market could be developed. First, private pass-throughs were being crowded out by agency issues. Second, private issuers faced federal and state laws or regulations that either limited the demand for private label products, or resulted in security structures that were not cost-efficient for issuers. Moreover, these restrictions had no economic justification. For example, federal or state regulators would not permit such securities to be treated as "qualified" investments for the institutions they regulated. Tax rules regarding how a transaction must be structured in order to qualify as a nontaxable conduit resulted in needlessly expensive security structures. Finally, private issues lacked standardization, and this deficiency limited liquidity.

The development of the private pass-through market has been the result of government intervention to foster the growth of this sector, as well as initiatives undertaken by the private sector to structure pass-throughs to enhance their credit quality.

***Government Intervention.***   Several legislative acts and regulatory changes helped foster the development of the private mortgage-backed securities market. The Secondary Mortgage Market Enhancement Act of 1984 (SMMEA) included provisions to improve the marketability of mortgage-related securities earning a double-A quality rating or better from one of the nationally recognized commercial rating companies.[3] More specifically, SMMEA made such securities legal investments for federally chartered banks and thrifts. These investments are referred to as *SMMEA-qualified securities*.

This legislation also made SMMEA-qualified securities permissible investments for state-regulated financial institutions (depository institutions and insurance companies), which are permitted to invest in Treasury securities or federal agency securities. This action opened the door to enormous pools of investment capital. The SMMEA grants individual states the right to override this particular provision of the act by October 1991. As many states have exercised their prerogative and overridden this provision of the act, they have reduced funds from the entities they regulate that could invest in the private sector market. The Department of Labor, which has the responsibility of regulating pension funds, has since made private pass-throughs acceptable assets for pension plans.

The peculiarities of creating pass-throughs made it difficult for issuers to comply with SEC registration regulations. The SEC, for example, requires that a prospectus provide pertinent information about the underlying pool of mortgages. In the creation of mortgage-backed securities, however, issuers sell the securities while they are assembling the underlying pool of mortgage loans.

---

[3] This is the reason why the private pass-throughs are also referred to as *AA pass-throughs*.

Thus, the final pool would be unknown at the time of registration and could not be indicated in the prospectus. SEC regulations prevented the registration of these "blind pools" and refused to allow such underwriting on a shelf registration basis (Rule 415). Issuers also had to contend with the periodic reporting requirements after a mortgage-backed security was issued. None of these actions was required for agency mortgage-backed securities, because such securities are exempt from SEC registration. All these factors—the increased cost associated with the inability to time issuances through shelf registration, the lost flexibility to assemble pools prior to the offering, and the ongoing reporting requirements—made private issuance unattractive and impeded development of the private label pass-through market.

Recognizing this, the SEC significantly modified the requirements for private pass-through issuers in 1983 by permitting the registration of securities backed by blind pools, so long as the issuer commits to obtain a specified quality rating and provides sufficient information about the potential pool in the prospectus. When the final pool is assembled, that information must be sent to investors. Private mortgage-backed security issuers can now also qualify for shelf registration, and the periodic reporting requirements are less stringent than for corporate issuers.

The Tax Reform Act of 1986 also made the structuring of private mortgage-related securities less costly from a tax perspective. The 1986 act expanded the types of structures that could be issued, and exempted from separate taxation the legal entity that distributes the cash flow if certain conditions are satisfied. Finally, brokers and dealers could use agency pass-throughs as collateral for margin transactions. Prior to 1983, private pass-throughs were not marginable. In January 1983, the Federal Reserve Board amended Regulation T to allow the same margin requirements as for over-the-counter nonconvertible bonds.

***The Issuers.*** Private pass-throughs have been issued by commercial banks, insurance companies, and savings institutions. As can be seen from Table 24-2, private pass-throughs made up only $14.3 billion of the $249.5 billion (or about 6%) of pass-throughs originated in 1990, roughly the same percentage as in 1989.

Prior to 1990, the five private issuers that dominated the market included subsidiaries of one commercial bank (Citicorp), two investment banking firms (Salomon Brothers and Merrill Lynch), one savings institution (Home Savings), and one life insurance company (The Travelers). Today, the two active issuers are Citicorp and General Electric. Citicorp has been by far the largest issuer of private label pass-throughs.

The newest player in the private issuance market might become the Resolution Trust Corporation (RTC), which has worked with investment banking firms in creating private pass-throughs backed by real estate loans from failed S&Ls. The complication is that the RTC portfolio includes nonperforming loans or lower-quality loans that would not be acceptable collateral for obtaining a double-A credit rating. Thus, a device to enhance the credit of the issue is needed.

***Credit Enhancement.***   Unlike agency pass-through securities, conventional mortgage pass-through securities are rated. Often they are supported by credit enhancements so that they can obtain a high rating. Most conventional mortgage pass-through securities have a rating of at least double-A. The development of private credit enhancement is the key to the success of this market and, indeed, the key to the development of all asset securitization. Credit enhancement may take the form of either (1) corporate guarantees; (2) pool insurance from a mortgage insurance company; (3) a bank letter of credit; or (4) senior/subordinated interests.

In the case of a corporate guarantee, the issuer of a conventional pass-through uses its own credit rating to back the security. Under the second approach to credit enhancement, a mortgage pool policy is obtained to cover defaults up to a specified amount. The rating of the mortgage insurance company that writes the policy must be equal to or higher than the rating that the issuer seeks for the pass-through security. For example, if an issuer seeks a double-A rating for the pass-through, it cannot obtain a pool insurance policy from a single-A rated mortgage insurance company. The cost of a letter of credit is relatively high because of the limited number of financial institutions willing to issue such guarantees, and therefore this form of credit enhancement is not common.

The fourth approach to credit enhancement is the senior/subordinated structure, also known as the A/B pass-through. In this structure, a mortgage pool is partitioned into senior certificates and subordinated certificates. The senior certificate holder has priority on the cash flow from the underlying collateral. It is the senior certificates that are rated and sold to investors as conventional pass-throughs. The subordinated certificates absorb the default risk. The amount of subordinated certificates relative to senior certificates that a mortgage pool is divided into will determine its credit rating. The greater the portion of subordinated certificates relative to senior certificates, the higher the credit rating that can be obtained.[4]

## Prepayment Risks Associated with Pass-Through Securities

An investor who owns pass-through securities does not know what the cash flow will be because cash flow depends on prepayments. The risk associated with prepayments is called *prepayment risk*.

To understand prepayment risk, suppose an investor buys a 10% coupon Ginnie Mae at a time when mortgage rates are 10%. Let's consider what will happen to prepayments if mortgage rates decline to, say, 6%. There will be two

---

[4] For a more detailed description of this structure, see Anand K. Bhattacharya and Peter J. Cannon, "Senior-Subordinated Mortgage Pass-Throughs," in Frank J. Fabozzi (ed.), *Advances and Innovations in the Bond and Mortgage Markets* (Chicago: Probus Publishing, 1989).

adverse consequences. First, as we explained in Chapter 11, the price of an option-free bond such as a Treasury bond will rise. In the case of a pass-through security, the rise in price will not be as large as that of an option-free bond, because a fall in interest rates will increase the probability that the market rate will fall below the rate the borrower is paying. This fall in rates gives the borrower an incentive to prepay the loan and refinance the debt at a lower rate. To the extent that this happens, the securityholder will be repaid not at a price incorporating the premium but at par value. The holder risks capital loss, which reflects the fact that the anticipated reimbursements at par will not yield the initial cash flow.

The adverse consequences when mortgage rates decline are the same as those faced by holders of callable corporate and municipal bonds. As in the case of those instruments, the upside price potential of a pass-through security is truncated because of prepayments. This should not be surprising, because a mortgage loan effectively grants the borrower the right to call the loan at par value. The adverse consequence when mortgage rates decline is referred to as *contraction risk*.

Now let's look at what happens if mortgage rates rise to 15%. The price of the pass-through, like the price of any bond, will decline. But again it will decline more because the higher rates will tend to slow down the rate of prepayment, in effect increasing the amount invested at the coupon rate, which is lower than the market rate. Prepayments will slow down, because homeowners will not refinance or partially prepay their mortgages when mortgage rates are higher than the contractual rate of 10%. Of course this is just the time when investors want prepayments to speed up so that they can reinvest the prepayments at the higher market interest rate. This adverse consequence of rising mortgage rates is called *extension risk*.

Therefore, prepayment risk encompasses contraction risk and extension risk. Prepayment risk makes pass-throughs unattractive for certain financial institutions to hold from an asset/liability perspective. Let's look at why particular institutional investors may find pass-throughs unattractive:

1. Thrifts and commercial banks, as we explained in Chapter 4, want to lock in a spread over their cost of funds. Their funds are raised on a short-term basis. If they invest in fixed-rate pass-through securities, they will be mismatched because a pass-through is a longer-term security. In particular, depository institutions are exposed to extension risk when they invest in pass-through securities.

2. To satisfy certain obligations of insurance companies, pass-through securities may be unattractive. More specifically, consider a life insurance company that has issued a four-year GIC. The uncertainty about the cash flow from a pass-through security, and the likelihood that slow prepayments will result in the instrument being long-term, make it an unappealing investment vehicle for such accounts. In such instances, a pass-through security exposes the insurance company to extension risk.

3. Consider a pension fund that wants to fund a 15-year liability. Buying a pass-through security exposes the pension fund to the risk that prepayments will speed up and that the maturity of the investment will shorten to considerably less than 15 years. Prepayments will speed up when interest rates decline, thereby forcing reinvestment of the prepaid amounts at a lower interest rate. In this case, the pension fund is open to contraction risk.

We can see that some institutional investors are concerned with extension risk and others with contraction risk when they purchase a pass-through security. Is it possible to alter the cash flow of a pass-through so as to reduce the contraction risk and extension risk for institutional investors? This is the subject of the next section.

▶ KEY POINTS THAT YOU SHOULD UNDERSTAND BEFORE PROCEEDING:

1. A mortgage pass-through security is created when one or more holders of mortgages form a collection (pool) of mortgages and sell shares or participation certificates in the pool.

2. The cash flow of a mortgage pass-through security depends on the cash flow of the underlying mortgages, which consists of monthly mortgage payments representing interest, the scheduled repayment of principal, and any prepayments.

3. The three major types of pass-through securities are guaranteed by either Ginnie Mae (a federally related entity), Fannie Mae (a government-sponsored entity), or Freddie Mac (a government-sponsored entity), and are referred to as agency pass-through securities.

4. There are private issuers of mortgage pass-through securities that are not explicitly or implicitly guaranteed by the U.S. government; these securities are called conventional pass-through or private label pass-through securities.

5. Of the mortgage pass-through securities guaranteed by one of the three agencies, only those guaranteed by Ginnie Mae carry the full faith and credit of the U.S. government; conventional pass-through securities are rated by a commercial rating company, and often they are supported by credit enhancements so that they can obtain a high rating.

6. There have been several legislative acts and regulatory changes to foster the development of the private label mortgage-backed securities market.

7. An investor in a mortgage pass-through security is exposed to prepayment risk which can be decomposed into two types of risk, contraction risk and extension risk.

## COLLATERALIZED MORTGAGE OBLIGATIONS

A *collateralized mortgage obligation* (CMO) reduces uncertainty concerning the maturity of a mortgage-backed security, thereby providing a risk/return pattern not available with typical mortgage pass-through securities.

A CMO is a security backed by a pool of mortgage pass-through securities or mortgages.[5] Because CMOs derive their cash flow from the underlying mortgage collateral, they are referred to as "derivative" securities. CMOs are structured so that there are several classes of bondholders with varying stated maturities. The principal payments from the underlying collateral in the earlier CMO structures were used to retire the bonds sequentially.

A "plain vanilla" CMO may be structured with four classes of bonds, which we shall refer to as Class A, Class B, Class C, and Class Z. (The classes are commonly referred to as "tranches.") The first three classes, with Class A representing the shortest-maturity bond, receive periodic interest payments from the underlying collateral; Class Z is an accrual bond that receives no periodic interest until the other three classes are retired. When principal payments, both scheduled and through prepayment, are received by the CMO trustee, they are applied to retire the Class A bonds. After all the Class A bonds are retired, all principal payments received are applied to retire the Class B bonds. Once all the Class B bonds are retired, Class C bonds are paid off from all principal payments. Finally, after the first three classes of bonds are retired, the cash flow payments from the remaining underlying collateral are used to satisfy the obligations on the Z-bonds (original principal plus accrued interest). Figure 24-2 shows how a CMO is created.

The CMO market has seen phenomenal growth since the first publicly issued CMO was introduced in June of 1983 by Freddie Mac.[6] By 1986, CMO issuance was $48 billion. From 1986, issuance more than doubled to $118 billion by 1990. The two major issuers of CMOs are Freddie Mac and Fannie Mae. In 1990, for example, Freddie Mac issued $39 billion and Fannie Mae $59 billion.

So far, we have discussed the "plain vanilla" CMO structure. Other CMO structures introduced since June 1983 include CMOs with a floating-rate class and an inverse floating-rate class. The truly important innovation was in the development of a *planned amortization class* (PAC) bond, which under all but extreme prepayment rates provides a more stable cash flow.

PAC bonds were created in March 1987, when the M.D.C. Mortgage Funding Corporation, CMO Series 0, included a class of bonds referred to as

---

[5] The overwhelming bulk of CMOs are backed by pass-through securities.

[6] One provision of the Tax Reform Act of 1986, the Real Estate Mortgage Investment Conduit (REMIC), facilitates the issuance of CMOs from a tax perspective. The issuer does this by electing to have the CMO treated as a REMIC. A REMIC CMO is not a new security but a tax election made by an issuer.

## FIGURE 24-2

ILLUSTRATION OF THE CREATION OF A CMO

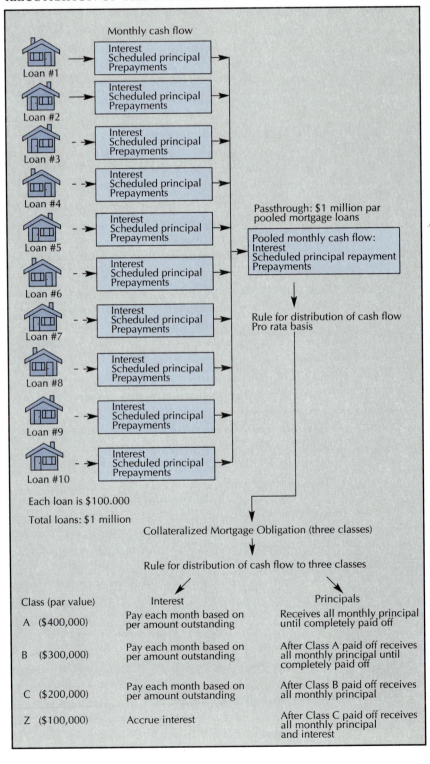

"stabilized mortgage reduction term bonds" or "SMRT" bonds. The same company included in its CMO Series P a class referred to as "planned amortization class bonds" or "PAC" bonds. Also in the late 1980s, the Oxford Acceptance Corporation III, Series C, CMOs included a class of bonds referred to as "planned redemption obligation bonds" or "PRO" bonds. A characteristic common to all three bonds is that, within a specified range of prepayment rates, the cash flow pattern is known with greater certainty than the cash flow for other classes in a typical CMO issue.

The greater predictability of the cash flow for these classes of bonds, referred to generically as PAC bonds, occurs because there is a specified schedule to retire the principal owed to this class (much like a sinking fund schedule for a corporate bond). The PAC class bondholders therefore have priority over all other classes in the CMO issue in receiving principal payments from the underlying collateral when prepayments are within the prespecified prepayment range. The greater certainty of the cash flow for the PAC bonds comes at the expense of the non-PAC bonds, called *companion bond* or *support bond* classes. Should the actual prepayment speed be faster than the upper limit of the PAC range, the companion bonds receive the excess. This means that the companion bonds absorb the contraction risk. Should the actual prepayment speed be slower than the lower limit of the range, the PAC bondholders have priority on principal payments (both scheduled and through prepayments) in subsequent periods. This means that extension risk is also absorbed by the companion bondholders.

In 1988, PaineWebber introduced a variant of the PAC bond in its PaineWebber CMO Trust Series L, with a class called the *targeted amortization class*, or TAC bond. A TAC bond is designed to provide protection against contraction risk while exposing the investor to extension risk. This is done by specifying a narrower prepayment range or just a single prepayment rate over which the principal is guaranteed.[7]

▶ KEY POINTS THAT YOU SHOULD UNDERSTAND BEFORE PROCEEDING:

1. A CMO is a security backed by a pool of mortgage pass-through securities or mortgages and is referred to as a derivative security.
2. A CMO reduces the uncertainty concerning the maturity of a mortgage-backed security, thereby providing a risk/return pattern not available with typical mortgage pass-through securities.
3. In a CMO structure there are several bond classes, called tranches.
4. A PAC bond is a class of bonds designed to reduce prepayment risk by specifying a schedule for the amortization of the principal owed to the bondholder; the reduction in the prepayment risk comes at the

[7] For a more detailed explanation of TACs, see William J. Curtin and Paul T. Van Valkenburg, "CMO PAC and TAC Bonds: Call Protected Mortgage Securities," in Frank J. Fabozzi (ed.), *Managing Institutional Assets* (New York: Harper & Row, 1990).

expense of non-PAC bond classes called companion or support bonds.

5. The PAC bond is designed to provide protection against both contraction risk and extension risk, while a TAC bond is designed to provide protection against contraction risk but exposes the investor to extension risk.

## STRIPPED MORTGAGE-BACKED SECURITIES

Stripped mortgage-backed securities, introduced by Fannie Mae in 1986, are another example of derivative mortgage securities. A mortgage pass-through security divides the cash flow from the underlying pool of mortgages on a pro rata basis to the securityholders. A stripped mortgage-backed security is created by altering that distribution of principal and interest from a pro rata distribution to an unequal distribution. The result is that some of the securities created will have a price/yield relationship that is different from the price/yield relationship of the underlying mortgage pool. Stripped mortgage-backed securities, if properly used, provide a means by which investors can hedge prepayment risk.

The first generation of stripped mortgage-backed securities were "partially stripped." We can see this by looking at the stripped mortgage-backed securities issued by Fannie Mae in mid-1986. The Class B stripped mortgage-backed securities were backed by FNMA pass-through securities with a 9% coupon. The mortgage payments from the underlying mortgage pool are distributed to Class B-1 and Class B-2 so that both classes receive an equal amount of the principal, but Class B-1 receives one-third of the interest payments while Class B-2 receives two-thirds.

In a subsequent issue, Fannie Mae distributed the cash flow from the underlying mortgage pool in a far different way. Using FNMA 11% coupon pools, Fannie Mae created Class A-1 and Class A-2. Class A-1 was given 4.95% of the 11% coupon interest, while Class A-2 received the other 6.05%. Class A-1 was given almost all of the principal payments, 99%, while Class A-2 was allotted only 1% of the principal payments.

In early 1987, stripped mortgage-backed securities began to be issued allocating all the interest to one class (called the *interest only* or IO class) and all the principal to the other class (called the *principal only* or PO class). The IO class receives no principal payments.

The PO security is purchased at a substantial discount from par value. The yield an investor realizes depends on the speed at which prepayments are made. The faster the prepayments, the higher the investor's yield. For example, suppose there is a mortgage pool consisting of only 30-year mortgages, with $400 million in principal, and that investors can purchase POs backed by this mortgage pool for $175 million. The dollar return on this investment will be $225 million. How quickly that dollar return is recovered by PO investors determines the yield that will be realized. In the extreme case, if all homeowners in the underlying mortgage pool decide to prepay their mortgage loans immediately, PO investors will realize the $225 million immediately. At the other extreme, if all homeowners decide to remain in their homes for 30 years and make no prepayments, the $225 million will be spread out over 30 years, which would result in a lower yield for PO investors.

A PO is a security whose price would rise when interest rates decline and fall when interest rates rise. This is typical of all the bonds we have discussed thus far in this book. A characteristic of a PO is that its price is very sensitive to changes in interest rates.

An IO has no par value. In contrast to the PO investor, the IO investor wants prepayments to be slow. The reason is that the IO investor receives interest only on the amount of the principal outstanding. When prepayments are made, less dollar interest will be received as the outstanding principal declines. In fact, if prepayments are too fast, the IO investor may not recover the amount paid for the IO. The unique aspect of an IO is that its price changes in the *same* direction as the change in interest rates. Moreover, as in the case of the PO, its price is highly responsive to a change in interest rates.

Because of these price volatility characteristics of stripped mortgage-backed securities, institutional investors have used them to control the risk of a portfolio of mortgage-backed securities so as to create a risk/return pattern that better fits their needs.

▶ KEY POINTS THAT YOU SHOULD UNDERSTAND BEFORE PROCEEDING:

1. A stripped mortgage-backed security is created by distributing the principal and interest from a pool of underlying mortgages on an unequal basis to two classes of securityholders.
2. A stripped mortgage-backed security is another example of a derivative mortgage security.
3. Stripped mortgage-backed securities can be used to hedge a portfolio exposed to prepayment risk.
4. There are two types of stripped mortgage-backed securities: partially stripped, and interest only/principal only securities.

## INVESTORS IN MORTGAGE-BACKED SECURITIES

To illustrate the broad appeal of mortgage-backed securities, Table 24-3 shows the estimated proportion of these securities held by U.S. institutions. It is interesting to note that less than 25% of these securities are held by thrifts. The large number of mortgage-backed securities held by the other kinds of institutions—banks, mutual funds, and so on—function either as investments or as hedging instruments for investments in mortgages.

The increasing appeal of these securities for non-U.S. investors is apparent in the distribution of the agency mortgage-backed securities that were issued in 1990: Japanese investors purchased about 11.25%, and European and U.K. investors purchased about 3.75%.[8] Again, the investors purchasing

[8] This information was provided by Bear Stearns & Co., Inc.

| TABLE 24-3 | |
|---|---|
| **PERCENTAGE DISTRIBUTION OF HOLDINGS OF MORTGAGE-BACKED SECURITIES BY U.S. INSTITUTIONS, 1991** | |
| Thrifts | 23.4% |
| Banks | 21.0 |
| Pension funds | 9.7 |
| Life insurance companioes | 14.4 |
| Dealers, mutual funds, asset managers, and property and casualty insurance companies | 31.5 |

*Source:* Bear Stearns & Co., Inc.

these securities may use them as investments or as instruments for hedging various kinds of risk arising from investments in mortgages.

## YIELDS ON MORTGAGE-BACKED SECURITIES

While many of the securities issued in the mortgage-backed securities market carry the explicit or implicit guarantee of the U.S. government, this does not mean that they will offer the same yield as U.S. Treasury securities or other government agency securities. The primary reason for a difference in yields lies in the uncertainty of the cash flow of a mortgage-backed security and the exposure to prepayment risk. This risk arises because the investor has granted the homeowner/borrower the right to prepay a loan at any time without penalty. Of course, investors require a higher potential yield as compensation for prepayment risk. This situation is not any different from that of an investor who buys a callable corporate bond and seeks compensation for the call risk associated with such a bond. In a CMO structure, classes that are exposed to less prepayment risk are willing to accept a lower yield than other classes such as the support bond classes that are exposed to greater prepayment risk.

The problem of calculating a yield for a mortgage-backed security is a complex one. As explained in Chapter 11, calculating the yield requires a determination of the cash flow. In the case of a mortgage-backed security, the cash flow is not known because of prepayments. This means that, to calculate the potential yield, projections of prepayments must be made for a mortgage-backed security. The conventions and practices for doing this are beyond the scope of this chapter.[9] What is important, however, is recognition that the yield on any mortgage-backed security is based on some assumption about prepayments.

---

[9] For an explanation of how this is done, see Chapters 9 and 10 in Frank J. Fabozzi and Franco Modigliani, *Mortgage and Mortgage-Backed Securities* (Boston, MA: Harvard Business School Publications, 1992).

**SUMMARY**

In this chapter we have discussed the market for mortgage-backed securities and the important role that securitization played in the development of the secondary mortgage market. The basic mortgage-backed security is the mortgage pass-through security. The types of mortgage pass-through securities are agency and conventional (private label) pass-through securities. The latter require private credit enhancements in order to receive a high credit rating.

To address the prepayment risk associated with investing in mortgage pass-through securities—contraction risk and extension risk—collateralized mortgage obligations (CMOs) were created. Another derivative mortgage-backed security, the stripped mortgage-backed security, was created for better controlling the risk of a portfolio of mortgage-backed securities.

The market for agency pass-through securities is now the second most liquid long-term fixed-income market in the U.S., the first being the U.S. Treasury securities market. The greater liquidity, coupled with new mortgage designs and security structures, has resulted in increased participation by a greater number of nondepository financial institutions. This development, in turn, has assured a supply of funds to the mortgage market so that mortgage rates are in line with rates in other sectors of the long-term debt market. Rates in the mortgage market therefore more nearly reflect supply and demand in the capital markets rather than the fortunes or misfortunes of the thrifts that historically have been the primary suppliers of funds to the mortgage market.

**GLOSSARY**

**Agency pass-through security:** A mortgage-pass through issued or guaranteed by either Ginnie Mae, Fannie Mae, or Freddie Mac.

**Collateralized mortgage obligation (or CMO):** A mortgage-backed security with multiple bond classes that is backed by one or more pools of pass-through securities or mortgages.

**Companion (or support) bond:** A type of CMO bond class that provides support for the PAC bonds in the structure.

**Contraction risk:** A form of prepayment risk resulting from a decline in mortgage rates that will shorten the life of a mortgage or mortgage-backed security.

**Conventional (or private-label) pass-through security:** A mortgage pass-through security not issued or guaranteed by an agency.

**Extension risk:** A form of prepayment risk resulting from a rise in mortgage rates that will lengthen the life of a mortgage or mortgage-backed security.

**Interest only (or IO) class:** A stripped mortgage-backed security that receives all the interest payments.

**Jumbo loan:** A mortgage loan that is nonconforming because the amount of the loan is greater than the maximum permissible loan size specified by an agency.

**Mortgage pass-through security:** Security created when one or more holders of mortgages form a collection (pool) of mortgages and sell shares or participation certificates in the pool.

**Participation certificate (or PC):** Pass-through security issued by Freddie Mac.

**Planned amortization class (or PAC) bond:** A type of CMO bond class providing a specified schedule to retire the original principal of the bondholders.

**Prepayment risk:** The risk associated with the ownership of a mortgage or mortgage-backed security due to the uncertainty of the cash flow arising from prepayments.

**Principal only (or PO) class:** A stripped mortgage-backed security that receives all the principal payments.

**Secondary Mortgage Market Enhancement Act of 1984 (or SMMEA):** Legislation qualifying mortgage-backed securities earning a high quality rating from one of the main commercial rating agencies as legal investments for federally chartered banks and thrifts.

**Securitized mortgage:** A mortgage included in a pool of mortgages that is used as collateral for a mortgage-backed security.

**Stripped mortgage-backed securities:** A mortgage-backed security created by distributing the principal and interest from a pool of underlying mortgages on an unequal basis to two classes of securityholders.

**Targeted amortization class (or TAC) bond:** A type of CMO bond that is designed to provide protection against contraction risk but exposes the investor to extension risk.

1. How has securitization enhanced the liquidity of mortgages?
2. a. What is a mortgage pass-through security?
   b. Describe the investment characteristics of a mortgage pass-through security.
   c. Why is the cash flow of a mortgage pass-through less than the cash flow of the underlying mortgage pool?
3. What are the different types of agency pass-through securities?
4. a. What is a conventional pass-through security?
   b. Describe various ways that issuers have enhanced the credit quality of a conventional pass-through security.
5. What is the difference between the Freddie Mac Cash Program and the Freddie Mac Swap program?

6. What are meant by prepayment risk, contraction risk, and extension risk?

7. a. How does a collateralized mortgage obligation alter the cash flow from mortgages so as to shift the prepayment risk across various classes of bondholders?

    b. "By creating a CMO, an issuer eliminates the prepayment risk associated with the underlying mortgages." Do you agree with this statement?

8. This quotation is taken from a 1991 issue of *Bondweek:*

    *First Interstate Bank of Texas will look into buying several different types of collateralized mortgage obligation tranches when it starts up its buy program sometime after the second quarter of 1991, according to Jules Pollard, v.p. Pollard said he will consider replacing maturing adjustable-rate mortgage pass-throughs with short companion tranches and planned and targeted amortization classes because the ARMS have become rich. . . . Pollard did not provide a dollar figure on the planned investments, which will be made to match fund the bank's liabilities. When he does invest he said he prefers government-guaranteed securities or those with implied guarantees.*

    a. Explain the types of securities that Pollard is buying and selling.

    b. Given the preference Pollard states in the last sentence of the quotation, what issuers is he likely to prefer? What issuers would he reject?

9. Why would you expect the yield offered on a Ginnie Mae pass-through to be higher than the yield on a Treasury security?

10. In what way is the risk of investing in a callable corporate bond similar to the risk of investing in a mortgage-backed security?

11. What are the complications in calculating the yield on a mortgage-backed security?

CHAPTER TWENTY-FIVE

# Financial Futures Markets

## LEARNING OBJECTIVES

*After reading this chapter you will understand:*

- what a futures contract is.
- the basic economic function of a futures contract.
- the differences between futures and forward contracts.
- the role of the clearinghouse.
- the mark-to-market and margin requirements of a futures contract.
- the role of futures markets in the economy.
- features of U.S. stock index futures contracts.
- features of interest rate futures contracts.
- Japanese financial futures markets.

In this chapter, we describe the financial futures market and the various contracts traded in it. The basic economic function of futures markets is to provide an opportunity for market participants to hedge against the risk of adverse price movements.

Futures contracts are products created by exchanges. To create a particular futures contract, an exchange must obtain approval from the Commodity Futures Trading Commission (CFTC), a government regulatory agency. In its application to the CFTC, the exchange must demonstrate that there is an economic purpose for the contract. While numerous futures contracts obtain approval for trading, only those contracts that spark investor interest and serve investor needs ultimately succeed.

Prior to 1972, only futures contracts involving traditional agricultural commodities (such as grain and livestock), imported foodstuffs (such as coffee, cocoa, and sugar), or industrial commodities were traded. Collectively, such futures contracts are known as *commodity futures*. Futures contracts based on a financial instrument or a financial index are known as *financial futures*. Financial futures can be classified as (1) stock index futures; (2) interest rate futures; and (3) currency futures.

As the value of a futures contract is derived from the value of the underlying instrument, futures contracts are commonly called *derivative instruments*. Options, discussed in the next chapter, are another example of derivative instruments. The pricing of derivative contracts and their uses by market participants are the topics of Chapters 27 and 28, respectively.

In the United States, the development of the markets for futures and options on stock indexes and debt obligations was a response to the need for an efficient risk-transference mechanism as stock price and interest rate volatility in the United States increased. Other countries have shared the U.S. experience with volatility and, as a result, developed derivative markets.

## FUTURES CONTRACTS

A futures contract is a firm legal agreement between and a buyer and a seller, in which:

1.  The buyer agrees to take delivery of something at a specified price at the end of a designated period of time.
2.  The seller agrees to make delivery of something at a specified price at the end of a designated period of time.

Of course, no one buys or sells anything when entering into a futures contract. Rather, the parties to the contract agree to buy or sell a specific amount of a specific item at a specified future date. When we speak of the "buyer" or the "seller" of a contract, we are simply adopting the jargon of the futures market, which refers to parties of the contract in terms of the future obligation they are committing themselves to.

Let's look closely at the key elements of this contract.

The price at which the parties agree to transact in the future is called the *futures price*. The designated date at which the parties must transact is called the *settlement date* or *delivery date*. The "something" that the parties agree to exchange is called the *underlying*.

To illustrate, suppose there is a futures contract traded on an exchange where the underlying to be bought or sold is Asset XYZ, and the settlement is three months from now. Assume further that Bob buys this futures contract, and Sally sells this futures contract, and the price at which they agree to transact in the future is $100. Then $100 is the futures price. At the settlement date, Sally will deliver Asset XYZ to Bob. Bob will give Sally $100, the futures price.

When an investor takes a position in the market by buying a futures contract (or agreeing to buy at the future date), the investor is said to be in a *long position* or to be *long futures*. If, instead, the investor's opening position is the sale of a futures contract (which means the contractual obligation to sell something in the future), the investor is said to be in a *short position* or to be *short futures*.

The buyer of a futures contract will realize a profit if the futures price increases; the seller of a futures contract will realize a profit if the futures price decreases. For example, suppose that one month after Bob and Sally take their positions in the futures contract, the futures price of Asset XYZ increases to $120. Bob, the buyer of the futures contract, could then sell the futures contract and realize a profit of $20. Effectively, he has agreed to buy, at the settlement date, Asset XYZ for $100 and to sell Asset XYZ for $120. Sally, the seller of the futures contract, will realize a loss of $20.

If the futures price falls to $40 and Sally buys the contract, she realizes a profit of $60 because she agreed to sell Asset XYZ for $100 and now can buy it for $40. Bob would realize a loss of $60. Thus, if the futures price decreases, the buyer of the futures contract realizes a loss while the seller of a futures contract realizes a profit.

## Liquidating a Position

Most financial futures contracts have settlement dates in the months of March, June, September, or December. This means that at a predetermined time in the contract settlement month the contract stops trading, and a price is determined by the exchange for settlement of the contract. The contract with the closest settlement date is called the *nearby futures contract*. The next futures contract is the one that settles just after the nearby contract. The contract farthest away in time from settlement is called the *most distant futures contract*.

A party to a futures contract has two choices on liquidation of the position. First, the position can be liquidated prior to the settlement date. For this purpose, the party must take an offsetting position in the same contract. For the buyer of a futures contract, this means selling the same number of identical futures contracts; for the seller of a futures contract, this means buying the same number of identical futures contracts.

The alternative is to wait until the settlement date. At that time the party purchasing a futures contract accepts delivery of the underlying; the party that sells a futures contract liquidates the position by delivering the underlying at the agreed-upon price. For some futures contracts that we shall describe later in this chapter, settlement is made in cash only. Such contracts are referred to as *cash settlement contracts*.

A useful statistic measuring the liquidity of a contract is the number of contracts that have been entered into but not yet liquidated. This figure is called the contract's *open interest*. An open interest figure is reported by an exchange for all the futures contracts traded on the exchange.

## The Role of the Clearinghouse

Associated with every futures exchange is a clearinghouse, which performs several functions. One of these functions is to guarantee that the two parties to the transaction will perform. To see the importance of this function, consider potential problems in the futures transaction described earlier from the perspective of the two parties—Bob the buyer and Sally the seller. Each must be concerned with the other's ability to fulfill the obligation at the settlement date. Suppose that at the settlement date the price of Asset XYZ in the cash market is $70. Sally can buy Asset XYZ for $70 and deliver it to Bob, who in turn must pay her $100. If Bob does not have the capacity to pay $100 or refuses to pay, however, Sally has lost the opportunity to realize a profit of $30. Suppose, instead, that the price of Asset XYZ in the cash market is $150 at the settlement date. In this case, Bob is ready and willing to accept delivery of Asset XYZ and pay the agreed-upon price of $100. If Sally cannot deliver or refuses to deliver Asset XYZ, Bob has lost the opportunity to realize a profit of $50.

The clearinghouse exists to meet this problem. When someone takes a position in the futures market, the clearinghouse takes the opposite position and agrees to satisfy the terms set forth in the contract. Because of the clearinghouse, the two parties need not worry about the financial strength and integrity of the party taking the opposite side of the contract. After initial execution of an order, the relationship between the two parties ends. The clearinghouse interposes itself as the buyer for every sale and the seller for every purchase. Thus, the two parties are then free to liquidate their positions without involving the other party in the original contract, and without worry that the other party may default.

Besides its guarantee function, the clearinghouse makes it simple for parties to a futures contract to unwind their positions prior to the settlement date. Suppose that Bob wants to get out of his futures position. He will not have to seek out Sally and work out an agreement with her to terminate the original agreement. Instead, Bob can unwind his position by selling an identical futures contract. As far as the clearinghouse is concerned, its records will show that Bob has bought and sold an identical futures contract. At the settlement date, Sally will not deliver Asset XYZ to Bob but will be instructed by the clearinghouse to deliver to someone who bought and still has an open futures position. In the same way, if Sally wants to unwind her position prior to the settlement date, she can buy an identical futures contract.

## Margin Requirements

When a position is first taken in a futures contract, the investor must deposit a minimum dollar amount per contract as specified by the exchange. This amount, called *initial margin*, is required as a deposit for the contract. Individual brokerage firms are free to set margin requirements above the minimum established by the exchange. The initial margin may be in the form of an interest-bearing security such as a Treasury bill. As the price of the futures contract fluctuates each trading day, the value of the investor's *equity* in the position changes. The equity in a futures account is the sum of all margins posted and all daily gains less all daily losses to the account. We develop this important concept throughout this section.

At the end of each trading day, the exchange determines the "settlement price" for the futures contract. The settlement price is different from the closing price, which many people know from the stock market and which is the price of the security in the final trade of the day (whenever that trade occurred during the day). The settlement price by contrast is that value that the exchange considers to be representative of trading at the end of the day. The representative price may in fact be the price in the day's last trade. But, if there is a flurry of trading at the end of the day, the exchange looks at all trades in the last few minutes and identifies a median or average price among those trades. The exchange uses the settlement price to mark to market the investor's position, so that any gain or loss from the position is quickly reflected in the investor's equity account.

*Maintenance margin* is the minimum level (specified by the exchange) to which an investor's equity position may fall as a result of an unfavorable price movement before the investor is required to deposit additional margin. The additional margin deposited is called *variation margin*, and it is an amount necessary to bring the equity in the account back to its initial margin level. Unlike initial margin, the variation margin must be in cash rather than interest-bearing instruments. Any excess margin in the account may be withdrawn by the investor. If a party to a futures contract who is required to deposit variation margin fails to do so within 24 hours, the exchange closes the futures position out.

Although there are initial and maintenance margin requirements for buying securities on margin, the concept of margin differs for securities and futures. When securities are acquired on margin, the difference between the price of the security and the initial margin is borrowed from the broker. The security purchased serves as collateral for the loan, and the investor pays interest. For futures contracts, the initial margin, in effect, serves as "good faith" money, an indication that the investor will satisfy the obligation of the contract. Normally, no money is borrowed by the investor who takes a futures position.

To illustrate the mark-to-market procedure, let's assume the following margin requirements for Asset XYZ:

Initial margin            $ 7 per contract
Maintenance margin    $ 4 per contract

Let's assume that Bob buys 500 contracts at a futures price of $100, and Sally sells the same number of contracts at the same futures price. The initial margin for both Bob and Sally is $3,500, which is determined by multiplying the initial margin of $7 by the number of contracts, which is 500. Bob and Sally must put up $3,500 in cash or Treasury bills or other acceptable collateral. At this time, $3,500 is also called the equity in the account. The maintenance margin for the two positions is $2,000 (the maintenance margin per contract of $4 multiplied by 500 contracts). The equity in the account may not fall below $2,000. If it does, the party whose equity falls below the maintenance margin must put up additional margin, which is the variation margin. There are two things to note here. First, the variation margin must be cash. Second, the amount of variation margin required is the amount to bring the equity up to the initial margin, not to the maintenance margin.

To illustrate the mark-to-market procedure, we assume the following settlement prices at the end of several trading days after the transaction was entered into. Those prices are:

| *Trading Day* | *Settlement Price* |
| --- | --- |
| 1 | $ 99 |
| 2 | 97 |
| 3 | 98 |
| 4 | 95 |

First, consider Bob's position. At the end of trading day 1, Bob realizes a loss of $1 per contract or $500 for the 500 contracts he bought. Bob's initial equity of $3,500 is reduced by $500 to $3,000. No action is taken by the clearinghouse because Bob's equity is still above the maintenance margin of $2,000. At the end of the second day, Bob realizes a further loss as the price of the futures contract has declined another $2 to $97, resulting in an additional reduction in his equity position by $1,000. Bob's equity is then $2,000: the equity at the end of trading day 1 of $3,000 minus the loss on trading day 2 of $1,000. Despite the loss, no action is taken by the clearinghouse, because the equity still meets the $2,000 maintenance requirement. At the end of trading day 3, Bob realizes a profit from the previous trading day of $1 per contract or $500. Bob's equity increases to $2,500. The drop in price from 98 to 95 at the end of trading day 4 results in a loss for the 500 contracts of $1,500 and consequent reduction of Bob's equity to $1,000. As Bob's equity is now below the $2,000 maintenance margin, Bob is required to put up additional margin of $2,500 (variation margin) to bring the equity up to the initial margin of $3,500. If Bob cannot put up the variation margin, his position will be liquidated.

Now, let's look at Sally's position. Sally as the seller of the futures contract benefits if the price of the futures contract declines. As a result, her equity increases at the end of the first two trading days. In fact, at the end of trading day 1, she realizes a profit of $500, which increases her equity to

$4,000. She is entitled to take out the $500 profit and use these funds elsewhere. Suppose she does, and her equity therefore remains at $3,500 at the end of trading day 1. At the end of trading day 2, she realizes an additional profit of $1,000 that she also withdraws. At the end of trading day 3, she realizes a loss of $500 with the increase of the price from $97 to $98. This results in a reduction of her equity to $3,000. Finally, on trading day 4, she realizes a profit of $1,000, making her equity $4,000. She can withdraw $500.

### Leveraging Aspect of Futures

A party taking a position in a futures contract need not put up the entire amount of the investment. Instead, the exchange and/or clearinghouse requires only the initial margin to be put up. To see the crucial consequences of this fact, suppose Bob has $100 and wants to invest in Asset XYZ because he believes its price will appreciate. If Asset XYZ is selling for $100, he can buy one unit of the asset. His payoff will then be based on the price action of one unit of Asset XYZ.

Suppose further that the exchange where the futures contract for Asset XYZ is traded requires an initial margin of only 5%, which in this case would be $5. This means Bob can purchase 20 contracts with his $100 investment. (We ignore the fact that Bob may need funds for variation margin.) His payoff will then depend on the price action of 20 units of Asset XYZ. Thus, he can leverage the use of his funds. (The degree of leverage equals 1/margin rate. In this case, the degree of leverage equals 1/0.05 or 20.) While the degree of leverage available in the futures market varies from contract to contract, as the initial margin requirement varies, the leverage attainable is considerably greater than in the cash market.

At first, the leverage available in the futures market may suggest that the market benefits mainly those who want to speculate on price movements. As we shall see in Chapter 28, however, futures markets can also be used to reduce price risk. Without the leverage possible in futures transactions, the cost of reducing price risk using futures would be too high for many market participants.

### Market Structure

All futures exchanges in the U.S. trade more than one futures contract. On the exchange floor, each futures contract is traded at a designated location in a polygonal or circular platform called a *pit*. The price of a futures contract is determined by open outcry of bids and offers in an auction market. Because of the large number of traders attempting to communicate to other traders the price and quantity that they wish to transact at, pit traders are often forced to communicate using a system of hand signals. There is no designated market maker in the futures market as there is on an exchange where common stock is traded.

Trading on the floor of the exchange is restricted to members of the exchange. A membership is called a "seat on the exchange." Its price is determined by supply and demand. Nonexchange members can lease a seat, which conveys to them the right to trade on an exchange. Floor traders include two types: *locals* and *floor brokers* (also called *pit brokers*). Locals buy and sell futures contracts for their own account, thereby risking their own capital. They are professional risk takers whose presence in the futures market adds liquidity to the market and brings bid and offer prices closer together. Consequently, collectively they play the same effective role as the market maker. Most locals do not maintain an open position overnight. The number of locals and the amount of capital that they can commit to the market far exceeds that of the floor brokers.

Floor brokers, just like locals, buy and sell for their own account. They execute customer orders as well. These orders come through an authorized futures broker, called a *futures commissions merchant*, or in the form of orders requested by other floor traders. For trades that they execute on behalf of others, floor brokers receive a commission. While floor brokers can both execute orders for customers and trade for their own account, most of their trades involve the former. When floor brokers do trade for their own account, such trades must not conflict with the interests of customers for whom they are executing trades.

This system of trading in futures markets is not very different from the process that began in the nineteenth century. Monitoring this sort of system is difficult, which has led to allegations that floor traders profit at the expense of customers whose orders are to be executed.

Several approaches for improving the system of trading futures via electronic trading are at the experimental stage. One approach is a computerized, automated system for executing routine trades. Another approach is to automate the entire competitive trading system that now takes place in the pit. The Chicago Mercantile Exchange is working with Reuters Holdings to develop such a system (called the "Globex System") for trading of futures contracts globally when a futures exchange is closed. Outside the United States, various forms of electronic trading of futures contracts have already been introduced.

## Daily Price Limits

The exchange has the right to impose a limit on the daily price movement of a futures contract from the previous day's closing price. A *daily price limit* sets the minimum and maximum price at which the futures contract may trade that day. When a daily price limit is reached, trading does not stop but rather continues at a price that does not violate the minimum or maximum price.

The rationale offered for the imposition of daily price limits is that they provide stability to the market at times when new information may cause the futures price to exhibit extreme fluctuations. Those who support daily price limits argue that giving market participants time to digest or reassess such information if trading ceases when price limits would be violated gives them greater confidence in the market. Not all economists agree with this rationale.

The question of the role of daily price limits and whether they are necessary remains the subject of extensive debate.

▶ <u>KEY POINTS THAT YOU SHOULD UNDERSTAND BEFORE PROCEEDING</u>:

1. A futures contract is a firm legal agreement between a buyer and a seller in which the buyer agrees to take delivery of something at the futures price at the settlement date and the seller agrees to make delivery.

2. A party to a futures contract can liquidate a position prior to the settlement date by taking an offsetting position in the same contract.

3. Associated with every futures exchange is a clearinghouse, which provides a guarantee function.

4. Parties to a futures contract must satisfy margin requirements (initial, maintenance, and variation), and futures contracts are marked to market at the end of each trading day.

5. Futures contracts are leveraged instruments that can be used to control risk.

## FUTURES VERSUS FORWARD CONTRACTS

A *forward contract*, just like a futures contract, is an agreement for the future delivery of something at a specified price at the end of a designated period of time. Futures contracts are standardized agreements as to the delivery date (or month) and quality of the deliverable, and are traded on organized exchanges. A forward contract is usually nonstandardized because the terms of each contract are negotiated individually between buyer and seller. Also, there is no clearinghouse for trading forward contracts, and secondary markets are often nonexistent or extremely thin. Unlike a futures contract, which is an exchange-traded product, a forward contract is an over-the-counter instrument.

Although both futures and forward contracts set forth terms of delivery, futures contracts are not intended to be settled by delivery. In fact, generally fewer than 2% of outstanding contracts are settled by delivery. Forward contracts, in contrast, are intended for delivery.

Futures contracts are marked to market at the end of each trading day, while forward contracts typically are not. Consequently, futures contracts are subject to interim cash flows as additional margin may be required in the case of adverse price movements, or as an investor who has experienced favorable price movements withdraws any cash that exceeds the account's margin requirement. There are no interim cash flow effects with forward contracts because no variation margin is required.

Finally, the parties in a forward contract are exposed to credit risk because either party may default on the obligation. Credit risk is minimal in the case of futures contracts because the clearinghouse associated with the exchange guarantees the other side of any transaction.

Other than these differences, which reflect the institutional arrangements in the two markets, most of what we say about futures contracts applies equally to forward contracts.

## THE ROLE OF FUTURES IN FINANCIAL MARKETS

Without financial futures, investors would have only one trading location to alter portfolio positions when they get new information that is expected to influence the value of assets — the cash market. If they hear economic news that is expected to impact the value of an asset adversely, investors want to reduce their price risk exposure to that asset. The opposite would be true if the new information is expected to impact the value of an asset favorably: an investor would increase price risk exposure to that asset. There are, of course, transactions costs associated with altering exposure to an asset — explicit costs (commissions), and execution costs (bid–ask spreads and market impact costs), which we discussed in Chapter 18.

The futures market is an alternative market that investors can use to alter their risk exposure to an asset when new information is acquired. But which market — cash or futures — should the investor employ to alter a position quickly on the receipt of new information? The answer is simple: the one that most efficiently achieves the objective. The factors to consider are liquidity, transactions costs, taxes, and leverage advantages of the futures contract.

The market that investors consider more efficient for their investment objective should be the one where prices will first be established that reflect the new economic information. That is, this will be the market where price discovery takes place. Price information is then transmitted to the other market. For many of the financial assets that we have discussed, it is in the futures market that it is easier and less costly to alter a portfolio position. Therefore, it is the futures market that will be the market of choice and will serve as the price discovery market. It is in the futures market that investors send a collective message about how any new information is expected to impact the cash market.

How is this message sent to the cash market? To understand how, it is necessary to understand that there is a relationship between the futures price and the cash price. More specifically, in Chapter 27 we will demonstrate that the futures price and the cash market price are tied together by the cost of carry. If the futures price deviates from the cash market price by more than the cost of carry, arbitrageurs (in attempting to obtain arbitrage profits) would pursue a strategy to bring them back into line. Arbitrage is the mechanism that assures that the cash market price will reflect the information that has been collected in the futures market.

Some investors and the popular press consider that the introduction of a futures market for a financial asset will increase the price volatility of that financial asset in the cash market. That is, some market observers believe that, as a result of speculative trading of futures contracts, the cash market instrument does not reflect its fundamental economic value. The implication here is that the price of the financial asset would better reflect its true economic value in the absence of a futures market for that financial asset.

Whether the introduction of futures markets destabilizes prices of financial assets is an empirical question. Whether or not the introduction of futures contracts increases cash market price volatility, we might ask whether greater volatility has negative effects on financial markets. At first glance, it might seem that volatility has adverse effects from the points of view of allocative efficiency and participation in financial markets.

Actually, it has been pointed out that this inference may not be justified if, say, the introduction of futures markets lets prices respond more promptly to changes in factors that affect the economic value of a financial asset, and if these factors themselves are subject to large shocks.[1] Thus, the greater volatility resulting from an innovation may simply more faithfully reflect the actual variability of factors that affect the economic value of financial assets. In this case, "more" volatility of a financial asset's price need not be bad but, rather, may be a manifestation of a well-functioning market. Of course, to say that more volatility need not be bad does not mean that it is good.

For example, we describe below one type of futures contract in which the underlying is a stock market index. Critics of these futures contracts assert that their introduction has created greater volatility for stock market prices. While the empirical evidence has not supported this view, the key point is that increased volatility of stock market prices may be due to the greater quantity and frequency of information released by the government about important economic indicators that affect the value of the common stock of all companies. That information itself is subject to a great deal of variability. Thus, if there is any observed increase in the volatility of stock prices, that volatility may be due to the substantial variability of economic information, not to the presence of a futures contract on a stock market index.

Clearly, price volatility greater than what can be justified by relevant new information is undesirable. By definition, it makes prices inefficient. This is referred to as "excess volatility."[2]

▶ KEY POINTS THAT YOU SHOULD UNDERSTAND BEFORE PROCEEDING:

1.  The key role of futures contracts is that, in a well-functioning futures market, these contracts provide a more efficient means for investors to alter their risk exposure to an asset.

2.  A futures market will be the price discovery market when market participants prefer to use this market rather than the cash market to change their risk exposure to an asset.

---

[1] Eugene F. Fama, "Perspectives on October 1987, or What Did We Learn from the Crash?" in Robert J. Barro, et al. (eds.), *Black Monday and the Future of Financial Markets* (Homewood, IL: Dow Jones-Irwin, 1989), p. 72.

[2] Franklin R. Edwards, "Futures Trading and Cash Market Volatility: Stock Index and Interest Rate Futures," *The Journal of Futures Markets*, Vol. 8, No. 4 (1988), p. 423.

3. The futures market and the cash market for an asset are tied together by an arbitrage process.

4. The argument that futures markets destabilize the prices of the underlying financial assets is an empirical question, but greater price volatility by itself is not an undesirable attribute of a financial market.

## UNITED STATES FINANCIAL FUTURES MARKETS

In this section we review the more important financial futures markets in the United States.

### Stock Index Futures Markets

In 1982, three futures contracts on broadly based common stock indexes made their debut: the Standard & Poor's 500 futures contract traded on the International Monetary Market of the Chicago Mercantile Exchange, the New York Stock Exchange Composite futures contract traded on the New York Futures Exchange, and the Value Line Average traded on the Kansas City Board of Trade. Since then, broad-based and specialized stock index futures contracts have been introduced. Table 25-1 shows the currently traded major stock index futures contracts. The most actively traded contract is the S&P 500 futures contract.

Stock index futures contracts are regulated by the Commodity Futures Trading Commission, although in recent years there have been proposals to shift regulatory authority to the SEC.

The dollar value of a stock index futures contract is the product of the futures price and the contract's *multiple*; that is,

## TABLE 25-1

SUMMARY OF MAJOR STOCK INDEX FUTURES CONTRACTS TRADED IN THE U.S. (AS OF JUNE 1991)

| Contract | Exchange | Multiple | Initial margin | | Last Trading Day in Delivery |
| | | | Speculator | Hedger | |
|---|---|---|---|---|---|
| S&P 500 Index | CBOE | $500 | $22,000 | $9,000 | Thurs. prior to 3rd Friday |
| NYSE Index | NYSE | 500 | 9,000 | 4,000 | Thurs. prior to 3rd Friday |
| Major Market Index | AMEX | 250 | 21,000 | 7,500 | 3rd Friday |
| Value Line Maxi Index | KCBT | 500 | 7,000 | 5,000 | 3rd Friday |

Features common to all contracts:

1. The contract value is the index value x the multiple.

2. All contracts settle in cash.

3. The contract months are March, June, September and December. With the exception of the Major Market Index, three months trade at one time. For the Major Market Index the contract months are the 3 near months and the next month in the cycle.

4. Initial margin requirements are subject to change by the exchange.

$$\text{Dollar value of a stock index futures contract} =$$
$$\text{Futures price} \times \text{Multiple}$$

The multiples for the key contracts are indicated in Table 25-1. For all contracts except the Major Market index, the multiple is $500. For the Major Market index it is $250. For example, if the futures price for the S&P 500 is 310, the dollar value of a stock index futures contract is:

$$310 \times \$500 = \$155,000$$

If an investor buys (takes a long position in) an S&P 500 futures contract at 310 and sells it at 330, the investor realizes a profit of 20 times $500, or $10,000. If the futures contract is sold instead for 260, the investor will realize a loss of 50 times $500, or $25,000.

Stock index futures contracts are *cash settlement contracts*. This means that, at the settlement date, cash will be exchanged to settle the contract. For example, if an investor buys an S&P 500 futures contract at 310 and the settlement index is 350, settlement would be as follows. The investor has agreed to buy the S&P 500 for 310 times $500, or $155,000. The S&P 500 value at the settlement date is 350 times $500, or $175,000. The seller of this futures contract must pay the investor $20,000 ($175,000 − $155,000). Had the index at the settlement date been 240 instead of $350, the value of the S&P 500 would be $120,000 (240 × $500). The investor must pay the seller of the contract $35,000 ($155,000 − $120,000).

## Interest Rate Futures Markets

In October 1975, the Chicago Board of Trade (CBT) pioneered trading in a futures contract based on a fixed-income instrument—Government National Mortgage Association certificates. Three months later, the International Monetary Market (IMM) of the Chicago Mercantile Exchange (CME) began trading futures contracts based on 13-week Treasury bills. Other exchanges soon followed with their own interest rate futures contracts. The more actively traded interest rate futures contracts are described below.

*Treasury Bill Futures.* The Treasury bill futures contract, which is traded on the IMM, is based on a 13-week (three-month) Treasury bill with a face value of $1 million. More specifically, the seller of a Treasury bill futures contract agrees to deliver to the buyer at the settlement date a Treasury bill with 13 weeks remaining to maturity and a face value of $1 million. The Treasury bill that would be delivered by the terms of this contract can be newly issued or seasoned. The futures price is the price at which the Treasury bill will be sold by the short and purchased by the buyer. For example, a nine-month Treasury bill futures contract requires that, nine months from now, the short deliver to the long $1 million face value of a Treasury bill with 13 weeks remaining to maturity. The Treasury bill could be a newly issued 13-week Treasury bill or a Treasury bill that was issued one year prior to the settlement date and that therefore, at the settlement, has only 13 weeks remaining to maturity.

As we explained in Chapter 16, Treasury bills are quoted in the cash market in terms of the annualized yield on a bank discount basis. The Treasury bill futures contract is not quoted directly in terms of yield but instead on an index basis that is related to the yield on a bank discount basis as follows:

$$\text{Index price} = 100 - (\text{Yield on a bank discount basis} \times 100)$$

For example, if the yield on a bank discount basis is 8%, then

$$\text{Index price} = 100 - (0.08 \times 100) = 92.$$

***Eurodollar CD Futures.***   As we explained in Chapter 22, Eurodollar certificates of deposit (CDs) are denominated in dollars but represent the liabilities of banks outside the United States. The rate paid on Eurodollar CDs is the London Interbank Offered Rate (LIBOR). The three-month Eurodollar CD is the underlying for the Eurodollar CD futures contract. As with the Treasury bill futures contract, this contract is for $1 million of face value and is traded on an index price basis. The contract is traded on both the International Monetary Market of the Chicago Mercantile Exchange and the London International Financial Futures Exchange.

The unique feature of the Eurodollar CD futures contract is that the settlement procedure requires the parties to settle in cash for the value of a Eurodollar CD based on LIBOR at the settlement date. Of the two futures contracts based on short-term instruments, Eurodollar CD futures are more commonly employed by institutional investors than Treasury bill futures.

***Treasury Bond Futures.***   The underlying for a Treasury bond futures contract is $100,000 par value of a hypothetical 20-year, 8% coupon bond. While prices and yields of the Treasury bond futures contract are quoted in terms of this hypothetical Treasury bond (see Chapter 16 for details on price quotations of Treasury bonds), the seller of the futures contract has the choice of several actual Treasury bonds that are acceptable to deliver. The Chicago Board of Trade (where the contract is traded) allows the seller to deliver any Treasury bond that has at least 15 years to maturity from the date of delivery if it is not callable; in the case of callable bonds, the issue must not be callable for at least 15 years from the first day of the delivery month. Settling a contract calls for an acceptable bond to be delivered. That is, the contract is not a cash settlement contract.

The delivery process for the Treasury bond futures contract makes the contract interesting. At the settlement date, the seller of a futures contract (the short) is required to deliver to the buyer (the long) $100,000 par value of an 8%, 20-year Treasury bond. Since no such bond exists, the seller must choose from the list of acceptable, deliverable bonds that the exchange has specified. But this choice raises a problem. Suppose the seller is entitled to deliver $100,000 of a 6%, 20-year Treasury bond to settle the futures contract. The value of this bond, of course, is less than the value of an 8%, 20-year bond. If the seller delivers the 6%, 20-year, this would be unfair to the buyer of the futures contract who contracted to receive $100,000 of an 8%, 20-year Treasury bond. Alternatively, suppose the seller delivers $100,000 of a 10%, 20-year Treasury bond. The value of a 10%, 20-year Treasury bond is greater than that of an 8%, 20-year bond, so this would be a disadvantage to the seller.

How can this problem be resolved? To make delivery equitable to both parties, and to tie cash prices to futures prices, the CBT has introduced *conversion factors* for determining the invoice price of each acceptable deliverable Treasury issue against the Treasury bond futures contract. The conversion factor is determined by the CBT before a contract with a specific settlement date begins trading. The conversion factor is based on the price that a deliverable bond would sell for, at the beginning of the delivery month, if it were to yield 8%. The conversion factor is constant throughout the trading period of the futures contract. The short must notify the long, one day before the delivery date, of the actual bond that will be delivered.

The invoice price paid by the buyer of the Treasury bonds which the seller delivers is determined using the formula:

$$\text{Invoice price} = \text{Contract size} \times \text{Futures contract settlement price} \times \text{Conversion factor}$$

Suppose the Treasury bond futures contract settles at 96 (0.96 in decimal form) and that the short elects to deliver a Treasury bond issue with a conversion factor of 1.15. As the contract size is $100,000, the invoice price is:

$$\$100,000 \times 0.96 \times 1.15 = \$110,400$$

The invoice price in the formula is just for the principal. The buyer of the futures contract must also pay the seller accrued interest on the bond delivered.

In selecting the issue to be delivered, the short will select from all the deliverable issues the bond that is cheapest to deliver. This issue is referred to as the *cheapest-to-deliver issue*. It plays a key role in the pricing of this futures contract. The cost to deliver is the difference between the cost of purchasing the Treasury issue and the invoice price for the principal. That is,

$$\text{Cost to deliver} = \text{Cost of purchasing issue} - \text{Invoice price}.$$

Of course, choosing the cheapest to deliver is equivalent to selecting the issue that would generate the greatest profit, as measured by the invoice price for the principal minus the cost of purchasing the issue. Notice that computation of the cost of delivery does not consider the accrued interest that the seller (the short position) must pay to acquire the issue. The reason is that this cost would be offset when the long purchases the issue from the short.

In addition to the option of which acceptable Treasury issue to deliver — sometimes referred to as the *quality* or *swap option* — the short position has two more options granted under CBT delivery guidelines. First, the short position is permitted to decide when in the delivery month actually to make the delivery. This is called the *timing option*. The second option is the right of the short position to give notice of intent to deliver up to 8:00 p.m. Chicago time after the closing of the exchange (3:15 p.m. Chicago time) on the date when the futures settlement price has been fixed. This option is referred to as the *wild card option*. The quality option, the timing option, and the wild card option (in sum referred to as the "delivery options") mean that the long position can never be sure which Treasury bond will be delivered or when it will be delivered.

**Treasury Note Futures.** Modeled after the Treasury bond futures contract, the Treasury note futures contract underlying is $100,000 par value of a hypothetical ten-year, 8% Treasury note. There are several acceptable Treasury issues that may be delivered by the short. An issue is acceptable if the maturity is not less than 6.5 years and not more than 10.0 years from the first day of the delivery month. The delivery options granted to the short position are the same as for the Treasury bond futures contract.

**Bond Buyer's Municipal Bond Index Futures.** The underlying product for this contract traded on the CBT is a basket, or index, of 40 municipal bonds. The Bond Buyer, publisher of *The Bond Buyer* (a trade publication of the municipal bond industry), serves as the index manager for the contract and prices each bond in the index according to prices received from five municipal bond brokers. It is necessary to obtain several independent prices from brokers because municipal bonds trade in the over-the-counter market.

Once the prices for a given issue are received from the five pricing brokers, the lowest and the highest prices are dropped. The remaining three prices then are averaged, with the resulting value referred to as the *appraisal value*. As delivery on all 40 bonds in the index is not practicable, the contract is a cash settlement contract, with settlement price based on the value of the index on the delivery date.

The contract is quoted in points and 32nds of a point. For example, suppose the settlement price for the contract is 93-21. This translates into a price of 93 and 21/32, or 93.65635. The dollar value of a contract is equal to $1,000 times the Bond Buyer Municipal Bond Index. For example, the dollar value based on the settlement price is:

$$\$1,000 \times 93.65635 = \$93,656.35$$

▶ KEY POINTS THAT YOU SHOULD UNDERSTAND BEFORE PROCEEDING:

1. Stock index futures contracts are cash settlement contracts whose underlying is a common stock index.
2. The dollar value of a stock index futures contract is the product of the futures price and the contract's multiple.

3. An interest rate futures contract is one whose underlying asset is a fixed-income instrument or an interest rate.

4. The more actively traded interest rate futures contracts are the Treasury bill futures contract, the Eurodollar CD futures contract (a cash settlement contract), the Treasury bond and note futures contracts, and the Bond Buyer's Municipal Bond Index futures contract (a cash settlement contract).

5. The Treasury bond and note futures contracts are unique in that the short is granted options as to which issue to deliver and when to deliver.

## FINANCIAL FUTURES MARKETS IN OTHER COUNTRIES

Other countries have developed financial futures exchanges that have introduced a wide range of contracts. Many of these contracts are modeled after those developed in the U.S. futures markets. Many of the stock index futures contracts, for example, are cash settlement contracts, which is the settlement procedure used in the U.S. In the case of futures on government bonds, the short (the seller of the futures contract) has the right to deliver one of several acceptable government issues. Japanese futures contracts are worth discussing at some length because of the size of this financial market and because several of these contracts are traded in the United States.

### *Japanese Stock Index Futures*

There are three stock index futures contracts traded in Japan: the Nikkei 225 Stock Average (which began trading on the Osaka Stock Exchange in September 1988), the Tokyo Stock Price Index (TOPIX) (which began trading on the Tokyo Stock Exchange in September 1988), and the Osaka Stock Futures 50 (which began trading on the Osaka Stock Exchange in June 1987). In fact, the Osaka Stock Futures 50 began trading on the Singapore Exchange (SIMEX) in September 1986 before stock index futures trading was authorized in Japan.

As we explained earlier in this chapter, one of the major reasons for using stock index futures is the significantly lower costs of transactions in the futures market compared to the cash market. Total round-trip futures costs for the TOPIX futures contract are less than 5% of trading costs in the underlying stocks.[3] In Japan, in particular, there is another advantage of transacting in stock index futures rather than in the underlying stocks. Shorting stocks in Japan is difficult, so selling stock index futures is the only effective way of going short in the equities market.

---

[3] Gary L. Gastineau, Mark M. Arimura, Michael J. Belkin, Eric A. Clausen, Tak Kyokuta, Tatsuya Higashino, and Christopher M. Mitchinson, "Japanese Stock Index Futures—Structure and Applications" (New York: Salomon Brothers Inc, August 29, 1988), Figure 4.

In September of 1990, stock index futures on Japanese stock market indexes began trading on U.S. exchanges. The Chicago Mercantile Exchange trades stock index futures on the Nikkei 225 and options on futures based on the same index. (Options on futures, also called "futures options," are explained in the next chapter.) The Nikkei 225, also known as the Nikkei Stock Average, is constructed like the Dow Jones Industrial Average and is a price-weighted average. For the futures contract, the dollar value is determined by multiplying $5 by the futures price. That is, the multiple for this contract is $5. Consequently, if the futures price is 27,000, the dollar value of the contract would be $135,000 ($5 times 27,000).

The Chicago Board of Trade trades futures and futures options on the Tokyo Stock Price Index (TOPIX), which is a value-weighted index and resembles the S&P 500 in its structure. The multiple for this futures contract is 5,000 yen, so if the index value is 2,450, the contract's yen value is 12,250,000 yen (5,000 yen times 2,450). According to volume through mid-1992, investors in U.S. markets seem to prefer the Nikkei contract to the TOPIX contract.

## *Japanese Interest Rate Futures*

The Japanese government bond futures market opened on the Tokyo Stock Exchange in October 1985, with trading on the 10-year JGB (long-term government bond) and in July 1988, on the 20-year JGB (super-long government bond). Actually, the underlying JGBs for these two contracts are fictional 10-year and 20-year bonds with coupon rates of 6% and a face value of 100 million yen. By daily trading volume, the JGB futures contract is now the most actively traded contract in the world. In September, 1990, the JGB futures contract began trading on the Chicago Board of Trade.

The options granted to the seller of a JGB futures contract are the same as those granted to the seller of a U.S. Treasury bond or note futures contract. Specifically, the seller has the right to select the JGB issue to deliver from among issues that the exchange has designated as acceptable for delivery. The short seller also has delivery date and wild card options.

▶ KEY POINTS THAT YOU SHOULD UNDERSTAND BEFORE PROCEEDING:

1. Non-U.S. exchanges have introduced a wide-range of contracts.
2. Many of these contracts are modeled after those developed in the U.S. futures markets.
3. There are three stock index futures contracts traded in Japan: the Nikkei 225 Stock Average, the Tokyo Stock Price Index (TOPIX), and the Osaka Stock Futures 50.
4. Stock index futures on Japanese stock market indexes are also traded on U.S. exchanges.
5. The Japanese government bond futures contract is modeled after the U.S. Treasury bond futures contract.

## SUMMARY

The traditional purpose of futures markets is to provide an important opportunity to hedge against the risk of adverse future price movements. Futures contracts are creations of exchanges, which require initial margin from parties. Each day positions are marked to market. Additional (variation) margin is required if the equity in the position falls below the maintenance margin. The clearinghouse guarantees that the parties to futures contracts will satisfy their obligations.

A buyer (seller) of a futures contract realizes a profit if the futures price increases (decreases). The buyer (seller) of a futures contract realizes a loss if the futures price decreases (increases). Because only initial margin is required when an investor takes a futures position, futures markets provide investors with substantial leverage for the money invested.

A forward contract differs in several important ways from a futures contract. In contrast to a futures contract, the parties to a forward contract are exposed to the risk that the other party to the contract will fail to perform. The positions of the parties are not marked to market, so there are no interim cash flows associated with a forward contract. Finally, unwinding a position in a forward contract may be difficult.

Investors can use the futures market or the cash market to react to economic news that is expected to change the value of an asset. Well-functioning futures markets are typically the market of choice for altering asset positions, and therefore represent the price discovery market, because of the lower transactions costs involved and the greater speed with which orders can be executed. The actions of arbitrageurs assure that price discovery in the futures markets will be transmitted to the cash market.

Critics of futures markets believe that these contracts are the source of greater price volatility in the cash market for the underlying asset. Although this is an empirical question not fully discussed here, even if price volatility in the cash market were greater because of the introduction of futures markets, this does not necessarily mean that greater volatility is bad for the economy.

The financial futures contracts traded in the U.S. include stock index futures contracts (with the most actively traded contract the S&P 500 futures contract), short-term interest rate futures contracts (Treasury bill and Eurodollar CD futures contracts), and Treasury bond and note futures contracts. Other countries have developed their financial futures markets with many of the contract features similar to those in the U.S.

Financial futures markets have become an important part of the Japanese financial system, as the instruments have proven popular and useful. Japanese futures contracts may be based on major stock indexes or on selected classes of government bonds. The interesting feature of these contracts, as well as the structure of their markets, is the extent to which their structure and trading resemble futures in the United States.

**Cash settlement futures contract:** A futures contract in which settlement is made in cash only.

**Cheapest-to-deliver issue:** The Treasury issue that is the cheapest to deliver to satisfy the delivery requirements of a Treasury bond or Treasury note futures contract.

**Clearinghouse:** The corporation that is associated with an exchange and that guarantees that the two parties to the transaction will perform.

**Conversion factor for a Treasury bond or note futures contracts:** The factor that must be multiplied by the price of the futures contract to arrive at the invoice price for a particular deliverable Treasury bond or note.

**Daily price limit:** A limit set by the exchange on the minimum and maximum price at which a futures contract may trade that day.

**Equity in a futures account:** The sum, in a futures account, of all margins posted and all daily gains less all daily losses to the account.

**Floor brokers (also called pit brokers):** Floor traders who not only buy and sell for their own account but also execute customer orders.

**Forward contract:** A nonstandardized contract (nonexchange-traded contract) calling for the future delivery of something at a specified price at the end of a designated period of time.

**Futures commissions merchant:** An authorized futures broker.

**Futures contract:** A standardized, exchange-traded, legal agreement between a buyer and a seller in which the buyer agrees to take delivery of something at a specified price at the end of a designated period of time and the seller agrees to make delivery.

**Futures price:** The price at which the parties to a futures contract agree to transact at the settlement date.

**Initial margin:** When a position is first taken in a futures contract, the amount per contract specified by the exchange that must be put up as margin.

**Locals:** Floor traders who buy and sell futures contracts for their own account.

**Long futures position:** When an investor takes an initial position in the market by buying a futures contract.

**Maintenance margin:** The minimum margin level to which an investor's equity position may fall as a result of an unfavorable price movement before the investor is required to deposit additional margin.

**Marking to market:** The requirement that the market value of a futures position be determined at the end of each trading day so as to realize losses and gains.

**Most distant futures contract:** The futures contract for a given underlying farthest away in time from settlement.

**Multiple of an index futures contract:** The dollar value, for the futures contract, of a point in the index.

**Nearby futures contract:** The futures contract for a given underlying with the closest settlement date.

**Open interest:** The number of contracts that have been entered into but not yet liquidated.

**Quality option (also called swap option).** The option granted to the short of a Treasury bond (or note) futures contract to select the Treasury issue to deliver.

**Settlement date (or delivery date):** The designated date at which the parties to a futures contract must transact.

**Settlement price:** At the end of each trading day, the closing price determined by the exchange for the futures contract.

**Short futures position:** When an investor takes an initial position in the market by selling a futures contract.

**Timing option:** The option granted to the short of a Treasury bond (or note) futures contract to decide when in the delivery month to deliver.

**Underlying:** The asset or instrument that the parties agree to exchange in a futures contract.

**Variation margin:** The additional margin that must be deposited to bring the equity in the account back to its initial margin level.

**Wild card option:** The right of the short position, under CBT rules, to give notice of intent to deliver after the closing of the exchange, on the date when the futures settlement price has been fixed.

## QUESTIONS

1. The chief financial officer of the corporation you work for recently told you that he had a strong preference to use forward contracts rather than futures contracts to hedge: "You can get contracts tailor-made to suit your needs." Comment on the CFO's statement. What other factors influence the decision to use futures or forward contracts?

2. Explain the functions of a clearinghouse associated with a futures exchange.

3. On April 1, 1992, you bought a stock index futures contract for 200 and were required to put up initial margin of $10,000. The value of the contract is 200 times the $500 multiple, or $100,000. On the next three days, the contract's settlement price was at these levels: day 1, 205; day 2, 197; day 3, 190.

    a. Calculate the value of your margin account on each day.

    b. If the maintenance margin for the contract is $7,000, how much variation margin did the exchange require you to put up at the end of the third day?

    c. If you had failed to put up that much, what would the exchange have done?

4. How do margin requirements in the futures market differ from margin requirements in the cash market?

5. "The futures market is where price discovery takes place." Do you agree with this statement? If so, why? If not, why not?

6. a. What is meant by a cash settlement futures contract?

   b. What two contracts in the U.S. are cash settlement futures contracts?

7. *Two years ago Osaka became the first Japanese exchange to come out with a financial future—a stock-index future known as the Osaka 50. It was only a modest success, mainly because it had to be delivered in shares rather than cash.*

   This claim comes from the September 1989 issue of Institutional Investor. Why is cash settlement preferred for stock index futures?

8. On April 28, 1992, a portfolio manager who wanted to hedge a position was considering both the June and December contracts on the S&P 500. The open interest for the S&P 500 June '92 futures contract was 129,623. Open interest for the December '92 contract was 1,244. What is open interest, and why would the portfolio manager want to know the open interest figures for the June and December contracts?

9. a. In the Treasury bond futures contract, there are choices or options granted to one of the parties to the contract. Which party has these choices, the buyer or seller?

   b. What are the options that are granted to the party?

10. On September 1, you sold 100 S&P 500 futures contracts at 250 with multiples of $500, expiration date in three months, and an initial margin of 10%. After that date, the index fell steadily and you were not required to post any additional margin, but you also did not withdraw any of the cash profits you were earning. On November 1, the futures price of the contract was 225, and you reversed your position by buying 100 contracts.

    a. How much money did you make (ignoring taxes and commissions)?

    b. What was the rate of return on your invested funds?

    c. In those two months the S&P 500 futures price fell 10%. Explain why your rate of return is so much higher than this level.

11. Suppose you bought five Nikkei 225 contracts (with multiples of $5 each) on the Chicago Board of Trade when the futures price was 17,400. Suppose the futures price went to 18,200 over the next month. How many dollars did you earn on this investment?

# CHAPTER TWENTY-SIX

# Options Markets

*After reading this chapter you will understand:*

- what an option contract is, and the basic features of an option.
- the difference between a call option and a put option.
- why an option is a derivative instrument.
- the difference between an American option and a European option.
- the difference between an exchange-traded option and options traded in the over-the-counter market.
- the difference between a futures contract and an option contract.
- the risk/return characteristics of call and put options, to both the seller and the buyer of the options.
- the hedging role of options in financial markets.
- the extensive role that the organized exchanges play in standardizing and guaranteeing option contracts traded on exchanges.
- how stock options can change the risk/return profile of a portfolio.
- the basic features of stock index options.

- the basic features of interest rate options.
- some key aspects of non-U.S. options markets.
- the basic features of options on futures or futures options.

In the previous chapter, we introduced our first derivative instrument, a futures contract. In this chapter we introduce a second derivative contract, an options contract, and we discuss the differences between the two. In Chapter 27 we show how to determine the price of an option, and in Chapter 28 we explain how market participants can use these contracts.

## OPTIONS CONTRACTS

There are two parties to an option contract: the *buyer* and the *writer* (also called the *seller*). In an option contract, the writer of the option grants the buyer of the option the right, but not the obligation, to purchase from or sell to the writer something at a specified price within a specified period of time (or at a specified date). The writer grants this right to the buyer in exchange for a certain sum of money, which is called the *option price* or *option premium*. The price at which the underlying (that is, the asset or commodity) may be bought or sold is called the *exercise price* or *strike price*. The date after which an option is void is called the *expiration date* or *maturity date*. Our focus in this chapter is on options where the underlying is a financial instrument or financial index.

When an option grants the buyer the right to purchase the underlying from the writer (seller), it is referred to as a *call option*, or simply, a *call*. When the option buyer has the right to sell the underlying to the writer, the option is called a *put option*, or simply, a *put*.

The timing of the possible exercise of an option is an important characteristic of the contract. There are options that may be exercised at any time up to and including the expiration date. Such options are referred to as *American options*. Other options may be exercised only at the expiration date; these are called *European options*.

Let's use an illustration to demonstrate the fundamental option contract. Suppose that Jack buys a call option for $3 (the option price) with the following terms:

1. The underlying asset is one unit of Asset XYZ.
2. The exercise price is $100.
3. The expiration date is three months from now, and the option can be exercised any time up to and including the expiration date (that is, it is an American option).

At any time up to and including the expiration date, Jack can decide to buy from the writer (seller) of this option one unit of Asset XYZ, for which he will pay a price of $100. If it is not beneficial for Jack to exercise the option, he will not, and we'll explain shortly how he decides whether it will be beneficial. Whether Jack exercises the option or not, the $3 he paid for the option will be kept by the option writer. If Jack buys a put option rather than a call option, then he would be able to sell Asset XYZ to the option writer for a price of $100.

The maximum amount that an option buyer can lose is the option price. The maximum profit that the option writer (seller) can realize is the option price. The option buyer has substantial upside return potential, while the option writer has substantial downside risk. We will investigate the risk/reward relationship for option positions later in this chapter.

There are no margin requirements for the buyer of an option once the option price has been paid in full. Because the option price is the maximum amount that the investor can lose, no matter how adverse the price movement of the underlying asset, no margin is needed. Because the writer (seller) of an option has agreed to accept all of the risk (and none of the reward) of the position in the underlying asset, the writer is generally required to put up the option price received as margin. In addition, as price changes occur that adversely affect the writer's position, the writer is required to deposit additional margin (with some exceptions) as the position is marked to market.

Options, like other financial instruments, may be traded either on an organized exchange or in the over-the-counter market. An exchange that wants to create an options contract must obtain approval from either the Commodity Futures Trading Commission or the Securities and Exchange Commission.[1] Exchange-traded options have three advantages. The first is standardization of the exercise price, the quantity of the underlying, and the expiration date of the contract. Second, as in the case of futures contracts, the direct link between buyer and seller is severed after the order is executed because of the interchangeability of exchange-traded options. The clearinghouse associated with the exchange where the option trades performs the same function in the options market it does in the futures market. Finally, the transactions costs are lower for exchange-traded options than for OTC options.

The higher cost of an OTC option reflects the cost of customizing the option for the common situation where an institutional investor needs to have a tailor-made option because the standardized exchange-traded option does not satisfy its investment objectives. Investment banking firms and commercial banks act as principals as well as brokers in the OTC options market. Most institutional investors are not concerned that an OTC option is less liquid than an exchange-traded option because they use OTC options as part of an asset/liability strategy in which they intend to hold them to expiration.

---

[1] By an agreement between the CFTC and the SEC and pursuant to an act of Congress, options on futures (discussed later in this chapter) are regulated by the former.

► KEY POINTS THAT YOU SHOULD UNDERSTAND BEFORE PROCEEDING:

1. An option is a contract in which the writer of the option grants the buyer the right, but not the obligation, to purchase from or sell to the writer something at the exercise (or strike) price within a specified period of time (until the expiration date).

2. The price paid by the option buyer is called the option price or option premium.

3. A call option grants the option buyer the right to buy something from the option writer, and a put option grants the option buyer the right to sell something to the option writer.

4. The maximum amount that an option buyer can lose is the option price, while the maximum profit that the option writer can realize is the option price; the option buyer has substantial upside return potential, while the option writer has substantial downside risk.

5. Options may be traded either on an organized exchange or in the over-the-counter market.

## DIFFERENCES BETWEEN OPTIONS AND FUTURES CONTRACTS

One distinction between futures and options contracts, is that one party to an option contract is not obligated to transact at a later date. Specifically, the option buyer has the right but not the obligation to exercise the option. The option writer (seller), though, does have the obligation to perform, if the buyer of the option insists on exercising it. In the case of a futures contract, both buyer and seller are obligated to perform. Of course, a futures buyer does not pay the seller to accept the obligation, while an option buyer pays the seller an option price.

Consequently, the risk/reward characteristics of the two contracts are also different. In the case of a futures contract, the buyer of the contract realizes a dollar-for-dollar gain when the price of the futures contract increases, and suffers a dollar-for-dollar loss when the price of the futures contract drops. The opposite occurs for the seller of a futures contract. Options do not provide this symmetric risk/reward relationship. The most that the buyer of an option can lose is the option price. While the buyer of an option retains all the potential benefits, the gain is always reduced by the amount of the option price. The maximum profit that the writer (seller) may realize is the option price; this is offset against substantial downside risk. This difference between options and futures is extremely important because, as we shall see in subsequent chapters, investors can use futures to protect against symmetric risk and options to protect against asymmetric risk.

We will return to the difference between options and futures later in this chapter when we discuss the application of these derivative contracts for hedging purposes.

▶ KEY POINTS THAT YOU SHOULD UNDERSTAND BEFORE PROCEEDING:

1. Unlike a futures contract, only one party to an option contract is obligated to transact at a later date: the option writer.
2. Futures have a symmetric risk/reward relationship, while options do not because the buyer of an option retains all the potential benefits, but the gain is always reduced by the amount of the option price.

## RISK AND RETURN CHARACTERISTICS OF OPTIONS

Here we illustrate the risk and return characteristics of the four basic option positions: buying a call option (which market participants refer to as "being long a call option"), selling a call option (short a call option), buying a put option (long a put option), and selling a put option (short a put option). The illustrations assume that each option position is held to the expiration date and not exercised early. Also, to simplify the illustrations, we ignore transactions costs.

### *Buying Call Options*

Assume that there is a call option on Asset XYZ that expires in one month and has a strike price of $100. The option price is $3. Suppose that the current price of Asset XYZ is $100. What is the profit or loss for the investor who purchases this call option and holds it to the expiration date?

The profit and loss from the strategy will depend on the price of Asset XYZ at the expiration date. A number of outcomes are possible.

1. If Asset XYZ's price at the expiration date is less than $100, the investor will not exercise the option. It would be foolish to pay the option writer $100 when Asset XYZ can be purchased in the market at a lower price. In this case, the option buyer loses the entire, original option price of $3. Notice, however, that this is the maximum loss that the option buyer will realize regardless of how low Asset XYZ's price declines.
2. If Asset XYZ's price is equal to $100 at the expiration date, again, there is no economic value in exercising the option. As in the case where the price is less than $100, the buyer of the call option will lose the entire option price, $3.
3. If Asset XYZ's price is more than $100 but less than $103 at the expiration date, the option buyer will exercise the option. By exercising, the option buyer can purchase Asset XYZ for $100 (the strike price) and sell it in the market for the higher price. Suppose, for example, that Asset XYZ's price is $102 at the expiration date. The buyer of the call option will realize a $2 gain by exercising the option. Of course, the cost of purchasing the call option was $3, so $1 is lost on this position. By failing to exercise the option, the investor loses $3 instead of only $1.

4. If Asset XYZ's price is equal to $103 at the expiration date, the investor will exercise the option. In this case, the investor breaks even, realizing a gain of $3 that offsets the cost of the option, $3.

5. If Asset XYZ's price is more than $103 at the expiration date, the investor will exercise the option and realize a profit. For example, if the price is $113, exercising the option will generate a profit on Asset XYZ of $13. Reducing this gain by the cost of the option ($3), the investor will realize a net profit of $10 from this position.

Table 26-1 shows the profit and loss for the buyer of the hypothetical call option in tabular form, while Figure 26-1 graphically portrays the result. While the break-even point and the size of the loss depend on the option price and the strike price, the profile shown in Figure 26-1 will hold for all buyers of call options. The shape indicates that the maximum loss is the option price and that there is substantial upside potential.

It is worthwhile to compare the profit and loss profile of the call option buyer to that of someone taking a long position in one unit of Asset XYZ. The payoff from the position depends on Asset XYZ's price at the expiration date. Consider again the five price outcomes given above (and again ignore transactions costs):

1. If Asset XYZ's price at the expiration date is less than $100, the investor in the call option loses the entire option price of $3. In contrast, a long position in Asset XYZ will have one of three possible losses:
   a. If Asset XYZ's price is less than $100 but greater than $97, the loss on the long position in Asset XYZ will be less than $3.
   b. If Asset XYZ's price is $97, the loss on the long position in Asset XYZ will be $3.
   c. If Asset XYZ's price is less than $97, the loss on the long position in Asset XYZ will be greater than $3. For example, if the price at the expiration date is $80, the long position in Asset XYZ will result in a loss of $20.

2. If Asset XYZ's price is equal to $100, the buyer of the call option will realize a loss of $3 (option price). Similarly, there will be no gain or loss on the long position in Asset XYZ.

3. If Asset XYZ's price is more than $100 but less than $103, the option buyer will realize a loss of less than $3, while the long position in Asset XYZ will realize a profit.

4. If the price of Asset XYZ at the expiration date is equal to $103, there will be no loss or gain from buying the call option. The long position in Asset XYZ, however, will produce a gain of $3.

5. If Asset XYZ's price at the expiration date is greater than $103, both the call option buyer and the long position in Asset XYZ will post a profit. However, the profit for the buyer of the call option will be $3 less than that for the long position. For example, if Asset XYZ's price is $113, the profit from the call position is $10, while the profit from the long position in Asset XYZ is $13.

| TABLE 26-1 | |
|---|---|
| **PROFIT/LOSS PROFILE FOR A LONG CALL POSITION** | |

**Assumptions:**
**Option price = $3**
**Strike price = $100**
**Time to expiration = 1 month**

| Price of Asset XYZ at Expiration Date | Net Profit/Loss* |
|---|---|
| $150 | $47 |
| 140 | 37 |
| 130 | 27 |
| 120 | 17 |
| 115 | 12 |
| 114 | 11 |
| 113 | 10 |
| 112 | 9 |
| 111 | 8 |
| 110 | 7 |
| 109 | 6 |
| 108 | 5 |
| 107 | 4 |
| 106 | 3 |
| 105 | 2 |
| 104 | 1 |
| 103 | 0 |
| 102 | −1 |
| 101 | −2 |
| 100 | −3 |
| 99 | −3 |
| 98 | −3 |
| 97 | −3 |
| 96 | −3 |
| 95 | −3 |
| 94 | −3 |
| 93 | −3 |
| 92 | −3 |
| 91 | −3 |
| 90 | −3 |
| 89 | −3 |
| 88 | −3 |
| 87 | −3 |
| 86 | −3 |
| 85 | −3 |
| 80 | −3 |
| 70 | −3 |
| 60 | −3 |

*Price at expiration − $100 − $3.
Maximum loss = −$3.

FIGURE 2 6 - 1

PROFIT/LOSS PROFILE FOR A LONG CALL
POSITION

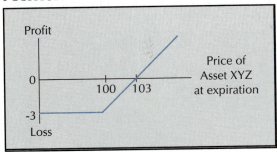

Table 26-2 compares the long call strategy and the long position in Asset XYZ. This comparison clearly demonstrates the way in which an option can change the risk/return profile for investors. An investor who takes a long position in Asset XYZ realizes a profit of $1 for every $1 increase in Asset XYZ's price. As Asset XYZ's price falls, however, the investor loses dollar-for-dollar. If the price drops by more than $3, the long position in Asset XYZ results in a loss of more than $3. The long call strategy, in contrast, limits the loss to only the option price of $3 but retains the upside potential, which will be $3 less than for the long position in Asset XYZ.

Which alternative is better, buying the call option or buying the asset? The answer depends on what the investor is attempting to achieve. This will become clearer in Chapter 28 where we explain various strategies using either option positions or cash market positions.

This hypothetical example demonstrates another important feature of options: their speculative appeal. Suppose an investor has strong expectations that Asset XYZ's price will rise in one month. At an option price of $3, the speculator can purchase 33.33 call options for each $100 invested. If Asset XYZ's price rises, the investor realizes the price appreciation associated with 33.33 units of Asset XYZ, while with the same $100, the investor could have bought only one unit of Asset XYZ selling at $100, realizing the appreciation associated with only one unit if Asset XYZ's price increases. For example, suppose that in one month the price of Asset XYZ rises to $120. The long call position will result in a profit of $566.50 [($20 × 33.33) − $100)] or a return of 566.5% on the $100 investment in the call option. By comparison, a $100 investment in the long position in Asset XYZ results in a profit of $20, for only a 20% return on $100.

It is this greater leverage that attracts investors to options when they wish to speculate on price movements. There are some drawbacks of leverage, however. Suppose that Asset XYZ's price is unchanged at $100 at the expiration date. The long call position (33.33 options) results, in this case, in a loss of the entire investment of $100, while the long position in Asset XYZ produces neither a gain nor a loss.

## TABLE 26-2

### COMPARISON OF LONG CALL POSITION AND LONG ASSET POSITION

**Assumptions:**
Initial price of Asset XYZ = $100
Option price = $3
Strike price = $100
Time to expiration = 1 month

| Price of Asset XYZ at Expiration Date | Net Profit/Loss for | |
|---|---|---|
| | Long Call | Long Asset XYZ |
| $150 | $47 | $50 |
| 140 | 37 | 40 |
| 130 | 27 | 30 |
| 120 | 17 | 20 |
| 115 | 12 | 15 |
| 114 | 11 | 14 |
| 113 | 10 | 13 |
| 112 | 9 | 12 |
| 111 | 8 | 11 |
| 110 | 7 | 10 |
| 109 | 6 | 9 |
| 108 | 5 | 8 |
| 107 | 4 | 7 |
| 106 | 3 | 6 |
| 105 | 2 | 5 |
| 104 | 1 | 4 |
| 103 | 0 | 3 |
| 102 | −1 | 2 |
| 101 | −2 | 1 |
| 100 | −3 | 0 |
| 99 | −3 | −1 |
| 98 | −3 | −2 |
| 97 | −3 | −3 |
| 96 | −3 | −4 |
| 95 | −3 | −5 |
| 94 | −3 | −6 |
| 93 | −3 | −7 |
| 90 | −3 | −8 |
| 91 | −3 | −9 |
| 90 | −3 | −10 |
| 89 | −3 | −11 |
| 88 | −3 | −12 |
| 87 | −3 | −13 |
| 86 | −3 | −14 |
| 85 | −3 | −15 |
| 80 | −3 | −20 |
| 70 | −3 | −30 |
| 60 | −3 | −40 |

## Writing (Selling) Call Options

To illustrate the option seller's (writer's) position, we use the same call option as in the example of buying a call option. The profit and loss profile of the short call position (that is, the position of the call option writer) is the mirror image of the profit and loss profile of the long call position (the position of the call option buyer). Consequently, the profit of the short call position for any given price of Asset XYZ at the expiration date is the same as the loss of the long call position. Further, the maximum profit that the short call position can produce is the option price. The maximum loss is not limited because it is the highest price reached by Asset XYZ on or before the expiration date, less the option price; this price can be indefinitely high. These relationships can be seen in Figure 26-2, which shows the profit/loss profile for a short call position.

## Buying Put Options

To illustrate the position of the buyer of a put option, we assume a hypothetical put option on one unit of Asset XYZ with one month to maturity and a strike price of $100. Assume the put option is selling for $2 and that the current price of Asset XYZ is $100. The profit or loss for this position at the expiration date depends on the market price of Asset XYZ. The possible outcomes are:

1.  If Asset XYZ's price is greater than $100, the buyer of the put option will not exercise it because exercising would mean selling Asset XYZ to the writer for a price that is less than the market price. In this case, a loss of $2 (the original price of the option) will result from buying the put option. Once again, the option price represents the maximum loss to which the buyer of the put option is exposed.

2.  If Asset XYZ's price at expiration is equal to $100, the put will not be exercised, leaving the put buyer with a loss equal to the option price of $2.

### FIGURE 26-2

PROFIT/LOSS PROFILE FOR A SHORT CALL POSITION

3. If Asset XYZ's price is less than $100 but greater than $98, the option buyer will experience a net loss on the position; exercising the put option, however, limits the loss to less than the option price of $2. For example, suppose that the price is $99 at the expiration date. By exercising the option, the option buyer will realize a loss of only $1. This is because the buyer of the put option can sell Asset XYZ, purchased in the market for $99, to the writer for $100, realizing a gain of $1. Deducting the $2 cost of the option results in a net loss of $1 to the position.

4. If Asset XYZ's price is $98 at the expiration date, the put buyer will break even. The investor will realize a gain of $2 by selling Asset XYZ to the writer of the option for $100, and this gain exactly offsets the cost of the option ($2).

5. If Asset XYZ's price is below $98 at the expiration date, the long put position (the put buyer) will realize a profit. For example, suppose the price falls at expiration to $80. The long put position will produce a profit of $18: a gain of $20 for exercising the put option less the $2 option price.

The profit and loss profile for the long put position is shown in tabular form in the second column of Table 26-3 and in graphical form in Figure 26-3. As with all long option positions, the loss is limited to the option price. The profit potential, however, is substantial: the theoretical maximum profit is generated if Asset XYZ's price falls to zero. Contrast this profit potential with that of the buyer of a call option. The theoretical maximum profit for a call buyer cannot be determined beforehand, because it depends on the highest price that can be reached by Asset XYZ before or at the option expiration date, a price that is indeterminate.

To see how an option alters the risk/return profile for an investor, we again compare it to a position in Asset XYZ. The long put position is compared to taking a short position in Asset XYZ because this is the position that would realize a profit if the price of the asset falls.[2] Suppose an investor sells Asset XYZ short for $100. The short position in Asset XYZ would produce the following profit or loss compared with the long put position (without considering transactions costs):

1. If Asset XYZ's price rises above $100, the long put option results in a loss of $2, but the short position in Asset XYZ realizes one of the following:
   a. If the price of Asset XYZ is less than $102, there will be a loss of less than $2, which is the loss to the long put position.
   b. If the price of Asset XYZ is equal to $102, the loss will be $2, the same as the maximum loss of the long put position.
   c. If the price of Asset XYZ is greater than $102, the loss will be greater than $2. For example, if the price is $125, the short po-

---

[2] See Chapter 18 for more detail on selling short in a securities market.

| TABLE 26-3 | | |
|---|---|---|

**PROFIT/LOSS PROFILE FOR A LONG PUT POSITION IN COMPARISON TO A SHORT ASSET POSITION**

**Assumptions:**
**Initial price of Asset XYZ = $100**
**Option price = $2**
**Strike price = $100**
**Time to expiration = 1 month**

| Price of Asset XYZ at Expiration Date | Net Profit/Loss for | |
|---|---|---|
| | Long Put* | Short Asset XYZ** |
| $150 | −$2 | −$50 |
| 140 | −2 | −40 |
| 130 | −2 | −30 |
| 120 | −2 | −20 |
| 115 | −2 | −15 |
| 110 | −2 | −10 |
| 105 | −2 | −5 |
| 100 | −2 | 0 |
| 99 | −1 | 1 |
| 98 | 0 | 2 |
| 97 | 1 | 3 |
| 96 | 2 | 4 |
| 95 | 3 | 5 |
| 94 | 4 | 6 |
| 93 | 5 | 7 |
| 92 | 6 | 8 |
| 91 | 7 | 9 |
| 90 | 8 | 10 |
| 89 | 9 | 11 |
| 88 | 10 | 12 |
| 87 | 11 | 13 |
| 86 | 12 | 14 |
| 85 | 13 | 15 |
| 84 | 14 | 16 |
| 83 | 15 | 17 |
| 82 | 16 | 18 |
| 81 | 17 | 19 |
| 80 | 18 | 20 |
| 75 | 23 | 25 |
| 70 | 28 | 30 |
| 65 | 33 | 35 |
| 60 | 38 | 40 |

*$100 − Price at expiration − $2.
  Maximum loss = − $2.
**$100 − Price of Asset XYZ.

**FIGURE  26-3**

PROFIT/LOSS PROFILE FOR A LONG PUT
POSITION

sition will realize a loss of $25, because the short seller must now pay
$125 for Asset XYZ that he sold short at $100.

2.   If Asset XYZ's price at expiration is equal to $100, the long put po-
sition will realize a $2 loss, while there will be no profit or loss on the
short position in Asset XYZ.

3.   If Asset XYZ's price is less than $100 but greater than $98, the long
put position will experience a loss of less than $2, but the short po-
sition will realize a profit. For example, a price of $99 at the expira-
tion date will result in a loss of $1 for the long put position but a profit
of $1 for the short position.

4.   If Asset XYZ's price is $98 at the expiration date, the long put posi-
tion will break even, but the short position in Asset XYZ will generate a $2 profit.

5.   If Asset XYZ's price is below $98, both positions will generate a
profit; however, the profit for the long put position will always be $2
less than the profit for the short position.

Table 26-3 presents a detailed account of this comparison of the profit
and loss profiles for the long put position and short position in Asset XYZ.
While the investor who takes a short position in Asset XYZ faces all the downside risk as well as the upside potential, the long put position limits the downside risk to the option price while still maintaining upside potential (reduced
only by an amount equal to the option price).

### Writing (Selling) Put Options

The profit and loss profile for a short put option is the mirror image of the long
put option. The maximum profit from this position is the option price. The theoretical maximum loss can be substantial should the price of the underlying
asset fall; at the outside, if the price were to fall all the way to zero, the loss
would be as large as the strike price less the option price. Figure 26-4 graphically depicts this profit and loss profile.

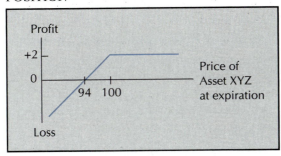

FIGURE 26-4

PROFIT/LOSS PROFILE FOR A SHORT PUT
POSITION

To summarize these illustrations of the four option positions, we can say
the following: buying calls or selling puts allows the investor to gain if the price
of the underlying asset rises; and selling calls and buying puts allows the investor to gain if the price of the underlying asset falls.

## Considering the Time Value of Money

Our illustrations of the four option positions do not take into account the time
value of money. Specifically, the buyer of an option must pay the seller the option price at the time the option is purchased. Thus, the buyer must finance
the purchase price of the option or, assuming the purchase price does not have
to be borrowed, the buyer loses the income that can be earned by investing
the amount of the option price until the option is sold or exercised. In contrast,
assuming that the seller does not have to use the option price amount as margin for the short position or can use an interest-earning asset as security, the
seller has the opportunity to earn income from the proceeds of the option sale.

The time value of money changes the profit/loss profile of the option positions we have discussed. The break-even price for the buyer and the seller
of an option will not be the same as in our illustrations. The break-even price
for the underlying asset at the expiration date is higher for the buyer of the
option; for the seller, it is lower.

Our comparisons of the option position with long and short positions in
the underlying asset also ignore the time value of money. We have not considered the fact that the underlying asset may generate interim cash flows (dividends in the case of common stock, interest in the case of bonds). The buyer
of a call option is not entitled to any interim cash flows generated by the underlying asset. The buyer of the underlying asset, however, would receive any
interim cash flows and would have the opportunity to reinvest them. A complete comparison of the long call option position and the long position in the
underlying asset must take into account the additional dollars from reinvesting any interim cash flows. Moreover, any effect on the price of the underlying asset as a result of the distribution of cash must be considered. This occurs,

for example, when the underlying asset is common stock and, as a result of a dividend payment, the stock declines in price.

▶ KEY POINTS THAT YOU SHOULD UNDERSTAND BEFORE PROCEEDING:

1. There are four basic option positions: buying a call option, selling a call option, buying a put option, and selling a put option.
2. An option can be used to alter the risk/reward relationship from that of a position in the underlying.
3. The buyer of a call option benefits if the price of the underlying rises; the writer (seller) of a call option benefits if the price of the underlying is unchanged or falls.
4. The buyer of a put option benefits if the price of the underlying falls; the writer (seller) of a put option benefits if the price of the underlying is unchanged or rises.
5. In determining the payoff from an option, the time value of money as a result of having to finance the option price must be considered.

## ECONOMIC ROLE OF THE OPTION MARKETS

Futures contracts allow investors to hedge the risks associated with adverse price movements. Hedging with futures lets a market participant lock in a price, and thereby eliminates price risk. In the process, however, the investor gives up the opportunity to benefit from a favorable price movement. In other words, hedging with futures involves trading off the benefits of a favorable price movement for protection against an adverse price movement.

Hedging with options has a variety of potential benefits, which we discuss in Chapter 28. For now, we provide an overview of how options can be used for hedging, and how the outcomes of hedging with options differ from those of hedging with futures. A good way to show the hedging uses of options is to return to the initial illustration in this chapter where the underlying for the option is Asset XYZ.

First let's consider an investor who owns Asset XYZ, currently selling for $100, which she expects to sell one month from now. The investor's concern is that, one month from now, Asset XYZ's price may decline below $100. One alternative available to this investor is to sell Asset XYZ now. Suppose, however, the investor does not want to sell this asset now because either some restrictions prevent this or she thinks that the price may rise during the month. Suppose also that an insurance company offers to sell the investor an insurance policy providing that, if at the end of one month Asset XYZ's price is less than $100, the insurance company will make up the difference between $100 and the market price. For example, if one month from now Asset XYZ's price is $80, the insurance company will pay the investor $20.

The insurance company naturally charges the investor a premium to write this policy. Let's suppose that the premium is $2. Holding aside the cost of the insurance policy, the payoff that this investor then faces is as follows. The minimum price for Asset XYZ that the investor can receive is $100 because, if the price is less, the insurance company will make up the difference. If Asset XYZ's price is greater than $100, however, the investor will receive the higher price. The premium of $2 that is required to purchase this insurance policy effectively assures the investor of a minimum price of $98 ($100 minus $2), while if the price is above $100 the investor realizes the benefits of a higher price (reduced always by the $2 for the insurance policy). In buying this policy, the investor has purchased protection against an adverse price movement, while maintaining the opportunity to benefit from a favorable price movement.

Insurance companies do not offer such policies, but we have described an option strategy that provides the same protection. Consider the put option on Asset XYZ with one month to expiration, a strike price of $100, and an option price of $2 that we discussed earlier in this chapter. The payoff to a long position in this put is identical to the insurance policy. The option price resembles the hypothetical insurance premium; this is the reason why the option price is referred to as the option premium. Thus, a put option can be used to hedge against a decline in the price of the underlying instrument.

The long put's payoff is quite different from that of a futures contract. Suppose that a futures contract with Asset XYZ as the underlying instrument has a futures price equal to $100 and a settlement date one month from now. By selling this futures contract, the investor would be agreeing to sell Asset XYZ for $100 one month from now. If Asset XYZ's price falls below $100, the investor is protected because she will receive $100 upon delivery of the asset to satisfy the futures contract. If Asset XYZ's price rises above $100, however, the investor will not realize the price appreciation because she must deliver the asset for an agreed-upon amount of $100. By selling the futures contract, the investor has locked in a price of $100, and fails to realize a gain if the price rises while avoiding a loss if the price declines.

Call options, too, are useful for hedging. A call option can be used to protect against a rise in the price of the underlying instrument while maintaining the opportunity to benefit from a decline in the price of the underlying instrument. Suppose, for example, that an investor expects to receive $100 one month from now, and plans to use that money to purchase Asset XYZ, which is selling currently for $100. The risk that the investor faces is that Asset XYZ's price will rise above $100 one month from now. Let us further suppose there is a call option such as we described earlier in the chapter: the option costs $3 and has a strike price of $100 and a month to expiration. By purchasing that call option, the investor has hedged the risk of a rise in the price of Asset XYZ.

The hedge outcome is as follows. If the price rises above $100 one month from now, the investor would exercise the call option and realize the difference between the market price of Asset XYZ and $100. Thus, if we hold aside the cost of the option for the moment, we can see that the investor is insuring that the maximum price she will have to pay for Asset XYZ is $100. Should the asset's price fall below $100, the call option expires worthless, but the investor benefits by being able to purchase Asset XYZ at a price less than $100. Once the $3 cost of the option is considered, the payoff is as follows. Regardless of the eventual price of the asset, the maximum price that the investor will have to pay for Asset XYZ is $103 (the strike price plus the option price). If the price of the asset declines below $100, the investor will benefit by the amount of the price decline less $3.

Compare this situation to a futures contract where Asset XYZ is the underlying instrument, the settlement is in one month, and the futures price is $100. Suppose that the investor buys this futures contract. If one month from now the price of Asset XYZ rises above $100, the investor has contracted to buy the asset for $100, thereby eliminating the risk of a price rise; if the price falls below $100, however, the investor cannot benefit because she has contracted to pay $100 for the asset.

It should be clear now how hedging with options differs from hedging with futures. This difference cannot be overemphasized—options and futures are not interchangeable instruments.

While our focus has been on hedging price risk, options also allow investors an efficient way to expand the range of return characteristics available. That is, investors can use options to "mold" a return distribution for a portfolio to fit particular investment objectives.[3]

▶ KEY POINTS THAT YOU SHOULD UNDERSTAND BEFORE PROCEEDING:

1. Hedging with futures involves trading off the benefits of a favorable price movement for protection against an adverse price movement.
2. Hedging with options allows the option buyer to limit risk but maintain the potential to benefit from a favorable price movement.
3. Options allow the investor to mold a risk/return relationship.

## U.S. OPTIONS MARKETS

There are a variety of options traded in the United States. Here, we provide a survey of the major ones.

### Stock Options

Options on individual shares of common stock have been traded for many years. Trading of standardized call options on common stock began on the Chicago Board Options Exchange (CBOE) in April 1973. Since then, the Securities and Exchange Commission (SEC) has granted permission to other exchanges to trade options: the American Stock Exchange in 1974, the Philadelphia Exchange in 1975, the Pacific and the Midwest Stock Exchanges in 1976, and the New York Stock Exchange in 1982. SEC permission to trade

---

[3] See Stephen A. Ross, "Options and Efficiency," *Quarterly Journal of Economics* (February 1976), pp. 75–89, and Fred Arditti and Kose John, "Spanning the State Space with Options," *Journal of Financial and Quantitative Analysis* (March 1980), pp. 1–9.

put options on common stocks on organized exchanges was not granted until March 1977.

The SEC approved the creation of a national clearing system for options, the Options Clearing Corporation (OCC), jointly established by the CBOE and the American Stock Exchange. Since its establishment in 1974, the OCC has issued, guaranteed, registered, cleared, and settled all transactions involving listed options on all exchanges.

Exchange-traded stock options have a standardized quantity: one contract applies to 100 shares of the designated common stock. While most underlying stocks are those of listed companies, stock options on a number of over-the-counter stocks are also available. However, all the companies are large and their shares are actively traded.

The Options Clearing Corporation has established standard strike price guidelines for listed options. For stocks with a price above $100, option strike prices are set at $10 intervals; for stocks with a price below $100 and above $30, strike prices are set at $5 intervals; and for stocks priced between $10 and $30 the interval is $2.50. While the strike price of exchange-traded options is not changed because of cash dividends paid to common stockholders, the strike price is adjusted for stock splits, stock dividends, reorganization, and other recapitalizations affecting the value of the underlying stock.

All exchange-traded stock options in the U.S. may be exercised any time before the expiration date; that is, they are American options. They expire at 11:59 p.m. Eastern Standard Time on the Saturday following the third Friday of the expiration month. Exchange rules require that investors wishing to exercise an expiring option must instruct a broker about the exercise no later than 5:30 p.m. Eastern time on the business day immediately preceding the expiration date. Notices to exercise a nonexpiring option on a date other than the expiration date must be made between 10:00 a.m. and 8:00 p.m. Eastern Standard Time. When a nonexpiring option is exercised, the OCC assigns the obligation the next day to someone who has an outstanding short position in an option of the same exercise price, expiration date, and underlying stock. This assignment is on a random basis.

Options are designated by the name of the underlying common stock, the expiration month, the strike price, and the type of option (put or call). Thus, an IBM call option expiring in October with a strike price of 55 is referred to as the "IBM October 55 call."

## Stock Index Options

In March 1983, a revolution in stock options and investments in general occurred. At that time, trading in an option whose underlying instrument was a stock index, the S&P 100 (originally called the CBOE 100), began on the Chicago Board Options Exchange. Shortly afterward, the American Stock Exchange initiated trading in an option based on what the exchange called "the Major Market Index" (MMI).[4] These index options have proven useful and popular with many kinds of investors. The total put-and-call volume for all broad- and narrow-based index options is large, and may in fact account for as much as 30% to 35% of all option contracts traded on exchanges. As in the case of options on individual stocks, stock index options are regulated by the Securities and Exchange Commission.

Table 26-4 lists the major stock index options traded in the U.S. and summarizes their key features. Besides the contracts shown here, which are based on broad-based indexes, there are traded options which are based on narrow indexes. These include the Computer Technology Index and the Oil Index, both traded on the AMEX, and the Utilities Index, traded on the Philadelphia Stock Exchange.

The level of trading volume, as measured by open interest, differs across the various contracts. For example, on April 30, 1992, the open interest for the call and put options on the S&P 100 was 342,373 contracts and 379,912 contracts, respectively; in contrast, open interest on the Major Market Index option was 55,319 contracts for the call options and 70,579 contracts for the put options. The most successful stock index futures contract has been the S&P 100 contract, which is traded on the CBOE.

## TABLE 26-4

### SUMMARY OF MAJOR STOCK INDEX OPTION CONTRACTS TRADED IN THE UNITED STATES (AS OF JANUARY 1993)

| Contract | Exchange | Exercise Provision | Delivery Months |
|---|---|---|---|
| S&P 100 Index (OEX) | CBOE | American | Nearest 4 months |
| S&P 500 Index (SPX) | CBOE | European | Nearest 3 months + next month in March cycle |
| S&P 500 Index (NSX) | CBOE | European | March, June, September, December |
| NYSE Index (NYA) | NYSE | American | Nearest 3 months |
| Major Market Index (XMI) | AMEX | American | Nearest 3 months |
| Institutional Index (XII) | AMEX | European | Nearest 3 months + next month in December cycle |
| Value Line Index (XVL) | Phil. | European | Nearest 3 months |

Features common to all contracts:

1. The contract size is the futures price × the multiple. The multiple for each contract is $100.

2. All contracts settle in cash.

3. The expiration day is the Saturday after the third Friday of the expiration month. For the S&P 500 NSX it is at the open.

4. The minimum price change is (a) 1/8 of a point (=$12.50) for option prices greater than $3; (b) 1/16 of a point (= $6.25) for option prices less than $3.

---

[4] The index includes 20 stocks and was constructed to be similar to the Dow Jones Industrial Average.

If a stock option is exercised, a stock must be delivered. It would be complicated, to say the least, to settle a stock index option by delivering all the stocks that make up the index. Instead, stock index options are cash settlement contracts. This means that, if the option is exercised, the exchange-assigned option writer pays cash to the option buyer. There is no delivery of any stock.

The value of a stock index option contract is equal to the index value multiplied by $100. The $100 is referred to as the *multiple for the contract*. That is,

Dollar value of a stock index option contract = Index value × $100

For example, if the cash index value for the S&P 100 is 300, then the dollar value of the S&P 500 contract is:

$$300 × \$100 = \$30,000$$

A one-point movement in the index value, say, from 300 to 301, is therefore equal to $100.

The option price is found by multiplying the quoted option price by $100. For example, if the quoted option price is 4 1/4, then the dollar price is $425 (4.25 times $100).

The strike index is converted into a dollar value by multiplying the strike index by the multiple for the contract. For example, if the strike index is 290, the dollar value is $29,000 (290 × $100). An option-holder wishing to exercise receives the difference between the strike index and the value of the actual index in the cash market at the time of exercise. For example, suppose that an investor purchases a call option on the S&P 100 with a strike index of 290 and decides to exercise the option when the index value is 300. In fact, the investor has the right to purchase the index for $29,000 when the market value of the index is $30,000. This option is clearly worth $1,000. Upon exercise, the buyer of the call option would receive $1,000 from the option writer assigned by the exchange to meet this obligation.

Exercise provisions for stock index options come in both the American and European variety. The S&P 100 and the NYSE index options are American options. The S&P 500, the Major Market, and the Institutional index options are European options (which means that they cannot be exercised until expiration). Institutional investors find European options attractive because they need not fear that a short position they take in an option in order to accomplish an investment objective will be exercised early. Index options expire on the Saturday following the third Friday of the contract month.

There are also options on stock index futures. These options are not as widely used as options on stock indexes. Options on futures contracts are the contracts of choice in the interest rate options market, so we will postpone our discussion of options on futures until later in this chapter.

### Interest Rate Options

Interest rate options can be written on cash instruments or futures. At one time, there were several exchange-traded option contracts whose underlying instrument was a debt instrument. These contracts are referred to as *options on physicals*. For reasons explained later, options on futures that are based on debt instruments have been far more popular than options on physicals.

In recent years, market participants have made increasingly greater use of over-the-counter options on Treasury and mortgage-backed securities.[5] Certain institutional investors who want to purchase an option on a specific Treasury security or a Ginnie Mae pass-through can do so on an over-the-counter basis. There are government and mortgage-backed securities dealers who make a market in options on specific securities. Typically, the maturity of the option coincides with the time period over which the buyer of the option wants to hedge, so the buyer is not concerned with the option's liquidity.

Besides options on fixed-income securities, investors can obtain OTC options on a yield spread (such as the spread between mortgage pass-through securities and Treasuries or between double-A corporates and Treasuries).

▶ KEY POINTS THAT YOU SHOULD UNDERSTAND BEFORE PROCEEDING:

1. There are options traded on individual shares of common stock and options traded on common stock indexes.
2. The value of a stock index option contract is equal to the index value multiplied by $100.
3. There are interest rate options in which the underlying is a debt instrument (called an option on a physical) and a futures contract (called a futures option).
4. Exchange-traded options on futures that are based on debt instruments have been far more popular than exchange-traded options on physicals.
5. There has been increased use by institutional investors of over-the-counter options on Treasury and mortgage-backed securities.

## OPTIONS MARKETS OUTSIDE THE UNITED STATES

Options markets have developed in many countries. In the United Kingdom, the London Traded Options Market is part of the International Stock Exchange and hosts trading in options on stocks and on indexes. In Canada, numerous options are traded on both the Toronto Stock Exchange and the Montreal Exchange. The European Options Exchange is in Amsterdam and it sponsors trading in a wide variety of European equity options and index options.

---

[5] For a more detailed discussion of over-the-counter options, see Chapter 2 of Mark Pitts and Frank J. Fabozzi, *Interest Rate Futures and Options* (Chicago: Probus Publishing, 1989).

Option trading has proven very popular in Japan. Both the Osaka Stock Exchange and the Tokyo Stock Exchange play host to large volumes of trading in stock index options.[6] The Nikkei 225 Stock Average Index Option is traded on Osaka's exchange and is a cash settlement contract, with a multiple of 1,000 yen. Its maturity structure has been described as "modified American style," and is rather interesting: the option can be exercised before expiration but only on one day a week.[7] The TOPIX option (the Tokyo Stock Price Index Option) trades on Tokyo's exchange: it has a modified American exercise structure, a cash settlement provision, and a multiple of 10,000 yen. Both index options are available for each of the four succeeding months, and the expiration date is the second Friday in the expiration month.

Options on interest rate futures (discussed next) are also traded in Japan.

# FUTURES OPTIONS

An option on a futures contract, commonly referred to as a *futures option*, gives the buyer the right to buy from or sell to the writer a designated futures contract at a designated price at any time during the life of the option. If the futures option is a call option, the buyer has the right to purchase one designated futures contract at the exercise price. That is, the buyer has the right to acquire a long futures position in the designated futures contract. If the buyer exercises the call option, the writer (seller) acquires a corresponding short position in the futures contract.

A put option on a futures contract grants the buyer the right to sell one designated futures contract to the writer at the exercise price. That is, the option buyer has the right to acquire a short position in the designated futures contract. If the put option is exercised, the writer acquires a corresponding long position in the designated futures contract.

There are futures options on all the interest rate futures contracts reviewed in the previous chapter.

## *Mechanics of Trading Futures Options*

As the parties to the futures option will realize a position in a futures contract when the option is exercised, the question is: what will the futures price be? That is, at what price will the long be required to pay for the instrument underlying the futures contract, and at what price will the short be required to sell the instrument underlying the futures contract?

Upon exercise, the futures price for the futures contract will be set equal to the exercise price. The position of the two parties is then immediately

---

[6] The American Stock Exchange trades a European-type option on an index of Japanese stocks. The index, called the Japanese Index, was created by the AMEX and consists of 210 stocks actively traded on the Tokyo Stock Exchange.

[7] Keith K.H. Park and Steven A. Schoenfeld, *The Pacific Rim Futures and Options Markets* (Chicago: Probus Publishing, 1992).

marked to market based on the then-current futures price. Thus, the futures position of the two parties will be at the prevailing futures price. At the same time, the option writer or seller must pay the option buyer the economic benefit from exercising. In the case of a call futures option, the option writer must pay the difference between the current futures price and the exercise price to the buyer of the option. In the case of a put futures option, the option writer must pay the option buyer the difference between the exercise price and the current futures price.

For example, suppose an investor buys a call option on some futures contract in which the exercise price is 85. Assume also that the futures price is 95, and that the buyer exercises the call option. Upon exercise, the call buyer is given a long position in the futures contract at 85, and the call writer is assigned the corresponding short position in the futures contract at 85. The futures position of the buyer and the writer is immediately marked to market by the exchange. Since the prevailing futures price is 95, and the exercise price is 85, the long futures position (the position of the call buyer) realizes a gain of 10 while the short futures position (the position of the call writer) realizes a loss of 10. The call writer pays the exchange 10 and the call buyer receives 10 from the exchange. The call buyer, who now has a long futures position at 95, can either liquidate the futures position at 95 or maintain a long futures position. If the former course of action is taken, the call buyer sells a futures contract at the prevailing futures price of 95. There is no gain or loss from liquidating the position. Overall, the call buyer realizes a gain of 10. If the call buyer elects to hold the long futures position, then he or she will face the same risk and reward of holding such a position. But the call buyer still has realized a gain of 10 from the exercise of the call option.

Suppose, instead, that the futures option is a put rather than a call, and the current futures price is 60 rather than 95. If the buyer of this put option exercises it, the buyer would have a short position in the futures contract at 85; the option writer would have a long position in the futures contract at 85. The exchange then marks the position to market at the then-current futures price of 60, resulting in a gain to the put buyer of 25 and a loss to the put writer of the same amount. The put buyer, now having a short futures position at 60, can either maintain that position or liquidate it by buying a futures contract at the prevailing futures price of 60. In either case the put buyer realizes a gain of 25 from exercising the put option.

The exchange imposes no margin requirements for the buyer of a futures option once the option price has been paid in full. Because the maximum amount the buyer can lose is the option price, regardless of how adverse the price movement of the underlying instrument, there is no need for margin.

Because the writer (seller) of an option has agreed to accept all of the risk (and none of the reward) of the position in the underlying instrument, the writer (seller) is required to deposit not only the margin required on the interest rate futures contract position if that is the underlying instrument, but, with certain exceptions, also the option price that is received for writing the option. In addition, if prices for the underlying futures contract adversely affect the writer's position, the writer would be required to deposit variation margin as it is marked to market.

### Reasons for the Popularity of Futures Options

There are three reasons why futures options on fixed-income securities have largely supplanted options on physicals as the options vehicle used by institutional investors.[8] First, unlike options on fixed-income securities, futures options on Treasury coupon futures do not require payments for accrued interest to be made. Consequently, when a futures option is exercised, the call buyer and the put writer need not compensate the other party for accrued interest.

Second, futures options are believed to be "cleaner" instruments because of the reduced likelihood of delivery squeezes. Market participants who must deliver an instrument are concerned that the instrument to be delivered will be in short supply at the time of delivery, resulting in a higher price to acquire it. As the deliverable supply of futures contracts is more than adequate for futures options currently traded, there is no concern about a delivery squeeze.

Finally, in order to price any option, it is imperative to know at all times the price of the underlying instrument. As we mentioned in our discussions of the various bond markets, current bond prices are not easily available. In contrast, futures prices are readily available.

▶ KEY POINTS THAT YOU SHOULD UNDERSTAND BEFORE PROCEEDING:

1. A futures option gives the buyer the right to buy from or sell to the writer a designated futures contract at a designated price at any time during the life of the option.
2. If the buyer of the futures option exercises, the futures price for the futures contract will be set equal to the exercise price, but the position of the two parties is then immediately marked to market based on the then-current futures price.
3. There are several reasons why futures options on fixed-income securities have been used more by institutional investors than options on physicals.

SUMMARY

An option is a contract between two parties, the buyer and the seller (or writer). The buyer pays a price or premium to the seller for the right (but not the obligation) to buy or sell a certain amount of a specified item at a set price for a specified period of time. The right to buy is a call option, and the right to sell is a put option. The set price is the exercise or strike price. The period ends on the maturity or expiration date. If the right cannot be exercised until that date, the option is called a European option. If

---

[8] Laurie Goodman, "Introduction to Debt Options," Chapter 1 in Frank J. Fabozzi (editor), *Winning the Interest Rate Game: A Guide to Debt Options* (Chicago: Probus Publishing, 1985), pp. 13-14.

the option can be exercised at any time before the maturity date, the option is an American option. The item to which the option applies is the underlying asset, and its value determines the value of the option. Hence, options are called derivative instruments.

Options traded on exchanges are standardized and guaranteed by the exchange and its clearing house, and trading in these options is monitored by the Securities and Exchange Commission. Customized options are traded in the unregulated OTC market.

Options differ from futures in several key ways. First, both parties to a futures contract accept an obligation to transact, but only the writer of an option has an obligation, and that occurs if the buyer wishes to exercise the option. Second, the option buyer has a limited, known maximum loss. Third, the risk/return profile of an option position is asymmetric, while that of a futures position is symmetric.

The risk/return profile of the option buyer is the mirror image of the risk/return profile of the option writer, whether the option is a put or a call, American or European. The purchase of a call option is like taking a long position in the underlying asset but with a fixed, maximum loss. The purchase of a put option resembles the short sale of the underlying asset but with a known maximum loss.

The essence of hedging with options is that it minimizes loss while reducing gains only by the price of the option. Thus, hedging with options is very much like taking out an insurance policy. Hedging with options differs from hedging with futures because the latter establishes a known, future price and does not allow the hedger to participate in gains that price changes might generate for the investor.

Options may be written on individual stocks or on bundles and groups of stocks. Those written on groups are called index options because the groups contain all or most of the stocks in popular stock market indexes such as the Standard & Poor's 500 Common Stock Index. Several stock index options are traded on major exchanges around the world. The exercise of stock options involves an exchange of cash for shares. By contrast, stock index options are cash settlement contracts, where the buyer receives the cash value of the difference between the exercise price (called the strike index) and the actual level of the stock market index. Options based on important government debt securities are also traded on major exchanges.

A complex but popular option is one that has a futures contract as its underlying instrument. These futures on options, or options futures, give the buyer, upon exercise, the right to assume a specified position in a specific futures contract.

GLOSSARY

**American option:** An option that the buyer may exercise at any time up to and including the expiration date.

**Call option:** An option where the buyer has the right to purchase the underlying from the option writer.

**European option:** An option that the buyer may exercise only at the expiration date.

**Exchange-traded option:** An option traded on an organized exchange.

**Exercise (or strike) price:** The price at which the underlying of an option may be bought or sold.

**Expiration (or maturity) date:** The date after which an option expires.

**Futures option:** An option on a futures contract, which gives the buyer the right to buy from or sell to the writer a designated futures contract at a designated price.

**Long option position:** The position of one owning the option and, hence, the right to exercise it.

**Option:** A contract in which the writer of the option grants the buyer the right, but not the obligation, to purchase from or sell to the writer something at a specified price within a specified period of time (or at a specified date).

**Option on a physical:** An interest rate option whose underlying is a fixed-income instrument.

**Option price (or option premium):** The price of an option.

**Options Clearing Corporation (or OCC):** Established in 1974, the OCC is the SEC-approved corporation that issues, guarantees, registers, clears, and settles all transactions involving listed options on all exchanges.

**Over-the-counter option (also called customized option):** A nonstandardized option contract that is traded in the over-the-counter market.

**Put option:** An option where the buyer has the right to sell the underlying to the option writer.

**Short option position:** The obligation to perform according to the specifications of an option if the long position chooses to exercise the option.

**Writer of option:** The entity that sells the option contract.

QUESTIONS

1. Identify and explain the key features of an option contract.
2. What is the difference between a put option and a call option?
3. What is the difference between an American option and a European option?
4. Why does an option writer need to post margin?

5. Identify two important ways in which an exchange-traded option differs from a typical over-the-counter option.

6. a. What are the main ways in which an option differs from a futures contract?

   b. Why are options and futures labeled "derivative securities"?

7. Explain how this statement can be true: "A long call position offers potentially unlimited gains, if the underlying asset's price rises, but a fixed, maximum loss if the underlying asset's price drops to zero."

8. Suppose a call option on a stock has an exercise price of $70 and a cost of $2, and suppose you buy the call. Identify the profit to your investment, at the call's expiration, for each of these values of the underlying stock: $25, $70, $100, $400.

9. Consider again the situation in question 8. Suppose you had sold the call option. What would your profit be, at expiration, for each of the stock prices?

10. Explain why you agree or disagree with this statement: "Buying a put is just like short selling the underlying asset. You gain the same thing from either position, if the underlying asset's price falls. If the price goes up, you have the same loss."

11. Why do stock index options involve cash settlement rather than delivery of the underlying stocks?

12. Suppose you bought an index call option for 5.50 that has a strike price of 200 and that, at expiration, you exercised it. Suppose, too, that, at the time you exercised the call option, the index has a value of 240.

    a. If the index option has a multiple of $100, how much money does the writer of this option pay you?

    b. What profit did you realize from buying this call option?

13. Suppose you have a long position in a call option on a futures contract, and the exercise price is 80. The futures contract price is now 87, and you want to exercise your option. Identify the gains from exercise, specifying any cash inflow and the futures position you get (and the price of the futures contract). Also, describe what the writer of the call must do.

# CHAPTER TWENTY-SEVEN

# Pricing of Futures and Options Contracts

*After reading this chapter you will understand:*

- the theory of pricing a futures contract.

- how arbitrage between the futures market and the cash or spot market links the prices of those markets.

- the meaning of the terms "cost of carry" and "net financing cost."

- the convergence of the futures and cash prices for a particular asset at the settlement date of the futures contract.

- why the actual futures price may differ from the theoretical futures price.

- how the market price of an option can be decomposed into an intrinsic value and a time premium.

- why arbitrage ensures that the prices of calls and puts on the same underlying asset with the same exercise price and expiration date have a certain relationship to each other.

- the factors that affect the price of an option: the underlying asset's current price and expected price volatility, the contract's expiration date and exercise price, the short-term rate of interest, and any cash flows from the underlying asset.

- the principles of the binomial option pricing model and how it is derived.

In the previous two chapters, we described the various types of futures and options contracts. In this chapter, we explain how to determine the theoretical price of these contracts using arbitrage arguments. A close examination of the underlying assumptions necessary to derive the theoretical price indicates how it must be modified to price the specific contracts described in the previous two chapters.

## PRICING OF FUTURES CONTRACTS

To understand what determines the futures price, consider once again the futures contract in Chapter 25 where the underlying instrument is Asset XYZ. We make several assumptions:

1. Asset XYZ is selling for $100 in the cash market.
2. Asset XYZ pays the holder (with certainty) $12 per year in four quarterly payments of $3, and the next quarterly payment is exactly three months from now.
3. The futures contract requires delivery three months from now.
4. The current three-month interest rate at which funds can be lent or borrowed is 8% per year.

What should the price of this futures contract be? That is, what should the futures price be? Suppose the price of the futures contract is $107. Consider this strategy:

Sell the futures contract at $107
Purchase Asset XYZ in the cash market for $100
Borrow $100 for three months at 8% per year

The borrowed funds are used to purchase Asset XYZ, resulting in no initial cash outlay for this strategy. At the end of three months, $3 will be received from holding Asset XYZ. Three months from now, Asset XYZ must be delivered to settle the futures contract, and the loan must be repaid. This strategy produces an outcome as follows:

1. From Settlement of the Futures Contract:
   Proceeds from sale of Asset XYZ to settle the futures
   contract                                                    = 107
   Payment received from investing in Asset XYZ for 3 month   =   3
                                                              -----
   Total proceeds                                             = 110

2. From the Loan:

| | |
|---|---|
| Repayment of principal of loan | = 100 |
| Interest on loan (2% for 3 months) | = 2 |
| Total outlay | = 102 |

3. Profit: 8

Notice that this strategy guarantees a profit of $8. Moreover, this profit is generated with no investment outlay; the funds needed to buy Asset XYZ were borrowed. The profit is realized regardless of what the futures price at the settlement date is. In financial terms, the profit arises from a riskless arbitrage between the price of Asset XYZ in the cash or spot market and the price of Asset XYZ in the futures market. Obviously, in a well-functioning market, arbitrageurs who could get this riskless gain for a zero investment would sell the futures and buy Asset XYZ, forcing the futures price down and bidding up Asset XYZ's price so as to eliminate this profit.

Suppose instead that the futures price is $92 and not $107. Let's consider this strategy:

Buy the futures contract at $92
Sell (short) Asset XYZ for $100
Invest (lend) $100 for three months at 8% per year[1]

Once again, there is no initial cash outlay for the strategy: the cost of the long position in the futures contract is zero, and there is no cost to selling the asset short and lending the money. Three months from now, Asset XYZ must be purchased to settle the long position in the futures contract. Asset XYZ accepted for delivery will then be used to cover the short position—to cover the short sale of Asset XYZ in the cash market. Shorting Asset XYZ requires the short seller to pay the lender of Asset XYZ the proceeds that the lender would have earned for the quarter. Therefore, the strategy requires a payment of $3 to the lender of Asset XYZ. The outcome in three months would be as follows:

1. From Settlement of the Futures Contract:

| | |
|---|---|
| Price paid for purchase of Asset XYZ to settle futures contract = | 92 |
| Proceeds to lender of Asset XYZ to borrow the asset | = 3 |
| Total outlay | = 95 |

2. From the Loan:

| | |
|---|---|
| Principal from maturing of investment | = 100 |
| Interest earned on loan ($2 for 3 months) | = 2 |
| Total proceeds | = 102 |

3. Profit 7

---

[1] Technically, a short seller may not be entitled to the full use of the proceeds resulting from the sale. We will discuss this later in this section.

The $7 profit from this strategy is also a riskless arbitrage profit. This strategy requires no initial cash outlay, but will generate a profit whatever the price of Asset XYZ is at the settlement date. Clearly, this opportunity would lead arbitrageurs to buy futures and short Asset XYZ, and the effect of these two actions would be to raise the futures price and lower the cash price until the profit again disappeared.

At what futures price would the arbitraging stop? Another way to ask this question is this: Is there a futures price that would prevent the opportunity for the riskless arbitrage profit? Yes, there is. There will be no arbitrage profit if the futures price is $99. Let's look at what happens if the two previous strategies are followed, now assuming a futures price of $99.

Consider the first strategy, which had these elements:
Sell the futures contract at $99
Purchase Asset XYZ in the cash market for $100
Borrow $100 for three months at 8% per year

In three months the outcome will be as follows:

1.  From Settlement of the Futures Contract:
    Proceeds from sale of Asset XYZ to settle the futures contract = 99
    Payment received from investing in Asset XYZ for 3 months  =  3
    Total proceeds                                            =102
2.  From the Loan:
    Repayment of principal of loan                            = 100
    Interest on loan (2% for 3 months)                        =  2
    Total outlay                                              = 102
3.  Profit:                                                    0

If the futures price is $99, the arbitrage profit has disappeared.

Next, consider the strategy consisting of these actions:
Buy the futures contract at $99
Sell (short) Asset XYZ for $100
Invest (lend) $100 for three months at 8% per year

The outcome in three months would be as follows:

1.  From Settlement of the Futures Contract:
    Price paid for purchase of Asset XYZ to settle futures contract   = 99
    Proceeds to lender of Asset XYZ to borrow the asset               =  3
    Total outlay                                                      = 102
2.  From the Loan:
    Principal from maturing of investment                            = 100

|  |  |
|---|---|
| Interest earned on loan ($2 for 3 months) | = 2 |
| Total proceeds | = 102 |
| 3. Profit | 0 |

Thus, if the futures price were $99, neither strategy would result in an arbitrage profit. Hence, a futures price of $99 is the equilibrium price, because any higher or lower futures price will permit riskless arbitrage profits.

## Theoretical Futures Price Based on Arbitrage Model

According to the arbitrage arguments we have just presented, we see that the equilibrium or theoretical futures price can be determined on the basis of the following information:

1. The price of the asset in the cash market.
2. The cash yield earned on the asset until the settlement date. In our example, the cash yield on Asset XYZ is $3 on a $100 investment or 3% quarterly (12% annual cash yield).
3. The "financing cost," which is the interest rate for borrowing and lending until the settlement date. In our example, the financing cost is 2% for the three months.

To develop a theory of futures pricing, we will use the notation following:

$$F = \text{futures price (\$)}$$
$$P = \text{cash market price (\$)}$$
$$r = \text{financing cost (\%)}$$
$$y = \text{cash yield (\%)}.$$

Now, consider this strategy:
Sell (or take a short position in) the futures contract at $F$
Purchase Asset XYZ for $P$
Borrow $P$, for a rate of $r$, until the settlement date.

The outcome at the settlement date would be:

1. From Settlement of the Futures Contract:

|  |  |
|---|---|
| Proceeds from sale of Asset XYZ to settle the futures contract | = $F$ |
| Payment received from investing in Asset XYZ | = $yP$ |
| Total proceeds | = $F + yP$ |

2. From the Loan:

|  |  |
|---|---|
| Repayment of principal of loan | = $P$ |
| Interest on loan | = $rP$ |
| Total outlay | = $P + rP$ |

The profit will equal:

$$\text{Profit} = \text{Total proceeds} - \text{Total outlay}$$
$$\text{Profit} = F + yP - (P + rP)$$

The equilibrium futures price is the price that insures that the profit from this arbitrage strategy is zero. Thus, equilibrium requires that:

$$0 = F + yP - (P + rP)$$

Solving for the theoretical futures price gives this equation:

$$F = P + P\,(r - y)$$

In other words, the equilibrium futures price is simply a function of the cash price, the financing cost, and the cash yield on the asset.

Alternatively, let us consider the second strategy illustrated in our example above, which looks like this:

Buy the futures contract at $F$
Sell (short) Asset XYZ for $P$
Invest (lend) $P$ at $r$ until the settlement date
The outcome at the settlement date would be:

1. From Settlement of the Futures Contract:
   Price paid for purchase of asset to settle futures contract $= F$
   Payment to lender of asset in order to borrow
   the asset $= yP$
   Total outlay $= F + yP$
2. From the Loan:
   Principal from maturing of investment $= P$
   Interest earned on loan $= rP$
   Total proceeds $= P + rP$

The profit will equal:

$$\text{Profit} = \text{Total proceeds} - \text{Total outlay}$$
$$\text{Profit} = P + rP - (F + yP)$$

Setting the profit equal to zero, so that there will be no arbitrage profit, and solving for the futures price, we obtain the same equation for the futures price as derived earlier:

$$F = P + P\,(r - y)$$

It is instructive to apply this equation to our previous example to determine the theoretical futures price. In that example, the key variables have these values:

$$r = 0.02$$
$$y = 0.03$$
$$P = \$100$$

Then, the theoretical futures price is:

$$F = \$100 - \$100\,(0.03 - 0.02)$$
$$= \$100 - \$1 = \$99$$

This agrees with the equilibrium futures price we proposed earlier.

The theoretical futures price may be at a premium to the cash market price (higher than the cash market price) or at a discount from the cash market price (lower than the cash market price), depending on the value of $P\,(r - y)$. The term, $r - y$, which reflects the difference between the cost of financing and the asset's cash yield, is called the *net financing cost*. The net financing cost is more commonly called the *cost of carry*, or simply, *carry*. *Positive carry* means that the yield earned is greater than the financing cost; *negative carry* means that the financing cost exceeds the yield earned. We can summarize the effect of carry on the difference between the futures price and the cash market price in this way:

| Carry | Futures Price |
|---|---|
| Positive $(y > r)$ | will sell at a discount to cash price $(F < P)$ |
| Negative $(y < r)$ | will sell at a premium to cash price $(F > P)$ |
| Zero $(r = y)$ | will be equal to the cash price $(F = P)$ |

### Price Convergence at the Delivery Date

At the delivery date, which is when the futures contract settles, the futures price must equal the cash market price, because a futures contract with no time left until delivery is equivalent to a cash market transaction. Thus, as the delivery date approaches, the futures price will converge to the cash market price. This fact is evident from the equation for the theoretical futures price. As the delivery date approaches, the financing cost approaches zero, and the yield that can be earned by holding the investment approaches zero. Hence, the cost of carry approaches zero, and the futures price will approach the cash market price.

### A Closer Look at the Theoretical Futures Price

To derive the theoretical futures price using the arbitrage argument, we made several assumptions. When the assumptions are violated, the actual futures price will diverge from the theoretical futures price. That is, the difference between the two prices will differ from the value of carry. Below, we examine those assumptions and identify practical reasons why the actual prices of all financial futures contracts tend to deviate from their theoretical prices.

***Interim Cash Flows.*** Our theoretical analysis assumes that no interim cash flows arise because of changes in futures prices and the variation margin of the organized exchanges on which futures are traded. In addition, our approach assumes implicitly that any dividends or coupon interest payments are paid at the delivery date rather than at some time between initiation of the cash position and expiration of the futures contract. However, we know that interim cash flows of either type can and do occur in practice.

In the case of stock index futures, incorporating interim dividend payments into the pricing model is necessary because a cash position in a set of 100 or 500 stocks (the number of stocks underlying an index) generates cash flows in the form of dividends from the stocks. The dividend rate and the pattern of dividend payments are not known with certainty. They must be projected from the historical dividend payments of the companies in the index. Once the dividend payments are projected, they can be incorporated into the pricing model. The only problem is that the value of the dividend payments at the settlement date will depend on the interest rate at which the dividend payments can be reinvested from the time they are projected to be received until the settlement date. The lower the dividend, and the closer the dividend payments to the settlement date of the futures contract, the less important the reinvestment income is in determining the futures price.

It is important to note that, in the absence of initial and variation margins, the theoretical price for the contract is technically the theoretical price for a forward contract, not the theoretical price for a futures contract. This is because, unlike a futures contract, a forward contract is not marked to market at the end of each trading day, and therefore does not require variation margin and does not generate cash inflows from gains or outflows from losses.

***Differences Between Lending and Borrowing Rates.***    In deriving the theoretical futures price, we assumed that the investor's borrowing rate and lending rate are equal. Typically, however, the borrowing rate is higher than the lending rate. The impact of this inequality is important and easy to identify. We will begin by adopting these symbols for the two rates:

$$r_B = \text{borrowing rate}$$
$$r_L = \text{lending rate}$$

Now, consider this familiar strategy:

Sell the futures contract at $F$
Purchase the asset for $P$
Borrow $P$ until the settlement date at $r_B$

Clearly, the futures price that would produce no arbitrage profit is:

$$F = P + P\,(r_B - y)$$

Recall that the second arbitrage strategy is:

Buy the futures contract at $F$
Sell (short) the asset for $P$
Invest (lend) $P$ at $r_L$ until the settlement date

The futures price that would prevent a riskless profit is:

$$F = P + P \, (r_L - y)$$

These two equations together provide boundaries between which the futures price will be in equilibrium. The first equation establishes the upper boundary, and the second equation the lower boundary. For example, assume that the borrowing rate is 8% per year, or 2% for three months, while the lending rate is 6% per year, or 1.5% for three months. According to the first equation, the upper boundary is:

$$F \text{ (upper boundary)} = \$100 + \$100 \, (0.02 - 0.03) = \$99$$

The lower boundary according to the second equation is:

$$F \text{ (lower boundary)} = \$100 + \$100 \, (0.015 - 0.03) = \$98.50$$

Thus, equilibrium is achieved if the futures price takes on any value between the two boundaries. In other words, equilibrium requires that $\$98.50 \le F \le \$99$.

***Transactions Costs.*** In deriving the theoretical futures price, we ignored transactions costs of the elements in the arbitrage strategies. In actuality, the costs of entering into and closing the cash position as well as round-trip transactions costs for the futures contract do affect the futures price. It is easy to show, as we do above for borrowing and lending rates, that transactions costs widen the boundaries for the equilibrium futures price. The details need not concern us here.

***Short Selling.*** In the strategy involving short selling of Asset XYZ when the futures price is below its theoretical value, we explicitly assumed that the proceeds from the short sale are received and reinvested. In practice, for individual investors, the proceeds are not received, and, in fact, the individual investor is required to put up margin (securities margin and not futures margin) to short sell. For institutional investors, the asset may be borrowed, but there is a cost to borrowing. This cost of borrowing can be incorporated into the model by reducing the yield on the asset.

For strategies applied to stock index futures, a short sale of the stocks in the index means that all stocks in the index must be sold simultaneously. The stock exchange rule for the short selling of stock, which we explained in Chapter 18, may prevent an investor from implementing the arbitrage strategy. The short selling rule for stocks specifies that a short sale can be made only at a price that is higher than the previous trade (referred to as an up-tick), or at a price that is equal to the previous trade (referred to as a zero-tick) but higher than the last trade at a different price. If the arbitrage requires selling the stocks in the index simultaneously, and the last transaction for some of the stocks is not an up-tick, the stocks cannot be shorted simultaneously. Thus, an institutional rule may in effect keep arbitrageurs from bringing the actual futures price in line with the theoretical futures price.

***Known Deliverable Asset and Settlement Date.*** Our example illustrating arbitrage strategies assumes that (1) only one asset is deliverable, and (2) the settlement date occurs at a known, fixed point in the future. Neither assumption is consistent with the delivery rules for some futures contracts. The case of U.S. Treasury bond and note futures contracts illustrates the point: an investor in a long position cannot know either the specific Treasury bond to be delivered or the specific date within the contract month when it might be delivered. This substantial uncertainty is a result of the delivery options that the short position in a futures contract has. As a reflection of the short positions' options and advantages, the actual futures price will be less than the theoretical futures price for the Treasury bond and note futures contracts.

***The Deliverable Is a Basket of Securities.*** Some futures contracts involve a single asset, but other contracts apply to a basket of assets or an index. Stock index futures and the municipal bond index futures contracts are examples. The problem in arbitraging these two futures contracts is that it is too expensive to buy or sell every security included in the index. Instead, a portfolio containing a smaller number of assets may be constructed to "track" the index (which means having price movements that are very similar to changes in the index). Nonetheless, arbitrage based on this tracking portfolio is no longer risk-free because of the risk that the portfolio will not track the index exactly. Clearly, then, the actual price of futures based on baskets of assets may diverge from the theoretical price because of transactions costs as well as uncertainty about the outcome of the arbitrage.

***Different Tax Treatment of Cash and Futures Transactions.*** The basic arbitrage model presented in this chapter ignores not only taxes but also different tax treatment of cash market transactions and futures transactions. Obviously, these factors can keep the actual futures price from being equal to the theoretical price.

▶ KEY POINTS THAT YOU SHOULD UNDERSTAND BEFORE PROCEEDING:

1. The equilibrium or theoretical futures price can be determined through arbitrage arguments.
2. The theoretical futures price depends on the price of the underlying asset in the cash market, the cost of financing a position in the underlying asset, and the cash yield on the underlying asset.
3. At the delivery date, the price of a futures contract converges to the cash market price.

4. The actual futures price will diverge from the theoretical futures price because of interim cash flows, differences between lending and borrowing rates, transactions costs, restrictions on short selling, and uncertainty about the deliverable asset and the date it will be delivered.

## PRICING OF OPTIONS

The theoretical price of an option is also derived from arbitrage arguments. However, the pricing of options is not as simple as the pricing of futures contracts.

### Basic Components of the Option Price

The option price is the sum of the option's *intrinsic value* and a premium over intrinsic value that is often referred to as the *time value* or *time premium*. While the former term is more common, we will use the term time premium to avoid confusion between the time value of money and the time value of the option.

***Intrinsic Value.*** The intrinsic value of an option, at any time, is its economic value if it is exercised immediately. If no positive economic value would result from exercising immediately, the intrinsic value is zero.

Computationally, the intrinsic value of a call option is the difference between the current price of the underlying asset and the strike price. If that difference is positive, then the intrinsic value equals that difference; if the difference is zero or negative, then the intrinsic value is set equal to zero. For example, if the strike price for a call option is $100 and the current asset price is $105, the intrinsic value is $5. That is, an option buyer exercising the option and simultaneously selling the underlying asset would realize $105 from the sale of the asset, which would be covered by acquiring the asset from the option writer for $100, thereby netting a $5 gain.

When an option has intrinsic value, it is said to be "in the money." When the strike price of a call option exceeds the current asset price, the call option is said to be "out of the money;" it has no intrinsic value. An option for which the strike price is equal to the current asset price is said to be "at the money." Both at-the-money and out-of-the-money options have intrinsic values of zero because it is not profitable to exercise them. Our call option with a strike price of $100 would be: (1) in the money when the current asset price is more than $100; (2) out of the money when the current asset price is less than $100; and (3) at the money when the current asset price is equal to $100.

For a put option, the intrinsic value is equal to the amount by which the current asset price is below the strike price. For example, if the strike price of a put option is $100, and the current asset price is $92, the intrinsic value is $8. That is, the buyer of the put option who simultaneously buys the underlying asset and exercises the put option will net $8 by exercising. The asset will be sold to the writer for $100 and purchased in the market for $92. For our put option with a strike price of $100, the option would be: (1) in the money when the current asset price is less than $100; (2) out of the money when the current asset price exceeds $100; (3) at the money when the current asset price is equal to $100.

***Time Premium.***    The time premium of an option is the amount by which the option's market price exceeds its intrinsic value. The option buyer hopes that, at some time prior to expiration, changes in the market price of the underlying asset will increase the value of the rights conveyed by the option. For this prospect, the option buyer is willing to pay a premium above the intrinsic value. For example, if the price of a call option with a strike price of $100 is $9 when the current asset price is $105, the time premium of this option is $4 ($9 minus its intrinsic value of $5). Had the current asset price been $90 instead of $105, then the time premium of this option would be the entire $9 because the option has no intrinsic value. Clearly, other things being equal, the time premium of an option will increase with the amount of time remaining to expiration.

An option buyer has two ways to realize the value of a position taken in the option. The first way is to exercise the option. The second way is to sell the call option for its market price. In the first example above, selling the call for $9 is preferable to exercising, because the exercise will realize a gain of only $5 but the sale will realize a gain of $9. As this example shows, exercise causes the immediate loss of any time premium. It is important to note that there are circumstances under which an option may be exercised prior to the expiration date. These circumstances depend on whether the total proceeds at the expiration date would be greater by holding the option or exercising and reinvesting any received cash proceeds until the expiration date.

## Put–Call Parity Relationship

There is an important relationship between the price of a call option and the price of a put option on the same underlying instrument, with the same strike price and the same expiration date. An example can illustrate this relationship, which is commonly referred to as the *put–call parity relationship*.

Our example comes from the previous chapter and assumes that a put option and a call option are available on the same underlying asset (Asset XYZ), and that both options have one month to expiration and a strike price of $100. The example assumes the price of the underlying asset to be $100. The call and put prices are assumed to be $3 and $2, respectively.

To see if the two prices have the right relationship, consider what happens if an investor pursues this strategy:

Buy Asset XYZ at a price of $100
Sell a call option at a price of $3
Buy a put option at a price of $2

| TABLE 27-1 |
|---|

## PROFIT/LOSS PROFILE FOR A STRATEGY INVOLVING A LONG POSITION IN ASSET XYZ, SHORT CALL OPTION POSITION, AND LONG PUT OPTION POSITION

Assumptions:
Price of Asset XYZ = $100
Call option price = $3
Put option price = $2
Strike price = $100
Time to expiration = 1 month

| Price of Asset XYZ at Expiration Date | Profit from Asset XYZ* | Price Received for Call | Price Paid for Put | Overall Profit |
|---|---|---|---|---|
| $150 | 0 | 3 | −2 | 1 |
| 140 | 0 | 3 | −2 | 1 |
| 130 | 0 | 3 | −2 | 1 |
| 120 | 0 | 3 | −2 | 1 |
| 115 | 0 | 3 | −2 | 1 |
| 110 | 0 | 3 | −2 | 1 |
| 105 | 0 | 3 | −2 | 1 |
| 100 | 0 | 3 | −2 | 1 |
| 95 | 0 | 3 | −2 | 1 |
| 90 | 0 | 3 | −2 | 1 |
| 85 | 0 | 3 | −2 | 1 |
| 80 | 0 | 3 | −2 | 1 |
| 75 | 0 | 3 | −2 | 1 |
| 70 | 0 | 3 | −2 | 1 |
| 65 | 0 | 3 | −2 | 1 |
| 60 | 0 | 3 | −2 | 1 |

*There is no profit, because at a price above $100, Asset XYZ will be called from the investor at a price of $100, and at a price below $100, Asset XYZ will be put by the investor at a price of $100.

This strategy generates these positions:

    Long Asset XYZ
    Short the call option
    Long the put option

Table 27-1 shows the profit and loss profile at the expiration date for this strategy. Notice that, no matter what Asset XYZ's price is at the expiration date, the strategy will produce a profit of $1. The net cost of creating this position is the cost of purchasing Asset XYZ ($100) plus the cost of buying the put ($2) less the cost from selling the call ($3), which is $101. Suppose that the net cost of creating the position for one month is less than $1. Then, by borrowing $101 to create the position so that no investment outlay is made by the investor, this strategy will produce a net profit of $1 (as shown in the last column of Table 27-1) less the cost of borrowing $101 which is assumed to be less than $1. This situation cannot exist in an efficient market. As market participants implement the strategy to capture the $1 profit, their actions will have one or more of the following consequences, which will tend to eliminate the $1 profit: (1) the price of Asset XYZ will increase; (2) the call option price will drop; and/or (3) the put option price will rise.

Our example clearly implies that, if Asset XYZ's price does not change, the call price and the put price must tend toward equality. But our example ignores the time value of money (financing and opportunity costs, cash payments, and reinvestment income). Also, our example does not consider the possibility of early exercise of the options. Thus, we have been considering a put–call parity relationship for only European options.

It can be shown that the put–call parity relationship for options where the underlying asset makes cash distributions and where the time value of money is recognized is:

Put option price − Call option price = Present value of strike price + Present value of cash distribution − Price of underlying asset

Once more, we note that this relationship is actually the put–call parity relationship for European options. However, the values of puts and calls that are American options do conform approximately to this relationship. If this relationship does not hold, arbitrage opportunities exist. That is, investors will be able to construct portfolios consisting of long and short positions in the asset and related options that will provide an extra return with (practical) certainty.

## Factors that Influence the Option Price

Six factors influence the price of an option:

1. Current price of the underlying asset.
2. Strike price.
3. Time to expiration of the option.
4. Expected price volatility of the underlying asset over the life of the option.
5. Short-term risk-free interest rate over the life of the option.
6. Anticipated cash payments on the underlying asset over the life of the option.

The impact of each of these factors may depend on whether (1) the option is a call or a put, and (2) the option is an American option or a European option. A summary of the effect of each factor on put and call option prices is presented in Table 27-2. Here we briefly explain why the factors have the particular effects.

***Current Price of the Underlying Asset.***  The option price will change as the price of the underlying asset changes. For a call option, as the price of the underlying asset increases (all other factors constant), the option price increases. The opposite holds for a put option: as the price of the underlying asset increases, the price of a put option decreases.

***Strike Price.*** The strike price is fixed for the life of the option. All other factors equal, the lower the strike price, the higher the price for a call option. For put options, the higher the exercise price, the higher the option price.

***Time to Expiration of the Option.*** An option is a "wasting asset." That is, after the expiration date the option has no value. All other factors equal, the longer the time to expiration of the option, the higher the option price. This is because, as the time to expiration decreases, less time remains for the underlying asset's price to rise (for a call buyer) or fall (for a put buyer), and therefore the probability of a favorable price movement decreases. Consequently, for American options, as the time remaining until expiration decreases, the option price approaches its intrinsic value.

***Expected Price Volatility of the Underlying Asset over the Life of the Option.*** All other factors equal, the greater the expected volatility (as measured by the standard deviation or variance) of the price of the underlying asset, the more an investor would be willing to pay for the option, and the more an option writer would demand for it. This occurs because the greater the volatility, the greater the probability that the price of the underlying asset will move in favor of the option buyer at some time before expiration.

Notice that it is the standard deviation or variance, not the systematic risk as measured by beta, as described in Chapter 13, that is relevant in the pricing of options.

***Short-Term Risk-Free Interest Rate over the Life of the Option.*** Buying the underlying asset ties up one's money. Buying an option on the same quantity of the underlying asset makes the difference between the asset price and the option price available for investment at an interest rate at least as high

---

**TABLE 27-2**

SUMMARY OF FACTORS THAT AFFECT THE PRICE OF AN OPTION

| Factor | Effect of an Increase of Factor on | |
| --- | --- | --- |
| | Call Price | Put Price |
| Current price of underlying asset | Increase | Decrease |
| Strike price | Decrease | Increase |
| Time to expiration of option | Increase | Increase |
| Expected price volatility | Increase | Increase |
| Short-term interest rate | Increase | Decrease |
| Anticipated cash payments | Decrease | Increase |

as the risk-free rate. Consequently, all other factors constant, the higher the short-term risk-free interest rate, the greater the cost of buying the underlying asset and carrying it to the expiration date of the call option. Hence, the higher the short-term risk-free interest rate, the more attractive the call option will be relative to the direct purchase of the underlying asset. As a result, the higher the short-term risk-free interest rate, the greater the price of a call option.

***Anticipated Cash Payments on the Underlying Asset over the Life of the Option.*** Cash payments on the underlying asset tend to decrease the price of a call option because the cash payments make it more attractive to hold the underlying asset than to hold the option. For put options, cash payments on the underlying asset tend to increase the price.

## Option Pricing Models

We have shown that the theoretical price of a futures contract can be determined on the basis of arbitrage arguments. An option pricing model uses a set of assumptions and arbitrage arguments to derive a theoretical price for an option. As we shall see below, deriving a theoretical option price is much more complicated than deriving a theoretical futures price because the option price depends on the expected price volatility of the underlying asset over the life of the option.

Several models have been developed to determine the theoretical value of an option. The most popular one was developed by Fischer Black and Myron Scholes in 1973 for valuing European call options.[2] Several modifications to their model have followed. We use another pricing model called the *binomial option pricing model* to see how arbitrage arguments can be used to determine a fair value for a call option.[3]

Basically, the idea behind the arbitrage argument is that if the payoff from owning a call option can be replicated by (1) purchasing the asset underlying the call option, and (2) borrowing funds, the price of the option is then (at most) the cost of creating the replicating strategy.

## Deriving the Binomial Option Pricing Model

To derive a one-period binomial option pricing model for a call option, we begin by constructing a portfolio consisting of: (1) a long position in a certain

---

[2] Fischer Black and Myron Scholes, "The Pricing of Corporate Liabilities," *Journal of Political Economy* (May–June 1973), pp. 637–659.

[3] John C. Cox, Stephen A. Ross, and Mark Rubinstein, "Option Pricing: A Simplified Approach," *Journal of Financial Economics* (September 1979), pp. 229–263; Richard J. Rendleman and Brit J. Bartter, "Two-State Option Pricing," *Journal of Finance* (December 1979), pp. 1093–1110; and William F. Sharpe, *Investments* (Englewood Cliffs, N.J.: Prentice-Hall, 1981), Chapter 16.

amount of the asset, and (2) a short call position in the underlying asset. The amount of the underlying asset purchased is such that the position will be hedged against any change in the price of the asset at the expiration date of the option. That is, the portfolio consisting of the long position in the asset and the short position in the call option is riskless and will produce a return that equals the risk-free interest rate. A portfolio constructed in this way is called a *hedged portfolio*.

We can show how this process works with an extended illustration. Let us assume first that there is an asset that has a current market price of $80, and that only two possible future states can occur one year from now. Each state is associated with one of only two possible values for the asset, and they can be summarized in this way:

| State | Price |
|-------|-------|
| 1 | $100 |
| 2 | 70 |

We assume further that there is a call option on this asset with a strike price of $80 (the same as the current market price), and that it expires in one year. Let us suppose an investor forms a hedged portfolio by acquiring ⅔ of a unit of the asset and selling one call option. The ⅔ of a unit of the asset is the so-called *hedge ratio* (how we derive the hedge ratio is explained later). Let us consider the outcomes for this hedged portfolio corresponding to the two possible outcomes for the asset.

If the price of the asset one year from now is $100, the buyer of the call option will exercise it. This means that the investor will have to deliver one unit of the asset in exchange for the strike price, $80. As the investor has only ⅔ of a unit of the asset, she has to buy ⅓ at a cost of $33 ⅓ (the market price of $100 times ⅓). Consequently, the outcome will equal the strike price of $80 received, minus the $33 ⅓ cost to acquire the ⅓ unit of the asset to deliver, plus whatever price the investor initially sold the call option for. That is, the outcome will be:

$$80 - 33 ⅓ + \text{Call option price} = 46 ⅔ + \text{Call option price.}$$

If, instead, the price of the asset one year from now is $70, the buyer of the call option will not exercise it. Consequently, the investor will own ⅔ of a unit of the asset. At the price of $70, the value of ⅔ of a unit is $46 ⅔. The outcome in this case is then the value of the asset plus whatever price the investor received when she initially sold the call option. That is, the outcome will be:

$$46 ⅔ + \text{Call option price.}$$

It is apparent that, given the possible asset prices, the portfolio consisting of a short position in the call option and ⅔ of a unit of the asset will generate an outcome that hedges changes in the price of the asset; hence, the hedged portfolio is riskless. Furthermore, this riskless hedge will hold regardless of the price of the call, which affects only the magnitude of the outcome.

***Deriving The Hedge Ratio.*** To show how to calculate the hedge ratio, we use the notation:

$S$ = current asset price

$u$ = 1 plus the percentage change in the asset's price if the price goes up in the next period

$d$ = 1 plus the percentage change in the asset's price if the price goes down in the next period

$r$ = a risk-free one-period interest rate (the risk-free rate until the expiration date)

$C$ = current price of a call option

$C_u$ = intrinsic value of the call option if the asset price goes up

$C_d$ = intrinsic value of the call option if the asset price goes down

$E$ = strike price of the call option

$H$ = hedge ratio, that is, the amount of the asset purchased per call sold.

In our illustration, $u$ and $d$ are:

$u$ = 1.250 ($100/$80)
$d$ = 0.875 ($70/$80)

Further, State 1 in our illustration means that the asset's price goes up, and State 2 means that the asset's price goes down.

The investment made in the hedged portfolio is equal to the cost of buying $H$ amount of the asset minus the price received from selling the call option. Therefore, because

$$\text{Amount invested in the asset} = HS,$$

then

$$\text{Cost of the hedged portfolio} = HS - C.$$

The payoff of the hedged portfolio at the end of one period is equal to the value of the $HS$ amount of the asset purchased minus the call option price. The payoffs of the hedged portfolio for the two possible states are defined in this way:

State 1, if the asset's price goes up: $uHS - C_u$
State 2, if the asset's price goes down: $dHS - C_d$

In our illustration, we have these payoffs:

If the asset's price goes up: $1.250\,H\,\$80 - C_u$ or $\$100\,H - C_u$
If the asset's price falls: $0.875\,H\,\$80 - C_d$ or $\$70\,H - C_d$

If the hedge is riskless, the payoffs must be the same. Thus,

$$uHS - C_u = dHS - C_d \qquad (1)$$

Solving equation (1) for the hedge ratio, $H$, we have

$$H = \frac{C_u - C_d}{(u - d)S} \qquad (2)$$

To determine the value of the hedge ratio, $H$, we must know $C_u$ and $C_d$. These two values are equal to the difference between the price of the asset and the strike price in the two possible states. Of course, the minimum value of the call option, in any state, is zero. Mathematically, the differences can be expressed as follows:

If the asset's price goes up: $C_u = \text{Max} [0, (uS - E)]$
If the asset's price goes down: $C_d = \text{Max} [0, (dS - E)]$

As the strike price in our illustration is \$80, the value of $uS$ is \$100, and the value of $dS$ is \$70. Then,

If the asset's price goes up: $C_u = \text{Max} [0, (\$100 - \$80)] = \$20$
If the asset's price goes down: $C_d = \text{Max} [0, (\$70 - \$80)] = \$0$

To continue with our illustration, we substitute the values of $u$, $d$, $S$, $C_u$ and $C_d$ into equation (2) to obtain the hedge ratio's value:

$$H = \frac{\$20 - \$0}{(1.25 - 0.875) \ \$80} = \tfrac{2}{3}$$

This value for $H$ agrees with the amount of the asset purchased when we introduced this illustration.

Now we can derive a formula for the call option price. Figure 27-1 diagrams the situation. The top left half of the figure shows the current price of the asset for the current period and at the expiration date. The lower left-hand portion of the figure does the same thing using the notation above. The upper right-hand side of the figure gives the current price of the call option and the value of the call option at the expiration date; the lower right-hand side does the same thing using our notation. Figure 27-2 uses the values in our illustration to construct the outcomes for the asset and the call option.

***Deriving the Price of a Call Option.***   To derive the price of a call option, we can rely on the basic principle that the hedged portfolio, being riskless, must have a return equal to the risk-free rate of interest. Given that the amount invested in the hedged portfolio is $HS - C$, the amount that should be generated one period from now is:

$$(1 + r) \ (HS - C) \qquad (3)$$

FIGURE 27-1

ONE-PERIOD OPTION PRICING MODEL

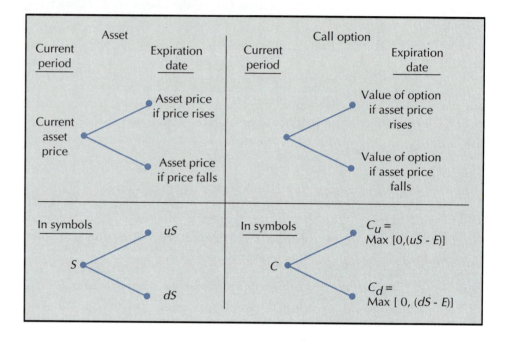

We also know what the payoff will be for the hedged portfolio if the asset's price goes up or down. Because the payoff of the hedged portfolio will be the same whether the asset's price rises or falls, we can use the payoff if it goes up, which is

$$uHS - C_u$$

The payoff of the hedged portfolio given above should be the same as the initial cost of the portfolio given by equation (3). Equating the two, we have:

$$(1 + r)\ (HS - C) = uHS - C_u \tag{4}$$

Substituting equation (2) for $H$ in equation (4), and solving for the call option price, $C$, we find

$$C = \left(\frac{1 + r - d}{u - d}\right) \left(\frac{C_u}{1 + r}\right) + \left(\frac{u - 1 - r}{u - d}\right) \left(\frac{C_d}{1 + r}\right) \tag{5}$$

Equation (5) is the formula for the one-period binomial option pricing model. We would have derived the same formula if we had used the payoff for a decline in the price of the underlying asset. This derivation is left as an exercise for the reader.

Applying equation (5) to our illustration where

FIGURE 27-2

ONE-PERIOD OPTION PRICING MODEL ILLUSTRATION

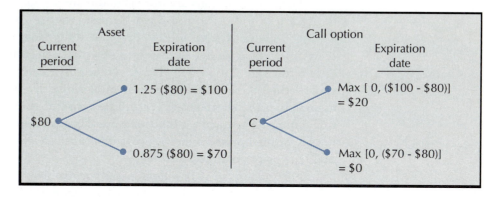

$u = 1.250$
$d = 0.875$
$r = 0.10$
$C_u = \$20$
$C_d = \$0$

we get

$$C = \left(\frac{1 + 0.10 - 0.875}{1.25 - 0.875}\right)\left(\frac{\$20}{1 + 0.10}\right) + \left(\frac{1.25 - 1 - 0.10}{1.25 - 0.875}\right)\left(\frac{\$0}{1 + 0.10}\right)$$

$$= \$10.90$$

The approach we present for pricing options may seem oversimplified, given that we assume only two possible future states for the price of the underlying asset. In fact, we can extend the procedure by making the period shorter and shorter, and in that way calculate a fair value for an option. It is important to note that extended and comprehensive versions of the binomial pricing model are in wide use throughout the world of finance. Moreover, the other popular option pricing model, the Black–Scholes model mentioned earlier, is in reality the mathematical equivalent of the binomial approach as the periods become very short. Thus, the approach we have described in detail here provides the conceptual framework for much of the analysis of option prices that today's financial market participants regularly perform.

## Fixed-Income Option Pricing Models

Because of the assumptions required for the binomial model described above, such models may have limited applicability to the pricing of options on fixed-income securities. More specifically, the binomial model assumes that (1) the price of the security can take on any positive value with some probability—

no matter how small; (2) the short-term interest rate is constant over the life of the option; and (3) the volatility of the price of the security is constant over the life of the option.

These assumptions are unreasonable for an option on a fixed-income security. First, the price of a fixed-income security cannot exceed the undiscounted value of the cash flow. Any possibility that the price can go higher than this value implies that interest rates can be negative. Second, the price of an interest rate option will change as interest rates change. A change in the short-term interest rate changes the rates along the yield curve. Therefore, to assume that the short-term rate will be constant is inappropriate for interest rate options. The third assumption, that the variance of prices is constant over the life of the option, is inappropriate because as a bond moves closer to maturity its price volatility declines.

Fortunately, it is possible to avoid the problem of negative interest rates. We can develop a binomial option pricing model that is based on the distribution of interest rates rather than prices. Once a binomial interest rate tree is constructed, it can be converted into a binomial price tree by using its interest rates to determine the prices of the bond at the end of the period. We can apply to these prices the same procedure described earlier to calculate the option price by working backward from the value of the call option at the expiration date.

While the binomial option pricing model based on yields is superior to models based on prices, it still has a theoretical drawback. All theoretically valid option pricing models must satisfy the put–call parity relationship. The problem with the binomial model based on yields is that it does not satisfy this relationship. It violates the relationship because it fails to take into consideration the yield curve, thereby allowing arbitrage opportunities.

The most elaborate models that take the yield curve into consideration, and as a result eliminate arbitrage opportunities, are called *yield curve option pricing models* or *arbitrage-free option pricing models*. These models can incorporate different volatility assumptions along the yield curve. While they are theoretically superior to the other models we have described, they require extensive computer time to solve.[4]

▶ KEY POINTS THAT YOU SHOULD UNDERSTAND BEFORE PROCEEDING:

1. The price of an option can be separated into two parts, its intrinsic value and its time premium.
2. The put–call parity relationship is the relationship between the price of a call option and the price of a put option on the same underlying instrument, with the same strike price and the same expiration date.

---

[4] For a discussion of yield curve or arbitrage-free option-pricing models see: Mark Pitts and Frank J. Fabozzi, *Interest Rate Futures and Options* (Chicago: Probus Publishing, 1989), Chapter 9; and Lawrence J. Dyer and David P. Jacob, "Guide to Fixed Income Option Pricing Models," in Frank J. Fabozzi (ed.) *The Handbook of Fixed Income Options* (Chicago: Probus Publishing, 1989).

3.  There are six factors that influence the price of an option: the current price of the underlying asset, the strike price, the time to expiration of the option, the expected price volatility of the underlying asset over the life of the option, the short-term risk-free interest rate over the life of the option, and the anticipated cash payments on the underlying asset over the life of the option.

4.  The theoretical price of an option can be determined on the basis of arbitrage arguments, but is much more complicated to determine than the theoretical price of a futures contract because the option price depends on the expected price volatility of the underlying asset over the life of the option.

5.  Several models have been developed to determine the theoretical value of an option.

6.  The value of an option is equal to the cost of creating a replicating hedge portfolio.

**SUMMARY**

Using arbitrage arguments, the theoretical or equilibrium price of a futures contract can be shown to be equal to the cash market price plus the cost of carry. The cost of carry is the net financing cost, that is, the difference between the financing rate and the cash yield on the underlying asset. The theoretical futures price will be less than the cash market price if the cost of carry is positive, equal to the cash market price if the cost of carry is zero, and more than the cash market price if the cost of carry is negative.

Developing the theoretical futures price with arbitrage arguments requires certain assumptions. When these assumptions are violated for a specific futures contract, the theoretical futures price must be modified. Because of the difference between borrowing and lending rates and because of transactions costs, there is not one theoretical futures price but, rather, a boundary around the theoretical futures price. So long as the actual futures price remains within this boundary, arbitrage profits cannot be realized.

The price of an option consists of two components: the intrinsic value and the time premium. The intrinsic value is the economic value of the option if it is exercised immediately. If there is no positive economic value resulting from exercising immediately, the intrinsic value is zero. The time premium is the amount by which the option price exceeds the intrinsic value. Six factors influence the option price: (1) the current price of the underlying asset; (2) the strike price of the option; (3) the time remaining to the expiration of the option; (4) the expected price volatility of the underlying asset; (5) the short-term risk-free interest rate over the life of the option; and (6) the anticipated cash payments on the underlying asset.

The relationship among the call option price, the put option price, and the price of the underlying asset is known as the put–call parity relationship. The theoretical option price can be calculated with the binomial option pricing model, which also employs arbitrage arguments. Application of the binomial model to the pricing of options on fixed-income securities poses problems because of the model's underlying assumptions.

**At-the-money option:** An option for which the strike price is equal to the current asset price.

**Cost of carry (or simply carry):** The net cost of financing a position in an asset; that is, the difference between the cost of financing a position in an asset and the asset's cash yield.

**Financing cost:** In the pricing of a futures contract, the interest rate for borrowing until the settlement date.

**In-the-money option:** An option that has intrinsic value.

**Intrinsic value:** The component of an option price that reflects its economic value if it is exercised immediately.

**Negative carry:** A net financing position in which the financing cost is greater than the cash yield earned on the asset.

**Net financing cost:** The difference between the cost of financing a position in an asset and the asset's cash yield. It is also called the cost of carry or simply carry.

**Out-of-the-money option:** A call option in which the current asset price is less than the strike price, or a put option in which the current asset price is greater than the strike price.

**Positive carry:** A net financing position in which the cash yield earned on the asset is greater than the financing cost.

**Put–call parity relationship:** The relationship between the price of a call option and the price of a put option on the same underlying instrument, with the same strike price and the same expiration date.

**Time premium:** The component of an option price that represents the amount by which the option's market price exceeds its intrinsic value.

1. Models for pricing futures and options are said to be based on arbitrage arguments.
   a. What does arbitrage mean?
   b. What is the investor's incentive to engage in arbitrage?
2. Suppose there is a financial asset ABC, which is the underlying asset

for a futures contract with settlement six months from now. You know the following about this financial asset and the futures contract:

1.  In the cash market, ABC is selling for $80.
2.  ABC pays $8 per year in two semiannual payments of $4, and the next semiannual payment is due exactly six months from now.
3.  The current six-month interest rate at which funds can be loaned or borrowed is 6%.

    a.   What is the theoretical (or equilibrium) futures price?

    b.   What action would you take if the futures price is $83?

    c.   What action would you take if the futures price is $76?

    d.   Suppose that ABC pays interest quarterly instead of semiannually. If you know that you can reinvest any funds you receive three months from now at 1% for three months, what would the theoretical futures price for six-month settlement be?

    e.   Suppose that the borrowing rate and lending rate are not equal. Instead, suppose that the current six-month borrowing rate is 8% and the six-month lending rate is 6%. What are the boundaries for the theoretical futures price?

3.   a.   Explain why restrictions on short-selling of stocks would cause the actual price of a stock index futures contract to diverge from its theoretical price.

    b.   Explain why creating a portfolio of stocks in which the number of stocks is less than the number of stocks in the index underlying a stock index futures contract would result in an arbitrage that is not riskless.

4.   Why do the delivery options in a Treasury bond futures contract cause the actual futures price to diverge from its theoretical price?

5.   "Of course the futures are more expensive than the cash price — there's positive carry." Do you agree with this statement?

6.   Consider the following call option with three months to expiration:

       strike price = $72
       current price of underlying asset = $87
       market price of option = $6

    a.   What is the intrinsic value for this call option?

    b.   What is the time premium for this call option?

7.   Suppose the option in the previous question is a put option rather than a call option.

    a.   What is the intrinsic value for this put option?

    b.   What is the time premium for this put option?

8.   You obtain the following price quotes for call options on Asset ABC. It is now December, with the near contract maturing in one month's time. Asset ABC's price is currently trading at $50.

| Strike | Jan. | March | June |
|--------|------|-------|------|
| $40 | $11 | $12 | $11.50 |
| 50 | 6 | 7 | 8.50 |
| 60 | 7 | 8 | 9.00 |

Glancing at the figures, you note that two of these quotes seem to violate some of the rules you learned regarding options pricing.

   a.  What are these discrepancies?

   b.  How could you take advantage of the discrepancies? What is the minimum profit you would realize by arbitraging based on these discrepancies?

9.  Indicate whether you agree or disagree with the statements following.

   a.  "To determine the theoretical value of an option, we will need some measure of the price volatility of the underlying asset. Because financial theorists tell us that the appropriate measure of risk is beta (that is, systematic risk), then we should use this value."

   b.  "If the expected price volatility of an option increases, the theoretical value of an option decreases?"

   c.  "It does not make sense that the price of a call option should rise in value if the price of the underlying asset falls."

10.  Consider two options with the same expiration date and for the same underlying asset. The two options differ only in the strike price. Option 1's strike price is greater than that of Option 2.

   a.  If the two options are call options, which option will have a higher price?

   b.  If the two options are put options, which option will have a higher price?

11.  Consider two options with the same strike price and for the same underlying asset. The two options differ only with respect to the time to expiration. Option A expires in three months and Option B expires in six months.

   a.  If the two options are call options, which option will have the higher intrinsic value (assuming the options are in the money)?

   b.  If the two options are call options, which option will have a higher time premium?

   c.  Would your answers to a and b be different if the option is a put rather than a call?

12.  In an option pricing model, what statistical measure is used as a measure of the price volatility of the underlying asset?

13.  For an asset that does not make cash distributions over the life of an option, it does not pay to exercise a call option prior to the expiration date. Why?

14.  Consider two strategies:

*Strategy 1:* Purchase one unit of Asset M currently selling for $103. A distribution of $10 is expected one year from now.

*Strategy 2:* (a) Purchase a call option on Asset M with an expiration date one year from now and a strike price of $100; and (b) place sufficient funds in a 10% interest-bearing bank account to exercise the option at expiration ($100) and to pay the cash distribution that would be paid by Asset M ($10).

a. What is the investment required under Strategy 2?

b. What are the payoffs of Strategy 1 and Strategy 2, assuming that the price of Asset M one year from now is:

    (i) $120

    (ii) $103

    (iii) $100

    (iv) $ 80

c. For the four prices of asset M one year from now, demonstrate that the following relationship holds:

$$\text{Call option price} \geq$$

Max [0, (Price of underlying asset − Present value of strike price − Present value of cash distribution)]

15. What is meant by a hedge ratio in developing an option pricing model?

16. a. Calculate the option value for a two-period European call option with the following terms:

    Current price of underlying asset = $100

    Strike price = $10

    One-period risk-free rate = 5%

The stock price can either go up or down by 10% at the end of one period.

b. Recalculate the value for the option when the stock price can move either up or down by 50% at the end of one period. Compare your answer with the calculated value in part (a).

17. What is the problem encountered in applying the binomial pricing model to the pricing of options on fixed-income securities?

# CHAPTER TWENTY-EIGHT

# The Applications of Futures and Options Contracts

*After reading this chapter, you will understand:*

- how participants use stock index futures to control a stock portfolio's risk and other portfolio applications.

- how investors in fixed-income securities employ interest rate futures to control the interest rate risk of a portfolio and other portfolio applications.

- how and under what circumstances futures can be used to enhance portfolio returns.

- how futures can be used to alter the allocation of a portfolio between equities and bonds.

- the differences in hedging with futures and options.

- how stock options and stock index options allow investors to protect the values of their stock portfolios.

- how interest rate options enable fixed income investors to hedge against adverse changes in interest rates.

- what is meant by the basis and that the basis can change over time.

- that hedging with futures eliminates price risk but exposes the hedged position to basis risk.
- what is meant by cross hedging and the risks associated with cross hedging.
- the difference between the long or buy hedge and the short or sell hedge, both in direct hedging and cross hedging.

In the previous three chapters, we focused on the general properties of financial futures and options contracts, the specific contracts available, and how they are priced. While we have alluded to various applications of these contracts, particularly their use in hedging, we did not cite specific applications. In this chapter, we provide an overview of how market participants can and do employ derivative instruments. The appendix to this chapter explains the general principles of hedging with futures contracts.

## APPLICATIONS OF FUTURES CONTRACTS

We begin with the various ways in which market participants can use stock index futures and interest rate futures.

### Stock Index Futures

Institutional investors can use stock index futures for seven distinct investment strategies. We describe these strategies below.

**Speculating on the Movement of the Stock Market.**   Prior to the development of stock index futures, an investor who wanted to speculate on the future course of aggregate stock prices had to buy or short individual stocks. Now, a stock index can be bought or sold in the futures market. However, making speculation easier for investors is not the main function of stock index futures contracts. The other strategies discussed below show how institutional investors can use stock index futures effectively to meet investment objectives.

**Controlling the Risk of a Stock Portfolio.**   An institution that wishes to alter its exposure to the market can do so by revising the portfolio's beta. This can be done by rebalancing the portfolio with stocks that will produce the target beta, but there are transactions costs associated with rebalancing a portfolio. Because of the leverage embedded in futures, institutions can use stock index futures to achieve a target beta at a considerably lower transaction cost. Buying stock index futures will increase a portfolio's beta, and selling futures will reduce it.

**Hedging against Adverse Stock Price Movements.**   Hedging is a special case of controlling a stock portfolio's exposure to adverse price changes. In a hedge, the objective is to alter a current or anticipated stock portfolio position so that its beta is zero. A portfolio with a beta of zero should generate a risk-free interest rate. Such a return from a zero-beta portfolio is consistent with the capital asset pricing model discussed in Chapter 13, and also consistent with our discussion of the pricing of futures contracts in the previous chapter.

Remember that using stock index futures for hedging locks in a price, and that the hedger cannot then benefit from a favorable movement in the portfolio's value. (As we explain later, using stock index options has downside protection but retains the upside potential reduced by the cost of the option.)

Two examples of how investment banking firms can use stock index futures to hedge their activities became known shortly after stock index futures began trading. In June 1982, International Harvester traded its stock portfolio to Goldman Sachs in exchange for a bond portfolio.[1] As recipient of the stock portfolio, Goldman Sachs was exposed to market risk. To protect itself against a decline in the value of the stock portfolio, Goldman Sachs placed a hedge on a "significant" portion of the stock portfolio, using all three stock index futures trading at the time to implement the hedge.

The second example involves Salomon Brothers, which used stock index futures to protect itself against a decline in stock prices in a transaction involving $400 million of stock. In that transaction, the New York City Pension Fund switched $400 million of funds that were being managed by Alliance Capital to Bankers Trust so that the latter could manage the funds with an indexing approach. Salomon Brothers guaranteed prices at which the Pension Fund and Bankers Trust could purchase or sell the stocks in the portfolio being transferred. To do this, Salomon Brothers used options on individual stocks to protect against price changes in certain stocks, but also used stock index futures to protect itself against broad market movements that would decrease the value of the stocks in the portfolio.

***Constructing Indexed Portfolios.***   As we explained in Chapter 18, an increasing number of institutional equity funds are indexed to some broad-based stock market index. Creating a portfolio that replicates a targeted stock index requires outlays for management fees and transactions costs. The higher these costs, the greater the divergence between the performance of the indexed portfolio and the target index. To control costs, many fund managers creating an indexed portfolio will not purchase all the stocks that comprise the index, but will purchase a group that "tracks the targeted index" or moves in much the same way as the index. As a result, the indexed portfolio produces *tracking error risk*, which is the chance that its movements will not precisely follow those of the index. To avoid the problems of using the cash market to construct an indexed portfolio, the manager can use stock index futures.

However, it is important to note that index fund managers can use stock index futures to create an index fund only if stock index futures contracts

[1] Kimberly Blanton, "Index Futures Contracts Hedge Big Block Trades," *Pension & Investments Age,* July 19, 1982, pp. 1, 38.

are fairly priced or cheap. If the futures price is less than the theoretical futures price (that is, the futures contracts are cheap), the index fund manager can enhance the indexed portfolio's return by buying the futures and buying the Treasury bills. That is, the return on the futures/Treasury bill portfolio will be greater than that on the underlying index when the position is held to the settlement date. In this case, the stock index futures contracts offer still another avantage to the manager.

***Index Arbitrage.***   Opportunities to enhance returns as a result of the mispricing of the futures contract are not restricted to index fund management. Money managers and arbitrageurs monitor the cash and futures market to see when the differences between the theoretical futures price and actual futures price are sufficiently large to generate an arbitrage profit. These investors respond to those opportunities by selling the futures index if it is expensive and buying stocks, or buying the futures index if it is cheap and selling the stocks. Index arbitrage plays an important role in linking futures prices and cash prices. Program trading is used to execute the buy and sell orders.[2]

***Creating Portfolio Insurance.***   As explained in the previous chapter, a put option can protect the value of an asset. At the expiration date of the put option, the minimum value for the asset will be the strike price minus the cost of the put option. Put options on stock indexes can do the same for a diversified portfolio of stocks.

Alternatively, an institutional investor can create a put option synthetically by using either (1) stock index futures, or (2) stocks and a riskless asset. Of course, the portfolio manager must change the allocation of the portfolio's funds to stock index futures or between stocks and a riskless asset, as market conditions change.[3] A strategy that seeks to insure the value of a portfolio through the use of a synthetic put option strategy is called *dynamic hedging*.

Given that put options on stock indexes are available to portfolio managers, why should they bother with dynamic hedging? There are four reasons. First, the size of the market for options on stock indexes is not as large as that for stock index futures and therefore may not easily accommodate a large portfolio insurance program without moving the price of the option substantially. Second, exchanges impose limits on the number of contracts in which an investor can have a position. Institutions wishing to protect large equity portfolios may find that position limits effectively prevent them from using exchange-traded index options to protect their portfolio. Third, existing exchange-traded index options contracts are of shorter maturity than the period over which some investors seek protection. Finally, the cost of a put option may be higher than the transactions costs associated with dynamic hedging.

---

[2] Program trading is discussed in Chapter 18.

[3] For a more detailed explanation of this strategy, see Mark Rubinstein and Hayne Leland, "Replicating Options with Positions in Stock and Cash," *Financial Analysts Journal* (July–August 1981), pp. 63–72.

In one way, however, hedging with put options does offer an advantage. While the cost of a put option is known (and is determined by expected price volatility), the cost of creating portfolio insurance by using stock index futures or stocks will be determined by actual price volatility in the market. The greater the market's price volatility, the more rebalancing of the portfolio is necessary, and the higher the cost of creating portfolio insurance.

***Asset Allocation.***   The decision on how to divide funds across the major asset classes (for example, equities, bonds, foreign securities, real estate) is referred to as the *asset allocation decision*. Futures and options can be used to implement an asset allocation decision more effectively than transacting in the cash markets.

For example, suppose that a pension fund sponsor with assets of $1 billion has allocated $300 million to the bond market and $700 million to the stock market. Suppose further that the sponsor has decided to alter that bond/stock mix to $600 million in bonds and $400 million in stock. Liquidation of $300 million in stock will involve significant transactions costs—both commissions and execution (market impact) costs.[4] Moreover, the external money managers who are managing the stock portfolios will face disruption as funds are withdrawn by the sponsor. Rather than liquidating the stock portfolio immediately, the sponsor can sell an appropriate number of stock index futures contracts. This effectively decreases the exposure of the pension fund to the stock market. To increase the fund's exposure to the bond market, the sponsor can buy interest rate futures contracts.

### Interest Rate Futures

Market participants can employ interest rate futures in various ways, which we will now discuss.

***Speculating on the Movement of Interest Rates.***   The price of a futures contract moves in the opposite direction from interest rates: when rates rise (fall), the futures price will fall (rise). An investor who wants to speculate that interest rates will rise (fall) can sell (buy) interest rate futures. Before interest rate futures were available, investors who wanted to speculate on interest rates did so with the long-term Treasury bond: shorting it if they expected interest rates to rise, and buying it if they expected interest rates to fall.

There are three advantages of using interest rate futures instead of the cash market (trading long-term Treasuries themselves). First, the transactions costs of using futures are lower than those in the corresponding cash market. Second, margin requirements are lower for futures than for Treasury securities; using futures thus permits greater leverage. Finally, it is easier to take a short position in the futures market than to sell short in the Treasuries mar-

---

[4] These costs are described in Chapter 18.

ket. We repeat here what we said when we discussed the use of stock index futures to speculate on stock price movements: making speculation easier for investors is not the function of interest rate futures contracts.

***Controlling the Interest Rate Risk of a Portfolio.*** Stock index futures can be used to change the market risk of a diversified stock portfolio; that is, to alter the beta of a portfolio. Likewise, interest rate futures can be used to alter the interest rate sensitivity of a portfolio. As we explained in Chapter 10, duration is a measure of the interest rate sensitivity.

Investment managers with strong expectations about the direction of the future course of interest rates will adjust the durations of their portfolios so as to capitalize on their expectations. Specifically, a manager expecting rates to increase will reduce the interest rate sensitivity of a portfolio. A manager expecting rates to decrease will raise the interest rate sensitivity of the portfolio. While investment managers can alter the interest rate sensitivity of their portfolios with cash market instruments, a quick and inexpensive means for doing so (on either a temporary or permanent basis) is to use futures contracts.

***Hedging against Adverse Interest Rate Movements.*** Interest rate futures can be used to hedge against adverse interest rate movements by locking in either a price or an interest rate. Some examples of hedging with interest rate futures will illustrate the basic concepts.

1.  Suppose that a pension fund manager knows that bonds must be liquidated in 40 days to make a $5 million payment to the beneficiaries of the pension fund. If interest rates rise in 40 days, more bonds will have to be liquidated to realize proceeds of $5 million. The pension fund manager can hedge by selling in the futures market to lock in a selling price.

2.  A pension fund manager expecting substantial cash contributions that must be invested, but concerned that interest rates may fall, can hedge against declining returns by buying interest rate futures. Also, a money manager who knows that bonds are maturing in the near future and who expects that interest rates will be lower at the time of reinvestment can buy interest rate futures. In both cases, interest rate futures are used to hedge against a fall in interest rates that would cause cash flows to be reinvested at a lower interest rate.

3.  A corporation planning to sell long-term bonds two months from now can protect itself against a rise in interest rates by selling or taking a short position in interest rate futures now.

4.  A thrift or commercial bank can hedge its cost of funds by locking in a rate using the Eurodollar CD futures contract.

5.  A corporation that plans to sell commercial paper one month from now can use Treasury bill futures or Eurodollar CD futures to lock in a commercial paper rate.

6.  Investment banking firms can use interest rate futures to protect both the value of positions held by their trading desks and positions assumed by the underwriting of new bond issues. An example of the latter is a 1979 Salomon Brothers underwriting of $1 billion of IBM bonds. To protect itself against a rise in interest rates, which would reduce the value of the IBM bonds, Salomon Brothers sold (shorted) Treasury futures. In October 1979, interest rates rose upon an announcement by the Federal Reserve Board that it was allowing interest rates more flexibility to move. While the value of the IBM bonds held by Salomon Brothers declined in value, so did the Treasury bond futures contracts. Because Salomon Brothers had sold these futures, it realized a gain and thus reduced the loss on the IBM bonds it underwrote.

***Enhancing Returns When Futures Are Mispriced.***   In our discussion of stock index futures earlier, we explained that institutional investors look for the mispricing of stock index futures to create arbitrage profits and thereby to enhance portfolio returns. We referred to this strategy as index arbitrage because it involves a stock index. If interest rate futures are mispriced (even after considering the pricing problems we discussed in the previous chapter), institutional investors can enhance returns in the same way that they do in equities.

***Asset Allocation.***   As noted earlier, interest rate futures and stock index futures are quick, cheap, and effective ways to change the composition of a portfolio between bonds and stocks.

▶ KEY POINTS THAT YOU SHOULD UNDERSTAND BEFORE PROCEEDING:

1.  Investors can use stock index futures to speculate on stock prices, control a portfolio's price risk exposure, hedge against adverse stock price movements, construct indexed portfolios, engage in index arbitrage, and create a synthetic put option.
2.  Market participants can employ interest rate futures to speculate on interest rate movements, control a portfolio's risk exposure to interest rate changes, hedge against adverse interest rate movements, and enhance returns when futures are mispriced.
3.  Because futures are highly leveraged and transactions costs are less than in the cash market, market participant can alter their risk exposure to a market (stock or bond) more efficiently in the futures market.
4.  Buying a futures contract increases a market participant's exposure to a market; selling a futures contract decreases a market participants exposure to a market.

5. A money manager can use both stock index futures and interest rate futures to more efficiently allocate funds between the stock market and the bond market.

## APPLICATIONS OF OPTIONS CONTRACTS

### *Stock Options and Stock Index Options*

Stock options can be used to take advantage of the anticipated price movement of individual stocks. Alternatively, they can help protect current or anticipated positions in individual stocks. For example, an investor can protect against a decline in the price of a stock in her portfolio by buying a put option on that stock. The put guarantees a minimum price equal to the strike price minus the cost of buying the option. This strategy is called a *protective put buying strategy*. Also, if an investor anticipates buying a stock in the future but fears that the stock price will rise over that time, she can buy a call option on the stock. This strategy guarantees that the maximum price that will be paid in the future is the strike price plus the option price.

Now consider an institutional investor that holds a portfolio consisting of a large number of stock issues. Using stock options to protect against an adverse price movement in the portfolio's value, the institutional investor would have to buy a put on every stock in the portfolio, which would be quite costly. By taking an appropriate position in a suitable stock index option, an institutional investor can create a protective put for the entire, diversified portfolio. For example, suppose that an institutional investor, who holds a diversified portfolio of common stock that is highly correlated with the S&P 100, is concerned that the stock market will decline in value over the next three months. Suppose, too, that a three-month put option on the S&P 100 is available. Because the put option buyer gains when the price of the underlying stock index declines, purchasing a put option will offset any adverse movements in the portfolio's value due to a decline in the stock market. This protective put buying strategy obviously offers a cheap, effective, and flexible alternative to either buying puts on the various stocks or liquidating the entire portfolio and converting holdings into cash.

When stock options or stock index options are used to protect an existing or anticipated position, the investor need not exercise the option if the prices of the held stocks move in the direction that the investor wants. This freedom not to exercise makes options more suited than futures to the task of protecting a cash position. An institutional investor can obtain downside protection using options at a cost equal to the option price, but preserve upside potential (reduced by the option price).

### *Interest Rate Options*

An institutional investor can use interest rate options or options on interest rate futures to speculate on fixed-income security price movements based on expectations of interest rate changes. Because a call option increases in price if interest rates decline, an investor can buy call options if he or she expects interest rates to move in that direction. Alternatively, because the writer of a put option will benefit if the price increases, an investor who expects interest rates to fall can write put options. Purchasing put options and/or selling call options would be appropriate for an investor who expects interest rates to rise. Remember that, unlike interest rate futures, interest rate options limit downside risk while permitting upside potential that is reduced only by the amount of the option price.

As noted, institutional investors can use interest rate options to hedge against adverse interest rate movements but still let the investor benefit from a favorable interest rate movement. It is important to recognize that hedging in this way can basically set a floor or ceiling on an institution's targeted interest rate. We will use the illustrations given earlier for interest rate futures to explain how this works using options.

1.   Suppose that a pension fund manager knows that bonds must be liquidated in 40 days to make a $5 million payment to the beneficiaries of the pension fund. If interest rates rise in 40 days, more bonds will have to be liquidated to realize $5 million. The hedger will buy put options (that is, follow a protective put buying strategy). Should interest rates rise, the value of the bonds to be sold will decline, but the put options purchased will rise in value. If the transaction is properly structured, the gain on the put options will offset the loss on the bonds. The cost of the safety bought by this strategy will then be the option price paid. If, in-stead, interest rates decline, the value of the bonds will rise. The pension fund manager will not exercise the put option. A gain equal to the rise in the bond value minus the put option price will be realized.

2.   Suppose a pension fund manager knows there will be substantial cash contributions flowing into the fund and is concerned that interest rates may fall. Or suppose that a money manager knows that bonds are maturing in the near future and expects interest rates to fall. In both cases, proceeds will be reinvested at a lower interest rate. Call options can be purchased in this situation. Should interest rates fall, the call options will increase in value, offsetting the loss in interest income that will result when the proceeds must be invested at a lower interest rate. The cost of this hedge strategy is the call option price. Should interest rates rise instead, the proceeds can be invested at a higher rate. The benefit of the higher rate will be reduced by the cost of the call option, which expires worthless.

3.   A corporation plans to issue long-term bonds two months from now. To protect itself against a rise in interest rates, the corporation can buy put options. If interest rates rise, the interest cost of the bonds issued two months from now will be higher, but the put option will have increased in value. Buying an appropriate number of put options yields a gain on the put options sufficient to offset the higher interest cost of the bond issue. Again,

the cost of this strategy is the price of the put options. Should interest rates decline instead, the corporation will benefit from a lower interest cost when the bonds are issued, a benefit reduced by the cost of the put options.

4.   A thrift or commercial bank wants to make sure that the cost of its funds will not exceed a certain level. This can be done by buying put options on Eurodollar CD futures.

5.   A corporation plans to sell commercial paper one month from now. Buying put options on Treasury bill futures or Eurodollar CD futures lets the corporation set a ceiling on its commercial paper interest cost.

▶   KEY POINTS THAT YOU SHOULD UNDERSTAND BEFORE PROCEEDING:

1.   Market participants can obtain downside protection using options at a cost equal to the option price, but preserve upside potential (reduced by the option price).

2.   A protective put buying strategy can be used to reduce the risk exposure of a stock portfolio to a decline in stock prices, guaranteeing a minimum price equal to the strike price minus the cost of buying the put option.

3.   The purchase of a call option can be used to guarantee that the maximum price that will be paid in the future is the strike price plus the option price.

4.   By taking an appropriate position in a suitable stock index option, an institutional investor can create a protective put for a diversified portfolio.

5.   Interest rate options or options on interest rate futures can be used by investors and issuers to hedge against adverse interest rate movements but still benefit from a favorable interest rate movement.

SUMMARY

Market participants, both investors and borrowers, can use derivative contracts in a variety of ways. The contracts can be used to speculate on stock prices or interest rates, to alter the risk exposure of a stock or bond portfolio, to hedge the risk associated with a stock position or bond position, to hedge the issuance of future debt, or to change the allocation of funds between stocks and bonds. When contracts are mispriced, a market participant can capitalize on this opportunity by enhancing returns, in the case of an investor, or reduce the cost of issuing an obligation, in the case of an issuer of securities.

| A P P E N D I X |
| --- |

## GENERAL PRINCIPLES OF HEDGING WITH FUTURES

■ ■ ■ ■

In this appendix, we explain the general principles of hedging with futures contracts. This explanation introduces numerous key concepts that underlie the applications and examples presented in this chapter.

The major function of futures markets is to transfer price risk from hedgers to speculators. That is, risk is transferred from those willing to pay to avoid risk to those wanting to assume the risk in the hope of gain. Hedging in this case is the employment of a futures transaction as a temporary substitute for a transaction in the cash market. The hedge position locks in a value for the cash position. As long as cash and futures prices move together, any loss realized on one position (whether cash or futures) will be offset by a profit on the other position. When the profit and loss are equal, the hedge is called a *perfect or textbook hedge*. In a market where the futures contract is correctly priced, a perfect hedge is risk-free and, therefore, should provide a return equal to the risk-free rate.

### *Risks Associated with Hedging*

In practice, hedging is not simple. The amount of the loss or profit on a hedge will depend on the relationship between the cash price and the futures price at two points in time, when a hedge is placed and when it is lifted. The difference between the cash price and the futures price is called the *basis*. That is,

$$\text{Basis} = \text{Cash price} - \text{Futures price}$$

As we explained in the previous chapter, if a futures contract is priced according to its theoretical value, the difference between the cash price and the futures price should be equal to the cost of carry. The risk that the hedger takes on is that the basis will change for some reason. This possibility of change is called *basis risk*. Therefore, hedging involves the substitution of basis risk for price risk; that is, the substitution of the risk that the basis will change for the risk that the cash price will change.

When a futures contract is used to hedge a position where either the portfolio or the individual financial instrument is not identical to the instrument underlying the futures, it is called *cross hedging*. Cross hedging is common in asset/liability and portfolio management and in hedging a corporate bond issuance. The reason it is so common is that there are no futures contracts on specific common stock shares and bonds. Cross hedging introduces another risk—the risk that the price movement of the underlying instrument of the futures contract may not accurately track the price movement of the portfolio or financial instrument to be hedged. This is called *cross-hedging risk*. Therefore, the effectiveness of a cross hedge will be determined by two factors:

1.  The relationship between the cash price of the underlying instrument and its futures price at the time when a hedge is placed and the time when it is lifted.
2.  The relationship between the market (cash) value of the portfolio and the cash price of the instrument underlying the futures contract when the hedge is placed and when it is lifted.

## Short and Long Hedges

A *short hedge* is used to protect against a decline in the cash price of a financial instrument or portfolio. To execute a short hedge, the hedger sells a futures contract (enters into the short side of a futures contract or agrees to make delivery). Consequently, a short hedge is also known as a *sell hedge*. By establishing a short hedge, the hedger has fixed the future cash price and transferred the price risk of ownership to the buyer of the futures contract.

A *long hedge* is undertaken to protect against an increase in the price of a financial instrument or portfolio to be purchased in the cash market at some future time. In a long hedge, the hedger buys a futures contract (enters into the long side of a futures contract or agrees to accept delivery). A long hedge is also known as a *buy hedge*.

## Hedging Illustrations

We illustrate the principles of hedging and cross hedging using an agricultural commodity, corn, rather than a financial instrument or portfolio, because a corn futures contract is not as complicated as a stock index futures contract or an interest rate futures contract. The principles we illustrate are equally applicable to these futures contracts but easier to grasp with a farm product example not involving financial contract nuances.

Suppose that a corn farmer expects to sell 30,000 bushels of corn three months from now. Assume further that the management of a food processing company plans to purchase 30,000 bushels of corn three months from now. Both the corn farmer and the management of the food processing company want to lock in a price today. That is, each wants to eliminate the price risk associated with corn three months from now. The cash or spot price for corn is currently $2.75 per bushel.

A corn futures contract is available with the following terms: (1) the settlement date for the contract is five months from now and (2) 5,000 bushels of corn must be delivered per contract. Notice that the settlement date is two months after the parties expect to lift their hedge. The futures price for this futures contract is currently $3.20 per bushel.

As the corn farmer seeks to lock in the price of corn to eliminate the risk of a decline in the price three months from now, he will place a short or sell hedge. That is, he will promise to make delivery of corn at the current futures price. The corn farmer will sell six futures contracts, because each contract

590 Part Nine / Markets for Derivative Securities

calls for the delivery of 5,000 bushels of corn. Three months from now, the corn farmer will do two things: deliver his corn at the prevailing price in the cash market and lift his short futures hedge by buying the corn futures contract, which will then have two months to settlement. The price at which the corn farmer will buy the corn futures contract depends on the futures contract price three months from now.

The management of the food processing company seeks to lock in the cost of corn to eliminate the risk of an increase in the price of corn three months from now. Consequently, management will place a buy or long hedge. That is, it will agree to accept delivery of corn at the futures price. Protection is sought against a price increase for 30,000 bushels of corn, so six contracts are bought. Three months from now, the food processing company will have to purchase corn in the cash market, paying the prevailing market price. To offset the long corn futures position, which has two months remaining until settlement, the food processing company will sell the contract at the then-prevailing futures price.

Let's look at what happens under various scenarios for the cash price and the futures price of corn three months from now when both parties lift their hedges by reversing their futures contract positions.

Suppose that, when the hedges are lifted, the cash price declines to $2.00 and the futures contract price declines to $2.45. Notice what happens to the basis under this scenario. At the time the hedge is placed, the basis is −$.45 ($2.75 − $3.20). When the hedge is lifted, the basis is still −$.45 ($2.00 − $2.45).

The corn farmer, when he placed the hedge, wanted to lock in a price of $2.75 per bushel of corn, or $82,500 for 30,000 bushels. He sold six futures contracts at a price of $3.20 per bushel, or $96,000 for 30,000 bushels. When he lifts his short hedge, the value of the farmer's corn is $60,000 ($2.00 × 30,000). The corn farmer realizes a decline in the cash market value of his corn of $22,500, but the futures price has declined to $2.45, so the cost to the corn farmer to liquidate his futures position is only $73,500 ($2.45 × 30,000). The corn farmer realizes a gain in the futures market of $22,500, or $96,000 − $73,500. The net result is that the gain in the futures market matches the loss in the cash market. Consequently, the corn farmer, by hedging, succeeds in ensuring a price per unit of $2.75, precisely equal to the initial price he had intended to realize for himself. This is an example of a perfect or textbook hedge.

Because there was a decline in the cash price, the food processing company would realize a gain in the cash market of $22,500 but would realize a loss in the futures market of the same amount. Therefore, this buy or long hedge is also a perfect or textbook hedge from the perspective of the food processing company, ensuring a cost per unit equal to the initial price of $2.75.

This scenario illustrates two important points. First, for both participants there was no overall gain or loss. The reason for this result is our assumption that the basis did not change while the hedges were in place. Thus, if the basis does not change, a perfect hedge will be achieved. Second, note that the management of the food processing company would have been better off if it had not hedged. The cost of corn would have fallen $22,500 in the cash market over the three months. This failure to gain from the decline in the cash price should not be interpreted as a sign of poor planning by management. Management is not in the business of speculating on the future price of corn. Hedging is a standard practice to insure the price to be paid at the delivery date, thus eliminating future price uncertainty.

Suppose that the cash price of corn, when the hedge is lifted increases to $3.55, and that the futures price increases to $4.00. Notice that the basis is unchanged at − $.45. As long as the basis is unchanged, the cash and futures price we have assumed in this scenario will produce a perfect hedge.

The corn farmer will gain in the cash market because the value of 30,000 bushels of corn is $106,500 ($3.55 × 30,000). This represents a $24,000 gain, compared to the cash value at the time the hedge was placed. However, the corn farmer must liquidate his position in the futures market by buying six futures contracts at a total cost of $120,000, which is $24,000 more than when the contracts were sold. The loss in the futures market offsets the gain in the cash market, which is the meaning of a perfect hedge. The food processing company would realize a gain in the futures market of $24,000 but would have to pay $24,000 more in the cash market to acquire 30,000 bushels of corn.

Note that the management of the food processing company under this scenario saved $24,000 in the cost of corn by employing a hedge. The corn farmer, though, would have been better off if he had not used a hedging strategy but rather simply sold his product on the market three months later. Again, it must be emphasized that the corn farmer, just like the management of the food processing company, employed a hedge to protect against unforeseen and adverse price changes in the cash market.

These scenarios assume that the basis does not change when the hedge is lifted. In the real world, the basis does, in fact, change between the time a hedge is placed and when it is lifted. Here is what happens when the basis changes.

Assume that the cash price of corn decreases to $2.00, just as in the first scenario; assume also that the futures price decreases to $2.70 rather than $2.45. The basis has now widened from −$.45 to −$.70 ($2.00 − $2.70). For the short (sell) hedge, the loss in the cash market of $22,500 is offset only partially by a $15,000 gain realized in the futures market (equal to 6 contracts × 5,000 bushels per contract × the per bushel price decline of $.50). Consequently, the hedge results in an overall loss of $7,500.

There are two points to note here. First, if the corn farmer had not employed the hedge, the loss would have been $22,500, because the value of 30,000 bushels of corn is $60,000, compared to $82,500 three months earlier. Although the hedge is not a perfect hedge because the basis widened, the loss of $7,500 on the hedged position is less than the loss of $22,500 which would have occurred in the absence of the hedge. So, the hedge did not eliminate all risk: as we said earlier, the hedge substitutes basis risk for price risk. Second, the management of the food processing company faces the same problem from the opposite perspective. An unexpected gain for either participant results in an unexpected loss of equal dollar value for the other. That is, the participants face a "zero-sum game." Consequently, the food processing company would realize an overall gain of $7,500 from its long (buy) hedge. This gain represents a gain of $22,500 in the cash market and a realized loss of $15,000 in the futures market.

### Illustrations of Cross Hedging

Suppose that a zucchini farmer plans to sell 37,500 bushels of zucchini three months from now and that a food processing company plans to purchase the same amount of zucchini three months from now. Each party wants to hedge against price risk, but zucchini futures contracts are not traded. Both parties believe there is a close price relationship between zucchini and corn. Specifically, both parties believe that the cash price of zucchini will be 80% of the cash price of corn. The cash price of zucchini is currently $2.20 per bushel, and the cash price of corn is currently $2.75 per bushel. The futures price of corn is currently $3.20 per bushel.

Let's examine various scenarios to see how effective the cross hedge will be. In each scenario, the difference between the cash price of corn and the futures price of corn will be assumed to remain unchanged at −$.45 over the interval between the time the cross hedge is placed and the time it is lifted. This assumption allows us to highlight the importance of the relationship between the two cash prices at the two times.

We must first determine how many corn futures contracts must be used in the cross hedge. The cash value of 37,500 bushels of zucchini at the cash price of $2.20 per bushel is $82,500. To protect a value of $82,500 using corn futures with a current cash price of $2.75, the price of 30,000 bushels of corn ($82,500/$2.75) must be hedged. Each corn futures contract involves 5,000 bushels, so six corn futures contracts are necessary.

Suppose that the cash prices of zucchini and corn decrease to $1.60 and $2.00 per bushel, respectively, and the futures price of corn decreases to $2.45 per bushel. The relationship between the cash price for zucchini and corn assumed when the cross hedge was placed holds at the time the cross hedge is lifted. That is, the cash price of zucchini is 80% of the cash price of corn. The basis for the cash price of corn and the futures price of corn is still −$.45 at the time the cross hedge is lifted.

The short cross hedge produces a gain in the futures market of $22,500 and an exactly offset loss in the cash market. The opposite occurs for the long cross hedge. There is neither overall gain nor loss from the cross hedge in this case. That is, we have a perfect cross hedge. The same would occur if we assume that the cash price of both commodities increases by the same percentage and the basis does not change.

Suppose that the cash prices of both commodities decrease, but the cash price of zucchini falls by a greater percentage than the cash price of corn. For example, suppose that the cash price of zucchini falls to $1.30 per bushel while the cash price of corn falls to $2.00 per bushel. The futures price of corn falls to $2.45 so that the basis is not changed. The cash price of zucchini at the time the cross hedge is lifted is 65% of the cash price of corn, rather than 80% as assumed when the cross hedge was constructed.

For the short cross hedge, the loss in the cash market exceeds the realized loss in the futures market by $11,200. For the long cross hedge, the opposite is true. There is an overall gain from the cross hedge of $11,200. Had the cash price of zucchini fallen by less than the decline in the cash price of corn, the short cross hedge would have produced an overall gain, while the long cross hedge would have generated an overall loss.

## GLOSSARY

**Asset allocation:** The investment decision concerning how to divide funds across major asset classes.

**Basis:** The difference between the cash price and the futures price.

**Basis risk:** In a hedge, the risk that the basis will change adversely.

**Cross hedging:** A hedging strategy in which a futures contract is used to hedge a position where either the portfolio or the individual financial instrument to be hedged is not identical to the instrument underlying the futures contract.

**Cross-hedging risk:** The risk associated with employing a strategy of cross hedging.

**Index arbitrage:** A strategy that seeks to enhance returns as a result of the mispricing of the futures contract relative to the cash index.

**Long hedge (also called a buy hedge):** A hedge in which futures are purchased to protect against a rise in the cash price of a financial instrument or portfolio.

**Perfect hedge (or textbook hedge):** A hedge in which the profit and loss on the cash and futures positions are equal.

**Portfolio strategy (also called dynamic hedging):** A strategy that seeks to synthetically create a put option.

**Protective put buying strategy:** A strategy of buying put options on securities held in a portfolio to insure a minimum price for the securities.

**Short hedge (also called a sell hedge):** A hedge in which futures are sold to protect against a decline in the cash price of a financial instrument or portfolio.

**Tracking error risk:** In an indexing strategy, the risk that the movement of a portfolio created to mimic an index does not match the targeted index.

1.  a.  If a stock portfolio's indicator of volatility is its beta, explain how stock index futures can be used to change the portfolio's volatility.

    b.  Suppose an institutional investor wants to increase the beta of a portfolio of stocks. Should the institutional investor buy or sell S&P 500 futures contracts?

2.  a.  What is the difference between an index arbitrage strategy and an indexing strategy?

    b.  Why would a portfolio manager find it advantageous to use stock index futures in an indexing strategy?

3.  Suppose a corporation plans to issue bonds three months from now and wants to protect against a rise in interest rates. Should the corporation buy or sell interest rate futures contracts?

4.  a.  What is meant by a synthetic put option?

    b.  What is meant by dynamic hedging?

5.  Assume you own an asset and there are both futures contracts and options contracts on that asset. Provide a clear account of the difference between hedging against a price decline with futures and hedging with options. Direct your analysis to the potential gains from options and the nature of losses from a futures position.

6.  a.  What is the basis of a futures contract?

    b.  Explain why hedging with futures contracts substitutes basis risk for price risk.

7.  Under what conditions would a perfect hedge occur?

8.  a.  Why is a short futures hedge called a sell hedge?

    b.  Why is a long futures hedge called a buy hedge?

9.  In the August 18, 1989, issue of *The Wall Street Journal* there appeared an article entitled "Program Trading Spreads From Just Wall Street Firms." Following are two quotations from that article:

    *Brokerage firms in the business, which tiptoed back into program trading after the post-crash furor died down, argue that such strategies as stock-index arbitrage — rapid trading between stock index futures and stocks to capture fleeting price differences — link two related markets and thus benefit both.*

    The second quotation in the article is from a senior vice president at Twenty-First Securities Corp:

    *Program trading is a product that is here, links markets, and it is not going to disappear. It is a function of the computerization of Wall Street.*

    Do you agree with these statements?

10. This quotation is from the June 8, 1987, issue of *Business Week.*

    *The idea sounds almost un-American. Instead of using your smarts to pick stocks that will reach the sky, you put money in a fund that merely tracks a broad market index. But that is precisely what institutional investors are doing. . . . Indexing is a new force in the stock market. . . . But the impact of index-funds reaches far beyond stock prices.*

Discuss how indexing may have contributed to the growth of the stock index derivatives markets.

11. This quotation appeared in the December 1988 issue of *Euromoney*

*The proliferation of futures and options markets has created new opportunities for international investors. It is now possible to change investment exposure from one country to another through the use of derivative instruments, augmented by a limited number of individual securities. Asset allocation in most major markets is now feasible using futures and options.*

Discuss this quotation and the reasons for using derivative rather than cash instruments to facilitate asset allocation decisions.

12. What are the risks associated with cross hedging?

13. Donald Singleton is an investment banker for a regional firm. One of his clients, Dolby Manufacturing, Inc., is a private company that will be making an initial public offering of 20 million shares of common stock. Mr. Singleton's firm will buy the issue at $10 per share. He has suggested to the managing director of the firm, John Wilson, that the firm should hedge the position using stock index futures contracts. What should Mr. Wilson's response be?

14. a. Explain why you agree or disagree with the following statement by Gary Gastineau ("A Short History of Program Trading," *Financial Analysts Journal*, September–October 1991):

*Stock index futures and options were introduced in the early 1980s. Their introduction was partly a response to institutional portfolio managers' preference for trading portfolios rather than individual stocks and partly a way of reducing transaction costs in the implementation of asset-allocation and market-timing decisions.*

b. In the same article, Gary Gastineau made the following statement:

*Long positions in stock index futures combined with short-term fixed income securities are an almost perfect substitute for a stock index portfolio. Conversely, selling futures contracts against a portfolio of stocks is a low-cost way to reduce market exposure.*

Explain the conditions that must hold for this statement to be true.

# CHAPTER TWENTY-NINE

# Interest Rate Swap and Interest Rate Agreement Market

## LEARNING OBJECTIVES

*After reading this chapter you will understand:*

- what an interest rate swap is.

- how an interest rate swap can be used by institutional investors and corporate borrowers.

- why the interest rate swap market has grown so rapidly.

- the risk/return characteristics of an interest rate swap.

- two ways to interpret an interest rate swap.

- reasons for the development of an interest rate swap market.

- determinants of the swap spread.

- what an interest rate agreement (cap or floor) is.

- how interest rate agreements can be used by institutional investors and corporate borrowers.

- the relationship between an interest rate agreement and options.

- how an interest rate collar can be created.

Interest rate futures and options can be used to control interest rate risk. Commercial banks and investment banks also customize other contracts useful for controlling such risk for their clients. These include interest rate swaps and interest rate agreements (caps and floors). In this chapter, we will review each contract and explain the way borrowers and institutional investors use them.

## INTEREST RATE SWAPS

An *interest rate swap* is an agreement whereby two parties (called *counterparties*) agree to exchange periodic interest payments. The dollar amount of the interest payments exchanged is based on some predetermined dollar principal, which is called the *notional principal amount*. The dollar amount each counterparty pays to the other is the agreed-upon periodic interest rate times the notional principal amount. The only dollars exchanged between the parties are the interest payments, not the notional principal amount. In the most common type of swap, one party agrees to pay the other party fixed interest payments at designated dates for the life of the contract. This party is referred to as the *fixed-rate payer*. The other party, referred to as the *floating-rate payer*, agrees to make interest rate payments that float with some reference interest rate (or, simply, reference rate).

For example, suppose that for the next five years party X agrees to pay party Y 10% per year, while party Y agrees to pay party X six-month LIBOR. Party X is a fixed-rate payer/floating-rate receiver, while party Y is a floating-rate payer/fixed-rate receiver. Assume that the notional principal amount is $50 million, and that payments are exchanged every six months for the next five years. This means that every six months, party X (the fixed-rate payer/floating-rate receiver) will pay party Y $2.5 million (10% times $50 million divided by 2). The amount that party Y (the floating-rate payer/fixed-rate receiver) will pay party X will be six-month LIBOR times $50 million divided by 2. For example, if six-month LIBOR is 7%, party Y will pay party X $1.75 million (7% times $50 million divided by 2). Note that we divide by two because one-half year's interest is being paid.

The reference rates that are commonly used for the floating rate in an interest rate swap are those on various money market instruments: Treasury bills, the London Interbank Offered Rate (LIBOR), commercial paper, bankers acceptances, certificates of deposit, federal funds rate, and prime rate.

As we illustrate later, market participants can use an interest rate swap to alter the cash flow character of assets or liabilities from a fixed-rate basis to a floating-rate basis or vice versa.

### *Risk/Return Characteristics of a Swap*

The value of an interest rate swap will fluctuate with market interest rates. To see how, let's analyze our hypothetical swap. Suppose that interest rates change immediately after parties X and Y enter into the swap. First, consider what would happen if the market demanded that the fixed-rate payer must pay

11% in order to receive six-month LIBOR in any five-year swap. If party X (the fixed-rate payer) wants to sell its position, say, to party A, then party A will benefit by only having to pay 10% (the original swap rate agreed upon) rather than 11% (the current swap rate) to receive six-month LIBOR. Party X will want compensation for this benefit. Consequently, the value of party X's position has increased. Thus, if interest rates increase, the fixed-rate payer will realize a profit and the floating-rate payer will realize a loss.

Next, consider what would happen if interest rates decline to, say, 6%. Now a five-year swap would require the fixed-rate payer to pay 6% rather than 10% to receive six-month LIBOR. If party X wants to sell its position to party B, the latter would demand compensation to take over the position. In other words, if interest rates decline, the fixed-rate payer will realize a loss, while the floating-rate payer will realize a profit.

The risk/return profile of the two positions when interest rates change is summarized in Table 29-1.

## Interpreting a Swap Position

There are two ways that a swap position can be interpreted: (1) as a package of forward/futures contracts, or (2) as a package of cash flows from buying and selling cash market instruments. We will evaluate both interpretations.

***Package of forward contracts.***   Contrast the position of the counterparties in the interest rate swap summarized in Table 29-1 to the position of the long and short futures (forward) contract discussed in Chapter 28. The long futures position gains if interest rates decline and loses if interest rates rise — this is similar to the risk/return profile of a floating-rate payer. The risk/return profile of a fixed-rate payer is similar to that of the short futures position: a gain if interest rates increase and a loss if interest rates decrease. By taking a closer look at the interest rate swap we can understand why the risk/return relationships of futures and swaps are similar.

Consider party X's position. Party X has agreed to pay 10% and receive six-month LIBOR. More specifically, based on a $50 million notional principal amount, X has agreed to buy a commodity called "six-month LIBOR" for $2.5 million. This is effectively a six-month forward contract where X agrees to pay $2.5 million in exchange for delivery of six-month LIBOR. If interest

| | TABLE  29 - 1 | |
|---|---|---|

RISK/RETURN PROFILE OF COUNTERPARTIES TO AN
INTEREST RATE SWAP

| | Interest Rates Decrease | Interest Rates Increase |
|---|---|---|
| Floating-rate payer | Gain | Loss |
| Fixed-rate payer | Loss | Gain |

rates increase to 11%, the price of that commodity (six-month LIBOR) is higher, resulting in a gain for the fixed-rate payer, who is effectively long a six-month forward contract on six-month LIBOR. The floating-rate payer is effectively short a six-month forward contract on six-month LIBOR. Accordingly, each planned exchange, over the life of a swap, constitutes a forward contract, which settles on the exchange date.

Now we can see why there is a similarity between the risk/return relationship for an interest rate swap and a forward contract. If interest rates increase to, say, 11%, the price of that commodity (six-month LIBOR) increases to $2.75 million (11% times $50 million divided by 2). The long forward position (the fixed-rate payer) gains, and the short forward position (the floating-rate payer) loses. If interest rates decline to, say, 9%, the price of our commodity decreases to $2.25 million (9% times $50 million divided by 2). The short forward position (the floating-rate payer) gains, and the long forward position (the fixed-rate payer) loses.

Consequently, interest rate swaps can be viewed as a package of more basic interest rate control tools, such as forwards. The pricing of an interest rate swap will then depend on the price of a package of forward contracts with the same settlement dates and in which the underlying for the forward contract is the same reference rate.

While an interest rate swap may be nothing more than a package of forward contracts, several important reasons suggest that it is not a redundant contract. First, the longest maturity of forward or futures contracts does not extend out as far as that of an interest rate swap. In fact, an interest rate swap with a term of 15 years or longer can be obtained. Second, an interest rate swap is a more transactionally efficient instrument. By this we mean that in one transaction two parties can effectively establish a payoff equivalent to a package of forward contracts. The forward contracts would each have to be negotiated separately. Third, the liquidity of the interest rate swap market has grown since its beginning in 1981; it is now more liquid than forward contracts, particularly long-dated (that is, long-term) forward contracts.

***Package of cash market instruments.*** To understand why a swap can also be interpreted as package of cash market instruments, consider the following. Suppose that an investor enters into a transaction to:

- buy $50 million par of a five-year floating-rate bond that pays six-month LIBOR every six months
- finance the purchase of the five-year floating-rate bond by borrowing $50 million for five years with a 10% annual interest rate and payments every six months.

The cash flow of this transaction is presented in Table 29-2. The second column of the exhibit sets out the cash flow from purchasing the five-year floating-rate bond. There is a $50 million cash outlay and then cash inflows. The amount of the cash inflows is uncertain because they depend on future

| TABLE 29-2 |
|:---:|

**CASH FLOW FOR THE PURCHASE OF A FIVE-YEAR FLOATING-RATE BOND FINANCED BY BORROWING ON A FIXED-RATE BASIS**

Transaction: Purchase for $50 million a five-year floating-rate bond:
floating rate = LIBOR, semiannual pay
Borrow $50 million for five years: fixed rate = 10%,
semi-annual payments

**Cash flow (in millions of dollars) from:**

| Six-month Period | Floating-rate Bond | Borrowing Cost | Net |
|:---:|:---:|:---:|:---:|
| 0 | − $ 50 | +$50.0 | $ 0 |
| 1 | +(LIBOR$_1$/2) × 50 | − 2.5 | +(LIBOR$_1$/2) × 50 − 2.5 |
| 2 | +(LIBOR$_2$/2) × 50 | − 2.5 | +(LIBOR$_2$/2) × 50 − 2.5 |
| 3 | +(LIBOR$_3$/2) × 50 | − 2.5 | +(LIBOR$_3$/2) × 50 − 2.5 |
| 4 | +(LIBOR$_4$/2) × 50 | − 2.5 | +(LIBOR$_4$/2) × 50 − 2.5 |
| 5 | +(LIBOR$_5$/2) × 50 | − 2.5 | +(LIBOR$_5$/2) × 50 − 2.5 |
| 6 | +(LIBOR$_6$/2) × 50 | − 2.5 | +(LIBOR$_6$/2) × 50 − 2.5 |
| 7 | +(LIBOR$_7$/2) × 50 | − 2.5 | +(LIBOR$_7$/2) × 50 − 2.5 |
| 8 | +(LIBOR$_8$/2) × 50 | − 2.5 | +(LIBOR$_8$/2) × 50 − 2.5 |
| 9 | +(LIBOR$_9$/2) × 50 | − 2.5 | +(LIBOR$_9$/2) × 50 − 2.5 |
| 10 | +(LIBOR$_{10}$/2)× 50 + 50 | − 52.5 | +(LIBOR$_{10}$/2)× 50 − 2.5 |

*Note:* The subscript for LIBOR indicates the six-month LIBOR as per the terms of the floating-rate bond at a particular time.

LIBOR. The third column shows the cash flow from borrowing $50 million on a fixed-rate basis. The last column shows the net cash flow from the entire transaction. As can be seen in the last column, there is no initial cash flow (no cash inflow or cash outlay). In all ten six-month periods the net position results in a cash inflow of LIBOR and a cash outlay of $2.5 million. This net position, however, is identical to the position of a fixed-rate payer/floating-rate receiver.

The net cash flow in Table 29-2 reveals that a fixed-rate payer has a cash market position that is equivalent to a long position in a floating-rate bond and borrowing the funds to purchase the floating-rate bond on a fixed-rate basis. But the borrowing can be viewed as issuing a fixed-rate bond, or equivalently, being short a fixed-rate bond. Consequently, the position of a fixed-rate payer can be viewed as being long a floating-rate bond and short a fixed-rate bond.

What about the position of a floating-rate payer? It can be demonstrated that the position of a floating-rate payer is equivalent to purchasing a fixed-rate bond and financing that purchase at a floating rate, with the floating rate being the reference interest rate for the swap. That is, the position of a floating-rate payer is equivalent to a long position in a fixed-rate bond and a short position in a floating-rate bond.

## Applications

So far we have merely described an interest rate swap and looked at its characteristics. With the help of two illustrations, we now explain how swaps can be used. Although we focus on basic or "plain vanilla" swaps, the illustrations will help us understand why other types of interest rate swaps have been developed.

### Application to Asset/Liability Management.

In the first illustration we look at how an interest rate swap can be used to alter the cash flow characteristics of an institution's assets so as to provide a better match between assets and liabilities. The two institutions are a commercial bank and a life insurance company.

Suppose a bank has a portfolio consisting of five-year term commercial loans with a fixed interest rate. The principal value of the portfolio is $50 million, and the interest rate on all the loans in the portfolio is 10%. The loans are interest only loans; interest is paid semi-annually, and the entire principal is paid at the end of five years. That is, assuming no default on the loans, the cash flow from the loan portfolio is $2.5 million every six months for the next five years and $50 million at the end of five years. To fund its loan portfolio, assume that the bank is relying on the issuance of six-month certificates of deposit. The interest rate that the bank plans to pay on its six-month CDs is the six-month Treasury bill rate plus 40 basis points.

The risk that the bank faces is that the six-month Treasury bill rate will be 9.6% or greater. To understand why, remember that the bank is earning 10% annually on its commercial loan portfolio. If the six-month Treasury bill rate is 9.6%, it will have to pay 9.6% plus 40 basis points to depositors for six-month funds, or 10%, and there will be no spread income. Worse, if the six-month Treasury bill rate rises above 9.6%, there will be a loss; that is, the cost of funds will exceed the interest rate earned on the loan portfolio. The bank's objective is to lock in a spread over the cost of its funds.

The other party in the interest rate swap illustration is a life insurance company that has committed itself to pay a 9% rate for the next five years on a guaranteed investment contract (GIC) it has issued. The amount of the GIC is $50 million. Suppose that the life insurance company has the opportunity to invest $50 million in what it considers an attractive five-year floating-rate instrument in a private placement transaction. The interest rate on this instrument is the six-month Treasury bill rate plus 160 basis points. The coupon rate is set every six months.

The risk that the life insurance company faces is that the six-month interest rate will fall so that it will not earn enough to realize a spread over the 9% rate that it has guaranteed to the GIC holders. If the six-month Treasury bill rate falls to 7.4% or less, no spread income will be generated. To understand why, suppose that the six-month Treasury bill rate at the date the floating-rate instrument resets its coupon is 7.4%. Then the coupon rate for the next six months will be 9% (7.4% plus 160 basis points). Because the life insurance company has agreed to pay 9% on the GIC policy, there will be no spread income. Should the six-month Treasury bill rate fall below 7.4%, the life insurance company will incur a loss.

We can summarize the asset/liability problem of the bank and life insurance company as follows:

*Bank:*

1.  Has lent long-term and borrowed short-term.
2.  If the six-month Treasury bill rate rises, spread income declines.

*Life insurance company:*

1.  Has effectively lent short-term and borrowed long-term.
2.  If the six-month Treasury bill rate falls, spread income declines.

Now let's suppose that an intermediary offers a five-year interest rate swap with a notional principal amount of $50 million to both the bank and life insurance company. The terms offered to the bank are as follows:

1.  Every six months the bank will pay 10% (annual rate) to the intermediary.
2.  Every six months the intermediary will pay the six-month Treasury bill rate plus 155 basis points to the bank.

The terms offered to the insurance company are as follows:

1.  Every six months the life insurance company will pay the six-month Treasury bill rate plus 160 basis points per year to the intermediary.
2.  Every six months the intermediary will pay the insurance company 10% (annual rate).

What has this interest rate contract done for the bank and the life insurance company? Consider first the bank. For every six-month period during the life of the swap agreement, the interest rate spread will be as follows:

### Annual Interest Rate Received:

| | |
|---|---|
| From commercial loan portfolio | = 10% |
| From interest rate swap | = 6-month T-bill rate + 155 b.p. |
| Total | = 11.55% + 6-month T-bill rate |

### Annual Interest Rate Paid:

| | |
|---|---|
| To CD depositors | = 6-month T-bill rate + 40 b.p. |
| On interest rate swap | = 10% |
| Total | = 10.40% + 6-month T-bill rate |

### Outcome:

| | |
|---|---|
| To be received | = 11.55% + 6-month T-bill rate |
| To be paid | = 10.40% + 6-month T-bill rate |
| Spread income | = 1.15% or 115 basis points |

Thus, regardless of what happens to the six-month Treasury bill rate, the bank locks in a spread of 115 basis points.

Now let's look at the effect of the interest rate swap on the life insurance company:

### Annual Interest Rate Received:

| | |
|---|---|
| From floating-rate instrument | = 6-month T-bill rate + 160 b.p. |
| From interest rate swap | = 10% |
| Total | = 11.6% + 6-month T-bill rate |

### Annual Interest Rate Paid:

| | |
|---|---|
| To GIC policyholders | = 9% |
| On interest rate swap | = 6-month T-bill rate + 160 b.p. |
| Total | = 10.6% + 6-month T-bill rate |

### Outcome:

| | |
|---|---|
| To be received | = 11.6% + 6-month T-bill rate |
| To be paid | = 10.6% + 6-month T-bill rate |
| Spread income | = 1.0% or 100 basis points |

Regardless of what happens to the six-month Treasury bill rate, the life insurance company locks in a spread of 100 basis points.

The interest rate swap has allowed each party to accomplish its asset/liability objective of locking in a spread.[1] The swap permits each financial institution to alter the cash flow characteristics of its assets: from fixed to floating in the case of the bank, and from floating to fixed in the case of the life insurance company. This type of transaction is referred to as an *asset swap*. The bank and the life insurance company could have used the swap market instead to change the cash flow nature of their liabilities. Such a swap is called a *liability swap*. While in our illustration we used a bank, an interest rate swap obviously would be appropriate for savings and loan associations that, because of regulation, borrow short term—on a floating-rate basis—and lend long term—on fixed-rate mortgages.

Of course there are other ways that the two institutions could have chosen to match the cash flow characteristics of their assets and liabilities. The bank might refuse to make fixed-rate commercial loans and insist only on floating-rate loans. This approach has a major pitfall: if borrowers can find another source willing to lend on a fixed-rate basis, the bank would lose these customers. The life insurance company might refuse to purchase a floating-rate instrument. But suppose that the terms offered on the private placement instrument were more attractive than what would have been offered on a floating-rate instrument of comparable credit risk. Thus, by using the

---

[1] Whether the size of the spread is adequate is not an issue to us in this illustration.

swap market, the life insurance company can earn a yield higher than what it would earn if it invested directly in a five-year fixed-rate security. For example, suppose the life insurance company can invest in a comparable credit risk five-year fixed-rate security with a yield of 9.8%. Given the funding through the GIC with a 9% rate, this investment would result in spread income of 80 basis points—less than the 100 basis point spread income the life insurance company achieved by purchasing the floating-rate instrument and entering into the swap.

Consequently, an interest rate swap performs two important functions: (1) it can change the risk of a financial position by altering the cash flow characteristics of assets or liabilities, and (2) under certain circumstances, it also can be used to enhance returns. Obviously, this second function arises only if there are market imperfections.

There is a final point to be made in this illustration. Look at the floating-rate payments that the life insurance company makes to the intermediary and the floating-rate payments that the intermediary makes to the bank. The life insurance company pays the six-month Treasury bill rate plus 160 basis points, but the intermediary pays the bank the six-month Treasury bill rate plus only 155 basis points. The difference of 5 basis points represents the fee to the intermediary for the services of intermediation.

***Application to Debt Issuance.***   Our second illustration considers two U.S. entities, a triple-A rated commercial bank and a triple-B rated nonfinancial corporation; each wants to raise $100 million for 10 years. For various reasons, the bank wants to raise floating-rate funds, while the nonfinancial corporation wants to raise fixed-rate funds. The interest rates available to the two entities in the U.S. bond market are as follows:

> Bank: Floating rate = 6-month LIBOR + 30 b.p.
> Nonfinancial corporation: Fixed rate = 12%

Suppose also that both entities could issue securities in the Eurodollar bond market, if they wanted to. Let us assume that the following terms are available in the Eurodollar bond market for ten-year securities for these two entities:

> Bank: Fixed rate = 10.5%
> Nonfinancial corporation: Floating rate = 6-month LIBOR + 80 b.p.

Notice that we indicate the terms that the bank could obtain on fixed-rate financing and that the nonfinancial corporation could obtain on floating-rate securities. You will shortly see why we did this. First, let us summarize the situation for the two entities in the U.S. domestic and Eurodollar bond markets:

### FLOATING-RATE SECURITIES

| Entity | Bond Market | Rate |
|--------|-------------|------|
| Bank | U.S. domestic | 6-month LIBOR + 30 b.p. |
| Nonfinancial corp. | Eurodollar | 6-month LIBOR + 80 b.p |
| | | Quality spread = 50 b.p. |

### FIXED-RATE SECURITIES

| Entity | Bond Market | Rate |
|--------|-------------|------|
| Bank | Eurodollar | 10.5% |
| Nonfinancial corp. | U.S. domestic | 12.0% |
| | | Quality spread = 150 b.p. |

In this table, we use the term "quality spread." This term simply means the differential borrowing costs that reflect the difference in the creditworthiness of the two entities.

Notice that the quality spread for floating-rate securities (50 basis points) is narrower than the quality spread for fixed-rate securities (150 basis points). This difference in spreads provides an opportunity for both entities to reduce the cost of raising funds. To see how, suppose each entity issued securities in the Eurodollar bond market, and then simultaneously entered into the following ten-year interest rate swap with a $100 million notional principal amount offered by an intermediary:

#### Bank:

Pay floating rate of 6-month LIBOR + 70 b.p.
Receive fixed rate of 11.3%

#### Nonfinancial Corp.:

Pay fixed rate of 11.3%
Receive floating rate of 6-month LIBOR + 45 b.p.

The cost of the issue for the bank would then be:

#### Interest Paid:

| | |
|---|---|
| On fixed-rate Eurodollar bonds issued = 10.5% | |
| On interest rate swap | = 6-month LIBOR + 70 b.p. |
| Total | = 11.2% + 6-month LIBOR |

#### Interest Received:

| | |
|---|---|
| On interest rate swap | = 11.3% |

#### Net cost:

| | |
|---|---|
| Interest paid | = 11.2% + 6-month LIBOR |
| Interest received | = 11.3% |
| Total | = 6-month LIBOR − 10 b.p. |

The cost of the issue for the nonfinancial corporation would then be:

### Interest Paid:

| | |
|---|---|
| On floating-rate Eurodollar bonds issued | = 6-month LIBOR + 80 b.p. |
| On interest rate swap | = 11.3% |
| Total | = 12.1% + 6-month LIBOR |

### Interest Received:

| | |
|---|---|
| On interest rate swap | = 6-month LIBOR + 45 b.p. |

### Net Cost:

| | |
|---|---|
| Interest paid | = 12.1% + 6-month LIBOR |
| Interest received | = 6-month LIBOR + 45 b.p. |
| Total | = 11.65% |

The transactions are diagrammed in Figure 29-1. By issuing securities in the Eurodollar bond market and using the interest rate swap, both entities are able to reduce their cost of issuing securities. The bank was able to issue floating-rate securities for six-month LIBOR minus 10 basis points rather than issue floating-rate securities in the U.S. domestic bond market for six-month LIBOR plus 30 basis points, thereby saving 40 basis points. The nonfinancial corporation saved 35 basis points (11.65% versus 12%) by issuing floating-rate bonds in the Eurodollar bond market and using the interest rate swap.

The point of this illustration is to show that, if differences in quality

### FIGURE 29-1

DIAGRAM OF INTEREST RATE SWAP FOR DEBT ISSUANCE

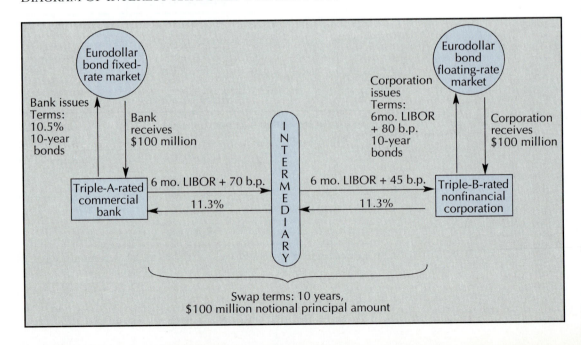

spreads exist in different sectors of the bond markets, borrowers can use the interest rate swap to arbitrage the inconsistency. Whether these differences do exist is another question, which we address below.

Finally, look once again at the intermediary in this transaction. The intermediary pays a floating rate of six-month LIBOR plus 45 basis points to the nonfinancial corporation, and receives six-month LIBOR plus 70 basis points from the bank, realizing 25 basis points for its intermediary services.

## *Reasons for the Development of the Interest Rate Swap Market*

The interest rate swap was first developed in late 1981. By December 1990, according to a survey by the International Swap Dealers Association, the swap market (consisting of interest rate swaps and currency swaps) totaled $2.9 trillion, as measured in terms of notional principal. (Currency swaps are discussed in Chapter 30.) The interest rate swap market grew by 50% over its 1989 level.[2]

What is behind this rapid growth? As our two illustrations have demonstrated, an interest rate swap is a quick way for institutional investors and corporate borrowers to change the nature of assets and liabilities or to exploit any perceived capital market imperfection.

The initial motivation for the interest rate swap market was borrower exploitation of what were perceived to be "credit arbitrage" opportunities. These opportunities were attributed to the fact that quality spreads, the difference in yields between lower- and higher-rated credits, were frequently not the same in the fixed-rate market as in the floating-rate market, and often the quality spreads were not the same in the U.S. debt markets as in the Eurodollar bond markets. Note that our second illustration assumes a spread of 50 basis points in the floating-rate markets and 150 basis points in the fixed-rate markets. Publications by dealer firms[3] and academic research have suggested this credit arbitrage motivation.[4]

Basically, this argument for swaps rested on the well-known economic principle of comparative advantage, which was developed in international economics. The argument takes this form: even though a high credit-rated issuer could borrow at a lower cost in both the fixed-rate and floating-rate markets (that is, have an absolute advantage in both), it will have a comparative advantage relative to a lower credit-rated issuer in one of the markets (and a comparative disadvantage in the other). Under these conditions, each borrower could benefit from issuing securities in the market in which it has a comparative advantage and then swapping obligations for the desired type of financing. The swap market developed as the vehicle for swapping obligations.

---

[2] As reported in Soma Biswas, "Derivative Pros See Growth in Customization," *BondWeek*, Special Supplement, October 14, 1991, p. 1.

[3] See, for example, a January 1986 Salomon Brothers publication: T. Lipsky and S. El-halaski, "Swap-Driven Primary Issuance in the International Bond Market."

[4] See, for example, James Bicksler and Andrew Chen, "An Economic Analysis of Interest Rate Swaps," *Journal of Finance* (July 1986), pp. 645–655.

Several observers have challenged the notion that "credit arbitrage" opportunities exist. They insist that the comparative advantage argument, while based on arbitrage, does not rely on irrational mispricing, but on assumptions of equilibrium in segmented markets. That is, two completely separate markets can be perfectly competitive unto themselves, but set different prices for risk. An economic agent transacting simultaneously in both markets would see an imperfectly competitive market and an opportunity to make money.

Those who challenge the "credit arbitrage" notion argue that the differences in quality spreads in the fixed-rate and floating-rate markets represent differences in the risks that lenders face in these two markets. Let us consider short- and long-term markets in this regard. The interest rate for a floating-rate note effectively represents a short-term interest rate, and the quality spread on floating-rate notes therefore is a spread in the short-term market. In contrast, the quality spread on fixed-rate medium- and long-term notes represents the spread in that maturity sector. There is no reason why the quality spreads across those two markets have to be the same.[5]

A serious obstacle to accepting the credit arbitrage explanation of the swap market is that opportunities for credit arbitrage should be rare in reasonably efficient international credit markets. Moreover, even if such opportunities arose, market participants would quickly exploit and eliminate them. How then can we explain the fact that the number of interest rate swap transactions has grown substantially over the last decade? The May 1984 edition of *Euromoney* contained a Citicorp-sponsored contribution that offered this intesting explanation of the swap market and its reason for being:

> *The nature of swaps is that they arbitrage market imperfections. As with any arbitrage opportunity, the more it is exploited, the smaller it becomes. . . .*
>
> *But some of the causes of market imperfections are unlikely to disappear quickly. For example, insurance companies in many countries are constrained to invest mainly in instruments that are domestic in that country. That requirement, tending to favor domestic issuers artificially, is unlikely to be changed overnight. And even in the world's most liquid markets there are arbitrage opportunities. They are small and exist only briefly, but they exist nevertheless.[6]*

As this opinion demonstrates, as early as 1984, some observers attributed the difference in quality spreads among markets to differences in regulations

---

[5] Two researchers demonstrate that differences in quality spreads between the fixed-rate and floating-rate markets are consistent with option-pricing theory. See Ian Cooper and Antonio Mello, "Default Spreads in the Fixed and in the Floating Rate Markets: A Contingent Claims Approach," *Advances in Futures and Options Research*, Vol. 3 (1988), pp. 269–290.

[6] "Swap Financing Techniques: A Citicorp Guide," Special Sponsored Section, *Euromoney* (May 1984), pp. S1–S7. Rather than relying exclusively on an arbitrage argument, one study suggests that the swaps market grew because it allowed borrowers to raise a type of financing that was not possible prior to the introduction of interest rate swaps. See: Marcelle Arak, Arturo Estrella, Laurie Goodman, and Andrew Silver, "Interest Rate Swaps: An Alternative Explanation," *Financial Management* (Summer 1988), pp. 12–18.

among countries. Similarly, differences in tax treatment across countries also create differences in the price of risk and in expected returns.[7] Thus, swaps can be used for regulatory or tax arbitrage and may be explained by such differences among national markets.

Finally, another argument suggested for the growth of the interest rate swap market is the increased volatility of interest rates that has led borrowers and lenders to hedge or manage their exposure. Even though risk/return characteristics can be replicated by a package of forward contracts, interest rate forward contracts are not as liquid as interest rate swaps. And entering into or liquidating swap transactions has been facilitated by the standardization of documentation published by the International Swap Dealers Association in early 1987. Moreover, a swap to hedge or manage a position costs less than a package of interest rate forward contracts.

Consequently, we can say that the swap market originally developed around the purpose of exploiting real or perceived imperfections in the capital market, but eventually evolved into a transactionally efficient market for accomplishing asset/liability objectives.

While there are no publicly available data on the users of swaps, a study by Leslie Lynn Rahl provides some insight into their identity.[8] She found that 25% of the end users of swaps are corporations, 60% are financial institutions that are not swap dealers, and 15% are government agencies and supranationals.

## Role of the Intermediary

The role of the intermediary in an interest rate swap sheds some light on the evolution of the market. Intermediaries in these transactions have been commercial banks and investment banks, who in the early stages of the market sought out end users of swaps. That is, commercial banks and investment banking firms found in their client bases those entities that needed swaps to accomplish funding or investing objectives, and they matched the two entities. In essence, the intermediary in this type of transaction performed the function of a broker.

In the early years of this market, the only time that the intermediary would take the opposite side of a swap (that is, would act as a principal) was when it had to do so in order to balance out the transaction. For example, if an intermediary had two clients that were willing to do a swap but one wanted the notional principal amount to be $100 million while the other wanted it to be $85 million, the intermediary might become the counterparty to the extent of $15 million. That is, the intermediary would warehouse or take a position

---

[7] This applies even more so to currency swaps, which we discuss in Chapter 30. Several examples of the way swaps can be used to exploit differences in taxes are given in Clifford W. Smith, Charles W. Smithson, and Lee MacDonald Wakeman, "The Evolving Market for Swaps," *Midland Corporate Finance Journal* (Winter 1986), pp. 20-32.

[8] Leslie Lynn Rahl, "Who is Using Swaps?" *BondWeek*, October 14, 1991, p. 4.

as a principal to the transaction in order to make up the $15 million difference between the clients' objectives. To protect itself against an adverse interest rate movement, the intermediary would hedge its position.

To explain how the intermediary's role developed over time, we need to address an important feature of the swap that we have not yet discussed. The parties to the swaps we have described had to be concerned that the other party would default on its obligation. While a default would not mean any principal was lost (because the notional principal amount had not been exchanged), a default would mean that the objective for which the swap was entered into would be impaired. As the early transactions involved a higher and a lower credit-rated entity, the former would be concerned with the potential for default of the latter. To reduce the risk of default, many early swap transactions required that the lower credit-rated entity obtain a guarantee from a highly rated commercial bank. Often, the intermediary in the swap was a bank of this type. Involvement as insurer or guarantor in this way led banks to accept the role of dealer or counterparty.

As the frequency and the size of the transactions increased, many intermediaries became comfortable with swap transactions and became principals instead of simply acting as brokers. As long as an intermediary had one entity willing to enter into a swap, the intermediary was willing to be the counterparty. Consequently, interest rate swaps became part of an intermediary's inventory of products. Advances in quantitative techniques and futures products for hedging complex positions such as swaps made the protection of large inventory positions feasible.

Yet another development encouraged intermediaries to become principals rather than brokers in swaps. As more intermediaries entered the swap market, bid–ask spreads on swaps narrowed sharply. To make money in the swaps market, intermediaries had to do a sufficient volume of business, which was possible only if they had (1) an extensive client base willing to use swaps, and (2) a large inventory of swaps. Accomplishing these objectives necessitated that the intermediaries act as principals. A survey by *Euromoney* asked 150 multinationals and supranationals to identify the characteristics that make a swap house efficient.[9] The results indicated that the speed at which a swap could be arranged for a client was the most important criterion. That speed depends on client base and inventory. The same survey also revealed clients to be less interested in brokered deals than in transactions in which the intermediary is a principal.

## Market Quotes

The convention that has evolved for quoting swaps levels is for a swap dealer to set the floating rate equal to the index and then quote the fixed rate that will apply. To illustrate this convention, we use the swap in our second example of the application of swaps. The terms for that ten-year swap are as follows:

---

[9] Special Supplement on Swaps, *Euromoney* (July 1987), p. 14.

*Bank*:
Pay floating rate of 6-month LIBOR + 70 b.p.
Receive fixed rate of 11.3%

*Nonfinancial corporation*:
Pay fixed rate of 11.3%
Receive floating rate of 6-month LIBOR + 45 b.p.

The offer price that the dealer would quote to the nonfinancial corporation (the fixed-rate payer) would be to pay 10.85% and receive LIBOR "flat." (The term "flat" means with no spread.) The 10.85% is obtained by subtracting from the fixed rate of 11.3% the 45-basis point spread over LIBOR. The bid price that the dealer would quote to the commercial bank would be to pay LIBOR flat and receive 10.6%. The 10.6% represents the payment to be received of 11.3% minus the 70-basis point spread over LIBOR.

The dealer determines or sets the quoted fixed rate by adding some spread to the Treasury yield curve with the same term to maturity as the swap. We refer to this spread as the "swap spread." In our illustration, suppose that the ten-year Treasury yield is 10.35%. In this case, the offer price that the dealer would quote to the fixed-rate payer is the ten-year Treasury rate plus 50 basis points versus receiving LIBOR flat. For the floating-rate payer, the bid price quoted would be LIBOR flat versus the ten-year Treasury rate plus 25 basis points. In the terminology of the market, the dealer would actually quote this particular swap as "25-50." This swap spread means that the dealer is willing to enter into a swap on either side: to receive LIBOR and pay a fixed rate equal to the ten-year Treasury rate plus 25 basis points, or to pay LIBOR and receive a fixed rate equal to the ten-year Treasury rate plus 50 basis points. The difference between the fixed rate paid and received is the bid–offer spread, which is 25 basis points. In practice, over recent years the bid–offer spread has fallen to a level of around 5 to 10 basis points.

## Primary Determinants of Swap Spreads

We mentioned earlier two interpretations of a swap: (1) a package of futures/forward contracts, and (2) a package of cash market instruments. The swap spread is determined by the same factors that influence the spread over Treasuries on financial instruments (futures/forward contracts or cash) that produce a similar return or funding profile. As we explain below, the key determinant of the swap spread for swaps with maturities of five years or less is the cost of hedging in the Eurodollar CD futures market. For longer-maturity swaps, the key determinant of the swap spread is the credit spreads in the corporate bond market.

Since a swap is a package of futures/forward contracts, the swap spread can be determined by looking for futures/forward contracts with the same risk/return profile. As explained in Chapter 25, a Eurodollar CD futures contract is an agreement in which a fixed dollar payment (that is, the futures price) is exchanged for three-month LIBOR. There are Eurodollar CD futures contracts that have maturities every three months for five years. A market participant can create a synthetic fixed-rate security or a fixed-rate funding vehicle of up to five years by taking a position in a strip of Eurodollar CD futures contracts (that is, a position in every three-month Eurodollar CD up to the desired maturity date).

For example, consider a financial institution that has fixed-rate assets and floating-rate liabilities. Assume that the assets and liabilities have a maturity of three years, and that the interest rate on the liabilities resets every three months to a level based on three-month LIBOR. This financial institution can hedge its mismatched asset/liability position by buying a three-year strip of Eurodollar CD futures contracts. In doing so, the financial institution is receiving LIBOR over the three-year period and paying a fixed dollar amount (or, the futures price). From the fixed dollar amount over the three years, an effective fixed interest rate that the financial institution pays can be calculated. The financial institution is now hedged because the assets are fixed-rate and the strip of long Eurodollar CD futures synthetically creates a fixed-rate funding arrangement.

Alternatively, the financial institution could have created a synthetic fixed-rate funding arrangement by entering into a three-year swap in which it pays fixed and receives three-month LIBOR. The financial institution will use the vehicle that gives it the lowest cost of hedging the mismatched position. This search for the low-cost method will drive the synthetic fixed rate in the swap market to what is available by hedging in the Eurodollar CD futures market.

For swaps with maturities greater than five years, the spread is determined primarily by the credit spreads in the corporate bond market. Since a swap can be interpreted as a package of long and short positions in a fixed-rate bond and a floating-rate bond, the credit spreads in those two market sectors will be the key determinant of the swap spread. Boundary conditions for swap spreads based on prices for fixed-rate and floating-rate corporate bonds can be determined.[10] Several technical factors, such as the relative supply of fixed-rate and floating-rate corporate bonds, and the cost to dealers of hedging their inventory position of swaps, influence where in the boundaries the actual swap spread will be.[11]

---

[10] These boundary conditions are derived in the appendix to Ellen Evans and Gioia Parente Bales, "What Drives Interest Rate Swap Spreads?" Chapter 13 in Carl R. Beidleman (ed.), *Interest Rate Swaps* (Homewood, IL: Richard D. Irwin, 1991).

[11] For a discussion of these other factors, see Evans and Bales, *ibid.*, pp. 293–301.

## Secondary Market for Swaps

There are three general types of transactions in the secondary market for swaps. These include (1) a swap reversal; (2) a swap sale (or assignment); and (3) a swap buy-back (or close-out or cancellation).

In a *swap reversal*, the party that wants out of the transaction will arrange for an additional swap in which (1) the maturity on the new swap is equal to the time remaining of the original swap; (2) the reference rate is the same; and (3) the notional principal amount is the same. For example, suppose party X enters into a five-year swap with a notional principal amount of $50 million in which it pays 10% and receives LIBOR, but that two years later, X wants out of the swap. In a swap reversal, X would enter into a three-year interest rate swap, with a counterparty different from the original counterparty, let's say Z, in which the notional principal amount is $50 million, and X pays LIBOR and receives a fixed rate. The fixed rate that X receives from Z will depend on prevailing swap terms for floating-rate receivers at the initiation of the three-year swap.

While party X has effectively terminated the original swap in economic terms, there is a major drawback to this approach: party X is still liable to the original counterparty Y, as well as to the new counterparty, Z. That is, party X now has two offsetting interest rate swaps on its books instead of one, and as a result it has increased its default risk exposure.

The *swap sale* or *swap assignment* overcomes this drawback. In this secondary market transaction, the party that wishes to close out the original swap finds another party that is willing to accept its obligations under the swap. In our illustration, this means that X finds another party, say, A, that will agree to pay 10% to Y and receive LIBOR from Y for the next three years. Party A might have to be compensated to accept the position of X, or A might have to be willing to compensate X. Who will receive compensation depends on the swap terms at the time. For example, if interest rates have risen so that, to receive LIBOR for three years, a fixed-rate payer would have to pay 12%, then A would have to compensate X because A has to pay only 10% to receive LIBOR. The compensation would be equal to the present value of a three-year annuity of 2% times the notional principal amount. If, instead, interest rates have fallen so that, to receive LIBOR for three years, a fixed-rate payer would have to pay 6%, then X would have to compensate A. The compensation would be equal to the present value of a three-year annuity of 4% times the notional principal amount. Once the transaction is completed, it is then A, not X, that is obligated to perform under the swap terms. (Of course an intermediary could act as principal and become party A.

In order to accomplish a swap sale, the original counterparty, Y in our example, must agree to the sale. A key factor in whether Y will agree is whether it is willing to accept the credit of A. For example, if A's credit rating is triple-B, while X's is double-A, Y would be unlikely to accept A as a counterparty.

A *buy-back* or *close-out sale* (or *cancellation*) involves the sale of the swap to the original counterparty. As in the case of a swap sale, one party might have to compensate the other, depending on how interest rates and credit spreads have changed since the inception of the swap.

These methods for getting into or out of a swap leave much to be desired for market participants. It is this illiquidity in the secondary market that will hamper swap market growth. There have been proposals to create a swap clearing corporation, similar to the clearing corporations for futures and options, in which case swaps could be marked to market and credit exposure to a swap could be reduced. So far, these proposals have not been implemented.

### Beyond the "Plain Vanilla" Swap

Thus far we have described the "plain vanilla" or generic interest rate swap. Nongeneric or individualized swaps have evolved as a result of the asset/liability needs of borrowers and lenders.

In a generic swap, the notional principal amount does not vary over the life of the swap. Thus, it is sometimes referred to as a *bullet swap*. In contrast, for amortizing, accreting, and roller coaster swaps, the notional principal amount varies over the life of the swap. An *amortizing swap* is one in which the notional principal amount decreases in a predetermined way over the life of the swap. An *accreting swap* is one in which the notional principal amount increases at a predetermined way over time. In a *roller coaster swap*, the notional principal amount can rise or fall from period to period.

The terms of a typical interest rate swap call for the exchange of fixed- and floating-rate payments. In a *basis rate swap*, both parties exchange floating-rate payments based on a different money market reference rate. As an example, assume a commercial bank has a portfolio of loans in which the lending rate is based on the prime rate, but the bank's cost of funds is based on LIBOR. The risk the bank faces is that the spread between the prime rate and LIBOR will change. This is referred to as "basis risk." The bank can use a basis rate swap to make floating-rate payments based on the prime rate and receive floating-rate payments based on LIBOR.

There are also options on swaps, which are called *swaptions*. The buyer of this option has the right to enter into an interest rate swap agreement on predetermined terms by some specified date in the future. The buyer of a put or call swaption pays the writer a premium.

▶ KEY POINTS THAT YOU SHOULD UNDERSTAND BEFORE PROCEEDING:

1. An interest rate swap is an agreement whereby two counterparties agree to exchange periodic interest payments based on a notional principal amount.

2. A position in an interest rate swap can be interpreted as a position in a package of forward contracts or a package of cash flows from buying and selling cash market instruments.

3. While the initial motivation for the swap market was borrower exploitation of what were perceived to be "credit arbitrage" oppor-

tunities, such opportunities are limited and depend on the presence of market imperfections.

4.  The swap market has evolved into a transactionally efficient market for accomplishing asset/liability objectives to alter the cash flow characteristics of assets (an asset swap) or liabilities (a liability swap).

5.  Commercial banks and investment banking firms take positions in swaps rather than act as simply intermediaries.

6.  For swaps with maturities of less than five years, the swap spread is driven by rates in the Eurodollar CD futures market, but for swaps with maturities greater than five years, the spread is determined primarily by the credit spreads in the corporate bond market.

7.  There are three general types of transactions in the secondary market for swaps: a swap reversal, a swap sale (or assignment), and a swap buy-back (or close-out or cancellation).

## INTEREST RATE AGREEMENTS

An interest rate agreement is an agreement between two parties in which one party, for an upfront premium, agrees to compensate the other if a designated interest rate, called the *reference rate*, is different from a predetermined level. When one party agrees to pay the other if the reference rate exceeds a predetermined level, the agreement is referred to as an *interest rate cap* or *ceiling*. The agreement is referred to as an *interest rate floor* when one party agrees to pay the other if the reference rate falls below a predetermined level. The predetermined level of the reference interest rate is called the *strike rate*.

The terms of an interest rate agreement include:

1.  The reference rate.
2.  The strike rate that sets the ceiling or floor.
3.  The length of the agreement.
4.  The frequency of settlement.
5.  The notional principal amount.

For example, suppose that C buys an interest rate cap from D with terms as follows:

1.  The reference rate is six-month LIBOR.
2.  The strike rate is 8%.
3.  The agreement is for seven years.
4.  Settlement is every six months.
5.  The notional principal amount is $20 million.

Under this agreement, every six months for the next seven years, D will pay C whenever six-month LIBOR exceeds 8%. The payment will equal the dollar value of the difference between six-month LIBOR and 8% times the notional principal amount divided by two. For example, if six months from now six-month LIBOR is 11%, then D will pay C 3% (11% minus 8%) times $20 million divided by 2, or $300,000. If six-month LIBOR is 8% or less, D does not have to pay anything to C.

As an example of an interest rate floor, assume the same terms as the interest rate cap we just illustrated. In this case, if six-month LIBOR is 11%, C receives nothing from D, but if six-month LIBOR is less than 8%, D compensates C for the difference. For example, if six-month LIBOR is 7%, D will pay C $100,000 (8% minus 7%, times $20 million divided by 2).

Interest rate caps and floors can be combined to create an *interest rate collar*. This is done by buying an interest rate cap and selling an interest rate floor. Some commercial banks and investment banking firms now write options on interest rate agreements for customers. Options on caps are called *captions*, and options on floors are called *flotions*.

### Risk/Return Characteristics

In an interest rate agreement, the buyer pays an upfront fee, which represents the maximum amount the buyer can lose and the maximum amount the writer of the agreement can gain. The only party that is required to perform is the writer of the interest rate agreement. The buyer of an interest rate cap benefits if the underlying interest rate rises above the strike rate because the seller (writer) must compensate the buyer. The buyer of an interest rate floor benefits if the interest rate falls below the strike rate, because the seller (writer) must compensate the buyer.

How can we better understand interest rate caps and interest rate floors? In essence these contracts are equivalent to a package of interest rate options. As the buyer benefits if the interest rate rises above the strike rate, an interest rate cap is similar to purchasing a package of put options; the seller of an interest rate cap has effectively sold a package of put options. As the buyer of an interest rate floor benefits from a decline in the interest rate below the strike rate, the buyer has effectively bought a package of call options from the writer of the option. An interest rate collar is equivalent to buying a package of put options and selling a package of call options.

It is important to note that, once again, a complex contract can be seen to be a package of basic contracts, or options in the case of interest rate agreements.

### Applications

To see how interest rate agreements can be used for asset/liability management, consider the problems faced by the commercial bank and the life insurance company in the first illustration in the chapter of the application of interest rate swaps.

Recall that the bank's objective is to lock in an interest rate spread over its cost of funds. Yet because it raises funds through a variable-rate instrument and is basically borrowing short term, the bank's cost of funds is uncertain. The bank may be able to purchase a cap so that the cap rate plus the cost of purchasing the cap is less than the rate it is earning on its fixed-rate commercial loans. If short-term rates decline, the bank does not benefit from the cap, but its cost of funds declines. The cap therefore allows the bank to impose a ceiling on its cost of funds while retaining the opportunity to benefit from a decline in rates. This use of a cap is consistent with the view of an interest rate cap as simply a package of call options.

The bank can reduce the cost of purchasing the cap by selling a floor. In this case, the bank agrees to pay the buyer of the floor if the underlying rate falls below the strike rate. The bank receives a fee for selling the floor, but it has sold off its opportunity to benefit from a decline in rates below the strike rate. By buying a cap and selling a floor, the bank has created a range for its cost of funds (or a collar).

Consider again from that same first example of the application of interest rate swaps the problem of the life insurance company that has guaranteed a 9% rate on a GIC for the next five years and is considering the purchase of an attractive floating-rate instrument in a private placement transaction. The risk that the company faces is that interest rates will fall so that it will not earn enough to realize the 9% guaranteed rate plus a spread. The life insurance company may be able to purchase a floor to set a lower bound on its investment return, yet retain the opportunity to benefit should rates increase. To reduce the cost of purchasing the floor, the life insurance company can sell an interest rate cap. By doing so, however, it gives up the opportunity of benefiting from an increase in the six-month Treasury bill rate above the strike rate of the interest rate cap.

▶ KEY POINTS THAT YOU SHOULD UNDERSTAND BEFORE PROCEEDING:

1. An interest rate agreement is an agreement between two parties in which one party, for an upfront premium, agrees to compensate the other if the reference rate is different from the strike rate.

2. A cap is an interest rate agreement in which one party agrees to pay the other if the reference rate exceeds the strike rate; an interest rate floor is an interest rate agreement in which one party agrees to pay the other if the reference rate falls below the strike rate.

3. A collar is created by buying an interest rate cap and selling an interest rate floor.

4. An interest rate floor can be used by a depository institution to lock in an interest rate spread over its cost of funds but maintain the opportunity to benefit if rates decline.

5. The buyer of a floating-rate asset can use an interest rate floor to establish a lower bound on its investment return, yet retain the opportunity to benefit should rates increase.

**SUMMARY**

An interest rate swap is an agreement specifying that the parties exchange interest payments at designated times. In a typical swap, one party will make fixed-rate payments, and the other will make floating-rate payments, with payments based on the notional principal amount. Participants in financial markets use interest rate swaps to alter the cash flow characteristics of their assets or liabilities, or to capitalize on perceived capital market inefficiencies. A swap has the risk/return profile of a package of forward contracts or a combination of positions in the cash bond market.

An interest rate agreement allows one party the right to receive compensation from the writer of the agreement for an upfront premium if a designated interest rate is different from a predetermined level. An interest rate cap calls for one party to receive a payment if a designated interest rate is above the predetermined level. An interest rate floor lets one party receive a payment if a designated interest rate is below the predetermined level. An interest rate cap can be used to establish a ceiling on the cost of funding; an interest rate floor can be used to establish a floor return. Buying a cap and selling a floor creates a collar.

**GLOSSARY**

**Accreting swap:** An interest rate swap in which the notional principal amount increases in a predetermined way over time.

**Amortizing swap:** An interest rate swap in which the notional principal amount decreases in a predetermined way over the life of the swap.

**Asset swap:** The use of an interest rate swap to change the cash flow characteristics of assets.

**Basis rate swap:** An interest rate swap in which both parties exchange floating-rate payments based on a different money market reference rate.

**Bullet swap:** An interest rate swap in which the notional principal amount does not vary over the life of the swap.

**Buy-back (or close-out swap or cancellation swap):** A secondary market transaction in the swap market in which a party that wishes to close out the original swap sells the swap to the original counterparty.

**Caption:** This is an option on an interest rate cap.

**Fixed-rate payer:** The party in an interest rate swap that agrees to pay a fixed rate and receive a floating rate.

**Floating-rate payer:** The party in an interest rate swap that agrees to pay a floating rate and receive a fixed rate.

**Flotion:** An option on an interest rate floor.

**Interest rate agreement:** An agreement between two parties in which one party, for an upfront premium, agrees to compensate the other if a reference rate is different from a predetermined level.

**Interest rate cap (or ceiling):** An interest rate agreement in which one party agrees to pay the other if the reference rate exceeds a predetermined level.

**Interest rate collar:** A position created by combining an interest rate cap and an interest rate floor that confines the reference rate to a particular range of possible values.

**Interest rate floor:** An interest rate agreement in which one party agrees to pay the other if the reference rate falls below a predetermined level.

**Interest rate swap:** An agreement in which two parties (called counterparties) agree to exchange periodic interest payments.

**Liability swap:** The use of an interest rate swap to change the cash flow characteristics of liabilities.

**Notional principal amount:** The dollar principal amount upon which the interest payments in an interest rate swap or interest rate agreement are based.

**Plain vanilla swap:** This is a generic interest rate swap in which the counterparties exchange a fixed rate for a floating rate, and the notional principal amount is the same over the life of the swap.

**Reference rate:** The benchmark interest rate used in an interest rate swap and interest rate agreement.

**Roller coaster swap:** An interest rate swap in which the notional principal amount can rise or fall from period to period.

**Strike rate:** In an interest rate cap or floor, the predetermined level of the reference rate that is used to determine when and how much the seller must compensate the buyer.

**Swap reversal:** A secondary market transaction in the swap market in which a party that wants to close out a swap position arranges for an additional swap in which the maturity on the new swap is equal to the time remaining of the original swap.

**Swap sale (or swap assignment):** A secondary market transaction in the swap market in which a party that wishes to close out the original swap finds another party that is willing to accept its obligations under the swap.

**Swaption:** An option on an interest rate swap that allows the buyer of the option to enter into an interest rate swap agreement on predetermined terms by some specified date in the future.

QUESTIONS

1. At any time in the life of the interest rate swap, does the notional principal become a cash flow to either party or to the intermediary?

2. Consider a swap with these features: maturity is five years, notional principal is $100 million, payments occur every six months, the fixed-rate payer pays a rate of 9.05% and receives LIBOR, while the

floating-rate payer pays LIBOR and receives 9%. Now, suppose that at a payment date, LIBOR is at 6.5%. What is each party's payment and receipt at that date?

3.  A bank borrows funds by issuing CDs that carry a variable rate equal to the yield of the six-month Treasury bill plus 50 basis points. The bank gets the chance to invest in a seven-year loan that will pay a fixed rate of 7%. So, the bank wants to engage in an interest rate swap designed to lock in an interest spread of 75 basis points. Give the outlines of two possible swaps: one designed to change the asset's cash flow into a variable rate, and the other designed to change the liability's cash flow into a fixed rate.

4.  Identify two factors that have contributed to the growth of the interest rate swap market.

5.  a.  Describe the role of the intermediary in a swap.

    b.  What are the two factors that led swap brokers/intermediaries to act as principals or dealers?

6.  Suppose a dealer quotes these terms on a five-year swap: fixed-rate payer to pay 9.5% for LIBOR flat and floating-rate payer to pay LIBOR flat for 9.2%.

    a.  What is the dealer's bid–ask spread?

    b.  How would the dealer quote the terms by reference to the yield on five-year Treasury notes, assuming this yield is 9%?

7.  Explain the three major ways in which a party to a swap can reverse that position in the secondary market for swaps.

8.  Why can a fixed-rate payer in an interest rate swap be viewed as being short the bond market, and the floating-rate payer be viewed as being long the bond market?

9.  a.  Why would a depository institution use an interest rate swap?

    b.  Why would a corporation that plans to raise funds in the debt market use an interest rate swap?

10.  Suppose that a life insurance company has issued a three-year GIC with a fixed rate of 10%. Under what circumstances might it be feasible for the life insurance company to invest the funds in a floating-rate security and enter into a three-year interest rate swap in which it pays a floating rate and receives a fixed rate?

11.  This is an excerpt taken from an article entitled "IRS Rule to Open Swaps to Pension Funds," that appeared in the November 18, 1991, issue of *BondWeek*, pp. 1 and 2:

     *A proposed Internal Revenue Service rule that gives tax-free status to income earned on swaps by pension funds and other tax-exempt institutions is expected to spur pension fund use of these products, say swap and pension fund professionals. . . .*

     *UBS Asset Management has received permission from most of its pension fund clients to use interest rate and currency swaps in its fixed-income portfolios and is awaiting the IRS regulation before stepping into the market, says Kenneth Choie, v.p. and head of research and product development. . . . "The IRS' proposed rule is great news for pension fund managers," as the use of swaps can enhance returns and lower transaction costs, Choie says. . . .*

*While some pension funds are exploring the swap market, pension fund consultants underscore that the funds' entrance into the market is likely to be slow. Counterparty risk has been a more formidable obstacle than the ambiguity of the tax status of income from interest rate and currency swaps, says Paul Burik, director of research at Ennis, Knupp & Associates, a pension fund consulting firm.*

    a.   In the article, Choie indicates that one "possible application that UBS is considering is to switch between fixed- and floating-rate income streams without incurring the transaction costs of trading chunks of securities." Explain how an interest rate swap can be used for this application.

    b.   What is meant by counterparty risk?

    c.   How can counterparty risk be reduced?

12.   Suppose a savings and loan association buys an interest rate cap that has these terms: the reference rate is the six-month Treasury bill rate; the cap will last for five years; payment is semi-annual; the strike rate is 5.5%; and the notional principal amount is $10 million. Suppose further that at the end of some six-month period, the six-month Treasury bill rate is 6.1%.

    a.   What is the amount of the payment that the savings and loan association will receive?

    b.   What would the writer of this cap pay if the six-month Treasury rate were 5.45% instead of 6.1%?

13.   What is the relationship between an interest rate agreement and an interest rate option?

14.   How can an interest rate collar be created?

# CHAPTER THIRTY

# The Market for Foreign Exchange Rate Risk Control Instruments

## LEARNING OBJECTIVES

*After reading this chapter you will understand:*

- what is meant by a foreign exchange rate.
- the different ways that a foreign exchange rate can be quoted (direct versus indirect).
- the conventions for quoting foreign exchange rates.
- what foreign exchange risk is.
- a cross rate and how to calculate a theoretical cross rate.
- what triangular arbitrage is.
- the foreign exchange market structure.
- what the European Currency Unit is.
- the fundamental determinants of exchange rates: purchasing power parity and interest rate parity.
- the different instruments for hedging foreign exchange risk: forwards, futures, options, and swaps.
- the limitations of forward and futures contracts for hedging long-dated foreign exchange risk.
- how a forward exchange rate is determined, and covered interest arbitrage.

■ the basic currency swap structure and the motivation for using currency swaps.

The fundamental fact of international finance is that different countries issue different currencies, and the relative values of those currencies may change quickly, substantially, and without warning. The change, moreover, may either reflect economic developments or be a response to political events that make no economic sense. As a result, the risk that a currency's value may change adversely, which is called *foreign exchange risk* or *currency risk*, is an important consideration for all participants in the international financial markets. Investors who purchase securities denominated in a currency different from their own must worry about the return from those securities after adjusting for changes in the exchange rate. Firms that issue obligations denominated in a foreign currency face the risk that the effective value of the cash payments they owe to investors is very uncertain.

In this chapter, we provide a review of the instruments that can be used to control the risk of an adverse movement in a foreign currency. These instruments include forward contracts, futures contracts, options, and currency swaps. We begin our discussion with a review of the foreign exchange rate market.

## FOREIGN EXCHANGE RATES

An *exchange rate* is defined as the amount of one currency that can be exchanged for a unit of another currency. In fact, the exchange rate is the price of one currency in terms of another currency. And, depending on circumstances, one could define either currency as the price for the other. So, exchange rates can be quoted "in either direction." For example, the exchange rate between the U.S. dollar and the Swiss franc could be quoted in one of two ways:

1.  The amount of U.S. dollars necessary to acquire one Swiss franc, and this is the dollar price of one Swiss franc; or
2.  The number of Swiss francs necessary to acquire one U.S. dollar, or the Swiss franc price of one dollar.

### *Exchange Rate Quotation Conventions*

Exchange rate quotations may be either *direct* or *indirect*. The difference depends on identifying one currency as a local currency and the other as a foreign currency. For example, from the perspective of a U.S. participant, the local currency would be U.S. dollars, and any other currency, such as Swiss francs, would be the foreign currency. From the perspective of a Swiss participant, the local currency would be Swiss francs, and other currencies, such as U.S. dollars, the foreign currency. A direct quote is the number of units of a local currency exchangeable for one unit of a foreign currency.

An indirect quote is the number of units of a foreign currency that can be exchanged for one unit of a local currency. Looking at this from a U.S. participant's perspective, a quote indicating the number of dollars exchangeable for one unit of a foreign currency is a direct quote. An indirect quote from the same participant's perspective would be the number of units of the foreign currency that can be exchanged for one U.S. dollar. Obviously, from the point of view of a non-U.S. participant, the number of U.S. dollars exchangeable for one unit of a non-U.S. currency is an indirect quote; the number of units of a non-U.S. currency exchangeable for a U.S. dollar is a direct quote.

Given a direct quote, we can obtain an indirect quote (which is simply the reciprocal of the direct quote), and vice versa. For example, suppose that a U.S. participant is given a direct quote of 0.7880 U.S. dollars for a Swiss franc. That is, the price of a Swiss franc is $0.7880. The reciprocal of the direct quote is 1.2690, which would be the indirect quote for the U.S. participant; that is, one U.S. dollar can be exchanged for 1.2690 Swiss francs, which is the Swiss franc price of a dollar.

The financial press reports quotes both ways, as Figure 30-1 shows. The figure reproduces foreign exchange quotes reported in the *Wall Street Journal* on October 22, 1990. All the exchange rates in the figure are between the country indicated in the first column and the U.S. dollar. Look down the first column that shows the countries until you get to "Switzerland (Franc)." Switzerland has four lines devoted to it. The first of the four lines refers to the *spot* or *cash market exchange rate*. (We will explain the other three lines—"30-Day Forward," "90-Day Forward," and "180-Day Forward"—later in the chapter.)

The first two columns show the U.S. dollar equivalent (labeled "U.S. $ equiv.") on the most recent two trading days. That is, the columns indicate how many U.S. dollars were exchangeable for one Swiss franc on those days. So, from a U.S. participant's perspective, these are direct quotes; from that of a Swiss participant, they are indirect. Look at the Friday number: "0.7880." This means that 78.80 cents can be exchanged for one Swiss franc; in other words, this was the price of one Swiss franc on Friday. The last two columns show how much of the foreign currency was necessary to exchange for one U.S. dollar—the foreign currency price of a dollar on each of the two days. Thus, these are indirect quotes from a U.S. participant's position, but direct quotes from the perspective of a non-U.S. participant. Once again, focusing on the Friday value, we see "1.2690." This means that 1.2690 Swiss francs could be exchanged for one U.S. dollar on that day.

If the number of units of a foreign currency that can be obtained for one dollar—the price of a dollar in that currency or indirect quotation—rises, the dollar is said to appreciate relative to the currency, and the currency is said to depreciate. Thus, appreciation means a decline in the direct quotation.

## FIGURE 30-1

EXCHANGE RATES REPORTED IN
*THE WALL STREET JOURNAL* FOR OCTOBER 19, 1990.

### EXCHANGE RATES

Friday, October 19, 1990
The New York foreign exchange selling rates below apply to trading among banks in amounts of $1 million and more, as quoted at 3 p.m. Eastern time by Bankers Trust Co. Retail transactions provide fewer units of foreign currency per dollar.

| Country | U.S. $ equiv. Fri. | Thurs. | Currency per U.S. $ Fri. | Thurs. |
|---|---|---|---|---|
| Argentina (Austral) ... | .0001890 | .0001859 | 5292.00 | 5380.00 |
| Australia (Dollar) | .7756 | .7705 | 1.2893 | 1.2979 |
| Austria (Schilling) | .09456 | .09483 | 10.57 | 10.55 |
| Bahrain (Dinar) | 2.6532 | 2.6532 | .3769 | .3769 |
| Belgium (Franc) | | | | |
| Commercial rate | .03231 | .03240 | 30.95 | 30.86 |
| Brazil (Cruzeiro) | .01068 | .01097 | 93.61 | 91.18 |
| Britain (Pound) | 1.9590 | 1.9701 | .5105 | .5076 |
| 30-Day Forward | 1.9495 | 1.9602 | .5130 | .5102 |
| 90-Day Forward | 1.9323 | 1.9438 | .5175 | .5145 |
| 180-Day Forward | 1.9093 | 1.9214 | .5238 | .5205 |
| Canada (Dollar) | .8525 | .8540 | 1.1730 | 1.1710 |
| 30-Day Forward | .8493 | .8508 | 1.1775 | 1.1754 |
| 90-Day Forward | .8439 | .8450 | 1.1850 | 1.1835 |
| 180-Day Forward | .8361 | .8375 | 1.1960 | 1.1940 |
| Chile (Official rate) | .003046 | .003046 | 328.35 | 328.35 |
| China (Renmimbi) | .211864 | .211864 | 4.7200 | 4.7200 |
| Colombia (Peso) | .001912 | .001912 | 523.00 | 523.00 |
| Denmark (Krone) | .1743 | .1750 | 5.7378 | 5.7156 |
| Ecuador (Sucre) | | | | |
| Floating rate | .001168 | .001168 | 856.00 | 856.00 |
| Finland (Markka) | .28019 | .28149 | 3.5690 | 3.5525 |
| France (Franc) | .19853 | .19906 | 5.0370 | 5.0235 |
| 30-Day Forward | .19826 | .19877 | 5.0440 | 5.0309 |
| 90-Day Forward | .19765 | .19818 | 5.0595 | 5.0459 |
| 180-Day Forward | .19670 | .19723 | 5.0840 | 5.0703 |
| Germany (Mark) | .6649 | .6671 | 1.5040 | 1.4990 |
| 30-Day Forward | .6648 | .6670 | 1.5042 | 1.4992 |
| 90-Day Forward | .6642 | .6665 | 1.5055 | 1.5003 |
| 180-Day Forward | .6629 | .6653 | 1.5085 | 1.5031 |
| Greece (Drachma) | .006601 | .006623 | 151.50 | 151.00 |
| Hong Kong (Dollar) | .12850 | .12858 | 7.7820 | 7.7770 |
| India (Rupee) | .05556 | .05556 | 18.00 | 18.00 |
| Indonesia (Rupiah) | .0005365 | .0005365 | 1864.00 | 1864.00 |
| Ireland (Punt) | 1.7845 | 1.7890 | .5604 | .5590 |
| Israel (Shekel) | .5089 | .5089 | 1.9650 | 1.9650 |
| Italy (Lira) | .0008874 | .0008901 | 1126.86 | 1123.51 |
| Japan (Yen) | .007940 | .008016 | 125.95 | 124.75 |
| 30-Day Forward | .007942 | .008019 | 125.92 | 124.71 |
| 90-Day Forward | .007938 | .008018 | 125.97 | 124.72 |
| 180-Day Forward | .007933 | .008015 | 126.06 | 124.77 |
| Jordan (Dinar) | 1.5485 | 1.5485 | .6458 | .6458 |
| Kuwait (Dinar) | z | z | z | z |

| Country | U.S. $ equiv. Fri. | Thurs. | Currency per U.S. $ Fri. | Thurs. |
|---|---|---|---|---|
| Lebanon (Pound) | .000947 | .000947 | 1055.97 | 1055.97 |
| Malaysia (Ringgit) | .3706 | .3709 | 2.6985 | 2.6965 |
| Malta (Lira) | 3.3445 | 3.3445 | .2990 | .2990 |
| Mexico (Peso) | | | | |
| Floating rate | .0003442 | .0003442 | 2905.00 | 2905.00 |
| Netherland (Guilder) . | .5901 | .5919 | 1.6945 | 1.6895 |
| New Zealand (Dollar) | .6060 | .6010 | 1.6502 | 1.6639 |
| Norway (Krone) | .1708 | .1715 | 5.8560 | 5.8315 |
| Pakistan (Rupee) | .0462 | .0462 | 21.65 | 21.65 |
| Peru (Inti) | .00000225 | .00000225 | 445037.83 | 445037.83 |
| Philippines (Peso) | .04032 | .04032 | 24.80 | 24.80 |
| Portugal (Escudo) | .007536 | .007450 | 132.70 | 134.22 |
| Saudi Arabia (Riyal) | .26667 | .26667 | 3.7500 | 3.7500 |
| Singapore (Dollar) | .5845 | .5865 | 1.7110 | 1.7050 |
| South Africa (Rand) | | | | |
| Commercial rate | .3938 | .3947 | 2.5394 | 2.5336 |
| Financial rate | .2688 | .2674 | 3.7202 | 3.7397 |
| South Korea (Won) | .0013985 | .0013985 | 715.05 | 715.05 |
| Spain (Peseta) | .010599 | .010633 | 94.35 | 94.05 |
| Sweden (Krona) | .1789 | .1794 | 5.5900 | 5.5750 |
| Switzerland (Franc) .. | .7880 | .7933 | 1.2690 | 1.2605 |
| 30-Day Forward | .7882 | .7935 | 1.2687 | 1.2602 |
| 90-Day Forward | .7883 | .7936 | 1.2685 | 1.2601 |
| 180-Day Forward | .7878 | .7931 | 1.2694 | 1.2608 |
| Taiwan (Dollar) | .037313 | .037327 | 26.80 | 26.79 |
| Thailand (Baht) | .03995 | .03995 | 25.03 | 25.03 |
| Turkey (Lira) | .0003690 | .0003700 | 2710.00 | 2703.00 |
| United Arab (Dirham) | .2723 | .2723 | 3.6725 | 3.6725 |
| Uruguay (New Peso) | | | | |
| Financial | .000733 | .000733 | 1365.00 | 1365.00 |
| Venezuela (Bolivar) | | | | |
| Floating rate | .02119 | .02119 | 47.20 | 47.20 |
| | | --- | | |
| SDR | 1.44202 | 1.44588 | .69347 | .69162 |
| ECU | 1.36477 | 1.36524 | .... | .... |

Special Drawing Rights (SDR) are based on exchange rates for the U.S., German, British, French and Japanese currencies. Source: International Monetary Fund.

European Currency Unit (ECU) is based on a basket of community currencies. Source: European Community Commission.

z-Not quoted.

*Source*: Reprinted by permission of *The Wall Street Journal*, © October 19, 1990. Dow Jones & Company Inc. All Rights Reserved Worldwide.

### Foreign Exchange Risk

From the perspective of a U.S. investor, the cash flows of assets denominated in a foreign currency expose the investor to uncertainty as to the actual level of the cash flow measured in U.S. dollars. The actual number of U.S. dollars that the investor eventually gets depends on the exchange rate between the U.S. dollar and the foreign currency at the time the non-dollar cash flow is received and exchanged for U.S. dollars. If the foreign currency depreciates (declines in value) relative to the U.S. dollar (that is, the U.S. dollar appreciates), the dollar value of the cash flows will be proportionately less. This risk is referred to as *foreign exchange risk*.

Any investor who purchases an asset denominated in a currency that is not the medium of exchange in the investor's country faces foreign exchange risk. For example, a Greek investor who acquires a yen-denominated Japanese bond is exposed to the risk that the Japanese yen will decline in value relative to the Greek drachma.

Foreign exchange risk is a consideration for the issuer, too. Suppose that IBM issues bonds denominated in Japanese yen. IBM's foreign exchange risk is that, at the time the coupon interest payments must be made and the principal repaid, the U.S. dollar will have depreciated relative to the Japanese yen, requiring that IBM pay more dollars to satisfy its obligation.

▶ ### KEY POINTS THAT YOU SHOULD UNDERSTAND BEFORE PROCEEDING:

1. An exchange rate is defined as the amount of one currency that can be exchanged for a unit of another currency and can be expressed as either a direct or indirect quote.

2. Any investor who purchases an asset denominated in a currency that is not the medium of exchange of the investor's country faces foreign exchange risk.

3. A borrower who has liabilities denominated in a currency that is not the medium of exchange of the borrower's country faces foreign exchange risk.

## SPOT MARKET

The *spot exchange rate market* is the market for settlement of a foreign exchange transaction within two business days. (The spot exchange rate is also known as the *cash exchange rate*.) Since the early 1970s, exchange rates among major currencies have been free to float, with market forces determining the relative value of a currency.[1] Thus, each day a currency's price relative to that of another freely floating currency may stay the same, increase, or decrease.

A key factor affecting the expectation of changes in a country's exchange rate with another currency is the relative expected inflation rate of the two countries. Spot exchange rates adjust to compensate for the relative inflation rate. This adjustment reflects the so-called *purchasing power parity* relationship, which posits that the exchange rate—the domestic price of the foreign currency—is proportional to the domestic inflation rate, and inversely proportional to foreign inflation.

Let's look at the spot exchange rate reported in Figure 30-1 between the U.S. dollar and the Australian dollar. The exchange rate in U.S. dollar equivalents on Thursday was *0.7705*; on Friday it was *0.7756*. Consequently, on Thursday, one Australian dollar cost *0.7705* U.S. dollars. On Friday, it cost more U.S. dollars, *0.7756*. Thus, the Australian dollar appreciated relative to the U.S. dollar, or, what amounts to the same thing, the U.S. dollar depreci-

---

[1] In practice, national monetary authorities can intervene in the foreign exchange market for their currency for a variety of economic reasons, so the current foreign exchange system is sometimes referred to as a "managed" floating rate system.

ated relative to the Australian dollar. Figure 30-1 also shows that the U.S. dollar appreciated relative to the Swiss franc between Thursday and Friday in the cash market. In terms of U.S. dollar equivalents, one Swiss franc cost 0.7933 U.S. dollars on Thursday; on Friday it cost fewer U.S. dollars, 0.7880.

While quotes can be either direct or indirect, the problem is defining from whose perspective the quote is given. Foreign exchange conventions in fact standardize the ways quotes are given. Because of the importance of the U.S. dollar in the international financial system, currency quotations are all relative to the U.S. dollar. When dealers quote, they either give U.S. dollars per unit of foreign currency (a direct quote from the U.S. perspective) or the number of units of the foreign currency per U.S. dollar (an indirect quote from the U.S. perspective). Quoting in terms of U.S. dollars per unit of foreign currency is called "American terms," while quoting in terms of the number of units of the foreign currency per U.S. dollar is called "European terms." The dealer convention is to use European terms in quoting foreign exchange with a few exceptions. The British pound, the Irish pound, the Australian dollar, the New Zealand dollar, and the European Currency Unit (discussed later) are exceptions that are quoted in American terms.

### Cross Rates

Barring any government restrictions, riskless arbitrage will assure that the exchange rate between two countries will be the same in both countries. The theoretical exchange rate between two countries other than the United States can be inferred from their exchange rates with the U.S. dollar. Rates computed in this way are referred to as *theoretical cross rates*. They would be computed as follows for two countries, X and Y:

$$\frac{\text{Quote in American terms of currency X}}{\text{Quote in American terms of currency Y}}$$

To illustrate how this is done, let's calculate the theoretical cross rate between German marks and Japanese yen using the exchange rates shown in Figure 30-1 for Friday, October 19, 1990. The exchange rate for the two currencies in American terms is $0.6649 per German mark and $0.007940 per Japanese yen. Then, the number of units of yen (Y) per unit of German marks (X) is:

$$\frac{\$0.66490}{\$0.00794} = 83.74 \quad \text{yen/mark}$$

Taking the reciprocal gives the number of German marks exchangeable for one Japanese yen. In our example, it is 0.01194.

In the real world, it is rare that the theoretical cross rate, as computed from actual dealer dollar exchange rate quotes, will differ from the actual cross rate quoted by dealers. When the discrepancy is large by comparison with the transactions costs of buying and selling the currencies, a riskless arbitrage opportunity arises. Arbitraging to take advantage of cross rate mispricing is called *triangular arbitrage*, so named because it involves positions in three currencies—the U.S. dollar and the two foreign currencies. The arbitrage keeps actual cross rates in line with theoretical cross rates.

## Dealers

Exchange rates reported in *The Wall Street Journal* are indications of the rate at which a foreign currency can be purchased in the spot market. They are the rates for which the dealer is willing to sell foreign exchange. Foreign exchange dealers, however, do not quote one price. Instead, they quote an exchange rate at which they are willing to buy a foreign currency and one at which they are willing to sell a foreign currency. That is, they quote a bid–ask spread. Consequently, a U.S. investor who has received Swiss francs and wants to exchange those francs into U.S. dollars will request a quote on the bid price for Swiss francs. Another U.S. investor who wants to purchase Swiss francs in order, say, to buy a bond denominated in that foreign currency will request an offer quote.

Dealers in the foreign exchange market are large international banks and other financial institutions that specialize in making markets in foreign exchange. Commercial banks dominate the market. There is no organized exchange where foreign currency is traded, but dealers are linked by telephone and cable, and by various information transfer services. Consequently, the foreign exchange market can best be described as an interbank over-the-counter market. Most transactions between banks are done through foreign exchange brokers. Brokers are agents that do not take a position in the foreign currencies involved in the transaction. The normal size of a transaction is $1 million or more.

Dealers in the foreign exchange market realize revenue from one or more sources: (1) the bid–ask spread; (2) commissions charged on foreign exchange transactions; and (3) trading profits (appreciation of the currencies that dealers hold a long position in, or depreciation of the currencies that they have a short position in), or trading losses (depreciation of the currencies that they hold a long position in, or appreciation of the currencies that they have a short position in).

## The European Currency Unit

Since the inception of floating exchange rates in the early 1970s, there have been several attempts to develop a currency unit composed of a basket of foreign currencies that would be accepted as the unit of denomination for international capital market transactions. The most widely used composite currency unit for capital market transactions today is the European Currency Unit (ECU), created in 1979 by the European Economic Community (EEC). The ECU is actually a weighted average of selected currencies. The currencies included in the ECU are those of the members of the European Monetary System (EMS): Germany, the United Kingdom, France, Italy, the Netherlands, Belgium, Luxembourg, Denmark, Ireland, Greece, Spain, and Portugal. The weight of each country's currency in this basket is an administrative and political decision of the EEC and depends upon the relative importance of a country's economic trade and financial sector within the European Economic Community.[2] Exchange rates between the ECU and those countries not part of the EEC float freely. The exchange rate between countries in the EEC, however, may fluctuate only within a narrow range that is, in effect, a cross rate determined by the weights of the ECU.

The increased use of ECU-denominated loans, and, more recently, the issuance of ECU-denominated government bonds by some members of the EMS, suggests the growing importance of this composite currency in international capital market transactions.

> ### ▶ KEY POINTS THAT YOU SHOULD UNDERSTAND BEFORE PROCEEDING:
>
> 1. The spot exchange rate market is the market for settlement of a foreign exchange transaction within two business days.
> 2. Foreign exchange rates between major currencies are free to float, with market forces determining the relative value of a currency.
> 3. Spot exchange rates adjust to compensate for the relative inflation rate between two countries.
> 4. Dealers in the foreign exchange market are large international banks and other financial institutions that specialize in making markets in foreign exchange.
> 5. The most widely used composite currency unit for capital market transactions today is the European Currency Unit (ECU).

## INSTRUMENTS FOR HEDGING FOREIGN EXCHANGE RISK

There are four instruments that borrowers and investors can use to protect against adverse foreign exchange rate movements: (1) currency forward contracts; (2) currency futures contracts; (3) currency options; and (4) currency swaps.

### Currency Forward Contracts

Earlier we discussed the spot rate for the Swiss franc, which appears on the first line in the Switzerland entry in Figure 30-1. Now let's look at the other three lines for the Swiss franc. Each line represents the exchange rate for a forward contract that expires a certain number of days in the future.

Recall that a forward contract is one in which one party agrees to buy the underlying, and another party agrees to sell that same underlying, for a specific price at a designated date in the future. Each line indicates a different

---

[2] As this is being written (in late 1992), the European currency arrangements are undergoing extensive and largely unexpected changes.

number of days until settlement or expiration of a forward contract: 30-day settlement for the first line below "Switzerland (Franc)," 90-day settlement for the second line below, and 180-day settlement for the third line. Consider Friday's quote for the 90-day forward exchange rate. In the U.S. dollar equivalent column, the quote is "0.7883." This means that an American who will receive Swiss francs 90 days from now can, by selling forward francs, be assured of receiving 0.7883 U.S. dollars per franc. Similarly, a Swiss firm wanting to convert U.S. dollars into francs 90 days from now can count on paying $0.7883 for francs (if it enters into a forward contract).

Although most daily newspapers report forward contracts with these three maturity dates, other maturities are available. Most forward contracts have a maturity of less than two years. Longer-dated forward contracts have relatively large bid–ask spreads; that is, the size of the bid–ask spread for a given currency increases with the maturity of the contract. Consequently, forward contracts are not attractive for hedging long-dated foreign currency exposure.

As Chapter 25 emphasizes, both forward and futures contracts can be used to lock in a certain price, which in this case would be the foreign exchange rate. By locking in a rate and eliminating downside risk, the user forgoes the opportunity to benefit from any advantageous foreign exchange rate movement. Futures contracts, which are creations of an exchange, have certain advantages over forward contracts in many cases, such as stock indexes and Treasury securities. For foreign exchange, by contrast, the forward market is the market of choice, and trading there is much larger than trading on exchanges. However, as the foreign exchange forward market is an interbank market, reliable information on the amount of contracts outstanding at any time, or open interest, is not publicly available.

*Pricing Currency Forward Contracts.* In Chapter 25, we showed the relationship between spot prices and forward prices, and explained how arbitrage ensures that the relationship holds. We now apply similar considerations to the pricing of foreign exchange futures contracts on the basis of the spot exchange rate, using an extended example.

Consider a U.S. investor with a one-year investment horizon who has two choices:

*Alternative 1:* Deposit $100,000 in a U.S. bank that pays 7% compounded annually for one year.

*Alternative 2:* Deposit the U.S. dollar equivalent of $100,000 in German marks ("Deutsche marks" or DM) in a German bank that pays 9% compounded annually for one year.

The two alternatives and their outcomes one year from now are depicted in Figure 30-2. Which is the better alternative? It will be the alternative that produces the most U.S. dollars one year from now. Ignoring U.S. and German taxes on interest income or any other taxes, we need to know two things in order to determine the better alternative: (1) the spot exchange rate between

FIGURE 30-2

OUTCOME OF TWO ALTERNATIVES: DETERMINATION
OF THEORETICAL FORWARD RATE

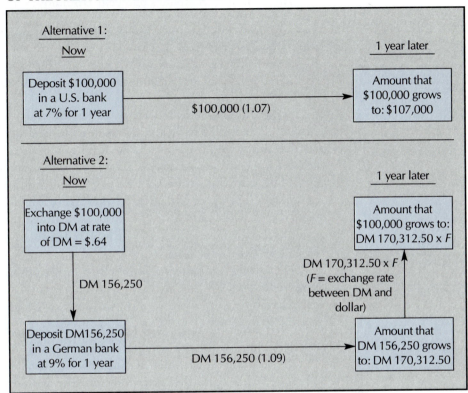

U.S. dollars and German marks, and (2) the spot exchange rate one year from
now between U.S. dollars and German marks. The former is known; the latter is not.

We can determine, however, the spot rate one year from now between
U.S. dollars and German marks that will make the investor indifferent between the two alternatives.

*For alternative 1:* The amount of U.S. dollars available one year from now
would be $107,000 ($100,000 times 1.07).

*For alternative 2:* Assume that the spot rate is $0.6400 for one Deutsche
mark at this time. Then, ignoring commissions, $100,000 can be exchanged
for DM 156,250 ($100,000 divided by 0.6400). The amount of German marks
available at the end of one year would be DM 170,312.50 (DM 156,250 times
1.09).

The number of U.S. dollars that the DM 170,312.50 can be exchanged
for will depend on the exchange rate one year from now. Let *F* denote the exchange rate between these two currencies one year from now. Specifically, *F*
will denote the number of U.S. dollars that can be exchanged for one German

mark. Thus, the number of U.S. dollars at the end of one year from the second alternative is:

$$\text{Amount of U.S. dollars one year from now} = \text{DM } 170{,}312.50 \times F$$

The investor will be indifferent between the two alternatives if the number of U.S. dollars is $107,000; that is,

$$\$107{,}000 = \text{DM } 170{,}312.50 \times F$$

Solving, we find that $F$ is equal to $0.6283. Thus, if one year from now the spot exchange rate is $0.6283 for one German mark, then the two alternatives will produce the same number of U.S. dollars. If more than $0.6283 can be exchanged for one German mark, then there will be more than $107,000 at the end of one year. An exchange rate of $0.6300 for one German mark, for example, would produce $107,296.88 (DM 170,312.50 times $0.6300). The opposite is true if less than $0.6283 can be exchanged for one German mark. For example, if the future exchange rate is $0.6200, there will be $105,593.75 (DM 170,312.50 times $0.6200).

Let us now look at this situation from a German investor's perspective. Suppose that the German investor with a one-year investment horizon has two alternatives:

*Alternative 1:* Deposit DM 156,250 in a German bank that pays 9% compounded annually for one year.

*Alternative 2:* Deposit the German mark equivalent of DM 156,250 in U.S. dollars in a U.S. bank that pays 7% compounded annually for one year.

Once again, assume that the spot exchange rate is $0.6400 for one German mark. The German investor will select the alternative that generates the most marks at the end of one year. The first alternative would generate DM 170,312.50 (DM 156,250 times 1.09). The second alternative requires that Deutsche marks be exchanged for U.S. dollars at the spot exchange rate at this time. Given the spot exchange rate assumed, DM 156,250 can be exchanged for $100,000 (DM 156,250 multiplied by $0.6400). At the end of one year, the second alternative would generate $107,000 ($100,000 times 1.07). Letting $F$ continue to denote the number of U.S. dollars needed to purchase one German mark one year from now, the German investor following Alternative 2 will realize the following amount of Deutsche marks one year from now:

$$\text{Amount of German marks one year from now} = \$107{,}000/F$$

The investor will be indifferent between the two alternatives if

$$\$107{,}000/F = \text{DM } 170{,}312.50$$

The equation yields a value for $F$ of $0.6283, the same exchange rate that we found when we sought the exchange rate one year from now that would make the U.S. investor indifferent between the two alternatives facing that investor.

Now suppose that a dealer quotes a one-year forward exchange rate between the two currencies. The one-year forward exchange rate fixes today the exchange rate one year from now. Thus, if the one-year forward exchange rate quoted is $0.6283 for one German mark, investing in the German bank will provide no arbitrage opportunity for the U.S. investor. If the one-year forward rate quoted is more than $0.6283 for one German mark, the U.S. investor can arbitrage the situation by selling German marks forward (and buying U.S. dollars forward for marks).

To see how this arbitrage opportunity can be exploited, suppose that the one-year forward exchange rate is $0.6300 for one German mark. Also assume that the borrowing and the lending rates within each currency's country are the same. Suppose that the U.S. investor borrows $100,000 for one year at 7% compounded annually and enters into a forward contract agreeing to deliver DM 170,312.50 one year from now at $0.6300 per German mark. That is, one year from now the investor is agreeing to deliver DM 170,312.50 in exchange for $107,296.88 (DM 170,312.50 multiplied by $0.6300).

The $100,000 that was borrowed can be exchanged for DM 156,250 at the spot rate of $0.6400 to one German mark, which can be invested in Germany at 9%. One year from now the U.S. investor will have DM 170,312.50 from the investment in Germany, which can be delivered against the forward contract. The U.S. investor will receive $107,296.88 and repay $107,000 to satisfy the bank loan, netting $296.88. Assuming that the counterparty to the forward contract does not default, this is a riskless arbitrage situation, because a $296.88 profit is generated with no initial investment.[3] This riskless profit will prompt many arbitrageurs to follow this strategy and will, obviously, result in the U.S. dollar rising relative to the German mark in the forward exchange rate market, or possibly some other adjustment.[4]

On the other hand, if the one-year forward exchange rate quoted is less than $0.6283, a German investor can arbitrage the situation by buying German marks forward (and by selling U.S. dollars forward). This riskless arbitrage will again lead arbitrageurs to act, with the result that the forward exchange rate of U.S. dollars relative to German marks will fall.[5] The conclu-

---

[3] A German investor could also arbitrage this situation.

[4] Actually, a combination of things may occur when U.S. investors attempt to exploit this situation: (1) the spot exchange rate of U.S. dollars relative to German marks will fall as U.S. investors sell dollars and buy marks; (2) U.S. interest rates will rise in the United States as investors borrow in the United States and invest in Germany; (3) German interest rates will fall as more is invested in Germany; and (4) the one-year forward rate of U.S. dollars relative to German marks will fall. In practice, the last will dominate.

[5] A combination of things may occur when German investors attempt to exploit this situation: (1) the spot exchange rate of U.S. dollars relative to German marks will rise as German investors buy dollars and sell marks; (2) German interest rates will rise as investors borrow in Germany and invest in the United States; (3) U.S. interest rates will fall as more is invested in the United States; and (4) the one-year forward rate of U.S. dollars relative to German marks will rise. In practice, the last will dominate.

sion of this argument is that the one-year forward exchange rate must be $0.6283, because any other forward exchange rate would result in an arbitrage opportunity for either the U.S. or the German investor.

Thus, the spot exchange rate and the interest rates in two countries will determine the forward exchange rate of their currencies. The relationship among the spot exchange rate, the interest rates in two countries, and the forward rate is called *interest rate parity*. The parity relationship implies that an investor, by hedging in the forward exchange rate market, will realize the same sure domestic return whether investing domestically or in a foreign country. The arbitrage process that forces interest rate parity is called *covered interest arbitrage*.

Mathematically, interest rate parity between the currencies of two countries, A and B, can be expressed in this way:

Let $I$ = amount of A's currency to be invested for a time period of length $t$

$S$ = spot exchange rate: price of foreign currency in terms of domestic currency (units of domestic currency per unit of foreign currency)

$F$ = $t$-period forward rate: price of foreign currency $t$ periods from now

$i_A$ = interest rate on an investment maturing at time $t$ in country A.

$i_B$ = interest rate on an investment maturing at time $t$ in country B.

Then:

$$I (1 + i_A) = (I/S) (1 + i_B) F$$

To illustrate, let country A be the United States and country B represent Germany. In our example we have:

$I$ = $100,000 for one year
$S$ = $0.6400
$F$ = $0.6283
$i_A$ = 0.07
$i_B$ = 0.09

Then, according to interest rate parity, this relationship holds:

$$\$100,000 (1.07) = (\$100,000/\$0.6400) (1.09) (\$0.6283)$$
$$\$107,000 = \$107,000$$

Alternatively, interest rate parity can also be expressed as:

$$(1 + i_A) = (F/S) (1 + i_B)$$

Rewriting the equation, we obtain the theoretical forward exchange rate that is implied by the interest rates and spot exchange rate:

$$F = S \left( \frac{(1 + i_A)}{(1 + i_B)} \right)$$

While we have referred so far to investors, we could use borrowers as well to illustrate interest rate parity. That is, a borrower has the choice of obtaining funds in a domestic or foreign market. Interest rate parity provides that a borrower who hedges in the forward exchange rate market will realize the same domestic borrowing rate whether borrowing domestically or in a foreign country.

To derive the theoretical forward exchange rate using the arbitrage argument, we made several assumptions. When the assumptions are violated, the actual forward exchange rate may deviate from the theoretical forward exchange rate. First, in deriving the theoretical forward exchange rate, we assumed the investor faced no commissions or bid–ask spread when exchanging in the spot market today and at the end of the investment horizon. In practice, investors incur such costs, which cause the actual forward exchange rate to lie within a plus or minus small amount of the theoretical rate.

Second, we assumed that the borrowing and lending rates in each currency are the same. Dropping this unrealistic assumption means that there is not a single theoretical forward exchange rate, but a band around a level reflecting borrowing and lending rates. The actual rate should be within this band.

Third, we ignored taxes. In fact, the divergence between actual and theoretical forward exchange rates can be the result of the different tax structures of the two countries. Finally, we assumed that arbitrageurs could borrow, and invest in another country, as much as they wanted in order to exploit mispricing in the exchange market. It should be noted, however, that any restrictions on foreign investing or borrowing in each country impede arbitrage and may cause a divergence between actual and theoretical forward exchange rates.

***Link between Eurocurrency Market and Forward Prices.*** In deriving interest rate parity, we looked at the interest rates in both countries. In fact, market participants in most countries look to one interest rate in order to perform covered interest arbitrage, and that is the interest rate in the Eurocurrency market. The *Eurocurrency market* is the name of the unregulated and informal market for bank deposits and bank loans denominated in a currency other than that of the country where the bank initiating the transaction is located. Examples of transactions in the Eurocurrency market are a British bank in London that lends U.S. dollars to a French corporation, and a Japanese corporation that deposits Swiss francs in a German bank. An investor seeking covered interest arbitrage will accomplish it with short-term borrowing and lending in the Eurocurrency market.

The largest sector of the Eurocurrency market involves bank deposits and bank loans in U.S. dollars and is called the Eurodollar market. (We discussed the Eurodollar CD market in Chapter 22.) The seed for the Eurocurrency market was, in fact, the Eurodollar market. As international capital market transactions increased, the market for bank deposits and bank loans in other currencies developed.

### Currency Futures Contracts

Foreign exchange futures contracts for the major currencies are traded on the International Monetary Market (IMM), a division of the Chicago Mercantile Exchange. The futures contracts traded on the IMM are for the Japanese yen, the German mark, the Canadian dollar, the British pound, the Swiss franc, and the Australian dollar. The amount of each foreign currency that must be delivered for a contract varies by currency. For example, the British pound futures contract calls for delivery of 62,500 pounds, while the Japanese yen futures contract is for delivery of 12.5 million yen. The maturity cycle for currency futures is March, June, September, and December. The longest maturity is one year. Consequently, as in the case of a currency forward contract, currency futures do not provide a good vehicle for hedging long-dated foreign exchange risk exposure.

Other exchanges trading currency futures in the United States are the Midamerica Commodity Exchange (a subsidiary of the Chicago Board of Trade) and the Financial Instrument Exchange (a subsidiary of the New York Cotton Exchange). The latter trades a futures contract in which the underlying is a U.S. dollar index. Outside the United States, currency futures are traded on the London International Financial Futures Exchange, the Singapore International Monetary Exchange, the Toronto Futures Exchange, the Sydney Futures Exchange, and the New Zealand Futures Exchange.

### Currency Option Contracts

In contrast to a forward or futures contract, an option gives the option buyer the opportunity to benefit from favorable exchange rate movements but establishes a maximum loss. The option price is the cost of arranging such a risk/return profile.

There are two types of foreign currency options: options on the foreign currency and futures options. The latter are options to enter into foreign exchange futures contracts. (We described the features of futures options in Chapter 26.) Futures options are traded on the IMM, the trading location of the currency futures contracts.

Options on foreign currencies have been traded on the Philadelphia Exchange since 1982. The foreign currencies underlying the options are the same as for the futures. There are two sorts of options traded on the Philadelphia Exchange for each currency: an American-type option and a European-type option. Recall from Chapter 26 that the former permits exercise at any time up to and including the expiration date, while the latter permits exercise only at the expiration date. The number of units of foreign currency underlying each option contract traded on the Philadelphia Exchange is one-half the amount of the futures contract. For example, the Japanese yen option is for

6.25 million yen and the British pound option is for 31,250 pounds. Options on currencies are also traded on the London Stock Exchange and the London International Financial Futures Exchange.

In addition to the organized exchanges, there is also an over-the-counter market for options on currencies. Trading in these products is dominated by commercial banks and investment banking firms. As we explained in Chapter 26, over-the-counter options are tailor-made products that accommodate the specific needs of clients. Only options on the major currencies are traded on the organized exchanges. An option on any other currency must be purchased in the over-the-counter market.

The factors that affect the price of any option were discussed in Chapter 26. One key factor is the expected volatility of the underlying over the life of the option. In the case of currency options, the underlying is the foreign currency specified by the option contract. So, the volatility that affects the option's value is the expected volatility of the exchange rate between the two currencies from the present time to the expiration of the option. The strike price also is an exchange rate, and it affects the option's value: the higher the strike price, the lower the value of a call, and the higher the value of a put. Another factor that influences the option price is the relative risk-free interest rate in the two countries.[6]

## Currency Swaps

In Chapter 29, we discussed interest rate swaps—a transaction where two counterparties agree to exchange interest payments with no exchange of principal. In a currency swap, there is an exchange of both interest and principal. The best way to explain a currency swap is with an illustration.

Assume two companies, a U.S. company and a Swiss company. Each company seeks to borrow for ten years in its domestic currency; that is, the U.S. company seeks $100 million U.S. dollar-denominated debt, and the Swiss company seeks debt in the amount of 127 million Swiss francs (SF). For reasons that we will explore later, let's suppose that each wants to issue ten-year bonds in the bond market of the other country, and those bonds are denominated in the other country's currency. That is, the U.S. company wants to issue the Swiss franc equivalent of $100 million in Switzerland, and the Swiss company wants to issue the U.S. dollar equivalent of SF 127 million in the United States.

---

[6] To understand why, recall the portfolio we created in Chapter 26 to replicate the payoff of a call option on an asset. A portion of the asset is purchased with borrowed funds. In the case of a currency option, this involves purchasing a portion of the foreign currency underlying the option. However, the foreign currency acquired can be invested at a risk-free interest rate in the foreign country. Consequently, the pricing of a currency option is similar to the pricing of an option on an income-earning asset such as a dividend-paying stock or an interest-paying bond. At the same time, the amount that must be set aside to meet the strike price depends on the domestic rate. Thus the option price, just like interest rate parity, reflects both rates.

Let's also assume the following:

1. At the time when both companies want to issue their ten-year bonds, the spot exchange rate between U.S. dollars and Swiss francs is one U.S. dollar for 1.27 Swiss francs.
2. The coupon rate that the U.S. company would have to pay on the ten-year Swiss franc-denominated bonds issued in Switzerland is 6%.
3. The coupon rate that the Swiss company would have to pay on the ten-year U.S. dollar-denominated bonds issued in the U.S. is 11%.

By the first assumption, if the U.S. company issues the bonds in Switzerland, it can exchange the SF 127 million for $100 million. By issuing $100 million of bonds in the United States, the Swiss company can exchange the proceeds for SF 127 million. Therefore, both get the amount of financing they seek. Assuming the coupon rates given by the last two assumptions, and assuming for purposes of this illustration that coupon payments will be made annually, the cash outlays that the companies must make for the next ten years are summarized as:

| Year | U.S. Company | Swiss Company |
|---|---|---|
| 1-10 | SF 7,620,000 | $ 11,000,000 |
| 10 | 127,000,000 | 100,000,000 |

Each issuer faces the risk that, at the time a payment on its liability must be made, its domestic currency will have depreciated relative to the other currency. Such a depreciation would require a greater outlay of the domestic currency to satisfy the liability. That is, both firms are exposed to foreign exchange risk.

In a currency swap, the two companies will issue bonds in the other's bond market and enter into an agreement requiring that:

1. The two parties exchange the proceeds received from the sale of the bonds.
2. The two parties make the coupon payments to service the debt of the other party.
3. At the termination date of the currency swap (which coincides with the maturity of the bonds), both parties agree to exchange the par value of the bonds.

In our illustration this means:

1. The U.S. company issues ten-year, 6% coupon bonds with a par value of SF 127 million in Switzerland and gives the proceeds to the Swiss company. At the same time, the Swiss company issues ten-year, 11% bonds with a par value of $100 million in the United States and gives the proceeds to the U.S. company.
2. The U.S. company agrees to service the coupon payments of the Swiss company by paying $11,000,000 per year for the next ten years

to the Swiss company; the Swiss company agrees to service the coupon payments of the U.S. company by paying SF 7,620,000 for the next ten years to the U.S. company.

3. At the end of ten years (this would be the termination date of this currency swap and the maturity of the two bond issues), the U.S. company would pay $100 million to the Swiss company, and the Swiss company would pay SF 127 million to the U.S. company.

This complex agreement is diagrammed in Figure 30-3.

Now let's assess what this transaction has done. Each party received the amount of financing it sought. The U.S. company's coupon payments are in dollars, not Swiss francs; the Swiss company's coupon payments are in Swiss francs, not U.S. dollars. At the termination date, both parties will receive an

**FIGURE 30-3**

ILLUSTRATION OF A CURRENCY SWAP

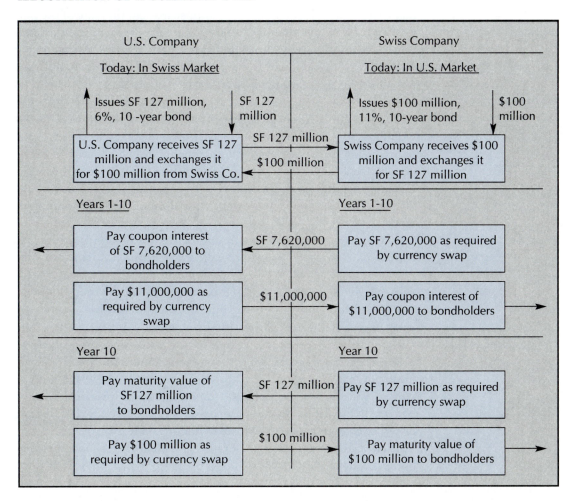

amount sufficient in their local currency to pay off the holders of their bonds. With the coupon payments and the principal repayment in their local currency, neither party faces foreign exchange risk.

In practice, the two companies would not deal directly with each other. Instead, either a commercial bank or investment banking firm would function as an intermediary (as either broker or dealer) in the transaction. As a broker, the intermediary simply brings the two parties together, receiving a fee for the service. If instead the intermediary serves as a dealer, it would not only bring the two parties together, but would also guarantee payment to both parties. Thus, if one party were to default, the counterparty would continue to receive its payments from the dealer. Of course, in this arrangement, both parties are concerned with the credit risk of the dealer. When the currency swap market started, transactions were typically brokered. The more prevalent arrangement today is that the intermediary acts as a dealer.

As we explained in Chapter 29, an interest rate swap is nothing more than a package of forward contracts. The same is true for a currency swap; it is simply a package of currency forward contracts.

***Currency Coupon Swap.*** In our illustration, we assumed that both parties made fixed cash flow payments. Suppose instead that one of the parties sought floating-rate rather than fixed-rate financing. Returning to the same illustration, assume that instead of fixed-rate financing, the Swiss company wanted LIBOR-based financing. In this case, the U.S. company would issue floating-rate bonds in Switzerland. Suppose that it could do so at a rate of LIBOR plus 50 basis points. Because the currency swap would call for the Swiss company to service the coupon payments of the U.S. company, the Swiss company would make annual payments of LIBOR plus 50 basis points. The U.S. company would still make fixed-rate payments in U.S. dollars to service the debt obligation of the Swiss company in the United States. Now, however, the Swiss company would make floating-rate payments (LIBOR plus 50 basis points) in Swiss francs to service the debt obligation of the U.S. company in Switzerland.

Currency swaps in which one of the parties pays a fixed rate and the counterparty a floating rate are called *currency coupon swaps*.

***Reasons for Development of the Currency Swap Market.*** Now we turn to the question of why the companies in this illustration may find a currency swap beneficial. In a global financial market where there are no market imperfections because of regulations, taxes, and transactions costs, the cost of borrowing should be the same whether the issuer raises funds domestically or in any foreign capital market. In a world with market imperfections, it may be possible for an issuer to reduce its borrowing cost by borrowing funds denominated in a foreign currency and hedging the associated exchange rate risk. This is what is meant by an arbitrage opportunity. The currency swap allows borrowers to capitalize on any such arbitrage opportunities.

Prior to the establishment of the currency swap market, capitalizing on such arbitrage opportunities required use of the currency forward market. The market for long-dated forward exchange rate contracts is thin, however, which increases the cost of eliminating foreign exchange risk. Eliminating foreign exchange risk in our U.S.-Switzerland illustration would have required each issuer to enter ten currency forward contracts (one for each yearly cash payment that the issuer was committed to make in the foreign currency). The currency swap provides a more transactionally efficient means for protecting against foreign exchange risk when an issuer (or its investment banker) has identified an arbitrage opportunity and seeks to benefit from it.

As the currency swap market has developed, the arbitrage opportunities for reduced funding costs that were available in the early days of the swap market have become less common. In fact, it was the development of the swap market that reduced arbitrage opportunities. When these opportunities do arise, they last for only a short period of time, usually less than a day.

There is another motivation for currency swaps. Some companies seek to raise funds in foreign countries as a means of increasing their recognition by foreign investors, despite the fact that the cost of funding is the same as in the United States. The U.S. company in our illustration might have been seeking to expand its potential sources of future funding by issuing bonds today in Switzerland.

As noted in Chapter 29, the estimated size of the swap market (interest rate and currency swaps) was $2.9 billion as of December 1990. Data on usage of each type of swap are not available. One study suggests that the currency swaps market has increased by 33% since 1989.[7]

---

▶ KEY POINTS THAT YOU SHOULD UNDERSTAND BEFORE PROCEEDING:

1. The four instruments that market participants have available to control foreign exchange risk are currency forward contracts, currency futures contracts, currency options, and currency swaps.

2. Because longer-dated forward contracts have relatively large bid–ask spreads, these contracts are not attractive for hedging long-dated foreign currency exposure.

3. The forward exchange rate between two countries is determined from the spot exchange rate and the interest rates in the two countries.

4. Interest rate parity implies that, by hedging in the forward exchange rate market, an investor will realize the same sure domestic return whether investing domestically or in a foreign country, and a bor-

---

[7] Soma Biswas, "Derivative Pros See Growth in Customization," *BondWeek*, Special Supplement, October 14, 1991, p. 1.

rower will realize the same domestic borrowing rate whether borrowing domestically or in a foreign country.

5. There are exchange-traded options on foreign exchange and exchange-traded futures options in which the underlying is foreign exchange.

6. A currency swap is an agreement in which two counterparties agree to the exchange of both interest and principal payments.

**SUMMARY**

We have reviewed the spot foreign exchange market and markets for hedging foreign exchange risk. An exchange rate is defined as the amount of one currency that can be exchanged for another currency. A direct exchange rate quote is the domestic price of a foreign currency; an indirect quote is the foreign price of the domestic currency. An investor or issuer whose cash flows are denominated in a foreign currency is exposed to foreign exchange risk.

The spot exchange rate market is the market for settlement of a currency within two business days. In the developed countries, and some of the developing ones, exchange rates are free to float. According to the purchasing power parity relationship, the exchange rate between two countries—the price of the foreign currency in terms of the domestic currency—is proportional to the domestic price level and inversely proportional to the price level in the foreign country. Exchange rates are typically quoted in terms of the U.S. dollar.

The foreign exchange market is an over-the-counter market dominated by large international banks that act as dealers. Foreign exchange dealers quote one price at which they are willing to buy a foreign currency and one at which they are willing to sell a foreign currency. The difference between those prices is one cost a user of the market must pay; another cost is the explicit fee or commission to brokers arranging the purchase or sale of currency.

Today, the European Currency Unit is the global capital market's most widely used composite currency unit. It is continuing to grow in importance as an increasing number of loans have been denominated in ECU, and some members of the European Monetary System have been issuing ECU-denominated government bonds.

Currency forward contracts, currency futures contracts, currency options, and currency swaps are four instruments that borrowers and investors can use to protect against adverse foreign exchange rate movements.

Interest rate parity gives the relationship among the spot exchange rate, the interest rates in two countries, and the forward rate. The relationship is assured by a covered interest arbitrage. Interest rate parity implies that investors and borrowers who hedge in the forward exchange rate market will realize the same domestic return or face the same domestic borrowing rate whether investing or borrowing domestically or in a foreign country.

In implementing covered interest arbitrage, the relevant interest rates are those in the Eurocurrency market, the market for bank deposits and bank loans denominated in a currency other than that of the country where the bank initiating the transaction is located. The Eurodollar market is the largest sector of this market.

There are exchange-traded options on major foreign currencies and futures options on the same currencies traded in the United States. An option on any other currency must be purchased in the over-the-counter market.

A currency swap is effectively a package of currency forward contracts, with the advantage that it allows hedging of long-dated foreign exchange risk and it is more transactionally efficient than futures or forward contracts. Currency swaps are used to arbitrage the increasingly rare opportunities in the global financial market for raising funds at less cost than in the domestic market.

## GLOSSARY

**Covered interest arbitrage:** The arbitrage process that forces interest rate parity to hold.

**Cross rate:** The exchange rate between two countries other than the United States

**Currency coupon swap:** A currency swap in which one of the parties pays a fixed rate and the counterparty a floating rate.

**Currency swap:** An agreement whereby two counterparties agree to swap interest and principal in two different currencies.

**Direct quote:** The convention in quoting an exchange rate expressed in terms of the number of units of a local currency exchangeable for one unit of a foreign currency.

**Eurocurrency Market:** The unregulated and informal market for bank deposits and bank loans denominated in a currency other than that of the country where the bank initiating the transaction is located.

**European Currency Unit:** The most widely used composite currency unit for capital market transactions, created by the European Economic Community.

**Exchange rate:** The amount of one currency that can be exchanged for a unit of another currency.

**Foreign exchange risk:** The risk of an adverse foreign exchange rate movement.

**Indirect quote:** The convention in quoting an exchange rate expressed in terms of the number of units of a foreign currency that can be exchanged for one unit of a local currency.

**Interest rate parity:** The relationship among the spot exchange rate, the interest rates in two countries, and the forward rate.

**Purchasing power parity:** The relationship that posits that the exchange rate of a foreign currency is proportional to the domestic inflation rate, and inversely proportional to foreign inflation.

**Spot (or cash) exchange rate market:** The market for settlement of a foreign exchange transaction within two business days.

**Triangular arbitrage:** An arbitrage strategy employed to take advantage of cross rate mispricing between the U.S. dollar and the two foreign currencies.

**QUESTIONS**

1. A U.S. life insurance company that buys British government bonds faces foreign exchange risk. Specify the nature of that risk in terms of the company's expected return in U.S. dollars.

2. Explain the difference between a spot exchange rate and a forward exchange rate.

3. These spot foreign exchange rates were reported on February 8, 1991:

|  | German Mark | Japanese Yen | British Pound |
|---|---|---|---|
| U.S. $ | 0.6874 | 0.00779 | 1.9905 |

The exchange rates indicate the number of U.S. dollars necessary to purchase one unit of the foreign currency.

   a. From the perspective of a U.S. investor, are the foreign exchange rates above direct or indirect quotes?

   b. How much of each of the foreign currencies is needed to buy one U.S. dollar?

   c. Calculate the theoretical cross rates between: (i) the German mark and the Japanese yen; (ii) the German mark and the British pound; and (iii) the Japanese yen and the British pound.

4. Explain the meaning of "triangular arbitrage," and show how it is related to cross rates.

5. On February 8, 1991, the U.S. dollar/British pound spot rate was U.S. $1.9905 per pound and the U.S. dollar/Japanese yen spot rate was U.S. $0.00779 per yen. The following forward rates were also quoted:

|  | British Pound | Japanese Yen |
|---|---|---|
| 30 days | 1.9908 | 0.007774 |
| 60 | 1.9597 | 0.007754 |
| 90 | 1.9337 | 0.007736 |

    a.   Explain what someone who enters into a 30-day forward contract to deliver British pounds is agreeing to do.

    b.   Explain what someone who enters into a 90-day forward contract to buy Japanese yen is agreeing to do.

    c.   What can you infer about the relationship between U.S. and British short-term interest rates and U.S. and Japanese short-term interest rates?

6.   The European Economic Community expects to revise the weights of the currencies comprising the ECU every five years. Why is it necessary to revise the weights?

7.   What is the drawback of using currency forward contracts for hedging long-dated positions?

8.   How does covered interest arbitrage relate to interest rate parity?

9.   Why are the interest rates in the Eurocurrency market important in covered interest arbitrage?

10.   Suppose you know the following items: you can borrow and lend $500,000 at the one-year interest rate in the United States of 7.5%; in France both the borrowing and lending rates are 9.2%; the spot exchange rate between the U.S. dollar and the French franc is now $.1725 per franc; and the one-year forward exchange rate is $.2 per franc.

    a.   Explain how you could make a profit without risk and without investing any of your own money. (Assume commissions, fees, etc., to be equal to zero.)

    b.   Aside from assuming commissions, fees, etc., to be zero, we have made several unrealistic assumptions. What are they?

    c.   Even if we incorporated realistic considerations regarding commissions, and so on, the interest rate and exchange rate numbers in this question would probably produce a profit of some size. Why do you think opportunities like the one in this question are unlikely to come along very often in the real world?

11.   If the one-year borrowing and lending rates in Japan were 5% and they were 7% in the United States, and if the forward exchange rate between dollars and yen were $.007576 per yen (i.e., one dollar could buy 131.99 yen), then what should the spot exchange rate of dollars for yen be?

12.   For which currencies are options and futures traded on organized U.S. exchanges?

13.   What is the major difference between a currency swap and an interest rate swap?

14.   The excerpt following appeared in the January 14, 1991, issue of *Wall Street Letter:*

> *The Philadelphia Stock Exchange plans to list the first non-dollar denominated options to trade in the United States, according to sources at the exchange. The Phlx will list cross-currency options based on the relationships between the Deutsche mark and the Japanese yen, as well as British pound/yen and pound/mark options, a spokesman confirmed. . . .*
>
> *The exchange currently lists currency options that are based on the relationship between that currency and the dollar, one Phlx member explained. "If you're not American," he added, "then the dollar doesn't do it for you." The three new cross-currency options should be attractive to the same banks and broker-dealers that currently trade dollar-based currency options, as well as non-U.S. entities that have interests in other currencies.*
>
> *Cross-currency options are "a very big part of international trade and international capital markets," and are big over-the-counter products, but none currently trades on an exchange. The advantage of exchange-traded options, the Phlx member said, is that "99% of the customers don't have the credit" to trade such a product over-the-counter with a big bank.*

a.  What does the representative of the Phlx mean by saying: "If you're not American then the dollar doesn't do it for you."?

b.  Why is the credit of customers critical in the over-the-counter market but not for an exchange-traded contract?

c.  When the Philadelphia Stock Exchange filed with the SEC to list cross-currency options, the exchange indicated that the demand for this product has been "spawned by recent large fluctuations and dramatic increases in volatility levels for cross-rate options." Why would this increase the demand for cross-currency options?

# Index